LUTHERAN WORSHIP

LUTHERAN WORSHIP

Prepared by
The Commission on Worship
of
The Lutheran Church—Missouri Synod

Publishing House
St. Louis

Copyright © 1982 by
Concordia Publishing House

All rights reserved. No part of this book may be reproduced in any manner whatsoever without written permission from the publisher (for material with Concordia Publishing House copyright) or from the other copyright holders. The copyright holders are identified in Acknowledgements, page 969.

Manufactured in the United States of America

3   4   5   6   7   8   9   10   KK   91   90   89   88   87   86   85   84   83   82

CONTENTS

INTRODUCTION

Our Lord speaks and we listen. His Word bestows what it says. Faith that is born from what is heard acknowledges the gifts received with eager thankfulness and praise. Music is drawn into this thankfulness and praise, enlarging and elevating the adoration of our gracious giver God.

Saying back to him what he has said to us, we repeat what is most true and sure. Most true and sure is his name, which he put upon us with the water of our Baptism. We are his. This we acknowledge at the beginning of the Divine Service. Where his name is, there is he. Before him we acknowledge that we are sinners, and we plead for forgiveness. His forgiveness is given us, and we, freed and forgiven, acclaim him as our great and gracious God as we apply to ourselves the words he has used to make himself known to us.

The rhythm of our worship is from him to us, and then from us back to him. He gives his gifts, and together we receive and extol them. We build one another up as we speak to one another in psalms, hymns, and spiritual songs. Our Lord gives us his body to eat and his blood to drink. Finally his blessing moves us out into our calling, where his gifts have their fruition. How best to do this we may learn from his Word and from the way his Word has prompted his worship through the centuries. We are heirs of an astonishingly rich tradition. Each generation receives from those who went before and, in making that tradition of the Divine Service its own, adds what best may serve in its own day—the living heritage and something new.

Lutheran Worship, within its compass, seeks to carry forward the great heritage and add something new. The Common Service (Divine Service I), familiar to all Lutherans, is carried forward with no great changes and with some improvements where these seemed needed. This will serve the continuity of our worship with an order of long-proven worth. In addition there is a service in two settings that derives from the work of the Inter-Lutheran Commission on Worship (Divine Service II, First Setting, and Divine Service II, Second Setting). Divine Service III draws on our treasury of chorales and revives the historical *Liedmesse,* a typically Lutheran contribution to worship form in which chorales largely replace chant.

There is also continuity with our familiar Matins and Vespers. In some places a better musical setting has been provided. In addition there are the Morning Prayer, Evening Prayer, and Prayer at the Close of the Day from the work of the Inter-Lutheran Commission on Worship. There are further orders for various occasions, so that altogether *Lutheran Worship* provides orders of service with a faithfulness to the Lutheran tradition and understanding of worship in the widest range of orders of service for English-speaking Lutherans.

In its hymnody each age of the Church reflects what it returns to God for the great blessings it has received from him. Some of the Church's song is always derived from a previous era.

The early Church developed its music from the psalmody of the synagog, to which it added the strophic hymns of Greek and Roman converts. When the liturgy became the sole property of the clergy, there arose a need for hymns in the language of the people. Thus there came into being the great body of Latin hymns introduced and promoted by Bishop Ambrose of Milan and his followers. In time these again became the property of the clergy and hierarchy. The Lutheran Reformation once more restored the Church's song to the people in their native tongue. From then on the Lutheran Church became known as the "singing Church." The song of this Church has weathered and withstood such influences as pietism, rationalism, modernism, and universalism in one form or another.

The hymns in *Lutheran Worship* draw on the vast treasury of Christian hymnody old and new, with words that speak God's law and Gospel and express our faith's response and with music that nourishes both memory and heart.

Directed by the 1979 convention of The Lutheran Church—Missouri Synod in St. Louis, the Commission on Worship offers this book for the enlivening and strengthening of worship, with gratitude for all those who have served the worship of our Lord and with the prayer that it may be serviceable to him and his people for the saving Gospel's sake.

THE CHURCH YEAR

SUNDAYS AND MAJOR FESTIVALS

The Time of Christmas

Advent Season
First Sunday in Advent P/B*
Second Sunday in Advent P/B
Third Sunday in Advent P/B
Fourth Sunday in Advent P/B

Christmas Season
THE NATIVITY OF OUR LORD W
 Christmas Eve
 Christmas Dawn
 Christmas Day
First Sunday after Christmas W
Second Sunday after Christmas W

Epiphany Season
The Epiphany of Our Lord W
The Baptism of Our Lord W
 First Sunday after the Epiphany
Second Sunday after the Epiphany G
Third Sunday after the Epiphany G
Fourth Sunday after the Epiphany G
Fifth Sunday after the Epiphany G
Sixth Sunday after the Epiphany G
Seventh Sunday after the Epiphany G
Eighth Sunday after the Epiphany G
The Transfiguration of Our Lord W
 Last Sunday after the Epiphany

The Time of Easter

Lenten Season
Ash Wednesday BK/P
First Sunday in Lent P
Second Sunday in Lent P
Third Sunday in Lent P
Fourth Sunday in Lent P
Fifth Sunday in Lent P

Holy Week
PALM SUNDAY S/P
 Sunday of the Passion
Monday in Holy Week S/P
Tuesday in Holy Week S/P
Wednesday in Holy Week S/P
Maundy Thursday S/W
GOOD FRIDAY BK

Easter Season
THE RESURRECTION OF
OUR LORD
 Easter Eve W
 Easter Day W/GO
 Easter Evening W/GO
Second Sunday of Easter W
Third Sunday of Easter W
Fourth Sunday of Easter W
Fifth Sunday of Easter W
Sixth Sunday of Easter W
The Ascension of Our Lord W
Seventh Sunday of Easter W

*The letters indicate the suggested colors: P = purple, B = blue,
W = white, G = green, BK = black, S = scarlet, GO = gold, R = red*

PENTECOST R
Pentecost Eve
The Day of Pentecost
Pentecost Evening

The Time of the Church

The Season after Pentecost
The Holy Trinity W
First Sunday after Pentecost
Second through Twenty-seventh Sunday
after Pentecost G
Sunday of the Fulfillment G
Last Sunday after Pentecost

MINOR FESTIVALS

November
30 St. Andrew, Apostle* R

December
21 St. Thomas, Apostle R
26 St. Stephen, The First Martyr R
27 St. John, Apostle and Evangelist W
28 The Holy Innocents, Martyrs R
31 New Year's Eve W
Eve of the Name of Jesus

January
1 New Year's Day W
The Circumcision of Our Lord
18 The Confession of St. Peter W
24 St. Timothy, Pastor and
Confessor W
25 The Conversion of St. Paul W
26 St. Titus, Pastor and Confessor W

February
2 The Presentation of Our Lord W
18 Martin Luther, Doctor and
Confessor W
24 St. Matthias, Apostle R

March
25 The Annunciation of Our Lord W

April
25 St. Mark, Evangelist R

May
1 St. Philip and St. James,
Apostles R
7 C. F. W. Walther, Doctor W
31 The Visitation W

June
11 St. Barnabas, Apostle R
24 The Nativity of St. John
the Baptist W
25 Presentation of the Augsburg
Confession W
29 St. Peter and St. Paul, Apostles R

July
22 St. Mary Magdalene W
25 St. James the Elder, Apostle R

August
10 St. Laurence, Martyr R
15 St. Mary, Mother of Our Lord W
24 St. Bartholomew, Apostle R

September
14 Holy Cross Day R
21 St. Matthew, Apostle and
Evangelist R
29 St. Michael and All Angels W

October
18 St. Luke, Evangelist R
28 St. Simon and St. Jude, Apostles R
31 Reformation Day R

November
1 All Saints' Day W
2 Commemoration of the Faithful
Departed W

OCCASIONS

Dedication of a Church R
Anniversary of a Congregation R
Mission Festival W
Harvest Festival Color of Season
Day of Supplication and Prayer P
Day of Special or National
Thanksgiving W

---

*St. Andrew's Day determines the First Sunday in Advent and
therefore begins the enumeration of the minor festivals.*

PROPERS OF THE DAY

FIRST SUNDAY IN ADVENT

INTROIT

See, your King comes to you,*
  righteous and having salvation.

To you, O Lord, I lift up my soul;*
  in you I trust, O my God.
Do not let me be put to shame,*
  nor let my enemies triumph over me.
No one whose hope is in you will ever
be put to shame,*
  but they will be put to shame who are
  treacherous without excuse.

Glory be to the Father and to the Son*
  and to the Holy Spirit;
as it was in the beginning,*
  is now, and will be forever. Amen

See, your King comes to you,*
  righteous and having salvation.

*(Antiphon, Zech. 9:9b;
Ps. 25:1-3)*

COLLECT OF THE DAY

Stir up, we implore you, your power, O Lord, and come that by your protection we
may be rescued from the threatening perils of our sins and be saved by your mighty
deliverance; for you live and reign with the Father and the Holy Spirit, one God, now
and forever. (1)

NOTE: *All Scripture references indicate the versification according to* The Holy Bible, New International Version. *Bracketed entries indicate
slight deviation from* The Holy Bible, New International Version. *More extensive changes were made in Luke 24:32 and Romans 10:10.*

When the chant tone for an Introit is separated from its text, the tone appears also on a facing page, thus avoiding an awkward page turn.

READINGS

One-Year Series		Three-Year Series	
Psalm 25:1-7	A. Psalm 50:1-15	B. Psalm 98	C. Psalm 25:1-9
Isaiah 62:10-12	Isaiah 2:1-5	Isaiah 63:16b-17; 64:1-8	Jeremiah 33:14-16
Romans 13:10-14a	Romans 13:11-14	I Corinthians 1:3-9	1 Thessalonians 3:9-13
Luke 19:29-38	Matthew 24:37-44	Mark 13:33-37	Luke 21:25-36
	or Matthew 21:1-11	or Mark 11:1-10	or Luke 19:28-40

GRADUAL

Rejoice greatly, O daughter of Zion!*
   Shout, daughter of Jerusalem!
See, your King comes to you,*
   righteous and having salvation.
Blessed is he who comes in the name of the Lord.*
   From the house of the Lord we bless you.   *(Zech. 9:9; Ps. 118:26)*

VERSE

Alleluia. Alleluia. Lift up your heads, O you gates; lift them up, you ancient doors,
that the King of glory may come in. Alleluia.   *(Ps. 24:9)*

SECOND SUNDAY IN ADVENT

INTROIT

Restore us, O God;*
   make your face shine upon us,
   that we may be saved.

Hear us, O Shepherd of Israel,
you who lead Joseph like a flock;*
   you who sit enthroned between the
   cherubim.
You brought a vine out of Egypt;*
   and it took root and filled the land.
Restore us, O God Almighty;*
   make your face shine upon us,
   that we may be saved.

Glory be to the Father and to the Son*
   and to the Holy Spirit;
as it was in the beginning,*
   is now, and will be forever. Amen

Restore us, O God;*
   make your face shine upon us,
   that we may be saved.

*(Antiphon, Ps. 80:3;
Ps. 80:1, 8a, 9b, 7)*

COLLECT OF THE DAY

Stir up our hearts, O Lord, to make ready the way of your only-begotten Son that at
his second coming we may worship him in purity; who lives and reigns with you and
the Holy Spirit, one God, now and forever. (2)

READINGS

One-Year Series

Psalm 105:1-7
Malachi 4:1-6
Hebrews 12:25-29
Mark 13:19-27

A. Psalm 72:1-14(15-19)
Isaiah 11:1-10
Romans 15:4-13
Matthew 3:1-12

Three-Year Series

B. Psalm 19
Isaiah 40:1-11
2 Peter 3:8-14
Mark 1:1-8

C. Psalm 126
Malachi 3:1-4
Philippians 1:3-11
Luke 3:1-6

GRADUAL

Rejoice greatly, O daughter of Zion!*
    Shout, daughter of Jerusalem!
See, your King comes to you,*
    righteous and having salvation.
Blessed is he who comes in the name of the Lord.*
    From the house of the Lord we bless you.   *(Zech. 9:9; Ps. 118:26)*

VERSE

Alleluia. Alleluia. Prepare the way for the Lord, make straight paths for him; all mankind will see God's salvation. Alleluia.   *(Luke 3:4, 6)*

THIRD SUNDAY IN ADVENT

INTROIT

Show us your unfailing love, O Lord,*
    and grant us your salvation.

I will listen to what God the Lord will say;*
    he promises peace to his people, his
    saints—but let them not return to folly.
Surely his salvation is near those who
fear him,*
    that his glory may dwell in our land.
The Lord will indeed give what is good,*
    and our land will yield its harvest.
Righteousness goes before him*
    and prepares the way for his steps.

Glory be to the Father and to the Son*
    and to the Holy Spirit;
as it was in the beginning,*
    is now, and will be forever. Amen

Show us your unfailing love, O Lord,*
    and grant us your salvation.

*(Antiphon, Ps. 85:7;
Ps. 85:8-9, 12-13)*

COLLECT OF THE DAY

Almighty God, through John the Baptist, the forerunner of Christ, you once proclaimed salvation; now grant that we may know this salvation and serve you in holiness and righteousness all the days of our lives; through Jesus Christ, our Lord, who lives and reigns with you and the Holy Spirit, one God, now and forever. (3)

READINGS

One-Year Series		Three-Year Series	
Psalm 50:1-6	A. Psalm 146	B. Luke 1:46b-55	C. Isaiah 12:2-6
Isaiah 40:1-8	Isaiah 35:1-10	Isaiah 61:1-3, 10-11	Zephaniah 3:14-18a
Romans 15:4-13	James 5:7-10	1 Thessalonians 5:16-24	Philippians 4:4-7(8-9)
Matthew 3:1-12	Matthew 11:2-11	John 1:6-8, 19-28	Luke 3:7-18

GRADUAL

Rejoice greatly, O daughter of Zion!*
   Shout, daughter of Jerusalem!
See, your King comes to you,*
   righteous and having salvation.
Blessed is he who comes in the name of the Lord.*
   From the house of the Lord we bless you.　*(Zech. 9:9; Ps. 118:26)*

VERSE

Alleluia. Alleluia. I will send my messenger ahead of you, who will prepare your way before you. Alleluia.　*(Matt. 11:10)*

FOURTH SUNDAY IN ADVENT

INTROIT

You heavens above, rain down righteousness; let the clouds shower it down.*
   Let the earth open wide,
   let salvation spring up.

The heavens declare the glory of God;*
   the skies proclaim the work
   of his hands.
In the heavens he has pitched
a tent for the sun,*
   which is like a bridegroom coming
   forth from his pavilion, like a champion
   rejoicing to run his course.
It rises at one end of the heavens

and makes its circuit to the other;*
   nothing is hidden from its heat.

Glory be to the Father and to the Son*
   and to the Holy Spirit;
as it was in the beginning,*
   is now, and will be forever. Amen

You heavens above, rain down righteousness; let the clouds shower it down.*
   Let the earth open wide,
   let salvation spring up.

*(Antiphon, Is. 45:8a and b;
Ps. 19:1, 4c, 5-6)*

13

COLLECT OF THE DAY

Stir up your power, O Lord, and come among us with great might; and because we are sorely hindered by our sins, let your bountiful grace and mercy speedily help and deliver us; through Jesus Christ, our Lord, who lives and reigns with you and the Holy Spirit, one God, now and forever. (4)

READINGS

One-Year Series		Three-Year Series	
Psalm 19:1-6	A. Psalm 24	B. Psalm 98	C. Psalm 96
Jeremiah 23:5-6	Isaiah 7:10-14(15-17)	2 Samuel 7:(1-7)8-11, 16	Micah 5:2-4
Philippians 4:4-7	Romans 1:1-7	Romans 16:25-27	Hebrews 10:5-10
Luke 1:26-38	Matthew 1:18-25	Luke 1:26-38	Luke 1:39-45(46-55)
or Luke 1:46-55			

GRADUAL

Rejoice greatly, O daughter of Zion!*
    Shout, daughter of Jerusalem!
See, your King comes to you,*
    righteous and having salvation.
Blessed is he who comes in the name of the Lord.*
    From the house of the Lord we bless you. *(Zech. 9:9; Ps. 118:26)*

VERSE

Alleluia. Alleluia. The virgin will be with child and will give birth to a Son, and they will call him Immanuel. Alleluia. *(Matt. 1:23)*

THE NATIVITY OF OUR LORD
The First Service (Christmas Eve)

INTROIT

XI A: Ionian

When all was still, and it was midnight,*
    your almighty Word, O Lord,
    descended from the royal throne.

Sing to the Lord a new song;*
    sing to the Lord, all the earth.
Sing to the Lord, praise his name;*
    proclaim his salvation day after day.
Declare his glory among the nations,*

his marvelous deeds among all peoples.
For great is the Lord and most
worthy of praise;*
    he is to be feared above all gods.
Let the heavens rejoice, let the
earth be glad;*
    let the sea resound, and all that is in it;

Introit continues on the next page

14

let the fields be jubilant, and
everything in them.*
  Then all the trees of the forest will
  sing for joy.

Glory be to the Father and to the Son*
  and to the Holy Spirit;
as it was in the beginning,*
  is now, and will be forever. Amen

When all was still, and it was midnight,*
  your almighty Word, O Lord,
  descended from the royal throne.

*(Antiphon, liturgical text;
Ps. 96:1-4, 11-12)*

COLLECT OF THE DAY

O God, because you once caused this holy night to shine with the brightness of the true
Light, grant that we who have known the mystery of that Light here on earth may
come to the full measure of its joys in heaven; through Jesus Christ, our Lord, who
lives and reigns with you and the Holy Spirit, one God, now and forever. (5)

READINGS

One-Year Series

Psalm 96:1-10
Isaiah 9:2(3-5)6-7
Titus 2:11-14
Luke 2:1-20

Three-Year Series

A, B, C. Psalm 96
  Isaiah 9:2-7
  Titus 2:11-14
  Luke 2:1-20

GRADUAL

To us a child is born, to us a son is given,*
  and the government will be on his shoulders.
And he will be called Wonderful Counselor, Mighty God,*
  Everlasting Father, Prince of Peace.
Sing to the Lord a new song,*
  for he has done marvelous things. *(Is. 9:6; Ps. 98:1)*

VERSE

Alleluia. Alleluia. Today in the town of David a Savior has been born to you; he is
Christ the Lord. Alleluia. *(Luke 2:11)*

THE NATIVITY OF OUR LORD
The Second Service (Christmas Dawn)

INTROIT

XI A: Ionian

The Lord reigns, he is robed in majesty;*
  the Lord is robed in majesty
  and is armed with strength.

The Lord reigns, let the earth be glad;*
  let the distant shores rejoice.
Clouds and thick darkness
surround him;*
  righteousness and justice are the
  foundation of his throne.
The heavens proclaim his righteousness,*
  and all the peoples see his glory.
Let those who love the Lord hate evil,*
  for he guards the lives of his faithful
  ones and delivers them from the
  hand of the wicked.

Light is shed upon the righteous*
  and joy on the upright in heart.
Rejoice in the Lord, you
who are righteous,*
  and praise his holy name.

Glory be to the Father and to the Son*
  and to the Holy Spirit;
as it was in the beginning,*
  is now, and will be forever. Amen

The Lord reigns, he is robed in majesty;*
  the Lord is robed in majesty
  and is armed with strength.

  (Antiphon, Ps. 93:1a;
  Ps. 97:1-2, 6, 10-12)

COLLECT OF THE DAY

O God, as you make us glad by the yearly festival of the birth of your only-begotten Son Jesus Christ, grant that we, who joyfully receive him as our Redeemer, may with sure confidence behold him when he comes to be our judge; who lives and reigns with you and the Holy Spirit, one God, now and forever. (6)

READINGS

One-Year Series

Psalm 98:1-7
Ezekiel 37:24-28
Titus 3:4-8a
John 1:1-14

Three-Year Series

A, B, C. Psalm 2
  Isaiah 52:7-10
  Hebrews 1:1-9
  John 1:1-14

GRADUAL

To us a child is born, to us a son is given,*
  and the government will be on his shoulders.
And he will be called Wonderful Counselor, Mighty God,*
  Everlasting Father, Prince of Peace.
Sing to the Lord a new song,*
  for he has done marvelous things. *(Is. 9:6; Ps. 98:1)*

VERSE

Alleluia. Alleluia. The Lord said to me, "You are my Son; today I have become your Father." Alleluia. *(Ps. 2:7b)*

THE NATIVITY OF OUR LORD
The Third Service (Christmas Day)

INTROIT

* XI A: Ionian

The Lord has made his salvation known*
  and revealed his righteousness
to the ñations.

Sing to the Lord a ñew song,*
  for he has done marvelous things.
He has remembered his love and his
faithfulness to the house of Israel;*
  all the ends of the earth have seen
  the salvation of our God.
Shout for joy to the Lord, all the earth,*
  burst into jubilant song with music;
with trumpets and the blast
of the ram's horn—*
  shout for joy before the Lord, the King.

Glory be to the Father and to the Son*
  and to the Holy Spirit;
as it was in the beginning,*
  is now, and will be forever. Amen

The Lord has made his salvation known*
  and revealed his righteousness
to the ñations.

*(Antiphon, Ps. 98:2;
Ps. 98:1a, 3-4, 6)*

COLLECT OF THE DAY

Grant, almighty God, that the birth of your only-begotten Son in human flesh may
set us free, who through sin are held in bondage; through Jesus Christ, your
Son, our Lord, who lives and reigns with you and the Holy Spirit, one God, now and
forever. (7)

READINGS

One-Year Series

Psalm 98:1-7
Micah 5:2-4
Hebrews 1:1-6
Luke 2:1-20

Three-Year Series

A, B, C. Psalm 98
    Isaiah 62:10-12
    Titus 3:4-7
    Luke 2:1-20

GRADUAL

To us a child is born, to us a son is given,*
  and the government will be on his shoulders.
And he will be called Wonderful Counselor, Mighty God,*
  Everlasting Father, Prince of Peace.
Sing to the Lord a ñew song,*
  for he has done marvelous things.   *(Is. 9:6; Ps. 98:1)*

VERSE

Alleluia. Alleluia. Let the peace of Christ rule in your hearts. Alleluia.   *(Col. 3:15a)*

FIRST SUNDAY AFTER CHRISTMAS

INTROIT

XI A: Ionian

For to us a child is born,*
 to us a son is given.
And he will be called*
 Wonderful Counselor, Mighty God.

Sing to the Lord a new song,*
 for he has done marvelous things;
his right hand and his holy arm*
 have worked salvation for him.
He has remembered his love*
 and his faithfulness to the
 house of Israel;
all the ends of the earth have seen*
 the salvation of our God.

Shout for joy to the Lord, all the earth,*
 shout for joy before
 the Lord, the King.

Glory be to the Father and to the Son*
 and to the Holy Spirit;
as it was in the beginning,*
 is now, and will be forever. Amen

For to us a child is born,*
 to us a son is given.
And he will be called*
 Wonderful Counselor, Mighty God.

*(Antiphon, Is. 9:6;
Ps. 98:1, 3-4a, 6b)*

COLLECT OF THE DAY

Direct us, O Lord, in all our actions by your gracious favor, and further us with your continual help that in all our works, begun, continued, and ended in your name, we may glorify your holy name and finally by your mercy receive eternal life; through Jesus Christ, your Son, our Lord, who lives and reigns with you and the Holy Spirit, one God, now and forever.(8)

READINGS

One-Year Series | Three-Year Series

Psalm 111
Isaiah 63:7-9
1 Corinthians 1:(18-20) 21-25
Luke 2:25-38

A. Psalm 111
 Isaiah 63:7-9
 Galatians 4:4-7
 Matthew 2:13-15, 19-23

B. Psalm 111
 Isaiah 45:22-25
 Colossians 3:12-17
 Luke 2:25-40

C. Psalm 111
 Jeremiah 31:10-13
 Hebrews 2:10-18
 Luke 2:41-52

GRADUAL

To us a child is born, to us a son is given,*
 and the government will be on his shoulders.
And he will be called Wonderful Counselor, Mighty God,*
 Everlasting Father, Prince of Peace.
Sing to the Lord a new song,*
 for he has done marvelous things. *(Is. 9:6; Ps. 98:1)*

VERSE

Alleluia. Alleluia. Let the peace of Christ rule in your hearts. Alleluia. *(Col. 3:15a)*

SECOND SUNDAY AFTER CHRISTMAS

INTROIT

The Word became flesh and lived
for a while among us.*
  We have seen his glory, the glory of the
  one and only Son, who came from the
  Father, full of grace and truth.

How good it is to sing praises
to our God,*
  how pleasant and fitting to praise him!
Great is our Lord and mighty in power;*
  his understanding has no limit.
The Lord delights in those who fear him,*
  who put their hope in
his unfailing love.

Extol the Lord, O Jerusalem;*
  praise your God, O Zion.

Glory be to the Father and to the Son*
  and to the Holy Spirit;
as it was in the beginning,*
  is now, and will be forever. Amen

The Word became flesh and lived
for a while among us.*
  We have seen his glory, the glory of the
  one and only Son, who came from the
  Father, full of grace and truth.

(Antiphon, John 1:14;
Ps. 147:1, 5, 11-12)

COLLECT OF THE DAY

O God, our Maker and Redeemer, who wonderfully created us and in the incarnation of your Son yet more wondrously restored our human nature, grant that we may ever be alive in him who made himself to be like us; through Jesus Christ, our Lord, who lives and reigns with you and the Holy Spirit, one God, now and forever. (9)

READINGS

One-Year Series

Psalm 148
1 Samuel 2:1-10
1 John 5:11-13
Luke 2:39-52

Three-Year Series

A, B, C. Psalm 147:12-20
Isaiah 61:10—62:3
Ephesians 1:3-6, 15-18
John 1:1-18

GRADUAL

To us a child is born, to us a son is given,*
  and the government will be on his shoulders.
And he will be called Wonderful Counselor, Mighty God,*
  Everlasting Father, Prince of Peace.
Sing to the Lord a new song,*
  for he has done marvelous things. *(Is. 9:6; Ps. 98:1a)*

VERSE

Alleluia. Alleluia. All the ends of the earth have seen the salvation of our God. Alleluia. *(Ps. 98:3b)*

THE EPIPHANY OF OUR LORD

INTROIT

All kings will bow down to him*
and all nations will serve him.

Endow the king with your justice,
O God,*
the royal son with your righteousness.
He will judge your people in
righteousness,*
your afflicted ones with justice.
For he will deliver the needy who
cry out,*
the afflicted who have no one to help.
He will take pity on the
weak and the needy*
and save the needy from death.

He will rescue them from
oppression and violence,*
for precious is their blood in his sight.
May his name endure forever;*
may it continue as long as the sun.

Glory be to the Father and to the Son*
and to the Holy Spirit;
as it was in the beginning,*
is now, and will be forever. Amen

All kings will bow down to him*
and all nations will serve him.

(Antiphon, Ps. 72:11;
Ps. 72:1-2, 12-14, 17a)

COLLECT OF THE DAY

O God, by the leading of a star you once made known to all nations your only-begotten Son; now lead us, who know you by faith, to know in heaven the fullness of your divine goodness; through Jesus Christ, our Lord, who lives and reigns with you and the Holy Spirit, one God, now and forever.(10)

READINGS

One-Year Series
Psalm 72:1-11
Isaiah 60:1(2-4)5-6
Ephesians 3:1-12
Matthew 2:1-12

Three-Year Series
A, B, C. Psalm 72
Isaiah 60:1-6
Ephesians 3:2-12
Matthew 2:1-12

GRADUAL

Praise the Lord, all you nations;*
extol him, all you peoples.
For great is his love toward us,*
and the faithfulness of the Lord endures forever.
Ascribe to the Lord the glory due his name;*
bring an offering and come into his courts. *(Ps. 117; 96:8)*

VERSE

Alleluia. Alleluia. We saw his star in the east and have come to worship him. Alleluia. *(Matt. 2:2b)*

THE BAPTISM OF OUR LORD
First Sunday after the Epiphany

INTROIT

Praise be to the Lord God, the God of Israel, who alone does marvelous deeds.*
Praise be to his glorious name forever.

You are the most excellent of men*
and your lips have been anointed with grace, since God has blessed you forever.
Your throne, O God, will last for ever and ever;*
a scepter of justice will be the scepter of your kingdom.
You love righteousness and hate wickedness;*
therefore God, your God, has set you above your companions by anointing you with the oil of joy.

Glory be to the Father and to the Son*
and to the Holy Spirit;
as it was in the beginning,*
is now, and will be forever. Amen

Praise be to the Lord God, the God of Israel, who alone does marvelous deeds.*
Praise be to his glorious name forever.

*(Antiphon, Ps. 72:18-19a;
Ps. 45:2, 6-7)*

COLLECT OF THE DAY

Father in heaven, as at the baptism in the Jordan river you once proclaimed Jesus your beloved Son and anointed him with the Holy Spirit, grant that all who are baptized in his name may faithfully keep the covenant into which they have been called, boldly confess their Savior, and with him be heirs of life eternal; through Jesus Christ, who lives and reigns with you and the Holy Spirit, one God, now and forever.(11)

READINGS

One-Year Series

Psalm 45:2-7
Isaiah 42:1(2-4)5-7
1 Corinthians 1:26-31
Mark 1:9-11
or Matthew 3:13-17

Three-Year Series

A. Psalm 45:7-9
Isaiah 42:1-7
Acts 10:34-38
Matthew 3:13-17

B. Psalm 45:7-9
Isaiah 42:1-7
Acts 10:34-38
Mark 1:4-11

C. Psalm 45:7-9
Isaiah 42:1-7
Acts 10:34-38
Luke 3:15-17, 21-22

GRADUAL

Praise the Lord, all you ñations;*
    extol him, all you peoples.
For great is his love toward us,*
    and the faithfulness of the Lord endures forever.
Ascribe to the Lord the glory due his name;*
    bring an offering and come into his courts. *(Ps. 117; 96:8)*

VERSE

Alleluia. Alleluia. You are my Son, whom I love; with you I am well pleased.
Alleluia. *(Mark 1:11b)*

SECOND SUNDAY AFTER THE EPIPHANY

INTROIT

V Eb: Lydian

I do not hide your righteousness in my
heart; I speak of your faithfulness
and salvation.*
    To do your will, O my God,
    is my desire.

I waited patiently for the Lord;*
    he turned to me and heard my cry.
He lifted me out of the slimy pit,*
    out of the mud and mire;
he set my feet on a rock*
    and gave me a firm place to stand.
He put a new song in my mouth,*
    a hymn of praise to our God.
Many will see and fear*
    and put their trust in the Lord.
Blessed is the man*
    who makes the Lord his trust.
Many, O Lord my God,*
    are the wonders you have done.

I do not conceal your love
and your truth*
    from the great assembly.
Do not withhold your mercy
from me, O Lord;*
    may your love and your truth
    always protect me.

Glory be to the Father and to the Son*
    and to the Holy Spirit;
as it was in the beginning,*
    is now, and will be forever. Amen

I do not hide your righteousness
in my heart; I speak of your
faithfulness and salvation.*
    To do your will, O my God,
    is my desire.

*(Antiphon, Ps 40:10a, 8a;
Ps. 40:1-4a, 5a, 10b-11)*

COLLECT OF THE DAY

Almighty and eternal God, Governor of all things in heaven and on earth, mercifully
hear the prayers of your people, and grant us your peace in our days; through Jesus
Christ, our Lord, who lives and reigns with you and the Holy Spirit, one God, now and
forever.(12)

READINGS

One-Year Series		Three-Year Series	
Psalm 36:5-10	A. Psalm 92:1-5	B. Psalm 67	C. Psalm 36:5-10
Isaiah 61:1-3	Isaiah 49:1-6	1 Samuel 3:1-10	Isaiah 62:1-5
James 1:17-18	1 Corinthians 1:1-9	1 Corinthians 6:12-20	1 Corinthians 12:1-11
John 2:1-11	John 1:29-41	John 1:43-51	John 2:1-11

GRADUAL

Praise the Lord, all you ñations;*
  extol him, all you peoples.
For great is his love toward us,*
  and the faithfulness of the Lord endures forever.
Ascribe to the Lord the glory due his name;*
  bring an offering and come into his courts.   *(Ps. 117; 96:8)*

VERSE

Alleluia. Alleluia. He said to me, "You are my servant, Israel, in whom I will display my splendor." Alleluia.   *(Is. 49:3)*

THIRD SUNDAY AFTER THE EPIPHANY

INTROIT

From the rising of the sun
to the place where it sets*
  the name of the Lord is to be praised.

Praise, O servants of the Lord,*
  praise the name of the Lord.
Let the name of the Lord be praised,*
  both now and forevermore.
The Lord is exalted over all the ñations,*
  his glory above the heavens.
He raises the poor from the dust*
  and lifts the needy from the ash heap;
he seats them with princes,*
  with the princes of their people.

He settles the barren woman
in her home*
  as a happy mother of children.

Glory be to the Father and to the Son*
  and to the Holy Spirit;
as it was in the beginning,*
  is now, and will be forever. Amen

From the rising of the sun
to the place where it sets*
  the name of the Lord is to be praised.

(Antiphon, Ps. 113:3;
Ps. 113:1-2, 4, 7-9)

COLLECT OF THE DAY

O Lord God Almighty, because you have always supplied your servants with the several gifts which come from your Holy Spirit alone, leave also us not destitute

23

of your manifold gifts nor of grace to use them always to your honor and glory and the good of others; through Jesus Christ, your Son, our Lord, who lives and reigns with you and the Holy Spirit, one God, now and forever.(13)

READINGS

One-Year Series		Three-Year Series	
Psalm 18:1-6	A. Psalm 27:1-9	B. Psalm 62:5-12	C. Psalm 146
Jeremiah 9:23-24	Isaiah 9:1-4	Jonah 3:1-5, 10	Isaiah 61:1-6
1 Corinthians 9:19-27	*or* Amos 3:1-8	1 Corinthians 7:29-31	1 Corinthians 12:12-21,
Matthew 20:1-16	1 Corinthians 1:10-17	Mark 1:14-20	26-27
	Matthew 4:12-23		Luke 4:14-21

GRADUAL

Praise the Lord, all you ñations;*
   extol him, all you p̄eoples.
For great is his love toward us,*
   and the faithfulness of the Lord endures forēver.
Ascribe to the Lord the glory due his name;*
   bring an offering and come into his courts.   *(Ps. 117; 96:8)*

VERSE

Alleluia. Alleluia. Jesus went throughout Galilee, teaching in their synagogues, preaching the good news of the kingdom, and healing every disease and sickness among the people. Alleluia.   *(Matt. 4:23)*

FOURTH SUNDAY AFTER THE EPIPHANY

INTROIT

The Lord watches over the way
of the r̄ighteous,*
   but the way of the wicked will p̄erish.

Blessed is the man who does not
walk in the counsel of the w̄icked*
   or stand in the way of sinners
   or sit in the seat of m̄ockers.
But his delight is in the law ōf the Lord,*
   and on his law he meditates
   day and night.

He is like a tree planted by streams of
water, which yields its fruit in season and
whose leaf does not w̄ither.*
   Whatever he does p̄rospers.
Not so the w̄icked!*
   They are like chaff that
   the wind blows away.

Introit continues on the next page

Therefore the wicked will not stand
in the judgment,*
    nor sinners in the assembly
    of the righteous.

Glory be to the Father and to the Son*
    and to the Holy Spirit;
as it was in the beginning,*
    is now, and will be forever. Āmen

The Lord watches over the way
of the righteous,*
    but the way of the wicked will perish.

*(Antiphon, Ps. 1:6;
Ps. 1:1-5)*

COLLECT OF THE DAY

Almighty God, because you know that we are set among so many and great dangers that by reason of the weakness of our fallen nature we cannot always stand upright, grant us your strength and protection to support us in all dangers and carry us through all temptations; through our Lord Jesus Christ, your Son, who lives and reigns with you and the Holy Spirit, one God, now and forever. (14)

READINGS

One-Year Series		Three-Year Series	
Psalm 126	A. Psalm 1	B. Psalm 1	C. Psalm 36
Amos 8:11-12	Micah 6:1-8	Deuteronomy 18:15-20	Jeremiah 1:4-10
Hebrews 4:12-13	1 Corinthians 1:26-31	1 Corinthians 8:1-13	1 Corinthians 12:27—
Luke 8:4-15	Matthew 5:1-12	Mark 1:21-28	13:13
			Luke 4:21-32

GRADUAL

Praise the Lord, all you nations;*
    extol him, all you peoples.
For great is his love toward us,*
    and the faithfulness of the Lord endures forever.
Ascribe to the Lord the glory due his name;*
    bring an offering and come into his courts. *(Ps. 117; 96:8)*

VERSE

Alleluia. Alleluia. The Spirit of the Lord is on me, because he has anointed me to preach good news to the poor. Alleluia. *(Luke 4:18a)*

FIFTH SUNDAY AFTER THE EPIPHANY

INTROIT

V Eb: Lydian

Even in darkness light dawns
for the upright,*
    for the gracious and compassionate
    and righteous man.

Praise the Lord. Blessed is the man
who fears the Lord,*
    who finds great delight
    in his commands.
Wealth and riches are in his house,*
    and his righteousness endures forever.
He will have no fear of bad news;*
    his heart is steadfast, trusting
    in the Lord.
His heart is secure, he will have no fear;*
    in the end he will look in triumph
    on his foes.

He has scattered abroad his gifts
to the poor,*
    his righteousness endures forever;
    his horn will be lifted high in honor.

Glory be to the Father and to the Son*
    and to the Holy Spirit;
as it was in the beginning,*
    is now, and will be forever. Amen

Even in darkness light dawns
for the upright,*
    for the gracious and compassionate
    and righteous man.

*(Antiphon, Ps. 112:4;
Ps. 112:1, 3, 7-9)*

COLLECT OF THE DAY

O God, our loving Father, through the grace of your Holy Spirit you plant the gifts of your love into the hearts of your faithful people. Grant to your servants soundness of mind and body, so that they may love you with their whole strength and with their whole heart do these things that are pleasing in your sight; through Jesus Christ, your Son, our Lord, who lives and reigns with you and the Holy Spirit, one God, now and forever.(15)

READINGS

One-Year Series		Three-Year Series	
Psalm 121	A. Psalm 119:17-24	B. Psalm 147:1-12	C. Psalm 136
Isaiah 49:1-6	Isaiah 58:5-9a	Job 7:1-7	Isaiah 6:1-8(9-13)
Romans 1:16-17	1 Corinthians 2:1-5	1 Corinthians 9:16-23	1 Corinthians 14:12b-20
Matthew 8:5-17	Matthew 5:13-20	Mark 1:29-39	Luke 5:1-11

GRADUAL

Praise the Lord, all you nations;*
    extol him, all you peoples.
For great is his love toward us,*
    and the faithfulness of the Lord endures forever.
Ascribe to the Lord the glory due his name;*
    bring an offering and come into his courts. *(Ps. 117; 96:8)*

VERSE

Alleluia. Alleluia. When Jesus spoke again to the people, he said, "I am the light of the world. Whoever follows me will never walk in darkness, but will have the light of life." Alleluia. *(John 8:12)*

SIXTH SUNDAY AFTER THE EPIPHANY

INTROIT

Many are the woes of the wicked,*
 but the Lord's unfailing love
 surrounds the man who trusts in him.

Blessed is he whose transgressions
are forgiven,*
 whose sins are covered.
Blessed is the man whose sin the Lord
does not count against him*
 and in whose spirit is no deceit.
I acknowledged my sin to you
and did not cover up my iniquity.*
 I said, "I will confess my
 transgressions to the Lord"—and you
 forgave the guilt of my sin.
Therefore let everyone who is godly pray
to you while you may be found;*
 surely when the mighty waters rise,
 they will not reach him.

You are my hiding place; you will protect
me from trouble*
 and surround me with songs
 of deliverance.

Glory be to the Father and to the Son*
 and to the Holy Spirit;
as it was in the beginning,*
 is now, and will be forever. Amen

Many are the woes of the wicked,*
 but the Lord's unfailing love
 surrounds the man who trusts in him.

*(Antiphon, Ps 32:10;
Ps. 32:1-2, 5-7)*

COLLECT OF THE DAY

O Lord, mercifully receive the prayers of your people who call upon you, and grant
that they may know and understand the things they ought to do and also may have
grace and strength to accomplish them; through Jesus Christ, your Son, who lives and
reigns with you and the Holy Spirit, one God, now and forever.(16)

READINGS

One-Year Series		Three-Year Series	
Psalm 92:1-7	A. Psalm 119:1-16	B. Psalm 32	C. Psalm 1
Exodus 15:1-13(14-18)	Deuteronomy 30:15-20	2 Kings 5:1-14	Jeremiah 17:5-8
Ephesians 1:15-23	1 Corinthians 2:6-13	1 Corinthians 9:24-27	1 Corinthians 15:12,
Matthew 8:23-27	Matthew 5:20-37	Mark 1:40-45	16-20
			Luke 6:17-26

GRADUAL

Praise the Lord, all you nations;*
 extol him, all you peoples.

Gradual continues on the next page

For great is his love toward us,*
  and the faithfulness of the Lord endures forever.
Ascribe to the Lord the glory due his name;*
  bring an offering and come into his courts. *(Ps. 117; 96:8)*

VERSE

Alleluia. Alleluia. Lord, to whom shall we go? You have the words of eternal life. Alleluia. *(John 6:68)*

SEVENTH SUNDAY AFTER THE EPIPHANY

INTROIT

V E♭: Lydian

The Lord is compassionate and gracious,*
  slow to anger, abounding in love.

Praise the Lord, O my soul;*
  all my inmost being,
  praise his holy name.
Praise the Lord, O my soul,*
  and forget not all his benefits.
He forgives all my sins*
  and heals all my diseases;
he redeems my life from the pit*
  and crowns me with love
  and compassion.
He satisfies my desires with good things,*
  so that my youth is renewed
  like the eagle's.
He does not treat us as our sins deserve*
  or repay us according to our iniquities.

For as high as the heavens are above
the earth,*
  so great is his love for those
  who fear him;
as far as the east is from the west,*
  so far has he removed our
  transgressions from us.

Glory be to the Father and to the Son*
  and to the Holy Spirit;
as it was in the beginning,*
  is now, and will be forever. Amen

The Lord is compassionate and gracious,*
  slow to anger, abounding in love.

*(Antiphon, Ps. 103:8;
Ps. 103:1-5, 10-12)*

COLLECT OF THE DAY

O Lord, keep your family and Church continually in the true faith that they who lean on the hope of your heavenly grace may ever be defended by your mighty power; through our Lord Jesus Christ, your Son, who lives and reigns with you and the Holy Spirit, one God, now and forever.(17)

READINGS

One-Year Series		Three-Year Series	
Psalm 1	A. Psalm 103:1-13	B. Psalm 130	C. Psalm 103:1-13
Deuteronomy 7:6-9	Leviticus 19:1-2, 17-18	Isaiah 43:18-25	Genesis 45:3-8a, 15
1 Corinthians 1:4-9	1 Corinthians 3:10-11,	2 Corinthians 1:18-22	1 Corinthians 15:35-
Matthew 13:24-30(36-43)	16-23	Mark 2:1-12	38a, 42-50
	Matthew 5:38-48		Luke 6:27-38

GRADUAL

Praise the Lord, all you ñations;*
   extol him, all you p̄eoples.
For great is his love toward us,*
   and the faithfulness of the Lord endures forēver.
Ascribe to the Lord the glory d̊ue his name;*
   bring an offering and come into his courts.   *(Ps. 117; 96:8)*

VERSE

Alleluia. Alleluia. Bless those who persecute you; bless and do not curse.
Alleluia.   *(Rom. 12:14)*

EIGHTH SUNDAY AFTER THE EPIPHANY

INTROIT

Find rest, O my soul, in G̊od alone;*
   my salvation and my honor
   dep̊end on God.

My soul finds rest in G̊od alone;*
   my salvation c̊omes from him.
He alone is my rock and my salv̄ation;*
   he is my fortress, I will
      never be s̄haken.
Trust in him at all times, O p̄eople;*
   pour out your hearts to him,
      for God is our r̄efuge.
One thing God has spoken,
two things h̊ave I heard:*
   that you, O God, are strong,
   and that you, O Lord, are l̄oving.

Surely you will reward each p̄erson*
   according to what h̊e has done.

Glory be to the Father and t̊o the Son*
   and to the Holy S̄pirit;
as it was in the beḡinning,*
   is now, and will be forever. Āmen

Find rest, O my soul, in G̊od alone;*
   my salvation and my honor
   dep̊end on God.

*(Antiphon, Ps. 62:5a, 7a;
Ps. 62:1-2, 8, 11-12)*

29

COLLECT OF THE DAY

O Lord, mercifully hear our prayers, and having set us free from the bonds of our sins, defend us from all evil; through Jesus Christ, your Son, our Lord, who lives and reigns with you and the Holy Spirit, one God, now and forever.(18)

READINGS

One-Year Series

Psalm 34:17-22
Isaiah 50:4-7(8-9)
1 Corinthians 13:1-13
Mark 8:31-38

A. Psalm 62
Isaiah 49:13-18
1 Corinthians 4:1-13
Matthew 6:24-34

Three-Year Series

B. Psalm 103:1-13
Hosea 2:14-16(17-18)
19-20
2 Corinthians 3:1b-6
Mark 2:18-22

C. Psalm 92
Jeremiah 7:1-7(8-15)
1 Corinthians 15:51-58
Luke 6:39-49

GRADUAL

Praise the Lord, all you ñations;*
 extol him, all you peoples.
For great is his love toward us,*
 and the faithfulness of the Lord endures forĕver.
Ascribe to the Lord the glory due his name;*
 bring an offering and come into his courts. *(Ps. 117; 96:8)*

VERSE

Alleluia. Alleluia. Because of the Lord's great love we are not consumed, for his compassions never fail. Alleluia. *(Lam. 3:22)*

THE TRANSFIGURATION OF OUR LORD
Last Sunday after the Epiphany

INTROIT

Exalt the Lord our God and worship
at his holy ñountain,*
 for the Lord our God is holy.

The Lord reigns,*
 let the nations tremble;
he sits enthroned between the cherubim,*
 let the ĕarth shake.
Great is the Lord in Žion;*
 he is exalted over all the ñations.

Let them praise your great
and awesome name—*
 he is holy.
The King is mighty, he loves justice—*
 you have established equity;
in Jacob you have done*
 what is just and right.

Introit continues on the next page

Exalt the Lord our God and worship
at his footstool;*
  he is holy.

Glory be to the Father and to the Son*
  and to the Holy Spirit;
as it was in the beginning,*
  is now, and will be forever. Amen

Exalt the Lord our God and worship
at his holy mountain,*
  for the Lord our God is holy.

*(Antiphon, Ps. 99:9;
Ps. 99:1-5)*

COLLECT OF THE DAY

O God, in the glorious transfiguration of your only-begotten Son you once confirmed the mysteries of the faith by the testimony of the ancient fathers, and in the voice that came from the bright cloud you wondrously foreshowed our adoption by grace. Therefore mercifully make us coheirs with our King of his glory, and bring us to the fullness of our inheritance in heaven; through Jesus Christ, our Lord, who lives and reigns with you and the Holy Spirit, one God, now and forever.(19)

READINGS

One-Year Series

Psalm 84:1-10
Exodus 24:4b-18
2 Peter 1:16-21
or 2 Corinthians 4:
  6-10
Luke 9:28-36

Three-Year Series

A. Psalm 2:6-12
  Exodus 24:12, 15-18
  2 Peter 1:16-19
    (20-21)
  Matthew 17:1-9

B. Psalm 50:1-6
  2 Kings 2:1-12c
  2 Corinthians 3:12—
    4:2
  Mark 9:2-9

C. Psalm 77
  Deuteronomy 34:1-12
  2 Corinthians 4:3-6
  Luke 9:28-36

GRADUAL

Praise the Lord, all you nations;*
  extol him, all you peoples.
For great is his love toward us,*
  and the faithfulness of the Lord endures forever.
Ascribe to the Lord the glory due his name;*
  bring an offering and come into his courts.   *(Ps. 117; 96:8)*

VERSE

Alleluia. Alleluia. You are the most excellent of men and your lips have been anointed with grace. Alleluia.   *(Ps. 45:2a)*

ASH WEDNESDAY

INTROIT

31

The sacrifices of God are a broken spirit; *
  a broken and contrite heart,
  O God, you will not despise.

Have mercy upon me, O God, *
  according to your unfailing love;
according to your great compassion *
  blot out my transgressions.
Wash away all my iniquity *
  and cleanse me from my sin.
For I know my transgressions, *
  and my sin is always before me.
Surely you desire truth in the inner parts; *
  you teach me wisdom in
  the inmost place.
Cleanse me with hyssop,
and I will be clean; *
  wash me, and I will be
  whiter than snow.
Let me hear joy and gladness; *
  let the bones you have crushed rejoice.

Hide your face from my sins *
  and blot out all my iniquity.
Create in me a pure heart, O God, *
  and renew a steadfast spirit within me.
Do not cast me from your presence *
  or take your Holy Spirit from me.
Restore to me the joy of your salvation *
  and grant me a willing spirit,
  to sustain me.

Glory be to the Father and to the Son *
  and to the Holy Spirit;
as it was in the beginning, *
  is now, and will be forever. Amen

The sacrifices of God are a broken spirit; *
  a broken and contrite heart,
  O God, you will not despise.

(Antiphon, Ps. 51:17;
Ps. 51:1-3, 6-12)

COLLECT OF THE DAY

Almighty and everlasting God, because you hate nothing you have made and forgive the sins of all who are penitent, create in us new and contrite hearts that we, worthily repenting our sins and acknowledging our wretchedness, may obtain from you, the God of all mercy, perfect remission and forgiveness; through Jesus Christ, your Son, our Lord, who lives and reigns with you and the Holy Spirit, one God, now and forever. (20)

READINGS

One-Year Series

Psalm 51:1-13
Isaiah 59:12-20
2 Corinthians 5:19—6:2
Matthew 11:20-30

Three-Year Series

A, B, C. Psalm 51:1-13
  Joel 2:12-19
  2 Corinthians 5:20b—6:2
  Matthew 6:1-6, 16-21

GRADUAL

[Oh, come,] let us fix our eyes on Jesus, *
  the author and perfecter of our faith,
who for the joy set before him endured the cross,
scorning its shame, *
  and sat down at the right hand of the throne of God.   *(Heb. 12:2)*

VERSE

Return to the Lord your God, for he is gracious and compassionate, slow to anger and abounding in love.   *(Joel 2:13b)*

FIRST SUNDAY IN LENT

INTROIT

*   IX g: Aeolian

He will call upon me,
and I will answer him;*
   I will be with him in trouble,
   I will deliver him and honor him.
With long life will I satisfy him*
   and show him my salvation.

If you make the Most High
your dwelling—*
   even the Lord, who is my refuge—
then no harm will befall you,*
   no disaster will come near your tent.
For he will command his angels
concerning you*
   to guard you in all your ways;
they will lift you up in their hands,*
   so that you will not strike your foot
   against a stone.
You will tread upon the lion and
the cobra;*
   you will trample the great lion and
   the serpent.

"Because he loves me," says the Lord,
"I will rescue him;*
   I will protect him, for he
   acknowledges my name.
He will call upon me, and I will
answer him;*
   I will be with him in trouble,
   I will deliver him and honor him."

Glory be to the Father and to the Son*
   and to the Holy Spirit;
as it was in the beginning,*
   is now, and will be forever. Amen

He will call upon me,
and I will answer him;*
   I will be with him in trouble,
   I will deliver him and honor him.
With long life will I satisfy him*
   and show him my salvation.

(Antiphon, Ps. 91:15-16;
Ps. 91:9-15)

COLLECT OF THE DAY

O almighty and eternal God, we implore you to direct, sanctify, and govern our hearts and bodies in the ways of your laws and the works of your commandments that through your mighty protection, both now and ever, we may be preserved in body and in soul; through our Lord Jesus Christ, your Son, who lives and reigns with you and the Holy Spirit, one God, now and forever.(21)

READINGS

One-Year Series

Psalm 91:9-16
Genesis 3:1-19
Hebrews 4:14-16
Matthew 4:1-11

A. Psalm 130
   Genesis 2:7-9, 15-
     17; 3:1-7
   Romans 5:12 (13-16)
     17-19
   Matthew 4:1-11

Three-Year Series

B. Psalm 6
   Genesis 22:1-18
   Romans 8:31-39
   Mark 1:12-15

C. Psalm 91
   Deuteronomy 26:5-10
   Romans 10:8b-13
   Luke 4:1-13

GRADUAL

[Oh, come,] let us fix our eyes on Jesus,*
   the author and perfecter of our faith,
who for the joy set before him endured the cross,
scorning its shame,*
   and sat down at the right hand of the throne of God.   *(Heb. 12:2)*

VERSE

Put on the full armor of God so that you can take your stand against the devil's schemes.   *(Eph. 6:11)*

SECOND SUNDAY IN LENT

INTROIT

IX g: Aeolian

Remember, O Lord, your great mercy
and love,*
   for they are from of old.

You who fear him, trust in the Lord—*
   he is their help and shield.
The Lord remembers us and
will bless us:*
   He will bless the house of Israel,
   he will bless the house of Aaron,
he will bless those who fear the Lord—*
   small and great alike.
It is we who extol the Lord,*
   both now and forevermore.
   Praise the Lord.

Glory be to the Father and to the Son*
   and to the Holy Spirit;
as it was in the beginning,*
   is now, and will be forever. Amen

Remember, O Lord, your great mercy
and love,*
   for they are from of old.

*(Antiphon, Ps. 25:6;
Ps. 115:11-13, 18)*

COLLECT OF THE DAY

O God, whose glory it is always to have mercy, be gracious to all who have gone astray from your ways, and bring them again with penitent hearts and steadfast faith to embrace and hold fast the unchangeable truth of your Word; through Jesus Christ, your Son, our Lord, who lives and reigns with you and the Holy Spirit, one God, now and forever.(22)

READINGS

One-Year Series		Three-Year Series	
Psalm 27:7-14	A. Psalm 105:4-11	B. Psalm 142	C. Psalm 4
Isaiah 5:1-7	Genesis 12:1-8	Genesis 28:10-17	Jeremiah 26:8-15
Romans 5:6-11	Romans 4:1-5, 13-17	(18-22)	Philippians 3:17—4:1
Mark 12:1-12	John 4:5-26 (27-30,	Romans 5:1-11	Luke 13:31-35
	39-42)	Mark 8:31-38	

GRADUAL

[Oh, come,] let us fix our eyes on Jesus,*
    the author and perfecter of our faith,
who for the joy set before him endured the cross,
scorning its shame,*
    and sat down at the right hand of the throne of God. *(Heb. 12:2)*

VERSE

Jesus humbled himself and became obedient to death—even death on a cross!
(Phil. 2:8b)

THIRD SUNDAY IN LENT

INTROIT

IX g: Aeolian

My eyes are ever on the Lord,*
    for only he will release my feet
from the snare.

I cry aloud to the Lord;*
    I lift up my voice to the Lord
    for mercy.
I cry to you, O Lord;*
    I say, "You are my refuge,
    my portion in the land of the living."
Listen to my cry, for I am
in desperate need;*
    rescue me from those who pursue me,
    for they are too strong for me.
Set me free from my prison that
I may praise your name.*

Then the righteous will gather
about me because of your
goodness to me.

Glory be to the Father and to the Son*
    and to the Holy Spirit;
as it was in the beginning,*
    is now, and will be forever. Amen

My eyes are ever on the Lord,*
    for only he will release my feet
from the snare.

*(Antiphon, Ps. 25:15;
Ps. 142:1, 5-7)*

35

COLLECT OF THE DAY

Almighty God, because you know that we of ourselves have no strength, keep us both outwardly and inwardly that we may be defended from all adversities that may happen to the body and from all evil thoughts that may assault and hurt the soul; through Jesus Christ, your Son, our Lord, who lives and reigns with you and the Holy Spirit, one God, now and forever. (23)

READINGS

One-Year Series

Psalm 90:1-12
Jeremiah 20:7-12
Romans 12:1-2
or Ephesians 5:1-2, 6-9
Luke 9:51-62

A. Psalm 142
   Isaiah 42:14-21
   Ephesians 5:8-14
   John 9:1-41
   or John 9:13-17, 34-39

Three-Year Series

B. Psalm 19:7-14
   Exodus 20:1-17
   1 Corinthians 1:22-25
   John 2:13-22

C. Psalm 126
   Exodus 3:1-8a, 10-15
   1 Corinthians 10:1-13
   Luke 13:1-9

GRADUAL

[Oh, come,] let us fix our eyes on Jesus,*
    the author and perfecter of our faith,
who for the joy set before him endured the cross,
scorning its shame,*
    and sat down at the right hand of the throne of God.   *(Heb. 12:2)*

VERSE

Just as Moses lifted up the snake in the desert, so the Son of Man must be lifted up, that everyone who believes in him may have eternal life.   *(John 3:14-15)*

FOURTH SUNDAY IN LENT

INTROIT (One-Year Series)   INTROIT (Three-Year Series)

Rejoice with Jerusalem and
be glad for her,*
    all you who love her;
rejoice greatly with her,*
    all you who mourn over her.

Praise be to the Lord,*
    for he has heard my cry for mercy.

Wait for the Lord;*
    be strong and take heart
    and wait for the Lord.

One thing I ask of the Lord, this is
what I seek: that I may dwell in the
house of the Lord all the days of my life,*
    to gaze upon the beauty of the Lord
    and to seek him in his temple.

Introit continues on the next page   *Introit continues on the next page*

The Lord is my strength and my shield;*
  my heart trusts in him, and
  I am helped.
The Lord is the strength of his people,*
  a fortress of salvation for his
  anointed one.
Save your people and bless
your inheritance;*
  be their shepherd and carry
  them forever.

Glory be to the Father and to the Son*
  and to the Holy Spirit;
as it was in the beginning,*
  is now, and will be forever. Amen

Rejoice with Jerusalem and
be glad for her,*
  all you who love her;
rejoice greatly with her,*
  all you who mourn over her.

(Antiphon, Is. 66:10;
Ps. 28:6-7a, 8-9)

For in the day of trouble he will keep me
safe in his dwelling;*
  he will hide me in the shelter of his
  tabernacle and set me high
  upon a rock.
At his tabernacle will I sacrifice
with shouts of joy;*
  I will sing and make music to the Lord.

Glory be to the Father and to the Son*
  and to the Holy Spirit;
as it was in the beginning,*
  is now, and will be forever. Amen

Wait for the Lord;*
  be strong and take heart
  and wait for the Lord.

(Antiphon, Ps. 27:14;
Ps. 27:4-5, 6b)

COLLECT OF THE DAY

Almighty God, our heavenly Father, your mercies are new every morning, and though we have in no way deserved your goodness, you still abundantly provide for all our wants of body and soul. Give us, we pray, your Holy Spirit that we may heartily acknowledge your merciful goodness toward us, give thanks for all your benefits, and serve you in willing obedience; through Jesus Christ, your Son, our Lord, who lives and reigns with you and the Holy Spirit, one God, now and forever. (24)

READINGS

One-Year Series

Psalm 146
Isaiah 55:1-7
Acts 2:41a, 42-47
John 6:1-14(15)

A. Psalm 138
   Hosea 5:15—6:2
   Romans 8:1-10
   Matthew 20:17-28

Three-Year Series

B. Psalm 27:1-6(7-14)
   Numbers 21:4-9
   Ephesians 2:4-10
   John 3:14-21

C. Psalm 32
   Isaiah 12:1-6
   1 Corinthians 1:18-31
     or 1 Corinthians 1:18,
     22-25
   Luke 15:1-3, 11-32

GRADUAL

[Oh, come,] let us fix our eyes on Jesus,*
  the author and perfecter of our faith,
who for the joy set before him endured the cross,
scorning its shame,*
  and sat down at the right hand of the throne of God. *(Heb. 12:2)*

VERSE

For God so loved the world that he gave his one and only Son, that whoever believes in him shall not perish but have eternal life. *(John 3:16)*

FIFTH SUNDAY IN LENT

INTROIT

Vindicate me, O God,*
    and plead my cause against an ungodly
    nation; rescue me from deceitful
    and wicked men.

I love the Lord, for he heard my voice;*
    he heard my cry for mercy.
Because he turned his ear to me,*
    I will call on him as long as I live.
The cords of death entangled me,
the anguish of the grave came upon me;*
    I was overcome by trouble and sorrow.
Then I called on the name of the Lord:*
    "O Lord, save me!"
For you, O Lord, have delivered my soul
from death,*
    my eyes from tears, my feet
    from stumbling.

Glory be to the Father and to the Son*
    and to the Holy Spirit;
as it was in the beginning,*
    is now, and will be forever. Amen

Vindicate me, O God,*
    and plead my cause against an ungodly
    nation; rescue me from deceitful
    and wicked men.

*(Antiphon, Ps. 43:1;
Ps. 116:1-4, 8)*

COLLECT OF THE DAY

Almighty and eternal God, because it was your will that your Son should bear the pains of the cross for us and thus remove from us the power of the adversary, help us so to remember and give thanks for our Lord's Passion that we may receive remission of sins and redemption from everlasting death; through Jesus Christ, your Son, our Lord, who lives and reigns with you and the Holy Spirit, one God, now and forever. (25)

READINGS

One-Year Series

Psalm 143:1-10
Genesis 18:20-21, 22b-33
Hebrews 9:15-22
or Romans 5:1-5
Mark 10:32-45

Three-Year Series

A. Psalm 116:1-9
    Ezekiel 37:1-3(4-10)11-14
    Romans 8:11-19
    John 11:1-53
    or John 11:47-53

B. Psalm 51:10-15
    Jeremiah 31:31-34
    Hebrews 5:7-9
    John 12:20-33

C. Psalm 28:1-3, 6-9
    Isaiah 43:16-21
    Philippians 3:8-14
    Luke 20:9-19

GRADUAL

[Oh, come,] let us fix our eyes on Jesus,*
   the author and perfecter of our faith,
who for the joy set before him endured the cross,
scorning its shame,*
   and sat down at the right hand of the throne of God. *(Heb. 12:2)*

VERSE

The Son of Man did not come to be served, but to serve, and to give his life as a ransom for many. *(Mark 10:45)*

PALM SUNDAY
Sunday of the Passion

INTROIT

Into your hands I commit my spirit;*
   redeem me, O Lord, the God of truth.

In you, O Lord, I have taken refuge;*
   let me never be put to shame;
   deliver me in your righteousness.
Since you are my rock and my fortress,*
   for the sake of your name lead and
   guide me.
Into your hands I commit my spirit;*
   redeem me, O Lord, the God of truth.
I hate those who cling to worthless idols;*
   I trust in the Lord.

My times are in your hands;*
   deliver me from my enemies
   and from those who pursue me.
Let your face shine on your servant;*
   save me in your unfailing love.

Into your hands I commit my spirit;*
   redeem me, O Lord, the God of truth.

*(Antiphon, Ps. 31:5;
Ps. 31:1, 3, 5-6, 15-16)*

COLLECT OF THE DAY

Almighty and everlasting God the Father, who sent your Son to take our nature upon him and to suffer death on the cross that all mankind should follow the example of his great humility, mercifully grant that we may both follow the example of our Savior Jesus Christ in his patience and also have our portion in his resurrection; through Jesus Christ, our Lord, who lives and reigns with you and the Holy Spirit, one God, now and forever.(26)

READINGS

One-Year Series   Three-Year Series

Psalm 24   A. Psalm 92   B. Psalm 92   C. Psalm 92
Isaiah 52:13—53:4   Isaiah 50:4-9b   Zechariah 9:9-10   Deuteronomy 32:36-39
or Zechariah 9:9-12   Philippians 2:5-11   Philippians 2:5-11   Philippians 2:5-11
Philippians 2:5-11   Matthew 26:1—27:66   Mark 14:1—15:47   Luke 22:1—23:56
John 12:12-24   or Matthew 27:11-54   or Mark 15:1-39   or Luke 23:1-49
or Matthew 21:1-9

GRADUAL

[Christ] entered the Most Holy Place once for all*
    by his own blood, having obtained eternal redemption.
He is the mediator of a new covenant,*
    that those who are called may receive the promised
    eternal inheritance.
He provided redemption for his people;*
    he ordained his covenant forever.   *(Heb. 9:12b, 15a; Ps. 111:9a)*

VERSE

The hour has come for the Son of Man to be glorified.   *(John 12:23)*

MONDAY IN HOLY WEEK

INTROIT

* III f♯: Phrygian

Continue your love to those
who know you,*
    your righteousness to the upright
    in heart.

Your love, O Lord, reaches to
the heavens,*
    your faithfulness to the skies.
Your righteousness is like the mighty
mountains, your justice like
the great deep.*
    O Lord, you preserve both man
    and beast.
How priceless is your unfailing love!*
    Both high and low among men
    find refuge in the shadow
    of your wings.

They feast on the abundance
of your house;*
    you give them drink from your river
    of delights.
For with you is the fountain of life;*
    in your light we see light.

Continue your love to those
who know you,*
    your righteousness to the upright
    in heart.

*(Antiphon, Ps. 36:10;
Ps. 36:5-9)*

COLLECT OF THE DAY

Almighty God, whose Son Jesus Christ chose to suffer pain before going up to joy, and crucifixion before entering into glory, mercifully grant that we, walking in the way of the cross, may find this path to be the way of life and peace; through Jesus Christ, your Son, our Lord, who lives and reigns with you and the Holy Spirit, one God, now and forever.(27)

READINGS

One-Year Series	Three-Year Series
Psalm 36:5-10	A, B, C. Psalm 36:5-10
Jeremiah 17:13-17	Isaiah 42:1-9
Isaiah 50:5-10	Hebrews 9:11-15
John 12:1-23	John 12:1-11

GRADUAL

[Christ] entered the Most Holy Place once for all*
    by his own blood, having obtained eternal redemption.
He is the mediator of a new covenant,*
    that those who are called may receive the promised
    eternal inheritance.
He provided redemption for his people;*
    he ordained his covenant forever.   *(Heb. 9:12b, 15a; Ps. 111:9a)*

VERSE

May I never boast except in the cross of our Lord Jesus Christ.   *(Gal. 6:14)*

TUESDAY IN HOLY WEEK

INTROIT

In you, O Lord, I have taken refuge;*
    let me never be put to shame.

Rescue me and deliver me in your
righteousness;*
    turn your ear to me and save me.
Be my rock of refuge,*
    to which I can always go;
give the command to save me,*
    for you are my rock and my fortress.

Deliver me, O my God, from the hand of the wicked,*
    from the grasp of evil and cruel men.

In you, O Lord, I have taken refuge;*
    let me never be put to shame.

(Antiphon, Ps. 71:1; Ps. 71:2-4)

41

COLLECT OF THE DAY

Almighty and everlasting God, grant us grace so to pass through this holy time of our Lord's Passion that we may receive the pardon of our sins; through Jesus, Christ, your Son, our Lord, who lives and reigns with you and the Holy Spirit, one God, now and forever. (28)

READINGS

One-Year Series

Psalm 28
Lamentations 1:1, 12-17, 20-21a
Hebrews 9:16-28
John 12:24-43

Three-Year Series

A, B, C. Psalm 18:1-7, 17-20
Isaiah 49:1-6
1 Corinthians 1:18-25
John 12:20-36

GRADUAL

[Christ] entered the Most Holy Place once for all*
  by his own blood, having obtained eternal redemption.
He is the mediator of a new covenant,*
  that those who are called may receive the promised
  eternal inheritance.
He provided redemption for his people;*
  he ordained his covenant forever.   *(Heb. 9:12b, 15a; Ps. 111:9a)*

VERSE

May I never boast except in the cross of our Lord Jesus Christ.   *(Gal. 6:14a)*

WEDNESDAY IN HOLY WEEK

INTROIT

Hasten, O God, to save me*
  O Lord, come quickly to help me.

May those who seek my life*
  be put to shame and confusion;
may all who desire my ruin*
  be turned back in disgrace.
But may all who seek you*
  rejoice and be glad in you;
may those who love your salvation
always say,*
  "Let God be exalted!"

Yet I am poor and needy;*
  come quickly to me, O God.
You are my help and my deliverer;*
  O Lord, do not delay.

Hasten, O God, to save me;*
  O Lord, come quickly to help me.

*(Antiphon, Ps. 70:1;
Ps. 70:2, 4-5)*

COLLECT OF THE DAY

Merciful and everlasting God the Father, who did not spare your only Son but delivered him up for us all that he might bear our sins on the cross, grant that our hearts may be so fixed with steadfast faith in our Savior that we may not fear the power of any adversaries; through Jesus Christ, your Son, our Lord, who lives and reigns with you and the Holy Spirit, one God, now and forever. (29)

READINGS

One-Year Series	Three-Year Series
Psalm 25:14-20	A, B, C. Psalm 18:21-30
Jeremiah 15:15-21	Isaiah 50:4-9b
Isaiah 62:11; 63:1-7	Romans 5:6-11
Luke 22:1—23:42	Matthew 26:14-25

GRADUAL

[Christ] entered the Most Holy Place once for all*
 by his own blood, having obtained eternal redemption.
He is the mediator of a new covenant,*
 that those who are called may receive the promised
 eternal inheritance.
He provided redemption for his people;*
 he ordained his covenant forever. *(Heb. 9:12b, 15a; Ps. 111:9a)*

VERSE

May I never boast except in the cross of our Lord Jesus Christ. *(Gal. 6:14a)*

MAUNDY THURSDAY

INTROIT

I will lift up the cup of salvation*
 and call on the name of the Lord.

How can I repay the Lord*
 for all his goodness to me?
I will lift up the cup of salvation*
 and call on the name of the Lord.
Precious in the sight of the Lord*
 is the death of his saints.
O Lord, truly I am your servant;*

I am your servant, the son of
 your maidservant; you have freed me
 from my chains.
I will sacrifice a thank offering to you*
 and call on the name of the Lord.

I will lift up the cup of salvation*
 and call on the name of the Lord.

*(Antiphon, Ps. 116:13;
Ps. 116:12-13, 15-17)*

43

COLLECT OF THE DAY

O Lord Jesus, since you have left us a memorial of your Passion in a wonderful sacrament, grant, we pray, that we may so use this sacrament of your body and blood that the fruits of your redeeming work may continually be manifest in us; for you live and reign with the Father and the Holy Spirit, one God, now and forever.(30)

READINGS

One-Year Series		Three-Year Series	
Psalm 116:12-19	A. Psalm 116:12-19	B. Psalm 116:12-19	C. Psalm 116:12-19
Exodus 12:1-14	Exodus 12:1-14	Exodus 24:3-11	Jeremiah 31:31-34
1 Corinthians 11:23-32	1 Corinthians 11:17-32	1 Corinthians 10:16-17	Hebrews 10:15-39
or 1 Corinthians 11:17-32	or 1 Corinthians 11:23-26	(18-21)	Luke 22:7-20
John 13:1-15	John 13:1-17, 34	Mark 14:12-26	

GRADUAL

[Christ] entered the Most Holy Place once for all*
  by his own blood, having obtained eternal redemption.
He is the mediator of a new covenant,*
  that those who are called may receive the promised
  eternal inheritance.
He provided redemption for his people;*
  he ordained his covenant forever. *(Heb. 9:12b, 15a; Ps. 111:9a)*

VERSE

For whenever you eat this bread and drink this cup, you proclaim the Lord's death until he comes. *(1 Cor. 11:26)*

GOOD FRIDAY

INTROIT

O Lord, be not far off;*
  O my Strength, come quickly
  to help me.

My God, my God, why have you
forsaken me?*
  Why are you so far from saving me,
  so far from the words of
  my groaning?

In you our fathers put their trust;*
  they trusted and you delivered them.
But I am a worm and not a man,*
  scorned by men and despised by the
  people.

Introit continues on the next page

Yet you brought me out of the womb;*
  you made me trust in you
  even at my mother's breast.
From birth I was cast upon you;*
  from my mother's womb you have
  been my God.
Do not be far from me,*

for trouble is near and there
  is no one to help.

O Lord, be not far off;*
  O my Strength, come quickly
  to help me.

*(Antiphon, Ps. 22:19;
Ps. 22:1, 4, 6, 9-11)*

COLLECT OF THE DAY

Almighty God, graciously behold this your family, for whom our Lord Jesus Christ
was willing to be betrayed, to be given into the hands of sinners, and to suffer death on
the cross; who now lives and reigns with you and the Holy Spirit, one God, now and
forever.(31)

READINGS

One-Year Series

Psalm 22:1-11
Isaiah 53:4-12
or Hosea 6:1-6
2 Corinthians 5:14-21
or Hebrews 5:(1-6)7-9
John 18:1—19:42

Three-Year Series

A, B, C. Psalm 22:1-24
Isaiah 52:13—53:12
or Hosea 6:1-6
Hebrews 4:14-16; 5:7-9
John 18:1—19:42
or John 19:17-30

GRADUAL

[Christ] entered the Most Holy Place once for all*
  by his own blood, having obtained eternal redemption.
He is the mediator of a new covenant,*
  that those who are called may receive the promised
  eternal inheritance.
He provided redemption for his people;*
  he ordained his covenant forever. *(Heb. 9:12b, 15a; Ps. 111:9a)*

VERSE

Surely he took up our infirmities and carried our sorrows, yet we considered him
stricken by God, smitten by him, and afflicted. *(Is. 53:4)*

THE RESURRECTION OF OUR LORD
Easter Eve (Evening Prayer or Vespers)

PSALMODY

* VII E: Mixolydian

From the depths of the grave
I called for help,*
   and you listened to my cry.

In my distress I called to the Lord,
and he answered me.*
   From the depths of the grave I called
   for help, and you listened to my cry.
You hurled me into the deep, into the
very heart of the seas,*
   and the currents swirled about me;
   all your waves and breakers
   swept over me.
I said, "I have been banished
from your sight;*
   yet I will look again toward your
   holy temple."
To the roots of the mountains I sank
down; the earth beneath barred
me in forever.*

But you brought my life up from the
pit, O Lord my God.
When my life was ebbing away, I
remembered you, Lord,*
   and my prayer rose to you, to your
   holy temple.
Those who cling to worthless idols*
   forfeit the grace that could be theirs.
But I, with a song of thanksgiving, will
sacrifice to you.*
   What I have vowed I will
   make good. Salvation comes
   from the Lord.

From the depths of the grave I
called for help,*
   and you listened to my cry.

*(Antiphon, Jonah 2:2b;
Psalmody, Jonah 2:2-4, 6-9)*

READINGS

One-Year Series

Daniel 3:1, 3-9, 12-29
1 Peter 3:17-22
Matthew 27:57-66

ANTIPHON TO THE MAGNIFICAT

You will not abandon me to the grave,*
   nor will you let your Holy One see decay.   *(Ps. 16:10)*

COLLECT OF THE DAY

O God, who made this most holy night to shine with the glory of the resurrection of
our Lord, preserve in all your people the spirit of adoption which you have given that,
made alive in body and soul, they may serve you purely; through Jesus Christ,
your Son, our Lord, who lives and reigns with you and the Holy Spirit, one God, now
and forever.(32)

OR

Abide with us, Lord, for it is toward evening, and the day is far spent. Abide with us
and with your whole Church. Abide with us in the end of the day, in the end of our life,
in the end of the world. Abide with us with your grace and goodness, with your holy
Word and Sacrament, with your strength and blessing. Abide with us when the night of
affliction and temptation comes upon us, the night of fear and despair when death shall
come. Abide with us and with all the faithful through time and eternity.(33)

THE RESURRECTION OF OUR LORD
Easter Day

INTROIT

* VII E: Mixolydian

Alleluia. [Christ] has risen, as he said. *
  He has risen from the dead. Alleluia.

Give thanks to the Lord, for he is good; *
  his love endures forever.
Let Israel say: *
  "His love endures forever."
I was pushed back and about to fall, *
  but the Lord helped me.
I will give you thanks,
for you answered me; *
  you have become my salvation.
The stone the builders rejected *
  has become the capstone:
This is the day the Lord has made; *
  let us rejoice and be glad in it.

Blessed is he who comes in the name
of the Lord, *
  From the house of the Lord
  we bless you.

Glory be to the Father and to the Son *
  and to the Holy Spirit;
as it was in the beginning, *
  is now, and will be forever. Amen

Alleluia, [Christ] has risen, as he said. *
  He has risen from the dead. Alleluia.

(Antiphon, Matt. 28:6a, 7b;
Ps. 118:1-2, 13, 21-22, 24, 26)

COLLECT OF THE DAY

Almighty God the Father, through your only-begotten Son Jesus Christ you have overcome death and opened the gate of everlasting life to us. Grant that we, who celebrate with joy the day of our Lord's resurrection, may be raised from the death of sin by your life-giving Spirit; through Jesus Christ, our Lord, who lives and reigns with you and the Holy Spirit, one God, now and forever.(34)

OR

O God, for our redemption you have given your only-begotten Son to the death of the cross, and by his glorious resurrection you have delivered us from the power of our enemy. Therefore grant that all our sin may be drowned through daily repentance and that day by day a new man may arise to live before you in righteousness and purity forever; through Jesus Christ, your Son, our Lord, who lives and reigns with you and the Holy Spirit, one God, now and forever.(35)

READINGS

One-Year Series

1. Psalm 118:19-29
   Daniel 3:8-25
   1 Corinthians 15:55-58

A. Psalm 118:1-2, 15-24
   Acts 10:34-43
   Colossians 3:1-4

Three-Year Series

B. Psalm 118:1-2, 15-24
   Isaiah 25:6-9
   1 Corinthians 15:19-28

C. Psalm 118:1-2, 15-24
   Exodus 15:1-11
   or Psalm 118:14-24

Readings continue on the next page

Matthew 28:1-10   John 20:1-9(10-18)   Mark 16:1-8   1 Corinthians 15:1-11
2. Psalm 118:19-29   *or* Matthew 28:1-10   *or* John 20:1-9(10-18)   Luke 24:1-11
   Daniel 12:1c-3   *or* John 20:1-9(10-18)
   or Job 19:25-27
   Colossians 3:1-4
   or 1 Corinthians 5:6-8
   Mark 16:1-8
3. Psalm 118:19-29
   Jonah 2:2-9
   1 Corinthians 15:12-20
   or Acts 10:34-43
   John 20:1-9(10-18)
   or Luke 24:33-49

GRADUAL

Christ has risen from the dead.*
    God the Father has crowned him with glory and honor.
He has made him ruler over the works of his hands;*
    he has put everything under his feet.   *(Adapt. from Matt. 28:7; Heb. 2:7; Ps. 8:5-6)*

VERSE

Alleluia. Alleluia. Christ has destroyed death. Alleluia. And has brought life and immortality to light through the Gospel. Alleluia.   *(2 Tim. 1:10b)*

The Victimae Paschali Celebration (Canticles and Chants, No. 11) may follow.

THE RESURRECTION OF OUR LORD
Easter Evening (Evening Prayer or Vespers)

PSALMODY

* VII E: Mixolydian

[The angel spoke to them.] "Don't be alarmed," he said.*
    "You are looking for Jesus the Nazarene, who was crucified.
    He has risen!" Alleluia.

Shout for joy to the Lord, all the earth.*
    Serve the Lord with gladness; come before him with joyful songs.
Know that the Lord is God.*
    It is he who made us, and we are his;
    we are his people, the sheep
    of his pasture.
Enter his gates with thanksgiving and his courts with praise;*
    give thanks to him and praise his name.

For the Lord is good and his love endures forever;*
    his faithfulness continues through all generations.

Glory be to the Father and to the Son*
    and to the Holy Spirit;
as it was in the beginning,*
    is now, and will be forever. Amen

[The angel spoke to them.] "Don't be alarmed," he said.*
    "You are looking for Jesus the Nazarene, who was crucified.
    He has risen!" Alleluia.

(Antiphon, Mark 16:6a; Ps. 100)

READINGS

One-Year Series

Psalm 8
1 Corinthians 15:(1-9)20-26, 51-58
John 11:17-27

Three-Year Series

A, B, C. Psalm 146
    Daniel 12:1c-3
    or Jonah 2:2-9
    1 Corinthians 5:6-8
    Luke 24:13-49

ANTIPHON TO THE MAGNIFICAT

Christ, our Passover Lamb, *
    has been sacrificed for us. Alleluia. *(1 Cor. 5:7)*

COLLECT OF THE DAY

Almighty God the Father, through your only-begotten Son Jesus Christ you have overcome death and opened the gate of everlasting life to us. Grant that we, who celebrate with joy the day of our Lord's resurrection, may be raised from the death of sin by your life-giving Spirit; through Jesus Christ, our Lord, who lives and reigns with you and the Holy Spirit, one God, now and forever. (34)

SECOND SUNDAY OF EASTER

INTROIT

* VII E: Mixolydian

Like newborn babies, crave pure spiritual milk, *
    so that by it you may grow up in your salvation, now that you have tasted that the Lord is good. Alleluia!

Give thanks to the Lord, call on his name; *
    make known among the nations what he has done.
Sing to him, sing praise to him; *
    tell of all his wonderful acts.
Glory in his holy name; *
    let the hearts of those who seek the Lord rejoice.
Look to the Lord and his strength; *
    seek his face always.
Remember the wonders he has done, *
    his miracles, and the judgments he pronounced.

He remembers his covenant forever, *
    the word he commanded,
    for a thousand generations.

Glory be to the Father and to the Son *
    and to the Holy Spirit;
as it was in the beginning, *
    is now, and will be forever. Amen

Like newborn babies, crave pure spiritual milk *
    so that by it you may grow up in your salvation, now that you have tasted that the Lord is good. Alleluia!

(Antiphon, 1 Peter 2:2-3;
Ps. 105:1-5, 8)

49

COLLECT OF THE DAY

Grant, almighty God, that we who have celebrated the mystery of the Lord's resurrection may by the help of your grace bring forth the fruits thereof in our life and conduct; through Jesus Christ, your Son, our Lord, who lives and reigns with you and the Holy Spirit, one God, now and forever.(36)

READINGS

One-Year Series		Three-Year Series	
Psalm 16	A. Psalm 105:1-7	B. Psalm 148	C. Psalm 100
Ezekiel 37:1-14	Acts 2:14a, 22-32	Acts 3:13-15, 17-26	Acts 5:12, 17-32
1 Peter 1:3-9	1 Peter 1:3-9	1 John 5:1-6	Revelation 1:4-18
John 20:19-31	John 20:19-31	John 20:19-31	John 20:19-31

GRADUAL

Christ has risen from the dead.*
    God the Father has crowned him with glory and honor.
He has made him ruler over the works of his hands;*
    he has put everything under his feet.   *(Adapt. from Matt. 28:7; Heb. 2:7; Ps. 8:5-6)*

VERSE

Alleluia. Alleluia. Since Christ was raised from the dead, he cannot die again; death no longer has mastery over him. Alleluia. Blessed are those who have not seen and yet have believed. Alleluia.   *(Rom. 6:9; John 20:29b)*

THIRD SUNDAY OF EASTER

INTROIT (One-Year Series)   INTROIT (Three-Year Series)

"I am the vine; you are the branches.*
    If a man remains in me and I in him,
    he will bear much fruit;
    apart from me you can do nothing."

You who fear the Lord, praise him!*
    All you descendants of Jacob,
    honor him! Revere him, all you
    descendants of Israel!
I will declare your name to my brothers;*
    in the congregation I will praise you.

You will fill me with joy in your presence,*
    with eternal pleasures at your right hand.

I will exalt you, O Lord,*
    for you lifted me out of the depths
    and did not let my enemies
    gloat over me.
O Lord my God, I called to you for help*
    and you healed me.

Introit continues on the next page   *Introit continues on the next page*

All the rich of the earth will feast and
worship;*
    all who go down to the dust will kneel
    before him—those who cannot keep
    themselves alive.
They will proclaim his righteousness
to a people yet unborn—*
    for he has done it.

Glory be to the Father and to the Son*
    and to the Holy Spirit;
as it was in the beginning,*
    is now, and will be forever. Amen

"I am the vine; you are the branches.*
    If a man remains in me and I in him,
    he will bear much fruit;
    apart from me you can do nothing."

(Antiphon, John 15:5;
Ps. 22:23, 22, 29, 31)

O Lord, you brought me up
from the grave,*
    you spared me from going down
    into the pit.
Sing to the Lord, you saints of his;*
    praise his holy name.
For his anger lasts only a moment,*
    but his favor lasts a lifetime;
weeping may remain for a night,*
    but rejoicing comes in the morning.

Glory be to the Father and to the Son*
    and to the Holy Spirit;
as it was in the beginning,*
    is now, and will be forever. Amen

You will fill me with joy in your
presence,*
    with eternal pleasures at your
    right hand.

(Antiphon, Ps. 16:11b;
Ps. 30:1-5)

COLLECT OF THE DAY

O almighty and eternal God, now that you have assured us of the completion of our redemption through the resurrection of our Lord Jesus, give us the will to show forth in our lives what we profess with our lips; through Jesus Christ, your Son, our Lord, who lives and reigns with you and the Holy Spirit, one God, now and forever. (37)

READINGS

One-Year Series		Three-Year Series	
Psalm 22:22-31	A. Psalm 16	B. Psalm 139:1-12	C. Psalm 28:1-2, 6-9
Isaiah 40:25-31	Acts 2:14a, 36-47	Acts 4:8-12	Acts 9:1-20
1 John 5:1-13	1 Peter 1:17-21	1 John 1:1—2:2	Revelation 5:11-14
John 15:1-8	Luke 24:13-35	Luke 24:36-49	John 21:1-14

GRADUAL

Christ has risen from the dead.*
    God the Father has crowned him with glory and honor.
He has made him ruler over the works of his hands;*
    he has put everything under his feet.   *(Adapt. from Matt. 28:7; Heb. 2:7; Ps. 8:5-6)*

VERSE

Alleluia. Alleluia. Since Christ was raised from the dead, he cannot die again; death no longer has mastery over him. Alleluia. Our hearts were burning within us while he talked with us on the road and opened the Scriptures to us. Alleluia.   *(Rom. 6:9; Luke 24:32)*

FOURTH SUNDAY OF EASTER

INTROIT

* VII E: Mixolydian

"I am the good Shepherd; *
  I know my sheep and my sheep know
  me, and I lay down my life
  for the sheep."

The Lord is my shepherd, *
  I shall lack nothing.
He makes me to lie down
in green pastures, *
  he leads me beside quiet waters,
he restores my soul. *
  He guides me in paths of
  righteousness for his name's sake.
Even though I walk through the valley
of the shadow of death, I will fear
no evil, *
  for you are with me; your rod
  and your staff, they comfort me.
You prepare a table before me in the
presence of my enemies. *

You anoint my head with oil; my cup
overflows.
Surely goodness and love will follow
me all the days of my life, *
  and I will dwell in the house of the
  Lord forever.

Glory be to the Father and to the Son *
  and to the Holy Spirit;
as it was in the beginning, *
  is now, and will be forever. Amen

"I am the good Shepherd; *
  I know my sheep and my sheep know
  me, and I lay down my life
  for the sheep."

*(Antiphon, John 10:14, 15b;
Ps. 23)*

COLLECT OF THE DAY

Almighty God, merciful Father, since you have wakened from death the Shepherd of
your sheep, grant us your Holy Spirit that we may know the voice of our Shepherd and
follow him that sin and death may never pluck us out of your hand; through Jesus
Christ, our Lord, who lives and reigns with you and the Holy Spirit, one God, now
and forever.(38)

READINGS

One-Year Series		Three-Year Series	
Psalm 23	A. Psalm 23	B. Psalm 23	C. Psalm 23
Ezekiel 34:11-16	Acts 6:1-9; 7:2a, 51-60	Acts 4:23-33	Acts 13:15-16a, 26-33
1 Peter 2:21b- 25	1 Peter 2:19-25	1 John 3:1-2	Revelation 7:9-17
John 10:11-16	John 10:1-10	John 10:11-18	John 10:22-30

GRADUAL

Christ has risen from the dead. *
  God the Father has crowned him with glory and honor.

Gradual continues on the next page

He has made him ruler over the works of his hands; *

  he has put everything under his feet. *(Adapt. from Matt. 28:7; Heb. 2:7; Ps. 8:5-6)*

VERSE

Alleluia. Alleluia. Since Christ was raised from the dead, he cannot die again; death no longer has mastery over him. Alleluia. I am the good shepherd; I know my sheep and my sheep know me. Alleluia. *(Rom. 6:9; John 10:14)*

FIFTH SUNDAY OF EASTER

INTROIT

"In a little while you will see me
no more, *

  and then after a little while you will
  see me."

I will exalt you, my God the King; *

  I will praise your name for ever and
  ever.

Every day I will praise you*

  and extol your name for ever and
  ever.

The Lord is gracious and
compassionate, *

  slow to anger and rich in love.

All you have made will praise you,
O Lord; *

  your saints will extol you.

My mouth will speak in praise
of the Lord. *

  Let every creature praise his holy name
  for ever and ever.

Glory be to the Father and to the Son*
  and to the Holy Spirit;
as it was in the beginning, *
  is now, and will be forever. Amen

"In a little while you will see me
no more, *

  and then after a little while you will
  see me."

*(Antiphon, John 16:16;
Ps. 145:1-2, 8, 10, 21)*

COLLECT OF THE DAY

O God, you make the minds of your faithful to be of one will; therefore grant to your people that they may love what you command and desire what you promise, that among the manifold changes of this age our hearts may ever be fixed where true joys are to be found; through Jesus Christ, your Son, our Lord, who lives and reigns with you and the Holy Spirit, one God, now and forever.(39)

READINGS

One-Year Series		Three-Year Series	
Psalm 65:1-8	A. Psalm 146	B. Psalm 22:25-31	C. Psalm 110
1 Chronicles 16:23-31	Acts 17:1-15	Acts 8:26-40	Acts 13:44-52
Colossians 3:12-17	1 Peter 2:4-10	1 John 3:18-24	Revelation 21:1-5
John 16:4b-15	John 14:1-12	John 15:1-8	John 13:31-35

GRADUAL

Christ has risen from the dead.*
  God the Father has crowned him with glory and honor.
He has made him ruler over the works of his hands;*
  he has put everything under his feet.   *(Adapt. from Matt. 28:7; Heb. 2:7; Ps. 8:5-6)*

VERSE

Alleluia. Alleluia. Since Christ was raised from the dead, he cannot die again; death no longer has mastery over him. Alleluia. If anyone loves me, he will obey my teaching. My father will love him, and we will come to him and make our home with him. Alleluia.   *(Rom. 6:9; John 14:23)*

SIXTH SUNDAY OF EASTER

INTROIT

* VII E: Mixolydian

Come and listen, all you who fear God;*
  let me tell you what he has done
  for me.

Shout with joy to God, all the earth!*
  Sing to the glory of his name;
  offer him glory and praise!
Praise our God, O peoples,*
  let the sound of his praise be heard;
he has preserved our lives*
  and kept our feet from slipping.
Praise be to God,*
  who has not rejected my prayer
  or withheld his love from me!

Glory be to the Father and to the Son*
  and to the Holy Spirit;
as it was in the beginning,*
  is now, and will be forever. Amen

Come and listen, all you who fear God;*
  let me tell you what he has done
  for me.

  *(Antiphon, Ps. 66:16;
  Ps. 66:1-2, 8-9, 20)*

COLLECT OF THE DAY

Lord, because you have promised to give what we ask in the name of your only-begotten Son, teach us rightly to pray and with all your saints to offer you our adoration and praise; through Jesus Christ, our Lord, who lives and reigns with you and the Holy Spirit, one God, now and forever. (40)

READINGS

One-Year Series		Three-Year Series	
Psalm 67	A. Psalm 98	B. Psalm 98	C. Psalm 67
Isaiah 55:6-11	Acts 17:22-31	Acts 11:19-30	Acts 14:8-18
1 Timothy 2:1-8	1 Peter 3:15-22	1 John 4:1-11	Revelation 21:10-14,
John 16:23b-33	John 14:15-21	John 15:9-17	22-23
			John 14:23-29

GRADUAL

Christ has risen from the dead.*
   God the Father has crowned him with glory and honor.
He has made him ruler over the works of his hands;*
   he has put everything under his feet.   *(Adapt. from Matt. 28:7; Heb. 2:7; Ps. 8:5-6)*

VERSE

Alleluia. Alleluia. Since Christ was raised from the dead, he cannot die again; death no longer has mastery over him. Alleluia. If anyone loves me, he will obey my teaching. My Father will love him, and we will come to him and make our home with him. Alleluia.   *(Rom. 6:9; John 14:23)*

THE ASCENSION OF OUR LORD

INTROIT

* VII E: Mixolydian

God has ascended amid shouts of joy,*
   the Lord amid the sounding of
   trumpets.

The Lord says to my Lord:
"Sit at my right hand,*
   until I make your enemies a footstool
   for your feet."
The Lord has sworn and will not change
his mind:*
   "You are a priest forever,
   in the order of Melchizedek."
The Lord is at your right hand;*

he will crush kings on the day of his
wrath.

Glory be to the Father and to the Son*
   and to the Holy Spirit;
as it was in the beginning,*
   is now, and will be forever. Amen

God has ascended amid shouts of joy,*
   the Lord amid the sounding of
   trumpets.

   *(Antiphon, Ps. 47:5;
   Ps. 110:1, 4-5)*

COLLECT OF THE DAY

Grant, we pray, almighty God, that even as we believe your only-begotten Son, our Lord Jesus Christ, to have ascended into heaven, so we may also in heart and mind ascend and continually dwell there with him; who lives and reigns with you and the Holy Spirit, one God, now and forever. (41)

READINGS

One-Year Series

Psalm 110
Isaiah 45:18-25
or Daniel 7:13-14
Acts 1:1-11
or Ephesians 4:7-13
Matthew 28:16-20

Three-Year Series

A, B, C. Psalm 110
Acts 1:1-11
Ephesians 1:16-23
Luke 24:44-53

GRADUAL

Christ has risen from the dead.*
    God the Father has crowned him with glory and honor.
He has made him ruler over the works of his hands;*
    he has put everything under his feet.   *(Adapt. from Matt. 28:7; Heb. 2:7; Ps. 8:5-6)*

VERSE

Alleluia. Alleluia. Since Christ was raised from the dead, he cannot die again; death no longer has mastery over him. Alleluia. Surely I will be with you always, to the very end of the age. Alleluia.   *(Rom. 6:9; Matt. 28:20b)*

SEVENTH SUNDAY OF EASTER

INTROIT

Hear my voice when I call, O Lord;*
    be merciful to me and answer me.

The Lord is my light and my salvation—*
    whom shall I fear?
One thing I ask of the Lord, this is what I seek:*
    that I may dwell in the house of the Lord all the days of my life, to gaze upon the beauty of the Lord and to seek him in his temple.
For in the day of trouble he will keep me safe in his dwelling;*
    he will hide me in the shelter of his tabernacle and set me high upon a rock.

Though my father and mother forsake me,*
    the Lord will receive me.
Wait for the Lord;*
    be strong and take heart and wait for the Lord.

Glory be to the Father and to the Son*
    and to the Holy Spirit;
as it was in the beginning,*
    is now, and will be forever. Amen

Hear my voice when I call, O Lord;*
    be merciful to me and answer me.

*(Antiphon, Ps. 27:7;
Ps. 27:1a, 4-5, 10, 14)*

COLLECT OF THE DAY

O King of glory, Lord of hosts, uplifted in triumph far above all heavens, we pray, leave us not without consolation, but send us the Spirit of truth, whom you promised from the Father; for you live and reign with the Father and the Holy Spirit, one God, now and forever. (42)

READINGS

One-Year Series		Three-Year Series	
Psalm 8	A. Psalm 133	B. Psalm 133	C. Psalm 133
Ezekiel 36:24-27	Acts 1:(1-7)8-14	Acts 1:15-26	Acts 16:6-10
Ephesians 3:14-21	1 Peter 4:12-17;	1 John 4:13-21	Revelation 22:12-17, 20
John 15:26—16:4	5:6-11	John 17:11b-19	John 17:20-26
	John 17:1-11		

GRADUAL

Christ has risen from the dead.*
  God the Father has crowned him with glory and honor.
He has made him ruler over the works of his hands;*
  he has put everything under his feet. *(Adapt. from Matt. 28:7; Heb. 2:7; Ps. 8:5-6)*

VERSE

Alleluia. Alleluia. Since Christ was raised from the dead, he cannot die again; death no longer has mastery over him. Alleluia. I will not leave you as orphans; I will come to you. Alleluia. *(Rom. 6:9; John 14:18)*

PENTECOST
Pentecost Eve (Evening Prayer or Vespers)

PSALMODY

All of them were filled with the
Holy Spirit*
  and began to speak in other tongues.

Praise the Lord. Praise, O servants of
the Lord,*
  praise the name of the Lord.
Let the name of the Lord be praised,*
  both now and forevermore.
From the rising of the sun to the place
where it sets*

the name of the Lord is to be praised.
The Lord is exalted over all the nations,*
  his glory above the heavens.
Who is like the Lord our God,*
  the One who sits enthroned on high,
who stoops down to look*
  on the heavens and the earth?
He raises the poor from the dust*
  and lifts the needy from the ash heap;

Psalmody continues on the next page

he seats them with princes,*
  with the princes of their people.
He settles the barren woman in
her home*
  as a happy mother of children. Praise
  the Lord.

Glory be to the Father and to the Son*
  and to the Holy Spirit;

as it was in the beginning,*
  is now, and will be forever. Amen

All of them were filled with the
Holy Spirit*
  and began to speak in other tongues.

*(Antiphon, Acts 2:4a;
Ps. 113)*

READINGS

One-Year Series

Joel 3:1-5
Romans 8:12-17
John 14:15-21

Three-Year Series

A, B, C. Psalm 98
  Exodus 19:1-9
  or Acts 2:1-11
  Romans 8:14-17, 22-27
  John 7:37-39a

ANTIPHON TO THE MAGNIFICAT

I will not leave you as orphans. Alleluia.*
  I am going away and I am coming back to you. *(John 14:18a, 28a)*

COLLECT OF THE DAY

O God, on this day you once taught the hearts of your faithful people by sending them
the light of your Holy Spirit. Grant us in our day by the same Spirit to have a right
understanding in all things and evermore to rejoice in his holy consolation; through
Jesus Christ, your Son, our Lord, who lives and reigns with you in communion with
the same Holy Spirit, one God, now and forever. (43)

PENTECOST
The Day of Pentecost

INTROIT

* VII E: Mixolydian

Come, Holy Spirit, fill the hearts of the
faithful,*
  and kindle in them the fire of
  your love. Alleluia.

How many are your works, O Lord.*
  In wisdom you made them all;
  the earth is full of your creatures.

These all look to you*
  to give them their food at the proper
  time.
When you give it to them,*
  they gather it up.

Introit continues on the next page

58

When you send your Spirit, they are created,*
  and you renew the face of the earth.

Glory be to the Father and to the Son*
  and to the Holy Spirit;
as it was in the beginning,*
  is now, and will be forever. Amen

Come, Holy Spirit, fill the hearts of the faithful,*
  and kindle in them the fire of your love. Alleluia.

(Antiphon, liturgical text; Ps. 104:24, 27-28a, 30)

COLLECT OF THE DAY

O God, on this day you once taught the hearts of your faithful people by sending them the light of your Holy Spirit. Grant us in our day by the same Spirit to have a right understanding in all things and evermore to rejoice in his holy consolation; through Jesus Christ, your Son, our Lord, who lives and reigns with you in communion with the same Holy Spirit, one God, now and forever.(43)

READINGS

One-Year Series

1. Psalm 139:1-12
   Joel 2:28-29
   Acts 2:1-8(9-11)
   12-18
   John 14:23-27
2. Psalm 139:1-12
   Acts 2:1-8(9-13)
   14-18(19-20)21-24(25-31)
   32-33(34-35)36-42
   1 Corinthians 12:4-11
   John 3:16-21

A. Psalm 143
   or Veni, Creator Spiritus
   (Hymn 158)
   Joel 2:28-29
   Acts 2:1-21
   John 16:5-11

Three-Year Series

B. Psalm 143
   or Veni, Creator Spiritus
   (Hymn 158)
   Ezekiel 37:1-14
   Acts 2:22-36
   John 7:37-39a

C. Psalm 143
   or Veni, Creator Spiritus
   (Hymn 158)
   Genesis 11:1-9
   Acts 2:37-47
   John 15:26-27;
   16:4b-11

GRADUAL

I will pour out my Spirit on all people.*
  Your sons and daughters will prophesy.
It is with the heart that man believes and is justified,*
  and it is with his mouth that he confesses and is saved.   *(Acts 2:17b; Rom. 10:10)*

VERSE

Alleluia. Alleluia. Come, Holy Spirit, fill the hearts of your faithful people, and kindle in them the fire of your love. Alleluia.   *(From the antiphon: Come, Holy Spirit)*

PENTECOST
Pentecost Evening (Evening Prayer or Vespers)

PSALMODY

59

* VII E: Mixolydian

The Lord announced the Word,*
  and great was the company of those
  who proclaimed it.

Within your temple, O God,*
  we meditate on your unfailing love.
Like your name, O God,*
  your praise reaches to the ends of the
  earth; your right hand is filled with
  righteousness.
Mount Zion rejoices,*
  the villages of Judah are glad because
  of your judgments.

Glory be to the Father and to the Son*
  and to the Holy Spirit;
as it was in the beginning,*
  is now, and will be forever. Amen

The Lord announced the Word,*
  and great was the company of those
  who proclaimed it.

*(Antiphon, Ps. 68:11;
Ps. 48:9-11)*

READINGS

One-Year Series

Ezekiel 36:22-28
Revelation 21:1-5
Matthew 28:16-20

ANTIPHON TO THE MAGNIFICAT

Come, Holy Spirit, fill the hearts of the faithful,*
  and kindle in them the fire of your love. Alleluia.

COLLECT OF THE DAY

O God, on this day you once taught the hearts of your faithful people by sending them
the light of your Holy Spirit. Grant us in our day by the same Spirit to have a right
understanding in all things and evermore to rejoice in his holy consolation; through
Jesus Christ, your Son, our Lord, who lives and reigns with you in communion with
the same Holy Spirit, one God, now and forever. (43)

THE HOLY TRINITY
First Sunday after Pentecost

INTROIT

* I d: Dorian

Blessed be the Holy Trinity and the undivided Unity.*
    Let us give glory to him because he has shown his mercy to us.

Ascribe to the Lord, O mighty ones,*
    ascribe to the Lord glory and strength.
Ascribe to the Lord the glory due his name;*
    worship the Lord in the splendor of his holiness.
The voice of the Lord is powerful;*
    the voice of the Lord is majestic.
The Lord sits enthroned over the flood;*
    the Lord is enthroned as King forever.

The Lord gives strength to his people;*
    the Lord blesses his people with peace.

Glory be to the Father and to the Son*
    and to the Holy Spirit;
as it was in the beginning,*
    is now, and will be forever. Amen

Blessed be the Holy Trinity and the undivided Unity.*
    Let us give glory to him because he has shown his mercy to us.

(Antiphon, liturgical text; Ps. 29:1-2, 4, 10-11)

COLLECT OF THE DAY

Almighty and everlasting God, since you have given us, your servants, grace to acknowledge the glory of the eternal Trinity by the confession of a true faith, and to worship the true Unity in the power of your divine majesty, keep us also steadfast in this true faith and worship, and defend us ever from all our adversaries; for you, O Father, Son, and Holy Spirit, live and reign, one God, now and forever. (44)

READINGS

One-Year Series   Three-Year Series

Psalm 148	A. Psalm 135	B. Psalm 96	C. Psalm 8
Isaiah 6:1-8	Genesis 1:1—2:3	Deuteronomy 6:4-9	Proverbs 8:22-31
Ephesians 1:3-14	or Deuteronomy 4:32-	Romans 8:14-17	Romans 5:1-5
John 3:1-8	34, 39-40	John 3:1-17	John 16:12-15
or Matthew 28:16-20	2 Corinthians 13:11-14		
	Matthew 28:16-20		

GRADUAL

Great is the Lord and most worthy of praise;*
    his greatness no one can fathom.
I will meditate on your wonderful works,*
    and I will proclaim your great deeds. *(Ps. 145:3, 5b, 6b)*

VERSE

Alleluia. Alleluia. Holy, holy, holy is the Lord Almighty; the whole earth is full of his glory. Alleluia. *(Is. 6:3b)*

SECOND SUNDAY AFTER PENTECOST

INTROIT (One-Year Series)   INTROIT (Three-Year Series)

I trust in your unfailing love;*
    my heart rejoices in your salvation.

How long, O Lord? Will you hide
yourself forever?*
    How long will your wrath burn like
    fire?
Remember how fleeting is my life.*
    For what futility you have created all
    men!
Blessed are those who have learned to
acclaim you,*
    who walk in the light of your presence,
    O Lord.

Glory be to the Father and to the Son*
    and to the Holy Spirit;
as it was in the beginning,*
    is now, and will be forever. Amen

I trust in your unfailing love;*
    my heart rejoices in your salvation.

(Antiphon, Ps. 13:5;
Ps. 89:46-47, 15)

Be my rock of refuge,*
    a strong fortress to save me.

How great is your goodness,*
    which you have stored up for those
    who fear you,
which you bestow in the sight of men*
    on those who take refuge in you.
Love the Lord, all his saints!*
    The Lord preserves the faithful,
    but the proud he pays back in full.
Be strong and take heart,*
    all you who hope in the Lord.

Glory be to the Father and to the Son*
    and to the Holy Spirit;
as it was in the beginning,*
    is now, and will be forever. Amen

Be my rock of refuge,*
    a strong fortress to save me.

(Antiphon, Ps. 31:2b;
Ps. 31:19, 23-24)

COLLECT OF THE DAY

O God, whose never-failing providence sets in order all things both in heaven and earth, put away from us, we entreat you, all hurtful things, and give us those things that are profitable for us; through Jesus Christ, our Lord, who lives and reigns with you and the Holy Spirit, one God, now and forever. (45)

READINGS

One-Year Series

Psalm 62:5-12
Exodus 20:1-17
1 John 3:11-18
Luke 16:19-31

A. Psalm 4
    Deuteronomy 11:18-
        21, 26-28
    Romans 3:21-25a,
        27-28
    Matthew 7:(15-20)
        21-29

Three-Year Series

B. Psalm 142
    Deuteronomy 5:12-15
    2 Corinthians 4:5-12
    Mark 2:23-28

C. Psalm 117
    1 Kings 8:(22-23, 27-
        30)41-43
    Galatians 1:1-10
    Luke 7:1-10

GRADUAL

Great is the Lord and most worthy of praise;*
    his greatness no one can fathom.
I will meditate on your wonderful works,*
    and I will proclaim your great deeds. *(Ps. 145:3, 5b, 6b)*

VERSE

Alleluia. Alleluia. Your Word is a lamp to my feet and a light for my path. Alleluia. *(Ps. 119:105)*

THIRD SUNDAY AFTER PENTECOST

INTROIT (One-Year Series)

Sing to the Lord a new song;*
  sing to the Lord, all the earth.
It is we who extol the Lord,*
  both now and forevermore.

Praise the Lord, all you nations;*
  extol him, all you peoples.
For great is his love toward us,*
  and the faithfulness of the Lord
  endures forever. Praise the Lord.

Glory be to the Father and to the Son*
  and to the Holy Spirit;
as it was in the beginning,*
  is now, and will be forever. Amen

Sing to the Lord a new song;*
  sing to the Lord, all the earth.
It is we who extol the Lord,*
  both now and forevermore.

*(Antiphon, Ps. 96:1; 115:18;
Ps. 117)*

INTROIT (Three-Year Series)

He who sacrifices thank offerings
honors me,*
  and he prepares the way so that
  I may show him the salvation of God.

The Mighty One, God, the Lord,*
  speaks and summons the earth from
  the rising of the sun to the place
  where it sets.
"Hear, O my people, and I will speak,
O Israel, and I will testify against you:*
  I am God, your God.
I do not rebuke you for your sacrifices
or your burnt offerings,*
  which are ever before me.
I have no need of a bull from your
stall*
  or of goats from your pens,
for every animal of the forest is mine,*
  and the cattle on a thousand hills.
Sacrifice thank offerings to God,*
  fulfill your vows to the Most High,
and call upon me in the day of
trouble;*
  I will deliver you, and you will
  honor me."

Glory be to the Father and to the Son*
  and to the Holy Spirit;
as it was in the beginning,*
  is now, and will be forever. Amen

Introit continues on the next page

He who sacrifices thank offerings
honors me,*
    and he prepares the way so that
    I may show him the salvation of God.

(Antiphon, Ps. 50:23;
Ps. 50:1, 7-10, 14-15)

COLLECT OF THE DAY

O God, from whom all good proceeds, grant to us, your humble servants, that by your
holy inspiration we may think the things that are right and by your merciful guiding accomplish them; through Jesus Christ, our Lord, who lives and reigns with you and the
Holy Spirit, one God, now and forever.(46)

READINGS

One-Year Series

Psalm 117
Deuteronomy 8:11-20
or Zechariah 1:3-6
Ephesians 2:13-22
or Revelation 3:14-22
Luke 14:15-24

A. Psalm 119:65-72
   Hosea 5:15—6:6
   Romans 4:18-25
   Matthew 9:9-13

Three-Year Series

B. Psalm 28
   Genesis 3:9-15
   2 Corinthians 4:13-18
   Mark 3:20-35

C. Psalm 116:1-9
   1 Kings 17:17-24
   Galatians 1:11-24
   Luke 7:11-17

GRADUAL

Great is the Lord and most worthy of praise;*
   his greatness no one can fathom.
I will meditate on your wonderful works,*
   and I will proclaim your great deeds. *(Ps. 145:3, 5b, 6b)*

VERSE

Alleluia. Alleluia. God was reconciling the world to himself in Christ, not counting
men's sins against them. Alleluia. *(2 Cor. 5:19a)*

FOURTH SUNDAY AFTER PENTECOST

INTROIT

Serve the Lord with gladness;*
   come before him with joyful songs.

Shout for joy to the Lord,

all the earth.*
   Serve the Lord with gladness;

Introit continues on the next page

come before him with joyful songs.
Know that the Lord is God.*
  It is he who made us, and we are his;
  we are his people, the sheep of his
  pasture.
Enter his gates with thanksgiving and
his courts with praise;*
  give thanks to him and praise his name.
For the Lord is good and his love endures
forever;*
  his faithfulness continues through all
  generations.

Glory be to the Father and to the Son*
  and to the Holy Spirit;
as it was in the beginning,*
  is now, and will be forever. Amen

Serve the Lord with gladness;*
  come before him with joyful songs.

(Antiphon, Ps. 100:2;
Ps. 100)

COLLECT OF THE DAY

Almighty and everlasting God, give us an increase of faith, hope, and love; and that we may obtain what you have promised, make us love what you have commanded; through Jesus Christ, your Son, our Lord, who lives and reigns with you and the Holy Spirit, one God, now and forever.(47)

READINGS

One-Year Series

Psalm 100
Micah 7:18-20
1 Timothy 1:12-16
Luke 15:11-32

Three-Year Series

A. Psalm 100
   Exodus 19:2-8a
   Romans 5:6-11
   Matthew 9:35—10:8

B. Psalm 92:1-5(6-11)12-15
   Ezekiel 17:22-24
   2 Corinthians 5:1-10
   Mark 4:26-34

C. Psalm 32
   2 Samuel 11:26—12:10
   13-15
   Galatians 2:11-21
   Luke 7:36-50

GRADUAL

Great is the Lord and most worthy of praise;*
  his greatness no one can fathom.
I will meditate on your wonderful works,*
  and I will proclaim your great deeds. *(Ps. 145:3, 5b, 6b)*

VERSE

Alleluia. Alleluia. May your priests be clothed with righteousness; may your saints sing for joy. Alleluia. *(Ps. 132:9)*

FIFTH SUNDAY AFTER PENTECOST

INTROIT

* XI A: Ionian

The Lord is my light and my salvation—*
whom shall I fear?

One thing I ask of the Lord, this is what I
seek:*
    that I may dwell in the house of the
    Lord all the days of my life,
    to gaze upon the beauty of the Lord
    and to seek him in his temple.
For in the day of trouble he will keep me
safe in his dwelling;*
    he will hide me in the shelter of his
    tabernacle and set me high upon a
    rock.
Then my head will be exalted
above the enemies who surround me;*

at his tabernacle will I sacrifice with
shouts of joy; I will sing and make
music to the Lord.

Glory be to the Father and to the Son*
    and to the Holy Spirit;
as it was in the beginning,*
    is now, and will be forever. Amen

The Lord is my light and my salvation—*
whom shall I fear?

*(Antiphon, Ps. 27:1a;
Ps. 27:4-6)*

COLLECT OF THE DAY

O Lord, whose gracious presence never fails to guide and govern those whom you have
nurtured in your steadfast love and worship, make us ever revere and adore your holy
name; through Jesus Christ, your Son, our Lord, who lives and reigns with you and the
Holy Spirit, one God, now and forever. (48)

READINGS

One-Year Series

Psalm 138
Genesis 50:15-21
Romans 12:14-21
Luke 6:36-42

A. Psalm 91
Jeremiah 20:7-13
Romans 5:12-15
Matthew 10:24-33

Three-Year Series

B. Psalm 107:1-3, 23-32
Job 38:1-11
2 Corinthians 5:14-21
Mark 4:35-41

C. Psalm 119:41-48
Zechariah 12:7-10
Galatians 3:23-29
Luke 9:18-24

GRADUAL

Great is the Lord and most worthy of praise;*
    his greatness no one can fathom.
I will meditate on your wonderful works,*
    and I will proclaim your great deeds. *(Ps. 145:3, 5b, 6b)*

VERSE

Alleluia. Alleluia. Because you are sons, God sent the Spirit of his Son into our hearts,
the Spirit who calls out, "Abba, Father." Alleluia. *(Gal. 4:6)*

SIXTH SUNDAY AFTER PENTECOST

INTROIT

XI A: Ionian

Hear my voice when I call, O Lord; *
   be merciful to me and answer me.

The Lord is my light and my salvation—*
   whom shall I fear?
The Lord is the stronghold of my life—*
   of whom shall I be afraid?
Do not hide your face from me, do not
turn your servant away in anger;*
   you have been my helper.
Do not reject me or forsake me,*
   O God my Savior.

Glory be to the Father and to the Son*
   and to the Holy Spirit;
as it was in the beginning,*
   is now, and will be forever. Amen

Hear my voice when I call, O Lord;*
   be merciful to me and answer me.

(Antiphon, Ps. 27:7;
Ps. 27:1, 9)

COLLECT OF THE DAY

O God, because you have prepared for those who love you such good things as surpass our understanding, pour into our hearts such love towards you that we, loving you above all things, may obtain your promises, which exceed all that we can desire; through Jesus Christ, our Lord, who lives and reigns with you and the Holy Spirit, one God, now and forever. (49)

READINGS

One-Year Series

Psalm 147:1-14
Lamentations 3:22-26
or Exodus 3:1-15
1 Peter 2:4-10
Luke 5:1-11

A. Psalm 119:153-160
   Jeremiah 28:5-9
   Romans 6:1b-11
   Matthew 10:34-42

Three-Year Series

B. Psalm 121
   Lamentations 3:22-33
   2 Corinthians 8:1-9,
     13-14
   Mark 5:21-24a, 35-43
   or Mark 5:24b-34

C. Psalm 16
   1 Kings 19:14-21
   Galatians 5:1, 13-25
   Luke 9:51-62

GRADUAL

Great is the Lord and most worthy of praise;*
   his greatness no one can fathom.
I will meditate on your wonderful works,*
   and I will proclaim your great deeds. *(Ps. 145:3, 5b, 6b)*

VERSE

Alleluia. Alleluia. Submit to one another out of reverence for Christ. Alleluia. *(Eph. 5:21)*

67

SEVENTH SUNDAY AFTER PENTECOST

INTROIT (One-Year Series)   INTROIT (Three-Year Series)

I stay close to you, O Lord;*
  your right hand upholds me.

O God, you are my God,*
  earnestly I seek you;
my soul thirsts for you,*
  my body longs for you.
Because your love is better than life,*
  my lips will glorify you.
I will praise you as long as I live,*
  and in your name I will lift up my
  hands.
My soul will be satisfied as with the
  richest of foods;*
  with singing lips my mouth will praise
  you.

Glory be to the Father and to the Son*
  and to the Holy Spirit;
as it was in the beginning,*
  is now, and will be forever. Amen

I stay close to you, O Lord;*
  your right hand upholds me.

*(Antiphon, Ps. 63:8;
Ps. 63:1a, 3-5)*

For your name's sake, O Lord,
preserve my life;*
  in your righteousness, bring me out of
  trouble.

O Lord, hear my prayer, listen to
my cry for mercy;*
  in your faithfulness and righteousness
  come to my relief.

Do not bring your servant into judgment,*
  for no one living is righteous before
  you.

Let the morning bring me word of your
unfailing love,*
  for I have put my trust in you.

Glory be to the Father and to the Son*
  and to the Holy Spirit;
as it was in the beginning,*
  is now, and will be forever. Amen

For your name's sake, O Lord,
preserve my life;*
  in your righteousness, bring me out of
  trouble.

*(Antiphon, Ps. 143:11;
Ps. 143:1-2, 8a)*

COLLECT OF THE DAY

Grant, Lord, that the course of this world may be so governed by your direction that
your Church may rejoice in serving you in godly peace and quietness; through Jesus
Christ, our Lord, who lives and reigns with you and the Holy Spirit, one God, now and
forever. (50)

READINGS

One-Year Series

Psalm 107:1-9
Isaiah 43:1-7
or Jeremiah 17:9-13
Romans 6:1-11
John 4:5-15(16-26)

A. Psalm 119:137-144
  Zechariah 9:9-12
  Romans 7:15-25a
  Matthew 11:25-30

Three-Year Series

B. Psalm 143:1-2, 5-8
  Ezekiel 2:1-5
  2 Corinthians 12:7-10
  Mark 6:1-6

C. Psalm 19
  Isaiah 66:10-14
  Galatians 6:1-10,
  14-16
  Luke 10:1-12, 16
  (17-20)

GRADUAL

Great is the Lord and most worthy of praise;*
  his greatness no one can fathom.
I will meditate on your wonderful works,*
  and I will proclaim your great deeds.   *(Ps. 145:3, 5b, 6b)*

VERSE

Alleluia. Alleluia. This is to my Father's glory, that you bear much fruit, showing yourselves to be my disciples. Alleluia.   *(John 15:8)*

EIGHTH SUNDAY AFTER PENTECOST

INTROIT

XI A: Ionian

Taste and see that the Lord is good;*
  blessed is the man who takes refuge
in him.

The Lord has chosen Zion,*
  he has desired it for his dwelling:
"This is my resting place for ever
and ever;*
  here I will sit enthroned, for I have
  desired it—
I will bless her with abundant
provisions;*
  her poor will I satisfy with food.

I will clothe her priests with salvation,*
  and her saints will ever sing for joy."

Glory be to the Father and to the Son*
  and to the Holy Spirit;
as it was in the beginning,*
  is now, and will be forever. Amen

Taste and see that the Lord is good;*
  blessed is the man who takes refuge
in him.

(Antiphon, Ps. 34:8;
Ps. 132:13-16)

COLLECT OF THE DAY

O almighty and most merciful God, of your bountiful goodness keep us, we pray, from all things that may hurt us that we, being ready in both body and soul, may cheerfully accomplish whatever things you want done; through Jesus Christ, your Son, our Lord, who lives and reigns with you and the Holy Spirit, one God, now and forever. (51)

READINGS

One-Year Series		Three-Year Series	
Psalm 139:14-18	A. Psalm 65	B. Psalm 126	C. Psalm 25:1-10
Exodus 16:2-3, 11-18	Isaiah 55:10-11	Amos 7:10-15	Deuteronomy 30:9-14
Acts 2:41-47	Romans 8:18-25	Ephesians 1:3-14	Colossians 1:1-14
John 6:1-15	Matthew 13:1-9(18-23)	Mark 6:7-13	Luke 10:25-37

GRADUAL

Great is the Lord and most worthy of praise;*
    his greatness no one can fathom.
I will meditate on your wonderful works,*
    and I will proclaim your great deeds.   *(Ps. 145:3, 5b, 6b)*

VERSE

Alleluia. Alleluia. The word is very near you; it is in your mouth and in your heart so
you may obey it. Alleluia.   *(Deut. 30:14)*

NINTH SUNDAY AFTER PENTECOST

INTROIT

Your word is a lamp to my feet*
    and a light for my path.

Teach me your way, O Lord,*
    and I will walk in your truth;
give me an undivided heart,*
    that I may fear your name.
I will praise you, O Lord my God,
    with all my heart;*
    I will glorify your name forever.
For great is your love toward me;*
    you have delivered my soul from the
    depths of the grave.

Glory be to the Father and to the Son*
    and to the Holy Spirit;
as it was in the beginning,*
    is now, and will be forever. Amen

Your word is a lamp to my feet*
    and a light for my path.

*(Antiphon, Ps. 119:105;
Ps. 86:11-13)*

COLLECT OF THE DAY

Grant us, Lord, the Spirit to think and do always such things as are pleasing in your
sight that we, who without you cannot do anything that is good, may by you be enabled to live according to your will; through Jesus Christ, your Son, our Lord, who
lives and reigns with you and the Holy Spirit, one God, now and forever. (52)

READINGS

One-Year Series   Three-Year Series

Psalm 1   A. Psalm 119:57-64   B. Psalm 23   C. Psalm 27
Genesis 12:1-4a(4b-7)   Isaiah 44:6-8   Jeremiah 23:1-6   Genesis 18:1-10a
Galatians 5:16-25   Romans 8:26-27   Ephesians 2:13-22   (10-14)
Matthew 5:13-16   Matthew 13:24-30   Mark 6:30-34   Colossians 1:21-28
                               (36-43)   Luke 10:38-42

70

GRADUAL

Great is the Lord and most worthy of praise;*
  his greatness no one can fathom.
I will meditate on your wonderful works,*
  and I will proclaim your great deeds.   *(Ps. 145:3, 5b, 6b)*

VERSE

Alleluia. Alleluia. My word that goes out from my mouth: it will not return to me empty, but will accomplish what I desire and achieve the purpose for which I sent it.
Alleluia.   *(Is. 55:11)*

TENTH SUNDAY AFTER PENTECOST

INTROIT

Righteous are you, O Lord,*
  and your laws are right.

Oh, how I love your law!*
  I meditate on it all day long.
Your commands make me wiser than my enemies,*
  for they are ever with me.
How sweet are your promises to my taste,*
  sweeter than honey to my mouth!
Your word is a lamp to my feet*
  and a light for my path.
Accept, O Lord, the willing praise of my mouth,*
  and teach me your laws.

Your statutes are my heritage forever;*
  they are the joy of my heart.

Glory be to the Father and to the Son*
  and to the Holy Spirit;
as it was in the beginning,*
  is now, and will be forever. Amen

Righteous are you, O Lord,*
  and your laws are right.

*(Antiphon, Ps. 119:137;
Ps. 119:97-98, 103, 105, 108, 111)*

COLLECT OF THE DAY

O God, the Protector of all who trust in you, without whom nothing is strong and
nothing is holy, increase and multiply your mercy on us that with you as our Ruler
and Guide we may so pass through things temporal that we lose not the things eternal;
through Jesus Christ, your Son, our Lord, who lives and reigns with you and the Holy
Spirit, one God, now and forever. (53)

71

READINGS

One-Year Series

Psalm 119:105-112
Exodus 32:1-7(8-14)
15-20(30-34)
Philippians 3:7-11
Matthew 25:14-30

A. Psalm 119:129-136
1 Kings 3:5-12
Romans 8:28-30
Matthew 13:44-52

Three-Year Series

B. Psalm 136:1-9,
23-26
Exodus 24:3-11
Ephesians 4:1-7, 11-16
John 6:1-15

C. Psalm 138
Genesis 18:20-32
Colossians 2:6-15
Luke 11:1-13

GRADUAL

Great is the Lord and most worthy of praise,*
  his greatness no one can fathom.
I will meditate on your wonderful works,*
  and I will proclaim your great deeds. *(Ps. 145:3, 5b, 6b)*

VERSE

Alleluia. Alleluia. Lord, to whom shall we go? You have the words of eternal life.
Alleluia. *(John 6:68)*

ELEVENTH SUNDAY AFTER PENTECOST

INTROIT (One-Year Series)

We wait in hope for the Lord,*
  he is our help and our shield.

Blessed is the nation whose God is
the Lord,*
  the people he chose for his inheritance.
From heaven the Lord looks down*
  and sees all mankind;
from his dwelling place he watches*
  all who live on earth—
he who forms the hearts of all,*
  who considers everything they do.
The eyes of the Lord are on those who
fear him,*
  on those whose hope is in his
unfailing love.

Glory be to the Father and to the Son*
  and to the Holy Spirit;

Introit continues on the next page

INTROIT (Three-Year Series)

Be not far from me, O God,*
  come quickly, O my God, to help me.

Hear this, all you peoples,*
  listen, all who live in this world,
both low and high,*
  rich and poor alike:
My mouth will speak words of wisdom;*
  the utterance from my heart will give
  understanding.
I will turn my ear to a proverb;*
  with the harp I will expound my riddle.
God will redeem my soul from the
grave;*
  he will surely take me to himself.

Glory be to the Father and to the Son*
  and to the Holy Spirit;

Introit continues on the next page

as it was in the beginning,*
    is now, and will be forever. Amen

We wait in hope for the Lord;*
    he is our help and our shield.

(Antiphon, Ps. 33:20;
Ps. 33:12-15, 18)

as it was in the beginning,*
    is now, and will be forever. Amen

Be not far from me, O God;*
    come quickly, O my God, to help me.

(Antiphon, Ps. 71:12;
Ps. 49:1-4, 15)

COLLECT OF THE DAY

Let your continual mercy, O Lord, cleanse and defend your Church; and because it cannot continue in safety without your help, protect and govern it always by your goodness; for you live and reign with the Father and the Holy Spirit, one God, now and forever. (54)

READINGS

One-Year Series

Psalm 73:25-28	A. Psalm 136:1-9, 23-26
Daniel 9:15-18	Isaiah 55:1-5
Romans 9:1-5; 10:1-4	Romans 8:35-39
Luke 19:41-48	Matthew 14:13-21

Three-Year Series

B.	C.
Psalm 119:89-104	Psalm 100
Exodus 16:2-15	Ecclesiastes 1:2;
Ephesians 4:17-24	2:18-26
John 6:24-35	Colossians 3:1-11
	Luke 12:13-21

GRADUAL

Oh, the depth of the riches of the wisdom and knowledge of God!*
    How unsearchable his judgments, and his paths beyond tracing out!
For from him and through him and to him are all things.*
    To him be the glory forever! Amen   *(Rom. 11:33, 36)*

VERSE

Alleluia. Alleluia. Jesus replied, "If anyone loves me, he will obey my teaching. My Father will love him, and we will come to him and make our home with him." Alleluia.   *(John 14:23)*

TWELFTH SUNDAY AFTER PENTECOST

INTROIT (One-Year Series)

Surely God is my help;*
    the Lord is the one who sustains me.

Introit continues on the next page

INTROIT (Three-Year Series)

You open your hand*
    and satisfy the desires of every
    living thing.

Introit continues on the next page

Praise the Lord. Praise, O servants of
the Lord,*
 praise the name of the Lord.
Let the name of the Lord be praised,*
 both now and forevermore.
From the rising of the sun to the place
where it sets*
 the name of the Lord is to be
 praised.
He raises the poor from the dust*
 and lifts the needy from the ash heap;
he seats them with princes,*
 with the princes of their people.

Glory be to the Father and to the Son*
 and to the Holy Spirit;
as it was in the beginning,*
 is now, and will be forever. Amen

Surely God is my help;*
 the Lord is the one who sustains me.

*(Antiphon, Ps. 54:4;
Ps. 113:1-3, 7-8)*

I will extol the Lord at all times;*
 his praise will always be on my lips.
I sought the Lord, and he answered me;*
 he delivered me from all my fears.
Those who look to him are radiant;*
 their faces are never covered with
 shame.
This poor man called, and the Lord heard
him;*
 he saved him out of all his troubles.
The angel of the Lord encamps around
those who fear him,*
 and he delivers them.
Taste and see that the Lord is good;*
 blessed is the man who takes refuge in
 him.

Glory be to the Father and to the Son*
 and to the Holy Spirit;
as it was in the beginning,*
 is now, and will be forever. Amen

You open your hand*
 and satisfy the desires of every
 living thing.

*(Antiphon, Ps. 145:16;
Ps. 34:1, 4-8)*

COLLECT OF THE DAY

Almighty and everlasting God, always more ready to hear than we to pray and always
ready to give more than we either desire or deserve, pour down on us the abundance of
your mercy, forgiving us the things of which our conscience is afraid and giving us the
good things we are not worthy to ask but through the merits and mediation of Jesus
Christ, your Son, our Lord, who lives and reigns with you and the Holy Spirit, one
God, now and forever.(55)

READINGS

One-Year Series

Psalm 138
2 Chronicles 1:7-12
1 Peter 5:5b-11
Luke 18:9-14

A. Psalm 28
 1 Kings 19:9-18
 Romans 9:1-5
 Matthew 14:22-33

Three-Year Series

B. Psalm 34:1-8
 1 Kings 19:4-8
 Ephesians 4:30—5:2
 John 6:41-51

C. Psalm 50
 Genesis 15:1-6
 Hebrews 11:1-3, 8-16
 Luke 12:32-40

GRADUAL

Oh, the depth of the riches of the wisdom and knowledge of God!*
 How unsearchable his judgments, and his paths beyond tracing out!

Gradual continues on the next page

OKa

For from him and through him and to him are all things.*
To him be the glory forever! Amen *(Rom. 11:33, 36)*

VERSE

Alleluia. Alleluia. Now faith is being sure of what we hope for and certain of what we do not see. Alleluia. *(Heb. 11:1)*

THIRTEENTH SUNDAY AFTER PENTECOST

INTROIT (One-Year Series)

IX a: Aeolian

Hasten, O God, to save me;*
O Lord, come quickly to help me.

Why have you rejected us forever,
O God?*
Why does your anger smolder
against the sheep of your pasture?
Rise up, O God, and defend your
cause;*
remember how fools mock you all day
long.
Do not let the oppressed retreat in
disgrace;*
may the poor and needy praise your
name.

Glory be to the Father and to the Son*
and to the Holy Spirit;
as it was in the beginning,*
is now, and will be forever. Amen

Hasten, O God, to save me;*
O Lord, come quickly to help me.

*(Antiphon, Ps. 70:1;
Ps. 74:1, 22, 21)*

INTROIT (Three-Year Series)

IX a: Aeolian

The eyes of all look to you,*
and you give them their food at the
proper time.

Fear the Lord, you his saints,*
for those who fear him lack nothing.
The lions may grow weak and hungry,*
but those who seek the Lord lack
no good thing.
Come, my children, listen to me;*
I will teach you the fear of the Lord.
Turn from evil and do good;*
seek peace and pursue it.
The eyes of the Lord are on the
righteous*
and his ears are attentive to their cry.

Glory be to the Father and to the Son*
and to the Holy Spirit;
as it was in the beginning,*
is now, and will be forever. Amen

The eyes of all look to you,*
and you give them their food at the
proper time.

*(Antiphon, Ps. 145:15;
Ps. 34:9-11, 14-15)*

COLLECT OF THE DAY

Merciful Father, since you have given your only Son as the sacrifice for our sin, also give us grace to receive with thanksgiving the fruits of his redeeming work and daily follow in his way; through your Son, Jesus Christ, who lives and reigns with you and the Holy Spirit, one God, now and forever. (56)

READINGS

One-Year Series		Three-Year Series	
Psalm 146	A. Psalm 67	B. Psalm 34:9-14	C. Psalm 119:81-88
Isaiah 29:18-21	Isaiah 56:1, 6-8	Proverbs 9:1-6	Jeremiah 23:23-29
2 Corinthians 12:6-10	Romans 11:13-15, 29-32	Ephesians 5:15-20	Hebrews 12:1-13
Mark 7:31-37	Matthew 15:21-28	John 6:51-58	Luke 12:49-53

GRADUAL

Oh, the depth of the riches of the wisdom and knowledge of God!*
How unsearchable his judgments, and his paths beyond tracing out!
For from him and through him and to him are all things.*
To him be the glory forever! Amen *(Rom. 11:33, 36)*

VERSE

Alleluia. Alleluia. The word of God is living and active. Sharper than any double-edged sword, it penetrates even to dividing soul and spirit, joints and marrow; it judges the thoughts and attitudes of the heart. Alleluia. *(Heb. 4:12)*

FOURTEENTH SUNDAY AFTER PENTECOST

INTROIT (One-Year Series)

INTROIT (Three-Year Series)

We give thanks to you, O God,*
  we give thanks, for your name is near; men tell of your wonderful deeds.

Praise the Lord. Blessed is the man who fears the Lord,*
  who finds great delight in his commands.
He will have no fear of bad news;*
  his heart is steadfast, trusting in the Lord.
His heart is secure, he will have no fear;*

Splendor and majesty are before him.*
  We extol the Lord, both now and forevermore. Praise the Lord.

Praise the Lord, all you nations;*
  extol him, all you peoples.
For great is his love toward us,*
  and the faithfulness of the Lord endures forever. Praise the Lord.

Glory be to the Father and to the Son*
  and to the Holy Spirit;
as it was in the beginning,*
  is now, and will be forever. Amen

Introit continues on the next page

Introit continues on the next page

in the end he will look in triumph
on his foes.

Glory be to the Father and to the Son*
and to the Holy Spirit;
as it was in the beginning,*
is now, and will be forever. Amen

We give thanks to you, O God,*
we give thanks, for your name is
near; men tell of your wonderful
deeds.

*(Antiphon, Ps. 75:1;
Ps. 112:1, 7-8)*

Splendor and majesty are before him.*
We extol the Lord, both now and
forevermore. Praise the Lord.

*(Antiphon, Ps. 96:6a; 115:18;
Ps. 117)*

COLLECT OF THE DAY

O almighty God, whom to know is everlasting life, grant us without all doubt to
know your Son Jesus Christ to be the Way, the Truth, and the Life that, following
his steps, we may steadfastly walk in the way that leads to eternal life; through
Jesus Christ, our Lord, who lives and reigns with you and the Holy Spirit, one God,
now and forever. (57)

READINGS

One-Year Series

Psalm 142
Genesis 4:(1-7)8-16a
1 John 4:7-11
Luke 10:25-37

A. Psalm 138
 Exodus 6:2-8
 Romans 11:33-36
 Matthew 16:13-20

Three-Year Series

B. Psalm 34:15-22
 Joshua 24:1-2a,
  14-18
 Ephesians 5:21-31
 John 6:60-69

C. Psalm 117
 Isaiah 66:18-23
 Hebrews 12:18-24
 Luke 13:22-30

GRADUAL

Oh, the depth of the riches of the wisdom and knowledge of God!*
  How unsearchable his judgments, and his paths beyond tracing out!
For from him and through him and to him are all things.*
  To him be the glory forever! Amen   *(Rom. 11:33, 36)*

VERSE

Alleluia. Alleluia. Our Savior, Christ Jesus, has destroyed death and brought life and
immortality to light through the Gospel. Alleluia.   *(2 Tim. 1:10b)*

FIFTEENTH SUNDAY AFTER PENTECOST

INTROIT (One-Year Series)

INTROIT (Three-Year Series)

Look upon our shield, O God;*
  look with favor on your anointed
  one.

Hear, O Lord, and answer me,*
  for I am poor and needy.
Guard my life, for I am devoted
to you.*
  You are my God; save your servant
  who trusts in you.
Have mercy on me, O Lord,*
  for I call to you all day long.
Bring joy to your servant,*
  for to you, O Lord, I lift
  up my soul.

Glory be to the Father and to the Son*
  and to the Holy Spirit;
as it was in the beginning,*
  is now, and will be forever. Amen

Look upon our shield, O God;*
  look with favor on your anointed
  one.

(Antiphon, Ps. 84:9;
Ps. 86:1-4)

I love the house where you live,
O Lord,*
  the place where your glory dwells.

Vindicate me, O Lord,*
  for I have led a blameless life;
I have trusted in the Lord*
  without wavering.
Test me, O Lord, and try me,*
  examine my heart and my mind.
I wash my hands in innocence,*
  and go about your altar, O Lord,
proclaiming aloud your praise,*
  and telling of all your wonderful
  deeds.

Glory be to the Father and to the Son*
  and to the Holy Spirit;
as it was in the beginning,*
  is now, and will be forever. Amen

I love the house where you live,
O Lord,*
  the place where your glory dwells.

(Antiphon, Ps. 26:8;
Ps. 26:1-2, 6-7)

COLLECT OF THE DAY

Lord of all power and might, Author and Giver of all good things, graft in our hearts
the love of your name, increase in us true religion, nourish us with all goodness, and
bring forth in us the fruit of good works; through Jesus Christ, your Son, our Lord,
who lives and reigns with you and the Holy Spirit, one God, now and forever. (58)

READINGS

One-Year Series

Psalm 107:17-22
Genesis 28:10-19a
Romans 8:12-17
Luke 17:11-19

Three-Year Series

A. Psalm 119:105-112
    Jeremiah 15:15-21
    Romans 12:1-8
    Matthew 16:21-26

B. Psalm 119:129-136
    Deuteronomy 4:1-2, 6-8
    Ephesians 6:10-20
    Mark 7:1-8, 14-15,
      21-23

C. Psalm 119:161-168
    Proverbs 25:6-7
    Hebrews 13:1-8
    Luke 14:1, 7-14

GRADUAL

Oh, the depth of the riches of the wisdom and knowledge of God!*
    How unsearchable his judgments, and his paths beyond tracing out!
For from him and through him and to him are all things.*
    To him be the glory forever! Amen *(Rom. 11:33, 36)*

78

VERSE

Alleluia. Alleluia. When your words came, I ate them; they were my joy and my heart's delight. Alleluia. *(Jer. 15:16a)*

SIXTEENTH SUNDAY AFTER PENTECOST

INTROIT

XI C: Ionian

It is good to praise the Lord*
    and make music to your name,
    O Most High.

Trust in the Lord and do good;*
    dwell in the land and enjoy safe
    pasture.
Delight yourself in the Lord*
    and he will give you the desires of
    your heart.
Commit your way to the Lord;*
    trust in him and he will do this.
The salvation of the righteous comes
from the Lord;*

he is their stronghold in time of
trouble.

Glory be to the Father and to the Son*
    and to the Holy Spirit;
as it was in the beginning,*
    is now, and will be forever. Amen

It is good to praise the Lord*
    and make music to your name,
    O Most High.

    (Antiphon, Ps. 92:1;
    Ps. 37:3-5, 39)

COLLECT OF THE DAY

Grant, merciful Lord, to your faithful people pardon and peace that they may be cleansed from all their sins and serve you with a quiet mind; through Jesus Christ, your Son, our Lord, who lives and reigns with you and the Holy Spirit, one God, now and forever. (59)

READINGS

One-Year Series

Psalm 4
1 Kings 17:8-16
2 Corinthians 6:1-10
Matthew 6:25-33

A. Psalm 119:113-120
    Ezekiel 33:7-9
    Romans 13:1-10
    Matthew 18:15-20

Three-Year Series

B. Psalm 146
    Isaiah 35:4-7a
    James 1:17-22(23-
        25)26-27
    Mark 7:31-37

C. Psalm 119:169-176
    Proverbs 9:8-12
    Philemon 1(2-9)
        10-21
    Luke 14:25-33

GRADUAL

Oh, the depth of the riches of the wisdom and knowledge of God!*
    How unsearchable his judgments, and his paths beyond tracing out!
For from him and through him and to him are all things.*
    To him be the glory forever! Amen *(Rom. 11:33, 36)*

VERSE

Alleluia. Alleluia. Rejoice in the Lord always. I will say it again: Rejoice! Alleluia.
(Phil. 4:4)

SEVENTEENTH SUNDAY AFTER PENTECOST

INTROIT

The Lord is gracious and righteous;*
 our God is full of compassion.

I love the Lord, for he heard my voice;*
 he heard my cry for mercy.
Because he turned his ear to me,*
 I will call on him as long as I live.
The cords of death entangled me, the
anguish of the grave came upon me.*
 I was overcome by trouble and
 sorrow.
Then I called on the name of the Lord:*
 "O Lord, save me";
The Lord is gracious and righteous;*
 our God is full of compassion.
Be at rest once more, O my soul,*

for the Lord has been good to you.
For you, O Lord, have delivered my
soul from death,*
 my eyes from tears, my feet
 from stumbling,
that I may walk before the Lord*
 in the land of the living.

Glory be to the Father and to the Son*
 and to the Holy Spirit;
as it was in the beginning,*
 is now, and will be forever. Amen

The Lord is gracious and righteous;*
 our God is full of compassion.

*(Antiphon, Ps. 116:5;
Ps. 116:1-5, 7-9)*

COLLECT OF THE DAY

O God, without whose blessing we are not able to please you, mercifully grant that your Holy Spirit may in all things direct and govern our hearts; through Jesus Christ, your Son, our Lord, who lives and reigns with you and the Holy Spirit, one God, now and forever. (60)

READINGS

One-Year Series

Psalm 116:1-9
1 Kings 17:17-24
1 Corinthians 15:1-11
Luke 7:11-16
or John 11:17-27

A. Psalm 103:1-13
 Genesis 50:15-21
 Romans 14:5-9
 Matthew 18:21-35

Three-Year Series

B. Psalm 116:1-9
 Isaiah 50:4-10
 James 2:1-5, 8-10,
 14-18
 Mark 8:27-35

C. Psalm 51:1-17
 Exodus 32:7-14
 1 Timothy 1:12-17
 Luke 15:1-10

GRADUAL

Oh, the depth of the riches of the wisdom and knowledge of God!*
 How unsearchable his judgments, and his paths beyond tracing out!

Gradual continues on the next page

For from him and through him and to him are all things.*
  To him be the glory forever! Amen   *(Rom. 11:33, 36)*

VERSE

Alleluia. Alleluia. Everything that was written in the past was written to teach us, so
that through endurance and the encouragement of the Scriptures we might have hope.
Alleluia.   *(Rom. 15:4)*

EIGHTEENTH SUNDAY AFTER PENTECOST

INTROIT (One-Year Series)   INTROIT (Three-Year Series)

I will lift up the cup of salvation*
  and call on the name of the Lord.

How can I repay the Lord*
  for all his goodness to me?
I will lift up the cup of salvation*
  and call on the name of the Lord.
Precious in the sight of the Lord*
  is the death of his saints.
O Lord, truly I am your servant;*
  I am your servant, the son of your
  maidservant; you have freed me from
  my chains.
I will sacrifice a thank offering to you*
  and call on the name of the Lord.

Glory be to the Father and to the Son*
  and to the Holy Spirit;
as it was in the beginning,*
  is now, and will be forever. Amen

I will lift up the cup of salvation*
  and call on the name of the Lord.

(Antiphon, Ps. 116:13;
Ps. 116:12-13, 15-17)

Surely God is my help;*
  the Lord is the one who sustains me.

Save me, O God, by your name;*
  vindicate me by your might.
Hear my prayer, O God;*
  listen to the words of my mouth.
I will sacrifice a freewill offering
to you;*
  I will praise your name, O Lord,
  for it is good.
For he has delivered me from all my
troubles,*
  and my eyes have looked in triumph
on my foes.

Glory be to the Father and to the Son*
  and to the Holy Spirit;
as it was in the beginning,*
  is now, and will be forever. Amen

Surely God is my help;*
  the Lord is the one who sustains me.

(Antiphon, Ps. 54:4;
Ps. 54:1-2, 6-7)

COLLECT OF THE DAY

Keep, we pray you, O Lord, your Church with your perpetual mercy; and because
without you we cannot but fall, keep us ever by your help from all things hurtful, and

lead us to all things profitable to our salvation; for you live and reign with the Father and the Holy Spirit, one God, now and forever. (61)

READINGS

One-Year Series

Psalm 116:12-19
Genesis 8:18-22
Galatians 3:26-28
Matthew 26:26-29
or Mark 14:22-25

A. Psalm 27:1-9
   Isaiah 55:6-9
   Philippians 1:1-5(6-11)
   19-27
   Matthew 20:1-16

Three-Year Series

B. Psalm 119:25-32
   Jeremiah 11:18-20
   James 3:16—4:6
   Mark 9:30-37

C. Psalm 119:33-40
   Amos 8:4-7
   1 Timothy 2:1-8
   Luke 16:1-13

GRADUAL

Oh, the depth of the riches of the wisdom and knowledge of God!*
    How unsearchable his judgments, and his paths beyond tracing out!
For from him and through him and to him are all things.*
    To him be the glory forever! Amen   *(Rom. 11:33, 36)*

VERSE

Alleluia. Alleluia. My grace is sufficient for you, for my power is made perfect in weakness. Therefore I will boast all the more gladly about my weaknesses, so that Christ's power may rest on me. Alleluia.   *(2 Cor. 12:9)*

NINETEENTH SUNDAY AFTER PENTECOST

INTROIT

Your name, O Lord, endures forever,*
    your renown, O Lord, through all
    generations.

Praise the Lord. Praise the name
of the Lord;*
    Praise him, you servants of the Lord,
you who minister in the house of the
Lord,*
    in the courts of the house of
    our God.
Praise the Lord, for the Lord is good;*
    sing praise to his name, for that
    is pleasant.
Your name, O Lord, endures forever,*

your renown, O Lord, through all
generations.
For the Lord will vindicate his people*
    and have compassion on his servants.

Glory be to the Father and to the Son*
    and to the Holy Spirit;
as it was in the beginning,*
    is now, and will be forever. Amen

Your name, O Lord, endures forever,*
    your renown, O Lord, through all
    generations.

(Antiphon, Ps. 135:13;
Ps. 135:1-3, 13-14)

COLLECT OF THE DAY

O God, the Strength of all who put their trust in you, mercifully accept our prayer, and because through the weakness of our mortal nature we can do no good thing without your aid, grant us the help of your grace that, keeping your commandments, we may please you in both will and deed; through Jesus Christ, your Son, our Lord, who lives and reigns with you and the Holy Spirit, one God, now and forever. (62)

READINGS

One-Year Series

Psalm 103:1-14
Deuteronomy 6:4-15
Romans 13:1-10
Mark 12:28-34
or Matthew 22:34-40

Three-Year Series

A. Psalm 25:1-10
Ezekiel 18:1-4, 25-32
Philippians 2:1-5(6-11)
Matthew 21:28-32

B. Psalm 135:1-7, 13-14
Numbers 11:4-6, 10-
16, 24-29
James 4:7-12(13—5:6)
Mark 9:38-50

C. Psalm 146
Amos 6:1-7
1 Timothy 6:6-16
Luke 16:19-31

GRADUAL

Oh, the depth of the riches of the wisdom and knowledge of God!*
How unsearchable his judgments, and his paths beyond tracing out!
For from him and through him and to him are all things.*
To him be the glory forever! Amen   *(Rom. 11:33, 36)*

VERSE

Alleluia. Alleluia. At the name of Jesus every knee should bow, in heaven and on earth and under the earth, and every tongue confess that Jesus Christ is Lord, to the glory of God the Father. Alleluia.   *(Phil. 2:10-11)*

TWENTIETH SUNDAY AFTER PENTECOST

INTROIT (One-Year Series)

Heal me, O Lord, and I will be healed;*
  save me and I will be saved, for you
  are the one I praise.

Blessed is he whose transgressions are
forgiven,*
  whose sins are covered.
Blessed is the man whose sin the Lord
does not count against him*
  and in whose spirit is no deceit.

Introit continues on the next page

INTROIT (Three-Year Series)

May the Lord bless you from Zion*
  all the days of your life.

Blessed are all who fear the Lord,*
  who walk in his ways.
You will eat the fruit of your labor;*
  blessings and prosperity will be yours.
Your wife will be like a fruitful vine
within your house;*
    your sons will be like olive shoots
    around your table.

Introit continues on the next page

When I kept silent, my bones
wasted away*
    through my groaning all day long.
For day and night your hand was
heavy upon me;*
    my strength was sapped as in the
    heat of summer.
Then I acknowledged my sin to you
and did not cover up my iniquity.*
    I said, "I will confess my
    transgressions to the Lord"—and
    you forgave the guilt of my sin.

Glory be to the Father and to the Son*
    and to the Holy Spirit;
as it was in the beginning,*
    is now, and will be forever. Amen

Heal me, O Lord, and I will be healed;*
    save me and I will be saved, for you
    are the one I praise.

(Antiphon Jer. 17:14;
Ps. 32:1-5)

Thus is the man blessed*
    who fears the Lord.
May you see the prosperity of
Jerusalem,*
    and may you live to see your
    children's children.

Glory be to the Father and to the Son*
    and to the Holy Spirit;
as it was in the beginning,*
    is now, and will be forever. Amen

May the Lord bless you from Zion*
    all the days of your life.

(Antiphon, Ps. 128:5a;
Ps. 128:1-4, 5b-6a)

COLLECT OF THE DAY

O God, whose almighty power is made known chiefly in showing mercy and pity, grant us the fullness of your grace that we may be partakers of your heavenly treasures; through our Lord Jesus Christ, your Son, who lives and reigns with you and the Holy Spirit, one God, now and forever.(63)

READINGS

One-Year Series	Three-Year Series		
Psalm 32:1-7	A. Psalm 118:19-24	B. Psalm 119:49-56	C. Psalm 62
Exodus 34:4a-10	Isaiah 5:1-7	Genesis 2:18-24	Habakkuk 1:1-3; 2:1-4
Ephesians 4:22-30	Philippians 3:12-21	Hebrews 2:9-11(12-18)	2 Timothy 1:3-14
Mark 2:1-12	Matthew 21:33-43	Mark 10:2-16	Luke 17:1-10

GRADUAL

These are they who have come out of the great tribulation;*
    they have washed their robes and made them white in the
    blood of the Lamb.
Blessed are those whose strength is in you,*
    who have set their hearts on pilgrimage. *(Rev. 7:14; Ps. 84:5)*

VERSE

Alleluia. Alleluia. I will declare your name to my brothers; in the presence of the congregation I will sing your praises. Alleluia. *(Heb. 2:12)*

TWENTY-FIRST SUNDAY AFTER PENTECOST

INTROIT

Great is the Lord, and most worthy
of praise,*
   in the city of our God, his holy
   mountain.

I will extol the Lord at all times,*
   his praise will always be on my
lips.
My soul will boast in the Lord,*
   let the afflicted hear and rejoice.
Glorify the Lord with me;*
   let us exalt his name together.
I sought the Lord, and he answered
me;*
   he delivered me from all my fears.
The righteous cry out, and the Lord
hears them;*

he delivers them from all their
troubles.

Glory be to the Father and to the Son*
   and to the Holy Spirit;
as it was in the beginning,*
   is now, and will be forever. Amen

Great is the Lord, and most worthy of
praise,*
   in the city of our God, his holy
   mountain.

*(Antiphon, Ps. 48:1;
Ps. 34:1-4, 17)*

COLLECT OF THE DAY

Enlighten our minds, we pray, O God, by the Spirit who proceeds from you that, as
your Son has promised, we may be led into all truth; through Jesus Christ, your Son,
our Lord, who lives and reigns with you and the Holy Spirit, one God, now and
forever. (64)

READINGS

One-Year Series		Three-Year Series	
Psalm 34:1-8	A. Psalm 23	B. Psalm 119:73-80	C. Psalm 111
Exodus 33:17-23	Isaiah 25:6-9	Amos 5:6-7, 10-15	Ruth 1:1-19a
Romans 10:9-17	Philippians 4:4-13	Hebrews 3:1-6	2 Timothy 2:8-13
Matthew 15:21-28	Matthew 22:1-10	Mark 10:17-27	Luke 17:11-19
	(11-14)	(28-30)	

GRADUAL

These are they who have come out of the great tribulation;*
   they have washed their robes and made them white in the
   blood of the Lamb.
Blessed are those whose strength is in you,*
   who have set their hearts on pilgrimage. *(Rev. 7:14; Ps. 84:5)*

VERSE

Alleluia. Alleluia. This is the Lord, we trusted in him; let us rejoice and be glad in his salvation. Alleluia. *(Is. 25:9b)*

TWENTY-SECOND SUNDAY AFTER PENTECOST

INTROIT

The Lord watches over you—*
   the Lord is your shade at your right hand.

I will lift my eyes to the hills—*
   where does my help come from?
My help comes from the Lord,*
   the Maker of heaven and earth.
He will not let your foot slip—*
   he who watches over you will not slumber;
indeed, he who watches over Israel*
   will neither slumber nor sleep.
The Lord will keep you from all harm—*
   he will watch over your life;

the Lord will watch over your coming and going*
   both now and forevermore.

Glory be to the Father and to the Son*
   and to the Holy Spirit;
as it was in the beginning,*
   is now, and will be forever. Amen

The Lord watches over you—*
   the Lord is your shade at your right hand.

(Antiphon, Ps. 121:5;
Ps. 121:1-4, 7-8)

COLLECT OF THE DAY

Lord, we pray that your grace may always precede and follow us that we may continually be given to good works; through Jesus Christ, your Son, our Lord, who lives and reigns with you and the Holy Spirit, one God, now and forever. (65)

READINGS

One-Year Series		Three-Year Series	
Psalm 119:1-8	A. Psalm 96	B. Psalm 91:9-16	C. Psalm 121
Joshua 24:1-2a, 14-18	Isaiah 45:1-7	Isaiah 53:10-12	Genesis 32:22-30
(22-28)	1 Thessalonians 1:1-5a	Hebrews 4:9-16	2 Timothy 3:14—4:5
Acts 4:23-31	Matthew 22:15-21	Mark 10:35-45	Luke 18:1-8a
Matthew 5:38-48			

GRADUAL

These are they who have come out of the great tribulation;*
   they have washed their robes and made them white in the
   blood of the Lamb.

Gradual continues on the next page

Blessed are those whose strength is in you,*
  who have set their hearts on pilgrimage.   *(Rev. 7:14; Ps. 84:5)*

VERSE

Alleluia. Alleluia. He chose to give us birth through the word of truth, that we might be a kind of firstfruits of all he created. Alleluia.   *(James 1:18)*

TWENTY-THIRD SUNDAY AFTER PENTECOST

INTROIT

IX g²: Aeolian

The Lord watches over the way
of the righteous,*
  but the way of the wicked will perish.

Blessed is the man who does not walk in
the counsel of the wicked*
  or stand in the way of sinners or sit
  in the seat of mockers.
But his delight is in the law of the Lord,*
  and on his law he meditates
  day and night.
He is like a tree planted by streams
of water, which yields its fruit in
season and whose leaf does not wither.*
  Whatever he does prospers.

Glory be to the Father and to the Son*
  and to the Holy Spirit;
as it was in the beginning,*
  is now, and will be forever. Amen

The Lord watches over the way
of the righteous,*
  but the way of the wicked will perish.

*(Antiphon, Ps. 1:6;
Ps. 1:1-3)*

COLLECT OF THE DAY

Almighty God, we pray, show your humble servants your mercy that we, who put no trust in our own merits, may be dealt with not according to the severity of your judgment but according to your mercy; through Jesus Christ, your Son, our Lord, who lives and reigns with you and the Holy Spirit, one God, now and forever.(66)

READINGS

One-Year Series

Psalm 51:10-17
Micah 6:6-8
Acts 6:1-7
Mark 12:41-44

A. Psalm 1
Leviticus 19:1-2, 15-18
1 Thessalonians 1:5b-10
Matthew 22:34-40
  (41-46)

Three-Year Series

B. Psalm 126
Jeremiah 31:7-9
Hebrews 5:1-10
Mark 10:46-52

C. Psalm 34
Deuteronomy 10:12-22
2 Timothy 4:6-8, 16-18
Luke 18:9-14

GRADUAL

These are they who have come out of the great tribulation;*
   they have washed their robes and made them white in the
   blood ôf the Lamb.
Blessed are those whose strength is īn you,*
   who have set their hearts on p̄ilgrimage.   *(Rev. 7:14; Ps. 84:5)*

VERSE

Alleluia. Alleluia. The Lord will rescue me from every evil attack and will bring me
safely to his heavenly kingdom. Alleluia.   *(2 Tim. 4:18)*

TWENTY-FOURTH SUNDAY AFTER PENTECOST

INTROIT (One-Year Series)

You rule over the surging šea, [O
Lord;]*
   when its waves mount up, you ŝtill
   them.
I will sing of the love of the Lord
forĕver;*
   with my mouth I will make your
   faithfulness known through all
   generãtions.
The heavens are yours, and yours alšo
the earth;*
   you founded the world and all
   that ĩs in it.
Your arm is endued with power;*
   your hand is strong, your right
   hand exãlted.
Righteousness and justice are the
foundation ôf your throne;*
   love and faithfulness go befŏre you.
Indeed, our shield belongs t̃o the Lord,*
   our king to the Holy One of Ĩsrael.

Glory be to the Father and t̃o the Son*
   and to the Holy Špirit;

Introit continues on the next page

INTROIT (Three-Year Series)

I am laid low ĩn the dust;*
   renew my life according t̃o your
   word.

Blessed are they whose ways are
b̃lameless,*
   who walk according to the law ôf
   the Lord.
Blessed are they who keep his ŝtatutes*
   and seek him with ãll their heart.
I seek you with ãll my heart;*
   do not let me stray from ̃your
   commands.
I have hidden your word ĩn my heart*
   that I might not sin aǧainst you.
Praise be to ̃you, O Lord;*
   teach me ̃your decrees.
I delight in ̃your decrees;*
   I will not neǧlect your word.

Glory be to the Father and t̃o the Son*
   and to the Holy Špirit;
as it was in the beǧinning,*
   is now, and will be forever. Āmen

Introit continues on the next page

as it was in the beginning,*
  is now, and will be forever. Āmen

You rule over the surging sea, [O Lord;]*
  when its waves mount up, you still
  them.

  (Antiphon, Ps. 89:9;
  Ps. 89:1, 11, 13-14, 18)

I am laid low in the dust;*
  renew my life according to your
  word.

  (Antiphon, Ps. 119:25;
  Ps. 119:1-2, 10-12, 16)

COLLECT OF THE DAY

O Lord, we pray that the visitation of your grace may so cleanse our thoughts and minds that your Son Jesus, when he shall come, may find in us a fit dwelling place; through Jesus Christ, our Lord, who lives and reigns with you and the Holy Spirit, one God, now and forever.(67)

READINGS

One-Year Series

Psalm 46
Exodus 14:10, 26-31
Colossians 1:9-14(15-23)
Mark 4:35-41

Three-Year Series

A. Psalm 84:1-7
  Amos 5:18-24
  1 Thessalonians 4:13-
    14(15-18)
  Matthew 23:37-39
  or Matthew 25:1-13

B. Psalm 119:121-128
  Deuteronomy 6:1-9
  Hebrews 7:23-28
  Mark 12:28-34
  (35-37)

C. Psalm 119:145-152
  Exodus 34:5-9
  2 Thessalonians 1:1-
    5, 11-12
  Luke 19:1-10

GRADUAL

These are they who have come out of the great tribulation;*
  they have washed their robes and made them white in the
  blood of the Lamb.
Blessed are those whose strength is in you,*
  who have set their hearts on pilgrimage. *(Rev. 7:14; Ps. 84:5)*

VERSE

Alleluia. Alleluia. The Lord says, "Yes, I am coming soon." Amen. Come, Lord Jesus. Alleluia. *(Rev. 22:20b)*

TWENTY-FIFTH SUNDAY AFTER PENTECOST

INTROIT (One-Year Series)

INTROIT (Three-Year Series)

I sought the Lord, and he answered
me;*
  he delivered me from all my fears.

Give thanks to the Lord, call on his
name;*
  make known among the nations
  what he has done.
Sing to him, sing praise to him;*
  tell of all his wonderful acts.
Glory in his holy name;*
  let the hearts of those who seek
  the Lord rejoice.
Look to the Lord and his strength;*
  seek his face always.

Glory be to the Father and to the Son*
  and to the Holy Spirit;
as it was in the beginning,*
  is now, and will be forever. Amen

I sought the Lord, and he answered
me;*
  he delivered me from all my fears.

(Antiphon, Ps. 34:4;
Ps. 105:1-4)

Let them give thanks to the Lord for
his unfailing love*
  and his wonderful deeds for men.

Give thanks to the Lord, for he is
good;*
  his love endures forever.
Let the redeemed of the Lord say
this—*
  those he redeemed from the hand of
  the foe.
He lifted the needy out of their
affliction*
  and increased their families like
  flocks.
The upright see and rejoice,*
  but all the wicked shut their mouths.

Glory be to the Father and to the Son*
  and to the Holy Spirit;
as it was in the beginning,*
  is now, and will be forever. Amen

Let them give thanks to the Lord
for his unfailing love*
  and his wonderful deeds for men.

(Antiphon, Ps. 107:8;
Ps. 107:1-2, 41-42)

COLLECT OF THE DAY

O God, so rule and govern our hearts and minds by your Holy Spirit that, being ever
mindful of the end of all things and your just judgment, we may be stirred up to
holiness of living here and dwell with you forever hereafter; through Jesus Christ, your
Son, our Lord, who lives and reigns with you and the Holy Spirit, one God, now and
forever.(68)

READINGS

One-Year Series

Psalm 2
Ezekiel 33:10-16
Galatians 1:6-9
Matthew 13:44-52

A. Psalm 90:13-17
   Hosea 11:1-4, 8-9
   1 Thessalonians 5:
   1-11
   Matthew 24:3-14
   or Matthew 25:14-30

Three-Year Series

B. Psalm 107:1-3, 33-43
   1 Kings 17:8-16
   Hebrews 9:24-28
   Mark 12:41-44

C. Psalm 148
   1 Chronicles 29:10-13
   2 Thessalonians 2:13—
   3:5
   Luke 20:27-38

GRADUAL

These are they who have come out of the great tribulation;*
  they have washed their robes and made them white in the blood of the Lamb.

Gradual continues on the next page

Blessed are those whose strength is in you,*
who have set their hearts on pilgrimage. *(Rev. 7:14; Ps. 84:5)*

VERSE

Alleluia. Alleluia. Grow in the grace and knowledge of our Lord and Savior Jesus Christ. Alleluia. *(2 Peter 3:18a)*

THIRD-LAST SUNDAY IN THE CHURCH YEAR

INTROIT

IX g²: Aeolian

He who stands firm to the end*
will be saved.

You showed favor to your land,
O Lord;*
you restored the fortunes of Jacob.
You forgave the iniquity of your people*
and covered all their sins.
You set aside all your wrath*
and turned from your fierce anger.
Restore us again, O God our Savior,*
and put away your displeasure toward us.

Show us your unfailing love, O Lord,*
and grant us your salvation.

Glory be to the Father and to the Son*
and to the Holy Spirit;
as it was in the beginning,*
is now, and will be forever. Amen

He who stands firm to the end*
will be saved.

(Antiphon, Matt. 24:13; Ps. 85:1-4, 7)

COLLECT OF THE DAY

O Lord, absolve your people from their offenses that from the bonds of our sins, which by reason of our weakness we have brought upon us, we may be delivered by your bountiful goodness; through Jesus Christ, your Son, our Lord, who lives and reigns with you and the Holy Spirit, one God, now and forever. (69)

READINGS

One-Year Series

Psalm 114
Exodus 32:1-6(7-14)15-20
Romans 14:7-11
Matthew 24:15-28
or Luke 17:20-24
    (25-30)

Three-Year Series

A. Psalm 90:1-12
Job 14:1-6
or Malachi 2:1-2, 4-10
1 Thessalonians 3:11-13
or 1 Thessalonians 2:
    8-13
Matthew 24:15-28
or Matthew 23:1-12

B. Psalm 16
Daniel 12:1-3
Hebrews 12:26-29
or Hebrews 10:11-18
Mark 13:1-13

C. Psalm 98
Exodus 32:15-20
or Malachi 4:1-2a
2 Thessalonians 3:1-5
or 2 Thessalonians 3:
    6-13
Luke 17:20-30
or Luke 21:5-19

GRADUAL

These are they who have come out of the great tribulation;*
   they have washed their robes and made them white in the
   blood of the Lamb.
Blessed are those whose strength is in you,*
   who have set their hearts on pilgrimage. *(Rev. 7:14; Ps. 84:5)*

VERSE

Alleluia. Alleluia. Therefore keep watch, because you do not know on what day your
Lord will come. Alleluia. *(Matt. 24:42)*

SECOND-LAST SUNDAY IN THE CHURCH YEAR

INTROIT

With you there is forgiveness,
[O Lord;]*
   therefore you are feared.

O Lord, hear my prayer, listen to my
cry for mercy;*
   in your faithfulness and righteousness
   come to my relief.
I spread out my hands to you;*
   my soul thirsts for you like a
   parched land.
Answer me quickly, O Lord;*
   my spirit faints with longing.
Do not hide your face from me*
   or I will be like those who go down
   to the pit.
Rescue me from my enemies, O Lord,*
   for I hide myself in you.

For your name's sake, O Lord, preserve
my life;*
   in your righteousness, bring me out
   of trouble.

Glory be to the Father and to the Son*
   and to the Holy Spirit;
as it was in the beginning,*
   is now, and will be forever. Amen

With you there is forgiveness,
[O Lord;]*
   therefore you are feared.

(Antiphon, Ps. 130:4;
Ps. 143:1, 6-7, 9, 11)

COLLECT OF THE DAY

Almighty and ever-living God, since you have given exceedingly great and precious
promises to those who believe, grant us so perfectly and without all doubt to believe in
your Son Jesus Christ that our faith in your sight may never be reproved; through our
Savior, Jesus Christ, who lives and reigns with you and the Holy Spirit, one God, now
and forever. (70)

READINGS

One-Year Series		Three-Year Series	
Psalm 143:1-10	A. Psalm 105:1-7	B. Psalm 111	C. Psalm 92:1-8
Jeremiah 8:4-7	Jeremiah 25:30-32	Daniel 7:9-10	Jeremiah 8:4-7
Romans 8:18-23(24-25)	or Jeremiah 26:1-6	Hebrews 12:1-2	or Isaiah 52:1-6
Matthew 25:31-46	1 Thessalonians 1:3-10	or Hebrews 13:20-21	2 Corinthians 5:1-10
	or 1 Thessalonians 3:	Mark 13:24-31	or 1 Corinthians 15:
	7-13		54-58
	Matthew 25:31-46		Luke 19:11-27
	or Matthew 24:1-14		

GRADUAL

These are they who have come out of the great tribulation; *
　　they have washed their robes and made them white in the
　　blood of the Lamb.
Blessed are those whose strength is in you, *
　　who have set their hearts on pilgrimage.　*(Rev. 7:14; Ps. 84:5)*

VERSE

Alleluia. Alleluia. Be always on the watch, and pray that you may be able to escape
all that is about to happen, and that you may be able to stand before the Son of Man.
Alleluia.　*(Luke 21:36)*

LAST SUNDAY IN THE CHURCH YEAR
Sunday of the Fulfillment

INTROIT

* VII E: Mixolydian

We are looking forward to a new
heaven and a new earth, *
　　the home of righteousness.

Show me, O Lord, my life's end and
the number of my days; *
　　let me know how fleeting is my life.
You have made my days a mere
handbreadth; the span of my years is as
nothing before you. *
　　Each man's life is but a breath.
But now, Lord, what do I look for? *
　　My hope is in you.
Save me from all my transgressions; *
　　do not make me the scorn of fools.

Hear my prayer, O Lord, listen to my
cry for help; *
　　be not deaf to my weeping.

Glory be to the Father and to the Son *
　　and to the Holy Spirit;
as it was in the beginning, *
　　is now, and will be forever. Amen

We are looking forward to a new
heaven and a new earth, *
　　the home of righteousness.

(Antiphon, 2 Peter 3:13b;
Ps. 39:4-5, 7-8, 12a)

93

COLLECT OF THE DAY

Lord God, heavenly Father, send forth your Son, we pray, that he may lead home his bride, the Church, that we with all the redeemed may enter into your eternal kingdom; through Jesus Christ, your Son, our Lord, who lives and reigns with you and the Holy Spirit, one God, now and forever. (71)

READINGS

One-Year Series

Psalm 130
Isaiah 65:17-25
2 Peter 3:3-4, 8-10a, 13
or Revelation 21:1-7
Matthew 25:1-13

Three-Year Series

A. Psalm 130
 or Psalm 100
 Isaiah 65:17-25
 or Ezekiel 34:11-16,
 23-24
 2 Peter 3:3-4, 8-10a, 13
 or 1 Corinthians 15:
 20-28
 Matthew 25:1-13
 or Matthew 25:31-46

B. Psalm 130
 Isaiah 51:4-6
 or Daniel 7:13-14
 Jude 20-25
 or Revelation 1:4b-8
 Mark 13:32-37
 or John 18:33-37

C. Psalm 130
 Malachi 3:14-18
 or Jeremiah 23:2-6
 Revelation 22:6-13
 or Colossians 1:13-20
 Luke 12:42-48
 or Luke 23:35-43

GRADUAL

These are they who have come out of the great tribulation;*
 they have washed their robes and made them white in the blood of the Lamb.
Blessed are those whose strength is in you,*
 who have set their hearts on pilgrimage. *(Rev. 7:14; Ps. 84:5)*

VERSE

Alleluia. Alleluia. I am the Alpha and the Omega, the First and the Last, the Beginning and the End. Alleluia. *(Rev. 22:13)*

MINOR FESTIVALS

COMMEMORATION OF THE APOSTLES OF OUR LORD

INTROIT

I will speak of your statutes before
kings, [O Lord;]*
 and will not be put to shame.

I will sing of the love of the Lord
forever;*

with my mouth I will make your
faithfulness known through
all generations.

The heavens praise your wonders,
O Lord,*

Introit continues on the next page

your faithfulness too, in the assembly of the holy ones.

Glory be to the Father and to the Son* and to the Holy Spirit; as it was in the beginning,* is now, and will be forever. Amen

I will speak of your statutes before kings, [O Lord;]* and will not be put to shame.

(Antiphon Ps. 119:46; Ps. 89:1, 5)

ST. ANDREW
November 30

COLLECT OF THE DAY

Almighty God, by whose grace the blessed apostle Saint Andrew obeyed the call of your Son Jesus Christ, grant us also to follow him in heart and life; through Jesus Christ, your Son, our Lord, who lives and reigns with you and the Holy Spirit, one God, now and forever. (72)

READINGS

One-Year Series

Psalm 139:1-10
Deuteronomy 30:11-14
Romans 10:8-18
Matthew 4:18-22

Three -Year Series

A, B, C. Psalm 19:1-6
Ezekiel 3:16-21
Romans 10:10-18
John 1:35-42

ST. THOMAS
December 21

COLLECT OF THE DAY

Almighty and ever-living God, as you through the Word of your beloved Son mightily strengthened the faith of the apostle Saint Thomas, keep also us steadfast in the faith by that same Word through all our days; through Jesus Christ, your Son, our Lord, who lives and reigns with you and the Holy Spirit, one God, now and forever. (73)

READINGS

One-Year Series

Psalm 139:1-4, 17-18, 23-24
Habakkuk 2:1-4
Ephesians 1:3-6
John 20:24-31

Three-Year Series

A, B, C. Psalm 136:1-4, 23-26
Judges 6:36-40
Ephesians 4:11-16
John 14:1-7

THE CONFESSION OF ST. PETER
January 18

COLLECT OF THE DAY

Dear Father in heaven, as you revealed to the apostle Saint Peter the blessed truth that

Jesus is the Christ, the Son of the living God, strengthen us in that same faith in our Savior that we too may joyfully confess that there is salvation in no one else; through Jesus Christ, our Lord, who lives and reigns with you and the Holy Spirit, one God, now and forever. (74)

READINGS

One-Year Series	Three-Year Series
Psalm 23	A, B, C. Psalm 18:1-7, 16-19
Acts 2:22-24, 32-33	Acts 4:8-13
1 Peter 1:3-9	1 Corinthians 10:1-5
Matthew 16:13-19	Matthew 16:13-19

THE CONVERSION OF ST. PAUL
January 25

COLLECT OF THE DAY

Almighty God, as you turned the heart of him who persecuted the Church and by his preaching caused the light of the Gospel to shine throughout the world, grant us ever to rejoice in the saving light of your Gospel and to spread it to the uttermost parts of the earth; through Jesus Christ, your Son, our Lord, who lives and reigns with you and the Holy Spirit, one God, now and forever. (75)

READINGS

One-Year Series	Three-Year Series
Psalm 67	A, B, C. Psalm 67
Jeremiah 1:4-10	Acts 9:1-22
Acts 9:1-22	Galatians 1:11-24
Matthew 19:27-30	Luke 21:10-19

ST. MATTHIAS
February 24

COLLECT OF THE DAY

Lord God, heavenly King, whose chosen apostles have witnessed to us regarding your resurrection, grant that your Church, ever preserved from false teachers, may praise your wonderful works and walk in the power of your resurrection; for you live and reign with the Father and the Holy Spirit, one God, now and forever. (76)

READINGS

One-Year Series	Three-Year Series
Psalm 16	A, B, C. Psalm 133
Acts 1:15-26	Isaiah 66:1-2
1 John 2:15-17	Acts 1:15-26
Matthew 11:25-30	Luke 6:12-16

ST. PHILIP AND ST. JAMES
May 1

COLLECT OF THE DAY

Almighty God, whom to know is life everlasting, grant that, even as your Son gave knowledge of everlasting life to the apostles Saint Philip and Saint James by revealing himself to them as the only way to you, so we may by a true and lively faith know him as our only Savior now and ever; through our Lord Jesus Christ, who lives and reigns with you and the Holy Spirit, one God, now and forever. (77)

READINGS

One-Year Series

Psalm 25:1-10
Malachi 3:16-18
Ephesians 2:19-22
John 14:1-14

Three-Year Series

A, B, C. Psalm 36:5-10
Isaiah 30:18-21
2 Corinthians 4:1-6
John 14:8-14

ST. BARNABAS
June 11

COLLECT OF THE DAY

O almighty God, by your Son, our Savior, you have always given to your Church on earth faithful shepherds to guide and feed your flock. Therefore we pray, make all pastors diligent to preach your holy Word and minister your means of grace, and grant your people wisdom to follow in the way that leads to life eternal; through our Lord Jesus Christ, who lives and reigns with you and the Holy Spirit, one God, now and forever. (78)

READINGS

One-Year Series

Psalm 67
Isaiah 60:1-5
Acts 11:19-30; 13:1-3
Mark 6:7-13

Three-Year Series

A, B, C. Psalm 135:1-7
Isaiah 42:5-12
Acts 11:19-30; 13:1-3
Matthew 10:5-16

ST. PETER AND ST. PAUL
June 29

COLLECT OF THE DAY

Merciful and eternal God, from whom the holy apostles Saint Peter and Saint Paul received grace and strength to lay down their lives for the sake of your Son, grant that, strengthened by the Holy Spirit, we may with like constancy confess your truth and be at all times ready to lay down our lives for him who laid down his life for us; even Jesus Christ, our Lord, who lives and reigns with you and the Holy Spirit, one God, now and forever. (79)

READINGS

One-Year Series

Psalm 46
Ezekiel 34:11-16
Acts 12:1-11
Matthew 16:13-20

Three-Year Series

A, B, C. Psalm 18:25-32
Ezekiel 34:11-16
1 Corinthians 3:16-23
Mark 8:27-35

ST. JAMES THE ELDER
July 25

COLLECT OF THE DAY

Grant, O Lord, that, as Saint James the apostle readily followed the calling of your Son Jesus Christ, we may by your grace be enabled to forsake all false and passing allurements and follow him alone; through Jesus Christ, our Lord, who lives and reigns with you and the Holy Spirit, one God, now and forever. (80)

READINGS

One-Year Series

Psalm 16
1 Kings 19:9-18
Romans 8:28-39
Matthew 20:20-28

Three-Year Series

A, B, C. Psalm 103:19-22
1 Kings 19:9-18
Acts 11:27—12:3a
Mark 10:35-45

ST. BARTHOLOMEW
August 24

COLLECT OF THE DAY

Almighty God, whose Son Jesus Christ chose Saint Bartholomew to be an apostle to preach the blessed Gospel, grant to your Church also in our time faithful pastors and teachers to proclaim the glory of your name; through Jesus Christ, our Lord, who lives and reigns with you and the Holy Spirit, one God, now and forever. (81)

READINGS

One-Year Series

Psalm 121
Proverbs 3:1-7
2 Corinthians 4:7-10
Luke 22:24-30

Three-Year Series

A, B, C. Psalm 121
Exodus 19:1-6
1 Corinthians 12:27-31a
John 1:43-51

ST. SIMON AND ST. JUDE
October 28

COLLECT OF THE DAY

O almighty God, whose Church is built on the foundation of the apostles and prophets, Jesus Christ himself being the chief cornerstone, grant us to be joined together in unity of spirit by their doctrine that we may be made a holy temple acceptable in your sight; through Jesus Christ, your Son, our Lord, who lives and reigns with you and the Holy Spirit, one God, now and forever. (82)

READINGS

One-Year Series

Psalm 119:89-96
Deuteronomy 32:1-4
1 Peter 1:3-9
John 15:17-21

Three-Year Series

A, B, C. Psalm 119:73-80
Jeremiah 26:(1-6)7-16
1 John 4:1-6
John 14:21-27

GRADUAL

All you have made will praise you, O Lord;*
    your saints will extol you.
The Lord is faithful to all his promises*
    and loving toward all he has made.   *(Ps. 145:10, 13b)*

VERSE

Alleluia. Alleluia. You did not choose me, but I chose you to go and bear fruit—fruit that will last. Alleluia.   *(John 15:16a)*

COMMEMORATION OF THE EVANGELISTS

INTROIT

I am the vine;*
    you are the branches.
If a man remains in me and I in him,
he will bear much fruit;*
    apart from me you can do nothing.

It is good to praise the Lord*
    and make music to your name, O
    Most High,
to proclaim your love in the morning*

    and your faithfulness at night.
For you make me glad by your deeds,
O Lord;*
    How great are your works, O Lord.

Glory be to the Father and to the Son*
    and to the Holy Spirit;
as it was in the beginning,*
    is now, and will be forever. Amen

Introit continues on the next page

I ám the vine;*
   you are the branches.
If a man remains in me and I in him,
he will bear much fruit;*

apart from me you can do ñothing.

*(Antiphon, John 15:5;
Ps. 92:1-2, 4a, 5a)*

ST. JOHN
December 27

COLLECT OF THE DAY

Merciful Lord, cast the bright beams of your light upon your Church that, being instructed in the doctrine of your blessed apostle and evangelist Saint John, we may come to the light of everlasting life; for you live and reign with the Father and the Holy Spirit, one God, now and forever. (83)

READINGS

One-Year Series

Psalm 92:1-4, 12-15
Hosea 11:1-4
1 John 1:1-10
John 21:20-24

Three-Year Series

A, B, C. Psalm 116:12-19
Genesis 1:1-5, 26-31
1 John 1:1—2:2
John 21:20-25

ST. MARK
April 25

COLLECT OF THE DAY

O almighty God, as you have enriched your Church with the precious Gospel proclaimed by the evangelist Saint Mark, grant us firmly to believe your glad tidings of salvation and daily walk according to your Word; through Jesus Christ, your Son, our Lord,who lives and reigns with you and the Holy Spirit,one God,now and forever. (84)

READINGS

One-Year Series

Psalm 146
Isaiah 55:1-5
Ephesians 4:7-16
Luke 10:1-9

Three-Year Series

A, B, C. Psalm 146
Isaiah 52:7-10
2 Timothy 4:6-11, 18
Mark 1:1-15

ST. MATTHEW
September 21

COLLECT OF THE DAY

O almighty God, whose blessed Son has called us even as he called Saint Matthew the tax collector, grant that we also may forsake all sin, all covetous desires and inordinate love of riches, and, casting every care upon him, may follow our Lord Jesus Christ, who lives and reigns with you and the Holy Spirit, one God, now and forever. (85)

READINGS

One-Year Series

Psalm 119:33-40
Proverbs 3:1-6
Ephesians 4:7-16
Matthew 9:9-13

Three-Year Series

A, B, C. Psalm 119:33-40
Ezekiel 2:8—3:11
Ephesians 2:4-10
Matthew 9:9-13

ST. LUKE
October 18

COLLECT OF THE DAY

Almighty God, whose blessed Son called Saint Luke the physician to be an evangelist and physician of the soul, grant that the healing medicine of your Word and the sacraments may put to flight the diseases of our souls that with willing hearts we may ever love and serve you; through Jesus Christ, your Son, our Lord, who lives and reigns with you and the Holy Spirit, one God, now and forever. (86)

READINGS

One-Year Series

Psalm 147:1-7
Isaiah 35:5-8
2 Timothy 4:5-15
Luke 10:1-9

Three-Year Series

A, B, C. Psalm 138
Isaiah 43:8-13
or Isaiah 35:5-8
2 Timothy 4:5-11
Luke 1:1-4; 24:44-53

GRADUAL

Blessed is the man who fears the Lord,*
    who finds great delight in his commands.
Wealth and riches are in his house,*
    and his righteousness endures forever.   (Ps. 112:1, 3)

VERSE

Alleluia. Alleluia. My mouth will tell of your righteousness, O God, of your salvation all day long. Alleluia.   (Ps. 71:15a)

NEW YEAR'S EVE
Eve of the Name of Jesus
December 31

INTROIT

Our help is in the name òf the Lord,*
the Maker of heaven and earth.

Sing to the Lord a new song, for he has
done marvelous things;*
his right hand and his holy arm have
worked salvation for him.
The Lord has made his salvation known*
and revealed his righteousness to the
ñations.
He has remembered his love and his
faithfulness to the house of Israel;*
all the ends of the earth have seen
the salvation òf our God.

Glory be to the Father and to the Son*
and to the Holy Spirit;
as it was in the beginning,*
is now, and will be forever. Āmen

Our help is in the name òf the Lord,*
the Maker of heaven and earth.

*(Antiphon, Ps. 124:8;
Ps. 98:1-3)*

COLLECT OF THE DAY

Lord God, heavenly Father, because you sent us your only-begotten Son for our salvation and gave him the name of Jesus, grant that we may begin the New Year trusting in his saving name and live all our days in his service and praise to the glory of his holy name; who lives and reigns with you and the Holy Spirit, one God, now and forever. (87)

READINGS

One-Year Series
Psalm 8
Isaiah 51:1-6
Romans 8:31-39
Matthew 1:18-21

GRADUAL

All the ends of the earth have seen the
salvation òf our God.*
Shout for joy to the Lord, àll the earth.
The Lord has made his salvation known*
and revealed his righteousness to the ñations. *(Ps. 98:3b, 4a, 2)*

VERSE

Alleluia. Alleluia. Come, let us bow down in worship, let us kneel before the Lord our Maker. Alleluia. *(Ps. 95:6)*

NEW YEAR'S DAY
The Circumcision of Our Lord
January 1

INTROIT

The Word became flesh and lived for a while among us.*
> We have seen his glory, the glory of the one and only Son, who came from the Father, full of grace and truth.

I will praise you, O Lord, with all my heart;*
> I will tell of your wonders.

What is man that you are mindful of him,*
> the son of man that you care for him?

I trust in your unfailing love;*
> my heart rejoices in your salvation.

Glory be to the Father and to the Son*
> and to the Holy Spirit;

as it was in the beginning,*
> is now, and will be forever. Amen

The Word became flesh and lived for a while among us.*
> We have seen his glory, the glory of the one and only Son, who came from the Father, full of grace and truth.

(Antiphon, John 1:14; Ps. 9:1; 8:4; 13:5)

COLLECT OF THE DAY

Lord God, you made your blessed Son, our Savior, subject to the Law to shed his blood on our behalf. Grant us the true circumcision of the spirit that our hearts may be made pure from all sin; through Jesus Christ, our Lord, who lives and reigns with you and the Holy Spirit, one God, now and forever. (88)

READINGS

One-Year Series	Three-Year Series
Psalm 116	A, B, C. Psalm 8
Genesis 17:1-4	Numbers 6:22-27
Galatians 3:23-29	Romans 1:1-7
Luke 2:21	or Philippians 2:9-13
	Luke 2:21

GRADUAL

The Lord is with me; I will not be afraid.*
> What can man do to me?

The Lord is with me; he is my helper.*
> I will look in triumph on my enemies. *(Ps. 118:6-7)*

103

VERSE

Alleluia. Alleluia. I love the Lord, for he heard my voice; he heard my cry for mercy. Alleluia. *(Ps. 116:1)*

COMMEMORATION OF PASTORS AND CONFESSORS
St. Timothy   St. Titus
January 24   January 26

INTROIT

I will speak of your statutes before
kings, [O Lord,]*
   and will not be put to shame.

I will sing of the love of the
Lord forever;*
   with my mouth I will make your
   faithfulness known through
all generations.
The heavens praise your wonders,
O Lord,*
   your faithfulness too, in the
   assembly of the holy ones.

Glory be to the Father and to the Son*
   and to the Holy Spirit;
as it was in the beginning,*
   is now, and will be forever. Amen

I will speak of your statutes before
kings, [O Lord,]*
   and will not be put to shame.

(Antiphon Ps. 119:46;
Ps. 89:1, 5)

COLLECT OF THE DAY

O almighty God, by your Son, our Savior, you have always given to your Church on earth faithful shepherds to guide and feed your flock. Therefore we pray, make all pastors diligent to preach your holy Word and minister your means of grace, and grant your people wisdom to follow in the way that leads to life eternal; through our Lord Jesus Christ, who lives and reigns with you and the Holy Spirit, one God, now and forever. (78)

READINGS

Three-Year Series

A, B, C. Psalm 84
      Ezekiel 34:11-16
      or Acts 20:17-35
      1 Peter 5:1-4
      or Ephesians 3:14-21
      John 21:15-17
      or Matthew 24:42-47

GRADUAL

Blessed is the man who fears the Lord,*
  who finds great delight in his commands.
Wealth and riches are in his house,*
  and his righteousness endures forever.   *(Ps. 112:1, 3)*

VERSE

Alleluia. Alleluia. My mouth will tell of your righteousness, [O God,] of your salvation
all day long. Alleluia.   *(Ps. 71:15a)*

COMMEMORATION OF THE FAITHFUL DEPARTED
November 2

INTROIT

Precious in the sight of the Lord*
  is the death of his saints.

I love the Lord, for he heard my voice;*
  he heard my cry for mercy.
Because he turned his ear to me,*
  I will call on him as long as I live.
He has caused his wonders to be
remembered;*
  the Lord is gracious and
  compassionate.
Show me, O Lord, my life's end*
  and the number of my days.

Glory be to the Father and to the Son*
  and to the Holy Spirit;
as it was in the beginning,*
  is now, and will be forever. Amen

Precious in the sight of the Lord*
  is the death of his saints.

  (Antiphon, Ps. 116:15;
  Ps. 116:1-2; 111:4; 39:4a)

COLLECT OF THE DAY

Almighty God, in whose glorious presence live all who depart in the Lord and before
whom all the souls of the faithful who are delivered of the burden of the flesh are in joy
and felicity, we give you hearty thanks for your loving-kindness to all your servants
who have finished their course in faith and now rest from their labors, and we humbly
implore your mercy that we, together with all who have departed in the saving faith,
may have our perfect consummation and bliss, in both body and soul, in your eternal
and everlasting glory; through Jesus Christ, our Lord, who lives and reigns with you
and the Holy Spirit, one God, now and forever. (89)

READINGS

One-Year Series
Psalm 34:1-9
Isaiah 35:3-10
2 Peter 3:8-14
John 5:24-29

GRADUAL

I am the light of the world.*
   Whoever follows me will never walk
   in darkness, but will have the light
   of life.
The Spirit and the bride say, "Come!"*
   And let him who hears say, "Come!"
He who testifies to these things says, "Yes,
I am coming soon."*
   Amen. Come, Lord Jesus. *(John 8:12b; Rev. 22:17a, 20)*

VERSE

Alleluia. Alleluia. Blessed are the dead who die in the Lord from now on. They kept themselves pure. They follow the Lamb wherever he goes. Alleluia. *(Rev. 14:13b, 4b)*

THE PRESENTATION OF OUR LORD, THE ANNUNCIATION OF OUR LORD, AND THE VISITATION

INTROIT

Within your temple, O God,*
   we meditate on your unfailing love.

Great is the Lord, and most worthy
of praise,*
   in the city of our God, his holy
   mountain.
As we have heard, so have we seen*
   in the city of the Lord Almighty,
   in the city of our God.

Glory be to the Father and to the Son*
   and to the Holy Spirit;
as it was in the beginning,*
   is now, and will be forever. Amen

Within your temple, O God,*
   we meditate on your unfailing love.

   *(Antiphon, Ps. 48:9;
   Ps. 48:1, 8a)*

THE PRESENTATION OF OUR LORD
February 2

COLLECT OF THE DAY

Almighty and ever-living God, grant that as your only-begotten Son was this day presented in the temple in the substance of our human flesh, so by him we may be presented to you with pure and clean hearts; through Jesus Christ, our Lord, who lives and reigns with you and the Holy Spirit, one God, now and forever. (90)

READINGS

One-Year Series

Psalm 84
Malachi 3:1-4
Hebrews 2:14-18
Luke 2:22-32

Three-Year Series

A, B, C. Psalm 84
1 Samuel 1:21-28
Hebrews 2:14-18
Luke 2:22-40

THE ANNUNCIATION OF OUR LORD
March 25

COLLECT OF THE DAY

We implore you, O Lord, to pour forth your grace on us that, as we have known the incarnation of your Son Jesus Christ by the message of the angel, so by his cross and Passion we may be brought to the glory of his resurrection; through our Lord Jesus Christ, who lives and reigns with you and the Holy Spirit, one God, now and forever. (91)

READINGS

One-Year Series

Psalm 45
Isaiah 7:10-14
Hebrews 10:5-10
Luke 1:25-38

Three-Year Series

A, B, C. Psalm 45
Isaiah 7:10-14; 8:10c
1 Timothy 3:16
Luke 1:25-38

THE VISITATION
May 31

COLLECT OF THE DAY

Almighty God, as you dealt wonderfully with your servant, the blessed virgin Mary, in choosing her to be the mother of your dearly beloved Son and thus graciously made known your regard for the poor and lowly and despised, grant us grace in all humility and meekness to receive your Word with hearty faith and to rejoice in Jesus Christ, your Son, our Lord, who lives and reigns with you and the Holy Spirit, one God, now and forever. (92)

READINGS

One-Year Series

Psalm 138
Zephaniah 3:14-17
Isaiah 11:1-5
Luke 1:39-56

Three-Year Series

A, B, C. Psalm 138
Isaiah 11:1-5
Romans 12:9-16
Luke 1:39-47

GRADUAL

The Lord is my light and my salvation—*
  whom shall I fear?
The Lord is the stronghold of my life—*
  of whom shall I be afraid?   *(Ps. 27:1)*

VERSE

Alleluia. Alleluia. The Mighty One has done great things for me—holy is his name.
Alleluia.   *(Luke 1:49)*

OR (when the Minor Festival occurs during Lent)
My soul praises the Lord and my spirit rejoices in God my Savior. For my eyes have
seen your salvation, which you have prepared in the sight of all people.
(Luke 1:46b, 47a; 2:30-31)

THE NATIVITY OF ST. JOHN THE BAPTIST
June 24

INTROIT

See, I will send my messenger,*
  who will prepare the way before me.

Praise be to the Lord, the God of
Israel,*
  because he has come and has
  redeemed his people,
to rescue us from the hand of our
enemies,*
  and to enable us to serve him
  without fear
in holiness and righteousness*
  before him all our days.
And you, my child, will be called a
prophet of the Most High;*

for you will go on before the Lord
  to prepare the way for him.

Glory be to the Father and to the Son*
  and to the Holy Spirit;
as it was in the beginning,*
  is now, and will be forever. Amen

See, I will send my messenger,*
  who will prepare the way before me.

(Antiphon, Mal. 3:1;
Luke 1:68, 74-76)

COLLECT OF THE DAY

Almighty God, through John the Baptist, the forerunner of Christ, you once proclaimed salvation; now grant that we may know this salvation and serve you in holiness and righteousness all the days of our life; through our Lord Jesus Christ, your Son, who lives and reigns with you and the Holy Spirit, one God, now and forever. (3)

READINGS

One-Year Series	Three-Year Series
Psalm 141	A, B, C. Psalm 141
Malachi 3:1-4	Malachi 3:1-4
Isaiah 40:1-5	Acts 13:13-26
Luke 1:57-80	Luke 1:57-67(68-80)

GRADUAL

"Before I formed you in the womb I knew you,*
  before you were born I set you apart."
The Lord reached out his hand and touched my mouth
and said to me,*
  "Now, I have put my words in your mouth." *(Jer. 1:5a, 9)*

VERSE

Allelula. Alleluia. There came a man who was sent from God; his name was John. He came as a witness to testify concerning that light. Alleluia. *(John 1:6-7a)*

PRESENTATION OF THE AUGSBURG CONFESSION
June 25

COMMEMORATION OF THE DOCTORS OF THE CHURCH
Martin Luther	C.F.W. Walther
February 18	May 7

INTROIT

I will speak of your statutes before kings, [O Lord,]*
  and will not be put to shame.

God is our refuge and strength,*

an ever present help in trouble.
Therefore we will not fear, though
the earth give way*

Introit continues on the next page

and the mountains fall into the
heart of the sea,
though its waters roar and foam*
and the mountains quake with
their surging.
The Lord Almighty is with us;*
the God of Jacob is our fortress.

Glory be to the Father and to the Son*

and to the Holy Spirit;
as it was in the beginning,*
is now, and will be forever. Amen

I will speak of your statutes before
kings, [O Lord,]*
and will not be put to shame.

*(Antiphon, Ps. 119:46;
Ps. 46:1-3, 7)*

COLLECT OF THE DAY

O Lord God, heavenly Father, pour out your Holy Spirit on your faithful people, keep them steadfast in your grace and truth, protect and comfort them in all temptation, defend them against all enemies of your Word, and bestow on Christ's Church Militant your saving peace; through Jesus Christ, your Son, our Lord, who lives and reigns with you and the Holy Spirit, one God, now and forever. (93)

READINGS

One-Year Series

Psalm 46
Isaiah 55:6-11
Romans 10:5-17
John 15:1-11

GRADUAL

Blessed is he whose help is the God of Jacob,*
whose hope is in the Lord his God.
The Lord takes delight in his people;*
he crowns the humble with salvation.   *(Ps. 146:5; 149:4)*

VERSE

Alleluia. Alleluia. O Lord Almighty, blessed is the man who trusts in you. Alleluia.   *(Ps. 84:12)*

ST. MARY MAGDALENE
July 22

INTROIT

* VII E: Mixolydian

In you, O Lord, I have taken refuge;*
　let me never be put to shame.

I will exalt you, O Lord,*
　for you lifted me out of the depths.
O Lord my God, I called to you for help*
　and you healed me.
O Lord, you brought me up from the grave;*
　you spared me from going down
　into the pit.

O Lord my God,*
　I will give you thanks forever.

Glory be to the Father and to the Son*
　and to the Holy Spirit;
as it was in the beginning,*
　is now, and will be forever. Amen

In you, O Lord, I have taken refuge;*
　let me never be put to shame.

(Antiphon, Ps. 31:1a;
Ps. 30:1a, 2-3, 12b)

COLLECT OF THE DAY

O almighty God, whom to know is everlasting life, grant us perfectly to know your Son Jesus Christ to be the Way, the Truth, and the Life that, following his steps, we may steadfastly walk in the way that leads to eternal life; through Jesus Christ, our Lord, who lives and reigns with you and the Holy Spirit, one God, now and forever.(94)

READINGS

One-Year Series

Psalm 73:23-28
Ruth 1:6-18
2 Corinthians 5:14-18
John 20:1-2, 11-18

Three-Year Series

A, B, C. Psalm 73:23-28
Ruth 1:6-18
or Exodus 2:1-10
Acts 13:26-33a
John 20:1-2, 11-18

GRADUAL

The Lord is my shepherd,*
　I shall lack nothing.
He guides me in paths of righteousness*
　for his name's sake.
Surely goodness and love will follow me all the days of my life,*
　and I will dwell in the house of
　the Lord forever.　*(Ps. 23:1, 3b, 6)*

VERSE

Alleluia. Alleluia. Whoever serves me must follow me. My Father will honor the one who serves me. Alleluia.　*(John 12:26)*

ST. MARY, MOTHER OF OUR LORD
August 15

111

INTROIT

* VII E: Mixolydian

I will extol the Lord at all times;*
  his praise will always be on my lips.

My soul will boast in the Lord;*
  let the afflicted hear and rejoice.
Glorify the Lord with me;*
  let us exalt his name together.
I sought the Lord and he answered me;*
  he delivered me from all my fears.
Those who look to him are radiant;*

their faces are never covered with shame.

Glory be to the Father and to the Son*
  and to the Holy Spirit;
as it was in the beginning,*
  is now, and will be forever. Amen

I will extol the Lord at all times;*
  his praise will always be on my lips.

*(Antiphon, Ps. 34:1;
Ps. 34:2-5)*

COLLECT OF THE DAY

Grant, we humbly pray, O Lord, to your servants the gift of your heavenly blessing that, as the Son of the virgin Mary has granted us salvation, we may daily grow in your favor; through Jesus Christ, your Son, our Lord, who lives and reigns with you and the Holy Spirit, one God, now and forever. (95)

READINGS

One-Year Series

Psalm 34:1-9
Isaiah 61:10-11
Galatians 4:4-7
Luke 1:46-55

Three-Year Series

A, B, C. Psalm 45:10-15
Isaiah 61:7-11
Galatians 4:4-7
Luke 1:46-55

GRADUAL

Fear the Lord, you his saints,*
  for those who fear him lack nothing.
A righteous man may have many troubles,*
  but the Lord delivers him from them all. *(Ps. 34:9, 19)*

VERSE

Alleluia. Alleluia. Greetings, you who are highly favored! The Lord is with you. The Holy Spirit will come upon you. Alleluia. *(Luke 1:28a, 35a)*

HOLY CROSS DAY
September 14

INTROIT

*   XI A: Ionian

The Lord has made his salvation known*
   and revealed his righteousness to the ñations.

Sing to the Lord a new song, for he has done marvelous things;*
   his right hand and his holy arm have worked salvation for him.
Shout for joy to the Lord, all the earth,*
   burst into jubilant song with music;
with trumpets and the blast of the ram's horn—*
   shout for joy before the Lord, the King.

Glory be to the Father and to the Son*
   and to the Holy Spirit;
as it was in the beginning,*
   is now, and will be forever. Amen

The Lord has made his salvation known*
   and revealed his righteousness to the ñations.

(Antiphon, Ps. 98:2;
Ps. 98:1, 4, 6)

COLLECT OF THE DAY

Merciful and everlasting God, you did not spare your only Son but delivered him up for us all that he might bear our sins on the cross. Grant that our hearts may be so fixed with steadfast faith in him that we may not fear the power of any adversaries; through Jesus Christ, your Son, our Lord, who lives and reigns with you and the Holy Spirit, one God, now and forever. (29)

READINGS

Three-Year Series

A, B, C. Psalm 98:1-5
      Isaiah 45:21-25
      1 Corinthians 1:18-24
      John 12:20-33

GRADUAL

God was pleased to have all his fullness dwell in Christ,*
   and through him to reconcile to himself all things,
whether things on earth or things in heaven,*
   by making peace through his blood, shed on the cross. *(Col. 1:19-20)*

VERSE

Alleluia. Alleluia. May I never boast except in the cross of our Lord Jesus Christ. Alleluia. *(Gal. 6:14a)*

113

ST. MICHAEL AND ALL ANGELS
September 29

INTROIT

Praise the Lord, Ó my soul;*
 all my inmost being, praise
 his hóly name.

Praise the Lord, you his ángels,*
 you mighty ones who do his bidding,
 who obey his word.
Praise the Lord, all his heavenly hosts,*
 you his servants who do his will.
Praise the Lord, all his works*
 everywhere in his dominion.

Glory be to the Father and to the Son*
 and to the Holy Spirit;
as it was in the beginning,*
 is now, and will be forever. Āmen

Praise the Lord, Ó my soul;*
 all my inmost being, praise
 his hóly name.

*(Antiphon, Ps. 103:1;
Ps. 103:20-22)*

COLLECT OF THE DAY

O everlasting God, whose wise planning has ordained and constituted the ministry of
men and angels in a wonderful order, mercifully grant that, as your holy angels always
serve you in heaven, so by your appointment they may also help and defend us here on
earth; through Jesus Christ, your Son, our Lord, who lives and reigns with you and the
Holy Spirit, one God, now and forever. (96)

READINGS

One-Year Series

Psalm 103:19-22
Joshua 5:13-15
Revelation 12:7-12
Matthew 18:1-11

Three-Year Series

A, B, C. Psalm 103:1-5, 20-22
 Daniel 10:10-14; 12:1-3
 Revelation 12:7-12
 Luke 10:17-20

GRADUAL

God will command his angels concerning you*
 to guard you in all your ways.
Praise the Lord, Ó my soul;*
 all my inmost being, praise his hóly name. *(Ps. 91:11; 103:1)*

VERSE

Alleluia. Alleluia. Praise the Lord, all his works everywhere in his dominion. Praise the
Lord, O my soul. Alleluia. *(Ps. 103:22)*

REFORMATION DAY
October 31

INTROIT

I will speak of your statutes before kings, [O Lord,]*
and will not be put to shame.

God is our refuge and strength,*
an ever present help in trouble.
Therefore we will not fear, though the earth give way*
and the mountains fall into the heart of the sea,
though its waters roar and foam*
and the mountains quake with their surging.

The Lord Almighty is with us;*
the God of Jacob is our fortress.

Glory be to the Father and to the Son*
and to the Holy Spirit;
as it was in the beginning,*
is now, and will be forever. Amen

I will speak of your statutes before kings, [O Lord,]*
and will not be put to shame.

*(Antiphon, Ps. 119:46;
Ps. 46:1-3, 7)*

COLLECT OF THE DAY

Almighty God, gracious Lord, pour out your Holy Spirit on your faithful people. Keep them steadfast in your grace and truth, protect and comfort them in all temptations, defend them against all enemies of your Word, and bestow on the Church your saving peace; through Jesus Christ, your Son, our Lord, who lives and reigns with you and the Holy Spirit, one God, now and forever. (93)

READINGS

One-Year Series	Three-Year Series
Psalm 46	A, B, C. Psalm 46
Isaiah 55:1-11	Jeremiah 31:31-34
Revelation 14:6-7	Romans 3:19-28
Matthew 11:12-15	John 8:31-36

GRADUAL

Great is the Lord, and most worthy of praise,*
in the city of our God, his holy mountain.
Walk about Zion, go around her, count her towers,
consider well her ramparts, view her citadels.*
that you may tell of them to the next generation. *(Ps. 48:1, 12-13)*

VERSE

Alleluia. Alleluia. This God is our God for ever and ever; he will be our guide even to the end. Alleluia. *(Ps. 48:14)*

ALL SAINTS' DAY AND
COMMEMORATION OF MARTYRS

INTROIT

These are they who have come out of the great tribulation;*
    they have washed their robes and made them white in the blood of the Lamb.

In you, O Lord, I have taken refuge;*
    let me never be put to shame;
    deliver me in your righteousness.
Since you are my rock and my fortress,*
    for the sake of your name lead and guide me.
Into your hands I commit my spirit;*
    redeem me, O Lord, the God of truth.

Glory be to the Father and to the Son*
    and to the Holy Spirit;
as it was in the beginning,*
    is now, and will be forever. Amen

These are they who have come out of the great tribulation;*
    they have washed their robes and made them white in the blood of the Lamb.

*(Antiphon, Rev. 7:14;
Ps. 31:1, 3, 5)*

COLLECTS OF THE DAY

ALL SAINTS' DAY
November 1

O almighty God, by whom we are graciously knit together as one communion and fellowship in the mystical body of Jesus Christ, our Lord, grant us so to follow your blessed saints in all virtuous and godly living that we may come to those unspeakable joys which you have prepared for those who unfeignedly love you; through our Lord Jesus Christ, your Son, who lives and reigns with you and the Holy Spirit, one God, now and forever. (97)

ST. STEPHEN, FIRST MARTYR
December 26

Heavenly Father, grant us grace that in our sufferings for the sake of Christ we may follow the example of Saint Stephen, that we may look to him who suffered and was crucified on our behalf and pray for those who do us wrong; through our Lord Jesus Christ, who lives and reigns with you and the Holy Spirit, one God, now and forever. (98)

THE HOLY INNOCENTS
December 28

Almighty God, whose praise was proclaimed on this day by the wicked death of innocent children, giving us thereby a picture of the death of your beloved Son, mortify and destroy in us all that is in conflict with you that we who have been called in faith to be your children may in life and death bear witness to your salvation; through our Lord Jesus Christ, who lives and reigns with you and the Holy Spirit, one God, now and forever. (99)

ST. LAURENCE
August 10

Stir up, O merciful Father, your people to true brotherly affection that we may gladly do good and serve our neighbor, as did your servant Saint Laurence when he emptied the treasury of the Church to help the poor; through our Lord Jesus Christ, your Son, who lives and reigns with you and the Holy Spirit, one God, now and forever. (100)

READINGS

One-Year Series	Three-Year Series
Psalm 65:1-8	A, B, C. Psalm 34:1-10
Deuteronomy 33:1-3	Isaiah 26:1-4, 8-9, 12-13, 19-21
Revelation 7:2-17	Revelation 21:9-11, 22-27(22:1-5)
Matthew 5:1-12	Matthew 5:1-12

GRADUAL

Fear the Lord, you his saints,*
   for those who fear him lack nothing.
A righteous man may have many troubles,*
   but the Lord delivers him from them all.   *(Ps. 34:9, 19)*

VERSE

Alleluia. Alleluia. They are before the throne of God and serve him day and night in his temple. Alleluia.   *(Rev. 7:15a)*

OCCASIONS

DEDICATION OF A CHURCH
ANNIVERSARY OF A CONGREGATION

INTROIT

V E♭: Lydian

I will speak of your statutes before
kings, [O Lord,]*
  and will not be put to shame.

God is our refuge and strength,*
  an ever present help in trouble.
Therefore we will not fear, though the
earth give way*
  and the mountains fall into the
  heart of the sea,
though its waters roar and foam*
  and the mountains quake with their
  surging.

The Lord Almighty is with us;*
  the God of Jacob is our fortress.

Glory be to the Father and to the Son*
  and to the Holy Spirit;
as it was in the beginning,*
  is now, and will be forever. Amen

I will speak of your statutes before
kings, [O Lord,]*
  and will not be put to shame.

*(Antiphon, Ps. 119:46;
Ps. 46:1-3, 7)*

COLLECT OF THE DAY

Lord God, heavenly Father, the unfailing giver of every good gift, we beseech you to
dwell continually among us with your holy Word and sacraments, so that by grace we
poor sinners may be turned to you and be saved eternally; through Jesus Christ, your
Son, our Lord, who lives and reigns with you and the Holy Spirit, one God, now and
forever. (101)

READINGS

One-Year Series

Psalm 84:1-7
1 Kings 8:22-30
Revelation 21:1-5
Luke 19:1-10

Three-Year Series

A, B, C. Psalm 84
  1 Kings 8:22-30
  1 Peter 2:1-9
  John 10:22-30

GRADUAL

I rejoiced with those who said to me,*
  "Let us go to the house of the Lord."
That is where the tribes go up, the tribes
of the Lord,*
  to praise the name of the Lord according
  to the statute given to Israel. *(Ps. 122:1, 4)*

VERSE

Alleluia. Alleluia. How lovely is your dwelling place, O Lord Almighty! My soul
yearns, even faints for the courts of the Lord. Alleluia. *(Ps. 84:1-2a)*

MISSION FESTIVAL

INTROIT

IX a: Aeolian

Declare his glory among the nations,*
  his marvelous deeds among all
peoples.

Great is the Lord and most worthy of
praise;*
  he is to be feared above all gods.
Say among the nations, "The Lord
reigns." The world is firmly established,
it cannot be moved;*
  he will judge the peoples with
  equity.
Worship the Lord in the splendor of his
holiness;*
  tremble before him, all the earth.

Glory be to the Father and to the Son*
  and to the Holy Spirit;
as it was in the beginning,*
  is now, and will be forever. Amen

Declare his glory among the nations,*
  his marvelous deeds among all
peoples.

*(Antiphon, Ps. 96:3;
Ps. 96:4, 10, 9)*

COLLECT OF THE DAY

Almighty God, since you have called your Church to witness that in Christ you reconciled us to yourself, grant that by your Holy Spirit we may proclaim the good news of
your salvation that all who hear it may receive the gift of salvation; through Jesus
Christ, our Lord, who lives and reigns with you and the Holy Spirit, one God, now and
forever. (102)

READINGS

One-Year Series

Psalm 96
Isaiah 2:1-5
Romans 10:8b-17
Luke 14:16-24

Three-Year Series

A, B, C. Psalm 96
  Isaiah 62:1-7
  Romans 10:11-17
  Luke 24:44-53

GRADUAL

I will praise you, O Lord, among the nations;*
  I will sing of you among the peoples.
For great is your love, higher than the heavens;*
  your faithfulness reaches to the skies. *(Ps. 108:3-4)*

119

VERSE

Alleluia. Alleluia. Give thanks to the Lord, call on his name; make known among the nations what he has done. Alleluia. *(Ps. 105:1)*

HARVEST FESTIVAL

INTROIT

IX a: Aeolian

Praise the Lord, O my soul.
O Lord my God, you are very great;*
  you are clothed with splendor and
  majesty.

He makes grass grow for the cattle,
and plants for man to cultivate—*
  bringing forth food from the earth;
wine that gladdens the heart of man,
oil to make his face shine,*
  and bread that sustains his heart.
May the glory of the Lord endure
forever;*
  may the Lord rejoice in his works.

Glory be to the Father and to the Son*
  and to the Holy Spirit;
as it was in the beginning,*
  is now, and will be forever. Amen

Praise the Lord, O my soul.
O Lord my God, you are very great;*
  you are clothed with splendor and
  majesty.

*(Antiphon, Ps. 104:1;
Ps. 104:14-15, 31)*

COLLECT OF THE DAY

Lord God, heavenly Father, through whose kindness we have again received the fruits of the earth in their season, grant us ever to rejoice in your mercy that neither prosperity nor adversity may drive us from your presence; through Jesus Christ, our Lord, who lives and reigns with you and the Holy Spirit, one God, now and forever. (103)

READINGS

One-Year Series

Psalm 67
Malachi 3:10-12
2 Corinthians 9:6-15
Luke 12:13-21

Three-Year Series

A, B, C. Psalm 65
  Deuteronomy 26:1-11
  2 Corinthians 9:6-15
  Matthew 13:24-30(36-43)

GRADUAL

Taste and see that the Lord is good;*
  blessed is the man who takes refuge in him.
Fear the Lord, you his saints,*
  for those who fear him lack nothing. *(Ps. 34:8-9)*

VERSE

Alleluia. Alleluia. Praise the Lord, O my soul; all my inmost being, praise his holy name. Alleluia. *(Ps. 103:1)*

DAY OF SUPPLICATION AND PRAYER

INTROIT

I d: Dorian

Out of the depths I cry to you, O Lord;*
    O Lord, hear my voice.

Let your ears be attentive*
    to my cry for mercy.
If you, O Lord, kept a record of sins,*
    O Lord, who could stand?

But with you there is forgiveness;*
    therefore you are feared.
I wait for the Lord, my soul waits,*
    and in his word I put my hope.

Out of the depths I cry to you, O Lord;*
    O Lord, hear my voice.

(Antiphon, Ps. 130:1-2a;
Ps. 130:2b-5)

COLLECT OF THE DAY

Almighty God, our heavenly Father, because you desire not the death of a sinner but rather that he should turn from his evil way and live, graciously turn away from us the punishments which we by our sins have deserved and which have been borne for us by our Lord Jesus Christ, and grant us ever to serve you in holiness and pureness of living; through Jesus Christ, our Lord, who lives and reigns with you and the Holy Spirit, one God, now and forever. (104)

READINGS

One-Year Series

Psalm 130
Isaiah 1:2-18
Joel 2:12-19
Matthew 6:16-21

Three-Year Series

A, B, C. Psalm 6
Nehemiah 1:4-11a
1 John 1:5—2:2
Luke 15:11-32

GRADUAL

Seek the Lord while he may be found;*
    call on him while he is near.
Let the wicked forsake his way*
    and the evil man his thoughts.

Gradual continues on the next page

Let him turn to the Lord, and he will
have mercy on him,*
   and to our God, for he will freely pardon. *(Is. 55:6-7)*

VERSE

Search me, O God, and know my heart; test me and know my anxious thoughts. See if there is any offensive way in me, and lead me in the way everlasting. *(Ps. 139:23-24)*

DAY OF SPECIAL OR NATIONAL THANKSGIVING

INTROIT

* XI A: Ionian

I will sing to the Lord all my life;*
   I will sing praise to my God as long
as I live.

How many are your works, O Lord!*
   In wisdom you made them all;
   the earth is full of your creatures.
These all look to you*
   to give them their food at the
   proper time.
When you send your Spirit, they are
created,*
   and you renew the face of the
   earth.

Glory be to the Father and to the Son*
   and to the Holy Spirit;
as it was in the beginning,*
   is now, and will be forever. Amen

I will sing to the Lord all my life;*
   I will sing praise to my God as long
as I live.

*(Antiphon, Ps. 104:33;
Ps. 104:24, 27, 30)*

COLLECT OF THE DAY

Almighty God, whose mercies are new every morning and whose goodness, though undeserved, still abundantly provides for all our wants of body and soul, grant us, we humbly pray, your Holy Spirit that we may heartily acknowledge your merciful goodness toward us, give thanks for all your benefits, and serve you in willing obedience; through Jesus Christ, your Son, our Lord, who lives and reigns with you and the Holy Spirit, one God, now and forever. (24)

READINGS

One-Year Series

Psalm 65
Isaiah 61:10-11
1 Timothy 2:1-8
Luke 17:11-19
or Matthew 6:24-34

Three-Year Series

A, B, C. Psalm 65
   Deuteronomy 8:1-10
   Philippians 4:6-20
   or 1 Timothy 2:1-4
   Luke 17:11-19

GRADUAL

The eyes of all look to you,*
  and you give them their food at the proper time.
You open your hand*
  and satisfy the desires of every living thing.
Praise the Lord, O my soul,*
  and forget not all his benefits.   *(Ps. 145:15-16; 103:2)*

VERSE

Alleluia. Alleluia. Praise the Lord, O my soul; all my inmost being, praise his holy name. Alleluia.   *(Ps. 103:1)*

PETITIONS, INTERCESSIONS, AND THANKSGIVINGS

FOR DAILY PRAYER
Morning
Faithful God, whose mercies are new to us every morning, we humbly pray that you look upon us in mercy and renew us by your Holy Spirit; keep safe our going out and our coming in and let your blessing remain with us throughout this day; preserve us in your righteousness and grant us a portion in that eternal life which is in Christ Jesus; through whom be glory and praise to you and the Holy Spirit, now and forever. (105)

Evening
Merciful Father, whose guiding hand has brought us to the completion of this day, we humbly pray you to stay with us and shelter us in quiet hours of the night that we who are wearied by the changes and chances of this passing world may rest in your changeless peace; through Jesus Christ, our Lord. (106)

FOR THE CHURCH
Merciful God, we humbly implore you to cast the bright beams of your light upon your Church that we, being instructed by the doctrine of the blessed apostles, may walk in the light of your truth and at length attain to the light of everlasting life; through Jesus Christ, our Lord. (107)

FOR THE HOLY SPIRIT
Almighty and everlasting God, of your great mercy in Jesus Christ you have granted us forgiveness of sin and all things pertaining to life and godliness. Therefore send us your Holy Spirit that he may so rule our hearts that we, being ever mindful of your fatherly mercy, may strive to overcome the world and, serving you in holiness and pureness of living, may give you continual thanks for all your goodness; through Jesus Christ, our Lord. (108)

FOR THE HOLY MINISTRY
Almighty and everlasting God, whose infinite power alone does great wonders, send down on your ministers and on the congregations committed to their care the

healthful spirit of your grace, and that they may truly please you, pour on them the continual dew of your blessing; through Jesus Christ, our Lord.(109)

FOR THE RIGHT WORSHIP OF GOD

Heavenly Father, God of all grace, waken our hearts that we may never forget your blessings but steadfastly thank and praise you for all your goodness, that we may live in your fear until with all your saints we praise you eternally in your heavenly kingdom; through Jesus Christ, our Lord.(110)

FOR DIVINE PROTECTION

O God, because you justify the ungodly and desire not the death of the sinner, we humbly implore you graciously to assist by your heavenly aid, and evermore shield with your divine protection, your servants who trust in your mercy, that they may be separated from you by no temptations but may serve you without ceasing; through Jesus Christ, our Lord.(111)

FOR DIVINE GUIDANCE AND ASSISTANCE

Direct us, O Lord, in all our doings with your most gracious favor, and further us with your continual help that in all our works begun, continued, and ended in you we may glorify your holy name and finally by your mercy obtain eternal salvation; through Jesus Christ, our Lord.(8)

FOR GRACE TO USE OUR GIFTS

O Lord God Almighty, since you bless your servants with various and unusual gifts of the Holy Spirit, grant us grace to use them always to your honor and glory; through Jesus Christ, our Lord.(112)

FOR LIKENESS TO CHRIST

O God, by the patient suffering of your only-begotten Son you have beaten down the pride of the old enemy. Now help us, we humbly pray, rightly to treasure in our hearts all that our Lord has of his goodness borne for our sake that after his example we may bear with patience all that is adverse to us; through Jesus Christ, our Lord. (113)

FOR STEADFAST FAITH

Almighty God, our heavenly Father, of your tender love towards us sinners you have given us your Son that, believing in him, we might have everlasting life. Continue to grant us your Holy Spirit that we may remain steadfast in this faith to the end and come to life everlasting; through Jesus Christ, our Lord. (114)

FOR NEWNESS OF LIFE IN CHRIST

Almighty God, give us grace that we may cast away the works of darkness and put upon ourselves the armor of light, now in the time of this mortal life, in which your Son Jesus Christ came to visit us in great humility, that in the last day, when he shall come again in glory to judge both the living and the dead, we may rise to the life immortal; through Jesus Christ, our Lord.(115)

FOR THE RETURN OF THE WAYWARD AND ERRING

Almighty, merciful, and most gracious God and Father, we earnestly implore you to turn the hearts of all who have forsaken the faith once delivered to your Church, those who have wandered from it or are in doubt or temptation through the corruption of your truth; mercifully visit them and turn them again that in singleness of heart they may take pleasure in your Word and be made wise to salvation through faith in Jesus Christ, our Lord.(116)

FOR UNITY OF FAITH

O God, whose infinite love restores to the right way those who err, gathers the scattered, and preserves those whom you have gathered, of your tender mercy pour out on your Christian people the grace of unity that, all schisms being healed, your flock, gathered to the true Shepherd of your Church, may serve you in all faithfulness; through Jesus Christ, our Lord.(117)

FOR THE AFFLICTED AND DISTRESSED

Almighty and everlasting God, the consolation of the sorrowful and the strength of the weak, may the prayers of those who in any tribulation or distress cry to you graciously come before you, so that in all their necessities they may mark and receive your manifold help and comfort; through Jesus Christ, our Lord.(118)

FOR OUR ENEMIES

O almighty, everlasting God, through your only Son, our blessed Lord, you commanded us to love our enemies, to do good to those who hate us, and to pray for those who persecute us. Therefore we earnestly beseech you that by your gracious visitation our enemies may be led to true repentance, may have the same love toward us as we have toward them, and be of one accord and of one mind and heart with us and with your whole Church; through Jesus Christ, our Lord.(119)

FOR THE HOPE OF ETERNAL LIFE IN CHRIST

Almighty, everlasting God, whose Son has assured forgiveness of sins and deliverance from eternal death, strengthen us by your Holy Spirit that our faith in Christ increase daily and we hold fast the hope that we shall not die but fall asleep and on the last day be raised to eternal life; through Jesus Christ, our Lord.(120)

FOR GOOD GOVERNMENT

Eternal Lord, Ruler of all, graciously regard those who have been set in positions of authority among us that they may be guided by your Spirit, be high in purpose, wise in counsel, firm in good resolution, and unwavering in duty, that under them we may be governed quietly and peaceably; through Jesus Christ, our Lord.(121)

FOR RESPONSIBLE CITIZENSHIP

Lord, keep this nation under your care. Bless the leaders of our land that we may be a people at peace among ourselves and a blessing to the other nations of the earth. Help us provide trustworthy leaders, contribute to wise decisions for the general welfare, and thus serve you faithfully in our generation to the honor of your holy name; through Jesus Christ, our Lord.(122)

FOR OUR COUNTRY

Almighty God, you have given us this good land as our heritage. Grant that we remember your generosity and constantly do your will. Bless our land with honest industry, truthful education, and an honorable way of life. Save us from violence, discord, and confusion, from pride and arrogance, and from every evil course of action. Make us who came from many nations with many different languages a united people. Defend our liberties, and give those whom we have entrusted with the authority of government the spirit of wisdom that there may be justice and peace in our land. When times are prosperous, let our hearts be thankful; and in troubled times do not let our trust in you fail; through Jesus Christ, our Lord. (123)

FOR THE UNEMPLOYED

Heavenly Father, we remember before you those who suffer want and anxiety from lack of work. Lead us so to use the wealth and resources of this rich land that all persons may find suitable and fulfilling employment and receive just payment for their labor; through your Son, Jesus Christ, our Lord. (124)

FOR THOSE SUFFERING FROM ADDICTION

O blessed Jesus, since you minister to all who are afflicted, look with compassion on those who through addiction have lost their health and freedom. Restore to them the assurance of your unfailing mercy, remove the fears that attack them, strengthen them in the recovery of their self-possession and health, and give skill, patience, and understanding love to those who provide care for them; for your own mercy's sake. (125)

FOR RESTORATION OF HEALTH

Almighty and gracious God, we give thanks that you have restored the health of your servant, _____ name _____, on whose behalf we praise your name. Grant that _he/she_ may continue the mission you have given _him/her_ in this world and also share in eternal glory at the appearing of your Son, Jesus Christ, our Lord. (126)

AT THE BIRTH OF A CHILD

Heavenly Father, you sent your own Son into this world as the child of Mary and Joseph. We thank you for the life of this child, _____ name _____, entrusted to our care. Help us remember that we are all your children and so love and nurture _him/her_ that _he/she_ may attain to that full stature intended for _him/her_ in your eternal kingdom; for the sake of Jesus Christ, your Son, our Lord. (127)

FOR THE CARE OF CHILDREN

Almighty God, heavenly Father, you have blessed us with the joy and care of children. As we bring them up, give us calm strength and patient wisdom that we may teach them to love whatever is just and true and good, following the example of our Savior Jesus Christ. (128)

FOR YOUNG PERSONS

God our Father, your Son grew in wisdom and stature and in favor with God and men. Bless, guide, and govern the children and young people of your Church by your Holy Spirit that they may grow in grace and in the knowledge of your Word. Grant that they may serve you well and usefully, developing their talents not for their own sakes but for the glory of God and the welfare of their neighbor. Protect and defend them from all danger and harm, giving your holy angels charge over them; through Jesus Christ, our Lord. (129)

BEFORE WORSHIP

O Lord, our Creator, Redeemer, and Comforter, as we come together to worship you in spirit and in truth, we humbly pray that you may open our hearts to the preaching of your Word, so that we may repent of our sins, believe in Jesus Christ as our only Savior, and grow in grace and holiness. Hear us for his sake. (130)

AFTER WORSHIP

Almighty and merciful God, we have again worshiped in your presence and have received forgiveness for our many sins and the assurance of your love in Jesus Christ. We thank you for this undeserved grace and ask you to keep us in faith until we inherit eternal salvation; through Jesus Christ, our Lord.(131)

BEFORE RECEPTION OF HOLY COMMUNION

Dear Savior, we come to your table at your gracious invitation to eat and drink your holy body and blood. Let us find favor in your eyes to receive this holy sacrament in faith for the salvation of our souls and to the glory of your holy name; for you live and reign with the Father and the Holy Spirit, one God, now and forever.(132)

AFTER RECEPTION OF HOLY COMMUNION

Dear Lord Jesus, we thank and praise you that you have again refreshed us with the gift of your holy body and blood in this comforting sacrament. Bless our participation that we may depart from your presence with peace and joy in the knowledge that we are reconciled to God. We ask this in your name.(133)

FOR RIGHT RECEPTION OF HOLY COMMUNION

O Lord, our God, in the name of whose only-begotten Son we have been called to be Christians and have been blest with Baptism for the remission of sins, make us, we pray, ready to receive the most holy body and blood of Christ for the forgiveness of all our sins and to give thanks with grateful hearts to you, O Father, to your Son, and to the Holy Spirit, one God, now and forever. (134)

A GENERAL THANKSGIVING

Almighty God, our heavenly Father, we, your unworthy servants, give you most humble and hearty thanks for all your goodness and loving-kindness to us and to all mankind. We praise you for our creation, preservation, and all the blessings of this life, but above all for your inestimable love in the redemption of the world by our Lord and Savior Jesus Christ, for the means of grace, and for the hope of glory. We implore you to give us that due sense of all your mercies that our hearts may ever be deeply thankful and that we may show forth your praise with both our lips and our lives. Let us walk before you in holiness and righteousness all the days of our life and enjoy the testimony of a good conscience and the hope of your favor, be sustained and comforted in every time of trouble, and finally be received into your everlasting kingdom; through your infinite mercy in Christ Jesus, our Lord.(135)

A GENERAL INTERCESSION

Lord God, heavenly Father, we offer before you our common supplications for the well-being of your Church throughout the world that it may be so guided and governed by your good Spirit that all who profess themselves Christians may be led into the way of truth and hold the faith in unity of spirit, in the bond of peace, and in righteousness of life. Send down upon all ministers of the Gospel and upon the congregations committed to their care the healthful spirit of your grace, and that they may truly please you, pour upon them the continual dew of your blessing.

We further implore you to behold in mercy all who are in authority over us; replenish them with your blessing that they may be inclined to your will and walk according to your commandments. We humbly entreat you also for all sorts and conditions of men that you would make known your ways among us; preserve those who travel; satisfy the wants of your creatures; help those who call upon you in any need that they may have patience in the midst of suffering and a happy issue out of their afflictions; through Jesus Christ, our Lord.(136)

FOR PEACE

Grant peace, we pray, in mercy, Lord.
   Peace in our time, oh, send us!
   For there is none on earth but you,
   None other to defend us.
   You only, Lord, can fight for us.

O God, from whom all holy desires, all good counsels, and all just works proceed, give to your servants that peace which the world cannot give that our hearts may be set to obey your commandments and also that we, being defended by you, may pass our time in rest and quietness; through the merits of Jesus Christ, our Savior. (137)

FOR AN ANSWER TO PRAYER

Almighty God, since you have granted us the favor to call on you with one accord and have promised that where two or three are gathered together in your name you are in the midst of them, fulfill now the prayers of your servants, granting us in this world knowledge of your truth and in the world to come life everlasting; through Jesus Christ, our Lord. (138)

IN TIME OF BEREAVEMENT

O heavenly Father, into whose keeping we entrust our loved ones, grant us to look to you, remembering the cloud of faithful witnesses with which we are surrounded, and grant that we on earth may share your joys with those who rest in the joyful peace of your presence; through Jesus Christ, our Lord.(139)

FOR THOSE IN DISTRESS

Keep in remembrance, O Lord, the tempted, the distressed, and the erring; gently guide them and by your great goodness bring them into the way of peace and truth. Let the light of your truth shine on those who do not know you that they may be turned toward you and so find peace. Graciously regard all who are in trouble, danger, temptation, bondage of sin, and those to whom death draws near. In your mercy draw them to yourself; for the sake of Jesus Christ, our Lord.(140)

FOR HOME AND FAMILY

Visit, we implore you, O Lord, the homes in which your people dwell, and keep far from them all harm and danger. Grant us to dwell together in peace under the protection of your holy angels, and may your blessing be with us forever; through Jesus Christ, our Lord. (141)

FOR THOSE ENGAGED TO BE MARRIED

O heavenly Father, grant that your Holy Spirit may lead those who have pledged their love to one another that they may always know the joy of your great love and dwell within it to the ending of their days; through Jesus Christ, our Lord.(142)

129

FOR AGRICULTURE

Almighty God, you blessed the earth to make it fruitful, bringing forth in abundance whatever is needed for the support of our lives. Prosper, we implore you, the work of farmers, and grant us seasonable weather that we may gather in the fruits of the earth and proclaim your goodness with thanksgiving; through Jesus Christ, our Lord.(143)

FOR INDUSTRY

Lord Jesus Christ, as once you shared in human toil and thus hallowed the work of our hands, prosper those who maintain the industries of this land, and give them a right regard for their labors, granting them a just reward for their toil and joy in serving you and supplying our needs; for you live and reign with the Father and the Holy Spirit, one God, now and forever.(144)

FOR THE ARMED FORCES OF OUR NATION

O Lord God of hosts, stretch forth your almighty arm to strengthen and protect those who serve in the armed forces of our country. Support them in times of war, and in times of peace keep them from all evil, giving them courage and loyalty and granting that in all things they may serve honestly and without reproach; through Jesus Christ, our Lord.(145)

FOR THOSE WHO MINISTER IN THE ARMED FORCES

O Lord, almighty God, as you have always granted singular gifts of the Holy Spirit to your Church on earth, grant your special blessing, we pray, to all who minister in your name in the armed forces that by your gracious working they may honor Christ and advance the good of those committed to their care; through Jesus Christ, our Lord.(146)

FOR THE INCREASE OF THE HOLY MINISTRY

O Lord, the God of all grace, as you have called your Church to minister in the name of your Son, our great High Priest, so by your Word and Spirit inspire men's hearts and minds to offer themselves for the sacred ministry that, ministering in the name of Christ, they may draw many to your kingdom; through Jesus Christ, our Lord.(147)

FOR MISSIONARY WORK

Almighty God, since you have called your Church to witness that in Christ you have reconciled us to yourself, grant that by your Holy Spirit we may proclaim the good news of your salvation that all who hear it may receive the gift of salvation; through Jesus Christ, our Lord.(102)

FOR CALLING A FAITHFUL PASTOR

O gracious Father, as you led your holy apostles to ordain ministers for the proclamation of your Word and the faithful ministration of the sacraments of Christ, so grant to your Church today the guidance of the Holy Spirit to choose a suitable minister according to your will and to constantly uphold him in fervent prayer; through Jesus Christ, our Lord.(148)

FOR THE ESTRANGED AND THE DIVORCED

Regard in mercy, O Lord, your servants for whom the bond of wedded love and faithfulness has been broken, and grant that, repenting their part in their condition

130

and confessing before you, they may have the assurance of your compassion and the knowledge of your healing power; through Jesus Christ, our Lord. (149)

FOR CHRISTIAN SCHOOLS

Almighty God, our heavenly Father, since you have committed the care and nurture of children to your people, graciously enlighten those who teach and those who are committed to their instruction that they may know the truth and trust in you all the days of their lives; through Jesus Christ, our Lord. (150)

FOR SEMINARIES AND CHURCH COLLEGES

O God, Source of all abiding knowledge, through Word and Spirit you both enlighten the minds and sanctify the lives of those whom you draw to your service. Therefore look with favor on the seminaries and colleges of the Church, blessing those who teach and those who learn, that they may apply themselves with ready diligence to your will and faithfully fulfill their service according to your purpose; through Jesus Christ, our Lord. (151)

FOR BIRTHDAYS OF THE ELDERLY

Grant your continued blessing, O Lord, to your servant/servants, _____ name(s) _____ , to whom you have granted length of days in this present life, that he/she/they may know your loving-kindness, abide in the confession of your care and protection, and in all things give you thanks; through Jesus Christ, our Lord. (152)

FOR THOSE WHO HAVE PARTICULAR RESPONSIBILITY IN THE CHURCH

Lord and Shepherd, in all the many things that need to be done for your Church, grant to those entrusted with special responsibilities zeal and faithfulness to perform their tasks to the upbuilding of your Church and the glory of your saving name; who with the Father and the Holy Spirit lives and reigns, ever one God, world without end. (153)

FOR THOSE WHO HOLD SPECIAL OFFICES IN THE CHURCH

Lord of the Church, in whose name all who oversee and serve your flock have been called, grant your servants all the gifts necessary to the godly administration of their duties, for the upbuilding of your Church and the glory of your name; who with the Father and the Holy Spirit lives and reigns, ever one God, world without end. (154)

FOR AN ANNIVERSARY OF MARRIAGE

Your mercies are new every morning, O Lord Jesus. We thank you for another year of life together for _____ name _____ and _____ name _____ . We ask you to keep them open to receive always more of your love that their love for each other may never grow weary but deepen and grow through every joy and sorrow shared; who with the Father and the Holy Spirit lives and reigns, ever one God, world without end. (155)

FOR CALLING FAITHFUL TEACHERS, MUSICIANS, DEACONESSES, AND OTHERS

Merciful Lord, for the good of the Church you call faithful men and women to serve in all manner of offices. Grant, we implore you, that your Holy Spirit may lead and guide us in calling a _____ to serve among us according to your gracious will; through Christ Jesus, our Lord. (156)

COMMEMORATION OF THE FAITHFUL DEPARTED

Merciful Father, whose dear Son, our Lord Jesus Christ, rose Victor over death and the grave, we remember with thanksgiving your faithful people who have trusted in Christ, whose tears are gone, and whose sorrows you have turned to joy; and we humbly implore you to strengthen us in the confident hope of the resurrection of the dead and the life of the world to come; through our Lord Jesus Christ. (157)

FOR THE ADOPTION OF CHILDREN

Merciful Father, of your great love revealed in Christ you called us to the household of faith in your Son Jesus, our Savior, and chose us to be your own dear children. Grant your blessing to your people who take children into their homes and families that, loving them as their own, they may nurture them as your own; through Jesus Christ, our Lord. (158)

FOR THOSE WHO ARE LONELY

Almighty God, merciful Father, by Word and Sacrament you have created your Church in this world to be a godly communion and family. Grant your blessing to those who dwell in loneliness that they may find a place of solace and pleasant fellowship among people faithful to you; through Jesus Christ, our Lord. (159)

GENERAL PRAYER OF THE CHURCH

Almighty and eternal God, worthy to be held in reverence by all the children of men, we give you humble and hearty thanks for the innumerable blessings which without any merit or worthiness on our part you have bestowed on us.

We praise you especially that you have preserved for us your saving Word and the holy sacraments. And we implore you, O Lord, to grant and preserve to your holy Church throughout the world purity of doctrine and faithful pastors to preach your Word with power. Help all who hear the Word rightly to understand and truly to believe it. Send laborers into your harvest, and open the door of faith to those who do not know you. In mercy remember the enemies of your Church, and grant them repentance to life. Protect and defend your Church in all tribulation and danger. Strengthen us and all fellow Christians to set our hope fully on the grace revealed in Christ, and help us to fight the good fight of faith that in the end we may receive the salvation of our souls.

Bestow your grace on all nations of the earth. Bless especially our country and its inhabitants and all who are in authority. Let your glory dwell in our land that mercy and truth, righteousness and peace may everywhere abound. We commend to you the care of all our schools and ask you to grant that our children may grow in useful knowledge and Christian virtue and bring forth wholesome fruits of life.

Graciously defend us from all calamity by fire and water, from war and pestilence, from scarcity and famine, and from every other evil. Protect and prosper everyone in his rightful calling, and let all useful arts flourish among us. Be the God and Father of the widow and the fatherless, the helper of the sick and needy, and the comforter of the forsaken and distressed.

Accept, we implore you, our bodies and souls, our hearts and minds, our talents and powers, together with the offerings we bring before you, for your praise and service.

Grant your Holy Spirit to those who come to the Lord's Table today that they may receive the body and blood of Jesus Christ in sincere repentance and firm faith and to their abundant blessing.

(Here special supplications, intercessions, and prayers may be made.)

As we are strangers and pilgrims on earth, help us by true faith and a godly life to prepare for the world to come, doing the work you have given us to do while it is day, before the night comes when no one can work. And when our last hour comes, support us by your power, and receive us into your heavenly kingdom; through Jesus Christ, your Son, our Lord, who lives and reigns with you and the Holy Spirit, one God, now and forever. (160)

ATHANASIAN CREED
Quicunque Vult

Whoever will be saved
shall, above all else, hold
the catholic faith.
Which faith, except everyone keeps
whole and undefiled,
without doubt he will perish
eternally.
And the catholic faith is this,
that we worship one God in three
persons and three persons in
one God, neither confusing the
persons nor dividing the substance.
For there is one person of the Father,
another of the Son,
and another of the Holy Spirit.
But the Godhead of the Father, of
the Son, and of the Holy Spirit
is all one: the glory equal,
the majesty coeternal.
Such as the Father is,
such is the Son,
and such is the Holy Spirit.
The Father uncreated,
the Son uncreated,
and the Holy Spirit uncreated.
The Father incomprehensible,
the Son incomprehensible,
and the Holy Spirit
incomprehensible.
The Father eternal,
the Son eternal,
and the Holy Spirit eternal.
And yet they are not
three eternals
but one eternal.
As there are not
three uncreated nor
three incomprehensibles
but one uncreated
and one incomprehensible.
So likewise the Father is almighty,
the Son almighty,

and the Holy Spirit almighty.
And yet they are not
three almighties
but one almighty.
So the Father is God,
the Son is God,
and the Holy Spirit is God.
And yet they are not three Gods
but one God.
So likewise the Father is Lord,
the Son Lord,
and the Holy Spirit Lord.
And yet they are not three Lords
but one Lord.
For as we are compelled by the
Christian truth
to acknowledge every person
by himself to be both
God and Lord,
So we cannot by the catholic faith
say that there are three Gods
or three Lords.
The Father is made of none,
neither created nor begotten.
The Son is of the Father alone,
not made nor created but begotten.
The Holy Spirit is of the Father
and of the Son,
neither made nor created
nor begotten
but proceeding.
So there is one Father,
not three Fathers;
one Son, not three Sons;
one Holy Spirit,
not three Holy Spirits.
And in this Trinity
none is before or after another;
none is greater or
less than another;
But the whole three persons are
coeternal together and coequal,

134

so that in all things, as is aforesaid,
the Unity in Trinity
and the Trinity in Unity
is to be worshiped.
He, therefore, that will be saved is
compelled thus to think
of the Trinity.
Furthermore, it is necessary
to everlasting salvation
that he also believe faithfully the
incarnation of our
Lord Jesus Christ.
For the right faith is
that we believe and confess
that our Lord Jesus Christ,
the Son of God, is God and man;
God of the substance of the Father,
begotten before the worlds;
and man of the substance of his
mother, born in the world;
Perfect God and perfect man,
of a reasonable soul
and human flesh subsisting.
Equal to the Father as touching
his Godhead
and inferior to the Father as
touching his manhood;
Who, although he is God and man,
yet he is not two
but one Christ:

One, not by conversion of the
Godhead into flesh
but by taking the manhood
into God;
One altogether,
not by confusion of substance
but by unity of person.
For as the reasonable soul and flesh
is one man,
so God and man is one Christ;
Who suffered for our salvation,
descended into hell,
rose again the third day from
the dead.
He ascended into heaven,
he sits at the right hand
of the Father, God Almighty,
from whence he will come to judge
the living and the dead.
At whose coming
all men will rise again with
their bodies and will give an account
of their own works.
And they that have done good
will go into life everlasting;
and they that have done evil,
into everlasting fire.
This is the catholic faith which,
except a man believe faithfully
and firmly, he cannot be saved.

DIVINE SERVICE I

THE PREPARATION

1. A hymn of invocation may be sung.

Stand

℗ In the name of the Father and of the ☩ Son and of the Holy Spirit.

℗ **Amen**

2. The CONFESSION OF SINS

℗ Beloved in the Lord. Let us draw near with a true heart and confess our sins to God our Father, imploring him in the name of our Lord Jesus Christ to grant us forgiveness.

Kneel/Stand

℗ Our help is in the name of the Lord.

℗ **Who made heaven and earth.**

℗ I said, I will confess my transgressions to the Lord.

℗ **And you forgave the iniquity of my sin.**

℗ **O almighty God, merciful Father, I, a poor, miserable sinner, confess to you all my sins and iniquities with which I have ever offended you and justly deserved your punishment now and forever. But I am heartily sorry for them and sincerely repent of them, and I**

OR

℗ Almighty God, our Maker and Redeemer, we poor sinners confess to you that we are by nature sinful and unclean and that we have sinned against you by thought, word, and deed; therefore we flee for refuge to your boundless mercy, seeking and imploring your grace

pray you of your boundless mercy and for the sake of the holy, innocent, bitter sufferings and death of your beloved Son, Jesus Christ, to be gracious and merciful to me, a poor sinful being.

The minister stands and pronounces the absolution.

℗ Upon this your confession, I, as a called and ordained servant of the Word, announce the grace of God to all of you, and in the stead and by the command of my Lord Jesus Christ I forgive you all your sins in the name of the Father and of the ☩ Son and of the Holy Spirit.

for the sake of our Lord Jesus Christ.

℗ & ℂ O most merciful God, since you have given your only-begotten Son to die for us, have mercy on us and for his sake grant us forgiveness of all our sins; and by your Holy Spirit increase in us true knowledge of you and of your will and true obedience to your Word, to the end that by your grace we may come to everlasting life; through Jesus Christ, our Lord. Amen

The minister stands and pronounces the declaration of grace.

℗ Almighty God, our heavenly Father, has had mercy on us and has given his only Son to die for us and for his sake forgives us all our sins. To those who believe on his name he gives power to become the children of God and has promised them his Holy Spirit. He that believes and is baptized shall be saved. Grant this, Lord, to us all.

ℂ **Amen**

Stand

THE SERVICE OF THE WORD

3. The INTROIT OF THE DAY, the appointed PSALM, or an ENTRANCE HYMN is sung.

4. The KYRIE is sung. Hymn 209, "Kyrie, God Father," may be used as an alternate.

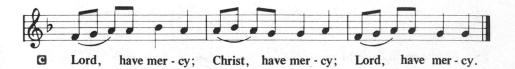

ℂ   Lord, have mer-cy; Christ, have mer-cy; Lord, have mer-cy.

5. The GLORIA IN EXCELSIS is sung. During Advent and Lent the Gloria in Excelsis is omitted. In its place "Oh, Come, Oh, Come, Emmanuel" (see Canticles and Chants, No. 1) may be sung during Advent, and "The Royal Banners Forward Go" (see Canticles and Chants, No. 2) during Lent.

℗ Glory be to God on high: ☧ and on earth peace, good will toward men.

We praise you, we bless you, we wor-ship you, we glorify you, we give you

thanks for your great glory. O Lord God, heav'n - ly King,

God the Fa - ther Al - mighty. O Lord, the only-begotten Son,

Je - sus Christ; O Lord God, Lamb of God, Son of the Father,

who takes away the sin of the world, have mer - cy;

who takes away the sin of the world, re - ceive our prayer;

who sits at the right hand of God the Father, have mer - cy.

For you on - ly are holy; you on - ly are the Lord;

you only, O Christ, with the Ho - ly Spirit, are most high in the

glo - ry of God the Father. A - men

6. *The COLLECT OF THE DAY is chanted or said; the salutation may precede it.*

℘ The Lord be with you.

ℂ And with your spir - it.

℘ Let us pray to the Lord.

The collect of the day is chanted according to the following model.

First Sunday in Advent

℘ Stir up, we implore you, your pow'r, O Lord, and come

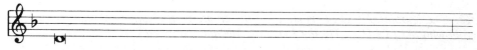

that by your protection we may be rescued from the
threatening perils of our sins and saved by your mighty deliverance;

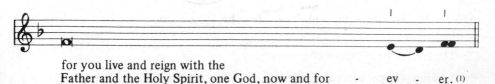

for you live and reign with the
Father and the Holy Spirit, one God, now and for - ev - er. (1)

DIVINE SERVICE I

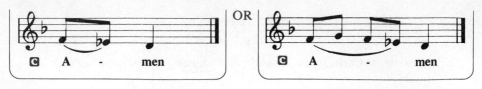

Sit

7. The OLD TESTAMENT READING (in the Three-Year Series, for Easter and its season: The Reading from the Book of Acts) is announced.

Ⓐ The Old Testament Reading for _____ is from the _____ chapter of _____.

8. After the reading the minister chants or says:

Ⓐ This is the Word of the Lord.

Ⓒ Thanks be to God.

9. The GRADUAL FOR THE SEASON or the appointed PSALM is sung or said.

10. The EPISTLE is announced.

Ⓐ The Epistle is from the _____ chapter of _____.

11. After the reading the minister chants or says:

Ⓐ This is the Word of the Lord.

Stand

12. The appointed VERSE is sung by the choir, or the congregation may sing the following ALLELUIA. During Lent the Alleluia is omitted.

Ⓒ Al - le - lu - ia, al - le - lu - ia.

13. The HOLY GOSPEL is announced.

Ⓟ The Holy Gospel according to St. _____, the _____ chapter.

140

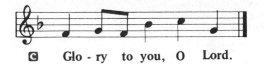

C Glo - ry to you, O Lord.

14. After the reading the minister chants or says:

P This is the Gospel of the Lord.

C Praise to you, O Christ.

15. The CREED. The Nicene Creed is said at celebrations of Holy Communion and on major festivals; the Apostles' Creed at other times. The Creeds may be sung (see Canticles and Chants, No. 4, and Hymns 212 and 213).

NICENE CREED

C **I believe in one God,**
    the Father Almighty,
    maker of heaven and earth
        and of all things visible and invisible.

  And in one Lord Jesus Christ,
    the only-begotten Son of God,
    begotten of his Father before all worlds,
    God of God, Light of Light,
    very God of very God,
    begotten, not made,
    being of one substance with the Father,
    by whom all things were made;
    who for us men and for our salvation
        came down from heaven
    and was incarnate by the Holy Spirit of the virgin Mary
    and was made man;
    and was crucified also for us under Pontius Pilate.
    He suffered and was buried.
    And the third day he rose again
        according to the Scriptures

and ascended into heaven
and sits at the right hand of the Father.
And he will come again with glory to judge
   both the living and the dead,
whose kingdom will have no end.

And I believe in the Holy Spirit,
   the Lord and giver of life,
   who proceeds from the Father and the Son,
   who with the Father and the Son together
      is worshiped and glorified,
   who spoke by the prophets.
   And I believe in one holy Christian and apostolic Church,*
   I acknowledge one Baptism for the remission of sins,
   and I look for the resurrection of the dead
   and the life of the world to come. Amen

*The ancient text: one holy catholic and apostolic Church

OR

APOSTLES' CREED

C I believe in God, the Father Almighty,
    maker of heaven and earth.

And in Jesus Christ, his only Son, our Lord,
   who was conceived by the Holy Spirit,
   born of the virgin Mary,
   suffered under Pontius Pilate,
   was crucified, died and was buried.
   He descended into hell.
   The third day he rose again from the dead.
   He ascended into heaven
      and sits at the right hand of God
      the Father Almighty.
   From thence he will come to judge the living and the dead.

I believe in the Holy Spirit,
   the holy Christian Church,*
   the communion of saints,
   the forgiveness of sins,

the resurrection of the body,
and the life everlasting. Amen

*The ancient text: the holy catholic Church

Sit

16. The *HYMN OF THE DAY* is sung (see Hymn of the Day index).

17. The *SERMON*

18. After the sermon the minister may say: "The peace of God, which passes all understanding, keep your hearts and minds in Christ Jesus."

19. The OFFERING is received and may be presented at the altar.

Stand

20. The OFFERTORY is sung. It may be sung to an alternate setting (see Canticles and Chants, No. 5).

C Cre - ate in me a clean heart, O God,

and re - new a right spir - it with - in me.

Cast me not a - way from your pres - ence,

and take not your Ho - ly Spir - it from me.

Re - store to me the joy of your sal - va - tion,

and up-hold me with your free Spir-it. A - men

21. The PRAYER OF THE CHURCH is said.

Ⓐ In peace let us pray to the Lord.

Ⓒ **Lord, have mercy.**

Petitions are included for the right use of Word and Sacrament, for the blessings associated with the appropriate season of the church year, for the Church and the proclamation of the Gospel, for good government, for special needs, for home and family, for the afflicted and needy, for the offerings of the people, and for the celebration of Holy Communion.

After each petition:

Ⓐ Let us pray to the Lord.

Ⓒ **Lord, have mercy.**

The Prayer of the Church concludes:

Ⓐ O Lord, heavenly Father, we here remember the sufferings and death of your dear Son, Jesus Christ, for our salvation. Praising his victorious resurrection from the dead, we draw strength from his ascension before you, where he ever stands for us as our own high priest. Gather us together, we pray, from the ends of the earth to celebrate with all the faithful the marriage feast of the Lamb in his kingdom, which has no end. Graciously receive our prayers, deliver and preserve us, for to you alone we give all glory, honor, and worship, Father, Son, and Holy Spirit, one God, now and forever. (161)

Ⓒ **Amen**

22. When there is no Communion, the service continues on page 155. ▶

THE SERVICE OF HOLY COMMUNION

23. The PREFACE is chanted or said.

Ⓟ The Lord be with you.

Ⓒ And with your spir-it.

P Lift up your hearts.

C We lift them to the Lord.

P Let us give thanks to the Lord, our God.

C It is good and right so to do.

24. The preface appropriate to the day or season is chanted (according to the following model) or said. The "Holy, holy, holy Lord" (SANCTUS) follows immediately (p. 148); it may be sung to an alternate setting (see Canticles and Chants, No. 6).

COMMON PREFACE (Sundays after Pentecost)

P It is truly good, right, and sal-u-tar-y that we should at all times

and in all places give thanks to you, ho-ly Lord, al-might-y Fa-ther,

ev-er-last-ing God, through Je-sus Christ, our Lord, ►

145

who on this day overcame death and the grave and by his glorious

resurrection o - pened to us the way of ev - er-last - ing life. There-

fore with angels and arch- an - gels and with all the company of

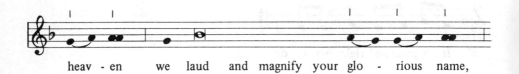

heav - en we laud and magnify your glo - rious name,

ev - er - more prais - ing you and say - ing:

ADVENT

It is truly good, right, and salutary that we should at all times and in all places give thanks to you, holy Lord, almighty Father, everlasting God, through Jesus Christ our Lord, whose way John the Baptist prepared, proclaiming him the Messiah, the very Lamb of God, and calling sinners to repentance that they might escape from the wrath to be revealed when he comes again in glory. Therefore with angels and archangels and with all the company of heaven we laud and magnify your glorious name, evermore praising you and saying:

CHRISTMAS

It is truly good, right, and salutary that we should at all times and in all places give thanks to you, holy Lord, almighty Father, everlasting God, for in the mystery of the Word made flesh you have given us a new revelation of your glory that, seeing you in the person of your Son, we may be drawn to the love of those things which are not seen. Therefore with angels and archangels and with all the company of heaven we laud and magnify your glorious name, evermore praising you and saying:

EPIPHANY

It is truly good, right, and salutary that we should at all times and in all places give thanks to you, holy Lord, almighty Father, everlasting God, and now we praise you that you sent us your only-begotten Son and that in him, being found in fashion as a man, you manifested the fullness of your glory. Therefore with angels and archangels and with all the company of heaven we laud and magnify your glorious name, evermore praising you and saying:

LENT

It is truly good, right, and salutary that we should at all times and in all places give thanks to you, holy Lord, almighty Father, everlasting God. You bid your people cleanse their hearts and prepare with joy for the paschal feast. Renew our zeal in faith and life, and bring us to the fullness of grace that belongs to the children of God. Therefore with angels and archangels and with all the company of heaven we laud and magnify your glorious name, evermore praising you and saying:

PASSION

It is truly good, right, and salutary that we should at all times and in all places give thanks to you, holy Lord, almighty Father, everlasting God. On the tree of the cross you gave salvation to mankind that, whence death arose, thence life also might rise again and that he who by a tree once overcame likewise by a tree might be overcome, through Jesus Christ our Lord. Therefore with angels and archangels and with all the company of heaven we laud and magnify your glorious name, evermore praising you and saying:

EASTER

It is truly good, right, and salutary that we should at all times and in all places give thanks to you, holy Lord, almighty Father, everlasting God; but chiefly are we bound to praise you for the glorious resurrection of your Son, Jesus Christ, our Lord; for he is the very Paschal Lamb, which was offered for us and has taken away the sins of the world. By his death he has destroyed death, and by his rising to life again he has restored to us everlasting life. Therefore with angels and archangels and with all the company of heaven we laud and magnify your glorious name, evermore praising you and saying:

ASCENSION

It is truly good, right, and salutary that we should at all times and in all places give thanks to you, holy Lord, almighty Father, everlasting God, through Jesus Christ our Lord, who after his resurrection appeared openly to all his disciples and in their sight was taken up to heaven that he might make us partakers of his divine nature. Therefore with angels and archangels and with all the company of heaven we laud and magnify your glorious name, evermore praising you and saying:

PENTECOST

It is truly good, right, and salutary that we should at all times and in all places give thanks to you, holy Lord, almighty Father, everlasting God, through Jesus Christ our Lord, who ascended above the heavens and, sitting at your right hand, poured out on this day as he had promised the Holy Spirit on the chosen disciples. At this the whole earth rejoices with exceeding joy. Therefore with angels and archangels and with all the company of heaven we laud and magnify your glorious name, evermore praising you and saying:

HOLY TRINITY

It is truly good, right, and salutary that we should at all times and in all places give thanks to you, holy Lord, almighty Father, everlasting God, who with your only-begotten Son and the Holy Spirit are one God, one Lord. In the confession of the only true God we worship the Trinity in person and the Unity in substance, of majesty coequal. Therefore with angels and archangels and with all the company of heaven we laud and magnify your glorious name, evermore praising you and saying:

APOSTLES AND EVANGELISTS

It is truly good, right, and salutary that we should at all times and in all places give thanks to you, holy Lord, almighty Father, everlasting God, because you have mightily governed and protected your holy Church, which the blessed apostles and evangelists instructed in your divine and saving truth. Therefore with angels and archangels and with all the company of heaven we laud and magnify your glorious name, evermore praising you and saying:

ALL SAINTS

It is truly good, right, and salutary that we should at all times and in all places give thanks to you, holy Lord, almighty Father, everlasting God, who in the multitude of your saints did surround us with so great a cloud of witnesses that we, rejoicing in their fellowship, may run with patience the race that is set before us and, together with them, may receive the crown of glory that does not fade away. Therefore with angels and archangels and with all the company of heaven we laud and magnify your glorious name, evermore praising you and saying:

C Ho - ly, ho - ly, ho - ly Lord, God of Sab - a - oth. Heav'n and earth are full of your glo - ry. Ho - san - na, ho - san - na, ho - san - na in the high - est.

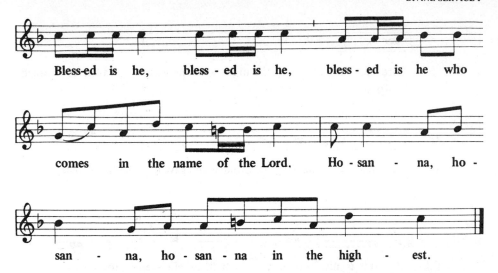

Bless-ed is he, bless-ed is he, bless-ed is he who comes in the name of the Lord. Ho-san-na, ho-san-na, ho-san-na in the high-est.

℗ Lord of heaven and earth, we praise and thank you for having had mercy on those whom you created, sending your only-begotten Son into our flesh to bear our sin and be our Savior. With repentant joy we receive the salvation accomplished for us by the all-availing sacrifice of his body and his blood on the cross.

Gathered in the name and the remembrance of Jesus, we beg you, O Lord, to forgive, renew, and strengthen us with your Word and Spirit. Grant us faithfully to eat his body and drink his blood as he bids us do in his own testament. Hear us as we pray in his name and as he has taught us. (162)

25. The LORD'S PRAYER is chanted or said. Appropriate chants appear on page 284.

☉ Our Father who art in heaven,
    hallowed be thy name,
    thy kingdom come,
    thy will be done
        on earth as it is in heaven.
Give us this day our daily bread;
and forgive us our trespasses
    as we forgive those
        who trespass against us;
and lead us not into temptation,
    but deliver us from evil.
For thine is the kingdom
    and the power and the glory
    forever and ever. Amen

OR

☉ Our Father in heaven,
    hallowed be your name,
    your kingdom come,
    your will be done
        on earth as in heaven.
Give us today our daily bread.
Forgive us our sins
    as we forgive those
        who sin against us.
Lead us not into temptation,
    but deliver us from evil.
For the kingdom, the power,
    and the glory are yours
    now and forever. Amen

26. The WORDS OF INSTITUTION are chanted or said.

℗ Our Lord Je - sus Christ, on the night when he was be - trayed, took bread,

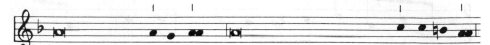

and when he had giv-en thanks, he broke it and gave it to the dis-ci - ples and said:

Take, eat; this is my ✠ bod - y, which is giv - en for you.

This do in re - mem-brance of me. In the same way al - so

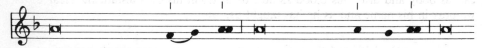

he took the cup after sup - per, and when he had giv - en thanks, he gave

it to them, say - ing: Drink of it, all of you; this is my ✠ blood of the

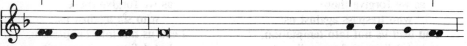

new tes - ta - ment, which is shed for you for the for - give - ness of sins.

This do, as often as you drink it, in re - mem-brance of me.

27. *The PEACE is chanted or said.*

P The peace of the Lord be with you al - ways.

C A - men

28. *The AGNUS DEI is sung. It may be sung to an alternate setting (see Canticles and Chants, No. 7).*

C O Christ, the Lamb of God, who takes a - way the sin of the world,

have mer - cy on us. O Christ, the Lamb of God,

who takes a - way the sin of the world, have mer - cy on us.

O Christ, the Lamb of God, who takes a - way the sin of the world,

grant us your peace. A - men

Sit

29. *The DISTRIBUTION. The minister and those who assist him receive the body and blood of Christ first and then distribute them to those who come to receive, saying:*

Take, eat; this is the true body of our Lord and Savior Jesus Christ, given into death for your sins.	OR	Take, eat; this is the very body of Christ, given for you.
Take, drink; this is the true blood of our Lord and Savior Jesus Christ, shed for the forgiveness of your sins.		Take, drink; this is the very blood of Christ, shed for you.

30. In dismissing the communicants, the minister says:

℗ The body and blood of our Lord strengthen and preserve you steadfast in the true faith to life everlasting. Go in peace.

31. The communicant may say: "Amen."

Stand

32. The POST-COMMUNION CANTICLE or an appropriate hymn may be sung. This canticle may be sung to an alternate setting (see Canticles and Chants, No. 11).

© Lord, now let your servant de - part in peace

ac - cord - ing to your word, for my eyes have

seen your sal - va - tion, which you have prepared before the

face of all peo - ple, a light to light - en the

Gen - tiles and the glory of your peo - ple Is - ra - el.

Glo - ry be to the Father and to the Son

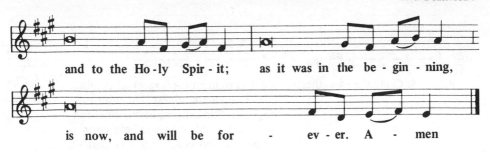

and to the Ho-ly Spir-it; as it was in the be-gin-ning,

is now, and will be for - ev-er. A - men

33. The minister continues:

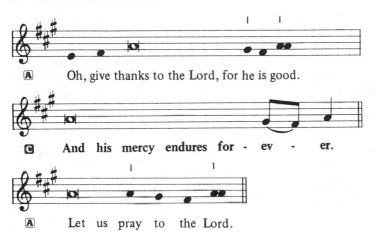

Ⓐ Oh, give thanks to the Lord, for he is good.

Ⓒ And his mercy endures for - ev - er.

Ⓐ Let us pray to the Lord.

34. One of the following POST-COMMUNION COLLECTS is chanted or said.

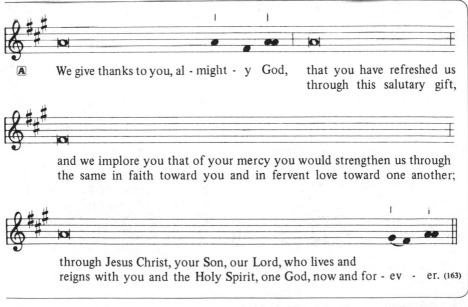

Ⓐ We give thanks to you, al - might - y God, that you have refreshed us through this salutary gift,

and we implore you that of your mercy you would strengthen us through the same in faith toward you and in fervent love toward one another;

through Jesus Christ, your Son, our Lord, who lives and reigns with you and the Holy Spirit, one God, now and for - ev - er. (163)

OR

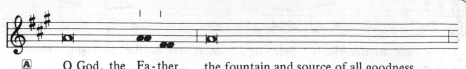

A O God, the Fa-ther, the fountain and source of all goodness,
who in loving-kindness sent your only-
begotten Son into the flesh, we thank
you that for his sake you have given
us pardon and peace in this sacrament,

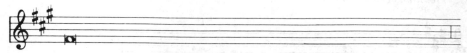

and we ask you not to forsake your children but always to rule our
hearts and minds by your Holy Spirit that we may be enabled to serve
you constantly;

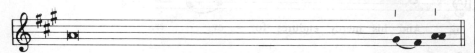

through Jesus Christ, your Son, our Lord, who lives and
reigns with you and the Holy Spirit, one God, now and for-ev - er. (164)

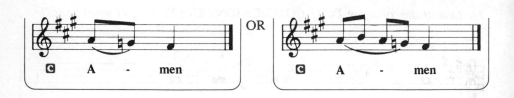

OR

C A - men   C A - men

35. *The minister continues:*

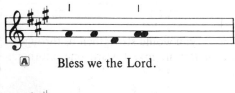

A Bless we the Lord.

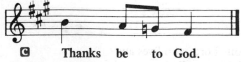

C Thanks be to God.

36. *The BENEDICTION is chanted or said.*

The Lord bless you and keep you. The Lord make

his face shine on you and be gra-cious to you.

The Lord lift up his countenance on you and ✠ give you peace.

A-men, a-men, a - men

Silent Prayer

37. ►*When there is no Communion, the service concludes as follows:*

𝕮 Our Father who art in heaven,	OR	𝕮 Our Father in heaven,

𝕮 Our Father who art in heaven,
   hallowed be thy name,
   thy kingdom come,
   thy will be done
      on earth as it is in heaven.
Give us this day our daily bread;
and forgive us our trespasses
   as we forgive those
      who trespass against us;
and lead us not into temptation,
   but deliver us from evil.
For thine is the kingdom
   and the power and the glory
   forever and ever. Amen

OR

𝕮 Our Father in heaven,
   hallowed be your name,
   your kingdom come,
   your will be done
      on earth as in heaven.
Give us today our daily bread.
Forgive us our sins
   as we forgive those
      who sin against us.
Lead us not into temptation,
   but deliver us from evil.
For the kingdom, the power,
   and the glory are yours
   now and forever. Amen

Sit

38. A hymn may be sung.

Stand

39. One of the following COLLECTS may be chanted or said.

A Let us pray to the Lord.

A Bless-ed Lord, since you have caused all Holy
Scriptures to be written for our learning,

grant that we may so hear them, read, mark, learn and take them
to heart that by patience and comfort of your holy Word we may
embrace and ever hold fast the blessed hope of everlasting life;

through Jesus Christ, your Son, our Lord, who lives and
reigns with you and the Holy Spirit, one God, now and for - ev - er. (165)

OR

A Grant, we implore you, al - might -y God, to your Church your Holy
Spirit and the wisdom which
comes down from above

that your Word may not be bound but have free course and be preached
to the joy and edifying of Christ's holy people, so that in steadfast faith
we may serve you and in the confession of your name abide to the end;

through Jesus Christ, your Son, our Lord, who lives and
reigns with you and the Holy Spirit, one God, now and for-ev - er. (166)

156

C A - men   OR   **C** A - men

40. *The BENEDICTION is chanted or said.*

P The Lord bless you and keep you. The Lord make

his face shine on you and be gra - cious to you.

The Lord lift up his countenance on you and ☩ give you peace.

C A-men, a-men, a - men

Silent Prayer

DIVINE SERVICE II

First Setting

1. A hymn of invocation may be sung.

Stand

ℙ In the name of the Father and of the ✠ Son and of the Holy Spirit.

𝐂 **Amen**

ℙ If we say we have no sin, we deceive ourselves, and the truth is not in us.

𝐂 **But if we confess our sins, God, who is faithful and just, will forgive our sins and cleanse us from all unrighteousness.**

Kneel/Stand

2. Silence for reflection on God's Word and for self-examination.

ℙ Let us then confess our sins to God our Father.

𝐂 **Most merciful God, we confess that we are by nature sinful and unclean. We have sinned against you in thought, word, and deed, by what we have done and by what we have left undone. We have not loved you with our whole heart; we have not loved our neighbors as ourselves. We justly deserve your present and eternal punishment. For the sake of your Son, Jesus Christ, have mercy on us. Forgive us, renew us, and lead us, so that we may delight in your will and walk in your ways to the glory of your holy name. Amen**

3. The minister stands and says:

ℙ Almighty God in his mercy has given his Son to die for you and for his sake forgives you all your sins. As a called and ordained servant of the Word I therefore forgive you all your sins in the name of the Father and of the ✠ Son and of the Holy Spirit.

OR

P In the mercy of almighty God, Jesus Christ was given to die for us, and for his sake God forgives us all our sins. To those who believe in Jesus Christ he gives the power to become the children of God and bestows on them the Holy Spirit. May the Lord, who has begun this good work in us, bring it to completion in the day of our Lord Jesus Christ.

C **Amen**

Stand

4. The INTROIT OF THE DAY, the appointed PSALM, or an ENTRANCE HYMN is sung.

5. The KYRIE may follow.

A In peace let us pray to the Lord.

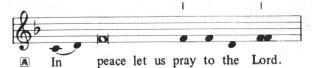

C Lord, have mer - cy.

A For the peace from above and for our salvation let us pray to the Lord.

C Lord, have mer - cy.

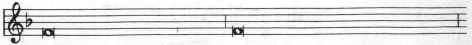

A For the peace of the whole world, for the well-being of the Church of God,

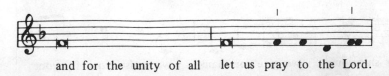

and for the unity of all let us pray to the Lord.

C Lord, have mer - cy.

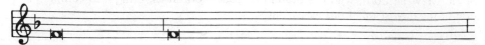

A For this holy house and for all who offer here their worship and praise

let us pray to the Lord.

C Lord, have mer - cy.

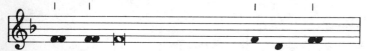

A Help, save, comfort, and defend us, gra-cious Lord.

C A - men

6. *The HYMN OF PRAISE is sung.*

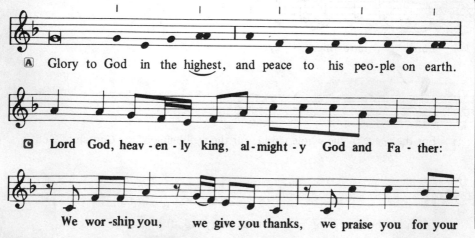

A Glory to God in the highest, and peace to his peo-ple on earth.

C Lord God, heav - en - ly king, al - might - y God and Fa - ther:

We wor -ship you, we give you thanks, we praise you for your

160

glo - ry. Lord Je - sus Christ, on - ly Son of the Fa - ther,

Lord God, Lamb of God: You take a - way the sin of the world;

have mer - cy on us. You are seat - ed at the right hand of the

Fa - ther; re - ceive our prayer. For you a -

lone are the Ho - ly One, you a - lone are the Lord,

you a - lone are the Most High, Je - sus Christ, with the Ho - ly Spir - it,

in the glo - ry of God the Fa - ther. A - men

OR

This is the feast of vic - to - ry for our God.

Al - le - lu - ia, al - le - lu - ia, al - le - lu - ia.

[I] Wor - thy is Christ, the Lamb who was slain, whose

blood set us free to be peo - ple of God.

[C] This is the feast of vic - to - ry for our God.

Al - le - lu - ia, al - le - lu - ia, al - le - lu - ia.

[II] Pow - er, rich - es, wis - dom, and strength, and

hon - or, bless - ing, and glo - ry are his.

[C] This is the feast of vic - to - ry for our God.

Al - le - lu - ia, al - le - lu - ia, al - le - lu - ia.

[I] Sing with all the peo - ple of God, and

join in the hymn of all cre - a - tion:

Bless - ing, hon - or, glo - ry, and might be to

God and the Lamb for - ev - er. A - men

C This is the feast of vic - to - ry for our God.

Al - le - lu - ia, al - le - lu - ia, al - le - lu - ia.

II For the Lamb who was slain has be -

gun his reign. Al - le - lu - ia.

C This is the feast of vic - to - ry for our God.

Al - le - lu - ia, al - le - lu - ia, al - le - lu - ia.

7. The COLLECT OF THE DAY is chanted or said; the salutation may precede it.

℗ The Lord be with you.

ℂ And al - so with you.

℗ Let us pray. . . .

ℂ **Amen**

Sit

8. The OLD TESTAMENT READING (in the Three-Year Series, for Easter and its season: The Reading from the Book of Acts) is announced.

Ⓐ The Old Testament Reading for _____ is from the _____ chapter of _____.

After the reading the minister says:

Ⓐ This is the Word of the Lord.

9. The GRADUAL FOR THE SEASON or the appointed PSALM is sung or said.

10. The EPISTLE is announced.

Ⓐ The Epistle is from the _____ chapter of _____.

After the reading the minister says:

Ⓐ This is the Word of the Lord.

Stand

11. The appointed VERSE is sung by the choir, or the congregation may sing the appropriate Verse below:

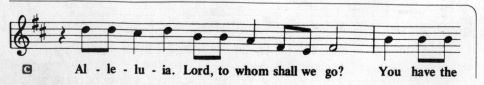

ℂ Al - le - lu - ia. Lord, to whom shall we go? You have the

164

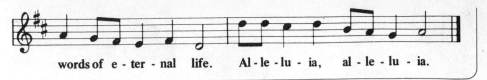

words of e - ter - nal life. Al - le - lu - ia, al - le - lu - ia.

OR

LENT

C Re - turn to the Lord, your God, for he is gra - cious and

mer - ci - ful, slow to an - ger, and a - bound-ing in

stead -fast love, and a - bound - ing in stead - fast love.

12. The HOLY GOSPEL is announced.

P The Holy Gospel according to St. _____, the _____ chapter.

C Glo - ry to you, O Lord.

13. After the reading the minister says:

P This is the Gospel of the Lord.

C Praise to you, O Christ.

Sit

14. The HYMN OF THE DAY is sung (see Hymn of the Day index).

15. The SERMON

Stand

16. *The CREED. The Nicene Creed is said at celebrations of Holy Communion and on major festivals; the Apostles' Creed at other times. The Creeds may be sung (see Canticles and Chants, No. 4, and Hymns 212 and 213).*

NICENE CREED

C I believe in one God,
> the Father Almighty,
> maker of heaven and earth
>> and of all things visible and invisible.

And in one Lord Jesus Christ,
> the only-begotten Son of God,
> begotten of his Father before all worlds,
> God of God, Light of Light,
> very God of very God,
> begotten, not made,
> being of one substance with the Father,
> by whom all things were made;
> who for us men and for our salvation
>> came down from heaven
> and was incarnate by the Holy Spirit of the virgin Mary
> and was made man;
> and was crucified also for us under Pontius Pilate.
> He suffered and was buried.
> And the third day he rose again
>> according to the Scriptures
>> and ascended into heaven
> and sits at the right hand of the Father.
> And he will come again with glory to judge
>> both the living and the dead,
> whose kingdom will have no end.

And I believe in the Holy Spirit,
> the Lord and giver of life,
> who proceeds from the Father and the Son,
> who with the Father and the Son together
>> is worshiped and glorified,
> who spoke by the prophets.
> And I believe in one holy Christian and apostolic Church,*

166

I acknowledge one Baptism for the remission of sins,
and I look for the resurrection of the dead
and the life of the world to come. Amen

*The ancient text: one holy catholic and apostolic Church

OR

APOSTLES' CREED

C I believe in God, the Father Almighty,
    maker of heaven and earth.

And in Jesus Christ, his only Son, our Lord,
    who was conceived by the Holy Spirit,
    born of the virgin Mary,
    suffered under Pontius Pilate,
    was crucified, died and was buried.
    He descended into hell.
    The third day he rose again from the dead.
    He ascended into heaven
        and sits at the right hand of God
        the Father Almighty.
    From thence he will come to judge the living and the dead.

I believe in the Holy Spirit,
    the holy Christian Church,*
    the communion of saints,
    the forgiveness of sins,
    the resurrection of the body,
    and the life everlasting. Amen

*The ancient text: the holy catholic Church

17. *When there is no Communion, the service continues on page 175.* ▶

18. *The PRAYERS are said.*

A Let us pray for the whole people of God in Christ Jesus and for all people according to their needs.

Prayers are included for the whole Church, the nations, those in need, the parish, special concerns.

The congregation may be invited to offer petitions and thanksgivings.

The minister gives thanks for the faithful departed, especially for those who recently have died.

After each portion of the prayers:

Ⓐ Lord, in your mercy,

Ⓒ **hear our prayer.**

OR

Ⓐ Let us pray to the Lord.

Ⓒ **Lord, have mercy.**

The prayers conclude:

Ⓟ Into your hands, O Lord, we commend all for whom we pray, trusting in your mercy; through your Son, Jesus Christ, our Lord.

Ⓒ **Amen**

Sit

19. *The OFFERING is received as the Lord's table is prepared.*

20. *The congregation may sing one of the following OFFERTORIES, or an appropriate hymn or psalm may be sung.*

Stand

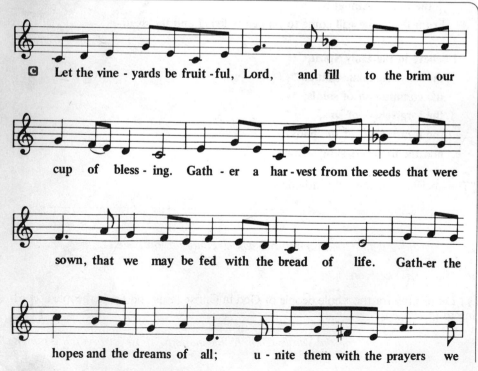

Ⓒ Let the vine-yards be fruit-ful, Lord, and fill to the brim our

cup of bless-ing. Gath-er a har-vest from the seeds that were

sown, that we may be fed with the bread of life. Gath-er the

hopes and the dreams of all; u-nite them with the prayers we

of - fer now. Grace our ta - ble with your pres - ence, and
give us a fore-taste of the feast to come.

OR

What shall I ren - der to the Lord for all his ben - e - fits to me? I will of - fer the sac - ri - fice of thanks-giv - ing and will call on the name of the Lord. I will take the cup of sal - va - tion and will call on the name of the Lord. I will pay my vows to the Lord now in the pres - ence of all his peo - ple, in the courts of the Lord's house, in the midst of you, O Je - ru - sa - lem.

21. The PREFACE is begun by the minister standing at the altar.

P   The   Lord   be   with   you.

C   And   al - so   with   you.

P   Lift   up   your   hearts.

C   We   lift   them   to   the Lord.

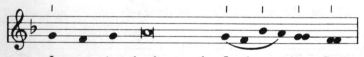

P   Let   us   give thanks   to   the   Lord   our   God.

C   It   is   right   to   give   him   thanks   and   praise.

22. The preface appropriate to the day or season is chanted or said.

P   It is truly good, right, and salutary . . . evermore praising you and saying:

C   Ho - ly,   ho - ly,   ho - ly   Lord,   God   of   pow'r and might:

Heav-en   and   earth   are   full   of   your   glo - ry.   Ho - san - na.   Ho -

san-na. Ho - san - na in the high - est. Bless-ed is he who

comes in the name of the Lord. Ho-san - na in the high - est.

23. The minister continues:

℗ Blessed are you, Lord of heaven and earth, for you have had mercy on us children of men and given your only-begotten Son that whoever believes in him should not perish but have eternal life. We give you thanks for the redemption you have prepared for us through Jesus Christ. Send your Holy Spirit into our hearts that he may establish in us a living faith and prepare us joyfully to remember our Redeemer and receive him who comes to us in his body and blood. (167)

☾ **Amen**

☾ **Our Father who art in heaven,**	OR	☾ **Our Father in heaven,**
hallowed be thy name,		**hallowed be your name,**
thy kingdom come,		**your kingdom come,**
thy will be done		**your will be done**
on earth as it is in heaven.		**on earth as in heaven.**
Give us this day our daily bread;		**Give us today our daily bread.**
and forgive us our trespasses		**Forgive us our sins**
as we forgive those		**as we forgive those**
who trespass against us;		**who sin against us.**
and lead us not into temptation,		**Lead us not into temptation,**
but deliver us from evil.		**but deliver us from evil.**
For thine is the kingdom		**For the kingdom, the power,**
and the power and the glory		**and the glory are yours**
forever and ever. Amen		**now and forever. Amen**

24. The minister continues with the Words of Institution:

℗ Our Lord Jesus Christ, on the night when he was betrayed, took bread, and when he had given thanks, he broke it and gave it to the disciples and said: Take, eat; this is my ✚ body, which is given for you. This do in remembrance of me. In the same way also he took the cup after supper, and when he had given thanks, he gave it to them, saying: Drink of it, all of you; this is my ✚ blood of the new testament, which is shed for you for the forgiveness of sins. This do, as often as you drink it, in remembrance of me.

25. The PEACE is given and shared at this time.

℗ The peace of the Lord be with you always.

☾ **And also with you.**

The ministers and congregation may greet one another in the name of the Lord.

Peace be with you. ℟ Peace be with you.

26. The AGNUS DEI is sung.

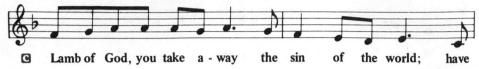

Lamb of God, you take a - way the sin of the world; have

mer-cy on us. Lamb of God, you take a-way the sin of the

world; have mer-cy on us. Lamb of God, you take a - way the

sin of the world; grant us peace.

Sit

27. The COMMUNION follows. Hymns and other appropriate music may be used during the ministration of Communion.

28. The minister and those who assist him are given the body and blood of Christ first and then give them to those who come to receive, saying:

Take, eat; this is the true body of our Lord and Savior Jesus Christ, given into death for your sins.	OR	Take, eat; this is the very body of Christ, given for you.
Take, drink; this is the true blood of our Lord and Savior Jesus Christ, shed for the forgiveness of your sins.		Take, drink; this is the very blood of Christ, shed for you.

29. In dismissing the communicants, the minister says:

℗ The body and blood of our Lord strengthen and preserve you steadfast in the true faith to life everlasting. Go in peace.

30. The communicant may say: "Amen."

Stand

31. The POST-COMMUNION canticle or an appropriate hymn is sung as the table is cleared. The "Thank the Lord . . ." is not sung during Lent.

Ⓒ Thank the Lord and sing his praise; tell ev-'ry-one what he has done.

Let all who seek the Lord re-joice and proud-ly bear his name.

He re-calls his prom-is-es and leads his peo-ple forth in joy with

shouts of thanks-giv-ing. Al-le-lu-ia, al-le-lu-ia.

OR

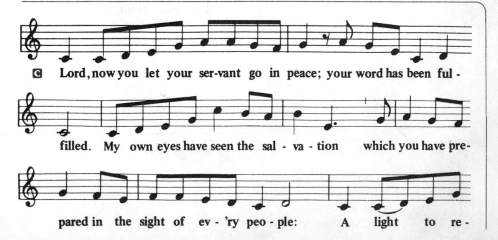

Ⓒ Lord, now you let your ser-vant go in peace; your word has been ful-

filled. My own eyes have seen the sal-va-tion which you have pre-

pared in the sight of ev-'ry peo-ple: A light to re-

▶

veal you to the na - tions   and the glo -ry of your peo-ple Is - ra - el.

Glo-ry be to the Fa - ther   and to the Son and to the Ho-ly Spir - it;

as it was in the be-gin - ning, is now, and will be for - ev - er. A -men

32. One of the following prayers is chanted or said.

Ⓐ Let us pray.

Ⓐ We give thanks to you, almighty God, that you have refreshed us through this salutary gift, and we implore you that of your mercy you would strengthen us through the same in faith toward you and in fervent love toward one another; through Jesus Christ, your Son, our Lord, who lives and reigns with you and the Holy Spirit, one God, now and forever. (163)

OR

Ⓐ O God the Father, the fountain and source of all goodness, who in loving-kindness sent your only-begotten Son into the flesh, we thank you that for his sake you have given us pardon and peace in this sacrament, and we ask you not to forsake your children but always to rule our hearts and minds by your Holy Spirit that we may be enabled to serve you constantly; through Jesus Christ, your Son, our Lord, who lives and reigns with you and the Holy Spirit, one God, now and forever. (164)

Ⓒ **Amen**

33. The minister blesses the congregation.

Ⓟ The Lord bless you and keep you.
The Lord make his face shine on you
    and be gracious to you.
The Lord look upon you with favor and ✠ give you peace.

174

A - men

34. ► *When there is no Communion, the service concludes as follows.*

35. *The OFFERING is received and may be presented at the altar.*

36. *The following Psalm or an appropriate hymn may be sung when the gifts are presented.*

Stand

Cre - ate in me a clean heart, O God, and re - new a right spir - it with - in me. Cast me not a - way from your pres - ence, and take not your Ho - ly Spir - it from me. Re - store to me the joy of your sal - va - tion, and up - hold me with your free Spir - it.

37. *THE PRAYERS are said. One of the following or another form of prayer may be used.*

Ⓐ Let us pray.

Ⓐ O Lord our God, you have commanded the light to shine out of darkness, and you have again brought us to your house of prayer to praise your goodness and ask for your gifts. Accept now in your endless mercy the sacrifice of our worship and thanksgiving, and grant us those requests which will be wholesome for us. Make us children of the light and of the day and heirs of your everlasting inheritance. Remember, O Lord, according to the multitude of your mercies, your whole Church, all who join with us in prayer, all our sisters and brothers wherever they may be in your vast kingdom who stand in need of your help and comfort. Pour out upon them the riches of your mercy, so that we, redeemed in soul and body and steadfast in faith, may ever praise your wonderful and holy name; through Jesus Christ, our Lord, who lives and reigns with you and the Holy Spirit, one God, now and always through all ages of ages. (168)

C Amen

OR

A Let us pray for the whole people of God in Christ Jesus and for all people according to their needs.

Prayers are included for the whole Church, the nations, those in need, the parish, special concerns.

The congregation may be invited to offer petitions and thanksgivings.

The minister gives thanks for the faithful departed, especially for those who recently have died.

After each portion of the prayers:

A Lord, in your mercy,	OR	**A** Let us pray to the Lord.
C hear our prayer.		**C Lord, have mercy.**

The prayers conclude:

P Into your hands, O Lord, we commend all for whom we pray, trusting in your mercy; through your Son, Jesus Christ, our Lord.

C Amen

C Our Father who art in heaven,	OR	**C Our Father in heaven,**
hallowed be thy name,		hallowed be your name,
thy kingdom come,		your kingdom come,
thy will be done		your will be done
on earth as it is in heaven.		on earth as in heaven.
Give us this day our daily bread;		Give us today our daily bread.
and forgive us our trespasses		Forgive us our sins
as we forgive those		as we forgive those
who trespass against us;		who sin against us.
and lead us not into temptation,		Lead us not into temptation,

176

but deliver us from evil.
For thine is the kingdom
and the power and the glory
forever and ever. Amen

but deliver us from evil.
For the kingdom, the power,
and the glory are yours
now and forever. Amen

38. *The minister blesses the congregation.*

P The Lord bless you and keep you.
The Lord make his face shine on you
and be gracious to you.
The Lord look upon you with favor
and ✠ give you peace.

C Amen

DIVINE SERVICE II

Second Setting

1. A hymn of invocation may be sung.

Stand

P In the name of the Father and of the ☩ Son and of the Holy Spirit.

C **Amen**

P If we say we have no sin, we deceive ourselves, and the truth is not in us.

C **But if we confess our sins, God, who is faithful and just, will forgive our sins and cleanse us from all unrighteousness.**

Kneel/Stand

2. Silence for reflection on God's Word and for self-examination.

P Let us then confess our sins to God our Father.

C **Most merciful God, we confess that we are by nature sinful and unclean. We have sinned against you in thought, word, and deed, by what we have done and by what we have left undone. We have not loved you with our whole heart; we have not loved our neighbors as ourselves. We justly deserve your present and eternal punishment. For the sake of your Son, Jesus Christ, have mercy on us. Forgive us, renew us, and lead us, so that we may delight in your will and walk in your ways to the glory of your holy name. Amen**

3. The minister stands and says:

P Almighty God in his mercy has given his Son to die for you and for his sake forgives you all your sins. As a called and ordained servant of the Word I therefore forgive you all your sins in the name of the Father and of the ✠ Son and of the Holy Spirit.

OR

P In the mercy of almighty God, Jesus Christ was given to die for us, and for his sake God forgives us all our sins. To those who believe in Jesus Christ he gives the power to become the children of God and bestows on them the Holy Spirit. May the Lord, who has begun this good work in us, bring it to completion in the day of our Lord Jesus Christ.

C Amen

Stand

4. The INTROIT OF THE DAY, the appointed PSALM, or an ENTRANCE HYMN is sung.

5. The KYRIE may follow.

A In peace let us pray to the Lord.

C Lord, have mer - cy.

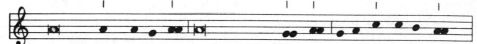

A For the peace from a - bove and for our sal - va - tion let us pray to the Lord.

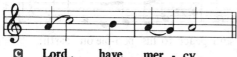

C Lord, have mer - cy.

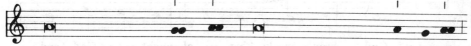

A For the peace of the whole world, for the well-being of the Church of God,

and for the uni-ty of all let us pray to the Lord.

C Lord, have mer - cy.

A For this holy house   and for all who offer here their wor - ship and praise

let us pray to the Lord.

C Lord, have mer - cy.

A Help, save, comfort, and de - fend us, gra - cious Lord.

C A - men

6. *The HYMN OF PRAISE is sung.*

A Glo - ry to God in the high - est,   and peace to his peo - ple on earth.

C Lord God, heav - en - ly king, al - might - y God and

Fa - ther: We wor - ship you, we   give you thanks, we

180

praise you for your glo - ry. Lord Je - sus Christ, on - ly

Son of the Fa - ther, Lord God, Lamb of God: You

take a - way the sin of the world; have mer - cy on

us. You are seat - ed at the right hand of the

Fa - ther; re - ceive our prayer. For you a - lone are the

Ho - ly One, you a - lone are the Lord, you a -

lone are the Most High, Je - sus Christ, with the Ho - ly Spir - it,

in the glo - ry of God the Fa - ther. A - men

OR

A This is the feast of vic-to-ry for our God. Al -le - lu - ia.

C Wor - thy is Christ, the Lamb who was slain, whose

blood set us free to be peo-ple of God.

Pow - er and rich - es and wis - dom and strength and

hon - or and bless-ing and glo - ry are his.

This is the feast of vic-to-ry for our God. Al - le -

lu - ia. Sing with all the peo - ple of

God, and join in the hymn of all cre - a - tion:

Bless - ing and hon - or and glo - ry and might be to

God and the Lamb for - ev - er. A - men

This is the feast of vic - to - ry for our God, for the

Lamb who was slain has be - gun his reign. Al -

- le - lu - ia, al - le - lu - ia.

7. *The COLLECT OF THE DAY is chanted or said; the salutation may precede it.*

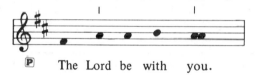

℗ The Lord be with you.

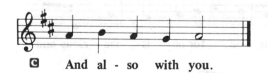

🅲 And al - so with you.

℗ Let us pray....

🅲 **Amen**

Sit

8. *The OLD TESTAMENT READING (in the Three-Year Series, for Easter and its season: The Reading from the Book of Acts) is announced.*

🅰 The Old Testament Reading for _____ is from the _____ chapter of _____.

After the reading the minister says:

Ⓐ This is the Word of the Lord.

9. The GRADUAL FOR THE SEASON or the appointed PSALM is sung or said.

10. The EPISTLE is announced.

Ⓐ The Epistle is from the _____ chapter of _____.

After the reading the minister says:

Ⓐ This is the Word of the Lord.

Stand

11. The appointed VERSE is sung by the choir, or the congregation may sing the appropriate Verse below:

Ⓒ Al - le - lu - ia. Lord, to whom shall we go?
You have the words of e - ter - nal life. Al - le - lu - ia.

OR

LENT

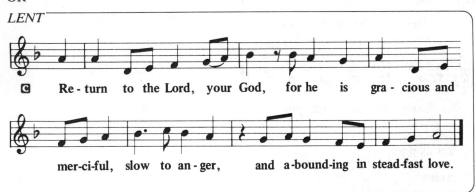

Ⓒ Re - turn to the Lord, your God, for he is gra - cious and
mer-ci-ful, slow to an - ger, and a-bound-ing in stead-fast love.

12. The HOLY GOSPEL is announced.

Ⓟ The Holy Gospel according to St. _____, the _____ chapter.

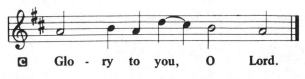

Ⓒ Glo - ry to you, O Lord.

184

13. After the reading the minister says:

℗ This is the Gospel of the Lord.

℅ Praise to you, O Christ.

Sit

14. The HYMN OF THE DAY is sung (see Hymn of the Day index).

15. The SERMON

Stand

16. The CREED. The Nicene Creed is said at celebrations of Holy Communion and on major festivals; the Apostles' Creed at other times. The Creeds may be sung (see Canticles and Chants, No. 4, and Hymns 212 and 213).

NICENE CREED

℅ I believe in one God,
the Father Almighty,
maker of heaven and earth
and of all things visible and invisible.

And in one Lord Jesus Christ,
the only-begotten Son of God,
begotten of his Father before all worlds,
God of God, Light of Light,
very God of very God,
begotten, not made,
being of one substance with the Father,
by whom all things were made;
who for us men and for our salvation
came down from heaven
and was incarnate by the Holy Spirit of the virgin Mary
and was made man;
and was crucified also for us under Pontius Pilate.
He suffered and was buried.
And the third day he rose again
according to the Scriptures
and ascended into heaven
and sits at the right hand of the Father.

And he will come again with glory to judge
   both the living and the dead,
whose kingdom will have no end.

And I believe in the Holy Spirit,
   the Lord and giver of life,
who proceeds from the Father and the Son,
who with the Father and the Son together
   is worshiped and glorified,
who spoke by the prophets.
And I believe in one holy Christian and apostolic Church,*
I acknowledge one Baptism for the remission of sins,
and I look for the resurrection of the dead
and the life of the world to come. Amen

*The ancient text: one holy catholic and apostolic Church

OR

APOSTLES' CREED

🅲 I believe in God, the Father Almighty,
   maker of heaven and earth.

And in Jesus Christ, his only Son, our Lord,
   who was conceived by the Holy Spirit,
born of the virgin Mary,
suffered under Pontius Pilate,
was crucified, died and was buried.
He descended into hell.
The third day he rose again from the dead.
He ascended into heaven
   and sits at the right hand of God
   the Father Almighty.
From thence he will come to judge the living and the dead.

I believe in the Holy Spirit,
   the holy Christian Church,*
the communion of saints,
the forgiveness of sins,
the resurrection of the body,
and the life everlasting. Amen

*The ancient text: the holy catholic Church

186

17. When there is no Communion, the service continues on page 194. ▶

18. The PRAYERS are said.

Ⓐ Let us pray for the whole people of God in Christ Jesus and for all people according to their needs.

Prayers are included for the whole Church, the nations, those in need, the parish, special concerns.

The congregation may be invited to offer petitions and thanksgivings.

The minister gives thanks for the faithful departed, especially for those who recently have died.

After each portion of the prayers:

Ⓐ Lord, in your mercy,

Ⓒ **hear our prayer.**

OR

Ⓐ Let us pray to the Lord.

Ⓒ **Lord, have mercy.**

The prayers conclude:

Ⓟ Into your hands, O Lord, we commend all for whom we pray, trusting in your mercy; through your Son, Jesus Christ, our Lord.

Ⓒ **Amen**

Sit

19. The OFFERING is received as the Lord's table is prepared.

20. The congregation may sing one of the following OFFERTORIES, or an appropriate hymn or psalm may be sung.

Stand

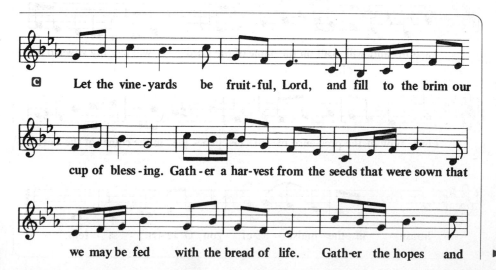

Ⓒ Let the vine-yards be fruit-ful, Lord, and fill to the brim our cup of bless-ing. Gath-er a har-vest from the seeds that were sown that we may be fed with the bread of life. Gath-er the hopes and ▶

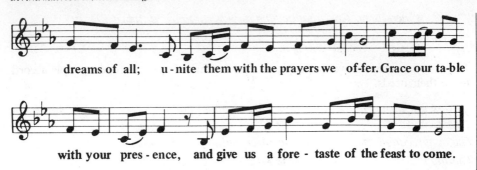

dreams of all; u-nite them with the prayers we of-fer. Grace our ta-ble

with your pres-ence, and give us a fore-taste of the feast to come.

OR

C What shall I ren-der to the Lord for all his ben-e-fits to

me? I will of-fer the sac-ri-fice of thanks-giv-ing and will

call on the name of the Lord. I will take the cup of sal-

va-tion and will call on the name of the Lord. I will pay my vows to the

Lord now in the pres-ence of all his peo-ple, in the courts of the Lord's

house, in the midst of you, O Je-ru-sa-lem.

21. The PREFACE is begun by the minister standing at the altar.

℗ The Lord be with you.

𝐂 And al - so with you.

℗ Lift up your hearts.

𝐂 We lift them to the Lord.

℗ Let us give thanks to the Lord our God.

𝐂 It is right to give him thanks and praise.

22. The preface appropriate to the day or season is chanted or said.

℗ It is truly good, right, and salutary ... evermore praising you and saying:

𝐂 Ho - ly, ho - ly, ho - ly Lord, Lord God of

pow'r and might: Heav'n and earth are full of your ▶

189

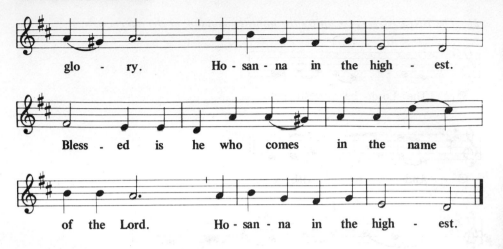

glo - ry. Ho - san - na in the high - est.

Bless - ed is he who comes in the name

of the Lord. Ho - san - na in the high - est.

23. *The minister continues:*

P Blessed are you, Lord of heaven and earth, for you have had mercy on us children of men and given your only-begotten Son that whoever believes in him should not perish but have eternal life. We give you thanks for the redemption you have prepared for us through Jesus Christ. Send your Holy Spirit into our hearts that he may establish in us a living faith and prepare us joyfully to remember our Redeemer and receive him who comes to us in his body and blood. (167)

C **Amen**

C **Our Father who art in heaven,**
    hallowed be thy name,
    thy kingdom come,
    thy will be done
        on earth as it is in heaven.
Give us this day our daily bread;
and forgive us our trespasses
    as we forgive those
        who trespass against us;
and lead us not into temptation,
    but deliver us from evil.
For thine is the kingdom
    and the power and the glory
    forever and ever. Amen

OR

C **Our Father in heaven,**
    hallowed be your name,
    your kingdom come,
    your will be done
        on earth as in heaven.
Give us today our daily bread.
Forgive us our sins
    as we forgive those
        who sin against us.
Lead us not into temptation,
    but deliver us from evil.
For the kingdom, the power,
    and the glory are yours
    now and forever. Amen

24. *The minister continues with the Words of Institution:*

P Our Lord Jesus Christ, on the night when he was betrayed, took bread, and when he had given thanks, he broke it and gave it to the disciples and said: Take, eat; this is my ✠ body, which is given for you. This do in remembrance of me. In the same way also he took the cup after supper, and when he had given thanks, he gave it to them, saying: Drink of it, all of you; this is my ☩ blood of the new testament, which is shed for you for the forgiveness of sins. This do, as often as you drink it, in remembrance of me.

25. The PEACE is given and shared at this time.

℗ The peace of the Lord be with you always.

℄ **And also with you.**

The ministers and congregation may greet one another in the name of the Lord.

Peace be with you.   ℝ Peace be with you.

26. The AGNUS DEI is sung.

℄ Lamb of God, you take a-way the sin of the world; have mer-cy on us. Lamb of God, you take a-way the sin of the world; have mer-cy on us. Lamb of God, you take a-way the sin of the world; grant us peace, grant us peace.

Sit

27. The COMMUNION follows. Hymns and other appropriate music may be used during the ministration of Communion.

28. The minister and those who assist him are given the body and blood of Christ first and then give them to those who come to receive, saying:

Take, eat; this is the true body of our Lord and Savior Jesus Christ, given into death for your sins.	OR	Take, eat; this is the very body of Christ, given for you.
Take, drink; this is the true blood of our Lord and Savior Jesus Christ, shed for the forgiveness of your sins.		Take, drink; this is the very blood of Christ, shed for you.

29. In dismissing the communicants, the minister says:

℗ The body and blood of our Lord strengthen and preserve you steadfast in the true faith to life everlasting. Go in peace.

30. The communicant may say: "Amen."

Stand

31. The POST-COMMUNION canticle or an appropriate hymn is sung as the table is cleared. The "Thank the Lord . . ." is not sung during Lent.

C Thank the Lord and sing his praise; tell ev-'ry-one what he has done. Let ev-'ry-one who seeks the Lord re-joice and proud-ly bear his name. He re-calls his prom-is-es and leads his peo-ple forth in joy with shouts of thanks-giv-ing. Al-le-lu-ia, al-le-lu-ia.

OR

Lord, now you let your ser-vant go in peace; your word has been ful-filled. My own eyes have seen the sal-va-tion which you have pre-pared in the sight of ev-'ry peo-ple: A light to re-veal you to the na-tions and the glo-ry of your peo-ple Is-ra-el. Glo-ry be to the Fa-ther and to the Son and to the Ho-ly Spir-it; as it was in the be-gin-ning, is now, and will be for-ev-er. A-men

32. One of the following prayers is chanted or said.

Ⓐ Let us pray.

Ⓐ We give thanks to you, almighty God, that you have refreshed us through this salutary gift, and we implore you that of your mercy you would strengthen us through the same in faith toward you and in fervent love toward one another; through Jesus Christ, your Son, our Lord, who lives and reigns with you and the Holy Spirit, one God, now and forever. (163)

OR

Ⓐ O God the Father, the fountain and source of all goodness, who in loving-kindness sent your only-begotten Son into the flesh, we thank you that for his sake you have given us pardon and peace in this sacrament, and we ask you not to forsake your children but always to rule our hearts and minds by your Holy Spirit that we may be enabled to serve you constantly; through Jesus Christ, your Son, our Lord, who lives and reigns with you and the Holy Spirit, one God, now and forever. (164)

Ⓒ **Amen**

33. The minister blesses the congregation.

Ⓟ The Lord bless you and keep you.
The Lord make his face shine on you
   and be gracious to you.
The Lord look upon you with favor and . . . . . ✛ give you peace.

Ⓒ A - men

34. ► When there is no Communion, the service concludes as follows.

35. The OFFERING is received and may be presented at the altar.

36. The following Psalm or an appropriate hymn may be sung when the gifts are presented.

Stand

Ⓒ Cre - ate in me a clean heart, O God, and re - new a

right spir - it with - in me. Cast me not a - way from your

pres - ence, and take not your Ho - ly Spir - it from

me. Re-store to me the joy of your sal - va - tion,

and up - hold me with your free Spir - it.

37. THE PRAYERS are said. One of the following or another form of prayer may be used.

Ⓐ Let us pray.

Ⓐ O Lord our God, you have commanded the light to shine out of darkness, and you have again brought us to your house of prayer to praise your goodness and ask for your gifts. Accept now in your endless mercy the sacrifice of our worship and thanksgiving, and grant us those requests which will be wholesome for us. Make us children of the light and of the day and heirs of your everlasting inheritance. Remember, O Lord, according to the multitude of your mercies, your whole Church, all who join with us in prayer, all our sisters and brothers wherever they may be in your vast kingdom who stand in need of your help and comfort. Pour out upon them the riches of your mercy, so that we, redeemed in soul and body and steadfast in faith, may ever praise your wonderful and holy name; through Jesus Christ, our Lord, who lives and reigns with you and the Holy Spirit, one God, now and always through all ages of ages. (168)

Ⓒ **Amen**

OR

Ⓐ Let us pray for the whole people of God in Christ Jesus and for all people according to their needs.

Prayers are included for the whole Church, the nations, those in need, the parish, special concerns.

The congregation may be invited to offer petitions and thanksgivings.

The minister gives thanks for the faithful departed, especially for those who recently have died.

After each portion of the prayers:

Ⓐ Lord, in your mercy,

Ⓒ hear our prayer.

OR

Ⓐ Let us pray to the Lord.

Ⓒ Lord, have mercy.

The prayers conclude:

Ⓟ Into your hands, O Lord, we commend all for whom we pray, trusting in your mercy; through your Son, Jesus Christ, our Lord.

Ⓒ Amen

Ⓒ Our Father who art in heaven,
    hallowed be thy name,
    thy kingdom come,
    thy will be done
        on earth as it is in heaven.
Give us this day our daily bread;
and forgive us our trespasses
    as we forgive those
        who trespass against us;
and lead us not into temptation,
    but deliver us from evil.
For thine is the kingdom
    and the power and the glory
    forever and ever. Amen

OR

Ⓒ Our Father in heaven,
    hallowed be your name,
    your kingdom come,
    your will be done
        on earth as in heaven.
Give us today our daily bread.
Forgive us our sins
    as we forgive those
        who sin against us.
Lead us not into temptation,
    but deliver us from evil.
For the kingdom, the power,
    and the glory are yours
    now and forever. Amen

38. The minister blesses the congregation.

Ⓟ The Lord bless you and keep you.
The Lord make his face shine on you
    and be gracious to you.
The Lord look upon you with favor
    and ✝ give you peace.

Ⓒ Amen

DIVINE SERVICE III

This Chorale Service follows the tradition of Luther's German Mass (1526), in which parts of the liturgy for Holy Communion are replaced with hymns (metrical paraphrases).

The numbers in parentheses correspond to the numbered rubrics in Divine Service I.

INTROIT OF THE DAY, appointed PSALM, or ENTRANCE HYMN (3)

KYRIE
  Lord, have mercy (4)
  or Hymn 209, Kyrie, God Father

GLORIA
  Hymn 215, All Glory Be to God on High
  or Hymn 210, All Glory Be to God Alone

COLLECT OF THE DAY (6)

EPISTLE (10)

GRADUAL
  Hymn 155, To God the Holy Spirit Let Us Pray
  or The Hymn of the Day (see Hymn of the Day index)

HOLY GOSPEL (13)

CREED
  Hymn 213, We All Believe in One True God

SERMON

PRAYER OF THE CHURCH (21)

OFFERING (19)

ADMONITION TO COMMUNICANTS
  P I exhort you in Christ that you give attention to the Testament of Christ in true faith, and above all take to heart the words with which Christ presents his

body and blood to us for forgiveness; that you take note of and give thanks for the boundless love that he showed us when he saved us from the wrath of God, sin, death, and hell by his blood; and that you then externally receive the bread and wine, that is, his body and blood, as a guarantee and pledge. Let us then in his name, according to his command, and with his own words administer and receive the Testament.

LORD'S PRAYER (25)

WORDS OF INSTITUTION (26)

SANCTUS
Hymn 214, Isaiah, Mighty Seer, in Spirit Soared

DISTRIBUTION (29)
O Christ, the Lamb of God (28)
Hymns 236, 237, Jesus Christ, Our Blessed Savior
Hymn 238, O Lord, We Praise You (or after the Benediction)

POST-COMMUNION COLLECT (34)

BENEDICTION (36)

HOLY BAPTISM

1. A hymn may be sung. The candidate/candidates and sponsors (and family/families) gather with the minister in the nave.

℗ In the name of the Father and of the ☩ Son and of the Holy Spirit.

🅒 **Amen**

2. The minister addresses the baptismal group and the congregation.

℗ Our Lord commanded Baptism, saying to his disciples in the last chapter of Matthew: "All authority in heaven and on earth has been given to me. Therefore go and make disciples of all nations, baptizing them in the name of the Father and of the Son and of the Holy Spirit and teaching them to obey everything I have commanded you. And surely I will be with you always, to the very end of the age." The holy apostles of the Lord have written: "The promise is for you and your children," and: "Baptism now saves you."

We also learn from the Word of God that we all are conceived and born sinful and so are in need of forgiveness. We would be lost forever unless delivered from sin, death, and everlasting condemnation. But the Father of all mercy and grace has sent his Son Jesus Christ, who atoned for the sin of the whole world that whoever believes in him shall not perish but have eternal life.

3. The minister turns to the candidate/candidates to be baptized.

℗ Receive the sign of the holy cross both upon your forehead ☩ and upon your heart ☩ to mark you as one redeemed by Christ the crucified.

4. For the baptism of infants and young children the minister says:

℗ Hear how our Lord Jesus Christ has opened the kingdom of God to little children.

People were bringing little children to Jesus to have him touch them, but the

199

disciples rebuked them. When Jesus saw this, he was indignant. He said to them, "Let the little children come to me, and do not hinder them, for the kingdom of God belongs to such as these. I tell you the truth, anyone who will not receive the kingdom of God like a little child will never enter it."

℗ This is the Gospel of the Lord.

Ⓒ **Praise to you, O Christ.**

OR

5. For the baptism of older children and adults the minister says:

℗ Hear the word of our Savior Jesus Christ telling of the new birth by water and the Spirit.

"I tell you the truth, unless a man is born of water and the Spirit, he cannot enter the kingdom of God. Flesh gives birth to flesh, but the Spirit gives birth to spirit."

℗ This is the Gospel of the Lord.

Ⓒ **Praise to you, O Christ.**

6. For the baptism of infants and young children the minister addresses the sponsors:

℗ It is your task as sponsors to confess with the whole Church the faith in our God, Father, Son, and Holy Spirit, in whose name this child is to be baptized.

After this child has been baptized you are at all times to remember him/her in your prayers, put him/her in mind of his/her Baptism, and, as much as in you lies, give your counsel and aid, especially if he/she should lose his/her parents, that he/she be brought up in the true knowledge and worship of God and be taught the Ten Commandments, the Creed, and the Lord's Prayer; and that, as he/she grows in years, you place in his/her hands the Holy Scriptures, bring him/her to the services of God's house, and provide for his/her further instruction in the Christian faith, that he/she come to the Sacrament of Christ's Body and Blood and thus, abiding in his/her baptismal grace and in communion with the Church, he/she may grow up to lead a godly life to the praise and honor of Jesus Christ.

This, then, you intend gladly and willingly to do?

ℝ **Yes.**

℗ God enable you both to will and to do this faithful and loving work and with his grace fulfill what we are unable to do.

℗ In order to implore the blessing of our Lord Jesus Christ upon the gathering of this child into the family of our Father, let us with all the family pray the prayer he gave us.

7. The minister lays his hand upon the head of the child. The congregation joins in praying:

<table>
<tr><td>

C Our Father who art in heaven,
    hallowed be thy name,
    thy kingdom come,
    thy will be done
        on earth as it is in heaven.
    Give us this day our daily bread;
    and forgive us our trespasses
        as we forgive those
           who trespass against us;
    and lead us not into temptation,
        but deliver us from evil.
    For thine is the kingdom
        and the power and the glory
        forever and ever. Amen

</td><td>

OR

</td><td>

C Our Father in heaven,
    hallowed be your name,
    your kingdom come,
    your will be done
        on earth as in heaven.
    Give us today our daily bread.
    Forgive us our sins
        as we forgive those
           who sin against us.
    Lead us not into temptation,
        but deliver us from evil.
    For the kingdom, the power,
        and the glory are yours
        now and forever. Amen

</td></tr>
</table>

P The Lord preserve your coming in and your going out from this time forth and even forevermore.

C **Amen**

8. The baptismal group gathers at the font.

9. For the baptism of infants and young children the minister says:

P Because this child cannot answer for <u>himself/herself</u> , we shall all, together with sponsors and parents, faithfully speak on <u>his/her</u> behalf in testimony of the forgiveness of sin and the birth of the life of faith which God our Father bestows in and through Baptism.

OR

10. For the baptism of older children and adults the minister says:

P Because you have been called by the Gospel and instructed in the faith, it is right and good that you should now confess with the Church what God works in and through Baptism.

P Do you renounce the devil and all his works and all his ways?

C **I do renounce them.**

P Do you believe in God, the Father Almighty?

C **Yes, I believe in God, the Father Almighty,**
    maker of heaven and earth.

P Do you believe in Jesus Christ, his only Son?

C Yes, I believe in Jesus Christ, his only Son, our Lord,
who was conceived by the Holy Spirit,
born of the virgin Mary,
suffered under Pontius Pilate,
was crucified, died, and was buried.
He descended into hell.
The third day he rose again from the dead.
He ascended into heaven
and sits at the right hand of God,
the Father Almighty.
From thence he will come to judge the living and the dead.

P Do you believe in the Holy Spirit?

C Yes, I believe in the Holy Spirit,
the holy Christian Church,
the communion of saints,
the forgiveness of sins,
the resurrection of the body,
and the life everlasting.

---

11. For the baptism of infants and young children the minister may address the parents:

P Who brings this child to be baptized?

R **We do.**

P How is this child to be named?

R _____ name _____

OR

---

12. For the baptism of older children and adults the minister may address the candidate:

P Do you wish to be baptized into this Christian faith?

R **I do.**

P How are you named?

R _____ name _____

---

13. The minister pours water three times on the head of the candidate saying:

P _____ name _____, I baptize you in the name of the Father and of the Son and of the Holy Spirit ✠.

C Amen

14. The minister lays his hand upon the one baptized and gives this blessing:

P̄ Almighty God, the Father of our Lord Jesus Christ, who has given you the new birth of water and of the Spirit and has forgiven you all your sins, strengthen you with his grace to life everlasting. Peace be with you.

C̄ **Amen**

15. A white garment may now be put upon the candidate.

P̄ Receive this white garment to show that Christ has taken away and borne your sin and put upon you his perfect righteousness. So shall you in faith ever stand before him.

16. A baptismal candle may now be lighted from the paschal or altar candle. In giving the candle the minister says:

P̄ Receive this burning light. Live always by the light of Christ, and be ever watchful for his coming that you may meet him with joy and enter with him to the marriage feast of the Lamb in his kingdom, which shall have no end.

17. The baptismal group gathers before the altar.

P̄ Let us pray.

P̄ Almighty and most merciful God and Father, we thank and praise you that you graciously preserve and enlarge your family and have granted ＿names＿ the new birth in Holy Baptism and made ＿him/her＿ a member of your Son, our Lord Jesus Christ, and an heir of your heavenly kingdom. We humbly beseech you that, as ＿he/she＿ has now become your child, you would keep ＿him/her＿ in ＿his/her＿ baptismal grace that according to all your good pleasure ＿he/she＿ may faithfully grow to lead a godly life to the praise and honor of your holy name and finally with all your saints obtain the promised inheritance in heaven; through Jesus Christ, our Lord.(169)

C̄ **Amen**

18. When infants and young children are baptized, this prayer may be said.

P̄ Lord and giver of life, look with kindness upon the father(s) and mother(s) of ＿this child/these children＿ , and upon all our parents. Let them ever rejoice in the gift you have given them. Enable them to be teachers and examples of righteousness for their children. Strengthen them in their own Baptism so that they may share eternally with their children the salvation you have given them; through Jesus Christ, our Lord.(170)

C̄ **Amen**

19. The baptismal group may turn toward the congregation; a representative of the congregation may say:

Through Baptism God has added ＿＿＿name(s)＿＿＿ to his own people to declare the wonderful deeds of our Savior, who has called us out of darkness into his marvelous light.

C **We welcome you into the Lord's family. We receive you as (a) fellow member(s) of the body of Christ, (a) child(ren) of the same heavenly Father, to work with us in his kingdom.**

P And you, _____name(s)_____ , the Lord bless you in all your ways from this time forth and even forevermore.

C **Amen**

20. All return to their places. The service continues with the Introit, Psalm, or Entrance Hymn.

CONFIRMATION

1. After a hymn of invocation of the Holy Spirit has been sung, the catechumens gather before the altar, and the minister addresses them:

℗ Beloved in the Lord, our Lord Jesus Christ said: "All authority in heaven and on earth has been given to me. Therefore go and make disciples of all nations, baptizing them in the name of the Father and of the Son and of the Holy Spirit and teaching them to obey everything I have commanded you. And surely I will be with you always, to the very end of the age."

You have been baptized and you have been taught the faith according to our Lord's bidding. The fulfillment of his bidding we now celebrate with thankful hearts, rejoicing to confess the faith into which you were baptized and which you yourselves will now confess before the Church.

Jesus said: "Whoever acknowledges me before men, I will also acknowledge him before my Father in heaven. But whoever disowns me before men, I will disown him before my Father in heaven."

Lift up your hearts therefore to the God of all grace and joyfully give answer to what, in the name of the Lord, as a minister of his Church, I now shall ask you.

℗ Do you this day in the presence of God and of this congregation acknowledge the gifts which God gave you in your Baptism?

℟ **I do.**

℗ Do you renounce the devil and all his works and all his ways?

℟ **I do.**

℗ Do you believe in God, the Father Almighty?

℟ **Yes, I believe in God, the Father Almighty,**
maker of heaven and earth.

℗ Do you believe in Jesus Christ, his only Son?

℟ Yes, I believe in Jesus Christ, his only Son, our Lord,
  who was conceived by the Holy Spirit,
  born of the virgin Mary,
  suffered under Pontius Pilate,
  was crucified, died, and was buried.
  He descended into hell.
  The third day he rose again from the dead.
He ascended into heaven
  and sits at the right hand of God
  the Father Almighty.
From thence he will come to judge the living and the dead.

℘ Do you believe in the Holy Spirit?

℟ Yes, I believe in the Holy Spirit,
  the holy Christian Church,
  the communion of saints,
  the forgiveness of sins,
  the resurrection of the body,
  and the life everlasting.

℘ Do you intend to continue steadfast in this confession and Church and to suffer all, even death, rather than fall away from it?

℟ I do so intend with the help of God.

℘ Do you hold all the prophetic and apostolic Scriptures to be the inspired Word of God and confess the doctrine of the Evangelical Lutheran Church, drawn from them, as you have learned to know it from the Small Catechism, to be faithful and true?

℟ I do.

℘ Do you desire to be a member of the Evangelical Lutheran Church and of this congregation?

℟ I do.

℘ Do you intend faithfully to conform all your life to the divine Word, to be faithful in the use of God's Word and Sacraments, which are his means of grace, and in faith, word, and action to remain true to God, Father, Son, and Holy Spirit, even to death?

℟ I do so intend by the grace of God.

℘ Give then your hand as pledge of your promise, and kneel to receive the blessing.

2. The catechumens, in turn, give their right hand and kneel. The minister lays his hands upon the head of each one and gives the following blessing. A confirmation text is then given to each.

℘ _____name_____, God, the Father of our Lord Jesus Christ, give you his Holy

Spirit, the Spirit of wisdom and knowledge, of grace and prayer, of power and strength, of sanctification and the fear of God.

3. After all catechumens have received the blessing and text of Scripture, the minister says:

℗ Upon this your profession and promise I invite and welcome you, as members of the Evangelical Lutheran Church and of this congregation, to share with us in all the gifts our Lord has for his Church and to live them out continually in his worship and service.

4. The minister invites the congregation to pray for the newly confirmed.

℗ Let us pray for the newly confirmed.

℗ Lord God, heavenly Father, we thank and praise you for your great goodness in bringing these your sons and daughters to the knowledge of your Son, our Savior, Jesus Christ, and enabling them both with the heart to believe and with the mouth to confess his saving name. Grant that, bringing forth the fruits of faith, they may continue steadfast and victorious to the day when all who have fought the good fight of faith shall receive the crown of righteousness; through Jesus Christ, your Son, our Lord, who lives and reigns with you and the Holy Spirit, one God, now and forever. (171)

☐ **Amen**

5. The minister dismisses the newly confirmed, saying:

℗ The almighty and most merciful God, Father, ✝ Son, and Holy Spirit, bless and keep you.

☐ **Amen**

MATINS

1. *A hymn of invocation of the Holy Spirit may be sung.*

2. *The Gloria Patri may be chanted to an alternate setting (see Canticles and Chants, No. 3).*

Stand

208

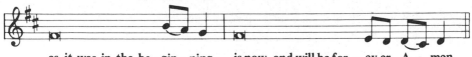

as it was in the be - gin - ning,   is now, and will be for - ev-er. A - men

3. *The following ascription of praise is chanted immediately following the Gloria Patri except during Advent and Lent.*

C   Praise to you, O Christ. Al - le - lu - ia.

ADVENT

C   Praise to you, O Christ, King who comes to save us.

LENT

C   Praise to you, O Christ, Lamb of our sal - va - tion.

4. *The INVITATORY introduces and concludes the VENITE. Proper invitatories for the minister are included in* Lutheran Worship, Altar Book.

COMMON INVITATORY

L   Blessed be God, the Fa - ther, the Son, and the Ho - ly Spir - it.

C   Oh, come,   let   us   wor - ship him.

THE VENITE

C   Oh, come, let us sing to the Lord, let us make a joyful noise to the rock of ▶

our sal - va - tion. Let us come into his presence with thanks - giv - ing,

let us make a joyful noise to him with songs of praise. For the Lord is a

great God and a great king a-bove all gods. The deep places of the earth are

in his hand; the strength of the hills is his al - so.

The sea is his, for he made it, and his hand formed the dry land.

Oh, come, let us worship and bow down, let us kneel before the

Lord our mak - er. For he is our God,

and we are the people of his pasture and the sheep of his hand.

Glory be to the Father and to the Son and to the Ho - ly Spir - it;

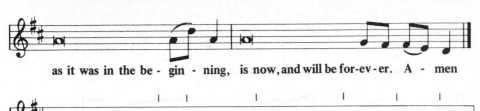

as it was in the be - gin - ning, is now, and will be for-ev-er. A - men

Ⓛ Blessed be God, the Fa - ther, the Son, and the Ho - ly Spir - it.

Ⓒ Oh, come, let us wor - ship him.

5. *The OFFICE HYMN is sung.*

6. *One or more PSALMS are sung or said, each concluding with the Gloria Patri.*

Sit

7. *One or two READINGS follow.*

8. *After the reading or readings the following is chanted or said.*

Ⓛ O Lord, have mer-cy on us.

Ⓒ Thanks be to God.

OR

COMMON RESPONSORY

Ⓛ For-ev-er, O Lord, your Word is firmly set in the heavens.

Ⓒ Lord, I love
the habitation of your house and the place where your glo-ry dwells.

▶

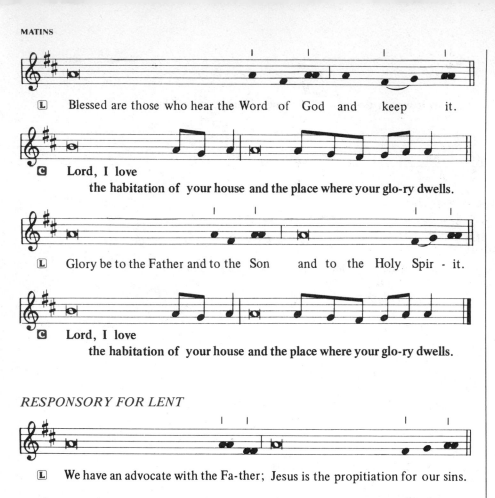

L   Blessed are those who hear the Word of God and keep it.

C   Lord, I love
the habitation of your house and the place where your glo-ry dwells.

L   Glory be to the Father and to the Son and to the Holy Spir - it.

C   Lord, I love
the habitation of your house and the place where your glo-ry dwells.

RESPONSORY FOR LENT

L   We have an advocate with the Fa-ther; Jesus is the propitiation for our sins.

C   He was delivered up to death; he was delivered for the sins of the peo - ple.

L   Blessed is he whose transgression is for - giv - en and whose sin is put a- way.

C   He was delivered up to death; he was delivered for the sins of the peo - ple.

L   We have an advocate with the Fa-ther; Jesus is the propitiation for our sins.

212

✠ HOLY COMMUNION ✠

Confession and Absolution

P In the name of the Father and of the ✠ Son and of the Holy Spirit.

C Amen.

P O almighty God, merciful Father,

C I, a poor, miserable sinner, confess unto You all my sins and iniquities with which I have ever offended You and justly deserved Your temporal and eternal punishment. But I am heartily sorry for them and sincerely repent of them, and I pray You of Your boundless mercy and for the sake of the holy, innocent, bitter sufferings and death of Your beloved Son, Jesus Christ, to be gracious and merciful to me, a poor, sinful being.

P Upon this your confession, I, by virtue of my office, as a called and ordained servant of the Word, announce the grace of God unto all of you, and in the stead and by the command of my Lord Jesus Christ I forgive you all your sins in the name of the Father and of the ✠ Son and of the Holy Spirit.

C Amen.

Nicene Creed

C I believe in one God,
   the Father Almighty,
   maker of heaven and earth
    and of all things visible and invisible.
And in one Lord Jesus Christ,
   the only-begotten Son of God,
   begotten of His Father before all worlds,
   God of God, Light of Light, very God of very God,
   begotten, not made,
   being of one substance with the Father,
   by whom all things were made;
   who for us men and for our salvation came down from

heaven and was incarnate by the Holy Spirit of the virgin
Mary and was made man; and was crucified also for us
under Pontius Pilate. He suffered and was buried.
And the third day He rose again according to the Scriptures
and ascended into heaven and sits at the right hand of the
Father. And He will come again with glory to judge both
the living and the dead, whose kingdom will have no end.
And I believe in the Holy Spirit,
the Lord and giver of life,
who proceeds from the Father and the Son,
who with the Father and the Son together is worshiped and
glorified, who spoke by the prophets.
And I believe in one holy Christian and apostolic Church,
I acknowledge one Baptism for the remission of sins,
and I look for the resurrection of the dead
and the life ✠ of the world to come. Amen.

Lord's Prayer

The Words of Our Lord

Distribution

Prayer
P Let us pray.
We give thanks to You, almighty God, that You have refreshed us
through this salutary gift, and we implore You that of Your mercy
You would strengthen us through the same in faith toward You
and fervent love toward one another; through Jesus Christ, Your
Son, our Lord, who lives and reigns with You and the Holy Spirit,
one God, now and forever.
C **Amen.**

Benediction
P The Lord bless you and keep you.
The Lord make His face shine on you and be gracious to you.
The Lord look upon you with favor and ✠ give you peace.
C **Amen.**

C He was delivered up to death; he was delivered for the sins of the peo - ple.

RESPONSORY FOR EASTER AND ITS SEASON

L Sing to the Lord and bless his name, proclaim his salvation from day to day.

C Give to the Lord all glo-ry and strength, give him the hon-or due his name.

Al - le - lu - ia,   al - le - lu - ia.

L Now is Christ risen from the dead and become the first fruits of them that sleep.

C Give to the Lord all glo- ry and strength, give him the hon-or due his name.

Al - le - lu - ia,   al - le - lu - ia.

L Glory be to the Father and to the Son   and to the Holy Spir - it.

C Give to the Lord all glo-ry and strength, give him the hon-or due his name.

213

Al - le - lu - ia,   al - le - lu - ia.

9. *The SERMON may follow.*

10. *The OFFERING may be received.*

Stand

11. *One of the following CANTICLES is sung. The Te Deum may be sung to an alternate setting (see Canticles and Chants, No. 8).*

TE DEUM

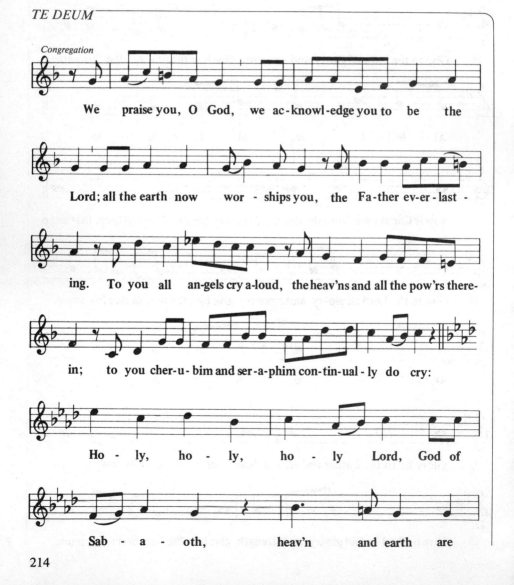

Congregation

We praise you, O God, we ac-knowl-edge you to be the

Lord; all the earth now wor - ships you, the Fa-ther ev-er-last -

ing. To you all an-gels cry a-loud, the heav'ns and all the pow'rs there-

in; to you cher-u-bim and ser-a-phim con-tin-ual-ly do cry:

Ho - ly, ho - ly, ho - ly Lord, God of

Sab - a - oth, heav'n and earth are

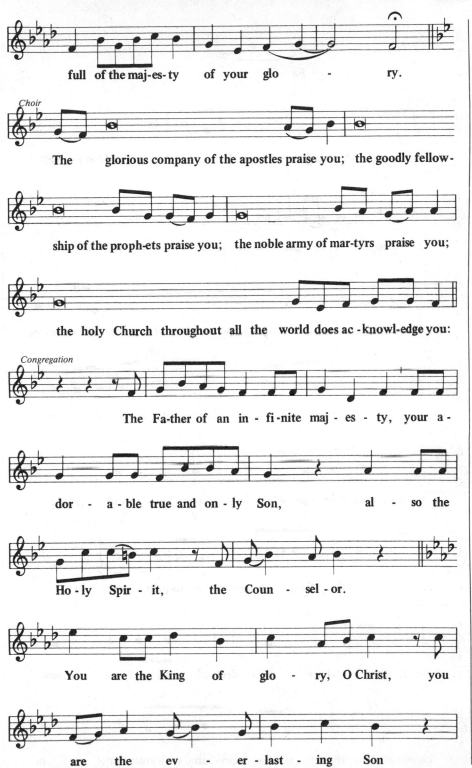

full of the maj-es-ty of your glo - ry.

Choir

The glorious company of the apostles praise you; the goodly fellow-

ship of the proph-ets praise you; the noble army of mar-tyrs praise you;

the holy Church throughout all the world does ac-knowl-edge you:

Congregation

The Fa-ther of an in - fi -nite maj - es - ty, your a -

dor - a - ble true and on - ly Son, al - so the

Ho - ly Spir - it, the Coun - sel - or.

You are the King of glo - ry, O Christ, you

are the ev - er - last - ing Son

of the Fa - ther.

Choir

When you took upon yourself to de-liv-er man, you humbled yourself

to be born of a vir-gin. When you had overcome the

sharp-ness of death, you opened the kingdom of heaven to all be-liev-ers.

You sit at the right hand of God in the glory of the Fa - ther.

We be - lieve that you will come to be our judge.

Congregation

We there - fore pray you to help your ser -

vants, whom you have re - deemed with your pre - cious

blood. Make them to be num- bered with your saints in

glo - ry ev - er - last - ing.

OR

BENEDICTUS

G Bless-ed be the Lord God of Is - ra - el; for he has visited and redeemed his

peo- ple and has raised up a horn of salvation for us in the house of his

ser-vant Da - vid, as he spoke by the mouth of his holy proph - ets,

who have been since the world be-gan: That we should be saved from our

en - e - mies and from the hand of all who hate us; to perform the mercy

promised to our fa - thers and to remember his holy cov - e - nant,

the oath that he swore to our father A -bra -ham, to grant us that we,

being delivered from the hand of our en-e-mies, might serve him with-out fear, ▶

217

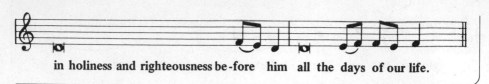

in holiness and righteousness be-fore him all the days of our life.

12. The Gloria Patri follows the Benedictus except during Advent.

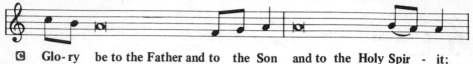

Glo-ry be to the Father and to the Son and to the Holy Spir - it;

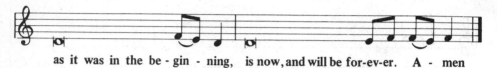

as it was in the be - gin - ning, is now, and will be for-ev-er. A - men

13. During Advent the following verses are added to the Benedictus, concluding with the Gloria Patri.

And you, child, will be called the prophet of the Most High; for you will go before

the Lord to pre-pare his ways; to give knowledge of salvation to his

peo - ple in the for-give-ness of their sins, through the tender mercy

of our God; when the day shall dawn upon us from on high

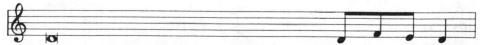

to give light to them who sit in darkness and in the shad - ow of death,

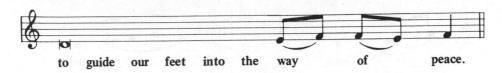

to guide our feet into the way of peace.

14. *The PRAYERS here following are chanted or said, beginning with the Kyrie.*
RESPONSIVE PRAYER 1 (page 270) may be used in place of the following.

Ⓒ Lord, have mer - cy; Christ, have mer - cy; Lord, have mer - cy.

Ⓒ Our Father who art in heaven,
    hallowed be thy name,
    thy kingdom come,
    thy will be done
        on earth as it is in heaven.
Give us this day our daily bread;
and forgive us our trespasses
    as we forgive those
        who trespass against us;
and lead us not into temptation,
    but deliver us from evil.
For thine is the kingdom
    and the power and the glory
    forever and ever. Amen

OR

Ⓒ Our Father in heaven,
    hallowed be your name,
    your kingdom come,
    your will be done
        on earth as in heaven.
Give us today our daily bread.
Forgive us our sins
    as we forgive those
        who sin against us.
Lead us not into temptation,
    but deliver us from evil.
For the kingdom, the power,
    and the glory are yours
    now and forever. Amen

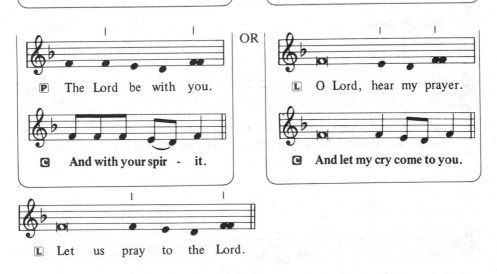

Ⓟ The Lord be with you.

OR

Ⓛ O Lord, hear my prayer.

Ⓒ And with your spir - it.

Ⓒ And let my cry come to you.

Ⓛ Let us pray to the Lord.

15. *The COLLECT OF THE DAY is chanted or said.*

16. *Additional prayers may be chanted or said by the minister with the congregation responding "Amen" to each.*

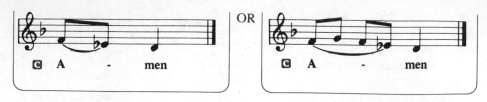

OR

17. *One of the following collects concludes the PRAYERS. The final collect ends with the full termination: "through Jesus Christ, your Son, our Lord, who lives and reigns with you and the Holy Spirit, one God, now and forever."*

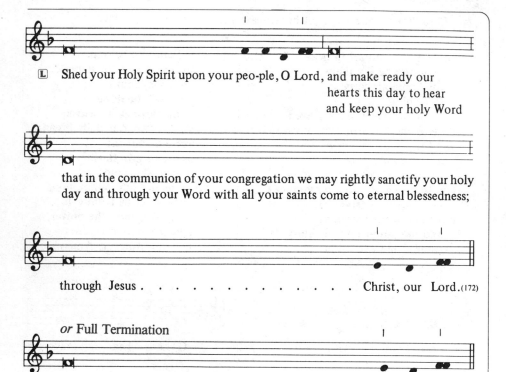

L Shed your Holy Spirit upon your peo-ple, O Lord, and make ready our
hearts this day to hear
and keep your holy Word

that in the communion of your congregation we may rightly sanctify your holy
day and through your Word with all your saints come to eternal blessedness;

through Jesus . . . . Christ, our Lord. (172)

or Full Termination

through Jesus Christ, your Son, our Lord, who lives and
reigns with you and the Holy Spirit, one God, now and for-ev - er.

OR

L Almighty God, heavenly Fa-ther, whose mercies are new to us every
morning and who, though we in no wise
deserve your goodness, abundantly
provides for all our wants of body and soul,

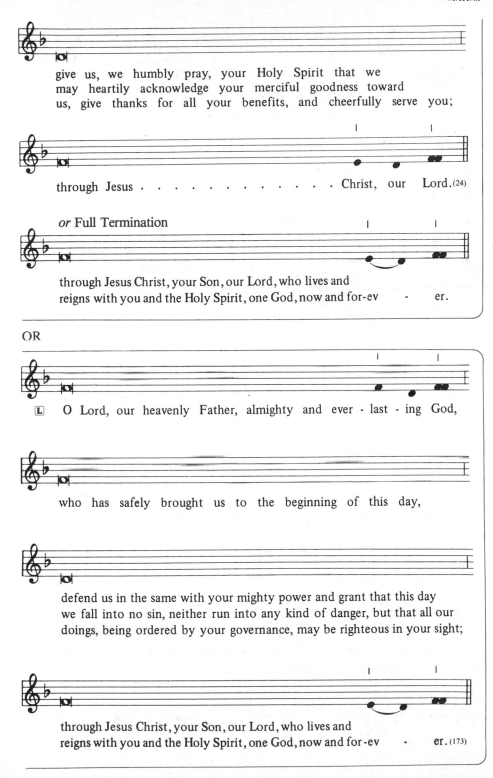

give us, we humbly pray, your Holy Spirit that we
may heartily acknowledge your merciful goodness toward
us, give thanks for all your benefits, and cheerfully serve you;

through Jesus . . . . Christ, our Lord. (24)

or Full Termination

through Jesus Christ, your Son, our Lord, who lives and
reigns with you and the Holy Spirit, one God, now and for-ev - er.

OR

Ⓛ O Lord, our heavenly Father, almighty and ever - last - ing God,

who has safely brought us to the beginning of this day,

defend us in the same with your mighty power and grant that this day
we fall into no sin, neither run into any kind of danger, but that all our
doings, being ordered by your governance, may be righteous in your sight;

through Jesus Christ, your Son, our Lord, who lives and
reigns with you and the Holy Spirit, one God, now and for-ev - er. (173)

221

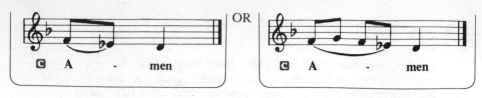

OR

18. *The BENEDICAMUS and BLESSING conclude the service.*

L Let us bless the Lord.

C Thanks be to God.

P The grace of our Lord Je - sus Christ and the love of God

and the communion of the Holy Spir - it ✠ be with you all.

OR

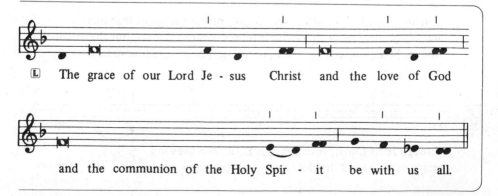

L The grace of our Lord Je - sus Christ and the love of God

and the communion of the Holy Spir - it be with us all.

C A - men

Silent Prayer

VESPERS

1. *A hymn of invocation of the Holy Spirit may be sung.*

2. *The Gloria Patri may be chanted to an alternate setting (see Canticles and Chants, No. 3).*

Stand

🅛 O Lord, o-pen my lips,

🅒 and my mouth will de - clare your praise.

🅛 Make haste, O God, to de - liv - er me;

🅒 make haste to help me, O Lord.

🅒 Glo-ry be to the Father and to the Son and to the Holy Spir - it;

as it was in the be - gin - ning,   is now, and will be for - ev - er. A - men

3. The following ascription of praise is chanted immediately following the Gloria Patri except during Advent and Lent.

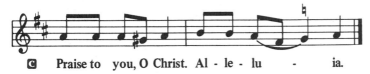

C   Praise to   you, O Christ. Al - le - lu   -   ia.

ADVENT

C   Praise to   you, O Christ, King who comes to save   us.

LENT

C   Praise to you,   O Christ, Lamb of   our sal - va - tion.

4. One or more PSALMS are sung or said, each concluding with the Gloria Patri.

Sit

5. One or two READINGS follow.

6. After the reading or readings the following is chanted or said.

L   O Lord, have mer-cy on   us.

C   Thanks   be   to   God.

OR

225

COMMON RESPONSORY

L Teach me your way, O Lord, that I may walk in your truth.

C Your Word is a lamp to my feet and a light to my path.

L Unite my heart to fear your name that I may walk in your truth.

C Your Word is a lamp to my feet and a light to my path.

L Glory be to the Father and to the Son and to the Holy Spir - it.

C Your Word is a lamp to my feet and a light to my path.

RESPONSORY FOR LENT

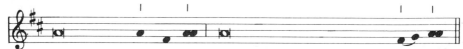

L Deliver me, O Lord, my God, for you are the God of my sal - va - tion.

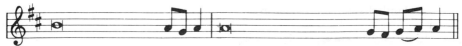

C Rescue me from my en-e-mies, protect me from those who rise a-gainst me.

L In you, O Lord, do I put my trust, leave me not, O Lord, my God.

226

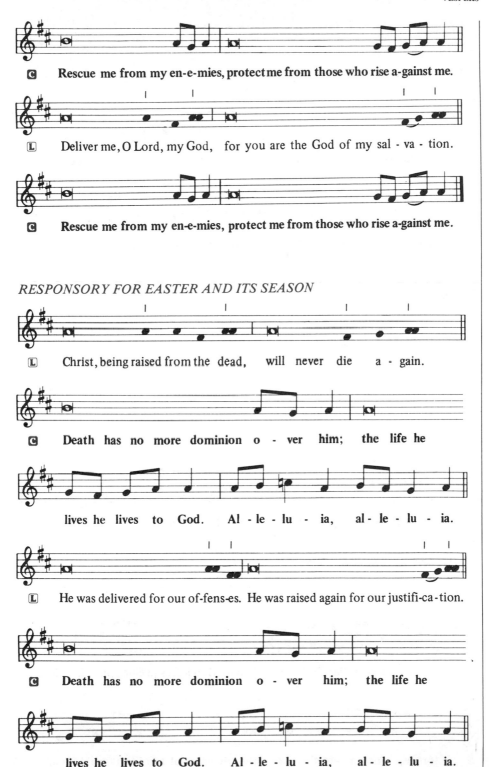

C Rescue me from my en-e-mies, protect me from those who rise a-gainst me.

L Deliver me, O Lord, my God, for you are the God of my sal - va - tion.

C Rescue me from my en-e-mies, protect me from those who rise a-gainst me.

RESPONSORY FOR EASTER AND ITS SEASON

L Christ, being raised from the dead, will never die a - gain.

C Death has no more dominion o - ver him; the life he

lives he lives to God. Al - le - lu - ia, al - le - lu - ia.

L He was delivered for our of-fens-es. He was raised again for our justifi-ca-tion.

C Death has no more dominion o - ver him; the life he

lives he lives to God. Al - le - lu - ia, al - le - lu - ia.

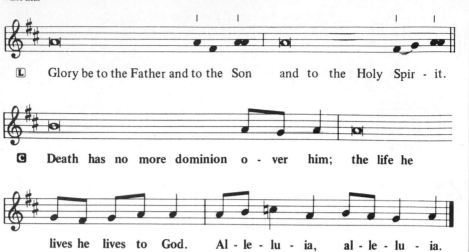

L Glory be to the Father and to the Son and to the Holy Spir - it.

C Death has no more dominion o - ver him; the life he

lives he lives to God. Al - le - lu - ia, al - le - lu - ia.

7. *The OFFICE HYMN is sung.*

8. *The SERMON may follow.*

9. *The OFFERING may be received.*

Stand

L Let my prayers rise before you as in - cense,

C and the lifting up of my hands as the eve - ning sac - ri - fice.

10. *One of the following CANTICLES is chanted.*

MAGNIFICAT

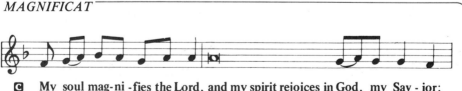

C My soul mag - ni - fies the Lord, and my spirit rejoices in God, my Sav - ior;

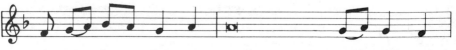

for he has re - gard - ed the lowliness of his hand - maid - en.

For be - hold, from this day   all generations will call   me bless - ed.

For he   who is mighty has done great things to me,   and holy is   his   name;

and his   mercy is on those who fear   him   throughout all gen - er - a - tions.

He has   shown   the   strength of   his   arm   and scattered the proud

in their own   con - ceit.   He   has   put down the

might-y   from   their seats   and exalted the hum - ble and   meek.

He   has   filled   the   hun - gry with good   things,

and   the   rich he   has   sent emp - ty   a - way.

He   has   remembered his mercy and sustained his ser-vant   Is - ra - el

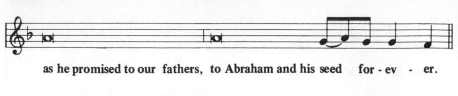

as he promised to our fathers, to Abraham and his seed for - ev - er.

Glo-ry be to the Fa-ther and to the Son and to the Ho - ly Spir - it;

as it was in the be-gin - ning, is now, and will be for-ev - er. A - men

OR

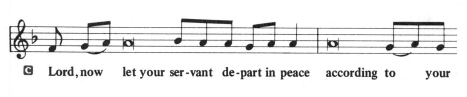

Lord, now let your ser-vant de-part in peace according to your

word. For my eyes have seen your sal - va - tion,

which you have prepared before the face of all peo - ple,

a light to light-en the Gen-tiles and the glory of your people Is- ra-el.

Glo-ry be to the Fa-ther and to the Son and to the Ho - ly Spir-it;

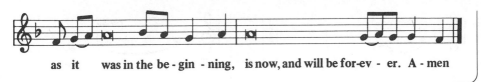

as it was in the be - gin - ning, is now, and will be for-ev - er. A - men

11. The PRAYERS here following are chanted or said, beginning with the Kyrie. RESPONSIVE PRAYER 2 (page 273) may be used in place of the following.

C Lord, have mer - cy; Christ, have mer - cy; Lord, have mer - cy.

C Our Father who art in heaven,
 hallowed be thy name,
 thy kingdom come,
 thy will be done
 on earth as it is in heaven.
Give us this day our daily bread;
and forgive us our trespasses
 as we forgive those
 who trespass against us;
and lead us not into temptation,
 but deliver us from evil.
For thine is the kingdom
 and the power and the glory
 forever and ever. Amen

OR

C Our Father in heaven,
 hallowed be your name,
 your kingdom come,
 your will be done
 on earth as in heaven.
Give us today our daily bread.
Forgive us our sins
 as we forgive those
 who sin against us.
Lead us not into temptation,
 but deliver us from evil.
For the kingdom, the power,
 and the glory are yours
 now and forever. Amen

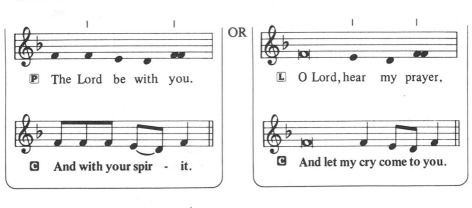

P The Lord be with you.

OR

L O Lord, hear my prayer,

C And with your spir - it.

C And let my cry come to you.

L Let us pray to the Lord.

12. The COLLECT OF THE DAY is chanted or said.

231

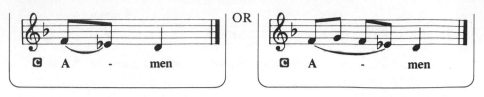

13. Additional prayers may be chanted or said by the minister with the congregation responding "Amen" to each.

14. One or more of the following collects concludes the PRAYERS. The final collect ends with the full termination: "through Jesus Christ, your Son, our Lord, who lives and reigns with you and the Holy Spirit, one God, now and forever."

AT VESPERS

L Di-rect us, O Lord, in all our doings with your most gracious favor, and further us with your continual help

that in all our works begun, continued, and ended in you we may glorify your holy name and finally by your mercy obtain eternal salvation;

through Jesus . . . . Christ, our Lord. (8)

or Full Termination

through Jesus Christ, your Son, our Lord, who lives and reigns with you and the Holy Spirit, one God, now and for-ev - er.

OR

IN LATE AFTERNOON

L O Lord, our dwelling place and our peace, who has pity on our weakness,

232

put far from us all worry and fearfulness that, having confessed
our sins and commending ourselves to your gracious mercy, we
may, when night shall come, commit ourselves, our work, and all
we love into your keeping, receiving from you the gift of quiet sleep;

through Jesus . . . . Christ,   our   Lord.(174)

or Full Termination

through Jesus Christ, your Son, our Lord, who lives and
reigns with you and the Holy Spirit, one God, now and for- ev   -   er.

OR

IN THE EVENING

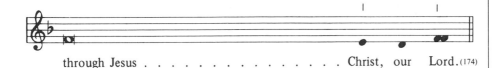

Ⓛ   O   Lord God,   the life of all the living, the light of the faithful, the
                       strength of those who labor, the repose of the blessed dead,

grant us a peaceful night free from all disturbance that after a time of
quiet slumber we may by your goodness be endued in the new day with
the guidance of your Holy Spirit and enabled in peace to render thanks to you;

through Jesus . . . . Christ,   our   Lord.(175)

or Full Termination

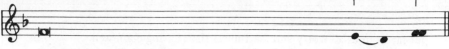

through Jesus Christ, your Son, our Lord, who lives and
reigns with you and the Holy Spirit, one God, now and for - ev - er.

OR

FOR PEACE

Ⓛ O God, from whom come all holy desires, all good counsels, and all just works,

give to us, your servants, that peace which the world cannot give, that
our hearts may be set to obey your commandments and also that we, being defended from the fear of our enemies, may live in peace and quietness;

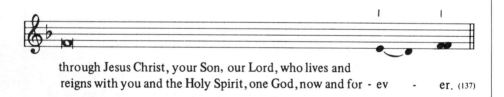

through Jesus Christ, your Son, our Lord, who lives and
reigns with you and the Holy Spirit, one God, now and for - ev - er. (137)

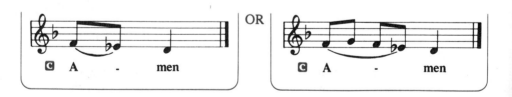

Ⓒ A - men   OR   Ⓒ A - men

15. The BENEDICAMUS and BLESSING conclude the service.

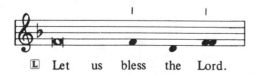

Ⓛ Let us bless the Lord.

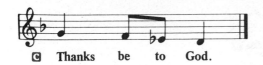

C   Thanks   be   to   God.

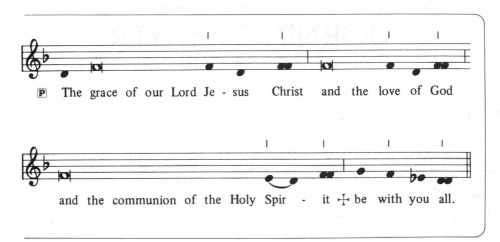

P   The grace of our Lord Je - sus   Christ   and   the   love   of   God

and   the   communion   of   the   Holy   Spir - it ✠ be   with   you   all.

OR

L   The grace of our Lord Je - sus Christ   and   the   love   of   God

and   the   communion   of   the   Holy   Spir - it   be   with   us   all.

C   A - men

Silent Prayer

235

MORNING PRAYER

A simplified form of Morning Prayer, suitable for family or small-group devotion, is indicated by the small circle.

Stand

○ Ⓛ O Lord, o-pen my lips,

○ Ⓒ and my mouth shall de - clare your praise.

○ Ⓒ Glo-ry be to the Fa - ther and to the Son and to the Ho-ly Spir - it;

as it was in the be-gin - ning, is now, and will be for- ev - er. A - men

The alleluia is omitted during Lent.

○ Ⓒ Al - le - lu - ia, al - le - lu - ia.

236

1. The PSALMODY begins with the Venite ("Oh, come, let us sing . . ."), introduced and concluded with the Invitatory. Another appropriate canticle may be used in place of the Venite.

L Give glory to God, our light and our life.

C Oh, come, let us wor - ship him.

C Oh, come, let us sing to the Lord;

let us make a joy - ful noise to the rock of our sal - va - tion.

I Let us come in - to his pres - ence with thanks-giv - ing;

let us make a joy - ful noise to him with songs of praise.

II For the Lord is a great God and a great king a - bove all gods.

I In his hand are the depths of the earth;

the heights of the moun-tains are his al - so.

II The sea is his, for he made it;

and his hand formed the dry land.

I Oh, come, let us wor-ship and bow down;

let us kneel be-fore the Lord, our mak - er.

II For he is our God, and we are the peo-ple of his

pas - ture and the sheep of his hand.

C Glo-ry be to the Fa-ther and to the Son and to the Ho-ly Spir-it;

as it was in the be-gin-ning, is now, and will be for-ev-er. A-men

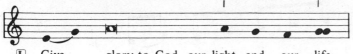

L Give glory to God, our light and our life.

C Oh, come, let us wor - ship him.

Sit

° 2. *Additional psalms may be sung or said, each concluding with the Gloria Patri. Silence for meditation may follow.*

Stand

3. *The HYMN is sung.*

Sit

° 4. *One or two READINGS follow. Silence for meditation may follow each reading.*

5. *The leader then continues:*

L In many and various ways God spoke to his people of old by the prophets.

C But now in these last days he has spoken to us by his Son.

Stand

° 6. *The GOSPEL CANTICLE is sung. If the Paschal Blessing is not used at the end of the service, the canticle "You are God, we praise you," page 246, or "We praise you, O God," page 214, may replace this canticle. An antiphon may be sung before (and after) the canticle.*

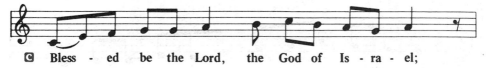

C Bless - ed be the Lord, the God of Is - ra - el;

he has come to his peo - ple and re - deemed them.

He has raised up for us a might - y Sav - ior, ▶

born of the house of his ser-vant Da - vid.

Through his ho - ly proph - ets he prom - ised of old

that he would save us from our en - e -mies, from the hands of all who

hate us. He prom-ised to show mer - cy to our fa -

thers and to re - mem- ber his ho - ly cov - e - nant.

This was the oath he swore to our fa - ther A - bra - ham:

to set us free from the hands of our en - e - mies,

free to wor - ship him with - out fear, ho - ly and

righ-teous in his sight all the days of our life.

L You, my child, shall be called the proph - et of the Most High,

for you will go be - fore the Lord to pre - pare his way,

to give his peo - ple knowl-edge of sal - va - tion by the for - give-ness

of their sins. In the ten - der com - pas - sion of our God,

the dawn from on high shall break up - on us

to shine on those who dwell in dark-ness and the shad - ow of death

and to guide our feet in - to the way of peace.

C Glo - ry be to the Fa - ther and to the Son and to the

Ho - ly Spir - it; as it was in the be - gin - ning,

241

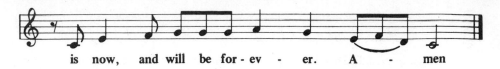

is now, and will be for-ev - er. A - men

7. The COLLECT OF THE DAY is chanted or said.

[C] A - men

8. Other prayers may be used by the leader with the congregation responding "Amen" to each, or members of the congregation may be invited to offer petitions and thanksgivings. Instead, the Litany, page 279, or Responsive Prayer 1, page 270, may be used. In concluding the prayers the leader chants or says:

○ [L] O Lord, almighty and everlasting God, you have brought us in safety to this new day; preserve us with your mighty power that we may not fall into sin nor be overcome in adversity; and in all we do, direct us to the fulfilling of your purpose; through Jesus Christ, our Lord. (173)

○ [C] A - men

○ [L] Lord, remember us in your kingdom, and teach us to pray:

○ [C] **Our Father who art in heaven,**
hallowed be thy name,
thy kingdom come,
thy will be done
on earth as it is in heaven.
Give us this day our daily bread;
and forgive us our trespasses
as we forgive those
who trespass against us;
and lead us not into temptation,
but deliver us from evil.
For thine is the kingdom
and the power and the glory
forever and ever. Amen

OR

[C] **Our Father in heaven,**
hallowed be your name,
your kingdom come,
your will be done
on earth as in heaven.
Give us today our daily bread.
Forgive us our sins
as we forgive those
who sin against us.
Lead us not into temptation,
but deliver us from evil.
For the kingdom, the power,
and the glory are yours
now and forever. Amen

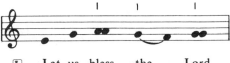

[L] Let us bless the Lord.

C   Thanks   be to God.

9. The BLESSING concludes the service when there is no sermon. A hymn may follow. On Sundays the service may be concluded with the Paschal Blessing, page 244. ▶

10. When there is a sermon, this blessing is omitted. The order of service continues below (11).

L   The Lord Al- mighty bless us and direct our days and our deeds in his peace.

C   A   -   men

Sit

11. An OFFERING may be received during which a hymn, psalm, or anthem may be sung.

12. A HYMN is sung.

13. The SERMON. After the sermon one of these prayers is chanted or said.

Stand

P Almighty God, grant to your Church your Holy Spirit and the wisdom which comes down from heaven that your Word may not be bound but have free course and be preached to the joy and edifying of Christ's holy people, that in steadfast faith we may serve you and in the confession of your name may abide to the end; through Jesus Christ, our Lord.(166)

OR

P Lord God, you have called your servants to ventures of which we cannot see the ending, by paths as yet untrodden, through perils unknown. Give us faith to go out with good courage, not knowing where we go but only that your hand is leading us and your love supporting us; through Jesus Christ, our Lord.(176)

OR

P Lord, we thank you that you have taught us what you would have us believe and do. Help us by your Holy Spirit, for the sake of Jesus Christ, to keep your Word in pure hearts that thereby we may be strengthened in faith, perfected in holiness, and comforted in life and in death.(177)

C Amen

14. The minister blesses the congregation. The Blessing is omitted here if the Paschal Blessing is to be used.

Ⓟ   The   al - mighty and merciful Lord, the Father,
          the ✠ Son, and the Holy Spirit, bless and pre - serve   you.

Ⓒ   A -   men

PASCHAL BLESSING

15. ►*The Paschal Blessing may be used on Sundays to conclude Morning Prayer. The service may be led from the font.*

Stand

Ⓛ   All   of   you who were baptized into Christ have been clothed with Christ.

Ⓒ   Al -   le - lu - ia.

Ⓛ   On the first day of the week, very early in the morn - ing,

the women took the spices they had prepared and went to the tomb.

They found the stone rolled a-way from the tomb, but when they

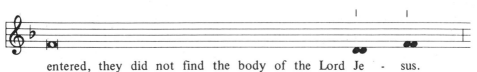

entered, they did not find the body of the Lord Je - sus.

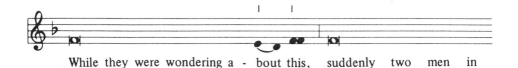

While they were wondering a - bout this,   suddenly   two   men   in

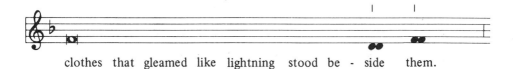

clothes that gleamed like lightning stood be - side   them.

In their fright the women bowed down with their fa - ces to the ground,

but   the   men said to them,   "Why do you look for the living a-mong

the   dead? Remember how he told you, while he was still with you in

Gal -   i - lee: 'The Son of Man must be delivered into the hands of

sin - ful men,   be crucified, and on the third day be raised a - gain.'"

16. The TE DEUM is sung.

mar-tyrs praise you. II Through-out the world the

ho - ly Church ac - claims you: C Fa - ther, of

maj - es - ty un - bound - ed; your true and on - ly Son,

wor - thy of all wor - ship; and the Ho - ly Spir - it,

ad - vo - cate and guide. II You, Christ, are the king of glo - ry,

the e - ter - nal Son of the Fa - ther.

II When you be - came man to set us free,

you did not spurn the vir - gin's womb.

I You o - ver - came the sting of death and
o - pened the king - dom of heav - en to all be - liev - ers.

II You are seat - ed at God's right hand in glo - ry.

We be - lieve that you will come and be our judge. C Come, then,

Lord, and help your peo - ple, bought with the price of your own blood,

and bring us with your saints to glo - ry ev - er - last - ing.

L O God, for our redemption you gave your only Son to suffer

death on the cross, and by his glorious resurrection you delivered us

from the power of death.   Make us die every day to sin so that we may rise to

live with Christ for-ev - er;   who lives and reigns with you

and   the   Holy   Spirit,   one   God,   now   and   for   -   ev   -   er. (178)

C   A   -   men

L   The Lord al - mighty bless us and direct our days and our deeds in his peace.

C   A   -   men

249

EVENING PRAYER

A simplified form of Evening Prayer, suitable for family or small group devotion, is indicated by the small circle.

1. The SERVICE OF LIGHT may be used to begin Evening Prayer. The service may be begun with a procession in which a large, lighted candle is carried to its stand in front of the congregation.

Stand

o [L] Jesus Christ is the Light of the world,

o [C] the light no darkness can o - ver - come.

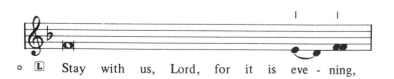

o [L] Stay with us, Lord, for it is eve - ning,

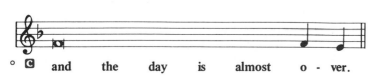

o [C] and the day is almost o - ver.

250

L Let your light scatter the dark - ness

C and il - lu - mine your Church.

2. As the hymn is sung, the candles on and near the altar are lighted. When the large candle is used, the candles are lighted from its flame.

L Joy-ous light of glo - ry:

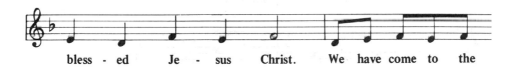

C of the im - mor - tal Fa - ther; heav - en - ly, ho - ly,

bless - ed Je - sus Christ. We have come to the

set - ting of the sun, and we look to the eve - ning light.

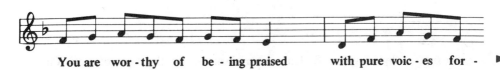

We sing to God, the Fa - ther, Son, and Ho - ly Spir - it:

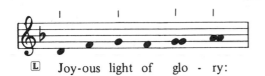

You are wor - thy of be - ing praised with pure voic - es for -

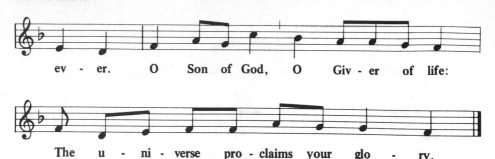

ev - er.   O   Son of God,   O   Giv - er   of life:

The   u - ni - verse pro - claims your   glo - ry.

3. *The thanksgiving concludes the Service of Light.*

L   The Lord be   with you.

C   And al - so   with you.

L   Let   us   give thanks to   the Lord our God.

C   It   is   right   to   give him thanks and praise.

L   Blessed are you, O Lord our God, king of the u - ni - verse,

who led your people Israel by a pillar of   cloud   by day   and a pillar of

fire   by night.   Enlighten our darkness by the light of your Christ;

may his Word be a lamp to our feet and a light to our path;

for you are mer - ci - ful, and you love your whole cre - a - tion

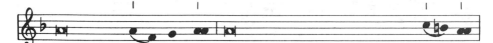

and we, your creatures, glo - ri - fy you, Father, Son, and Ho - ly Spir - it. (179)

C A - men

Kneel/Sit

° *4. The PSALMODY begins with this song for forgiveness and protection.*

C Let my prayer rise be - fore you as in - cense; the

lift - ing up of my hands as the eve - ning sac - ri - fice.

I O Lord, I call to you; come to me quick - ly; hear my voice

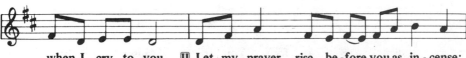

when I cry to you. II Let my prayer rise be - fore you as in - cense; ▶

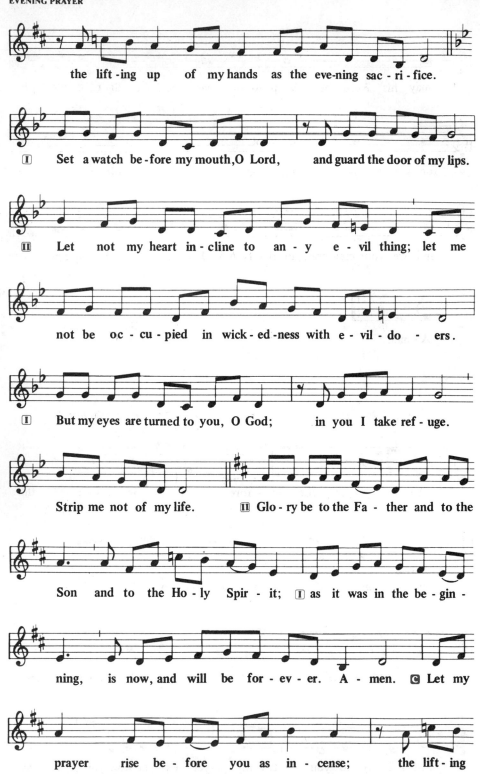

the lift -ing up   of my hands   as the eve-ning sac - ri - fice.

Ⅰ Set a watch be -fore my mouth, O Lord,   and guard the door of my lips.

Ⅱ Let   not my heart in - cline to an - y e - vil thing; let me

not be oc - cu - pied in wick - ed -ness with e - vil - do - ers.

Ⅰ But my eyes are turned to you, O God;   in you I take ref - uge.

Strip me not of my life.   Ⅱ Glo - ry be to the Fa - ther and to the

Son   and to the Ho - ly   Spir - it; Ⅰ as it was in the be - gin -

ning,   is now, and will be for - ev - er. A - men. C Let my

prayer   rise be - fore   you   as   in - cense;   the lift - ing

up of my hands as the eve - ning sac - ri - fice.

Silence for meditation.

○ Ⓛ Let the incense of our repentant prayer ascend before you, O Lord, and let your loving-kindness descend on us that with purified minds we may sing your praises with the Church on earth and the whole heavenly host and may glorify you forever and ever. (180)

Ⓒ **Amen**

Sit

5. Additional psalms may be sung or said, each concluding with the Gloria Patri. Silence for meditation may follow.

Stand

6. The HYMN is sung.

Sit

○ *7. One or two READINGS follow. Silence for meditation may follow each reading.*

8. The leader then continues:

Ⓛ In many and various ways God spoke to his people of old by the prophets.

Ⓒ **But now in these last days he has spoken to us by his Son.**

Stand

○ *9. The GOSPEL CANTICLE is sung. An antiphon may be sung before (and after) the canticle.*

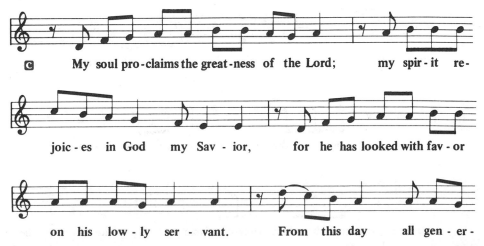

Ⓒ My soul pro-claims the great-ness of the Lord; my spir-it re-

joic-es in God my Sav-ior, for he has looked with fav-or

on his low-ly ser-vant. From this day all gen-er- ▶

a - tions will call me bless - ed. The Al - might - y has

done great things for me, and ho - ly is his name. He has

mer-cy on those who fear him in ev - 'ry gen- er - a - tion.

He has shown the strength of his arm; he has scat - tered the

proud in their con - ceit. He has cast down the might-y from their

thrones and has lift - ed up the low - ly. He has filled the

hun-gry with good things, and the rich he has sent a - way emp - ty.

He has come to the help of his ser - vant Is - ra - el,

for he has re-mem-bered his prom-ise of mer-cy, the prom-ise he

made to our fa-thers, to A-bra-ham and his chil-dren for-ev-er.

Glo-ry be to the Fa-ther and to the Son and to the Ho-ly Spir-it; as it

was in the be-gin-ning, is now, and will be for-ev-er. A - men

Kneel/Stand

10. The following LITANY is chanted or said. The classic Litany, page 279, may be used as an alternate.

Ⓛ   In peace let us pray to the Lord.

Ⓒ   Lord,   have mer - cy.

Ⓛ   For the peace from above and for our salvation let us pray to the Lord.

Ⓒ   Lord,   have mer - cy.

Ⓛ   For the peace of the whole world, for the well-being
of the Church of God, and for the unity of all let us pray to the Lord. ▶

257

C Lord, have mer - cy.

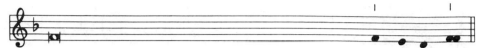

L For this holy house and for all who
   offer here their worship and praise let us . . . . pray to the Lord.

C Lord, have mer - cy.

L For _____names_____ , for our *pastor/pastors* in Christ,
   for all servants of the Church, and for all the people, let us pray to the Lord.

C Lord, have mer - cy.

L For our public servants, for the government
   and those who protect us, that they may be
   upheld and strengthened in every good deed, let us   pray to the Lord.

C Lord, have mer - cy.

L For those who work to bring peace, justice,
   health, and protection in this and every place let us   pray to the Lord.

C   Lord,   have mer - cy.

L   For those who bring offerings, those who do good
works in this congregation, those who toil, those
who sing, and all the people here present who
await from the Lord great and abundant mercy let us   pray to the Lord.

C   Lord,   have mer - cy.

L   For favorable weather, for an abundance of the
fruits of the earth, and for peaceful times let us . . . . pray to the Lord.

C   Lord,   have mer - cy.

L   For our deliverance from all
affliction, wrath, danger, and need let us . . . . pray to the Lord.

C   Lord,   have mer - cy.

L   For the faithful who have gone
before us and are with you let us give . . . . thanks to the Lord.

C Al - le - lu - ia.

L Help, save, comfort, and defend us, ... gra - cious Lord.

Silence for meditation.

L Rejoicing in the fellowship of all the saints, let us
commend ourselves, one another, and our whole life to Christ, our Lord.

C To you, O Lord.

L O God, from whom come all holy desires, all good counsels, and all just works, give to us, your servants, that peace which the world cannot give, that our hearts may be set to obey your commandments; and also that we, being defended from the fear of our enemies, may live in peace and quietness; through the merits of Jesus Christ, our Savior, who lives and reigns with you and the Holy Spirit, God forever.(137)

C A - men

L Lord, remember us in your kingdom, and teach us to pray:

C Our Father who art in heaven,	OR	**C** Our Father in heaven,
hallowed be thy name,		hallowed be your name,
thy kingdom come,		your kingdom come,
thy will be done		your will be done
on earth as it is in heaven.		on earth as in heaven.
Give us this day our daily bread;		Give us today our daily bread.
and forgive us our trespasses		Forgive us our sins
as we forgive those		as we forgive those

| who trespass against us;
and lead us not into temptation,
but deliver us from evil.
For thine is the kingdom
and the power and the glory
forever and ever. Amen | who sin against us.
Lead us not into temptation,
but deliver us from evil.
For the kingdom, the power,
and the glory are yours
now and forever. Amen |

Stand

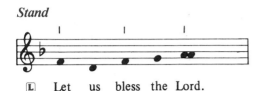

Ⓛ Let us bless the Lord.

Ⓒ Thanks be to God.

11. The BLESSING concludes the service when there is no sermon. A hymn may follow the blessing.

12. When there is a sermon, this blessing is omitted. The order of service continues below (13).

o Ⓛ The almighty and merciful Lord,
the Father, the Son, and the Holy Spirit, bless and pre - serve us.

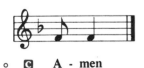

o Ⓒ A - men

Sit

13. An OFFERING may be received during which a hymn, psalm, or anthem may be sung.

14. A HYMN is sung.

15. The SERMON. After the sermon one of these prayers is chanted or said.

Stand

P Almighty God, grant to your Church your Holy Spirit and the wisdom which comes down from heaven that your Word may not be bound but have free course and be preached to the joy and edifying of Christ's holy people, that in steadfast faith we may serve you and in the confession of your name may abide to the end; through Jesus Christ, our Lord. (166)

OR

P Lord God, you have called your servants to ventures of which we cannot see the ending, by paths as yet untrodden, through perils unknown. Give us faith to go out with good courage, not knowing where we go but only that your hand is leading us and your love supporting us; through Jesus Christ, our Lord. (176)

OR

P Lord, we thank you that you have taught us what you would have us believe and do. Help us by your Holy Spirit, for the sake of Jesus Christ, to keep your Word in pure hearts that thereby we may be strengthened in faith, perfected in holiness, and comforted in life and in death. (177)

C **Amen**

16. The minister blesses the congregation.

P The almighty and merciful Lord,
the Father, the ✝Son, and the Holy Spirit, bless and pre - serve you.

C **A - men**

PRAYER AT THE
CLOSE OF THE DAY

Compline

1. The congregation assembles in silence.

Stand

L The Lord almighty grant us a qui - et night and peace at the last.

C A - men

L It is good to give thanks to the Lord,

C to sing praise to your name, O Most High;

L to herald your love in the morn - ing,

G your truth at the close of the day.

2. A HYMN appropriate for a night service is sung.

Kneel/Sit

3. The CONFESSION follows.

Ⓛ Let us confess our sin in the presence of God and of one another.

Silence for self-examination.

Ⓛ Holy and gracious God,

G I confess that I have sinned against you this day. Some of my sin I know—the thoughts and words and deeds of which I am ashamed—but some is known only to you. In the name of Jesus Christ I ask forgiveness. Deliver and restore me that I may rest in peace.

Ⓛ By the mercy of God we are redeemed by Jesus Christ, and in him we are forgiven. We rest now in his peace and rise in the morning to serve him.

OR

Ⓛ I confess to God Almighty, before the whole company of heaven and to you, my brothers and sisters, that I have sinned in thought, word, and deed by my fault, by my own fault, by my own most grievous fault; wherefore I pray God Almighty to have mercy on me, forgive me all my sins, and bring me to everlasting life.
Amen

G The almighty and merciful Lord grant you pardon, forgiveness, and remission of all your sins. Amen

G I confess to God Almighty, before the whole company of heaven and to you, my brothers and sisters, that I have sinned in thought, word, and deed by my fault, by my own fault, by my own most grievous fault; wherefore I pray God Almighty to have mercy on me, forgive me all my sins, and bring me to everlasting life. Amen

Ⓛ The almighty and merciful Lord grant you pardon, forgiveness, and remission of all your sins.

G Amen

Sit

4. The PSALMODY. One or more psalms (4, 34, 91, 134, 136) are sung or said, each concluding with the Gloria Patri. Silence for meditation may follow each psalm.

5. As a BRIEF READING one or more of the following are used.

You are among us, O Lord, and we bear your name; do not forsake us! (Jer. 14:9)

Come to me, all you who are weary and burdened, and I will give you rest. Take my yoke upon you and learn from me, for I am gentle and humble in heart, and you will find rest for your souls. For my yoke is easy and my burden is light. (Matt. 11:28-30)

Peace I leave with you; my peace I give you. I do not give to you as the world gives. Do not let your hearts be troubled, and do not be afraid. (John 14:27)

I am convinced that neither death nor life, neither angels nor demons, neither the present nor the future, nor any powers, neither height nor depth, nor anything else in all creation will be able to separate us from the love of God that is in Christ Jesus our Lord. (Rom. 8:38-39)

Humble yourselves, therefore, under God's mighty hand that he may lift you up in due time. Cast all your anxiety on him because he cares for you. Be self-controlled and alert. Your enemy the devil prowls around like a roaring lion looking for someone to devour. Resist him, standing firm in the faith. (1 Peter 5:6-9a)

6. The RESPONSORY follows the reading(s).

L In-to your hands, O Lord, I com-mend my spir - it.

C In-to your hands I com - mend my spir - it.

L You have re - deemed me, O Lord, God of truth.

C In-to your hands I com - mend my spir - it.

L Glory be to the Fa - ther and to the Son and to the Ho - ly Spir - it.

C In-to your hands I com - mend my spir - it.

Stand

7. The HYMN is sung.

Kneel/Sit

L Hear my prayer, O Lord;

C listen   to my cry.

L Keep me as the apple of your eye;

C hide me in the shadow of your wings.

L In righteousness I shall see you;

C when I awake, your presence will give me joy.

8. One or more of the following PRAYERS are chanted or said.

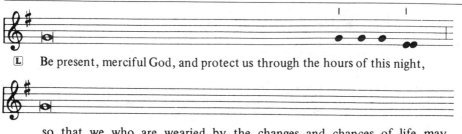

L Be present, merciful God, and protect us through the hours of this night,

so that we who are wearied by the changes and chances of life may

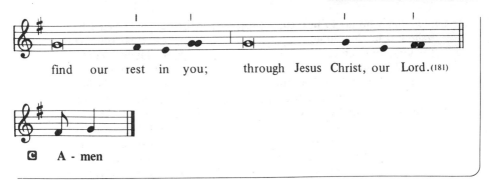

find our rest in you; through Jesus Christ, our Lord. (181)

C A - men

OR

L O Lord, support us all the day long of this troubled life, until the shadows lengthen and the evening comes and the busy world is hushed, the fever of life is over, and our work is done. Then, Lord, in your mercy grant us a safe lodging and a holy rest and peace at the last; through Jesus Christ, our Lord. (182)

OR

L Be our light in the darkness, O Lord, and in your great mercy defend us from all perils and dangers of this night; for the love of your only Son, our Savior Jesus Christ. (183)

OR

L Visit our dwellings, O Lord, and drive from them all the snares of the enemy; let your holy angels dwell with us to preserve us in peace; and let your blessing be on us always; through Jesus Christ, our Lord. (184)

OR

L Eternal God, the hours both of day and night are yours, and to you the darkness is no threat. Be present, we pray, with those who labor in these hours of night, especially those who watch and work on behalf of others. Grant them diligence in their watching, faithfulness in their service, courage in danger, and competence in emergencies. Help them to meet the needs of others with confidence and compassion; through Jesus Christ, our Lord. (185)

OR

L Gracious Lord, we give you thanks for the day, especially for the good we were permitted to give and to receive; the day is now past and we commit it to you. We entrust to you the night; we rest in surety, for you are our help, and you neither slumber nor sleep. (186)

C Amen

| C Our Father who art in heaven,
    hallowed be thy name,
    thy kingdom come,
    thy will be done
        on earth as it is in heaven.
Give us this day our daily bread;
and forgive us our trespasses
    as we forgive those
        who trespass against us;
and lead us not into temptation,
    but deliver us from evil.
For thine is the kingdom
    and the power and the glory
    forever and ever. Amen | OR | C Our Father in heaven,
    hallowed be your name,
    your kingdom come,
    your will be done
        on earth as in heaven.
Give us today our daily bread.
Forgive us our sins
    as we forgive those
        who sin against us.
Lead us not into temptation,
    but deliver us from evil.
For the kingdom, the power,
    and the glory are yours
    now and forever. Amen |

Stand

9. The GOSPEL CANTICLE is sung.

L   Guide us wak-ing, O Lord, and guard us sleep-ing that

a-wake we may watch with Christ and asleep we may rest in peace.

C   Lord, now you let your ser-vant go in peace; your word has been ful-filled.

My own eyes have seen the sal-va-tion which you have prepared in the

sight of ev-'ry peo-ple: a light to reveal you to the na-tions

and the glory of your peo-ple Is-ra-el. Glo-ry be to the

Fa-ther and to the Son and to the Ho-ly Spir-it;

as it was in the be-gin-ning, is now, and will be for-

ev-er. A-men. Guide us wak-ing, O Lord,

and guard us sleep-ing that a-wake we may

watch with Christ and asleep we may rest in peace.

10. The BLESSING concludes the service.

L The almighty and merciful Lord, the Fa-ther, the Son,

and the Holy Spir-it, bless us and keep us.

C A-men

269

RESPONSIVE PRAYER 1

Suffrages

1. Responsive Prayer 1 is for use in the morning. Responsive Prayer 2 is for use at other times of the day and before travel.

Ⓛ Holy God, holy and most gracious Father,

Ⓒ have mercy and hear us.

Ⓒ Our Father who art in heaven,
  hallowed be thy name,
  thy kingdom come,
  thy will be done
    on earth as it is in heaven.
Give us this day our daily bread;
and forgive us our trespasses
  as we forgive those
    who trespass against us;
and lead us not into temptation,
  but deliver us from evil.
For thine is the kingdom
  and the power and the glory
  forever and ever. Amen

OR

Ⓒ Our Father in heaven,
  hallowed be your name,
  your kingdom come,
  your will be done
    on earth as in heaven.
Give us today our daily bread.
Forgive us our sins
  as we forgive those
    who sin against us.
Lead us not into temptation,
  but deliver us from evil.
For the kingdom, the power,
  and the glory are yours
  now and forever. Amen

Ⓒ I believe in God, the Father Almighty,
  maker of heaven and earth.

And in Jesus Christ, his only Son, our Lord,
  who was conceived by the Holy Spirit,
  born of the virgin Mary,
  suffered under Pontius Pilate,
  was crucified, died and was buried.
He descended into hell.
The third day he rose again from the dead.

270

He ascended into heaven
    and sits at the right hand of God, the Father Almighty.
From thence he will come to judge the living and the dead.

I believe in the Holy Spirit,
    the holy Christian Church,
    the communion of saints,
    the forgiveness of sins,
    the resurrection of the body,
    and the life everlasting. Amen

L I cry to you for help, O Lord;

C in the morning my prayer comes before you.

L Restore to me the joy of your salvation,

C and grant me a willing spirit to sustain me.

L My mouth is filled with your praise,

C declaring your splendor all day long.

L Every day I will praise you

C and extol your name forever and ever.

L You answer us with awesome deeds of righteousness,

C O God our Savior, the hope of all the ends of the earth and of the farthest seas.

L Praise the Lord, O my soul;

C all my inmost being, praise his holy name.

L He redeems my life from the pit

C and crowns me with love and compassion.

L Lord, hear my prayer,

C and let my cry come before you.

2. The COLLECT OF THE DAY is said; the salutation may precede it. Additional prayers may be said also. The prayer beginning, "We give thanks to you . . . ," is always said.

L The Lord be with you.

C And also with you.

L Let us pray. . . .

C Amen

271

L We give thanks to you, heavenly Father, through Jesus Christ your dear Son, that you have protected us through the night from all danger and harm. We ask you to preserve and keep us, this day also, from all sin and evil that in all our thoughts, words, and deeds we may serve and please you. Into your hands we commend our bodies and souls and all that is ours. Let your holy angels have charge of us that the wicked one have no power over us. (187)

C **Amen**

3. *The BENEDICAMUS and BLESSING conclude the service.*

L Let us bless the Lord.

C **Thanks be to God.**

L The Lord Almighty order our days and our deeds in his peace.

C **Amen**

RESPONSIVE PRAYER 2

Suffrages

1. Responsive Prayer 1 is for use in the morning. Responsive Prayer 2 is for use at other times of the day and before travel.

Ⓛ Holy God, holy and most gracious Father,

Ⓒ have mercy and hear us.

Ⓒ Our Father who art in heaven,
  hallowed be thy name,
  thy kingdom come,
  thy will be done
    on earth as it is in heaven.
  Give us this day our daily bread;
  and forgive us our trespasses
    as we forgive those
      who trespass against us;
  and lead us not into temptation,
    but deliver us from evil.
  For thine is the kingdom
    and the power and the glory
    forever and ever. Amen

OR

Ⓒ Our Father in heaven,
  hallowed be your name,
  your kingdom come,
  your will be done
    on earth as in heaven.
  Give us today our daily bread.
  Forgive us our sins
    as we forgive those
      who sin against us.
  Lead us not into temptation,
    but deliver us from evil.
  For the kingdom, the power,
    and the glory are yours
    now and forever. Amen

Ⓒ I believe in God, the Father Almighty,
  maker of heaven and earth.

  And in Jesus Christ, his only Son, our Lord,
  who was conceived by the Holy Spirit,
  born of the virgin Mary,
  suffered under Pontius Pilate,
  was crucified, died and was buried.
  He descended into hell.
  The third day he rose again from the dead.

►

He ascended into heaven
    and sits at the right hand of God, the Father Almighty.
From thence he will come to judge the living and the dead.
I believe in the Holy Spirit,
    the holy Christian Church,
    the communion of saints,
    the forgiveness of sins,
    the resurrection of the body,
    and the life everlasting. Amen

Ⓛ Show us your unfailing love, O Lord,

Ⓒ **and grant us your salvation.**

Ⓛ May your priests be clothed with righteousness;

Ⓒ **may your saints sing for joy.**

Ⓛ I will grant peace in the land,

Ⓒ **and no one will make you afraid.**

Ⓛ Lord, keep this nation under your care,

Ⓒ **and guide us in the way of justice and truth.**

Ⓛ May your ways be known on earth,

Ⓒ **your salvation among all nations.**

Ⓛ The needy will not always be forgotten,

Ⓒ **nor the hope of the afflicted ever perish.**

Ⓛ Create in me a pure heart, O God,

Ⓒ **and renew a steadfast spirit within me.**

2. The COLLECT OF THE DAY is said; the salutation may precede it. Additional prayers may be said also.

Ⓛ The Lord be with you.

Ⓒ **And also with you.**

Ⓛ Let us pray. . . .

Ⓒ **Amen**

3. The final prayer is one appropriate to the time of day:

NOON

Ⓛ Gracious Jesus, our Lord and our God, at this hour you bore our sins in your own body on the tree so that we, being dead to sin, might live unto

274

righteousness. Have mercy upon us now and at the hour of our death, and grant to us, your servants, with all others who devoutly remember your blessed Passion, a holy and peaceful life in this world and through your grace eternal glory in the life to come, where, with the Father and the Holy Spirit, you live and reign, God forever. (188)

C **Amen**

OR

AFTERNOON

L Heavenly Father, in whom we live and move and have our being, we humbly pray you so to guide and govern us by your Word and Spirit that in all the cares and occupations of our life we may not forget you but remember that we are ever walking in your sight; through Jesus Christ, our Lord. (189)

C **Amen**

OR

EVENING

L We give thanks to you, heavenly Father, through Jesus Christ your dear Son, that you have this day so graciously protected us. We beg you to forgive us all our sins and the wrong which we have done. By your great mercy defend us from all the perils and dangers of this night. Into your hands we commend our bodies and souls and all that is ours. Let your holy angels have charge of us that the wicked one have no power over us. (190)

C **Amen**

OR

BEFORE TRAVEL

L Lord God our Father, you kept Abraham and Sarah in safety throughout the days of their pilgrimage, you led the children of Israel through the midst of the sea, and by a star you led the Wise Men to the infant Jesus. Protect and guide us now in this time as we set out to travel, make our ways safe and our homecomings joyful, and bring us at last to our heavenly home, where you dwell in glory with your Son and the Holy Spirit, God forever. (191)

C **Amen**

4. The BENEDICAMUS and BLESSING conclude the service.

L Let us bless the Lord.

C **Thanks be to God.**

L The Lord bless us, defend us from all evil, and bring us to everlasting life.

C **Amen**

THE BIDDING PRAYER

🅰 Let us pray for the whole Church, that our Lord God would defend her against all the assaults and temptations of the adversary and keep her perpetually on the true foundation, Jesus Christ:

🅟 Almighty and everlasting God, since you have revealed your glory to all nations in Jesus Christ and in the Word of his truth, keep, we ask you, in safety the works of your mercy so that your Church, spread throughout all nations, may be defended against the adversary and may serve you in true faith and persevere in the confession of your name; through Jesus Christ, our Lord.(192)

🅒 **Amen**

🅰 Let us pray for all the ministers of the Word and for all the people of God:

🅟 Almighty and everlasting God, by whose Spirit the whole body of the Church is governed and sanctified, receive the supplications and prayers which we offer before you for all your servants in your holy Church that every member of the same may truly serve you; through Jesus Christ, our Lord.(193)

🅒 **Amen**

🅰 Let us pray for our catechumens, that our Lord God would open their hearts and the door of his mercy that, having received the remission of all their sins by the washing of regeneration, they may be mindful of their Baptism and throughout their lives remain faithful to Christ Jesus, our Lord:

🅟 Almighty God and Father, because you always grant growth to your Church, increase the faith and understanding of our catechumens that, recalling the new birth by the water of Holy Baptism, they may forever continue in the family of those whom you adopt as your sons and daughters; through Jesus Christ, our Lord.(194)

🅒 **Amen**

🅰 Let us pray for all in authority that we may lead a quiet and peaceable life in all godliness and honesty:

Ⓟ O merciful Father in heaven, because you hold in your hand all the might of man and because you have ordained, for the punishment of evildoers and for the praise of those who do well, all the powers that exist in all the nations of the world, we humbly pray you graciously to regard your servants,

(USA) especially the President and Congress of the United States, the Governor of this State, and all those who make, administer, and judge our laws

(Canada) especially Her(His) Gracious Majesty, the Queen(King); the Governor General; the Prime Minister and the Parliament; the Governments of this Province and all who have authority over us

that all who receive the sword as your ministers may bear it according to your Word; through Jesus Christ, our Lord. (195)

Ⓒ Amen

Ⓐ Let us pray our Lord God Almighty that he would deliver the world from disease, ward off famine, set free those in bondage, grant health to the sick and a safe journey to all who travel:

Ⓟ Almighty and everlasting God, the consolation of the sorrowful and the strength of those who labor, may the prayers of those who in any tribulation or distress cry to you graciously come before you, so that in all their necessities they may rejoice in your manifold help and comfort; through Jesus Christ, our Lord. (196)

Ⓒ Amen

Ⓐ Let us pray for all who are outside the Church, that our Lord God would be pleased to deliver them from their error, call them to faith in the true and living God and his only Son, Jesus Christ, our Lord, and gather them into his family, the Church:

Ⓟ Almighty and everlasting God, because you seek not the death but the life of all, hear our prayers for all who have no right knowledge of you, free them from their error, and for the glory of your name bring them into the fellowship of your holy Church; through Jesus Christ, our Lord. (197)

Ⓒ Amen

Ⓐ Let us pray for our enemies, that God would remember them in mercy and graciously grant them such things as are both needful for them and profitable to their salvation:

Ⓟ O almighty, everlasting God, through your only Son, our blessed Lord, you have commanded us to love our enemies, to do good to those who hate us, and to pray for those who persecute us. We therefore earnestly implore you that by your gracious visitation all our enemies may be led to true repentance and may have the same love and be of one accord and of one mind and heart with us and with your whole Church; through Jesus Christ, our Lord. (198)

Ⓒ Amen

Ⓐ Let us pray for the fruits of the earth, that God would send down his blessing upon them and graciously dispose our hearts to enjoy them according to his own goodwill:

🅿 O Lord, Father Almighty, by your Word you created and you still continue to bless and uphold all things. We pray you so to reveal to us your Word, our Lord Jesus Christ, that he may dwell in our hearts and we may by your grace be made ready to receive your blessing on all the fruits of the earth and these things that pertain to our bodily need; through Jesus Christ, our Lord.(199)

🅲 **Amen**

🅰 Finally let us pray for all these things for which our Lord would have us ask, praying:

🅲 **Our Father who art in heaven,**	OR	🅲 **Our Father in heaven,**
hallowed be thy name,		**hallowed be your name,**
thy kingdom come,		**your kingdom come,**
thy will be done		**your will be done**
on earth as it is in heaven.		**on earth as in heaven.**
Give us this day our daily bread;		**Give us today our daily bread.**
and forgive us our trespasses		**Forgive us our sins**
as we forgive those		**as we forgive those**
who trespass against us;		**who sin against us.**
and lead us not into temptation,		**Lead us not into temptation,**
but deliver us from evil.		**but deliver us from evil.**
For thine is the kingdom		**For the kingdom, the power,**
and the power and the glory		**and the glory are yours**
forever and ever. Amen		**now and forever. Amen**

THE LITANY

L O Lord, R R have mer-cy.

L O Christ, R R have mer-cy.

L O Lord, R R have mer-cy.

L O Christ, R R hear us.

L God the Fa-ther in heaven, R R have mer-cy.

L God the Son, Redeemer of the world, R R have mer-cy.

279

Ⓛ God the Holy Spir - it, ℞   ℞ have mer-cy.

Ⓛ Be gra-cious to us. ℞   ℞ Spare us, good Lord.

Ⓛ Be gra-cious to us. ℞   ℞ Help us, good Lord.

Ⓛ From all sin, from all error, from all . . . . e - vil:

From the crafts and assaults of the devil; from sudden and e - vil death:

From pestilence and famine;
from war and bloodshed; from sedition and from re - bel - lion:

From lightning and tempest;
from all calamity by fire and water; and from ever - last-ing death: ℞

℞ Good Lord, de - liv-er us.

Ⓛ By the mystery of your holy incarnation; by your holy na - tiv - i - ty:

By your baptism, fasting, and temptation;
by your agony and bloody sweat; by your
cross and Passion; by your precious death and . . . . bur - i - al:

By your glorious resurrection and ascension;
and by the coming of the Holy Spirit, the . . . . . Com-for-ter: ℞

℞ Help us, good Lord.

L In all time of our tribulation; in all time
of our prosperity; in the hour of death; and in the day of judg-ment: R

R Help us, good Lord.

 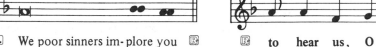

L We poor sinners im-plore you R   R to hear us, O Lord.

L To rule and govern your holy Christian Church;
to preserve all pastors and ministers of your
Church in the true knowledge and understanding
of your wholesome Word and to sustain them in holy . . . liv - ing:

To put an end to all schisms and causes of offense;
to bring into the way of truth all who have erred and are de - ceived:

To beat down Satan under our feet;
to send faithful laborers into your harvest;
and to accompany your Word with your grace and . . . . . . Spir - it: R

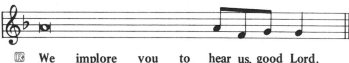

R We implore you to hear us, good Lord.

L To raise those that fall and to strengthen those that
stand; and to comfort and help the weakhearted and the dis - tressed: R

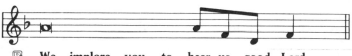

R We implore you to hear us, good Lord.

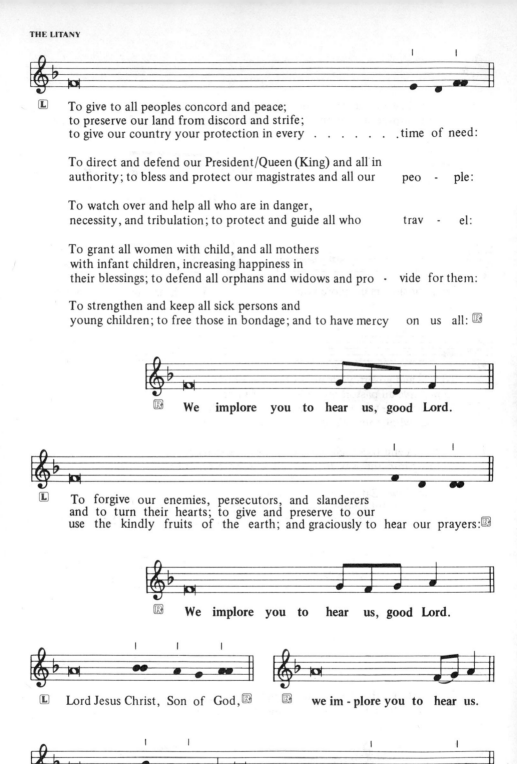

L To give to all peoples concord and peace;
to preserve our land from discord and strife;
to give our country your protection in every . . . . time of need:

To direct and defend our President/Queen (King) and all in
authority; to bless and protect our magistrates and all our   peo - ple:

To watch over and help all who are in danger,
necessity, and tribulation; to protect and guide all who   trav - el:

To grant all women with child, and all mothers
with infant children, increasing happiness in
their blessings; to defend all orphans and widows and pro · vide for them:

To strengthen and keep all sick persons and
young children; to free those in bondage; and to have mercy   on us all: ℞

℞ We implore you to hear us, good Lord.

L To forgive our enemies, persecutors, and slanderers
and to turn their hearts; to give and preserve to our
use the kindly fruits of the earth; and graciously to hear our prayers: ℞

℞ We implore you to hear us, good Lord.

L Lord Jesus Christ, Son of God, ℞   ℞ we im - plore you to hear us.

L Christ, the Lamb of God,   who takes away the sin of the world, ℞

R have mer - cy.

L Christ, the Lamb of God, who takes away the sin of the world, R

R have mer - cy.

L Christ, the Lamb of God, who takes away the sin of the world, R

R grant us your peace.

L O Christ, R

R hear us.

L O Lord, R

R have mer- cy.

L O Christ, R

R have mer- cy.

C O Lord, have mer - cy. A - men

The LORD'S PRAYER is chanted.

OR

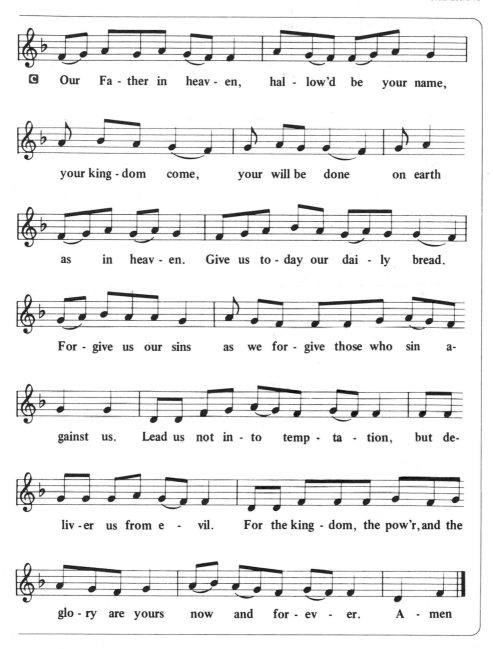

C Our Father in heaven, hallow'd be your name, your kingdom come, your will be done on earth as in heaven. Give us today our daily bread. Forgive us our sins as we forgive those who sin against us. Lead us not into temptation, but deliver us from evil. For the kingdom, the pow'r, and the glory are yours now and forever. Amen

One or more of the following LITANY COLLECTS may be chanted.

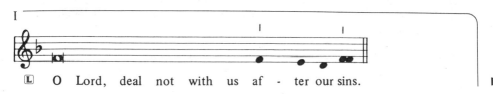

I

L O Lord, deal not with us after our sins.

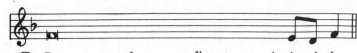

C Do not reward us according to our in-iq-ui-ties.

L Almighty God, our heavenly Fa - ther, because you desire not the

death of a sinner, but rather that we turn from our evil way and live,

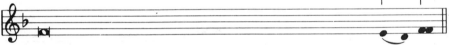

we implore you graciously to turn from us those punishments which we
by our sins have deserved and to grant us grace always to serve
you in holiness and pureness of living;

through Jesus Christ, your Son, our Lord, who lives and
reigns with you and the Holy Spirit, one God, now and for - ev - er. (104)

C A - men

OR

C A - men

OR

II

L Help us, O God of our salvation, for the glory of your name.

C **Deliver us and purge away our sins for your name's sake.**

L Almighty and everlasting God, since you govern and sanctify the whole
Christian Church by your Holy Spirit, hear our prayers for all its members, and
mercifully grant that by your grace we may serve you in true faith; through Jesus
Christ, our Lord. (200)

C **Amen**

OR

III

Ⓛ O Lord, deal not with us after our sins.

Ⓒ **Do not reward us according to our iniquities.**

Ⓛ O God, merciful Father, because you despise not the sighing of a contrite heart nor the desire of the sorrowful, mercifully assist our prayers which we make before you in all our troubles and adversities as they come upon us, and graciously hear us, so that those evils which the craft and subtlety of the devil or man work against us may by your good guidance be brought to naught that we, your servants, being hurt by no afflictions, may evermore give thanks to you in your holy Church; through Jesus Christ, our Lord. (201)

Ⓒ **Amen**

OR

IV

Ⓛ O Lord, enter not into judgment with your servant.

Ⓒ **For in your sight shall no man living be justified.**

Ⓛ Almighty God, since you know that we are set in the midst of so many and great dangers that by reason of the frailty of our nature we cannot always stand upright, grant us such strength and protection as may support us in all dangers and carry us through all temptations; through Jesus Christ, our Lord. (14)

Ⓒ **Amen**

OR

V

Ⓛ Call on me in the day of trouble.

Ⓒ **I will deliver you, and you will glorify me.**

Ⓛ Spare us, O Lord, and mercifully forgive us our sins, and though by our continual transgressions we have merited your punishments, be gracious to us and grant that all these evils which we have deserved may be turned from us and overruled to our everlasting good; through Jesus Christ, your Son, our Lord, who lives and reigns with you and the Holy Spirit, one God, now and forever. (202)

Ⓒ **Amen**

PROPERS FOR MORNING PRAYER AND EVENING PRAYER

ADVENT

Invitatory for Morning Prayer

Ⓛ Give glory to the coming King.

Ⓒ **Oh, come, let us worship him.**

Versicles (Service of Light) for Evening Prayer

Ⓛ The Spirit and the Church cry out:

Ⓒ **Come, Lord Jesus.**

Ⓛ All those who await his appearance pray:

Ⓒ **Come, Lord Jesus.**

Ⓛ The whole creation pleads:

Ⓒ **Come, Lord Jesus.**

Psalm Antiphons for Evening Prayer

In that day the mountains will drip
new wine,*
    and the hills will flow with milk.
    Alleluia.

OR

The rough ground shall become level,
the rugged places a plain.*
    Come, Lord, do not delay. Alleluia.

Antiphon to "Benedictus" and "Magnificat" in Evening Prayer

Do not be afraid, Mary, you have found
favor with God.*
    You will be with child and give
    birth to a son. Alleluia.

From December 17 the O Antiphons may be used.

December 17

O Wisdom, proceeding from the mouth
of the Most High, pervading and
permeating all creation, mightily
ordering all things:*
    Come and teach us the way of
    prudence.

December 18

O Adonai and ruler of the house of
Israel, who appeared to Moses in
the burning bush and gave him the
Law on Sinai:*
    Come with an outstretched arm and
    redeem us.

288

December 19

* I d: Dorian

O Root of Jesse, standing as an ensign
before the peoples, before whom all
kings are mute, to whom the nations
will do homage:*
    Come quickly to deliver us.

December 20

* I d: Dorian

O Key of David and scepter of the
house of Israel, you open and no one
can close, you close and no one
can open:*
    Come and rescue the prisoners who
    are in darkness and the shadow
    of death.

December 21

* I d: Dorian

O Dayspring, splendor of light
everlasting:*
    Come and enlighten those who sit
    in darkness and in the shadow
    of death.

December 22

* I d: Dorian

O King of the nations, the ruler
they long for, the cornerstone
uniting all people:*
    Come and save us all,
    whom you formed out of clay.

December 23

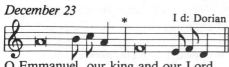

* I d: Dorian

O Emmanuel, our king and our Lord,
the anointed for the nations and
their Savior:*
    Come and save us, O Lord our God.

CHRISTMAS/EPIPHANY

Invitatory for Morning Prayer

Ⓛ The Word became flesh, and we
have seen his glory.

Ⓒ **Oh, come, let us worship him.**

*Versicles (Service of Light)
for Evening Prayer*

Ⓛ The people walking in darkness
have seen a great light.

Ⓒ **The light shines in the darkness,
but the darkness has not understood it.**

Ⓛ On those living in the land of the
shadow of death a light has dawned.

Ⓒ **We have seen his glory, the glory
of the one and only Son who came
from the Father.**

Ⓛ For to us a child is born, to
us a Son is given.

Ⓒ **In him was life, and that life was
the light of men.**

Psalm Antiphons for Evening Prayer

A prince from the day of your birth,*
    from the womb before daybreak
    have I begotten you.

OR

Come, you peoples of the earth;*
    drink from the wells of the Savior.

*Antiphon to "Benedictus" and
"Magnificat"*

Today Christ is born; today salvation
has appeared.*
    Today the just exult and say, Glory
    to God in the highest. Alleluia.

OR

289

Our Lord and Savior, begotten before all āges,*
> revealed himself to the world. Alleluia.

LENT

Invitatory for Morning Prayer

Ⓛ The Lord is near to all who call on him.

Ⓒ **Oh, come, let us worship him.**

Versicles (Service of Light) for Evening Prayer

Ⓛ Now is the time of God's favor;

Ⓒ **now is the day of salvation.**

Ⓛ Turn us again, O God of our salvation,

Ⓒ **that the light of your face may shine on us.**

Ⓛ May your justice shine like the sun;

Ⓒ **and may the poor be lifted up.**

Psalm Antiphons for Evening Prayer

Return to the Lord your God, for he is gracious and merciful,*
> slow to anger, and abounding in steadfast love.

OR

The Lord delivers us from the power of dārkness,*
> and leads us into the kingdom of his Son.

Antiphon to "Benedictus" and "Magnificat"

Let justice roll on like a rīver,*
> righteousness like a never-failing stream.

HOLY WEEK

The Invitatory and Venite in Morning Prayer are not sung during Holy Week.

The Service of Light in Evening Prayer is omitted during Holy Week. Instead begin the service with the Psalmody—Psalm 141.

Psalm Antiphons for Evening Prayer

Christ humbled himself and became obedient to death,*
> even death on a cross.

OR

He was pierced for our transgressions, he was crushed for our iniquities,*
> the punishment that brought us peace was upon him, and by his wounds we are healed.

Antiphon to "Benedictus" and "Magnificat"

Glory to the cross of our Lord Jesus Christ,*
> our salvation, life, and resurrection.

EASTER

Invitatory for Morning Prayer

Ⓛ The Lord is risen indeed.

Ⓒ **Oh, come, let us worship him.**

Versicles (Service of Light) for Evening Prayer

Ⓛ Jesus Christ is risen from the dead.

Ⓒ **Alleluia, alleluia, alleluia.**

Ⓛ We are illumined by the brightness of his rising.

Ⓒ **Alleluia, alleluia, alleluia.**

Ⓛ Death has no more dominion over us.

Ⓒ **Alleluia, alleluia, alleluia.**

Psalm Antiphons for Evening Prayer

The glory of the Lord shines on the city. Alleluia.*
Its lamp is the Lamb. Alleluia.

OR

God feeds us with the finest of wheat. Alleluia.*
He satisfies us with honey from the rock. Alleluia.

Antiphon to "Benedictus" and "Magnificat"

This is the day the Lord has made. Alleluia.*
Let us rejoice and be glad in it. Alleluia.

THANKSGIVING FOR LIGHT II

We praise and thank you, O God,
through your Son, Jesus Christ, our
Lord, through whom you have enlightened us by revealing the light that
never fades.
Night *is falling/has fallen,* and day's
allotted span draws to a close.
The daylight which you created for our
pleasure has fully satisfied us, and yet,
of your free gift, now the evening
lights do not fail us.
We praise you and glorify you through
your Son, Jesus Christ, our Lord;
through him be glory, honor, and
power to you in the Holy Spirit now
and always and forever and ever.
Amen

THANKSGIVING FOR LIGHT I

We praise and thank you, O God, for you
are without beginning and without end.
Through Christ you are the creator and
preserver of the whole world; but
above all, you are his God and
Father, the giver of the Spirit, and the
ruler of all that is, seen and unseen.
You made the day for the works of light
and the night for the refreshment of
our weakness.
O loving Lord and source of all that is
good, mercifully accept our evening
sacrifice of praise.
As you have conducted us through the day
and brought us to night's beginning,
keep us now in Christ; grant us a
peaceful evening and a night free from
sin; and at the end bring us to
everlasting life through Christ, our
Lord.
Through him we offer glory, honor, and
worship to you in the Holy Spirit
now and always and forever and ever.
Amen

PSALMS FOR DAILY PRAYER

MATINS AND MORNING PRAYER

Sundays and Festivals: 1, 2, 8, 19, 27, 45, 62, 67, 72, 84, 98

Other days: 18, 22, 24, 25, 28, 32, 36, 50, 65, 73, 90, 92, 96,
100, 107, 119, 147, 148

VESPERS AND EVENING PRAYER

Sundays and Festivals: 23, 110, 111, 114

Other days: 6, 38, 46, 51, 105, 116, 117, 118, 126, 130, 135,
136, 138, 139, 141, 142, 143, 146

COMPLINE

Sundays and Festivals: 4, 91, 133, 134

Other days: 16, 18, 34, 77, 103, 121

DAILY DEVOTION FOR FAMILY OR INDIVIDUAL USE

1. An appropriate HYMN may be sung here or at the conclusion.

Ⓛ In the name of the Father and of the ✢ Son and of the Holy Spirit.

Ⓡ **Amen**

2. A PSALM may be read.

> Morning Psalms: 1, 2, 8, 19, 27, 45, 62, 67, 72, 84, 98
> Evening Psalms: 23, 110, 111, 114, 4, 91, 133, 134
> Introit Psalmody may also be read from the Propers of the Day (pp. 10-123).

3. The SCRIPTURE READING may be from the Propers of the Day (pp. 10-123), the Daily Lectionary (pp. 295-299), or a book of devotions, followed by an exposition. On Saturday evening any reading for the morrow from the Propers of the Day is appropriate. The reading is introduced and concluded with the following.

Ⓛ Hear the Word of God as recorded in _____.

Ⓡ **Thanks be to God.**

4. The PRAYER(S) may dwell on any of the following:

> Reflection on this Word of God
> Prayer that grows out of this Word of God
> Collect of the Day from the Church Year (pp. 10-123)
> Prayers for the particular day*
> Morning Prayer (p. 236)
> Evening Prayer (p. 250)
> Lord's Prayer (p. 149)

Ⓛ May the almighty and most merciful God, Father, ✢ Son, and Holy Spirit, bless and preserve us.

Ⓡ **Amen**

*These may follow this weekly rhythm:

Sunday:	God's gifts to us through Word and Sacrament
Monday:	Our Baptism, calling, and daily work
Tuesday:	Facing temptation and struggle, witnessing
Wednesday:	Our homes, families, schools, country, and neighbor
Thursday:	The Lord's Supper, his fellowship and family around the world
Friday:	The Lamb of God, who takes away the sin of the world, from the cross forgiveness and salvation
Saturday:	Preparation for the Day of the Lord, for death and resurrection

DAILY LECTIONARY

This outline is a devotional reading plan that covers the entire Sacred Scriptures each year. The selections are based on ancient models and are generally in harmony with the liturgical church year. The average reading is three chapters daily. A seasonal canticle is assigned for each month and is scheduled to replace the psalm on the first and last days of the month. All of the psalms are read twice a year.

The lectionary is in accordance with Martin Luther's suggestions: "But let the entire Psalter, divided in parts, remain in use and the entire Scriptures, divided into lections, let this be preserved in the ears of the church." Also: "After that another book should be selected, and so on, until the entire Bible has been read through, and where one does not understand it, pass that by and glorify God."

December

1	Luke 1:46-55
	Revelation 1—2
2	Psalm 1
	Revelation 3—5
3	Psalm 2
	Revelation 6—8
4	Psalm 3
	Revelation 9—11
5	Psalm 4
	Revelation 12—14
6	Psalm 5
	Revelation 15—17
7	Psalm 6
	Revelation 18—20
8	Psalm 7
	Revelation 21—22
9	Psalm 8
	Isaiah 1—3
10	Psalm 9
	Isaiah 4—6
11	Psalm 10
	Isaiah 7—9
12	Psalm 11
	Isaiah 10—12
13	Psalm 12
	Isaiah 13—15
14	Psalm 13
	Isaiah 16—18
15	Psalm 14
	Isaiah 19—21
16	Psalm 15
	Isaiah 22—24
17	Psalm 16
	Isaiah 25—27

18	Psalm 17
	Isaiah 28—30
19	Psalm 18
	Isaiah 31—33
20	Psalm 19
	Isaiah 34—36
21	Psalm 20
	Isaiah 37—39
22	Psalm 21
	Isaiah 40—42
23	Psalm 22
	Isaiah 43—45
24	Psalm 23
	Isaiah 46—48
25	Psalm 24
	Isaiah 49—51
26	Psalm 25
	Isaiah 52—54
27	Psalm 26
	Isaiah 55—57
28	Psalm 27
	Isaiah 58—60
29	Psalm 28
	Isaiah 61—63
30	Psalm 29
	Isaiah 64—66
31	Luke 1:46-55
	Mark 1

January

1	Luke 1:68-79
	Mark 2
2	Psalm 30
	Mark 3

3	Psalm 31
	Mark 4
4	Psalm 32
	Mark 5
5	Psalm 33
	Mark 6
6	Psalm 34
	Mark 7
7	Psalm 35
	Mark 8
8	Psalm 36
	Mark 9
9	Psalm 37
	Mark 10
10	Psalm 38
	Mark 11
11	Psalm 39
	Mark 12
12	Psalm 40
	Mark 13
13	Psalm 41
	Mark 14
14	Psalm 42
	Mark 15—16
15	Psalm 43
	Genesis 1—3
16	Psalm 44
	Genesis 4—6
17	Psalm 45
	Genesis 7—9
18	Psalm 46
	Genesis 10—12
19	Psalm 47
	Genesis 13—15

20	Psalm 48	22	Psalm 79	27	Psalm 110
	Genesis 16—18		Leviticus 22—24		Luke 16—17
21	Psalm 49	23	Psalm 80	28	Psalm 111
	Genesis 19—21		Leviticus 25—27		Luke 18—19
22	Psalm 50	24	Psalm 81	29	Psalm 112
	Genesis 22—24		Numbers 1—3		Luke 20—21
23	Psalm 51	25	Psalm 82	30	Psalm 113
	Genesis 25—27		Numbers 4—6		Luke 22
24	Psalm 52	26	Psalm 83	31	Isaiah 64:1-9
	Genesis 28—30		Numbers 7—9		Luke 23—24
25	Psalm 53	27	Psalm 84		
	Genesis 31—33		Numbers 10—12		
26	Psalm 54	28	Luke 2:29-32	**April**	
	Genesis 34—36		Numbers 13—15	1	Isaiah 25:1-9
27	Psalm 55				Romans 1—3
	Genesis 37—39			2	Psalm 114
28	Psalm 56				Romans 4—6
	Genesis 40—42	**March**		3	Psalm 115
29	Psalm 57	1	Isaiah 64:1-9		Romans 7—9
	Genesis 43—45		Numbers 16—18	4	Psalm 116
30	Psalm 58	2	Psalm 85		Romans 10—13
	Genesis 46—48		Numbers 19—21	5	Psalm 117
31	Luke 1:68-79	3	Psalm 86		Romans 14—16
	Genesis 49—50		Numbers 22—24	6	Psalm 118
		4	Psalm 87		1 Corinthians 1—3
			Numbers 25—27	7	Psalm 119:1-8
February		5	Psalm 88		1 Corinthians 4—6
1	Luke 2:29-32		Numbers 28—30	8	Psalm 119:9-16
	Exodus 1—3	6	Psalm 89		1 Corinthians 7—9
2	Psalm 59		Numbers 31—33	9	Psalm 119:17-24
	Exodus 4—6	7	Psalm 90		1 Corinthians 10—11
3	Psalm 60		Numbers 34—36	10	Psalm 119:25-32
	Exodus 7—9	8	Psalm 91		1 Corinthians 12—14
4	Psalm 61		Deuteronomy 1—3	11	Psalm 119:33-40
	Exodus 10—12	9	Psalm 92		1 Corinthians 15—16
5	Psalm 62		Deuteronomy 4—6	12	Psalm 119:41-48
	Exodus 13—15	10	Psalm 93		2 Corinthians 1—4
6	Psalm 63		Deuteronomy 7—9	13	Psalm 119:49-56
	Exodus 16—18	11	Psalm 94		2 Corinthians 5—7
7	Psalm 64		Deuteronomy 10—12	14	Psalm 119:57-64
	Exodus 19—21	12	Psalm 95		2 Corinthians 8—10
8	Psalm 65		Deuteronomy 13—15	15	Psalm 119:65-72
	Exodus 22—24	13	Psalm 96		2 Corinthians 11—13
9	Psalm 66		Deuteronomy 16—18	16	Psalm 119:73-80
	Exodus 25—27	14	Psalm 97		Galatians 1—3
10	Psalm 67		Deuteronomy 19—21	17	Psalm 119:81-88
	Exodus 28—30	15	Psalm 98		Galatians 4—6
11	Psalm 68		Deuteronomy 22—24	18	Psalm 119:89-96
	Exodus 31—33	16	Psalm 99		Ephesians 1—3
12	Psalm 69		Deuteronomy 25—27	19	Psalm 119:97-104
	Exodus 34—36	17	Psalm 100		Ephesians 4—6
13	Psalm 70		Deuteronomy 28—30	20	Psalm 119:105-112
	Exodus 37—38	18	Psalm 101		Philippians 1—2
14	Psalm 71		Deuteronomy 31—34	21	Psalm 119:113-120
	Exodus 39—40	19	Psalm 102		Philippians 3—4
15	Psalm 72		Luke 1	22	Psalm 119:121-128
	Leviticus 1—3	20	Psalm 103		Colossians 1—2
16	Psalm 73		Luke 2—3	23	Psalm 119:129-136
	Leviticus 4—6	21	Psalm 104		Colossians 3—4
17	Psalm 74		Luke 4—5	24	Psalm 119:137-144
	Leviticus 7—9	22	Psalm 105		1 Thessalonians 1—3
18	Psalm 75		Luke 6—7	25	Psalm 119:145-152
	Leviticus 10—12	23	Psalm 106		1 Thessalonians 4—5
19	Psalm 76		Luke 8—9	26	Psalm 119:153-160
	Leviticus 13—15	24	Psalm 107		2 Thessalonians 1—3
20	Psalm 77		Luke 10—11	27	Psalm 119:161-168
	Leviticus 16—18	25	Psalm 108		1 Timothy 1—3
21	Psalm 78		Luke 12—13	28	Psalm 119:169-176
	Leviticus 19—21	26	Psalm 109		1 Timothy 4—6
			Luke 14—15		

29	Psalm 120	**June**		3	Psalm 29	
	2 Timothy 1—2	1	Isaiah 12:1-6		2 Samuel 4—6	
30	Isaiah 25:1-9		Acts 15—16	4	Psalm 30	
	2 Timothy 3—4	2	Psalm 150		2 Samuel 7—9	
			Acts 17—18	5	Psalm 31	
		3	Psalm 1		2 Samuel 10—12	
May			Acts 19—20	6	Psalm 32	
1	1 Samuel 2:1-10	4	Psalm 2		2 Samuel 13—15	
	Titus, Philemon		Acts 21—22	7	Psalm 33	
2	Psalm 121	5	Psalm 3		2 Samuel 16—18	
	Hebrews 1—4		Acts 23—24	8	Psalm 34	
3	Psalm 122	6	Psalm 4		2 Samuel 19—21	
	Hebrews 5—7		Acts 25—26	9	Psalm 35	
4	Psalm 123	7	Psalm 5		2 Samuel 22—24	
	Hebrews 8—10		Acts 27—28	10	Psalm 36	
5	Psalm 124	8	Psalm 6		1 Kings 1—2	
	Hebrews 11—13		Joshua 1—5	11	Psalm 37	
6	Psalm 125	9	Psalm 7		1 Kings 3—6	
	James 1—3		Joshua 6—8	12	Psalm 38	
7	Psalm 126	10	Psalm 8		1 Kings 7—8	
	James 4—5		Joshua 9—11	13	Psalm 39	
8	Psalm 127	11	Psalm 9		1 Kings 9—11	
	1 Peter 1—2		Joshua 12—16	14	Psalm 40	
9	Psalm 128	12	Psalm 10		1 Kings 12—14	
	1 Peter 3—5		Joshua 17—21	15	Psalm 41	
10	Psalm 129	13	Psalm 11		1 Kings 15—17	
	2 Peter		Joshua 22—24	16	Psalm 42	
11	Psalm 130	14	Psalm 12		1 Kings 18—20	
	1 John 1—3		Judges 1—3	17	Psalm 43	
12	Psalm 131	15	Psalm 13		1 Kings 21—22	
	1 John 4—5		Judges 4—6	18	Psalm 44	
13	Psalm 132	16	Psalm 14		2 Kings 1—3	
	2 John, 3 John, Jude		Judges 7—9	19	Psalm 45	
14	Psalm 133	17	Psalm 15		2 Kings 4—6	
	John 1—2		Judges 10—12	20	Psalm 46	
15	Psalm 134	18	Psalm 16		2 Kings 7—9	
	John 3—4		Judges 13—15	21	Psalm 47	
16	Psalm 135	19	Psalm 17		2 Kings 10—12	
	John 5—6		Judges 16—18	22	Psalm 48	
17	Psalm 136	20	Psalm 18		2 Kings 13—15	
	John 7—8		Judges 19—21	23	Psalm 49	
18	Psalm 137	21	Psalm 19		2 Kings 16—18	
	John 9—10		Ruth	24	Psalm 50	
19	Psalm 138	22	Psalm 20		2 Kings 19—22	
	John 11—12		1 Samuel 1—3	25	Psalm 51	
20	Psalm 139	23	Psalm 21		2 Kings 23—25	
	John 13—14		1 Samuel 4—6	26	Psalm 52	
21	Psalm 140	24	Psalm 22		1 Chronicles 1—5	
	John 15—16		1 Samuel 7—9	27	Psalm 53	
22	Psalm 141	25	Psalm 23		1 Chronicles 6—10	
	John 17—18		1 Samuel 10—12	28	Psalm 54	
23	Psalm 142	26	Psalm 24		1 Chronicles 11—15	
	John 19		1 Samuel 13—15	29	Psalm 55	
24	Psalm 143	27	Psalm 25		1 Chronicles 16—20	
	John 20—21		1 Samuel 16—18	30	Psalm 56	
25	Psalm 144	28	Psalm 26		1 Chronicles 21—25	
	Acts 1—2		1 Samuel 19—21	31	Deuteronomy 32:1-4	
26	Psalm 145	29	Psalm 27		1 Chronicles 26—29	
	Acts 3—4		1 Samuel 22—24			
27	Psalm 146	30	Isaiah 12:1-6			
	Acts 5—6		1 Samuel 25—27	**August**		
28	Psalm 147			1	Habakkuk 3:2-19	
	Acts 7—8				2 Chronicles 1—3	
29	Psalm 148			2	Psalm 57	
	Acts 9—10	**July**			2 Chronicles 4—6	
30	Psalm 149	1	Deuteronomy 32:1-4	3	Psalm 58	
	Acts 11—12		1 Samuel 28—31		2 Chronicles 7—9	
31	1 Samuel 2:1-10	2	Psalm 28	4	Psalm 59	
	Acts 13—14		2 Samuel 1—3		2 Chronicles 10—12	

5	Psalm 60 2 Chronicles 13—15	7	Psalm 91 Proverbs 8—10	10	Psalm 119:25-32 Ezekiel 1—3
6	Psalm 61 2 Chronicles 16—18	8	Psalm 92 Proverbs 11—13	11	Psalm 119:33-40 Ezekiel 4—6
7	Psalm 62 2 Chronicles 19—21	9	Psalm 93 Proverbs 14—16	12	Psalm 119:41-48 Ezekiel 7—9
8	Psalm 63 2 Chronicles 22—24	10	Psalm 94 Proverbs 17—19	13	Psalm 119:49-56 Ezekiel 10—12
9	Psalm 64 2 Chronicles 25—27	11	Psalm 95 Proverbs 20—22	14	Psalm 119:57-64 Ezekiel 13—15
10	Psalm 65 2 Chronicles 28—30	12	Psalm 96 Proverbs 23—25	15	Psalm 119:65-72 Ezekiel 16—18
11	Psalm 66 2 Chronicles 31—33	13	Psalm 97 Proverbs 26—28	16	Psalm 119:73-80 Ezekiel 19—21
12	Psalm 67 2 Chronicles 34—36	14	Psalm 98 Proverbs 29—31	17	Psalm 119:81-88 Ezekiel 22—24
13	Psalm 68 Ezra 1—5	15	Psalm 99 Ecclesiastes 1—3	18	Psalm 119:89-96 Ezekiel 25—27
14	Psalm 69 Ezra 6—10	16	Psalm 100 Ecclesiastes 4—6	19	Psalm 119:97-104 Ezekiel 28—30
15	Psalm 70 Nehemiah 1—3	17	Psalm 101 Ecclesiastes 7—9	20	Psalm 119:105-112 Ezekiel 31—33
16	Psalm 71 Nehemiah 4—6	18	Psalm 102 Ecclesiastes 10—12	21	Psalm 119:113-120 Ezekiel 34—36
17	Psalm 72 Nehemiah 7—9	19	Psalm 103 Song of Solomon 1—4	22	Psalm 119:121-128 Ezekiel 37—39
18	Psalm 73 Nehemiah 10—13	20	Psalm 104 Song of Solomon 5—8	23	Psalm 119:129-136 Ezekiel 40—42
19	Psalm 74 Esther 1—3	21	Psalm 105 Jeremiah 1—3	24	Psalm 119:137-144 Ezekiel 43—45
20	Psalm 75 Esther 4—6	22	Psalm 106 Jeremiah 4—6	25	Psalm 119:145-152 Ezekiel 46—48
21	Psalm 76 Esther 7—10	23	Psalm 107 Jeremiah 7—9	26	Psalm 119:153-160 Daniel 1—3
22	Psalm 77 Job 1—3	24	Psalm 108 Jeremiah 10—12	27	Psalm 119:161-168 Daniel 4—6
23	Psalm 78 Job 4—6	25	Psalm 109 Jeremiah 13—15	28	Psalm 119:169-176 Daniel 7—9
24	Psalm 79 Job 7—9	26	Psalm 110 Jeremiah 16—18	29	Psalm 120 Daniel 10—12
25	Psalm 80 Job 10—12	27	Psalm 111 Jeremiah 19—22	30	Psalm 121 Hosea 1—4
26	Psalm 81 Job 13—15	28	Psalm 112 Jeremiah 23—25	31	Jonah 2:2-9 Hosea 5—7
27	Psalm 82 Job 16—18	29	Psalm 113 Jeremiah 26—28		
28	Psalm 83 Job 19—21	30	1 Chronicles 29:10-13 Jeremiah 29—31		
29	Psalm 84 Job 22—24			**November**	
30	Psalm 85 Job 25—27			1	Exodus 15:1-18 Hosea 8—10
31	Habakkuk 3:2-19 Job 28—30	**October**		2	Psalm 122 Hosea 11—14
		1	Jonah 2:2-9 Jeremiah 32—34	3	Psalm 123 Joel
September		2	Psalm 114 Jeremiah 35—37	4	Psalm 124 Amos 1—5
1	1 Chronicles 29:10-13 Job 31—33	3	Psalm 115 Jeremiah 38—40	5	Psalm 125 Amos 6—9
2	Psalm 86 Job 34—36	4	Psalm 116 Jeremiah 41—43	6	Psalm 126 Obadiah, Jonah
3	Psalm 87 Job 37—39	5	Psalm 117 Jeremiah 44—47	7	Psalm 127 Micah 1—3
4	Psalm 88 Job 40—42	6	Psalm 118 Jeremiah 48—50	8	Psalm 128 Micah 4—7
5	Psalm 89 Proverbs 1—3	7	Psalm 119:1-8 Jeremiah 51—52	9	Psalm 129 Nahum
6	Psalm 90 Proverbs 4—7	8	Psalm 119:9-16 Lamentations 1—2	10	Psalm 130 Habakkuk
		9	Psalm 119:17-24 Lamentations 3—5	11	Psalm 131 Zephaniah

298

12 Psalm 132
   Haggai
13 Psalm 133
   Zechariah 1—5
14 Psalm 134
   Zechariah 6—10
15 Psalm 135
   Zechariah 11—14
16 Psalm 136
   Malachi
17 Psalm 137
   Matthew 1—2

18 Psalm 138
   Matthew 3—4
19 Psalm 139
   Matthew 5—6
20 Psalm 140
   Matthew 7—8
21 Psalm 141
   Matthew 9—10
22 Psalm 142
   Matthew 11—12
23 Psalm 143
   Matthew 13—14

24 Psalm 144
   Matthew 15—16
25 Psalm 145
   Matthew 17—18
26 Psalm 146
   Matthew 19—20
27 Psalm 147
   Matthew 21—22
28 Psalm 148
   Matthew 23—24
29 Psalm 149—150
   Matthew 25—26
30 Exodus 15:1-18
   Matthew 27—28

Dr. Martin Luther's
SMALL CATECHISM

SECTION I

The Ten Commandments

As the Head of the Family Should Teach Them in a Simple Way to His Household

The First Commandment

Thou shalt have no other gods before Me.

What does this mean? We should fear, love, and trust in God above all things.

The Second Commandment

Thou shalt not take the name of the Lord, thy God, in vain.

What does this mean? We should fear and love God that we may not curse, swear, use witchcraft, lie, or deceive by His name, but call upon it in every trouble, pray, praise, and give thanks.

The Third Commandment

Remember the Sabbath day, to keep it holy. (Thou shalt sanctify the holy day.)

What does this mean? We should fear and love God that we may not despise preaching and His Word, but hold it sacred and gladly hear and learn it.

The Fourth Commandment

Thou shalt honor thy father and thy mother, that it may be well with thee, and thou mayest live long on the earth.

What does this mean? We should fear and love God that we may not despise our parents and masters, nor provoke them to anger, but give them honor, serve and obey them, and hold them in love and esteem.

The Fifth Commandment

Thou shalt not kill.

What does this mean? We should fear and love God that we may not hurt nor harm our neighbor in his body, but help and befriend him in every bodily need.

The Sixth Commandment

Thou shalt not commit adultery.

What does this mean? We should fear and love God that we may lead a chaste and decent life in word and deed, and each love and honor his spouse.

The Seventh Commandment

Thou shalt not steal.

What does this mean? We should fear and love God that we may not take our neighbor's money or goods, nor get them by false ware or dealing, but help him to improve and protect his property and business.

The Eighth Commandment

Thou shalt not bear false witness against thy neighbor.

What does this mean? We should fear and love God that we may not deceitfully belie, betray, slander, nor defame our neighbor, but defend him, speak well of him, and put the best construction on everything.

The Ninth Commandment

Thou shalt not covet thy neighbor's house.

What does this mean? We should fear and love God that we may not craftily seek to get our neighbor's inheritance or house, nor obtain it by a show of right, but help and be of service to him in keeping it.

The Tenth Commandment

Thou shalt not covet thy neighbor's wife, nor his manservant, nor his maidservant, nor his cattle, nor anything that is thy neighbor's.

What does this mean? We should fear and love God that we may not estrange, force, or entice away from our neighbor his wife, servants, or cattle, but urge them to stay and do their duty.

The Close of the Commandments

What does God say of all these Commandments? He says thus: I, the Lord, thy God, am a jealous God, visiting the iniquity of the fathers upon the children unto the third and fourth generation of them that hate Me, and showing mercy unto thousands of them that love Me and keep My Commandments.

What does this mean? God threatens to punish all that transgress these Commandments. Therefore we should fear His wrath and not act contrary to them. But He promises grace and every blessing to all that keep these Commandments. Therefore we should also love and trust in Him and willingly do according to His Commandments.

The Creed

As the Head of the Family Should Teach It in a Simple Way to His Household

The First Article

Creation

I believe in God the Father Almighty, Maker of heaven and earth.

What does this mean? I believe that God has made me and all creatures; that He has given me my body and soul, eyes, ears, and all my members, my reason and all my senses, and still preserves them;

also clothing and shoes, meat and drink, house and home, wife and children, fields, cattle, and all my goods; that He richly and daily provides me with all that I need to support this body and life;

that He defends me against all danger, and guards and protects me from all evil;

and all this purely out of fatherly, divine goodness and mercy, without any merit or worthiness in me;

for all which it is my duty to thank and praise, to serve and obey Him.

This is most certainly true.

The Second Article

Redemption

And in Jesus Christ, His only Son, our Lord, who was conceived by the Holy Ghost, born of the Virgin Mary, suffered under Pontius Pilate, was crucified, dead, and buried;

He descended into hell; the third day He rose again from the dead; He ascended into heaven, and sitteth on the right hand of God the Father Almighty; from thence He shall come to judge the quick and the dead.

What does this mean? I believe that Jesus Christ, true God, begotten of the Father from eternity, and also true man, born of the Virgin Mary, is my Lord,

who has redeemed me, a lost and condemned creature, purchased and won me from all sins, from death, and from the power of the devil; not with gold or silver, but with His holy, precious blood and with His innocent suffering and death,

that I may be His own, and live under Him in His kingdom, and serve Him in everlasting righteousness, innocence, and blessedness,

even as He is risen from the dead, lives and reigns to all eternity.

This is most certainly true.

The Third Article

Sanctification

I believe in the Holy Ghost; the holy Christian Church, the communion of saints; the forgiveness of sins; the resurrection of the body; and the life everlasting. Amen.

What does this mean? I believe that I cannot by my own reason or strength believe in Jesus Christ, my Lord, or come to Him; but the Holy Ghost has called me by the Gospel, enlightened me with His gifts, sanctified and kept me in the true faith;

even as He calls, gathers, enlightens, and sanctifies the whole Christian Church on earth, and keeps it with Jesus Christ in the one true faith;

in which Christian Church He daily and richly forgives all sins to me and all believers,

and will at the Last Day raise up me and all the dead, and give unto me and all believers in Christ eternal life.

This is most certainly true.

The Lord's Prayer

As the Head of the Family Should Teach It in a Simple Way to His Household

Our Father who art in heaven. Hallowed be Thy name. Thy kingdom come. Thy will be done on earth as it is in heaven. Give us this day our daily bread. And forgive us our trespasses, as we forgive those who trespass against us. And lead us not into temptation, but deliver us from evil. For Thine is the kingdom and the power and the glory forever and ever. Amen.

The Introduction

Our Father who art in heaven.

What does this mean? God would by these words tenderly invite us to believe that He is our true Father, and that we are His true children, so that we may with all boldness and confidence ask Him as dear children ask their dear father.

The First Petition

Hallowed be Thy name.

What does this mean? God's name is indeed holy in itself; but we pray in this petition that it may be holy among us also.

How is this done? When the Word of God is taught in its truth and purity, and we, as the children of God, also lead a holy life according to it. This grant us, dear Father in heaven.

But he that teaches and lives otherwise than God's Word teaches, profanes the name of God among us. From this preserve us, Heavenly Father.

The Second Petition

Thy kingdom come.

What does this mean? The kingdom of God comes indeed without our prayer, of itself; but we pray in this petition that it may come unto us also.

How is this done? When our heavenly Father gives us His Holy Spirit, so that by His grace we believe His holy Word and lead a godly life, here in time and hereafter in eternity.

The Third Petition

Thy will be done on earth as it is in heaven.

What does this mean? The good and gracious will of God is done indeed without our prayer; but we pray in this petition that it may be done among us also.

How is this done? When God breaks and hinders every evil counsel and will which would not let us hallow God's name nor let His kingdom come, such as the will of the devil, the world, and our flesh; but strengthens and preserves us steadfast in His Word and faith unto our end. This is His gracious and good will.

The Fourth Petition

Give us this day our daily bread.

What does this mean? God gives daily bread indeed without our prayer, also to all the wicked; but we pray in this petition that He would lead us to know it, and to receive our daily bread with thanksgiving.

What is meant by daily bread? Everything that belongs to the support and wants of the body, such as food, drink, clothing, shoes, house, home, field, cattle, money, goods, a pious spouse, pious children, pious servants, pious and faithful rulers, good government, good weather, peace, health, discipline, honor, good friends, faithful neighbors, and the like.

The Fifth Petition

And forgive us our trespasses, as we forgive those who trespass against us.

What does this mean? We pray in this petition

that our Father in heaven would not look upon our sins, nor on their account deny our prayer; for we are worthy of none of the things for which we pray, neither have we deserved them; but that He would grant them all to us by grace; for we daily sin much and indeed deserve nothing but punishment. So will we also heartily forgive, and readily do good to, those who sin against us.

The Sixth Petition

And lead us not into temptation.

What does this mean? God indeed tempts no one; but we pray in this petition that God would guard and keep us, so that the devil, the world, and our flesh may not deceive us nor seduce us into misbelief, despair, and other great shame and vice; and though we be assailed by them, that still we may finally overcome and obtain the victory.

The Seventh Petition

But deliver us from evil.

What does this mean? We pray in this petition, as the sum of all, that our Father in heaven would deliver us from every evil of body and soul, property and honor, and finally, when our last hour has come, grant us a blessed end, and graciously take us from this vale of tears to Himself in heaven.

The Conclusion

For Thine is the kingdom and the power and the glory forever and ever. Amen.

What is meant by the word "Amen"? That I should be certain that these petitions are acceptable to our Father in heaven, and are heard by Him; for He Himself has commanded us so to pray, and has promised to hear us. Amen, Amen, that is, Yea, yea, it shall be so.

The Sacrament of Holy Baptism

As the Head of the Family Should Teach It in a Simple Way to His Household

I. The Nature of Baptism

What is Baptism?

Baptism is not simple water only, but it is the water comprehended in God's command and connected with God's word.

Which is that word of God?

Christ, our Lord, says in the last chapter of Matthew: Go ye and teach all nations, baptizing them in the name of the Father and of the Son and of the Holy Ghost.

II. The Blessings of Baptism

What does Baptism give or profit?

It works forgiveness of sins, delivers from death and the devil, and gives eternal salvation to all who believe this, as the words and promises of God declare.

Which are such words and promises of God?

Christ, our Lord, says in the last chapter of Mark: He that believeth and is baptized shall be saved; but he that believeth not shall be damned.

III. The Power of Baptism

How can water do such great things?

It is not the water indeed that does them, but the word of God which is in and with the water, and faith, which trusts such word of God in the water. For without the word of God the water is simple water and no Baptism. But with the word of God it is a Baptism, that is, a gracious water of life and a washing of regeneration in the Holy Ghost, as St. Paul says, Titus, chapter third:

[According to His mercy He saved us] By the washing of regeneration and renewing of the Holy Ghost, which He shed on us abundantly through Jesus Christ, our Savior, that, being justified by His grace, we should be made heirs according to the hope of eternal life. This is a faithful saying.

IV. The Significance of Baptizing with Water

What does such baptizing with water signify?

It signifies that the Old Adam in us should, by daily contrition and repentance, be drowned and die with all sins and evil lusts and, again, a new man daily come forth and arise, who shall live before God in righteousness and purity forever.

Where is this written?

St. Paul writes, Romans, chapter sixth: We are buried with Christ by Baptism into death, that, like as He was raised up from the dead by the glory of the Father, even so we also should walk in newness of life.

The Office of the Keys and Confession

As the Head of the Family Should Teach It in a Simple Way to His Household

What is the Office of the Keys?

It is the peculiar church power which Christ has given to His Church on earth to forgive the sins of penitent sinners, but to retain the sins of the impenitent as long as they do not repent.

Where is this written?

Thus writes the holy Evangelist John, chapter twentieth:

The Lord Jesus breathed on His disciples and saith unto them, Receive ye the Holy Ghost. Whosesoever sins ye remit, they are remitted unto them; and whosesoever sins ye retain, they are retained.

What do you believe according to these words?

I believe that, when the called ministers of Christ deal with us by His divine command, especially when they exclude manifest and impenitent sinners from the Christian congregation, and, again, when they absolve those who repent of their sins and are willing to amend, this is as valid and certain, in heaven also, as if Christ, our dear Lord, dealt with us Himself.

What is Confession?

Confession embraces two parts. One is that we confess our sins; the other, that we receive absolution, or forgiveness, from the pastor as from God Himself, and in no wise doubt, but firmly believe, that by it our sins are forgiven before God in heaven.

What sins should we confess?

Before God we should plead guilty of all sins, even of those which we do not know, as we do in the Lord's Prayer; but before the pastor we should confess those sins only which we know and feel in our hearts.

Which are these?

Here consider your station according to the Ten Commandments, whether you are a father, mother, son, daughter, master, mistress, servant; whether you have been disobedient, unfaithful, slothful; whether you have grieved any person by word or deed; whether you have stolen, neglected, or wasted aught, or done other injury.

The Sacrament of the Altar

As the Head of the Family Should Teach It in a Simple Way to His Household

What is the Sacrament of the Altar?

It is the true body and blood of our Lord Jesus Christ under the bread and wine, for us Christians to eat and to drink, instituted by Christ Himself.

Where is this written?

The holy Evangelists Matthew, Mark, Luke, and St. Paul [the Apostle] write thus:

Our Lord Jesus Christ, the same night in which He was betrayed, took bread; and when He had given thanks, He brake it and gave it to His disciples, saying, Take, eat; this is My body, which is given for you. This do in remembrance of Me.

After the same manner also He took the cup when He had supped, and when He had given thanks, He gave it to them, saying, Drink ye all of it; this cup is the new testament in My blood, which is shed for you for the remission of sins. This do, as oft as ye drink it, in remembrance of Me.

What is the benefit of such eating and drinking?

That is shown us by these words, "Given and shed for you for the remission of sins"; namely, that in the Sacrament forgiveness of sins, life, and salvation are given us through these words. For where there is forgiveness of sins, there is also life and salvation.

How can bodily eating and drinking do such great things?

It is not the eating and drinking indeed that does them, but the words here written, "Given and shed for you for the remission of sins"; which words, besides the bodily eating and drinking, are the chief thing in the Sacrament; and he that believes these words has what they say and express, namely, the forgiveness of sins.

Who, then, receives such Sacrament worthily?

Fasting and bodily preparation are indeed a fine outward training; but he is truly worthy and well prepared who has faith in these words, "Given and shed for you for the remission of sins."

But he that does not believe these words, or doubts, is unworthy and unprepared; for the words "for you" require all hearts to believe.

sins where I have done wrong, and graciously keep me this night. For into Thy hands I commend myself, my body and soul, and all things. Let Thy holy angel be with me, that the wicked Foe may have no power over me. Amen.

Then go to sleep at once and in good cheer.

SECTION II

How the Head of the Family Should Teach His Household to Pray Morning and Evening

Morning Prayer

In the morning, when you get up, make the sign of the holy cross and say:

In the name of ✚ the Father and of the Son and of the Holy Ghost. Amen.

Then, kneeling or standing, repeat the Creed and the Lord's Prayer. If you choose, you may also say this little prayer:

I thank Thee, my heavenly Father, through Jesus Christ, Thy dear Son, that Thou hast kept me this night from all harm and danger; and I pray Thee that Thou wouldst keep me this day also from sin and every evil, that all my doings and life may please Thee. For into Thy hands I commend myself, my body and soul, and all things. Let Thy holy angel be with me, that the wicked Foe may have no power over me. Amen.

Then go joyfully to your work, singing a hymn, like that of the Ten Commandments, or whatever your devotion may suggest.

Evening Prayer

In the evening, when you go to bed, make the sign of the holy cross and say:

In the name of ✚ the Father and of the Son and of the Holy Ghost. Amen.

Then, kneeling or standing, repeat the Creed and the Lord's Prayer. If you choose, you may also say this little prayer:

I thank Thee, my heavenly Father, through Jesus Christ, Thy dear Son, that Thou hast graciously kept me this day; and I pray Thee that Thou wouldst forgive me all my

How the Head of the Family Should Teach His Household to Ask a Blessing and Return Thanks

Asking a Blessing

The children and members of the household shall go to the table reverently, fold their hands, and say:

The eyes of all wait upon Thee, O Lord, and Thou givest them their meat in due season; Thou openest Thine hand and satisfiest the desire of every living thing.

Then shall be said the Lord's Prayer and the following:

Lord God, Heavenly Father, bless us and these Thy gifts which we receive from Thy bountiful goodness, through Jesus Christ, our Lord. Amen.

Returning Thanks

Also, after eating, they shall, in like manner, reverently and with folded hands say:

Oh, give thanks unto the Lord, for He is good, for His mercy endureth forever. He giveth food to all flesh; He giveth to the beast his food, and to the young ravens which cry. He delighteth not in the strength of the horse. He taketh not pleasure in the legs of a man. The Lord taketh pleasure in them that fear Him, in those that hope in His mercy.

Then shall be said the Lord's Prayer, and the following:

We thank Thee, Lord God, Heavenly Father, through Jesus Christ, our Lord, for all Thy benefits, who livest and reignest forever and ever. Amen.

305

SECTION IV

Christian Questions with Their Answers

Drawn Up by Dr. Martin Luther for Those Who Intend to Go to the Sacrament

After Confession and instruction in the Ten Commandments, the Creed, the Lord's Prayer, and the Sacraments of Baptism and the Holy Supper, the pastor may ask, or one may ask himself:

1. Do you believe that you are a sinner?

Yes, I believe it; I am a sinner.

2. How do you know this?

From the Ten Commandments; these I have not kept.

3. Are you also sorry for your sins?

Yes, I am sorry that I have sinned against God.

4. What have you deserved of God by your sins?

His wrath and displeasure, temporal death, and eternal damnation. Rom. 6:21, 23.

5. Do you also hope to be saved?

Yes, such is my hope.

6. In whom, then, do you trust?

In my dear Lord Jesus Christ.

7. Who is Christ?

The Son of God, true God and man.

8. How many Gods are there?

Only one; but there are three Persons: Father, Son, and Holy Ghost.

9. What, then, has Christ done for you that you trust in Him?

He died for me and shed His blood for me on the cross for the forgiveness of sins.

10. Did the Father also die for you?

He did not; for the Father is God only, the Holy Ghost likewise; but the Son is true God and true man; He died for me and shed His blood for me.

11. How do you know this?

From the holy Gospel and from the words of the Sacrament; and by His body and blood given me as a pledge in the Sacrament.

12. How do those words read?

Our Lord Jesus Christ, the same night in which He was betrayed, took bread; and when He had given thanks, He brake it and gave it to His disciples, saying, Take, eat; this is My body, which is given for you. This do in remembrance of Me.

After the same manner also He took the cup when He had supped, and when He had given thanks, He gave it to them, saying, Drink ye all of it; this cup is the new testament in My blood, which is shed for you for the remission of sins. This do, as oft as ye drink it, in remembrance of Me.

13. You believe, then, that the true body and blood of Christ are in the Sacrament?

Yes, I believe it.

14. What induces you to believe this?

The word of Christ, Take, eat, this is My body; Drink ye all of it, this is My blood.

15. What ought we to do when we eat His body and drink His blood, and thus receive the pledge?

We ought to remember and proclaim His death and the shedding of His blood, as He taught us: This do, as oft as ye drink it, in remembrance of Me.

16. Why ought we to remember and proclaim His death?

That we may learn to believe that no creature could make satisfaction for our sins but Christ, true God and man; and that we may learn to look with terror at our sins, and to regard them as great indeed, and to find joy and comfort in Him alone, and thus be saved through such faith.

17. What was it that moved Him to die and make satisfaction for your sins?

His great love to His Father and to me and other sinners, as it is written in John 14; Rom. 5; Gal. 2; Eph. 5.

18. Finally, why do you wish to go to the Sacrament?

That I may learn to believe that Christ died for *my* sin out of great love, as before said; and that I may also learn of Him to love God and my neighbor.

19. What should admonish and incite a Christian to receive the Sacrament frequently?

In respect to God, both the command and the promise of Christ the Lord should move him, and in respect to himself, the trouble that lies heavy on him, on account of which such command, encouragement, and promise are given.

20. But what shall a person do if he be not sensible of such trouble and feel no hunger and thirst for the Sacrament?

To such a person no better advice can be given than that, in the first place, he put his hand into his bosom, and feel whether he still have flesh and blood, and that he by all means believe what the Scriptures say of it in Gal. 5 and Rom. 7.

Secondly, that he look around to see whether he is still in the world, and keep in mind that there will be no lack of sin and trouble, as the Scriptures say in John 15 and 16; 1 John 2 and 5.

Thirdly, he will certainly have the devil also about him, who with his lying and murdering, day and night, will let him have no peace within or without, as the Scriptures picture him in John 8 and 16; 1 Peter 5; Eph. 6; 2 Tim. 2.

Note

These questions and answers are no child's play, but are drawn up with great earnestness of purpose by the venerable and pious Dr. Luther for both young and old. Let each one take heed and likewise consider it a serious matter; for St. Paul writes to the Galatians, chapter sixth: "Be not deceived; God is not mocked."

SERVICE OF
CORPORATE CONFESSION
AND ABSOLUTION

1. A HYMN may be sung.

Stand

P In the name of the Father and of the ✠ Son and of the Holy Spirit.

G **Amen**

2. The minister says the following or another appropriate prayer.

P Father of mercies and God of all consolation, come to the aid of your people, turning us from our sin to live for you alone. Give us the power of your Holy Spirit that we may attend to your Word, confess our sins, receive your forgiveness, and grow into the fullness of your Son Jesus Christ, our Lord and our Redeemer. (203)

G **Amen**

3. PSALM 51 or another appropriate psalm is sung or said.

Sit

4. Then may follow a CONFESSIONAL ADDRESS or an EXHORTATION after the following manner:

P Dearly beloved, since it is our intention to come to the Holy Supper of our Lord Jesus Christ, it is proper that we diligently examine ourselves as St. Paul tells us to do, for this Holy Sacrament has been instituted for the special comfort and strengthening of those who humbly confess their sins and hunger and thirst for righteousness.

But if we thus examine ourselves, we shall find nothing in us but sin and death, from which we cannot set ourselves free. Therefore our Lord Jesus Christ has had mercy on us and has taken on himself our nature that he might fulfill for us the whole will and law of God and for us and for our deliverance suffer death and all that we by our sins have deserved. And that we should the more confidently believe

308

this and be strengthened by our faith in cheerful obedience to his holy will, he has instituted the Holy Sacrament of his Supper, in which he feeds us with his body and gives us to drink of his blood.

Therefore whoever eats of this bread and drinks of this cup, firmly believing the words of Christ, dwells in Christ, and Christ in him, and has eternal life.

We should do this also in remembrance of him, showing his death, that he was delivered for our offenses and raised again for our justification and, giving him our most hearty thanks, take up our cross and follow him and according to his commandment love one another as he has loved us. For we are all one body, even as we all eat of his body and drink of his blood.

℗ Humble yourselves before God, confess your sins to him, and implore his forgiveness.

Kneel/Stand

℅ **O almighty God, merciful Father, I, a poor, miserable sinner, confess to you all my sins and iniquities with which I have ever offended you and justly deserved your punishment now and forever. But I am heartily sorry for them and sincerely repent of them, and I pray you of your boundless mercy and for the sake of the holy, innocent, bitter sufferings and death of your beloved Son, Jesus Christ, to be gracious and merciful to me, a poor sinful being. Forgive me all my sins and grant me the power of your Holy Spirit that I may amend my sinful life.**

5. The minister stands and says to the penitents:

℗ God be gracious to you and strengthen your faith.

℅ **Amen**

6. The minister shall preferably absolve the penitents individually at the altar, laying his hand on each and pronouncing the following absolution, or he may absolve all the penitents corporately from the altar.

℗ In the stead and by the command of my Lord Jesus Christ I forgive you all your sins in the name of the Father and of the ✠ Son and of the Holy Spirit.

℅ **Amen**

℗ The God of peace will sanctify you wholly and keep your spirit, soul, and body sound and blameless at the coming of our Lord Jesus Christ. He who calls you is faithful, and he will do it. Go in ✠ peace.

℅ **Amen**

INDIVIDUAL CONFESSION
AND ABSOLUTION

1. *When, during consultation with the pastor, a person desires individual confession and absolution, the following order may be used. The confession made by the penitent is protected from disclosure. The pastor is at all times obligated to respect the confidential nature of a confession.*

2. *The penitent, who may kneel, says:*

Dear pastor, hear my confession.

3. *The pastor responds:*

℗ Let us begin in the name of God, to whom all hearts are open and from whom no secrets are hid.

The pastor and penitent say:

In the name of God, the Father, the Son, and the Holy Spirit.
Hear my prayer, O Lord; let my cry for help come to you.
Do not hide your face from me when I am in distress.
Turn your ear to me; when I call, answer me quickly.   (Ps. 102:1-2)

Have mercy on me, O God, according to your unfailing love;
   according to your great compassion blot out my transgressions.
Wash away all my iniquity and cleanse me from my sin.
For I know my transgressions, and my sin is always before me.
Against you, you only, have I sinned and done what is evil in your sight.   (Ps. 51:1-4a)

The penitent continues:

I have lived as if God did not matter and as if I mattered most.
My Lord's name I have not honored as I should; my worship and prayers have
   faltered.
I have not let his love have its way with me, and so my love for others has failed.
There are those whom I have hurt, and those whom I failed to help.
My thoughts and desires have been soiled with sin.
What troubles me particularly is that . . .

4. Here the penitent confesses those sins which are known and those which disturb or grieve him/her.

5. The pastor may then offer admonition and comfort from the Holy Scriptures. Then they say together:

Create in me a clean heart, O God,
    and renew a right spirit within me.
Cast me not away from your presence,
    and take not your Holy Spirit from me.
Restore to me the joy of your salvation,
    and uphold me with your free Spirit.   (Ps. 51:10-12)

The penitent continues:

O Almighty God, merciful Father, I, a poor, miserable sinner, confess to you all my sins and iniquities with which I have ever offended you and justly deserved your punishment now and forever. But I am heartily sorry for them and sincerely repent of them, and I pray you of your boundless mercy and for the sake of the holy, innocent, bitter sufferings and death of your beloved son, Jesus Christ, to be gracious and merciful to me, a poor sinful being.

6. The pastor stands and says:

℗ Do you believe that the word of Christ's forgiveness I speak to you is from the Lord himself?

℟ Yes, I do.

7. The pastor lays his hand on the head of the penitent and says:

℗ Receive the forgiveness Christ won for you by his Passion, death, and resurrection. By the command of our Lord Jesus Christ I, a called and ordained servant of the Word, forgive you your sins in the name of the Father and of the ✠ Son and of the Holy Spirit.

℟ Amen

The penitent and pastor continue:

Sing to the Lord, you saints of his; praise his holy name. For his anger lasts only a moment, but his favor lasts a lifetime; weeping may remain for a night, but rejoicing comes in the morning. O Lord my God, I will give you thanks forever. (Ps. 30:4-5, 12b)

8. The pastor says:

℗ Go in the strength, the peace, and the joy of the Lord, and come soon to receive Christ's body and blood, and being joined to him, live toward the work and the beauty he would fulfill in you for himself and for others. Go, you are free.

HOLY BAPTISM

In Cases of Emergency

1. In urgent situations, in the absence of the pastor, any Christian may administer Holy Baptism.

2. Take water, pour or sprinkle the water on the head of the child, saying:

____name____, I baptize you in the name of the Father and of the Son and of the Holy Spirit ✠. Amen

3. If time permits, the Baptism may be preceded by the following prayer and the Lord's Prayer.

Eternal, merciful Father, we pray you, extend your goodness and mercy to this child that __he/she__ may enjoy the everlasting blessings of your heavenly washing and may come to the eternal kingdom which you have prepared through Jesus Christ, our Lord. Amen (204)

Our Father who art in heaven,
hallowed be thy name,
thy kingdom come,
thy will be done
on earth as it is in heaven.
Give us this day our daily bread;
and forgive us our trespasses
as we forgive those
who trespass against us;
and lead us not into temptation,
but deliver us from evil.
For thine is the kingdom
and the power and the glory
forever and ever. Amen

OR

Our Father in heaven,
hallowed be your name,
your kingdom come,
your will be done
on earth as in heaven.
Give us today our daily bread.
Forgive us our sins
as we forgive those
who sin against us.
Lead us not into temptation,
but deliver us from evil.
For the kingdom, the power,
and the glory are yours
now and forever. Amen

4. Baptism administered by a lay person shall immediately be reported to the pastor for its recognition in the congregation.

THE PSALMS

1

* V E♭: Lydian

[1]Blessed is the man who does not
walk in the counsel of the wicked*
 or stand in the way of sinners
 or sit in the seat of mockers.

[2]But his delight is in the law
of the Lord,*
 and on his law he meditates
 day and night.

[3]He is like a tree planted
by streams of water,
which yields its fruit in season
and whose leaf does not wither.*
 Whatever he does prospers.

[4]Not so the wicked!*
 They are like chaff
 that the wind blows away.

[5]Therefore the wicked
will not stand in the judgment,*
 nor sinners in the assembly
 of the righteous.

[6]For the Lord watches over
the way of the righteous,*

but the way of the wicked
will perish.

Glory be to the Father and to the Son*
 and to the Holy Spirit;
as it was in the beginning,*
 is now, and will be forever. Amen

2

* IX g²: Aeolian

[1]Why do the nations rage*
 and the peoples plot in vain?

[2]The kings of the earth take their stand
and the rulers gather together*
 against the Lord
 and against his Anointed One.

[3]"Let us break their chains," they say,*
 "and throw off their fetters."

[4]The One enthroned in heaven laughs;*
 the Lord scoffs at them.

[5]Then he rebukes them in his anger*
 and terrifies them in his wrath,
 saying,

313

⁶"I have installed my King*
  on Zion, my holy hill."

⁷I will proclaim the decree of the Lord:*
  He said to me, "You are my Son;
  today I have become your Father.

⁸Ask of me, and I will make
  the nations your inheritance,*
    the ends of the earth your
    possession.

⁹You will rule them with an iron
  scepter;*
    you will dash them to pieces
    like pottery."

¹⁰Therefore, you kings, be wise;*
  be warned, you rulers of the earth.

¹¹Serve the Lord with fear*
  and rejoice with trembling.

¹²Kiss the Son, lest he be angry
  and you be destroyed in your way,
  for his wrath can flare up in a
  moment.*
    Blessed are all
    who take refuge in him.

Glory be to the Father and to the Son*
  and to the Holy Spirit;
as it was in the beginning,*
  is now, and will be forever. Amen

Know that the Lord has set apart
  the godly for himself;*
    the Lord will hear
    when I call to him.

⁴In your anger do not sin;*
  when you are on your beds,
  search your hearts and be silent.

⁵Offer right sacrifices*
  and trust in the Lord.

⁶Many are asking, "Who can show us
  any good?"*
    Let the light of your face shine
    upon us, O Lord.

⁷You have filled my heart
  with greater joy*
    than when their grain and new
    wine abound.

⁸I will lie down and sleep in peace,*
  for you alone, O Lord,
  make me dwell in safety.

Glory be to the Father and to the Son*
  and to the Holy Spirit;
as it was in the beginning,*
  is now, and will be forever. Amen

6

I d: Dorian

¹O Lord, do not rebuke me in your
anger*
  or discipline me in your wrath.

²Be merciful to me, Lord, for I am
faint;*
  O Lord, heal me,
  for my bones are in agony.

³My soul is in anguish.*
  How long, O Lord, how long?

⁴Turn, O Lord, and deliver me;*

4

IX g: Aeolian

¹Answer me when I call to you,
  O my righteous God.*
    Give me relief from my distress;
    be merciful to me and hear my
    prayer.

²How long, O men, will you turn
  my glory into shame?*
    How long will you love delusions
    and seek false gods?

save me because of
your unfailing love.

⁵No one remembers you
when he is dead.*
    Who praises you from the grave?

⁶I am worn out from groaning;*
    all night long I flood my bed
    with weeping
    and drench my couch with tears.

⁷My eyes grow weak with sorrow;*
    they fail because of all my foes.

⁸Away from me, all you who do evil,*
    for the Lord has heard my weeping.

⁹The Lord has heard my cry for
mercy;*
    the Lord accepts my prayer.

¹⁰May all my enemies be ashamed
and dismayed;*
    may they turn back in sudden
    disgrace.

Glory be to the Father and to the Son*
    and to the Holy Spirit;
as it was in the beginning,*
    is now, and will be forever. Amen

the moon and the stars,
which you have set in place,

⁴what is man that you are
mindful of him,*
    the son of man that you
    care for him?

⁵You made him a little lower than the
heavenly beings*
    and crowned him with glory and
    honor.

⁶You made him ruler over the works
of your hands;*
    you put everything under his feet:

⁷all flocks and herds,*
    and the beasts of the field,

⁸the birds of the air,
and the fish of the sea,*
    all that swim the paths of the seas.

⁹O Lord, our Lord,*
    how majestic is your name
    in all the earth!

Glory be to the Father and to the Son*
    and to the Holy Spirit;
as it was in the beginning,*
    is now, and will be forever. Amen

8

III f♯: Phrygian

¹O Lord, our Lord, how majestic is your
name in all the earth!*
    You have set your glory
    above the heavens.

²From the lips of children and infants
you have ordained praise*
    because of your enemies,
    to silence the foe and the avenger.

³When I consider your heavens,
the work of your fingers,*

16

VII E: Mixolydian

¹Keep me safe, O God,*
    for in you I take refuge.

²I said to the Lord, "You are my Lord;*
    apart from you I have no good
    thing."

³As for the saints who are in the land,*
    they are the glorious ones
    in whom is all my delight.

⁴The sorrows of those will increase
who run after other gods.*

I will not pour out their libations
of blood or take up their names on
my lips.

⁵Lord, you have assigned me my
portion and my cup;*
  you have made my lot secure.

⁶The boundary lines have fallen for me
in pleasant places;*
  surely I have a delightful
  inheritance.

⁷I will praise the Lord,
who counsels me;*
  even at night
  my heart instructs me.

⁸I have set the Lord
always before me.*
  Because he is at my right hand,
  I will not be shaken.

⁹Therefore my heart is glad
and my tongue rejoices;*
  my body also will rest secure,

¹⁰because you will not abandon me
to the grave,*
  nor will you let your Holy One
  see decay.

¹¹You have made known to me the path
of life;*
  you will fill me with joy in your
  presence, with eternal pleasures at
  your right hand.

Glory be to the Father and to the Son*
  and to the Holy Spirit;
as it was in the beginning,*
  is now, and will be forever. Amen

¹I love you,*
  O Lord, my strength.

²The Lord is my rock, my fortress and
my deliverer; my God is my rock,
in whom I take refuge.*
  He is my shield and the horn of my
  salvation, my stronghold.

³I call to the Lord,
who is worthy of praise,*
  and I am saved from my enemies.

⁴The cords of death entangled me;*
  the torrents of destruction
  overwhelmed me.

⁵The cords of the grave
coiled around me;*
  the snares of death confronted me.

⁶In my distress I called to the Lord;
I cried to my God for help.*
  From his temple he heard my
  voice; my cry came before him,
  into his ears.

⁷The earth trembled and quaked, and
the foundations of the mountains
shook;*
  they trembled because he was
  angry.

⁸Smoke rose from his nostrils;
consuming fire came from his mouth,*
  burning coals blazed out of it.

⁹He parted the heavens
and came down;*
  dark clouds were under his feet.

¹⁰He mounted the cherubim and flew;*
  he soared on the wings of the wind.

¹¹He made darkness his covering,
his canopy around him—*
  the dark rain clouds of the sky.

¹²Out of the brightness of his presence
clouds advanced,*
  with hailstones
  and bolts of lightning.

18

IX g: Aeolian

¹³The Lord thundered from heaven;*
   the voice of the Most High
   resounded.

¹⁴He shot his arrows and
   scattered the enemies,*
      great bolts of lightning
      and routed them.

¹⁵The valleys of the sea were exposed
   and the foundations
   of the earth laid bare*
      at your rebuke, O Lord, at the
      blast of breath from your nostrils.

¹⁶He reached down from on high
   and took hold of me;*
      he drew me out of deep waters.

¹⁷He rescued me from my powerful
   enemy,*
      from my foes,
      who were too strong for me.

¹⁸They confronted me in the day
   of my disaster,*
      but the Lord was my support.

¹⁹He brought me out
   into a spacious place;*
      he rescued me because he delighted
      in me.

²⁰The Lord has dealt with me
   according to my righteousness;*
      according to the cleanness
      of my hands he has rewarded me.

²¹For I have kept the ways of the Lord;*
   I have not done evil
   by turning from my God.

²²All his laws are before me;*
   I have not turned away
   from his decrees.

²³I have been blameless before him*
   and have kept myself from sin.

²⁴The Lord has rewarded me
   according to my righteousness,*
      according to the cleanness
      of my hands in his sight.

²⁵To the faithful
   you show yourself faithful,*
      to the blameless
      you show yourself blameless,

²⁶to the pure you show yourself pure,*
   but to the crooked
   you show yourself shrewd.

²⁷You save the humble*
   but bring low those
   whose eyes are haughty.

²⁸You, O Lord, keep my lamp burning;*
   my God turns my darkness into
   light.

²⁹With your help I can advance
   against a troop;*
      with my God I can scale a wall.

³⁰As for God, his way is perfect;
   the word of the Lord is flawless.*
      He is a shield
      for all who take refuge in him.

³¹For who is God besides the Lord?*
   And who is the Rock
   except our God?

³²It is God who arms me with strength*
   and makes my way perfect.

³³He makes my feet like the feet
   of a deer;*
      he enables me to stand
      on the heights.

³⁴He trains my hands for battle;*
   my arms can bend a bow of
   bronze.

³⁵You give me your shield of victory,
   and your right hand sustains me;*
      you stoop down to make me great.

³⁶You broaden the path beneath me,*
   so that my ankles do not turn.

³⁷I pursued my enemies
   and overtook them;*
      I did not turn back till they
      were destroyed.

³⁸I crushed them so that they
could not rise;*
they fell beneath my feet.

³⁹You armed me with strength
for battle;*
you made my adversaries
bow at my feet.

⁴⁰You made my enemies
turn their backs in flight,*
and I destroyed my foes.

⁴¹They cried for help,
but there was no one to save them—*
to the Lord, but he did not answer.

⁴²I beat them as fine as dust
borne on the wind;*
I poured them out like mud
in the streets.

⁴³You have delivered me from the
attacks of the people;
you have made me the head of
nations;*
people I did not know
are subject to me.

⁴⁴As soon as they hear me,
they obey me;*
foreigners cringe before me.

⁴⁵They all lose heart;*
they come trembling
from their strongholds.

⁴⁶The Lord lives! Praise be to my Rock!*
Exalted be God my Savior!

⁴⁷He is the God who avenges me,*
who subdues nations under me,

⁴⁸who saves me from my enemies.*
You exalted me above my foes;
from violent men you rescued me.

⁴⁹Therefore I will praise you
among the nations, O Lord;*
I will sing praises to your name.

⁵⁰He gives his king great victories;*
he shows unfailing kindness to his
anointed, to David and his
descendants forever.

Glory be to the Father and to the Son*
and to the Holy Spirit;
as it was in the beginning,*
is now, and will be forever. Amen

19

XI D: Ionian

¹The heavens declare the glory of God;*
the skies proclaim the work
of his hands.

²Day after day they pour forth speech;*
night after night
they display knowledge.

³There is no speech or language*
where their voice is not heard.

⁴Their voice goes out
into all the earth,*
their words to the ends of the
world.

⁵In the heavens he has pitched a tent
for the sun,*
which is like a bridegroom coming
forth from his pavilion,
like a champion rejoicing
to run his course.

⁶It rises at one end of the heavens
and makes its circuit to the other;*
nothing is hidden from its heat.

⁷The law of the Lord is perfect,
reviving the soul.*
The statutes of the Lord
are trustworthy,
making wise the simple.

⁸The precepts of the Lord are right,
giving joy to the heart.*
The commands of the Lord are
radiant, giving light to the eyes.

⁹The fear of the Lord is pure,
enduring forever.*

The ordinances of the Lord
are sure and altogether righteous.

¹⁰They are more precious than gold,
than much pure gold;*
they are sweeter than honey,
than honey from the comb.

¹¹By them is your servant warned;*
in keeping them
there is great reward.

¹²Who can discern his errors?*
Forgive my hidden faults.

¹³Keep your servant
also from willful sins;
may they not rule over me.*
Then will I be blameless,
innocent of great transgression.

¹⁴May the words of my mouth
and the meditation of my heart
be pleasing in your sight,*
O Lord, my Rock
and my Redeemer.

Glory be to the Father and to the Son*
and to the Holy Spirit;
as it was in the beginning,*
is now, and will be forever. Amen

22

I d: Dorian

¹My God, my God, why have you
forsaken me?*
Why are you so far from saving
me, so far from the words of my
groaning?

²O my God, I cry out by day,
but you do not answer,*
by night, and am not silent.

³Yet you are enthroned
as the Holy One;*
you are the praise of Israel.

⁴In you our fathers put their trust;*
they trusted
and you delivered them.

⁵They cried to you and were saved;*
in you they trusted
and were not disappointed.

⁶But I am a worm and not a man,*
scorned by men
and despised by the people.

⁷All who see me mock me;*
they hurl insults, shaking their
heads:

⁸"He trusts in the Lord;
let the Lord rescue him.*
Let him deliver him,
since he delights in him."

⁹Yet you brought me out of the womb;*
you made me trust in you
even at my mother's breast.

¹⁰From birth I was cast upon you;*
from my mother's womb
you have been my God.

¹¹Do not be far from me,*
for trouble is near
and there is no one to help.

¹²Many bulls surround me;*
strong bulls of Bashan encircle me.

¹³Roaring lions tearing their prey*
open their mouths wide against me.

¹⁴I am poured out like water,
and all my bones are out of joint.*
My heart has turned to wax;
it has melted away within me.

¹⁵My strength is dried up like a
potsherd, and my tongue sticks to the
roof of my mouth;*
you lay me in the dust of death.

¹⁶Dogs have surrounded me;
a band of evil men has encircled me,*
they have pierced
my hands and my feet.

319

¹⁷I can count all my bones;*
   people stare and gloat over me.

¹⁸They divide my garments
among them*
   and cast lots for my clothing.

¹⁹But you, O Lord, be not far off;*
   O my Strength, come quickly to
   help me.

²⁰Deliver my life from the sword,*
   my precious life from the power
   of the dogs.

²¹Rescue me from the mouth of the
lions;*
   save me from the horns
   of the wild oxen.

²²I will declare your name to my
brothers;*
   in the congregation
   I will praise you.

²³You who fear the Lord, praise him!*
   All you descendants of Jacob,
   honor him! Revere him, all you
   descendants of Israel!

²⁴For he has not despised or disdained
the suffering of the afflicted one;*
   he has not hidden his face
   from him
   but has listened to his cry for help.

²⁵From you comes my praise
in the great assembly;*
   before those who fear you will I
   fulfill my vows.

²⁶The poor will eat and be satisfied;
they who seek the Lord
will praise him—*
   may your hearts live forever!

²⁷All the ends of the earth
will remember and turn to the Lord,*
   and all the families of the nations
   will bow down before him,

²⁸for dominion belongs to the Lord*
   and he rules over the nations.

²⁹All the rich of the earth
will feast and worship;*
   all who go down to the dust will
   kneel before him—those who
   cannot keep themselves alive.

³⁰Posterity will serve him;*
   future generations will
   be told about the Lord.

³¹They will proclaim his righteousness
to a people yet unborn—*
   for he has done it.

Glory be to the Father and to the Son*
   and to the Holy Spirit;
as it was in the beginning,*
   is now, and will be forever. Amen

23

V Eb: Lydian

¹The Lord is my shepherd,*
   I shall lack nothing.

²He makes me lie down in green
pastures,*
   he leads me beside quiet waters,

³he restores my soul.*
   He guides me in paths of
   righteousness for his name's sake.

⁴Even though I walk through the valley
of the shadow of death,
I will fear no evil,*
   for you are with me; your rod and
   your staff, they comfort me.

⁵You prepare a table before me
in the presence of my enemies.*
   You anoint my head with oil;
   my cup overflows.

⁶Surely goodness and love will follow
me all the days of my life,*

and I will dwell in the house
of the Lord forever.

Glory be to the Father and to the Son*
and to the Holy Spirit;
as it was in the beginning,*
is now, and will be forever. Amen

Glory be to the Father and to the Son*
and to the Holy Spirit;
as it was in the beginning,*
is now, and will be forever. Amen

24

XI A: Ionian

¹The earth is the Lord's,
and everything in it,*
the world, and all who live in it;

²for he founded it upon the seas*
and established it upon the waters.

³Who may ascend the hill of the Lord?*
Who may stand in his holy place?

⁴He who has clean hands
and a pure heart,*
who does not lift up his soul to an
idol or swear by what is false.

⁵He will receive blessing from the Lord*
and vindication from God his
Savior.

⁶Such is the generation of those
who seek him,*
who seek your face, O God of Jacob.

⁷Lift up your heads, O you gates;
be lifted up, you ancient doors,*
that the King of glory may come in.

⁸Who is this King of glory?*
The Lord strong and mighty,
the Lord mighty in battle.

⁹Lift up your heads, O you gates;
lift them up, you ancient doors,*
that the King of glory may come in.

¹⁰Who is he, this King of glory?*
The Lord Almighty—
he is the King of glory.

25

III f♯: Phrygian

¹To you, O Lord,*
I lift up my soul;

²in you I trust, O my God.*
Do not let me be put to shame, nor
let my enemies triumph over me.

³No one whose hope is in you
will ever be put to shame,*
but they will be put to shame
who are treacherous without excuse.

⁴Show me your ways, O Lord,*
teach me your paths;

⁵guide me in your truth and teach me,*
for you are God my Savior, and
my hope is in you all day long.

⁶Remember, O Lord,
your great mercy and love,*
for they are from of old.

⁷Remember not the sins of my youth
and my rebellious ways;*
according to your love remember
me, for you are good, O Lord.

⁸Good and upright is the Lord;*
therefore he instructs sinners
in his ways.

⁹He guides the humble in what is right*
and teaches them his way.

¹⁰All the ways of the Lord
are loving and faithful*
for those who keep the demands
of his covenant.

¹¹For the sake of your name, O Lord,*

forgive my iniquity,
though it is great.

¹²Who, then, is the man
that fears the Lord?*
    He will instruct him in the way
    chosen for him.

¹³He will spend his days in prosperity,*
and his descendants will
    inherit the land.

¹⁴The Lord confides in those
who fear him;*
    he makes his covenant
    known to them.

¹⁵My eyes are ever on the Lord,*
for only he will release my feet
    from the snare.

¹⁶Turn to me and be gracious to me,*
for I am lonely and afflicted.

¹⁷The troubles of my heart
have multiplied;*
    free me from my anguish.

¹⁸Look upon my affliction
and my distress*
    and take away all my sins.

¹⁹See how my enemies have increased*
and how fiercely they hate me!

²⁰Guard my life and rescue me;*
    let me not be put to shame,
    for I take refuge in you.

²¹May integrity and uprightness
protect me,*
    because my hope is in you.

²²Redeem Israel, O God,*
    from all their troubles!

Glory be to the Father and to the Son*
and to the Holy Spirit;
as it was in the beginning,*
is now, and will be forever. Amen

27

XI A: Ionian

¹The Lord is my light and my
salvation—whom shall I fear?*
    The Lord is the stronghold of my
    life—of whom shall I be afraid?

²When evil men advance against me
to devour my flesh,*
    when my enemies and my foes attack
    me, they will stumble and fall.

³Though an army besiege me,
my heart will not fear;*
    though war break out against me,
    even then will I be confident.

⁴One thing I ask of the Lord, this is
what I seek:*
    that I may dwell in the house of
    the Lord all the days of my life,
    to gaze upon the beauty of the
    Lord and to seek him in his
    temple.

⁵For in the day of trouble
he will keep me safe in his dwelling;*
    he will hide me in the shelter
    of his tabernacle and set me
    high upon a rock.

⁶Then my head will be exalted
above the enemies who surround me;*
    at his tabernacle will I sacrifice
    with shouts of joy;
    I will sing and make music
    to the Lord.

⁷Hear my voice when I call, O Lord;*
    be merciful to me and answer me.

⁸My heart says of you,
"Seek his face!"*
    Your face, Lord, I will seek.

⁹Do not hide your face from me,
do not turn your servant away in
anger; you have been my helper.*
  Do not reject me or forsake me,
  O God my Savior.

¹⁰Though my father and mother
forsake me,*
  the Lord will receive me.

¹¹Teach me your way, O Lord;*
  lead me in a straight path
  because of my oppressors.

¹²Do not turn me over to the desire
of my foes,*
  for false witnesses rise up against
  me, breathing out violence.

¹³I am still confident of this:*
  I will see the goodness of the Lord
  in the land of the living.

¹⁴Wait for the Lord;*
  be strong and take heart
  and wait for the Lord.

Glory be to the Father and to the Son*
  and to the Holy Spirit;
as it was in the beginning,*
  is now, and will be forever. Amen

28

IX g: Aeolian

¹To you I call, O Lord my Rock;
do not turn a deaf ear to me.*
  For if you remain silent, I will
  be like those who have gone down
  to the pit.

²Hear my cry for mercy
as I call to you for help,*
  as I lift up my hands
  toward your Most Holy Place.

³Do not drag me away with the
wicked, with those who do evil,*

who speak cordially with their
neighbors but harbor malice in
their hearts.

⁴Repay them for their deeds
and for their evil work;*
  repay them for what their hands
  have done and bring back upon
  them what they deserve.

⁵Since they show no regard
for the works of the Lord
and what his hands have done,*
  he will tear them down
  and never build them up again.

⁶Praise be to the Lord,*
  for he has heard my cry for
  mercy.

⁷The Lord is my strength
and my shield;*
  my heart trusts in him,
  and I am helped.
My heart leaps for joy*
  and I will give thanks
  to him in song.

⁸The Lord is the strength of his
people,*
  a fortress of salvation
  for his anointed one.

⁹Save your people
and bless your inheritance;*
  be their shepherd
  and carry them forever.

Glory be to the Father and to the Son*
  and to the Holy Spirit;
as it was in the beginning,*
  is now, and will be forever. Amen

32

I d: Dorian

¹Blessed is he
  whose transgressions are forgiven,*
  whose sins are covered.

²Blessed is the man whose sin the
Lord does not count against him*
and in whose spirit is no deceit.

³When I kept silent,
my bones wasted away*
through my groaning all day long.

⁴For day and night
your hand was heavy upon me;*
my strength was sapped
as in the heat of summer.

⁵Then I acknowledged my sin to you
and did not cover up my iniquity.*
I said, "I will confess my
transgressions to the Lord"—and
you forgave the guilt of my sin.

⁶Therefore let everyone who is godly
pray to you while you may be found;*
surely when the mighty waters rise,
they will not reach him.

⁷You are my hiding place;
you will protect me from trouble*
and surround me with
songs of deliverance.

⁸I will instruct you and teach you
in the way you should go;*
I will counsel you
and watch over you.

⁹Do not be like the horse
or the mule,*
which have no understanding but
must be controlled by bit and
bridle or they will not come to you.

¹⁰Many are the woes of the wicked,*
but the Lord's unfailing love
surrounds the man who trusts in him.

¹¹Rejoice in the Lord and be glad,
you righteous;*
sing, all you who are upright
in heart!

Glory be to the Father and to the Son*
and to the Holy Spirit;

as it was in the beginning,*
is now, and will be forever. Amen

34

XI C: Ionian

¹I will extol the Lord at all times;*
his praise will always be
on my lips.

²My soul will boast in the Lord;*
let the afflicted hear and rejoice.

³Glorify the Lord with me;*
let us exalt his name together.

⁴I sought the Lord,
and he answered me;*
he delivered me from all my fears.

⁵Those who look to him are radiant;*
their faces are never covered
with shame.

⁶This poor man called, and the Lord
heard him;*
he saved him out of all his
troubles.

⁷The angel of the Lord encamps
around those who fear him,*
and he delivers them.

⁸Taste and see that the Lord is good;*
blessed is the man who takes
refuge in him.

⁹Fear the Lord, you his saints,*
for those who fear him lack
nothing.

¹⁰The lions may grow weak and
hungry,*
but those who seek the Lord
lack no good thing.

¹¹Come, my children, listen to me;*
  I will teach you
    the fear of the Lord.

¹²Whoever of you loves life*
  and desires to see
    many good days,

¹³keep your tongue from evil*
  and your lips from speaking lies.

¹⁴Turn from evil and do good;*
  seek peace and pursue it.

¹⁵The eyes of the Lord are on the
  righteous*
    and his ears are attentive
    to their cry;

¹⁶the face of the Lord is against those
  who do evil,*
    to cut off the memory of them
    from the earth.

¹⁷The righteous cry out, and the
  Lord hears them;*
    he delivers them from all
    their troubles.

¹⁸The Lord is close to the
  brokenhearted*
    and saves those who are crushed
    in spirit.

¹⁹A righteous man may have many
  troubles,*
    but the Lord delivers him
    from them all;

²⁰he protects all his bones,*
  not one of them will be broken.

²¹Evil will slay the wicked;*
  the foes of the righteous
    will be condemned.

²²The Lord redeems his servants;*
  no one who takes refuge in him
    will be condemned.

Glory be to the Father and to the Son*
  and to the Holy Spirit;
as it was in the beginning,*
  is now, and will be forever. Amen

36

VII E: Mixolydian

¹An oracle is within my heart
concerning the sinfulness of the
wicked:*
  There is no fear of God
  before his eyes.

²For in his own eyes he flatters himself*
  too much to detect or hate his sin.

³The words of his mouth
are wicked and deceitful;*
  he has ceased to be wise
  and to do good.

⁴Even on his bed he plots evil;*
  he commits himself to a sinful
  course and does not reject what is
  wrong.

⁵Your love, O Lord,
reaches to the heavens,*
  your faithfulness to the skies.

⁶Your righteousness
is like the mighty mountains,
your justice like the great deep.*
  O Lord, you preserve both man
  and beast.

⁷How priceless is your unfailing love!*
  Both high and low among men
  find refuge in the shadow of your
  wings.

⁸They feast on the abundance
of your house;*
  you give them drink from your
  river of delights.

⁹For with you is the fountain of life;*
  in your light we see light.

¹⁰Continue your love
to those who know you,*
  your righteousness to the upright
  in heart.

¹¹May the foot of the proud
not come against me,*
 nor the hand of the wicked drive
 me away.

¹²See how the evildoers lie fallen—*
 thrown down, not able to rise!

Glory be to the Father and to the Son*
 and to the Holy Spirit;
as it was in the beginning,*
 is now, and will be forever. Amen

38

* III f♯: Phrygian

¹O Lord, do not rebuke me in your anger*
 or discipline me in your wrath.

²For your arrows have pierced me,*
 and your hand has come down
upon me.

³Because of your wrath
 there is no health in my body;*
 my bones have no soundness
 because of my sin.

⁴My guilt has overwhelmed me*
 like a burden too heavy to bear.

⁵My wounds fester and are loathsome*
 because of my sinful folly.

⁶I am bowed down
 and brought very low;*
 all day long I go about mourning.

⁷My back is filled with searing pain;*
 there is no health in my body.

⁸I am feeble and utterly crushed;*
 I groan in anguish of heart.

⁹All my longings lie open before you,
 O Lord;*

my sighing is not hidden
 from you.

¹⁰My heart pounds,
 my strength fails me;*
 even the light has gone from my eyes.

¹¹My friends and companions avoid me
 because of my wounds;*
 my neighbors stay far away.

¹²Those who seek my life set their traps,*
 those who would harm me talk of
 my ruin; all day long they plot
 deception.

¹³I am like a deaf man,
 who cannot hear,*
 like a mute, who cannot open his
 mouth;

¹⁴I have become like a man
 who does not hear,*
 whose mouth can offer no reply.

¹⁵I wait for you, O Lord;*
 you will answer, O Lord my God.

¹⁶For I said, "Do not let them gloat*
 or exalt themselves over me
 when my foot slips."

¹⁷For I am about to fall,*
 and my pain is ever with me.

¹⁸I confess my iniquity;*
 I am troubled by my sin.

¹⁹Many are those who are
 my vigorous enemies;*
 those who hate me without reason
 are numerous.

²⁰Those who repay my good with evil
 slander me*
 when I seek what is good.

²¹O Lord, do not forsake me;*
 be not far from me, O my God.

²²Come quickly to help me,*
 O Lord my Savior.

Glory be to the Father and to the Son*
 and to the Holy Spirit;

as it was in the beginning,*
  is now, and will be forever. Amen

45

*   XI C: Ionian

[1] My heart is stirred by a noble theme
  as I recite my verses for the king;*
    my tongue is the pen
    of a skillful writer.

[2] You are the most excellent of men*
  and your lips have been anointed
  with grace, since God has blessed
  you forever.

[3] Gird your sword upon your side,
  O mighty one;*
    clothe yourself with splendor
    and majesty,

[4] In your majesty ride forth victoriously
  in behalf of truth, humility
  and righteousness;*
    let your right hand
    display awesome deeds.

[5] Let your sharp arrows pierce
  the hearts of the king's enemies;*
    let the nations fall beneath
    your feet.

[6] Your throne, O God, will last
  for ever and ever;*
    a scepter of justice will be
    the scepter of your kingdom.

[7] You love righteousness
  and hate wickedness;*
    therefore God, your God,
    has set you above your

companions by anointing you with
  the oil of joy.

[8] All your robes are fragrant
  with myrrh and aloes and cassia;*
    from palaces adorned with ivory the
    music of the strings makes you glad.

[9] Daughters of kings are among
  your honored women;*
    at your right hand is the royal
    bride in gold of Ophir.

[10] Listen, O daughter,
  consider and give ear:*
    Forget your people and
    your father's house.

[11] The king is enthralled
  by your beauty;*
    honor him, for he is your lord.

[12] The Daughter of Tyre will come
  with a gift,*
    men of wealth will seek your favor.

[13] All glorious is the princess
  within her chamber;*
    her gown is interwoven with gold.

[14] In embroidered garments
  she is led to the king;*
    her virgin companions follow her
    and are brought to you.

[15] They are led in with joy and gladness;*
    they enter the palace of the king.

[16] Your sons will take the place
  of your fathers;*
    you will make them princes
    throughout the land.

[17] I will perpetuate your memory
  through all generations;*
    therefore the nations will praise
    you for ever and ever.

Glory be to the Father and to the Son*
  and to the Holy Spirit;
as it was in the beginning,*
  is now, and will be forever. Amen

46

50

¹God is our refuge and strength,*
    an ever present help in trouble.

²Therefore we will not fear,
    though the earth give way*
        and the mountains fall
        into the heart of the sea,

³though its waters roar and foam*
    and the mountains quake
    with their surging.

⁴There is a river whose streams
    make glad the city of God,*
        the holy place where the
        Most High dwells.

⁵God is within her, she will not fall;*
    God will help her at break of day.

⁶Nations are in uproar, kingdoms fall;*
    he lifts his voice, the earth melts.

⁷The Lord Almighty is with us;*
    the God of Jacob is our fortress.

⁸Come and see the works of the Lord,*
    the desolations he has
    brought on the earth.

⁹He makes wars cease to the ends
    of the earth;*
        he breaks the bow and shatters
        the spear, he burns the shields
        with fire.

¹⁰"Be still, and know that I am God;*
    I will be exalted among the nations,
    I will be exalted in the earth."

¹¹The Lord Almighty is with us;*
    the God of Jacob is our fortress.

Glory be to the Father and to the Son*
    and to the Holy Spirit;
as it was in the beginning,*
    is now, and will be forever. Amen

¹The Mighty One, God, the Lord,*
    speaks and summons the earth
    from the rising of the sun to the
    place where it sets.

²From Zion, perfect in beauty,*
    God shines forth.

³Our God comes and will not be silent;*
    a fire devours before him,
    and around him a tempest rages.

⁴He summons the heavens above,
    and the earth,*
        that he may judge his people:

⁵"Gather to me my consecrated ones,*
    who made a covenant with me
    by sacrifice."

⁶And the heavens
    proclaim his righteousness,*
        for God himself is judge.

⁷"Hear, O my people, and I will speak,
    O Israel, and I will testify
    against you:*
        I am God, your God.

⁸I do not rebuke you for your sacrifices
    or your burnt offerings,*
        which are ever before me.

⁹I have no need of a bull
    from your stall*
        or of goats from your pens,

¹⁰for every animal of the forest is mine,*
    and the cattle on a thousand hills.

¹¹I know every bird in the mountains,*
    and the creatures of the field
    are mine.

¹²If I were hungry
    I would not tell you,*

for the world is mine,
and all that is in it.

¹³Do I eat the flesh of bulls*
or drink the blood of goats?

¹⁴Sacrifice thank offerings to God,*
fulfill your vows to the Most High,

¹⁵and call upon me in the day
of trouble;*
I will deliver you, and you
will honor me."

¹⁶But to the wicked, God says:*
"What right have you to recite
my laws or take my covenant on
your lips?

¹⁷You hate my instruction*
and cast my words behind you.

¹⁸When you see a thief,
you join with him;*
you throw in your lot with
adulterers.

¹⁹You use your mouth for evil*
and harness your tongue to deceit.

²⁰You speak continually
against your brother*
and slander your own mother's son.

²¹These things you have done
and I kept silent;
you thought I was altogether like you.*
But I will rebuke you
and accuse you to your face.

²²"Consider this, you who forget God,*
or I will tear you to pieces,
with none to rescue:

²³He who sacrifices thank offerings
honors me,*
and he prepares the way so that
I may show him the salvation
of God."

Glory be to the Father and to the Son*
and to the Holy Spirit;
as it was in the beginning,*
is now, and will be forever. Amen

51

I d: Dorian

¹Have mercy on me, O God,
according to your unfailing love;*
according to your great compassion
blot out my transgressions.

²Wash away all my iniquity*
and cleanse me from my sin.

³For I know my transgressions,*
and my sin is always before me.

⁴Against you, you only, have I sinned
and done what is evil in your sight,*
so that you are proved right when
you speak and justified when you
judge.

⁵Surely I have been a sinner from
birth,*
sinful from the time
my mother conceived me.

⁶Surely you desire truth in the inner
parts;*
you teach me wisdom
in the inmost place.

⁷Cleanse me with hyssop,
and I will be clean;*
wash me, and I will be whiter
than snow.

⁸Let me hear joy and gladness;*
let the bones you have crushed
rejoice.

⁹Hide your face from my sins*
and blot out all my iniquity.

¹⁰Create in me a pure heart, O God,*
and renew a steadfast spirit
within me.

¹¹Do not cast me from your presence*
or take your Holy Spirit from me.

¹²Restore to me the joy of your
salvation*

and grant me a willing spirit,
to sustain me.

¹³Then I will teach transgressors
your ways,*
and sinners will turn back to you.

¹⁴Save me from bloodguilt, O God,
the God who saves me,*
and my tongue will sing
of your righteousness.

¹⁵O Lord, open my lips,*
and my mouth will declare your
praise.

¹⁶You do not delight in sacrifice,
or I would bring it;*
you do not take pleasure
in burnt offerings.

¹⁷The sacrifices of God
are a broken spirit;*
a broken and contrite heart,
O God, you will not despise.

¹⁸In your good pleasure make Zion
prosper;*
build up the walls of Jerusalem.

¹⁹Then there will be righteous sacrifices,
whole burnt offerings to delight you;*
then bulls will be offered
on your altar.

Glory be to the Father and to the Son*
and to the Holy Spirit;
as it was in the beginning,*
is now, and will be forever. Amen

62

*   I d: Dorian

¹My soul finds rest in God alone;*
my salvation comes from him.

²He alone is my rock and my
salvation;*

he is my fortress,
I will never be shaken.

³How long will you assault a man?
Would all of you throw him down—*
this leaning wall,
this tottering fence?

⁴They fully intend to topple him
from his lofty place;
they take delight in lies.*
With their mouths they bless,
but in their hearts they curse.

⁵Find rest, O my soul, in God alone;*
my hope comes from him.

⁶He alone is my rock and my
salvation;*
he is my fortress,
I will not be shaken.

⁷My salvation and my honor
depend on God;*
he is my mighty rock, my refuge.

⁸Trust in him at all times, O people;*
pour out your hearts to him,
for God is our refuge.

⁹Lowborn men are but a breath,
the highborn are but a lie;*
if weighed on a balance,
they are nothing;
together they are only a breath.

¹⁰Do not trust in extortion
or take pride in stolen goods;*
though your riches increase,
do not set your heart on them.

¹¹One thing God has spoken,
two things have I heard:*
that you, O God, are strong,
and that you, O Lord, are loving.

¹²Surely you will reward each person*
according to what he has done.

Glory be to the Father and to the Son*
and to the Holy Spirit;
as it was in the beginning,*
is now, and will be forever. Amen

65

XI A: Ionian

¹Praise awaits you, O God, in Zion;*
to you our vows will be fulfilled.

²O you who hear prayer,*
to you all men will come.

³When we were overwhelmed by sins,*
you atoned for our transgressions.

⁴Blessed is the man you choose and
bring near to live in your courts!*
We are filled with the good things
of your house, of your holy
temple.

⁵You answer us with awesome deeds
of righteousness, O God our Savior,*
the hope of all the ends of the
earth and of the farthest seas,

⁶who formed the mountains by your
power,*
having armed yourself with strength,

⁷who stilled the roaring of the seas,*
the roaring of their waves,
and the turmoil of the nations.

⁸Those living far away fear your
wonders;*
where morning dawns and evening
fades you call forth songs of joy.

⁹You care for the land and water it;
you enrich it abundantly.*
The streams of God are filled with
water to provide the people with
grain, for so you have ordained it.

¹⁰You drench its furrows and level its
ridges;*
you soften it with showers
and bless its crops.

¹¹You crown the year with your bounty,*
and your carts overflow with
abundance.

¹²The grasslands of the desert overflow;*
the hills are clothed with gladness.

¹³The meadows are covered with flocks
and the valleys are mantled with
grain;*
they shout for joy and sing.

Glory be to the Father and to the Son*
and to the Holy Spirit;
as it was in the beginning,*
is now, and will be forever. Amen

67

V E♭: Lydian

¹May God be gracious to us
and bless us*
and make his face shine upon us;

²may your ways be known on earth,*
your salvation among all nations.

³May the peoples praise you, O God;*
may all the peoples praise you.

⁴May the nations be glad
and sing for joy,*
for you rule the peoples justly
and guide the nations of the earth.

⁵May the peoples praise you, O God;*
may all the peoples praise you.

⁶Then the land will yield its harvest,*
and God, our God, will bless us.

⁷God will bless us,*
and all the ends of the earth
will fear him.

Glory be to the Father and to the Son*
and to the Holy Spirit;
as it was in the beginning,*
is now, and will be forever. Amen

72

III f#: Phrygian

¹Endow the king with your justice,
O God,*
   the royal son with your
   righteousness.

²He will judge your people in
righteousness,*
   your afflicted ones with justice.

³The mountains will bring prosperity to
the people,*
   the hills the fruit of righteousness.

⁴He will defend the afflicted among the
people and save the children of the
needy;*
   he will crush the oppressor.

⁵He will endure as long as the sun,*
   as long as the moon,
   through all generations.

⁶He will be like rain
falling on a mown field,*
   like showers watering the earth.

⁷In his days the righteous will flourish,*
   prosperity will abound
   till the moon is no more.

⁸He will rule from sea to sea*
   and from the River
   to the ends of the earth.

⁹The desert tribes will bow before him*
   and his enemies will lick the dust.

¹⁰The kings of Tarshish and of distant
shores will bring tribute to him;*
   the kings of Sheba and Seba
   will present him gifts.

¹¹All kings will bow down to him*
   and all nations will serve him.

¹²For he will deliver the needy
who cry out,*

the afflicted who have
no one to help.

¹³He will take pity on the weak
and the needy*
   and save the needy from death.

¹⁴He will rescue them from oppression
and violence,*
   for precious is their blood
   in his sight.

¹⁵Long may he live!
May gold from Sheba be given him.*
   May people ever pray for him
   and bless him all day long.

¹⁶Let grain abound
throughout the land;*
   on the tops of the hills
   may it sway.
Let its fruit flourish like Lebanon;*
   let it thrive like the grass
   of the field.

¹⁷May his name endure forever;*
   may it continue as long as the sun.
All nations will be blessed
through him,*
   and they will call him blessed.

¹⁸Praise be to the Lord God,
the God of Israel,*
   who alone does marvelous deeds.

¹⁹Praise be to his glorious name
forever;*
   may the whole earth be filled with
   his glory. Amen and Amen.

Glory be to the Father and to the Son*
   and to the Holy Spirit;
as it was in the beginning,*
   is now, and will be forever. Amen

73

V Eb: Lydian

¹Surely God is good to Israel,*
  to those who are pure in heart.

²But as for me, my feet had almost
  slipped;*
  I had nearly lost my foothold.

³For I envied the arrogant*
  when I saw the prosperity
  of the wicked.

⁴They have no struggles;*
  their bodies are healthy and
  strong.

⁵They are free from the burdens
  common to man;*
  they are not plagued
  by human ills.

⁶Therefore pride is their necklace;*
  they clothe themselves
  with violence.

⁷From their callous hearts
  comes iniquity;*
  the evil conceits of their minds
  know no limits.

⁸They scoff, and speak with malice;*
  in their arrogance
  they threaten oppression.

⁹Their mouths lay claim to heaven,*
  and their tongues take possession
  of the earth.

¹⁰Therefore their people turn to them*
  and drink up waters in abundance.

¹¹They say, "How can God know?*
  Does the Most High have
  knowledge?"

¹²This is what the wicked are like—*
  always carefree,
  they increase in wealth.

¹³Surely in vain have I kept
  my heart pure;*
  in vain have I washed my hands
  in innocence.

¹⁴All day long I have been plagued;*
  I have been punished every morning.

¹⁵If I had said, "I will speak thus,"*
  I would have betrayed this
  generation of your children.

¹⁶When I tried to understand all this,*
  it was oppressive to me

¹⁷till I entered the sanctuary of God;*
  then I understood their final
  destiny.

¹⁸Surely you place them on slippery
  ground;*
  you cast them down to ruin.

¹⁹How suddenly are they destroyed,*
  completely swept away by terrors!

²⁰As a dream when one awakes,*
  so when you arise, O Lord,
  you will despise them as fantasies.

²¹When my heart was grieved*
  and my spirit embittered,

²²I was senseless and ignorant;*
  I was a brute beast before you.

²³Yet I am always with you;*
  you hold me by my right hand.

²⁴You guide me with your counsel,*
  and afterward you will take me
  into glory.

²⁵Whom have I in heaven but you?*
  And being with you,
  I desire nothing on earth.

²⁶My flesh and my heart may fail,*
  but God is the strength of
  my heart and my portion forever.

²⁷Those who are far from you
  will perish;*
  you destroy all who are
  unfaithful to you.

²⁸But as for me, it is good
  to be near God.*
  I have made the Sovereign Lord my
  refuge; I will tell of all your deeds.

Glory be to the Father and to the Son*
  and to the Holy Spirit;

as it was in the beginning,*
   is now, and will be forever. Āmen

77

I d: Dorian

¹I cried out to God for help;*
   I cried out to God to hear me.

²When I was in distress,
I sought the Lord;*
   at night I stretched out untiring
   hands and my soul refused to be
   comforted.

³I remembered you, O God, and I
groaned;*
   I mused, and my spirit grew faint.

⁴You kept my eyes from closing;*
   I was too troubled to speak.

⁵I thought about the former days,*
   the years of long ago;

⁶I remembered my songs in the night.*
   My heart mused and my spirit
   inquired:

⁷"Will the Lord reject us forēver?*
   Will he never show his favor again?

⁸Has his unfailing love vanished
forēver?*
   Has his promise failed
   for all time?

⁹Has God forgotten to be merciful?*
   Has he in anger withheld his
   compassion?"

¹⁰Then I thought, "To this I will
appeal:*

the years of the right hand of the
   Most High."

¹¹I will remember the deeds
of the Lord;*
   yes, I will remember your miracles
   of long ago.

¹²I will meditate on all your works*
   and consider all your mighty
   deeds.

¹³Your ways, O God, are holy.*
   What god is so great as our God?

¹⁴You are the God who performs
miracles;*
   you display your power among the
   peoples.

¹⁵With your mighty arm you redeemed
your people,*
   the descendants of Jacob and
   Joseph.

¹⁶The waters saw you, O God,
the waters saw you and writhed;*
   the very depths were convulsed.

¹⁷The clouds poured down water,
the skies resounded with thunder;*
   your arrows flashed back and
   forth.

¹⁸Your thunder was heard in the
whirlwind, your lightning lit up the
world;*
   the earth trembled and quaked.

¹⁹Your path led through the sea,
your way through the mighty waters,*
   though your footprints
   were not seen.

²⁰You led your people like a flock*
   by the hand of Moses and Āaron.

Glory be to the Father and to the Son*
   and to the Holy Spirit;
as it was in the beginning,*
   is now, and will be forever. Āmen

84

XI A: Ionian

¹How lovely is your dwelling place,*
  O Lord Almighty!

²My soul yearns, even faints
for the courts of the Lord;*
  my heart and my flesh cry out
  for the living God.

³Even the sparrow has found a home,
and the swallow a nest for herself,
where she may have her young—*
  a place near your altar,
  O Lord Almighty, my King and
  my God.

⁴Blessed are those who dwell
in your house;*
  they are ever praising you.

⁵Blessed are those whose strength
is in you,*
  who have set their hearts
  on pilgrimage.

⁶As they pass through
the Valley of Baca,
they make it a place of springs;*
  the autumn rains also cover
  it with pools.

⁷They go from strength to strength*
  till each appears before God
  in Zion.

⁸Hear my prayer, O Lord God
Almighty;*
  listen to me, O God of Jacob.

⁹Look upon our shield, O God;*
  look with favor on your
  anointed one.

¹⁰Better is one day in your courts
than a thousand elsewhere;*

I would rather be a doorkeeper
in the house of my God
than dwell in the tents of the
wicked.

¹¹For the Lord God is a sun and
shield; the Lord bestows favor
and honor;*
  no good thing does he withhold
  from those whose walk is
  blameless.

¹²O Lord Almighty,*
  blessed is the man
  who trusts in you.

Glory be to the Father and to the Son*
  and to the Holy Spirit;
as it was in the beginning,*
  is now, and will be forever. Amen

90

XI C: Ionian

¹Lord, you have been our dwelling
place*
  throughout all generations.

²Before the mountains were born
or you brought forth the earth
and the world,*
  from everlasting to everlasting
  you are God.

³You turn men back to dust, saying,*
  "Return to dust, O sons of men."

⁴For a thousand years in your sight
are like a day that has just gone by,*
  or like a watch in the night.

⁵You sweep men away in the sleep
of death;*
  they are like the new grass
  of the morning—

⁶though in the morning
it springs up new,*
    by evening it is dry and withered.

⁷We are consumed by your anger*
    and terrified by your indignation.

⁸You have set our iniquities
before you,*
    our secret sins in the light
    of your presence.

⁹All our days pass away
under your wrath;*
    we finish our years with a moan.

¹⁰The length of our days
is seventy years—
or eighty, if we have the strength;*
    yet their span is but trouble
    and sorrow,
    for they quickly pass,
    and we fly away.

¹¹Who knows the power of your
anger?*
    For your wrath is as great
    as the fear that is due you.

¹²Teach us to number our days
aright,*
    that we may gain a heart of
    wisdom.

¹³Relent, O Lord!
How long will it be?*
    Have compassion on your
    servants.

¹⁴Satisfy us in the morning
with your unfailing love,*
    that we may sing for joy
    and be glad all our days.

¹⁵Make us glad for as many days
as you have afflicted us,*
    for as many years
    as we have seen trouble.

¹⁶May your deeds be shown
to your servants,*
    your splendor to their children.

¹⁷May the favor of the Lord our God
rest upon us;*
    establish the work of our hands
    for us—yes, establish the work of
    our hands.

Glory be to the Father and to the Son*
    and to the Holy Spirit;
as it was in the beginning,*
    is now, and will be forever. Amen

91

III f♯: Phrygian

¹He who dwells in the shelter of the
Most High*
    will rest in the shadow
    of the Almighty.

²I will say of the Lord,
"He is my refuge and my fortress,*
    my God, in whom I trust."

³Surely he will save you from the
fowler's snare*
    and from the deadly pestilence.

⁴He will cover you with his feathers,
and under his wings you will find
refuge;*
    his faithfulness will be your shield
    and rampart.

⁵You will not fear the terror of
night,*
    nor the arrow that flies by day,

⁶nor the pestilence that stalks
in the darkness,*
    nor the plague that destroys at
    midday.

⁷A thousand may fall at your side,
ten thousand at your right hand,*
    but it will not come near you.

⁸You will only observe
with your eyes*

and see the punishment of the
wicked.

⁹If you make the Most High your
dwelling—*
even the Lord, who is my refuge—

¹⁰then no harm will befall you,*
no disaster will come
near your tent.

¹¹For he will command his angels
concerning you*
to guard you in all your ways;

¹²they will lift you up in their hands,*
so that you will not strike your
foot against a stone.

¹³You will tread upon the lion and the
cobra;*
you will trample the great lion
and the serpent.

¹⁴"Because he loves me," says the
Lord, "I will rescue him;*
I will protect him,
for he acknowledges my name.

¹⁵He will call upon me, and I will
answer him;*
I will be with him in trouble,
I will deliver him and honor him.

¹⁶With long life will I satisfy him*
and show him my salvation."

Glory be to the Father and to the Son*
and to the Holy Spirit;
as it was in the beginning,*
is now, and will be forever. Amen

92

XI D: Ionian

¹It is good to praise the Lord*
and make music to your name,
O Most High,

²to proclaim your love in the
morning*
and your faithfulness at night,

³to the music of the ten-stringed lyre*
and the melody of the harp.

⁴For you make me glad by your
deeds, O Lord;*
I sing for joy at the works
of your hands.

⁵How great are your works, O Lord,*
how profound your thoughts!

⁶The senseless man does not know,*
fools do not understand,

⁷that though the wicked spring
up like grass and all evildoers
flourish,*
they will be forever destroyed.

⁸But you, O Lord,*
are exalted forever.

⁹For surely your enemies, O Lord,
surely your enemies will perish;*
all evildoers will be scattered.

¹⁰You have exalted my horn
like that of a wild ox;*
fine oils have been
poured upon me.

¹¹My eyes have seen the defeat
of my adversaries;*
my ears have heard the rout
of my wicked foes.

¹²The righteous will flourish
like a palm tree,*
they will grow like a cedar
of Lebanon;

¹³planted in the house of the Lord,*
they will flourish
in the courts of our God.

¹⁴They will still bear fruit
in old age,*
they will stay fresh and green,

¹⁵proclaiming, "The Lord is upright;*

he is my Rock, and there is
no wickedness in him.''

Glory be to the Father and to the Son*
and to the Holy Spirit;
as it was in the beginning,*
is now, and will be forever. Amen

96

XI A: Ionian

[1]Sing to the Lord a new song;*
sing to the Lord, all the earth.

[2]Sing to the Lord, praise his name;*
proclaim his salvation
day after day.

[3]Declare his glory among the
nations,*
his marvelous deeds among all
peoples.

[4]For great is the Lord
and most worthy of praise;*
he is to be feared above all gods.

[5]For all the gods of the nations
are idols,*
but the Lord made the heavens.

[6]Splendor and majesty
are before him;*
strength and glory are in his
sanctuary.

[7]Ascribe to the Lord, O families
of nations,*
ascribe to the Lord glory and
strength.

[8]Ascribe to the Lord
the glory due his name;*
bring an offering
and come into his courts.

[9]Worship the Lord in the splendor
of his holiness;*
tremble before him, all the earth.

[10]Say among the nations,
''The Lord reigns.''*
The world is firmly established,
it cannot be moved; he will judge
the peoples with equity.

[11]Let the heavens rejoice,
let the earth be glad;*
let the sea resound,
and all that is in it;

[12]let the fields be jubilant,
and everything in them.*
Then all the trees of the forest
will sing for joy;

[13]they will sing before the Lord,
for he comes,
he comes to judge the earth.*
He will judge the world
in righteousness
and the peoples in his truth.

Glory be to the Father and to the Son*
and to the Holy Spirit;
as it was in the beginning,*
is now, and will be forever. Amen

98

XI D: Ionian

[1]Sing to the Lord a new song,
for he has done marvelous things;*
his right hand and his holy arm
have worked salvation for him.

[2]The Lord has made his salvation
known*
and revealed his righteousness
to the nations.

³He has remembered his love
and his faithfulness to the house
of Israel;*
   all the ends of the earth have seen
   the salvation of our God.

⁴Shout for joy to the Lord,
all the earth,*
   burst into jubilant song with
   music;

⁵make music to the Lord
with the harp,*
   with the harp and the sound of
   singing,

⁶with trumpets
and the blast of the ram's horn—*
   shout for joy before the Lord,
   the King.

⁷Let the sea resound,
and all that is in it,*
   the world, and all who live in it.

⁸Let the rivers clap their hands,*
   let the mountains sing
   together for joy;

⁹let them sing before the Lord,*
   for he comes to judge the earth.
He will judge the world
in righteousness*
   and the peoples with equity.

Glory be to the Father and to the Son*
   and to the Holy Spirit;
as it was in the beginning,*
   is now, and will be forever. Amen

100

XI g²: Aeolian

¹Shout for joy to the Lord,*
all the earth.

²Serve the Lord with gladness;*

come before him with joyful
songs.

³Know that the Lord is God.*
   It is he who made us, and we are
   his; we are his people, the sheep
   of his pasture.

⁴Enter his gates with thanksgiving
and his courts with praise;*
   give thanks to him
   and praise his name.

⁵For the Lord is good
and his love endures forever;*
   his faithfulness continues
   through all generations.

Glory be to the Father and to the Son*
   and to the Holy Spirit;
as it was in the beginning,*
   is now, and will be forever. Amen

103

XI A: Ionian

¹Praise the Lord, O my soul;*
   all my inmost being,
   praise his holy name.

²Praise the Lord, O my soul,*
   and forget not all his benefits.

³He forgives all my sins*
   and heals all my diseases;

⁴he redeems my life from the pit*
   and crowns me with love
   and compassion.

⁵He satisfies my desires with good
things,*
   so that my youth is renewed like
   the eagle's.

⁶The Lord works righteousness*
   and justice for all the oppressed.

⁷He made known his ways to Moses,*
   his deeds to the people of Israel:

⁸The Lord is compassionate and
gracious,*
   slow to anger, abounding in love.

⁹He will not always accuse,*
   nor will he harbor his anger
   forever;

¹⁰he does not treat us as our sins
deserve*
   or repay us according to
   our iniquities.

¹¹For as high as the heavens are above
the earth,*
   so great is his love for those
   who fear him;

¹²as far as the east is from the west,*
   so far has he removed our
   transgressions from us.

¹³As a father has compassion on his
children,*
   so the Lord has compassion on
   those who fear him;

¹⁴for he knows how we are formed,*
   he remembers that we are dust.

¹⁵As for man, his days are like grass,*
   he flourishes like a flower
   of the field;

¹⁶the wind blows over it
and it is gone,*
   and its place remembers it
   no more.

¹⁷But from everlasting to everlasting
the Lord's love is with those who
fear him,*
   and his righteousness with their
   children's children—

¹⁸with those who keep his covenant*
   and remember to obey his
   precepts.

¹⁹The Lord has established his throne
in heaven,*
   and his kingdom rules over all.

²⁰Praise the Lord, you his angels,
you mighty ones who do his
bidding,*
   who obey his word.

²¹Praise the Lord, all his heavenly
hosts,*
   you his servants who do his will.

²²Praise the Lord, all his works
everywhere in his dominion.*
   Praise the Lord, O my soul.

Glory be to the Father and to the Son*
   and to the Holy Spirit;
as it was in the beginning,*
   is now, and will be forever. Amen

105

XI D: Ionian

¹Give thanks to the Lord,
call on his name;*
   make known among the nations
   what he has done.

²Sing to him, sing praise to him;*
   tell of all his wonderful acts.

³Glory in his holy name;*
   let the hearts of those
   who seek the Lord rejoice.

⁴Look to the Lord and his strength;*
   seek his face always.

⁵Remember the wonders
he has done,*
   his miracles,
   and the judgments he pronounced,

⁶O descendants of Abraham
his servant,*
   O sons of Jacob, his chosen ones.

⁷He is the Lord our God;*
   his judgments are in all the earth.

⁸He remembers his covenant forēver,*
   the word he commanded, for a
   thousand generātions,

⁹the covenant he made with
   Àbraham,*
   the oath he swore to Īsaac.

¹⁰He confirmed it to Jacob as à
   decree,*
   to Israel as an everlasting
   còvenant:

¹¹"To you I will give the land of
   Canaan*
   as the portion you will inḧerit."

¹²When they were but few in ñumber,*
   few indeed, and strangers īn it,

¹³they wandered from nation to
   ñation,*
   from one kingdom to anōther.

¹⁴He allowed no one
   to oppr̀ess them;*
   for their sake he rebùked kings:

¹⁵"Do not touch my anòinted ones;*
   do my prophèts no harm."

¹⁶He called down famine òn the land*
   and destroyed all their suppĺies
   of food;

¹⁷and he sent a man befōre them—*
   Joseph, sold às a slave.

¹⁸They bruised his feet with s̄hackles,*
   his neck was put in īrons,

¹⁹till what he foretold c̀ame to pass,*
   till the word of the Lord
   pr̀oved him true.

²⁰The king sent and rel̄eased him,*
   the ruler of peoples s̀et him free.

²¹He made him master of his
   ḧousehold,*
   ruler over all h̀e possessed,

²²to discipline his princes
   às he pleased*
   and teach his elders w̄isdom.

²³Then Israel entered Ēgypt;*
   Jacob lived as an alien
   in the l̀and of Ham.

²⁴The Lord made his people
   very f̄ruitful;*
   he made them too numerous
   f̀or their foes,

²⁵whose hearts he turned to hate
   his p̄eople,*
   to conspire against his s̄ervants.

²⁶He sent Moses his s̄ervant,*
   and Aaron, whom he had c̄hosen.

²⁷They performed his miraculous
   signs amōng them,*
   his wonders in the l̀and of Ham.

²⁸He sent darkness and made
   the īand dark—*
   for had they not rebelled
   aǵainst his words?

²⁹He turned their waters ìnto blood,*
   causing their f̀ish to die.

³⁰Their land t̀eemed with frogs,*
   which went up into the bedrooms
   of their r̄ulers.

³¹He spoke, and there came
   s̀warms of flies,*
   and gnats throughout their
   c̄ountry.

³²He turned their rain ìnto hail,*
   with lightning throughòut
   their land;

³³he struck down their vines
   and f̄ig trees*
   and shattered the trees
   of their c̄ountry.

³⁴He spoke, and the l̀ocusts came,*
   grasshoppers without ñumber;

³⁵they ate up every green thing
   ìn their land,*
   ate up the produce òf their soil.

³⁶Then he struck down
all the firstborn in their land,*
the firstfruits of all their
manhood.

³⁷He brought out Israel, laden with
silver and gold,*
and from among their tribes
no one faltered.

³⁸Egypt was glad when they left,*
because dread of Israel
had fallen on them.

³⁹He spread out a cloud as a
covering,*
and a fire to give light at night.

⁴⁰They asked, and he brought them
quail*
and satisfied them
with the bread of heaven.

⁴¹He opened the rock, and water
gushed out;*
like a river it flowed in the desert.

⁴²For he remembered his holy
promise*
given to his servant Abraham.

⁴³He brought out his people with
rejoicing,*
his chosen ones
with shouts of joy;

⁴⁴he gave them the lands of the
nations,*
and they fell heir
to what others had toiled for—

⁴⁵that they might keep his precepts*
and observe his laws.
Praise the Lord.

Glory be to the Father and to the Son*
and to the Holy Spirit;
as it was in the beginning,*
is now, and will be forever. Amen

107

I d: Dorian

¹Give thanks to the Lord,
for he is good;*
his love endures forever.

²Let the redeemed of the Lord
say this—*
those he redeemed
from the hand of the foe,

³those he gathered from the lands,*
from east and west,
from north and south.

⁴Some wandered in desert wastelands,*
finding no way to a city
where they could settle.

⁵They were hungry and thirsty,*
and their lives ebbed away.

⁶Then they cried out to the Lord
in their trouble,*
and he delivered them
from their distress.

⁷He led them by a straight way*
to a city where they could settle.

⁸Let them give thanks to the Lord
for his unfailing love*
and his wonderful deeds for men,

⁹for he satisfies the thirsty*
and fills the hungry
with good things.

¹⁰Some sat in darkness
and the deepest gloom,*
prisoners suffering in iron chains,

¹¹for they had rebelled
against the words of God*
and despised the counsel
of the Most High.

¹²So he subjected them
to bitter labor;*

they stumbled,
and there was no one to help.

¹³Then they cried to the Lord
in their trouble,*
and he saved them
from their distress.

¹⁴He brought them out of darkness
and the deepest gloom*
and broke away their chains.

¹⁵Let them give thanks to the Lord
for his unfailing love*
and his wonderful deeds for men,

¹⁶for he breaks down gates of bronze*
and cuts through bars of iron.

¹⁷Some became fools
through their rebellious ways*
and suffered affliction
because of their iniquities.

¹⁸They loathed all food*
and drew near the gates of death.

¹⁹Then they cried to the Lord
in their trouble,*
and he saved them from
their distress.

²⁰He sent forth his word
and healed them;*
he rescued them from the grave.

²¹Let them give thanks to the Lord
for his unfailing love*
and his wonderful deeds for men.

²²Let them sacrifice thank offerings*
and tell of his works
with songs of joy.

²³Others went out on the sea in ships;*
they were merchants
on the mighty waters.

²⁴They saw the works of the Lord,*
his wonderful deeds in the deep.

²⁵For he spoke and stirred up a tempest*
that lifted high the waves.

²⁶They mounted up to the heavens
and went down to the depths;*

in their peril their courage
melted away.

²⁷They reeled and staggered
like drunken men;*
they were at their wits' end.

²⁸Then they cried out to the Lord
in their trouble,*
and he brought them
out of their distress.

²⁹He stilled the storm to a whisper;*
the waves of the sea were hushed.

³⁰They were glad when it grew calm,*
and he guided them
to their desired haven.

³¹Let them give thanks to the Lord
for his unfailing love*
and his wonderful deeds for men.

³²Let them exalt him
in the assembly of the people*
and praise him in the council
of the elders.

³³He turned rivers into a desert,*
flowing springs into thirsty ground,

³⁴and fruitful land into a salt waste,*
because of the wickedness
of those who lived there.

³⁵He turned the desert into pools of
water*
and the parched ground
into flowing springs;

³⁶there he brought the hungry to live,*
and they founded a city
where they could settle.

³⁷They sowed fields
and planted vineyards*
that yielded a fruitful harvest;

³⁸he blessed them,
and their numbers greatly increased,*
and he did not let their herds
diminish.

³⁹Then their numbers decreased,*
and they were humbled
by oppression, calamity and
sorrow;

⁴⁰he who pours contempt on nobles*
made them wander in a trackless
waste.

⁴¹But he lifted the needy
out of their affliction*
and increased their families
like flocks.

⁴²The upright see and rejoice,*
but all the wicked
shut their mouths.

⁴³Whoever is wise,
let him heed these things*
and consider the great love
of the Lord.

Glory be to the Father and to the Son*
and to the Holy Spirit;
as it was in the beginning,*
is now, and will be forever. Amen

110

XI A: Ionian

¹The Lord says to my Lord:
"Sit at my right hand*
until I make your enemies
a footstool for your feet."

²The Lord will extend your mighty
scepter from Zion;*
rule in the midst of your enemies.

³Your troops will be willing
on your day of battle.*
Arrayed in holy majesty,
from the womb of the dawn
you will receive the dew of your
youth.

⁴The Lord has sworn and will not
change his mind:*
"You are a priest forever,
in the order of Melchizedek."

⁵The Lord is at your right hand;*
he will crush kings
on the day of his wrath.

⁶He will judge the nations,
heaping up the dead*
and crushing the rulers
of the whole earth.

⁷He will drink from a brook
beside the way;*
therefore he will lift up his head.

Glory be to the Father and to the Son*
and to the Holy Spirit;
as it was in the beginning,*
is now, and will be forever. Amen

111

IX g²: Aeolian

¹Praise the Lord. I will extol the Lord
with all my heart*
in the council of the upright
and in the assembly.

²Great are the works of the Lord;*
they are pondered by all
who delight in them.

³Glorious and majestic are his deeds,*
and his righteousness endures
forever.

⁴He has caused his wonders
to be remembered;*
the Lord is gracious and
compassionate.

⁵He provides food
for those who fear him;*

he remembers his covenant
forēver.

⁶He has shown his people
the power óf his works,*
giving them the lands of other
ñations.

⁷The works of his hands
are faithful and just;*
all his precepts are trustworthy.

⁸They are steadfast for ever and ēver,*
done in faithfulness and
uprīghtness.

⁹He provided redemption for his
people;
he ordained his covenant forēver—*
holy and awesome is his name.

¹⁰The fear of the Lord
is the beginning of wīsdom;*
all who follow his precepts have
good understanding. To him belongs eternal praise.

Glory be to the Father and to the Son*
and to the Holy Spirit;
as it was in the beḡinning,*
is now, and will be forever. Āmen

⁵Why was it, O sea, that you fled,*
O Jordan, that you turned back,

⁶you mountains, that you skipped
like rams,*
you hills, like lambs?

⁷Tremble, O earth,
at the presence óf the Lord,*
at the presence of the God of
Jacob,

⁸who turned the rock into a pool,*
the hard rock into springs of
wāter.

Glory be to the Father and to the Son*
and to the Holy Spirit;
as it was in the beḡinning,*
is now, and will be forever. Āmen

116

IX a: Aeolian

¹I love the Lord, for he heard my
voice;*
he heard my cry for mercy.

²Because he turned his ear to me,*
I will call on him as long as I live.

³The cords of death entangled me,
the anguish of the grave came upōn
me;*
I was overcome by trouble and
sorrow.

⁴Then I called on the name
óf the Lord:*
"O Lord, save me!"

⁵The Lord is gracious and righteous;*
our God is full of compassion.

⁶The Lord protects the simplehearted;*

114

I d: Dorian

¹When Israel came out of Ēgypt,*
the house of Jacob
from a people of foreign tongue,

²Judah became God's sanctuāry,*
Israel his dominion.

³The sea looked and fled,*
the Jordan turned back;

⁴the mountains skipped like rams,*
the hills like lambs.

when I was in great need,
he šaved me.

⁷Be at rest once more, Ò my soul,*
for the Lord has been
good to you.

⁸For you, O Lord, have delivered
my šoul from death,*
my eyes from tears,
my feet from štumbling,

⁹that I may walk before the Lord*
in the land of the Iiving.

¹⁰I believed; therefore I said,*
"I am greatly afflicted."

¹¹And in my dismay I said,*
"All men are liars."

¹²How can I repay the Lord*
for all his goodness to me?

¹³I will lift up the cup of salvation*
and call on the name òf the Lord.

¹⁴I will fulfill my vows to the Lord*
in the presence of all his people.

¹⁵Precious in the sight òf the Lord*
is the death òf his saints.

¹⁶O Lord, truly I am your šervant;*
I am your servant,
the son of your maidservant;
you have freed me from my chains.

¹⁷I will sacrifice a thank offering
to you*
and call on the name òf the Lord.

¹⁸I will fulfill my vows to the Lord*
in the presence of all his people,

¹⁹in the courts of the house
òf the Lord—*
in your midst, O Jerusalem.
Praise the Lord.

Glory be to the Father and to the Son*
and to the Holy Špirit;
as it was in the beginning,*
is now, and will be forever. Āmen

117

XI A: Ionian

¹Praise the Lord, all you ñations;*
extol him, all you peoples.

²For great is his love toward us,*
and the faithfulness of the Lord
endures forever. Praise the Lord.

Glory be to the Father and to the Son*
and to the Holy Špirit;
as it was in the beginning,*
is now, and will be forever. Āmen

118

VII E: Mixolydian

¹Give thanks to the Lord,
for he is good;*
his love endures forever.

²Let İsrael say:*
"His love endures forever."

³Let the house of Åaron say:*
"His love endures forever."

⁴Let those who fear the Lord say:*
"His love endures forever."

⁵In my anguish I cried to the Lord,*
and he answered
by setting me free.

⁶The Lord is with me;
I will not be afraid.*
What can man do to me?

⁷The Lord is with me; he is my helper.*
I will look in triumph on my
enemies.

⁸It is better to take refuge
in the Lord*
  than to trust in man.

⁹It is better to take refuge
in the Lord*
  than to trust in princes.

¹⁰All the nations surrounded me,*
  but in the name of the Lord
  I cut them off.

¹¹They surrounded me on every side,*
  but in the name of the Lord
  I cut them off.

¹²They swarmed around me like bees,
but they died out as quickly
as burning thorns;*
    in the name of the Lord I cut
    them off.

¹³I was pushed back
and about to fall,*
  but the Lord helped me.

¹⁴The Lord is my strength
and my song;*
  he has become my salvation.

¹⁵Shouts of joy and victory resound
in the tents of the righteous:*
    "The Lord's right hand has done
    mighty things!

¹⁶The Lord's right hand
is lifted high;*
    the Lord's right hand has done
    mighty things!"

¹⁷I will not die but live,*
  and will proclaim what the Lord
  has done.

¹⁸The Lord has chastened me severely,*
  but he has not given me
  over to death.

¹⁹Open for me the gates
of righteousness;*
  I will enter and give thanks
  to the Lord.

²⁰This is the gate of the Lord*
  through which the righteous
  may enter.

²¹I will give you thanks,
for you answered me;*
  you have become my salvation.

²²The stone the builders rejected*
  has become the capstone;

²³the Lord has done this,*
  and it is marvelous in our eyes.

²⁴This is the day the Lord has made;*
  let us rejoice and be glad in it.

²⁵O Lord, save us:*
  O Lord, grant us success.

²⁶Blessed is he who comes in the name
of the Lord.*
  From the house of the Lord
  we bless you.

²⁷The Lord is God, and he has made
his light shine upon us.*
  With boughs in hand, join in the
  festal procession up to the horns
  of the altar.

²⁸You are my God,
and I will give you thanks;*
  you are my God,
  and I will exalt you.

²⁹Give thanks to the Lord,
for he is good;*
  his love endures forever.

Glory be to the Father and to the Son*
  and to the Holy Spirit;
as it was in the beginning,*
  is now, and will be forever. Amen

119

Aleph

I d: Dorian

¹Blessed are they whose ways are
blameless,*
  who walk according to the law
  of the Lord.

²Blessed are they who keep his statutes*
  and seek him with all their heart.

³They do nothing wrong;*
  they walk in his ways.

⁴You have laid down precepts*
  that are to be fully obeyed.

⁵Oh, that my ways were steadfast*
  in obeying your decrees!

⁶Then I would not be put to shame*
  when I consider
  all your commands.

⁷I will praise you
  with an upright heart*
    as I learn your righteous laws.

⁸I will obey your decrees;*
  do not utterly forsake me.

Glory be to the Father and to the Son*
  and to the Holy Spirit;
as it was in the beginning,*
  is now, and will be forever. Amen

Beth

III f♯: Phrygian

⁹How can a young man
  keep his way pure?*
    By living according to your word.

¹⁰I seek you with all my heart;*
  do not let me stray
  from your commands.

¹¹I have hidden your word in my heart*
  that I might not sin against you.

¹²Praise be to you, O Lord;*
  teach me your decrees.

¹³With my lips I recount*
  all the laws that come
  from your mouth.

¹⁴I rejoice in following your statutes*
  as one rejoices in great riches.

¹⁵I meditate on your precepts*
  and consider your ways.

¹⁶I delight in your decrees;*
  I will not neglect your word.

Glory be to the Father and to the Son*
  and to the Holy Spirit;
as it was in the beginning,*
  is now, and will be forever. Amen

Gimel

IX g: Aeolian

¹⁷Do good to your servant,
  and I will live;*
    I will obey your word.

¹⁸Open my eyes that I may see*
  wonderful things in your law.

¹⁹I am a stranger on earth;*
  do not hide your commands
  from me.

²⁰My soul is consumed with longing*
  for your laws at all times.

²¹You rebuke the arrogant, who are
cursed*
  and who stray from your
  commands.

²²Remove from me scorn and
contempt,*
    for I keep your statutes.

²³Though princes sit together
and slander me,*
    your servant will meditate
    on your decrees.

²⁴Your statutes are my delight;*
    they are my counselors.

Glory be to the Father and to the Son*
and to the Holy Spirit;
as it was in the beginning,*
    is now, and will be forever. Amen

Daleth

²⁵I am laid low in the dust;*
    renew my life
    according to your word.

²⁶I recounted my ways and you
answered me;*
    teach me your decrees.

²⁷Let me understand the teaching
of your precepts;*
    then I will meditate
    on your wonders.

²⁸My soul is weary with sorrow;*
    strengthen me according
    to your word.

²⁹Keep me from deceitful ways;*
    be gracious to me
    through your law.

³⁰I have chosen the way of truth;*
    I have set my heart on your laws.

³¹I hold fast to your statutes,
O Lord;*
    do not let me be put to shame.

³²I run in the path of your
commands,*
    for you have set my heart free.

Glory be to the Father and to the Son*
and to the Holy Spirit;
as it was in the beginning,*
    is now, and will be forever. Amen

He

³³Teach me, O Lord,
    to follow your decrees;*
        then I will keep them to the end.

³⁴Give me understanding,
    and I will keep your law*
        and obey it with all my heart.

³⁵Direct me in the path
of your commands,*
    for there I find delight.

³⁶Turn my heart toward your statutes*
    and not toward selfish gain.

³⁷Turn my eyes away from worthless
things;*
    renew my life
    according to your word.

³⁸Fulfill your promise to your
servant,*
    so that you may be feared.

³⁹Take away the disgrace I dread,*
    for your laws are good.

⁴⁰How I long for your precepts!*
    Renew my life in your
    righteousness.

Glory be to the Father and to the Son*
and to the Holy Spirit;
as it was in the beginning,*
    is now, and will be forever. Amen

Waw

*	V Eb: Lydian

⁴¹May your unfailing love come to me,
O Lord,*
    your salvation according
    to your promise;

⁴²then I will answer the one
who taunts me,*
    for I trust in your word.

⁴³Do not snatch the word of truth
from my mouth,*
    for I have put my hope
    in your laws.

⁴⁴I will always obey your law,*
    for ever and ever.

⁴⁵I will walk about in freedom,*
    for I have sought out your
    precepts.

⁴⁶I will speak of your statutes
before kings*
    and will not be put to shame,

⁴⁷for I delight
in your commandments*
    because I love them.

⁴⁸I reach out my hands for your
commandments, which I love,*
    and I meditate on your decrees.

Glory be to the Father and to the Son*
    and to the Holy Spirit;
as it was in the beginning,*
    is now, and will be forever. Amen

Zayin

*	VII E: Mixolydian

⁴⁹Remember your word
to your servant,*
    for you have given me hope.

⁵⁰My comfort in my suffering is this:*
    Your promise renews my life.

⁵¹The arrogant mock me without
restraint,*
    but I do not turn from your law.

⁵²I remember your ancient laws,
O Lord,*
    and I find comfort in them.

⁵³Indignation grips me because
of the wicked,*
    who have forsaken your law.

⁵⁴Your decrees are the theme
of my song*
    wherever I lodge.

⁵⁵In the night I remember your name,
O Lord,*
    and I will keep your law.

⁵⁶This has been my practice:*
    I obey your precepts.

Glory be to the Father and to the Son*
    and to the Holy Spirit;
as it was in the beginning,*
    is now, and will be forever. Amen

Heth

*	XI D: Ionian

⁵⁷You are my portion, O Lord;*
    I have promised to obey your
    words.

⁵⁸I have sought your face
with all my heart;*
    be gracious to me
    according to your promise.

⁵⁹I have considered my ways*
    and have turned my steps
    to your statutes.

⁶⁰I will hasten and not delay*
    to obey your commands.

61Though the wicked bind me with
ropes,*
   I will not forget your law.

62At midnight I rise to give you
thanks*
   for your righteous laws.

63I am a friend to all who fear you,*
   to all who follow your precepts.

64The earth is filled with your love,
O Lord;*
   teach me your decrees.

Glory be to the Father and to the Son*
   and to the Holy Spirit;
as it was in the beginning,*
   is now, and will be forever. Amen

72The law from your mouth
is more precious to me*
   than thousands of pieces
   of silver and gold.

Glory be to the Father and to the Son*
   and to the Holy Spirit;
as it was in the beginning,*
   is now, and will be forever. Amen

Yodh

XI A: Ionian

73Your hands made me
and formed me;*
   give me understanding to learn
   your commands.

74May they who fear you rejoice when
they see me,*
   for I have put my hope
   in your word.

75I know, O Lord, that your laws are
righteous,*
   and in faithfulness you have
   afflicted me.

76May your unfailing love
be my comfort,*
   according to your promise
   to your servant.

77Let your compassion come to me
that I may live,*
   for your law is my delight.

78May the arrogant be put to shame
for wronging me without cause;*
   but I will meditate on
   your precepts.

79May those who fear you
turn to me,*
   those who understand your
   statutes.

Teth

XI C: Ionian

65Do good to your servant*
   according to your word, O Lord.

66Teach me knowledge and good
judgment,*
   for I believe in your commands.

67Before I was afflicted I went astray,*
   but now I obey your word.

68You are good, and what you do
is good;*
   teach me your decrees.

69Though the arrogant have smeared
me with lies,*
   I keep your precepts with all my
   heart.

70Their hearts are callous and
unfeeling,*
   but I delight in your law.

71It was good for me to be afflicted*
   so that I might learn your decrees.

351

⁸⁰May my heart be blameless toward
your decrees,*
　　that I may not be put to shame.

Glory be to the Father and to the Son*
　and to the Holy Spirit;
as it was in the beginning,*
　　is now, and will be forever. Amen

and I will obey the statutes of
your mouth.

Glory be to the Father and to the Son*
　and to the Holy Spirit;
as it was in the beginning,*
　　is now, and will be forever. Amen

Kaph

XI A: Ionian

⁸¹My soul faints with longing for
your salvation,*
　　but I have put my hope
　　in your word.

⁸²My eyes fail, looking for your
promise;*
　　I say, "When will you
　　comfort me?"

⁸³Though I am like a wineskin in
the smoke,*
　　I do not forget your decrees.

⁸⁴How long must your servant wait?*
　　When will you punish my
　　persecutors?

⁸⁵The arrogant dig pitfalls for me,*
　　contrary to your law.

⁸⁶All your commands are
trustworthy;*
　　help me, for men persecute me
　　without cause.

⁸⁷They almost wiped me from the
earth,*
　　but I have not forsaken your
　　precepts.

⁸⁸Preserve my life according to
your love,*

Lamedh

XI C: Ionian

⁸⁹Your word, O Lord, is eternal;*
　　it stands firm in the heavens.

⁹⁰Your faithfulness continues
through all generations;*
　　you established the earth,
　　and it endures.

⁹¹Your laws endure to this day,*
　　for all things serve you.

⁹²If your law had not been my
delight,*
　　I would have perished
　　in my affliction.

⁹³I will never forget your precepts,*
　　for by them you have renewed
　　my life.

⁹⁴Save me, for I am yours;*
　　I have sought out your precepts.

⁹⁵The wicked are waiting
to destroy me,*
　　but I will ponder your statutes.

⁹⁶To all perfection I see a limit;*
　　but your commands are boundless.

Glory be to the Father and to the Son*
　and to the Holy Spirit;
as it was in the beginning,*
　　is now, and will be forever. Amen

Mem

XI D: Ionian

⁹⁷Oh, how I love your law!*
I meditate on it all day long.

⁹⁸Your commands make me wiser
than my enemies,*
for they are ever with me.

⁹⁹I have more insight than all
my teachers,*
for I meditate on your statutes.

¹⁰⁰I have more understanding
than the elders,*
for I obey your precepts.

¹⁰¹I have kept my feet from
every evil path*
so that I might obey your word.

¹⁰²I have not departed from your laws,*
for you yourself have taught me.

¹⁰³How sweet are your promises
to my taste,*
sweeter than honey to my mouth!

¹⁰⁴I gain understanding from your
precepts;*
therefore I hate
every wrong path.

Glory be to the Father and to the Son*
and to the Holy Spirit;
as it was in the beginning,*
is now, and will be forever. Amen

Nun

VII E: Mixolydian

¹⁰⁵Your word is a lamp to my feet*
and a light for my path.

¹⁰⁶I have taken an oath
and confirmed it,*
that I will follow your
righteous laws.

¹⁰⁷I have suffered much;*
renew my life, O Lord,
according to your word.

¹⁰⁸Accept, O Lord, the willing praise
of my mouth,*
and teach me your laws.

¹⁰⁹Though I constantly
take my life in my hands,*
I will not forget your law.

¹¹⁰The wicked have set a snare for me,*
but I have not strayed
from your precepts.

¹¹¹Your statutes are my heritage
forever;*
they are the joy of my heart.

¹¹²My heart is set on keeping
your decrees*
to the very end.

Glory be to the Father and to the Son*
and to the Holy Spirit;
as it was in the beginning,*
is now, and will be forever. Amen

Samekh

V E♭: Lydian

¹¹³I hate double-minded men,*
but I love your law.

¹¹⁴You are my refuge and my shield;*
I have put my hope
in your word.

¹¹⁵Away from me, you evildoers,*
that I may keep
the commands of my God!

[116]Sustain me according to your promise,
and I will live;*
do not let my hopes be dashed.

[117]Uphold me, and I will be delivered;*
I will always have regard
for your decrees.

[118]You reject all who stray
from your decrees,*
for their deceitfulness is in vain.

[119]All the wicked of the earth
you discard like dross;*
therefore I love your statutes.

[120]My flesh trembles in fear of you;*
I stand in awe of your laws.

Glory be to the Father and to the Son*
and to the Holy Spirit;
as it was in the beginning,*
is now, and will be forever. Amen

Ayin

IX g²: Aeolian

[121]I have done what is righteous
and just;*
do not leave me
to my oppressors.

[122]Ensure your servant's well-being;*
let not the arrogant oppress me.

[123]My eyes fail, looking for
your salvation,*
looking for your righteous
promise.

[124]Deal with your servant
according to your love*
and teach me your decrees.

[125]I am your servant;
give me discernment*
that I may understand
your statutes.

[126]It is time for you to act, O Lord;*
your law is being broken.

[127]Because I love your commands*
more than gold,
more than pure gold,

[128]and because I consider all your
precepts right,*
I hate every wrong path.

Glory be to the Father and to the Son*
and to the Holy Spirit;
as it was in the beginning,*
is now, and will be forever. Amen

Pe

IX a: Aeolian

[129]Your statutes are wonderful;*
therefore I obey them.

[130]The entrance of your words
gives light;*
it gives understanding
to the simple.

[131]I open my mouth and pant,*
longing for your commands.

[132]Turn to me and have mercy on me,*
as you always do to those who
love your name.

[133]Direct my footsteps according
to your word;*
let no sin rule over me.

[134]Redeem me from
the oppression of men,*
that I may obey your precepts.

[135]Make your face shine
upon your servant*
and teach me your decrees.

[136]Streams of tears flow from my eyes,*
for your law is not obeyed.

Glory be to the Father and to the Son*
 and to the Holy Spirit;
as it was in the beginning,*
 is now, and will be forever. Amen

Tsadhe

IX g: Aeolian

137Righteous are you, O Lord,*
 and your laws are right.

138The statutes you have laid down
 are righteous;*
 they are fully trustworthy.

139My zeal wears me out,*
 for my enemies ignore your
 words.

140Your promises have been thoroughly
 tested,*
 and your servant loves them.

141Though I am lowly and despised,*
 I do not forget your precepts.

142Your righteousness is everlasting*
 and your law is true.

143Trouble and distress
 have come upon me,*
 but your commands are my
 delight.

144Your statutes are forever right;*
 give me understanding
 that I may live.

Glory be to the Father and to the Son*
 and to the Holy Spirit;
as it was in the beginning,*
 is now, and will be forever. Amen

Qoph

III f♯: Phrygian

145I call with all my heart;*
 answer me, O Lord,
 and I will obey your decrees.

146I call out to you;*
 save me and I will keep
 your statutes.

147I rise before dawn and cry for help;*
 I have put my hope
 in your word.

148My eyes stay open
 through the watches of the night,*
 that I may meditate
 on your promises.

149Hear my voice
 in accordance with your love;*
 renew my life, O Lord,
 according to your laws.

150Those who devise wicked schemes
 are near,*
 but they are far from your law.

151Yet you are near, O Lord,*
 and all your commands are true.

152Long ago I learned from your
 statutes*
 that you established them
 to last forever.

Glory be to the Father and to the Son*
 and to the Holy Spirit;
as it was in the beginning,*
 is now, and will be forever. Amen

Resh

I d: Dorian

¹⁵³Look upon my suffering
and deliver me,*
    for I have not forgotten
    your law.

¹⁵⁴Defend my cause and redeem me;*
renew my life
    according to your promise.

¹⁵⁵Salvation is far from the wicked,*
for they do not seek
    out your decrees.

¹⁵⁶Your compassion is great, O Lord;*
renew my life
    according to your laws.

¹⁵⁷Many are the foes who persecute me,*
but I have not turned from
    your statutes.

¹⁵⁸I look on the faithless with loathing,*
for they do not obey your word.

¹⁵⁹See how I love your precepts;*
preserve my life, O Lord,
    according to your love.

¹⁶⁰All your words are true;*
all your righteous laws are
    eternal.

Glory be to the Father and to the Son*
and to the Holy Spirit;
as it was in the beginning,*
    is now, and will be forever. Amen

Sin and Shin

III f♯: Phrygian

¹⁶¹Rulers persecute me without cause,*
but my heart trembles
    at your word.

¹⁶²I rejoice in your promise*
like one who finds great spoil.

¹⁶³I hate and abhor falsehood*
but I love your law.

¹⁶⁴Seven times a day I praise you*
for your righteous laws.

¹⁶⁵Great peace have they who
love your law,*
    and nothing can make them
    stumble.

¹⁶⁶I wait for your salvation, O Lord,*
and I follow your commands.

¹⁶⁷I obey your statutes,*
for I love them greatly.

¹⁶⁸I obey your precepts
and your statutes,*
    for all my ways
    are known to you.

Glory be to the Father and to the Son*
and to the Holy Spirit;
as it was in the beginning,*
    is now, and will be forever. Amen

Taw

IX g: Aeolian

¹⁶⁹May my cry come before you,
O Lord;*
    give me understanding
    according to your word.

¹⁷⁰May my supplication
come before you;*
    deliver me according to
    your promise.

¹⁷¹May my lips overflow with praise,*
for you teach me your decrees.

¹⁷²May my tongue sing of your word,*
for all your commands
    are righteous.

¹⁷³May your hand be ready to help me,*
    for I have chosen your precepts.

¹⁷⁴I long for your salvation, O Lord,*
    and your law is my delight.

¹⁷⁵Let me live that I may praise you,*
    and may your laws sustain me.

¹⁷⁶I have strayed like a lost sheep.*
    Seek your servant, for I have not
    forgotten your commandments.

Glory be to the Father and to the Son*
    and to the Holy Spirit;
as it was in the beginning,*
    is now, and will be forever. Amen

⁸the Lord will watch over your
coming and going*
    both now and forevermore.

Glory be to the Father and to the Son*
    and to the Holy Spirit;
as it was in the beginning,*
    is now, and will be forever. Amen

126

IX g: Aeolian

¹When the Lord brought back the
captives to Zion,*
    we were like men who dreamed.

²Our mouths were filled with laughter,*
    our tongues with songs of joy.
Then it was said among the nations,*
    "The Lord has done great things
    for them."

³The Lord has done
great things for us,*
    and we are filled with joy.

⁴Restore our fortunes, O Lord,*
    like streams in the Negev.

⁵Those who sow in tears*
    will reap with songs of joy.

⁶He who goes out weeping,
carrying seed to sow,*
    will return with songs of joy,
    carrying sheaves with him.

Glory be to the Father and to the Son*
    and to the Holy Spirit;
as it was in the beginning,*
    is now, and will be forever. Amen

121

IX g²: Aeolian

¹I lift up my eyes to the hills—*
    where does my help come from?

²My help comes from the Lord,*
    the Maker of heaven and earth.

³He will not let your foot slip—*
    he who watches over you will not
    slumber;

⁴indeed, he who watches over Israel*
    will neither slumber nor sleep.

⁵The Lord watches over you—*
    the Lord is your shade at your
    right hand;

⁶the sun will not harm you by day,*
    nor the moon by night.

⁷The Lord will keep you
from all harm—*
    he will watch over your life;

130

III f♯: Phrygian

¹Out of the depths*
  I cry to you, O Lord;

²O Lord, hear my voice.*
  Let your ears be attentive
  to my cry for mercy.

³If you, O Lord, kept
a record of sins,*
  O Lord, who could stand?

⁴But with you there is forgiveness;*
  therefore you are feared.

⁵I wait for the Lord, my soul waits,*
  and in his word I put my hope.

⁶My soul waits for the Lord more than
watchmen wait for the morning,*
  more than watchmen
  wait for the morning.

⁷O Israel, put your hope in the Lord,*
  for with the Lord is unfailing love
  and with him is full redemption.

⁸He himself will redeem Israel*
  from all their sins.

Glory be to the Father and to the Son*
  and to the Holy Spirit;
as it was in the beginning,*
  is now, and will be forever. Amen

133

XI A: Ionian

¹How good and pleasant it is*
  when brothers live together in unity!

²It is like precious oil poured on the
head, running down on the beard,*

running down on Aaron's beard,
down upon the collar of his robes.

³It is as if the dew of Hermon
were falling on Mount Zion.*
  For there the Lord bestows his
  blessing, even life forevermore.

Glory be to the Father and to the Son*
  and to the Holy Spirit;
as it was in the beginning,*
  is now, and will be forever. Amen

134

XI C: Ionian

¹Praise the Lord, all you servants
of the Lord*
  who minister by night in the house
  of the Lord.

²Lift up your hands in the sanctuary*
  and praise the Lord.

³May the Lord, the Maker of heaven
and earth,*
  bless you from Zion.

Glory be to the Father and to the Son*
  and to the Holy Spirit;
as it was in the beginning,*
  is now, and will be forever. Amen

135

XI D: Ionian

¹Praise the Lord.
  Praise the name of the Lord;*

Praise him, you servants
of the Lord,

²you who minister in the house
of the Lord,*
in the courts of the house
of our God.

³Praise the Lord, for the Lord is good;*
sing praise to his name,
for that is pleasant.

⁴For the Lord has chosen Jacob to be
his own,*
Israel to be his treasured possession.

⁵I know that the Lord is great,*
that our Lord is greater
than all gods.

⁶The Lord does whatever pleases him,
in the heavens and on the earth,*
in the seas and all their depths.

⁷He makes clouds rise from the ends
of the earth;*
he sends lightning with the rain
and brings out the wind from
his storehouses.

⁸He struck down the firstborn of
Egypt,*
the firstborn of men and animals.

⁹He sent his signs and wonders
into your midst, O Egypt,*
against Pharaoh and all his servants.

¹⁰He struck down many nations*
and killed mighty kings—

¹¹Sihon king of the Amorites,
Og king of Bashan*
and all the kings of Canaan—

¹²and he gave their land as an
inheritance,*
an inheritance to his people Israel.

¹³Your name, O Lord, endures forever,*
your renown, O Lord, through all
generations.

¹⁴For the Lord will vindicate his people*
and have compassion on his servants.

¹⁵The idols of the nations are silver
and gold,*
made by the hands of men.

¹⁶They have mouths, but cannot speak,*
eyes, but they cannot see;

¹⁷they have ears, but cannot hear,*
nor is there breath in their
mouths.

¹⁸Those who make them
will be like them,*
and so will all who trust in them.

¹⁹O house of Israel, praise the Lord;*
O house of Aaron, praise the Lord;

²⁰O house of Levi, praise the Lord;*
you who fear him, praise the Lord.

²¹Praise be to the Lord from Zion,*
to him who dwells in Jerusalem.
Praise the Lord.

Glory be to the Father and to the Son*
and to the Holy Spirit;
as it was in the beginning,*
is now, and will be forever. Amen

136

IX g: Aeolian

¹Give thanks to the Lord,
for he is good.*
His love endures forever.

²Give thanks to the God of gods.*
His love endures forever.

³Give thanks to the Lord of lords:*
His love endures forever.

⁴to him who alone does great wonders,*
His love endures forever.

⁵who by his understanding made the
heavens,*
His love endures forever.

⁶who spread out the earth
upon the w̄aters,*
His love endures forēver.

⁷who made the ḡreat lights—*
His love endures forēver.

⁸the sun to govérn the day,*
His love endures forēver.

⁹the moon and stars to govérn the
night;*
His love endures forēver.

¹⁰to him who struck down
the firstborn of Ēgypt*
His love endures forēver.

¹¹and brought Israel out
from am̄ong them*
His love endures forēver.

¹²with a mighty hand
and óutstretched arm;*
His love endures forēver.

¹³to him who divided the Red Sea
as̄under*
His love endures forēver.

¹⁴and brought Israel
through the mídst of it,*
His love endures forēver.

¹⁵but swept Pharaoh and his army
into the R̄ed Sea;*
His love endures forēver.

¹⁶to him who led his people
through the d̄esert,*
His love endures forēver.

¹⁷who struck down ḡreat kings,*
His love endures forēver.

¹⁸and killed míghty kings—*
His love endures forēver.

¹⁹Sihon king of the Ámorites*
His love endures forēver.

²⁰and Og king of B̄ashan—*
His love endures forēver.

²¹and gave their land
as an inh̄eritance,*
His love endures forēver.

²²an inheritance to his servant Ísrael;*
His love endures forēver.

²³to the Ọne who remembered us
in our l̇ow estate*
His love endures forēver.

²⁴and freed us from our énemies,*
His love endures forēver.

²⁵and who gives food to every c̄reature.*
His love endures forēver.

²⁶Give thanks to the God of h̄eaven.*
His love endures forēver.

Glory be to the Father and t́o the Son*
and to the Holy S̄pirit;
as it was in the beḡinning,*
is now, and will be forever. Āmen

138

 * VII E: Mixolydian

¹I will praise you, O Lord,
with áll my heart;*
before the "gods"
I will s̀ing your praise.

²I will bow down toward your holy
temple and will praịse your name for
your love and your faithfulness,*
for you have exalted above all
things your name ȧnd your word.

³When I called, you ȧnswered me;*
you made me bold and s̀touthearted.

⁴May all the kings of the earth
praise ẏou, O Lord,*
when they hear the words óf your
mouth.

⁵May they sing of the ways
of the Lord,*
　for the glory of the Lord is great.

⁶Though the Lord is on high,
he looks upon the lowly,*
　but the proud he knows from afar.

⁷Though I walk in the midst of
trouble, you preserve my life;*
　you stretch out your hand
　against the anger of my foes,
　with your right hand you save me.

⁸The Lord will fulfill his purpose
for me;*
　your love, O Lord, endures
　forever—do not abandon the works
　of your hands.

Glory be to the Father and to the Son*
　and to the Holy Spirit;
as it was in the beginning,*
　is now, and will be forever. Amen

139

V E♭: Lydian

¹O Lord, you have searched me*
　and you know me.

²You know when I sit and when I rise;*
　you perceive my thoughts from afar.

³You discern my going out
and my lying down;*
　you are familiar with all my ways.

⁴Before a word is on my tongue*
　you know it completely, O Lord.

⁵You hem me in, behind and before;*
　you have laid your hand upon me.

⁶Such knowledge is too wonderful
for me,*
　too lofty for me to attain.

⁷Where can I go from your Spirit?*
　Where can I flee from your
　presence?

⁸If I go up to the heavens,
you are there;*
　if I make my bed in the depths,
　you are there.

⁹If I rise on the wings of the dawn,*
　if I settle on the far side of the sea,

¹⁰even there your hand will guide me,*
　your right hand will hold me fast.

¹¹If I say, "Surely the darkness
will hide me*
　and the light become night
　around me,"

¹²even the darkness will not be dark
to you;*
　the night will shine like the day,
　for darkness is as light to you.

¹³For you created my inmost being;*
　you knit me together
　in my mother's womb.

¹⁴I praise you because I am fearfully
and wonderfully made;*
　your works are wonderful,
　I know that full well.

¹⁵My frame was not hidden from you
when I was made in the secret place.*
　When I was woven together
　in the depths of the earth,

¹⁶your eyes saw my unformed body.*
　All the days ordained for me
　were written in your book
　before one of them came to be.

¹⁷How precious to me are your
thoughts, O God!*
　How vast is the sum of them!

¹⁸Were I to count them, they would
outnumber the grains of sand.*
　When I awake, I am still with you.

¹⁹If only you would slay the wicked,
O God!*

Away from me,
you bloodthirsty men!

²⁰They speak of you with evil intent;*
your adversaries
misuse your name.

²¹Do I not hate those who hate you,
O Lord,*
and abhor those who rise up
against you?

²²I have nothing but hatred for them;*
I count them my enemies.

²³Search me, O God, and know my
heart;*
test me and know
my anxious thoughts.

²⁴See if there is any offensive way
in me,*
and lead me in the way everlasting.

Glory be to the Father and to the Son*
and to the Holy Spirit;
as it was in the beginning,*
is now, and will be forever. Amen

⁴Let not my heart be drawn to what is
evil, to take part in wicked deeds with
men who are evildoers;*
let me not eat of their delicacies.

⁵Let a righteous man strike me—
it is a kindness; let him rebuke me—
it is oil on my head.*
My head will not refuse it.
Yet my prayer is ever against
the deeds of evildoers;

⁶their rulers will be thrown down
from the cliffs,*
and the wicked will learn
that my words were well spoken.

⁷They will say, "As one plows
and breaks up the earth,*
so our bones have been scattered
at the mouth of the grave."

⁸But my eyes are fixed on you,
O Sovereign Lord;*
in you I take refuge—do not give
me over to death.

⁹Keep me from the snares
they have laid for me,*
from the traps set by evildoers.

¹⁰Let the wicked fall
into their own nets,*
while I pass by in safety.

Glory be to the Father and to the Son*
and to the Holy Spirit;
as it was in the beginning,*
is now, and will be forever. Amen

141

IX g: Aeolian

¹O Lord, I call to you; come quickly
to me.*
Hear my voice when I call to you.

²May my prayer be set before you
like incense;*
may the lifting up of my hands
be like the evening sacrifice.

³Set a guard over my mouth, O Lord;*
keep watch over the door
of my lips.

142

I d: Dorian

¹I cry aloud to the Lord;*
I lift up my voice to the Lord
for mercy.

²I pour out my complaint before him;*
  before him I tell my trouble.

³When my spirit grows faint within me,
it is you who know my way.*
  In the path where I walk
  men have hidden a snare for me.

⁴Look to my right and see;
no one is concerned for me.*
  I have no refuge;
  no one cares for my life.

⁵I cry to you, O Lord;*
  I say, "You are my refuge, my
  portion in the land of the living."

⁶Listen to my cry,
for I am in desperate need;*
  rescue me from those who pursue
  me, for they are too strong for me.

⁷Set me free from my prison that I may
praise your name.*
  Then the righteous will gather about
  me because of your goodness to me.

Glory be to the Father and to the Son*
  and to the Holy Spirit;
as it was in the beginning,*
  is now, and will be forever. Amen

143

*   III f♯: Phrygian

¹O Lord, hear my prayer, listen to my
cry for mercy;*
  in your faithfulness and
  righteousness come to my relief.

²Do not bring your servant
into judgment,*
  for no one living is righteous
  before you.

³The enemy pursues me,
he crushes me to the ground;*
  he makes me dwell in darkness
  like those long dead.

⁴So my spirit grows faint within me;*
  my heart within me is dismayed.

⁵I remember the days of long ago;*
  I meditate on all your works
  and consider what your hands
  have done.

⁶I spread out my hands to you;*
  my soul thirsts for you
  like a parched land.

⁷Answer me quickly, O Lord;*
  my spirit faints with longing.
Do not hide your face from me*
  or I will be like those
  who go down to the pit.

⁸Let the morning bring me word
of your unfailing love,*
  for I have put my trust in you.
Show me the way I should go,*
  for to you I lift up my soul.

⁹Rescue me from my enemies, O Lord,*
  for I hide myself in you.

¹⁰Teach me to do your will,
for you are my God;*
  may your good Spirit
  lead me on level ground.

¹¹For your name's sake, O Lord,
preserve my life;*
  in your righteousness,
  bring me out of trouble.

¹²In your unfailing love,
silence my enemies;*
  destroy all my foes,
  for I am your servant.

Glory be to the Father and to the Son*
  and to the Holy Spirit;
as it was in the beginning,*
  is now, and will be forever. Amen

146

*   XI A: Ionian

¹Praise the Lord.*
  Praise the Lord, O my soul.

²I will praise the Lord all my life;*
  I will sing praise to my God
  as long as I live.

³Do not put your trust in princes,*
  in mortal men, who cannot save.

⁴When their spirit departs,
they return to the ground;*
  on that very day their plans
  come to nothing.

⁵Blessed is he whose help is the God of
Jacob,*
  whose hope is in the Lord his God,

⁶the Maker of heaven and earth,
the sea, and everything in them—*
  the Lord, who remains faithful
  forever.

⁷He upholds the cause of the oppressed
and gives food to the hungry.*
  The Lord sets prisoners free,

⁸the Lord gives sight to the blind, the
Lord lifts up those
who are bowed down,*
  the Lord loves the righteous.

⁹The Lord watches over the alien and
sustains the fatherless and the widow,*
  but he frustrates the ways of
  the wicked.

¹⁰The Lord reigns forever,*
  your God, O Zion, for all
  generations. Praise the Lord.

Glory be to the Father and to the Son*
  and to the Holy Spirit;
as it was in the beginning,*
  is now, and will be forever. Amen

147

*   XI D: Ionian

¹Praise the Lord. How good it is to sing
praises to our God,*
  how pleasant and fitting
  to praise him!

²The Lord builds up Jerusalem;*
  he gathers the exiles of Israel.

³He heals the brokenhearted*
  and binds up their wounds.

⁴He determines the number of the stars*
  and calls them each by name.

⁵Great is our Lord and mighty in
power;*
  his understanding has no limit.

⁶The Lord sustains the humble*
  but casts the wicked to the ground.

⁷Sing to the Lord with thanksgiving;*
  make music to our God on the harp.

⁸He covers the sky with clouds;*
  he supplies the earth with rain
  and makes grass grow on the hills.

⁹He provides food for the cattle*
  and for the young ravens
  when they call.

¹⁰His pleasure is not in the strength of
the horse,*
  nor his delight in the legs of a man;

¹¹the Lord delights in those
who fear him,*
  who put their hope in his
  unfailing love.

¹²Extol the Lord, O Jerusalem;*
  praise your God, O Zion,

¹³for he strengthens the bars of your
gates*
  and blesses your people within you.

¹⁴He grants peace to your borders*
and satisfies you with the finest
of wheat.

¹⁵He sends his command to the earth;*
his word runs swiftly.

¹⁶He spreads the snow like wool*
and scatters the frost like ashes.

¹⁷He hurls down his hail like pebbles.*
Who can withstand his icy blast?

¹⁸He sends his word and melts them;*
he stirs up his breezes,
and the waters flow.

¹⁹He has revealed his word to Jacob,*
his laws and decrees to Israel.

²⁰He has done this for no other nation;*
they do not know his laws.
Praise the Lord.

Glory be to the Father and to the Son*
and to the Holy Spirit;
as it was in the beginning,*
is now, and will be forever. Amen

148

*   XI A: Ionian

¹Praise the Lord. Praise the Lord
from the heavens,*
praise him in the heights above.

²Praise him, all his angels,*
praise him, all his heavenly hosts.

³Praise him, sun and moon,*
praise him, all you shining stars.

⁴Praise him, you highest heavens*
and you waters above the skies.

⁵Let them praise the name of the Lord,*
for he commanded and they were
created.

⁶He set them in place for ever and
ever;*
he gave a decree that will never
pass away.

⁷Praise the Lord from the earth,*
you great sea creatures
and all ocean depths,

⁸lightning and hail, snow and clouds,*
stormy winds that do his bidding,

⁹you mountains and all hills,*
fruit trees and all cedars,

¹⁰wild animals and all cattle,*
small creatures and flying birds,

¹¹kings of the earth and all nations,*
you princes and all rulers on earth,

¹²young men and maidens,*
old men and children.

¹³Let them praise the name of the Lord,
for his name alone is exalted;*
his splendor is above
the earth and the heavens.

¹⁴He has raised up for his people a horn,
the praise of all his saints,*
of Israel, the people close
to his heart. Praise the Lord.

Glory be to the Father and to the Son*
and to the Holy Spirit;
as it was in the beginning,*
is now, and will be forever. Amen

CHANTING THE PSALMS, INTROITS, GRADUALS, AND CANTICLES

The psalms, introits, graduals, and canticles may be carried by various extant systems of formulary chant. In this worship book 10 simple tones are provided for use by the congregation.

Each verse of text divides into half-verses at the asterisk (*); likewise, each tone divides into half-phrases at the asterisk over the single bar. The first half-phrase carries the first half-verse, and the second one carries the second. A few long verses (such as Ps. 98:9) are treated like the Gloria Patri with the entire tone repeated as shown by the markings.

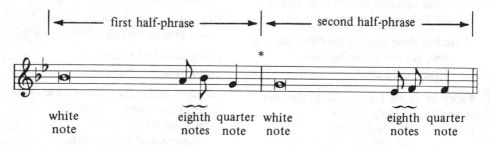

|← first half-phrase → | ← second half-phrase →|

white note — eighth quarter notes note — white note — eighth quarter notes note

Most of the text in each half-phrase is chanted to the white note (reciting note). Only the last syllable of each half-verse should be chanted to the one quarter note of the corresponding half-phrase. Accordingly, the three concluding notes of each half-phrase carry either:

a) *three* syllables of text (signaled by a vertical stroke (ı) over the third last syllable)—chant one syllable to each note—see Example 1; or

b) *two* syllables of text (signaled by a horizontal stroke (-) over the second last syllable)—slur the two eighth notes to carry the second last syllable, and chant the last syllable to the final quarter note—see Example 2.

Example 1. Verse 4 of Psalm 25 can be chanted to Tone I d:

Show me your ways, O Lord,* teach me your paths.

Example 2. Verse 1 of Psalm 23 can be chanted to Tone I d:

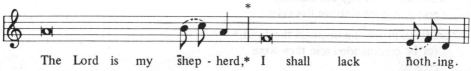

The Lord is my shep - herd,* I shall lack noth - ing.

Occasionally a two-syllable word is contracted to one syllable (heav'n, pow'r, blessed-blest), or a three-syllable word to two (ev-'ry, of-f'ring, mar-v'lous).

In this book the tones are assigned to the psalms and introits with their notes printed near and over the texts. The tones may also be assigned to the graduals, canticles, and similar texts.

Furthermore, for longer psalms or canticles, two closely related tones may be used, organized as in the *Benedicite, omnia opera* (see Canticles and Chants, No. 9). When chanting such arrangements, care should be exercised to pass from one tone to the other without unnecessary pause.

CONTENTS

CANTICLES AND CHANTS

HYMNS

The Church Year

The Divine Service

CANTICLES
AND CHANTS

Oh, Come, Oh, Come, Emmanuel   1
Veni, Emmanuel

Oh, come, oh, come, Em - man - u - el,   And ran - som cap - tive

Is - ra - el,   That mourns in lone - ly ex - ile here   Un - til the

Son of   God   ap - pear.   Re - joice!   Re - joice!   Em -

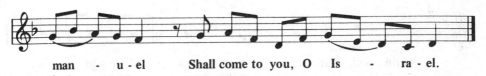

man - u - el   Shall come to you, O   Is - ra - el.

Text: Psalteriolum Cantionum Catholicarum, *Köln, 1710; tr. John M. Neale, 1818–66, alt.*
Tune: French processional, 15th cent.

2   The Royal Banners Forward Go

Vexilla regis

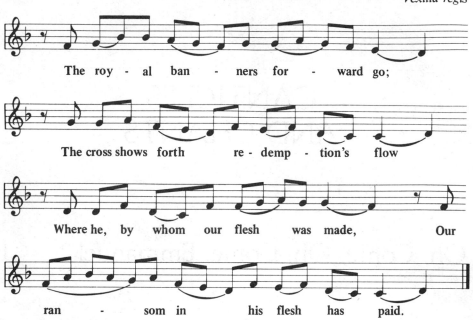

The roy - al ban - ners for - ward go;

The cross shows forth re - demp - tion's flow

Where he, by whom our flesh was made, Our

ran - som in his flesh has paid.

Text: Venantius Honorius Fortunatus, 530–609; tr. composite
Tune: Sarum plainsong, mode I

3   Glory Be to the Father

Gloria patri

Glory be to the Father and to the Son   and   to the Ho - ly Ghost;

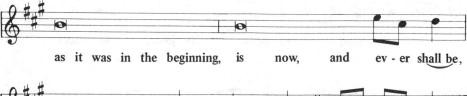

as it was in the beginning, is   now,   and   ev - er shall be,

world with - out end.   A - men.   Al - le - lu - ia.

Text: based on Rom. 16:27; Eph. 3:21; Phil. 4:20; Rev. 1:6
Tune: source unknown

I Believe in One God

Nicene Creed

4

I be-lieve in one God, ℂ the Fa-ther Al-might-y,

mak-er of heav-en and earth and all things vis - i -

ble and in-vis - i-ble. And in one Lord

Je - sus Christ, the on-ly - be-got-ten Son of God,

be - got-ten of his Fa - ther be - fore all worlds,

God of God, Light of Light, ver -y God of ver - y God,

be-got-ten, not made, be - ing of one sub-stance

with the Fa - ther, by whom all things were made; ▶

whose king-dom will have no end. And I be-lieve in the

Ho-ly Spir-it, the Lord and giv-er of life, who pro-

ceeds from the Fa-ther and the Son, who with the Fa-ther

and the Son to-geth-er is wor-shiped and glo-ri-fied,

who spoke by the proph - ets. And I be-lieve in one ho-ly

Chris-tian and ap-os-tol-ic Church, I ac-knowl-edge one

Bap - tism for the re-mis-sion of sins, and I look for the

res-ur-rec-tion of the dead and the life of the world to come.

A - men, a - men, a - men

Text: The Book of Common Prayer, *1549*
Tune: plainsong, Credo III, *17th cent.*

5

Create in Me

Offertory

Cre-ate in me a clean heart, O God, and re-new a

right spir - it with-in me. Cast me not a-way from your

pres-ence, and take not your Ho-ly Spir - it from me.

Re-store to me the joy of your sal - va-tion, and up-hold

me with your free Spir - it. A - men

Text: from Psalm 51
Tune: J. G. Winer, 1583–1651

6

Holy, Holy, Holy

Sanctus

Ho - ly, ho - ly, ho - ly is God,

the Lord of Sab - a - oth; all the heav - ens and all

the earth are full of your glo - ry. Ho -

- san - na, ho - san - na in the high - est. Bless -

ed is the vir - gin's Son, he who comes in the name of the
(Pas - chal Lamb,*)

Lord. Ho - san - na, ho - san - na in the high - est.

*During Easter and its season

Text: from Isaiah 6
Tune: Lucas Lossius, 1508–82; based on plainsong Sanctus, 11th cent.; adapt.

O Christ, the Lamb of God   7

Agnus Dei

O Christ, the Lamb of God, who takes a-way the sin of the world,

have mer-cy on us. O Christ, the Lamb of God, who takes a-way the

sin of the world, have mer-cy on us. O Christ, the Lamb of God, who

takes a-way the sin of the world, grant us your peace. A - men

Text: from John 1
Tune: Kirchenordnung, Braunschweig, 1528

We Praise You, O God

Te Deum laudamus

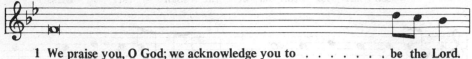

1 We praise you, O God; we acknowledge you to . . . . be the Lord.
2 Holy, holy, holy, Lord God of . . . . Sab-a - oth;
3 The noble army of martyrs . . . . praise you.

1 All the earth now worships you, the Fa - ther ev-er-last - ing.
2 heav'n and earth are full of the majes - ty of your glo - ry.
3 The holy Church throughout all the . . . . world does ac-knowledge you:

1 To you all angels cry aloud, the heav'ns and all the . . . . . pow'rs there-in.
2 The glorious company of the apostles . . . . praise you.
3 The Father of an infinite majesty; your adorable, true, and . .on - ly Son;
4 You are the king of glory, ...O   Christ;

1 To you cherubim and seraphim con - tin - ual - ly do cry:
2 The goodly fellowship of the . . . . . .proph-ets praise you.
3 also the Holy . . . . .Ghost, the Com-fort - er.
4 you are the everlasting Son . . . . . . .of   the   Fa - ther.

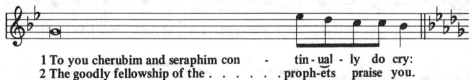

5 When you took upon yourself to de- . . . . liv - er man,
6 You sit at the right . . . . hand of God

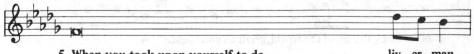

5 you humbled yourself to be born . . . . of a vir - gin.
6 in the glory . . . . of the Fa - ther.

5 When you had overcome the . . . . sharpness of death,
6 We believe that . . . . you will come

5 you opened the kingdom of heav'n to . . . . . all be-liev - ers.
6 to . . . . be our judge.

7 We therefore pray you to help your . . . . ser - vants,

7 whom you have redeem- . . . . .ed with your pre - cious blood.

7 Make them to be numbered . . . . with your saints

7 in glory . . . . .ev - er - last - ing.

Text: source unknown, 4th cent.; tr. from King's Primer, 1545
Chant: H. Lawes, 1596–1662, and R. Cooke, 1768–1814, adapt.

9 All You Works of the Lord

Benedicite, omnia opera

VII G: Mixolydian

1 All you works of the Lord, bless the Lord—praise him
and magnify him for - ev - er.

2 You angels of the Lord, bless the Lord; you heavens, ... bless the Lord;

3 all you powers of the Lord, bless the Lord—praise him
and magnify him for - ev - er.

4 You sun and moon, . . . bless the Lord; you stars of heaven, bless the Lord;

IX a²: Aeolian

5 you showers and dew, bless the Lord—praise him
and magnify him for - ev - er.

6 You winds of God, . . . bless the Lord; you fire and heat, ... bless the Lord;

7 you winter and summer, bless the Lord—praise him
and magnify him for - ev - er.

8 You dews and frost, bless the Lord; you frost and cold, . . . bless the Lord;

9 you ice and snow, . . . bless the Lord—praise him
and magnify him for - ev - er.

10 You nights and days, . . . bless the Lord; you light and darkness, bless the Lord;

11 you lightnings and clouds, bless the Lord—praise him
and magnify him for - ev - er.

VII G: Mixolydian

12 Let the earth . . . . bless the Lord; you mountains and hills, bless the Lord;

13 all you green things
   that grow on the earth, bless the Lord— praise him
                    and magnify him for - ev - er.

14 You wells and springs, bless the Lord; you rivers and seas, ... bless the Lord;

15 you whales and all who
   move in the waters, bless the Lord— praise him
                    and magnify him for - ev - er.

16 All you birds of the air, bless the Lord; all you beasts and cattle, bless the Lord;

IX a²: Aeolian

17 all you
   children of mortals, bless the Lord— praise him
                    and magnify him for - ev - er.

18 You people of God, bless the Lord; you priests of the Lord, bless the Lord;

19 you servants
   of the Lord, . . . bless the Lord— praise him
                    and magnify him for - ev - er.

20 You spirits and
   souls of the righteous, bless the Lord; you pure
                    and humble of heart, bless the Lord;

21 let us bless
   the Father and
   the Son and the Holy Spir - it— praise him
                    and magnify him for - ev - er.

VII G: Mixolydian

22 Glory be to the Father and to the Son   and   to   the   Holy Spir- it;

23 as it was in the be - gin - ning, is now, and will be forever. A - men

Text: from Song of the Three Young Men
© *Chant: Paul G. Bunjes, b. 1914*

10 Christians, to the Paschal Victim

The Victimae Paschali Celebration

Choir

Chris-tians, to the Pas-chal Vic-tim   Of - fer your thank-ful prais-es!

The Lamb the sheep has ran-somed: Christ, who on - ly   is   sin-less,

Rec - on - cil - ing sin - ners   to   the   Fa - ther. Death and life have con-

tend-ed   In that   com-bat stu - pen-dous: The Prince of life, who died,

Congregation

Reigns im - mor - tal.   **Christ   is   a - ris - en   From the grave's dark**

pris - on.   So let   our song ex - ult - ing rise: Christ   with   com-fort

Choir

lights our eyes. Al   - le - lu   - ia!   "Speak, Mar - y, de - clar - ing

What you saw when way-far-ing." "The tomb of Christ, who is liv - ing, The

glo - ry of Je-sus' res-ur - rec - tion; Bright an-gels at-test - ing, The shroud and

nap-kin rest-ing. Lord Christ, my hope, is a - ris -en; To Gal-i -lee he goes be-

Congregation

fore you." All our hopes were end - ed Had Je - sus not as -

cend - ed From the grave tri - um-phant-ly Our nev - er - end - ing

Choir

life to be. Al - le -lu - ia! Christ in-deed from death is

ris - en, Our new life ob -tain - ing. Have mer - cy, vic -tor King,

Congregation

ev - er reign - ing! Al - le - lu - ia, al - le -

lu - ia, al - le - lu - ia! So let our song ex -ult -

ing rise: Christ, our com-fort, fills the skies. Al - le - lu - ia!

© Texts: Latin sequence, attr. Wipo of Burgundy, 11th cent.; tr. unknown, alt.
   German hymn, c. 1100; tr. F. Samuel Janzow, b. 1913
Tunes: plainsong, mode I, attr. Wipo of Burgundy, 11th cent.
   J. Klug, Geistliche Lieder, 1533

11

Lord, Now Let Your Servant
Depart in Peace

Nunc dimittis

Lord, now let your servant de - part in peace ac-cord-ing to your

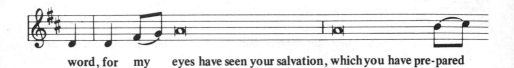

word, for my eyes have seen your salvation, which you have pre-pared

be - fore the face of all people, a light to light - en the

Gen-tiles and the glo - ry of your peo-ple Is - ra - el.

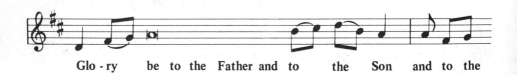

Glo - ry be to the Father and to the Son and to the

Ho - ly Ghost; as it was in the beginning, is now, and

ev - er shall be, world with - out end. A - men

Text: from Luke 2
Tune: plainsong, based on Psalm tone V

HYMNS

The Advent of Our God 12

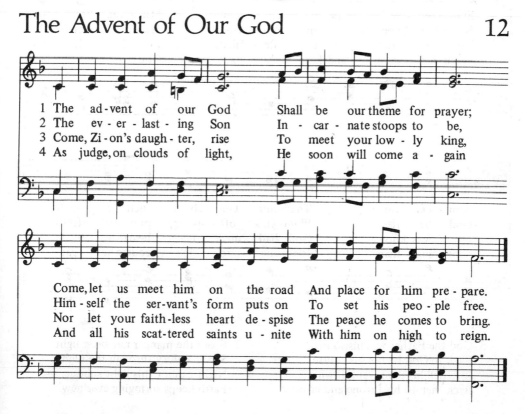

1 The ad-vent of our God Shall be our theme for prayer;
2 The ev-er-last-ing Son In-car-nate stoops to be,
3 Come, Zi-on's daugh-ter, rise To meet your low-ly king,
4 As judge, on clouds of light, He soon will come a-gain

Come, let us meet him on the road And place for him pre-pare.
Him-self the ser-vant's form puts on To set his peo-ple free.
Nor let your faith-less heart de-spise The peace he comes to bring.
And all his scat-tered saints u-nite With him on high to reign.

5 Before the dawning day
  Let sin be put to flight;
No longer let the law hold sway,
  But walk in freedom's light.

6 All glory to the Son,
  Who comes to set us free,
With Father, Spirit, ever one
  Through all eternity.

Text: Charles Coffin, 1676–1749; tr. John Chandler, 1806–76, alt.
Tune: Aaron Williams, 1731–76

ST. THOMAS
SM

13 Savior of the Nations, Come

1 Sav-ior of the na-tions, come,
2 No man's pow'r of mind or blood
3 Here a maid was found with child,
4 Then stepped forth the Lord of all

Show your-self the vir-gin's son. Mar-vel, heav-en,
But the Spir-it of our God Made the Word of
Vir-gin pure and un-de-filed. In her vir-tues
From his pure and king-ly hall; God of God, be-

won-der, earth, That our God chose such a birth.
God be flesh, Wom-an's off-spring, pure and fresh.
it was known God had made her heart his throne.
com-ing man, His he-ro-ic course be-gan.

5 God the Father was his source,
Back to God he ran his course.
Into hell his road went down,
Back then to his throne and crown.

6 Father's equal, you will win
Vict'ries for us over sin.
Might eternal, make us whole;
Heal our ills of flesh and soul.

7 From the manger newborn light
Sends a glory through the night.
Night cannot this light subdue,
Faith keeps springing ever new.

8 Glory to the Father sing,
Glory to the Son, our king,
Glory to the Spirit be
Now and through eternity.

© Text: attr. St. Ambrose, 340–97; German version,
Martin Luther, 1483–1546; tr. F. Samuel Janzow, b. 1913, alt.
Tune: Johann Walter, Geystliche gesangk Buchleyn, 1524

NUN KOMM, DER HEIDEN HEILAND
77 77

On Jordan's Bank the Baptist's Cry

1 On Jor-dan's bank the Bap - tist's cry An - nounc - es
2 Then cleansed be ev - 'ry life from sin; Make straight the
3 We hail you as our Sav - ior, Lord, Our ref - uge
4 Stretch forth your hand, our health re - store, And make us

that the Lord is nigh; A - wake and hear - ken,
way for God with - in, And let us all our
and our great re - ward; With-out your grace we
rise to fall no more; Oh, let your face up -

for he brings Glad tid - ings of the King of kings!
hearts pre - pare For Christ to come and en - ter there.
waste a - way Like flow'rs that with - er and de - cay.
on us shine And fill the world with love di - vine.

5 All praise to you, eternal Son,
Whose advent has our freedom won,
Whom with the Father we adore,
And Holy Spirit, evermore.

Text: Charles Coffin, 1676–1749; tr. composite
Tune: adapt. Michael Praetorius, 1571–1621

PUER NOBIS
L M

15 Lo, He Comes with Clouds Descending

1 Lo, he comes with clouds descending, Once for ev-'ry
2 Ev-'ry eye shall now be-hold him Robed in glo-rious
3 Those dear to-kens of his Pas-sion Still his daz-zling
4 Yea, a-men, let all a-dore thee, High on thine e-

sin - ner slain; Thou-sand thou-sand saints at-tend - ing
maj - es - ty; Those who set at nought and sold him,
bod - y bears, Cause of end-less ex-ul-ta - tion
ter - nal throne; Sav - ior, take the pow'r and glo - ry,

Swell the tri-umph of his train: Al - le - lu - ia,
Pierced and nailed him to the tree, Deep-ly wail - ing,
To his ran-somed wor - ship-ers. With what rap - ture,
Claim the king-dom for thine own. Al - le - lu - ia,

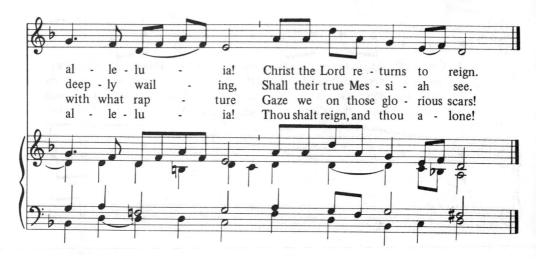

al - le - lu - ia! Christ the Lord re - turns to reign.
deep - ly wail - ing, Shall their true Mes - si - ah see.
with what rap - ture Gaze we on those glo - rious scars!
al - le - lu - ia! Thou shalt reign, and thou a - lone!

Text: Charles Wesley, 1707–88, alt.
Tune: French folk tune, 17th cent.

PICARDY
87 87 87

Hosanna Now Through Advent   16

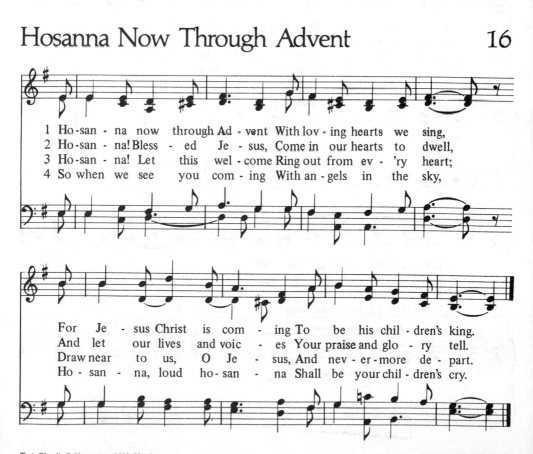

1 Ho-san - na now through Ad - vent With lov - ing hearts we sing,
2 Ho-san - na! Bless - ed Je - sus, Come in our hearts to dwell,
3 Ho-san - na! Let this wel - come Ring out from ev - 'ry heart;
4 So when we see you com - ing With an - gels in the sky,

For Je - sus Christ is com - ing To be his chil - dren's king.
And let our lives and voic - es Your praise and glo - ry tell.
Draw near to us, O Je - sus, And nev - er - more de - part.
Ho - san - na, loud ho - san - na Shall be your chil - dren's cry.

Text: Claudia F. Hernaman, 1838–98; alt.
Tune: Geistliche Kirchengesäng, Köln, 1623

MARIA IST GEBOREN
76 76

17 O Lord of Light, Who Made the Stars

1 O Lord of light, who made the stars, O Dawn, by whom we
2 In low - li - ness you came on earth To res - cue us from
3 To pay the debt we owed for sin, Your pain - ful cross was
4 But now you reign, the King of kings, A - dored in high - est

see the way, O Christ, re - deem - er of the world:
Sa - tan's snares; O won - drous love that healed our wounds
made the price; From bless - ed Mar - y's womb you came,
maj - es - ty; Your ver - y name is held in awe

Come now and lis - ten as we pray!
By tak - ing on our mor - tal cares!
A vic - tim pure for sac - ri - fice.
From pole to pole and sea to sea! A - men

5 Great judge of all, on earth's last day
   Have pity on your children's plight;
   Rise up to shield us with your grace;
   Deliver us from Satan's might.

6 To God the Father and the Son
   And Holy Spirit, Three in One,
   Praise, honor, might, and glory be
   From age to age eternally. Amen

© Text: Latin hymn, c. 9th cent.; tr. Melvin Farrell, b. 1930, alt.
Tune: Sarum plainsong, mode IV

CONDITOR ALME SIDERUM
L M

Hark! A Thrilling Voice Is Sounding 18

1 Hark! A thrill-ing voice is sound - ing! "Christ is near," we hear it say. "Cast a - way the works of dark - ness, All you chil-dren of the day!"

2 Star - tled at the sol-emn warn - ing, Let the earth-bound soul a - rise; "Christ, its sun, all sloth dis-pel - ling, Shines up - on the morn - ing skies.

3 See, the Lamb, so long ex - pect - ed, Comes with par-don down from heav'n. Let us haste, with tears of sor - row, One and all, to be for - giv'n;

4 So, when next he comes in glo - ry And the world is wrapped in fear, He will shield us with his mer - cy And with words of love draw near.

5 Honor, glory, might, dominion
  To the Father and the Son

With the everliving Spirit
While eternal ages run!

Text: Latin hymn, 1632; tr. Edward Caswall, 1814–78, alt.
Tune: Michael Weisse, c. 1480–1534

FREUEN WIR UNS ALL IN EIN
87 87

19 O Lord, How Shall I Meet You

1 O Lord, how shall I meet you, How wel-come you a-right? Your
2 Your Zi-on strews be-fore you Green boughs and fair-est palms; And
3 I lay in fet-ters, groan-ing; You came to set me free. I
4 Love caused your in-car-na-tion; Love brought you down to me. Your

peo-ple long to greet you, My hope, my heart's de-light! Oh,
I too will a-dore you With joy-ous songs and psalms. My
stood, my shame be-moan-ing; You came to hon-or me. A
thirst for my sal-va-tion Pro-cured my lib-er-ty. Oh,

kin - dle, Lord most ho - ly, Your lamp with-in my
heart shall bloom for-ev - er For you with prais-es
glo - rious crown you give me, A trea-sure safe on
love be - yond all tell-ing, That led you to em-

breast To do in spir-it low-ly All that may please you best.
new And from your name shall nev - er With-hold the hon-or due.
high That will not fail or leave me As earth-ly rich-es fly.
brace In love, all love ex-cel - ling, Our lost and fall-en race.

5 Rejoice, then, you sad-hearted,
   Who sit in deepest gloom,
Who mourn your joys departed
   And tremble at your doom.
Despair not; he is near you,
   There, standing at the door,
Who best can help and cheer you
   And bids you weep no more.

6 He comes to judge the nations,
   A terror to his foes,
A light of consolations
   And blessed hope to those
Who love the Lord's appearing.
   O glorious Sun, now come,
Send forth your beams so cheering,
   And guide us safely home.

Text: Paul Gerhardt, 1607–76; tr. The Lutheran Hymnal, *1941, alt.*
Tune: Johann Crüger, 1598–1662

WIE SOLL ICH DICH EMPFANGEN
76 76 D

O Bride of Christ, Rejoice   20

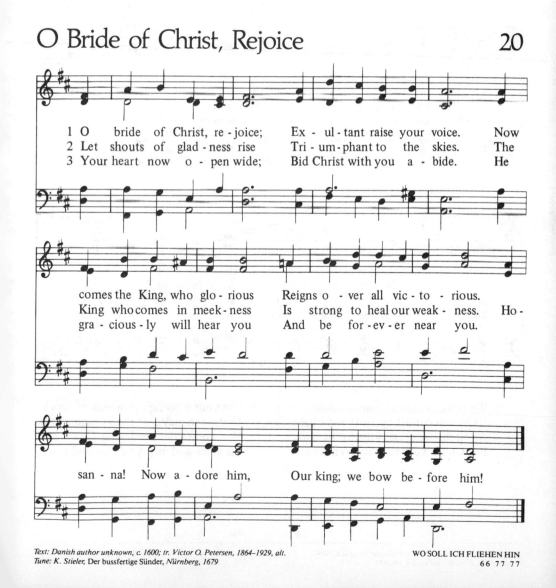

1 O bride of Christ, re-joice; Ex-ul-tant raise your voice. Now
2 Let shouts of glad-ness rise Tri-um-phant to the skies. The
3 Your heart now o-pen wide; Bid Christ with you a-bide. He

comes the King, who glo-rious Reigns o-ver all vic-to-rious.
King who comes in meek-ness Is strong to heal our weak-ness. Ho-
gra-cious-ly will hear you And be for-ev-er near you.

san-na! Now a-dore him, Our king; we bow be-fore him!

Text: Danish author unknown, c. 1600; tr. Victor O. Petersen, 1864–1929, alt.
Tune: K. Stieler, Der bussfertige Sünder, *Nürnberg, 1679*

WO SOLL ICH FLIEHEN HIN
66 77 77

21 "Comfort, Comfort," Says the Voice

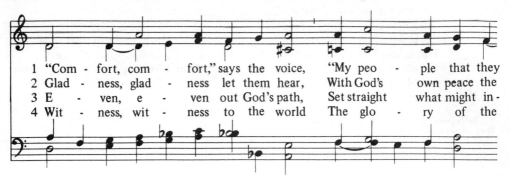

1 "Com - fort, com - fort," says the voice, "My peo - ple that they
2 Glad - ness, glad - ness let them hear, With God's own peace the
3 E - ven, e - ven out God's path, Set straight what might in -
4 Wit - ness, wit - ness to the world The glo - ry of the

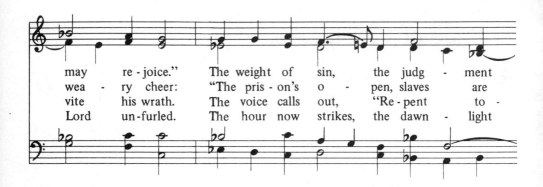

may re - joice." The weight of sin, the judg - ment
wea - ry cheer: "The pris - on's o - pen, slaves are
vite his wrath. The voice calls out, "Re - pent to -
Lord un - furled. The hour now strikes, the dawn - light

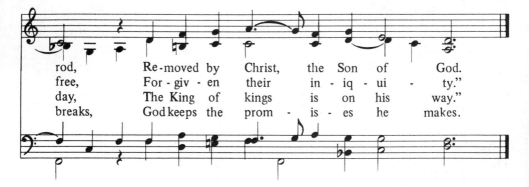

rod, Re - moved by Christ, the Son of God.
free, For - giv - en their in - iq - ui - ty."
day, The King of kings is on his way."
breaks, God keeps the prom - is - es he makes.

5 Withered, withered human might,
Its bloom cut off by frost and blight.
All flesh, like grass, wilts to the core,
But God's Word lives forevermore.

6 Lift your voice, speak words of pow'r
That none may fear the awesome hour.
Now comes the Lord, your God is here,
His grace and might rule far and near.

© Text: Waldemar Rode, b. 1903; tr. F. Samuel Janzow, b. 1913
© Tune: Hans Friedrich Micheelsen, 1902–73

TRÖSTET, TRÖSTET, SPRICHT DER HERR
78 88

Come, O Long-Expected Jesus

1 Come, O long-ex-pect-ed Je-sus, Born to set your peo-ple free;
2 Born your peo-ple to de-liv-er, Born a child and yet a king;

From our fears and sins re-lease us By your death on Cal-va-ry.
Born to reign in us for-ev-er, Now your gra-cious king-dom bring.

Is-rael's strength and con-so-la-tion, Hope to all the earth im-part,
By your own e-ter-nal Spir-it Rule in all our hearts a-lone;

Dear de-sire of ev-'ry na-tion, Joy of ev-'ry long-ing heart.
By your all-suf-fi-cient mer-it Raise us to your glo-rious throne.

Text: Charles Wesley, 1707–88, alt.
Tune: W. Walker, Southern Harmony, 1835

JEFFERSON
87 87 D

23 Lift Up Your Heads, You Mighty Gates

1 Lift up your heads, you might-y gates! Be-hold, the King of
2 The righ-teous King is bring-ing peace; He comes the pris-'ners
3 O hap-py town, O bless-ed land That keeps our gra-cious
4 Un-bar the gate, fling wide the door, Your heart to God's de-

glo-ry waits. The King of kings is draw-ing near, The
to re-lease. His roy-al crown, self-sac-ri-fice, Its
King's com-mand, And blest the heart when he comes in His
sign re-store. A-dorn its walls with all things right, With

Sav-ior of the world is here. He brings sal-va-tion
jew-el, mer-cy with-out price. He brings our sor-rows
ho-ly reign there to be-gin. His en-trance is the
peace and love and joy and light. Your King will then be

down to earth. Greet him with shouts of ho-ly mirth. Our
to an end. Shout out your joy to God, our friend. Our
dawn of bliss; He fills our lives and makes them his. Our
glad to come And live with-in you as his home. Our

high - est praise we bring, Our God, Cre - a - tor, King.
high - est praise we bring, Our God, Re - deem -er, King.
high - est praise we bring, God, Com - fort - er and King.
high - est praise we bring To God, our Lord and King.

5 Christ Jesus, Lord and Savior, come,
I open wide my heart, your home.
Oh, enter with your radiant grace,
On my life's pattern shine your face,
And let your Holy Spirit guide
To gracious vistas rich and wide.
Our God, we praise your name,
Forevermore the same.

© Text: Georg Weissel, 1590–1635; tr. F. Samuel Janzow, b. 1913
Tune: Johann A. Freylinghausen, Geistreiches Gesang-Buch, 1704

MACHT HOCH DIE TÜR
88 88 88 66

24 Lift Up Your Heads, You Mighty Gates

1 Lift up your heads, you might - y gates! Be - hold, the King of
2 The righ - teous King is bring - ing peace; He comes the pris - 'ners
3 O hap - py town, O bless - ed land That keeps our gra - cious
4 Un - bar the gate, fling wide the door, Your heart to God's de -

glo - ry waits. The King of kings is draw - ing near, The
to re - lease. His roy - al crown, self - sac - ri - fice, Its
King's com - mand, And blest the heart when he comes in His
sign re - store. A - dorn its walls with all things right, With

Sav - ior of the world is here. He brings sal - va - tion
jew - el, mer - cy with - out price. He brings our sor - rows
ho - ly reign there to be - gin. His en - trance is the
peace and love and joy and light. Your King will then be

down to earth. Greet him with shouts of ho - ly mirth. Our
to an end. Shout out your joy to God, our friend. Our
dawn of bliss; He fills our lives and makes them his. Our
glad to come And live with - in you as his home. Our

high - est praise we	bring,	Our God, Cre - a - tor,	King.
high - est praise we	bring,	Our God, Re-deem - er,	King.
high - est praise we	bring,	God, Com - fort - er, and	King.
high - est praise we	bring	To God, our Lord and	King.

5 Christ Jesus, Lord and Savior, come,
I open wide my heart, your home.
Oh, enter with your radiant grace,
On my life's pattern shine your face,
And let your Holy Spirit guide
To gracious vistas rich and wide.
Our God, we praise your name,
Forevermore the same.

© Text: Georg Weissel, 1590–1635; tr. F. Samuel Janzow, b. 1913
Tune: August Lemke, 1820–1913

MILWAUKEE
88 88 88 66

25   O People, Rise and Labor

1 O peo-ple, rise and la - bor To ren - o - vate the
2 Pre - pare with ear - nest rig - or The way for your great
3 A heart that hum - bly serves him Stands high - est in his
4 Dear Lord, in high com - pas - sion Bend down with Ad - vent

heart That man - kind's might - y Sav - ior, Whom
guest. Make straight his path with vig - or, Re -
sight. The haugh - ty heart, the proud whim Go
grace. My heart, I pray, re - fash - ion With

God's love set a - part To free you all from sin,
build your lives with zest. The sunk - en val - leys fill,
down in an-guished night. But those who love God's Word
mer - cy from your face. Come from the thank - less inn

May do the prom - ised won - der And with his life and
Re - store e - rod - ed plac - es, Where sin - bursts leave their
And go where he is point - ing Are fit by his a -
To make my heart your man - ger That I, no more a

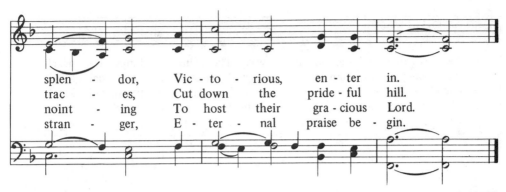

splen - dor, Vic - to - rious, en - ter in.
trac - es, Cut down the pride - ful hill.
noint - ing To host their gra - cious Lord.
stran - ger, E - ter - nal praise be - gin.

© Text: Valentin Thilo, 1607–62; tr. F. Samuel Janzow, b. 1913
Tune: Hamburg, 1598

AUS MEINES HERZENS GRUNDE
76 76 67 76

The King Shall Come 26

1 The King shall come when morn-ing dawns And light tri - um-phant breaks,
2 Not as of old a lit - tle child, To bear and fight and die,
3 Oh, bright-er than the ris - ing morn When Christ, vic - to - rious, rose
4 Oh, bright-er than that glo - rious morn Shall dawn up - on our race

When beau - ty gilds the east-ern hills And life to joy a - wakes.
But crowned with glo - ry like the sun That lights the morn-ing sky.
And left the lone-some place of death De - spite the rage of foes.
The day when Christ in splen-dor comes And we shall see his face.

5 The King shall come when morning dawns
   And light and beauty brings.
   Hail, Christ the Lord! Your people pray:
   Come quickly, King of kings.

Text: John Brownlie, 1859–1925, alt.
Tune: John Wyeth, Repository of Sacred Music, Part II, 1813

CONSOLATION
C M

27 Prepare the Royal Highway

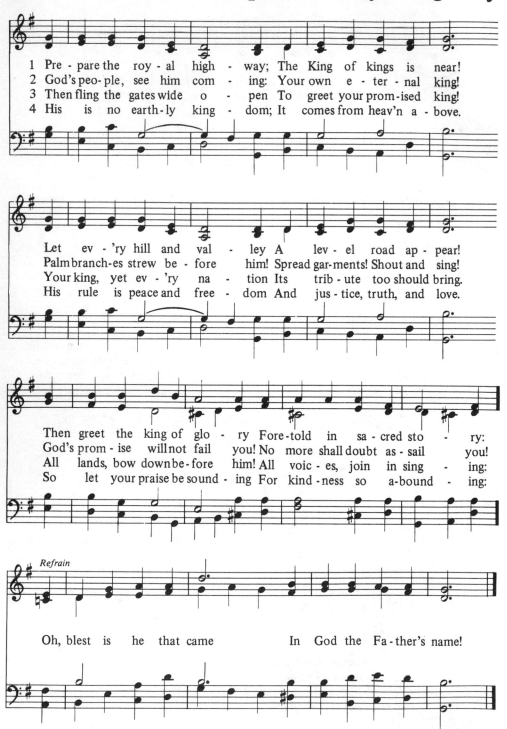

1 Pre - pare the roy - al high - way; The King of kings is near!
2 God's peo- ple, see him com - ing: Your own e - ter - nal king!
3 Then fling the gates wide o - pen To greet your prom-ised king!
4 His is no earth-ly king - dom; It comes from heav'n a - bove.

Let ev - 'ry hill and val - ley A lev - el road ap - pear!
Palm branch-es strew be - fore him! Spread gar-ments! Shout and sing!
Your king, yet ev - 'ry na - tion Its trib - ute too should bring.
His rule is peace and free - dom And jus - tice, truth, and love.

Then greet the king of glo - ry Fore-told in sa - cred sto - ry:
God's prom - ise will not fail you! No more shall doubt as - sail you!
All lands, bow down be - fore him! All voic - es, join in sing - ing:
So let your praise be sound - ing For kind - ness so a-bound - ing:

Refrain

Oh, blest is he that came In God the Fa - ther's name!

© Text: Frans Mikael Franzén, 1772–1847; tr. Lutheran Book of Worship, 1978, alt.
Tune: Swedish folk tune, 17th cent.

BEREDEN VÄG FÖR HERRAN
7 6 7 6 7 7 and refrain

Comfort, Comfort These My People

1 "Com - fort, com - fort these my peo - ple, Speak of peace!" so says our God.
2 Yes, our sins the Lord will par - don, Blot - ting out each dark mis - deed.
3 Now the her - ald's voice is cry - ing In the des - ert far and near,
4 Straight must be what long was crook - ed; Make the rough - est plac - es plain!

Com - fort these who sit in dark - ness Groan - ing un - der sin's dread rod.
All that well de - served his an - ger He no more will see nor heed.
Call - ing us to true re - pent - ance, For the king - dom now is here!
Let your hearts be true and hum - ble, Read - y for his ho - ly reign!

"To my peo - ple I pro - claim Par - don now in Je - sus' name.
We who lan - guished man - y a day Un - der guilt now washed a - way,
Oh, that warn - ing cry o - bey, Oh, pre - pare for God a way,
Here the glo - ry of the Lord Stands so gra - cious - ly re - vealed

Tell them that their sins I cov - er, That their war - fare now is o - ver!"
We ex - change our pin - ing sad - ness For his com - fort, peace, and glad - ness!
Let the val - leys rise to meet him, Let the hills bow down to greet him!
That all peo - ple see the to - ken That God's word is nev - er bro - ken!

Text: Johann Olearius, 1611–84; tr. Catherine Winkworth, 1829–78, alt.
Tune: Trente quatre pseaumes de David, Geneva, 1551

FREU DICH SEHR
87 87 77 88

Hark the Glad Sound

1 Hark the glad sound! The Sav - ior comes, The Sav - ior
2 He comes the pris - 'ners to re - lease, In Sa - tan's
3 He comes the bro - ken heart to bind, The bleed - ing
4 Our glad ho - san - nas, Prince of Peace, Your wel - come

prom - ised long; Let ev - 'ry heart pre -
bond - age held. The gates of brass be -
soul to cure, And with the trea - sures
shall pro - claim, And heav'n's e - ter - nal

pare a throne And ev - 'ry voice a song.
fore him burst, The i - ron fet - ters yield.
of his grace To en - rich the hum - ble poor.
arch - es ring With your be - lov - ed name.

Text: Philip Doddridge, 1702–51
Tune: attr. Thomas Haweis, 1734–1820

CHESTERFIELD
C M

Once He Came in Blessing

30

1 Once he came in bless-ing, All our sins re-dress-ing; Came in like-ness low-ly, Son of God most ho-ly; Bore the cross to save us; Hope and free-dom gave us.

2 Still he comes with-in us; Still his voice would win us From the sins that hurt us; Would to truth con-vert us From our fool-ish er-ror Ere he comes in ter-ror.

3 Thus, if we have known him, Not a-shamed to own him, Nor have spurned him cold-ly But will trust him bold-ly, He will then re-ceive us, Heal us, and for-give us.

4 Those who then are loy-al Find a wel-come roy-al. Come, then, O Lord Je-sus, From our sins re-lease us; Let us here con-fess you Till in heav'n we bless you.

Text: Johann Horn, c. 1490–1547; tr. Catherine Winkworth, 1829–78, alt.
Tune: Bohemian Brethren, Ein New Gesengbuchlen, 1531

GOTTES SOHN IST KOMMEN
66 66 66

31   Oh, Come, Oh, Come, Emmanuel

1 Oh, come, oh, come, Em - man - u - el, And ran - som
2 Oh, come, our Wis - dom from on high, Who or - dered
3 Oh, come, oh, come, our Lord of might, Who to your
4 Oh, come, O Rod of Jes - se's stem, From ev - 'ry

cap - tive Is - ra - el, That mourns in lone - ly ex - ile
all things might - i - ly; To us the path of knowl - edge
tribes on Si - nai's height In an - cient times gave ho - ly
foe de - liv - er them That trust your might - y pow'r to

here Un - til the Son of God ap - pear.
show, And teach us in her ways to go.
law, In cloud and maj - es - ty and awe.
save; Bring them in vic - t'ry through the grave.

Re-joice! Re-joice! Em - man - u - el Shall

come to you, O Is - ra - el!

5 Oh, come, O Key of David, come,
   And open wide our heav'nly home;
   Make safe the way that leads on high,
   And close the path to misery. *Refrain*

6 Oh, come, our Dayspring from on high,
   And cheer us by your drawing nigh;
   Disperse the gloomy clouds of night,
   And death's dark shadows put to flight. *Refrain*

7 Oh, come, Desire of nations, bind
   In one the hearts of all mankind;
   Oh, bid our sad divisions cease,
   And be yourself our King of Peace. *Refrain*

Text: Psalteriolum Cantionum Catholicarum, *Köln, 1710; tr. John M. Neale, 1818–66, alt.*
Tune: French processional, 15th cent.

VENI EMMANUEL
L M and refrain

32 O Savior, Rend the Heavens Wide

1 O Sav - ior, rend the heav - ens wide; Come down, come down with might - y stride; Un - lock the gates, the doors break down; Un - bar the way to heav - en's crown.

2 O Fa - ther, light from heav - en lend; As morn - ing dew, O Son, de - scend. Drop down, you clouds, the life of spring: To Ja - cob's line rain down the King.

3 O earth, in flow - 'ring bud be seen; Clothe hill and dale in garb of green. Bring forth, O earth, a blos - som rare, Our Sav - ior, sprung from mead - ow fair.

4 O Morn - ing Star, O ra - diant Dawn, When will we sing your morn - ing song? Come, Son of God! With - out your light We grope in dread and gloom of night.

5 Sin's dreadful doom upon us lies;
Grim death looms fierce before our eyes.
Oh, come, lead us with mighty hand
From exile to our promised land.

6 There shall we all our praises bring
And sing to you, our Savior King;
There shall we laud you and adore
Forever and forevermore.

© Text: Friedrich von Spee, 1591–1635; tr. Martin L. Seltz, 1909–67, alt.
Tune: Rheinfelsisches Gesangbuch, Augsburg, 1666

O HEILAND, REISS DIE HIMMEL AUF
L M

Let the Earth Now Praise the Lord 33

1 Let the earth now praise the Lord,
2 What the fa - thers most de - sired,
3 A - bram's prom - ised great re - ward,
4 Wel - come, O my Sav - ior, now!

Who has tru - ly kept his word And at last to
What the proph - ets' heart in - spired, What they longed for
Zi - on's help - er, Ja - cob's Lord— Him of two - fold
Joy - ful, Lord, to you I bow. Come in - to my

us did send Christ, the sin - ner's help and friend.
man - y a year, Stands ful - filled in glo - ry here.
race be - hold— Tru - ly came, as long fore - told.
heart, I pray; Oh, pre - pare your - self a way!

5 As your coming was in peace,
   Quiet, full of gentleness,
   Let the same mind dwell in me
   Which is yours eternally.

6 Bruise for me the Serpent's head
   That, set free from doubt and dread,
   I may cling to you in faith,
   Safely kept through life and death.

7 Then when you will come again
   As the glorious king to reign,
   I with joy will see your face,
   Freely ransomed by your grace.

Text: Heinrich Held, 1620–59; tr. Catherine Winkworth, 1829–78, alt.
Tune: Johann Walter, Geystliche gesangk Buchleyn, 1524

NUN KOMM, DER HEIDEN HEILAND
77 77

34 Come, O Precious Ransom

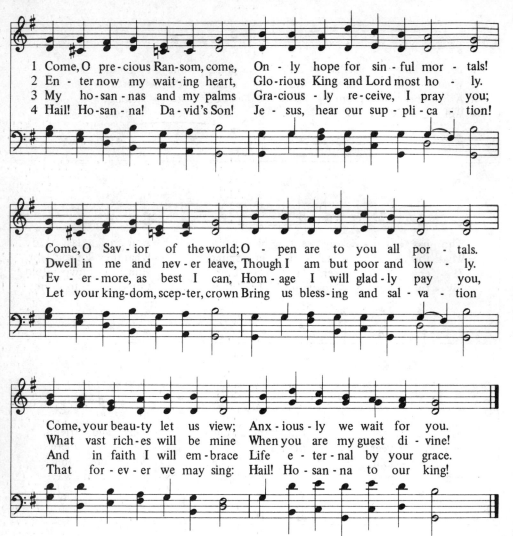

1 Come, O pre-cious Ran-som, come, / On - ly hope for sin - ful mor - tals.
2 En - ter now my wait-ing heart, / Glo-rious King and Lord most ho - ly.
3 My ho-san - nas and my palms / Gra-cious - ly re - ceive, I pray you;
4 Hail! Ho-san - na! Da - vid's Son! / Je - sus, hear our sup - pli - ca - tion!

Come, O Sav - ior of the world; O - pen are to you all por - tals.
Dwell in me and nev - er leave, Though I am but poor and low - ly.
Ev - er - more, as best I can, Hom - age I will glad - ly pay you,
Let your king-dom, scep-ter, crown Bring us bless-ing and sal - va - tion

Come, your beau-ty let us view; Anx - ious - ly we wait for you.
What vast rich - es will be mine When you are my guest di - vine!
And in faith I will em - brace Life e - ter - nal by your grace.
That for - ev - er we may sing: Hail! Ho - san - na to our king!

Text: Johann G. Olearius, 1635–1711; tr. August Crull, 1845–1923, alt.
Tune: Neuverfertigtes Gesangbuch, Darmstadt, 1699

MEINEN JESUM LASS ICH NICHT
78 78 77

We Praise, O Christ, Your Holy Name 35

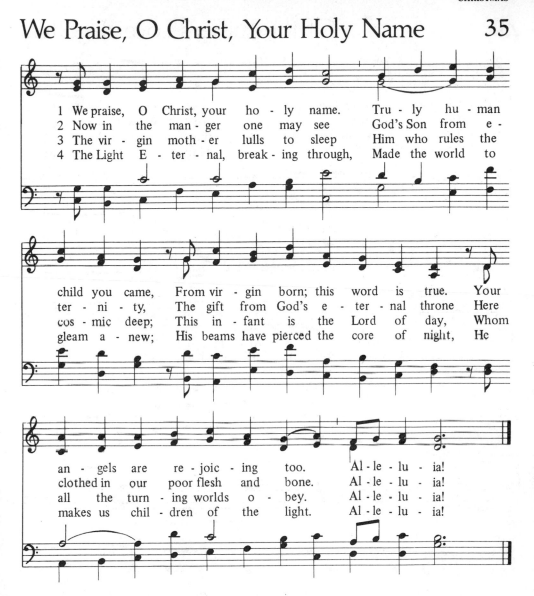

1 We praise, O Christ, your ho - ly name. Tru - ly hu - man
2 Now in the man - ger one may see God's Son from e -
3 The vir - gin moth - er lulls to sleep Him who rules the
4 The Light E - ter - nal, break - ing through, Made the world to

child you came, From vir - gin born; this word is true. Your
ter - ni - ty, The gift from God's e - ter - nal throne Here
cos - mic deep; This in - fant is the Lord of day, Whom
gleam a - new; His beams have pierced the core of night, He

an - gels are re - joic - ing too. Al - le - lu - ia!
clothed in our poor flesh and bone. Al - le - lu - ia!
all the turn - ing worlds o - bey. Al - le - lu - ia!
makes us chil - dren of the light. Al - le - lu - ia!

5 The Prince, God's very Son, came here,
Guest among the sons of fear.
His banner leads us out of woe,
And to his royal hall we go. Alleluia!

6 Such grace toward us now fills with light
Length and breadth and depth and height!
O endless ages, raise your voice;
O Christendom, rejoice, rejoice! Alleluia!

© *Text:* German hymn, 1370, st. 1; Martin Luther, 1483–1546, sts. 2–6; tr. F. Samuel Janzow, b. 1913
Tune: Enchiridion, Erfurt, 1524

GELOBET SEIST DU
87 88 4

36 Of the Father's Love Begotten

1 Of the Fa - ther's love be - got - ten Ere the worlds be -
2 Oh, that birth for - ev - er bless - ed, When the vir - gin,
3 This is he whom seers in old time Chant-ed of with
4 Let the heights of heav'n a - dore him; An - gel hosts, his

gan to be, He is Al - pha and O - me - ga,
full of grace, By the Ho - ly Ghost con - ceiv - ing,
one ac - cord, Whom the voic - es of the proph - ets
prais - es sing; Pow'rs, do - min - ions, bow be - fore him

He the source, the end - ing he, Of the things that are, that
Bore the Sav - ior of our race, And the babe, the world's re -
Prom-ised in their faith - ful word; Now he shines, the long - ex -
And ex - tol our God and King; Let no tongue on earth be

have been, And that fu-ture years shall see
deem - er, First re-vealed his sa-cred face
pect - ed; Let cre-a-tion praise its Lord
si - lent, Ev-'ry voice in con-cert ring

Ev - er - more and ev - er - more.
Ev - er - more and ev - er - more.
Ev - er - more and ev - er - more.
Ev - er - more and ev - er - more.

5 Christ, to you, with God the Father
   And the Spirit, there shall be
Hymn and chant and high thanksgiving
   And the shout of jubilee:
Honor, glory, and dominion
   And eternal victory
Evermore and evermore!

Text: Aurelius Prudentius Clemens, 348–c.413; tr. composite
Tune: plainsong, mode V, 13th cent.

DIVINUM MYSTERIUM
87 87 877

37 From Heaven Above to Earth I Come

Part I—The Angel's Message

1 From heav'n a-bove to earth I come To bring good
2 To you this night is born a child Of Mar - y,
3 This is the Christ, God's Son most high, Who hears your
4 The bless - ing which the Fa - ther planned The Son holds

news to ev - 'ry - one! Glad tid - ings of great joy I
cho - sen vir - gin mild; This new - born child of low - ly
sad and bit - ter cry; He will him - self your Sav - ior
in his in - fant hand That in his king - dom, bright and

bring To all the world and glad - ly sing:
birth Shall be the joy of all the earth.
be And from all sin will set you free.
fair, You may with us his glo - ry share.

5 These are the signs which you will see
To let you know that it is he:
In manger bed, in swaddling clothes
The child who all the earth upholds.

6 How glad we'll be to find it so!
Then with the shepherds let us go
To see what God for us has done
In sending us his own dear Son.

7 Look, look, dear friends, look over there!
What lies within that manger bare?
Who is that lovely little one?
The baby Jesus, God's dear Son.

© *Text: Martin Luther, 1483–1546; tr.* Lutheran Book of Worship, *1978*
Tune: Valentin Schumann, Geistliche Lieder, *1539*

VOM HIMMEL HOCH
L M

Welcome to Earth, O Noble Guest

Part II—Our Response

1 Wel - come to earth, O no - ble Guest, Through whom this
2 O Lord, you have cre - at - ed all! How did you
3 Were earth a thou - sand times as fair And set with
4 For vel - vets soft and silk - en stuff You have but

sin - ful world is blest! You turned not from our needs a -
come to be so small To sweet - ly sleep In man - ger
gold and jew - els rare, Still such a cra - dle would not
hay and straw so rough On which as king so rich and

way! How can our thanks such love re - pay?
bed Where low - ing cat - tle late - ly fed?
do To rock a prince so great as you.
great To be en - throned in hum - ble state.

5 O dearest Jesus, holy child,
Prepare a bed, soft, undefiled,
A holy shrine, within my heart,
That you and I need never part.

6 My heart for very joy now leaps;
My voice no longer silence keeps;
I too must join the angel throng
To sing with joy his cradlesong:

7 "Glory to God in highest heav'n,
Who unto us his Son has giv'n."
With angels sing in pious mirth:
A glad new year to all the earth!

© *Text: Martin Luther, 1483-1546; tr.* Lutheran Book of Worship, *1978*
Tune: Valentin Schumann, Geistliche Lieder, 1539

VOM HIMMEL HOCH
L M

39   Once Again My Heart Rejoices

1 Once a - gain my heart re - joic - es
2 Should we still fear God's dis - plea - sure,
3 Hark! his voice, our hearts de - light - ing,
4 Come, then, ban - ish all your sad - ness,

As I hear Far and near Sweet-est an - gel voic - es.
Who, to save, Free - ly gave His most pre - cious trea - sure?
Soft - ly greets, It en - treats, All the world in - vit - ing:
One and all, Great and small, Come with songs of glad - ness!

"Christ is born!" their choirs are sing - ing Till the air
To re - deem us, he has giv - en His own Son,
"Chil - dren, from the sins that grieve you You are freed;
Let your thank - ful hearts now hold him Sav - ior dear,

Ev - 'ry - where Now with joy is ring - ing!
Cher - ished one, From his throne in heav - en.
All you need I will sure - ly give you!"
Ev - er near, Lov - ing - ly en - fold him!

Text: Paul Gerhardt, 1607–76; tr. Catherine Winkworth, 1829–78, alt.
Tune: Johann Crüger, 1598–1662

FRÖHLICH SOLL MEIN HERZE SPRINGEN
8 3 3 6 D

Oh, Rejoice, All Christians, Loudly

40

Al - le - lu - ia, al - le - lu - ia, al - le - lu - ia,

al - le - lu - ia, al - le - lu - ia, al - le - lu - ia,

al - le - lu - ia, al - le - lu - ia, al - le - lu - ia,

al - le - lu - ia, al - le - lu - ia, al - le - lu - ia!

The twelvefold alleluia may be sung by the choir or the congregation before the first and after the last stanza.

Hymn continues on next page

1 Oh, re - joice, all Chris - tians, loud - ly, For our joys have
2 See, my soul, your Sav - ior choos - ing Pov - er - ty and
3 Lord, how shall I thank you right - ly? I am saved e -
4 Je - sus, guard and guide your mem - bers, Make us chil - dren

now be - gun: Christ is born as Mar - y's son.
weak - ness too, In such love he comes to you.
ter - nal - ly By your life and death for me.
of your grace, Hear our prayers in ev - 'ry place.

Tell a - broad his good - ness proud - ly, Who our race has
Nei - ther crib nor cross re - fus - ing, All he suf - fers
Let me not re - gard you light - ly But on you in
Quick - en now faith's glow - ing em - bers, Give all Chris - tians,

hon - ored so, That he lives with us be - low.
for your good, To re - deem you by his blood.
faith de - pend, Prais - ing you, my heav'n - ly friend.
far and near, Ho - ly peace, a glad new year.

Refrain

Joy, O joy, all hearts em - brac - ing, God in Christ him-

self a - bas - ing, Our a - dor - ing love en - shrin - ing,

Here the sun of grace lies shin - ing!

Text: Christian Keimann, 1607–62; tr. Catherine Winkworth, 1829–78, alt.
Tune: Andreas Hammerschmidt, c. 1611–75

FREUET EUCH, IHR CHRISTEN
877 877 and refrain

41 Oh, Come, All Ye Faithful

1 Oh, come, all ye faith - ful, Joy - ful and tri - um - phant! Oh,
2 High - est, most ho - ly, Light of light e - ter - nal,
3 Sing, choirs of an - gels, Sing in ex - ul - ta - tion,
4 Yea, Lord, we greet thee, Born this hap - py morn - ing;

come ye, oh, come . . ye to Beth - le - hem;
Born of a vir - gin, a mor - tal he comes;
Sing, all ye cit - i - zens of heav - en a - bove!
Je - sus, to thee . . be . . glo - ry giv'n!

Come and be - hold him Born the king of an - gels:
Son of the Fa - ther Now in flesh ap - pear - ing!
Glo - ry to God . . . In . . the . . high - est:
Word of the Fa - ther, Now in flesh ap - pear - ing!

Refrain

Oh, come, let us a - dore him, Oh, come, let us a - dore him,

Oh, come, let us a - dore him, Christ the Lord!

Text: attr. John F. Wade, c. 1711–86; tr. composite
Tune: John F. Wade, c. 1711–86

ADESTE FIDELES
irregular

Let Us All with Gladsome Voice   42

1 Let us all with glad-some voice   Praise the God of heav - en,
2 To this place of fears he came,   Ser - vant, heal - er, mend - er;
3 We are rich, for he was poor;   Is not this a won - der?
4 Christ, our Lord and Sav - ior dear,   Oh, be ev - er near us.

Who, to make our hearts re - joice,   His own Son has giv - en.
Through his death we heav -en claim,   There to reign in splen - dor.
There - fore praise God ev - er - more   Here on earth and yon - der.
Be our joy through-out each year.   A - men, Je - sus, hear us.

Text: author unknown, 1632; tr. Catherine Winkworth, 1829–78, alt.
Tune: Gesangbuch, Ander Teil, Dresden, 1632

LASST UNS ALLE
7 6 7 6 Trochaic

43

From East to West

1 From east to west, from shore to shore
Let ev - 'ry

2 Be - hold, the world's cre - a - tor wears
The form and

3 For this how won - drous - ly he wrought!
A maid - en,

4 And while the an - gels in the sky
Sang praise a -

heart a - wake and sing
The ho - ly child whom

fash - ion of a slave;
Our ver - y flesh our

in her low - ly place,
Be - came, in ways be -

bove the si - lent field,
To shep - herds poor the

Ma - ry bore,
The Christ, the ev - er - last - ing king.

mak - er shares,
His fall - en crea - tures all to save.

yond all thought,
The cho - sen ves - sel of his grace.

Lord most high,
The one great shep - herd, was re - vealed.

5 All glory for this blessed morn
To God the Father ever be;
All praise to you, O Virgin-born,
And Holy Ghost eternally.

Text: Coelius Sedulius, 5th cent.; tr. John Ellerton, 1826–93, alt.
Tune: Enchiridion, Erfurt, 1524

CHRISTUM WIR SOLLEN LOBEN SCHON
L M

Let All Together Praise Our God

44

1 Let all to-geth-er praise our God Be-fore his glo-rious
2 The Fa-ther sends him from his throne To be an in-fant
3 With-in an earth-born form he hides His all-cre-at-ing
4 He un-der-takes a great ex-change, Puts on our hu-man

throne; To-day he o-pens heav'n a-gain To
small And lie here poor-ly man-gered now In
light; To serve us all he hum-bly cloaks The
frame, And in re-turn gives us his realm, His

give us his own Son, To give us his own Son.
this cold, dis-mal stall, In this cold, dis-mal stall.
splen-dor of his might, The splen-dor of his might.
glo-ry, and his name, His glo-ry, and his name.

5 He is a servant, I a lord:
　How great a mystery!
　How strong the tender Christ child's love!
　No truer friend than he,
　No truer friend than he.

6 He is the key and he the door
　To blessed paradise;
　The angel bars the way no more.
　To God our praises rise,
　To God our praises rise.

7 Your grace in lowliness revealed,
　Lord Jesus, we adore
　And praise to God the Father yield
　And Spirit evermore;
　We praise you evermore.

© Text: Nikolaus Herman, c. 1480–1561; tr. F. Samuel Janzow, b. 1913
Tune: Nikolaus Herman, c. 1480–1561

LOBT GOTT, IHR CHRISTEN
86 866

45   O Savior of Our Fallen Race

1 O Sav - ior of our fall - en race, O Bright- ness
2 O Je - sus, ver - y Light of light, Our con - stant
3 Re-mem - ber, Lord of life and grace, How once, to
4 To - day, as year by year its light Bathes all the

of the Fa - ther's face, O Son who shared the Fa - ther's
star in sin's deep night: Now hear the prayers your peo - ple
save our fall - en race, You put our hu - man ves - ture
world in ra - diance bright, One pre - cious truth out - shines the

might Be - fore the world knew day or night,
pray Through-out the world this ho - ly day.
on And came to us as Mar -y's son.
sun: Sal - va - tion comes from you a - lone. A - men

5 For from the Father's throne you came,
His banished children to reclaim;
And earth and sea and sky revere
The love of him who sent you here.

6 And we are jubilant today,
For you have washed our guilt away.
Oh, hear the glad new song we sing
On this, the birthday of our king!

7 O Christ, redeemer virgin-born,
Let songs of praise your name adorn,
Whom with the Father we adore
And Holy Spirit evermore. Amen

© Text: Latin office hymn, c. 6th cent.; tr. Gilbert E. Doan, b. 1930
Tune: plainsong, mode I, c. 1200

CHRISTE REDEMPTOR
L M

Love Came Down at Christmas 46

1 Love came down at Christ - mas,
Love all love - ly, Love di - vine;
2 Wor - ship we the God - head,
Love in - car - nate, Love di - vine;
3 Love shall be our to - ken,
Love be yours and love be mine,

Love was born at Christ - mas,
Star and an - gels gave the sign.
Wor - ship we our Je - sus:
But where - with for sa - cred sign?
Love to God and all men,
Love for plea and gift and sign.

Text: Christina G. Rossetti, 1830–94
Tune: Irish traditional hymn melody

GARTAN
67 67

47

Now Sing We, Now Rejoice

1 Now sing we, now re-joice With heart and soul and voice.
2 God's Son, come from a-bove, Your grace and sav-ing love
3 We see God's love di-vine For us in Je-sus shine.
4 Where is that place so fair? Oh, no-where else but there

Life's most pre-cious trea-sure Here poor in man-ger lies;
To my spir-it bring-ing, O pure and ho-ly Child,
Guilt of sin had taught us But death and mis-er-y;
Where the an-gel voic-es With God's re-deemed u-nite,

He brings pur-er plea-sure Than sun-light from the skies.
Fill my heart with sing-ing For grace so great and mild.
Then our Ran-som bought us God's bright e-ter-ni-ty.
Awed that he re-joic-es To share his joy and light.

Christ is born to-day! Christ is born to-day!
Draw me, Lord, to you! Draw me, Lord, to you!
Oh, that we were there! Oh, that we were there!
Oh, that we were there! Oh, that we were there!

© Text: medieval Latin hymn; tr. F. Samuel Janzow, b. 1913
Tune: German carol, 14th cent.

IN DULCI JUBILO
66 66 66 55

Come, Your Hearts and Voices Raising 48

1 Come, your hearts and voic - es rais - ing, Christ the
2 Christ, from heav'n to us de - scend - ing And in
3 Ja - cob's star in all its splen - dor Beams with
4 From the bond - age that op - pressed us, From sin's

Lord with glad - ness prais - ing; Loud - ly sing his love
love our race be - friend - ing; In our need his help
com - fort sweet and ten - der, Forc - ing Sa - tan to
fet - ters that pos - sessed us, From the grief that sore

a - maz - ing, Wor - thy folk of Chris - ten - dom.
ex - tend - ing, Saved us from the wi - ly foe.
sur - ren - der, Break - ing all the pow'rs of hell.
dis - tressed us, We, the cap - tives, now are free.

5 Oh, the joy beyond expressing
When by faith we grasp this blessing
And to you we come confessing
Your great love has set us free.

6 Gracious Child, we pray, oh, hear us,
From your lowly manger cheer us,
Gently lead us and be near us
Till we join your choir above.

Text: Paul Gerhardt, 1607–76; tr. The Lutheran Hymnal, 1941, alt.
Tune: German carol, 14th cent.

QUEM PASTORES
8 8 87

49 Hark! The Herald Angels Sing

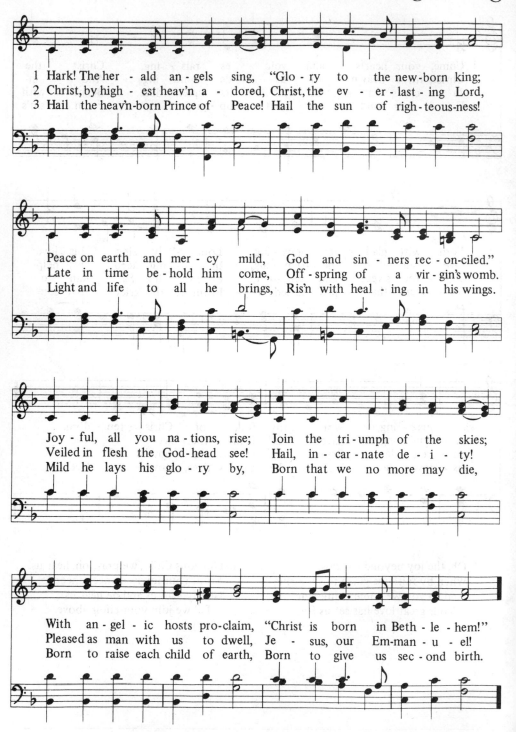

1 Hark! The her - ald an - gels sing, "Glo - ry to the new-born king;
2 Christ, by high - est heav'n a - dored, Christ, the ev - er - last - ing Lord,
3 Hail the heav'n-born Prince of Peace! Hail the sun of righ - teous-ness!

Peace on earth and mer - cy mild, God and sin - ners rec - on-ciled."
Late in time be - hold him come, Off - spring of a vir - gin's womb.
Light and life to all he brings, Ris'n with heal - ing in his wings.

Joy - ful, all you na - tions, rise; Join the tri - umph of the skies;
Veiled in flesh the God-head see! Hail, in - car - nate de - i - ty!
Mild he lays his glo - ry by, Born that we no more may die,

With an - gel - ic hosts pro-claim, "Christ is born in Beth - le - hem!"
Pleased as man with us to dwell, Je - sus, our Em-man - u - el!
Born to raise each child of earth, Born to give us sec - ond birth.

Refrain

Hark! The her-ald an-gels sing, "Glo-ry to the new-born king!"

Text: Charles Wesley, 1707–88, alt.
Tune: Felix Mendelssohn, 1809–47

MENDELSSOHN
77 77 D and refrain

Angels from the Realms of Glory   50

1 An - gels from the realms of glo-ry, Wing your flight o'er all the earth;
2 Shep-herds in the fields a - bid-ing, Watch-ing o'er your flocks by night,
3 Sa - ges, leave your con - tem-pla-tions, Bright-er vi-sions beam a - far;
4 All cre - a - tion, join in prais-ing God the Fa - ther, Spir-it, Son,

Once you sang cre - a - tion's sto - ry; Now pro-claim Mes - si - ah's birth:
God with us is now re - sid - ing, Yon-der shines the in - fant light.
Seek the great de - sire of na - tions, You have seen his na - tal star.
Ev - er-more your voic - es rais - ing To th'e - ter - nal Three in One.

Refrain

Come and wor-ship, come and wor-ship, Wor-ship Christ, the new-born king.

Text: James Montgomery, 1771–1854, sts. 1-3; Salisbury Hymn Book, 1857, st. 4; alt.
Tune: Henry T. Smart, 1813–79

REGENT SQUARE
87 87 87

51   A Great and Mighty Wonder

1 A great and might-y won-der, A full and ho - ly cure:
2 The Word be-comes in - car - nate And yet re - mains on high,
3 While thus they sing your mon - arch, Those bright an - gel - ic bands,
4 Since all he comes to ran - som, By all be he a - dored,

The vir - gin bears the in - fant With vir - gin hon - or pure!
And cher - u - bim sing an - thems To shep-herds from the sky.
Re - joice, O vales and moun - tains, And o - ceans, clap your hands.
The in - fant born in Beth - l'em, The Sav - ior and the Lord.

Refrain

Re - peat the hymn a - gain: "To God on high be

glo - ry And peace on earth to men!"

5 All idol forms shall perish,   And Christ shall wield his scepter,
     And error's arguing,   Our Lord, our God, our King! *Refrain*

Text: St. Germanus, c. 634–c. 734; tr. John M. Neale, 1818–66, alt.
Tune: Alte Catholische Geistliche Kirchengesäng, Köln, 1599

ES IST EIN ROS
7 6 7 6 and refrain

From Heaven Came the Angels Bright 52

1 From heav-en came the an-gels bright To shep-herds
2 To Beth-le-hem, King Da-vid's town, As Mi-cah
3 Re-joice there-fore that through his Son Your God with
4 God came to share him-self with you; Your sin and

watch-ing in the night. A new-born roy-al
saw, comes great re-nown; Your Lord Christ is in-
you is now at one. He took on hu-man
death he o-ver-threw. The foe may send his

child, they said, Lies yon-der in a man-ger bed.
car-nate there To save you all from sin and care.
flesh and bone, And you, his broth-ers, are God's own.
fier-y dart, Your friend, God's Son, will shield your heart.

5 He never will abandon you.
Trust King Immanuel the True.
Yield not to any evil might.
Walk in the Christ child's saving light.

6 Then in the end you will prevail;
God's friends and brothers cannot fail.
In praise to God then raise your voice,
Prepare forever to rejoice.

© Text: Martin Luther, 1483–1546; tr. F. Samuel Janzow, b. 1913, alt.
Tune: adapt. Michael Praetorius, 1571–1621

PUER NOBIS
L M

53

Joy to the World

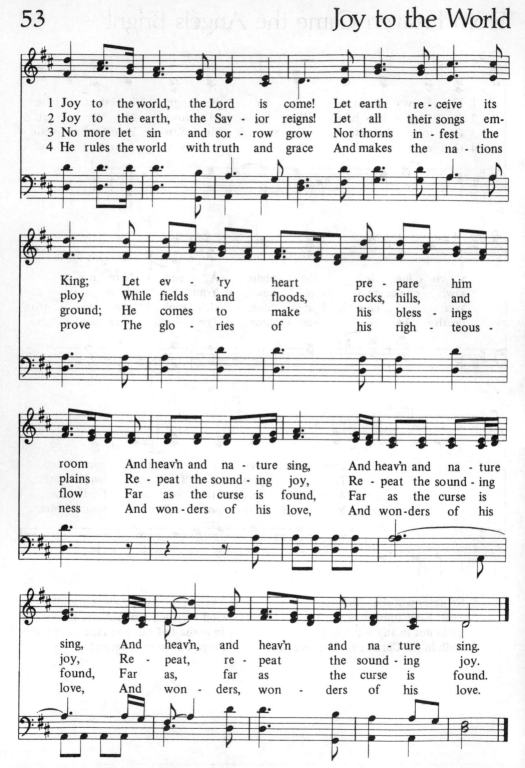

1 Joy to the world, the Lord is come! Let earth re-ceive its
2 Joy to the earth, the Sav-ior reigns! Let all their songs em-
3 No more let sin and sor-row grow Nor thorns in-fest the
4 He rules the world with truth and grace And makes the na-tions

King; Let ev-'ry heart pre-pare him
ploy While fields and floods, rocks, hills, and
ground; He comes to make his bless-ings
prove The glo-ries of his righ-teous-

room And heav'n and na-ture sing, And heav'n and na-ture
plains Re-peat the sound-ing joy, Re-peat the sound-ing
flow Far as the curse is found, Far as the curse is
ness And won-ders of his love, And won-ders of his

sing, And heav'n, and heav'n and na-ture sing.
joy, Re-peat, re-peat the sound-ing joy.
found, Far as, far as the curse is found.
love, And won-ders, won-ders of his love.

Text: Isaac Watts, 1674–1748, alt.
Tune: George F. Handel, 1685–1759, adapt.

ANTIOCH
C M and repeat

He Whom Shepherds Once Came Praising

The Quempas Celebration

Quem pastores
Children in groups

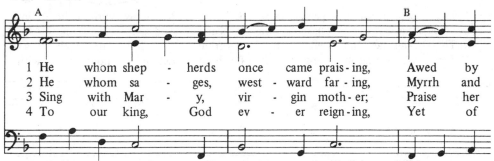

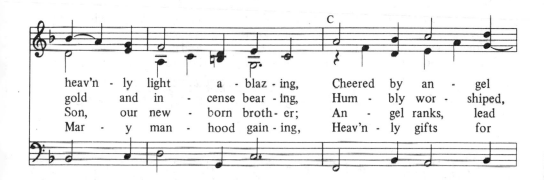

1 He whom shep - herds once came prais-ing, Awed by heav'n - ly light a - blaz-ing, Cheered by an - gel news a - maz-ing: "King of glo - ry, Christ is born!"

2 He whom sa - ges, west - ward far-ing, Myrrh and gold and in - cense bear-ing, Hum - bly wor - shiped, of - f'rings shar-ing, Ju - dah's li - on reigns this morn!

3 Sing with Mar - y, vir - gin moth-er; Praise her Son, our new - born broth-er; An - gel ranks, lead one an - oth - er, Hail - ing him in ho - ly joy!

4 To our king, God ev - er reign-ing, Yet of Mar - y man - hood gain-ing, Heav'n - ly gifts for us ob - tain-ing, Raise your hymns of hom - age high!

During a short prelude on the *Quempas* four groups of children station themselves in the four corners of the church. Group **A** sings the first phrase of the *Quempas* (preferably unaccompanied), group **B** the second phrase, group **C** the third phrase, and group **D** the fourth phrase. (This symbolizes the announcement of Christ's birth to the four corners of the world.)

While the adult choir sings the first stanza of the *Nunc angelorum,* the children move to new stations.

Congregation, choirs, and available instruments then join in the refrain *Resonet in laudibus.*

The remaining stanzas are sung in the same way.

Hymn continues on next page

Nunc angelorum
Choir in unison

1 The glo-rious an-gels came to-day, A-glow with light in-
2 "God's maj-es-ty has come to earth And sent his on-ly
3 Then sang the an-gels this re-frain: "To God on high a-
4 The won-d'ring shep-herds said: "Be-hold! Let us now go with

to the night of dark-ness deep, To shep-herds who by
Son to you in hu-man-kind; A cho-sen vir-gin
lone give praise and glo - ry, And peace on earth a-
all good speed to Beth - le - hem To see this thing the

moon's bright ray Did in the field o'er sheep their si - lent
gave him birth. In Da - vid's town the ho - ly in - fant
gain shall reign. Let all on earth with glad - ness heed this
Lord has told; The sheep are safe; he will in - deed take

vig - il keep. "Joy, great joy and tid - ings glad we
you will find, Ly - ing help - less in a man - ger,
sto - ry And re - joice in his good-will." The
care of them." There they found the won - der child, in

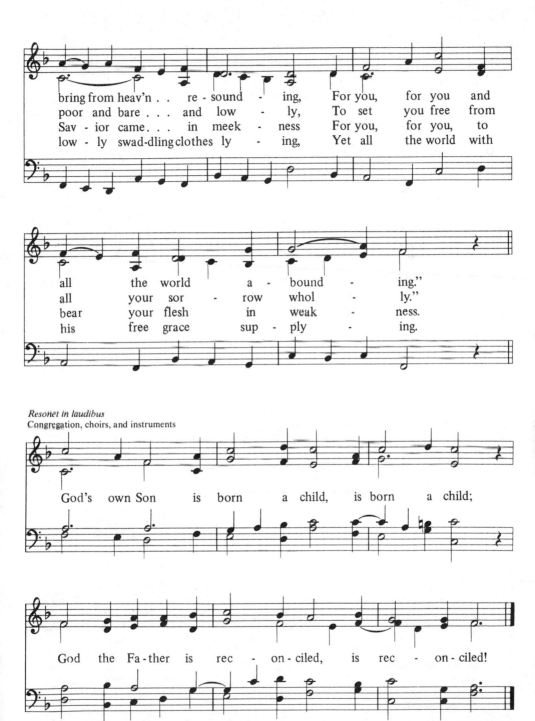

bring from heav'n . . re-sound - ing, For you, for you and
poor and bare . . . and low - ly, To set you free from
Sav - ior came . . . in meek - ness For you, for you, to
low - ly swad-dling clothes ly - ing, Yet all the world with

all the world a - bound - ing."
all your sor - row whol - ly."
bear your flesh in weak - ness.
his free grace sup - ply - ing.

Resonet in laudibus
Congregation, choirs, and instruments

God's own Son is born a child, is born a child;

God the Fa - ther is rec - on - ciled, is rec - on - ciled!

© *Text: German carols, 14th cent.; tr. composite*
Tunes: German carols, 14th cent.

QUEM PASTORES
8 8 8 7
NUNC ANGELORUM
irregular
RESONET IN LAUDIBUS
11 12

55 Angels We Have Heard on High

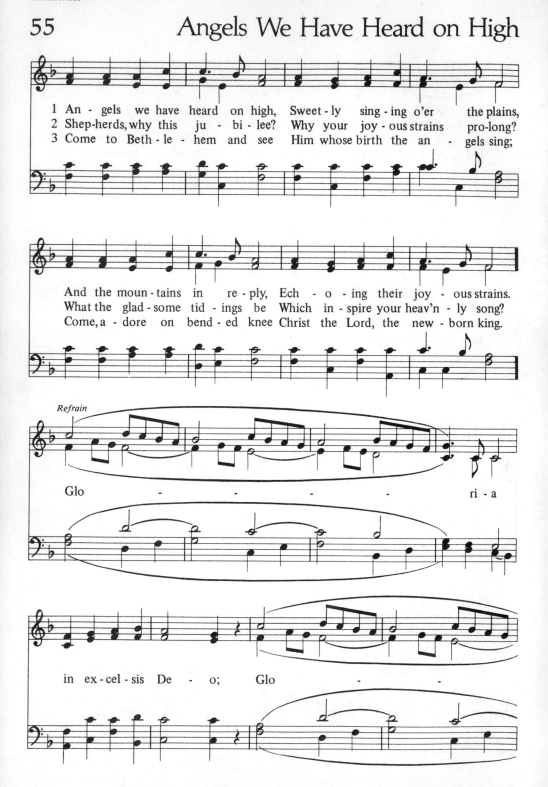

1 An - gels we have heard on high, Sweet - ly sing - ing o'er the plains,
2 Shep-herds, why this ju - bi - lee? Why your joy - ous strains pro-long?
3 Come to Beth - le - hem and see Him whose birth the an - gels sing;

And the moun - tains in re - ply, Ech - o - ing their joy - ous strains.
What the glad - some tid - ings be Which in - spire your heav'n - ly song?
Come, a - dore on bend - ed knee Christ the Lord, the new - born king.

Refrain

Glo - - - - ri - a

in ex - cel - sis De - o; Glo - -

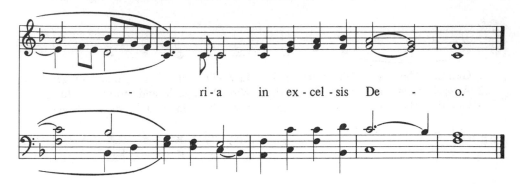

- ri - a   in ex - cel - sis De - o.

Text: French carol; tr. H.F. Hemy, Crown of Jesus Music, *Part II, 1862, alt.*
Tune: French carol

GLORIA
7 7 7 7 and refrain

I Am So Glad when Christmas Comes   56

1 I am so glad when Christ-mas comes, The night of Je - sus' birth,
2 The lit - tle child of Beth - le - hem, The King of heav'n - ly grace,
3 He's now re - turned to heav'n a - bove, God's Son he is al - way;
4 I too would sing my Sav - ior's praise, My joy, my crown, my Lord;

When Beth-l'em's star shone as the sun And an - gels sang with mirth.
Came down from his ex - alt - ed throne To save our fall - en race.
He ne'er for - gets his lit - tle ones But hears them when they pray.
For he has made me his own child By Wa - ter and the Word.

5 I love this precious Christmas eve
  And my dear Savior mild,
  And I shall not forget the truth:
  He loves me as his child.

6 I am so glad when Christmas comes:
  Let anthems fill the air!
  He opens wide for every child
  His paradise so fair.

© *Text: Marie Wexelsen, 1832-1911; tr. Norman A. Madson, 1886-1962*
Tune: Peder Knudsen, 1819-63

JEG ER SAA GLAD
C M

57

Gentle Mary Laid Her Child

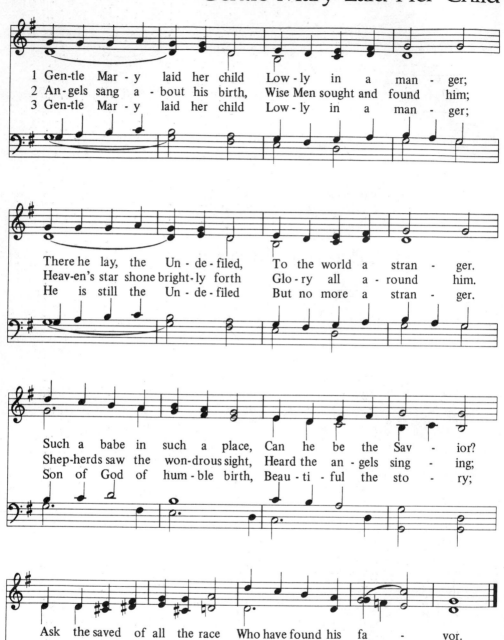

1 Gen-tle Mar-y laid her child   Low-ly in a man - ger;
2 An-gels sang a-bout his birth,   Wise Men sought and found   him;
3 Gen-tle Mar-y laid her child   Low-ly in a man - ger;

There he lay, the Un-de-filed,   To the world a stran - ger.
Heav-en's star shone bright-ly forth   Glo-ry all a-round   him.
He is still the Un-de-filed   But no more a stran - ger.

Such a babe in such a place,   Can he be the Sav - ior?
Shep-herds saw the won-drous sight,   Heard the an-gels sing - ing;
Son of God of hum-ble birth,   Beau-ti-ful the sto - ry;

Ask the saved of all the race   Who have found his fa - vor.
All the plains were lit that night,   All the hills were ring - ing.
Praise his name in all the earth;   Hail the King of glo - ry!

© Text: Joseph Simpson Cook, 1859–1933
Tune: Swedish, Piae Cantiones, 1582

TEMPUS ADEST FLORIDUM
76 76 D

Once in Royal David's City

1 Once in roy - al Da - vid's cit - y Stood a low - ly cat - tle shed, Where a moth - er laid her ba - by In a man - ger for his bed; Mar - y was that moth - er mild, Je - sus Christ her lit - tle child.

2 He came down to earth from heav - en Who is God and Lord of all, And his shel - ter was a sta - ble, And his cra - dle was a stall; With the poor and mean and low Lived our Sav - ior long a - go.

3 But our eyes in truth should see him Through his own re - deem - ing love, For that child so dear and gen - tle Is our Lord in heav'n a - bove, As he leads his chil - dren on To the place where he is gone.

4 Not in that poor low - ly sta - ble With the ox - en stand - ing by Shall we see him, but in heav - en, Set at God's right hand on high. Then like stars his chil - dren, crowned, All in white, his praise will sound!

Text: Cecil Frances Alexander, 1823-95, alt.
Tune: Henry J. Gauntlett, 1805-76

IRBY
87 87 77

59 O Little Town of Bethlehem

1 O lit-tle town of Beth-le-hem, How still we see thee lie!
2 For Christ is born of Mar - y, And, gath-ered all a-bove
3 How si-lent-ly, how si-lent-ly The won-drous gift is giv'n!
4 O ho-ly Child of Beth-le-hem, De-scend to us, we pray;

A-bove thy deep And dream-less sleep The si-lent stars go by;
While mor-tals sleep, The an-gels keep Their watch of won-d'ring love.
So God im-parts To hu-man hearts The bless-ings of his heav'n.
Cast out our sin, And en-ter in, Be born in us to-day.

Yet in thy dark streets shin - eth The ev-er-last-ing light.
O morn-ing stars, to - geth - er Pro-claim the ho-ly birth,
No ear may hear his com - ing; But in this world of sin,
We hear the Christ-mas an - gels The great glad tid-ings tell;

The hopes and fears Of all the years Are met in thee to-night.
And prais-es sing To God the king And peace to all the earth!
Where meek souls will Re-ceive him, still The dear Christ en-ters in.
Oh, come to us, A-bide with us, Our Lord Im-man-u-el!

Text: Phillips Brooks, 1835-93
© *Tune: English traditional melody; coll. and arr. Ralph Vaughan Williams, 1872-1958*

FOREST GREEN
86 86 76 86

O Little Town of Bethlehem

1 O lit - tle town of Beth - le - hem, How still we see thee lie!
2 For Christ is born of Mar - y, And, gath - ered all a - bove
3 How si - lent - ly, how si - lent - ly The won - drous gift is giv'n!
4 O ho - ly Child of Beth - le - hem, De - scend to us, we pray;

A - bove thy deep And dream - less sleep The si - lent stars go by;
While mor - tals sleep, The an - gels keep Their watch of won - d'ring love.
So God im - parts To hu - man hearts The bless - ings of his heav'n.
Cast out our sin, And en - ter in, Be born in us to - day.

Yet in thy dark streets shin - eth The ev - er - last - ing light.
O morn - ing stars, to - geth - er Pro - claim the ho - ly birth,
No ear may hear his com - ing; But in this world of sin,
We hear the Christ - mas an - gels The great glad tid - ings tell;

The hopes and fears Of all the years Are met in thee to - night.
And prais - es sing To God the king, And peace to all the earth!
Where meek souls will Re - ceive him, still The dear Christ en - ters in.
Oh, come to us, A - bide with us, Our Lord Im - man - u - el!

Text: Phillips Brooks, 1835–93
Tune: Lewis H. Redner, 1831–1908

ST. LOUIS
86 86 76 86

61 What Child Is This

1 What child is this, who, laid to rest, On Mar-y's lap is sleep-ing?
2 Why lies he in such mean es-tate Where ox and ass are feed-ing?
3 So bring him in-cense, gold, and myrrh; Come, peas-ant, king, to own him.

Whom an-gels greet with an-thems sweet While shep-herds watch are keep-ing?
Good Chris-tian, fear; for sin-ners here The si-lent Word is plead-ing.
The King of kings sal-va-tion brings; Let lov-ing hearts en-throne him.

This, this is Christ the king, Whom shep-herds guard and an-gels sing;
Nails, spear shall pierce him through, The cross be borne for me, for you;
Raise, raise the song on high, The vir-gin sings her lul-la-by;

Haste, haste to bring him laud, The babe, the son of Mar-y!
Hail, hail the Word made flesh, The babe, the son of Mar-y!
Joy, joy, for Christ is born, The babe, the son of Mar-y!

Text: William C. Dix, 1837–98
Tune: English ballad, 16th cent.

GREENSLEEVES
87 87 68 67

It Came upon the Midnight Clear

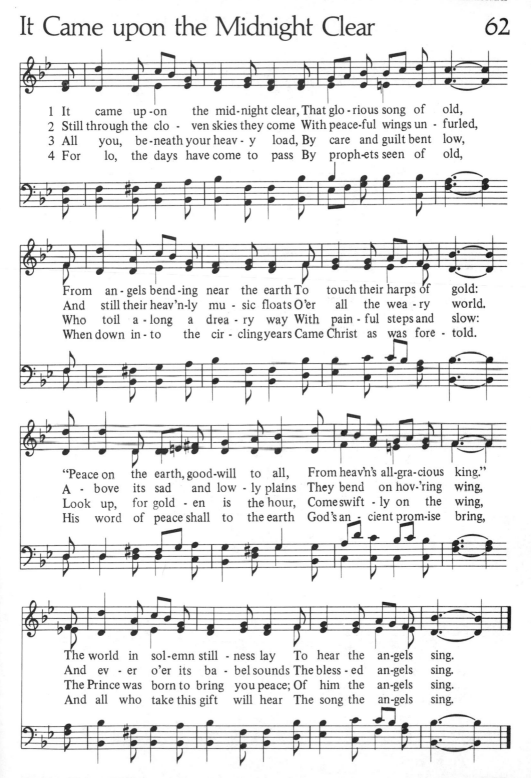

1 It came up-on the mid-night clear, That glo-rious song of old,
2 Still through the clo - ven skies they come With peace-ful wings un - furled,
3 All you, be-neath your heav - y load, By care and guilt bent low,
4 For lo, the days have come to pass By proph-ets seen of old,

From an - gels bend-ing near the earth To touch their harps of gold:
And still their heav'n-ly mu - sic floats O'er all the wea - ry world.
Who toil a - long a drea - ry way With pain - ful steps and slow:
When down in - to the cir - cling years Came Christ as was fore - told.

"Peace on the earth, good-will to all, From heav'n's all-gra-cious king."
A - bove its sad and low - ly plains They bend on hov-'ring wing,
Look up, for gold - en is the hour, Come swift - ly on the wing,
His word of peace shall to the earth God's an - cient prom-ise bring,

The world in sol-emn still - ness lay To hear the an-gels sing.
And ev - er o'er its ba - bel sounds The bless - ed an-gels sing.
The Prince was born to bring you peace; Of him the an-gels sing.
And all who take this gift will hear The song the an-gels sing.

Text: Edmund H. Sears, 1810–76, alt.
Tune: Richard S. Willis, 1819–1900

CAROL
C M D

63 Who Are These That Earnest Knock

1 Who are these that ear-nest knock, Seek-ing some safe ha - ven,
2 Who is this that doc-ile lies In a low-ly cra - dle?
3 Who are these that si-lent stand Filled with ho - ly won - der,

These in lone - ly streets that walk, Weak and heav-y - la - den?
Who is this that dig - ni - fies This rude, com-mon sta - ble?
Pros - e - lyte and pil - grim band, Thou-sand with-out num - ber?

Jo - seph and the vir - gin mild Seek-ing shel - ter for the child
Christ the ev - er - liv - ing Lord, By the an - gel hosts a - dored,
Shep-herds, sa - ges, saints whose eyes See the new - born sac - ri - fice

Yet un - born but near; Let me read - y room for him,
Come to meet his death. O Re - deem - er of my sin,
With dis - cern - ing faith. All un - wor - thy, yet make me

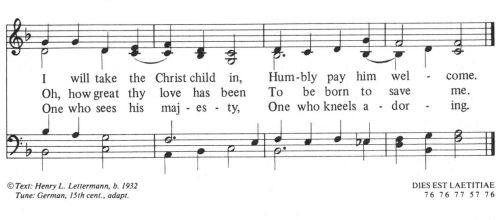

I will take the Christ child in, Hum-bly pay him wel - come.
Oh, how great thy love has been To be born to save me.
One who sees his maj - es - ty, One who kneels a - dor - ing.

© Text: Henry L. Lettermann, b. 1932
Tune: German, 15th cent., adapt.

DIES EST LAETITIAE
76 76 77 57 76

Away in a Manger
64

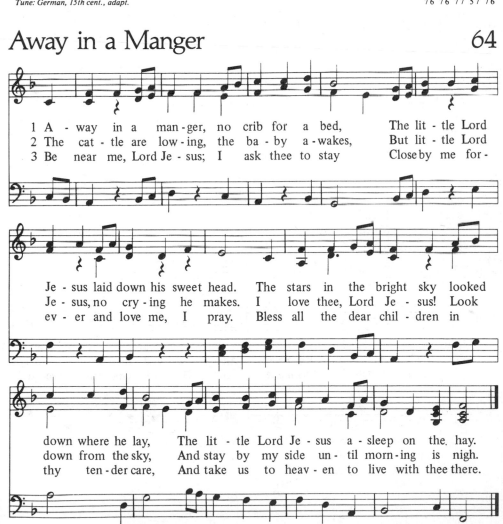

1 A - way in a man - ger, no crib for a bed, The lit - tle Lord
2 The cat - tle are low - ing, the ba - by a - wakes, But lit - tle Lord
3 Be near me, Lord Je - sus; I ask thee to stay Close by me for -

Je - sus laid down his sweet head. The stars in the bright sky looked
Je - sus, no cry - ing he makes. I love thee, Lord Je - sus! Look
ev - er and love me, I pray. Bless all the dear chil - dren in

down where he lay, The lit - tle Lord Je - sus a - sleep on the hay.
down from the sky, And stay by my side un - til morn - ing is nigh.
thy ten - der care, And take us to heav - en to live with thee there.

Text: author unknown, c. 1883, sts. 1-2; John T. McFarland, 1851-1913, st. 3, alt.
Tune: William J. Kirkpatrick, 1838-1921

CRADLE SONG
11 11 11 11

65 On Christmas Night All Christians Sing

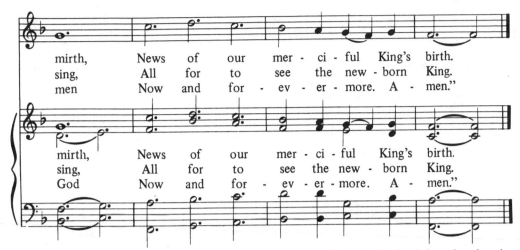

mirth, News of our mer - ci - ful King's birth.
sing, All for to see the new - born King.
men Now and for - ev - er - more. A - men."

mirth, News of our mer - ci - ful King's birth.
sing, All for to see the new - born King.
God Now and for - ev - er - more. A - men."

Ordinarily this carol will be sung in unison; however, a text is provided also for the choir to sing along in parts.

© *Text: English carol*
© *Tune: traditional carol*

SUSSEX CAROL
L M

Every Year the Christ Child 66

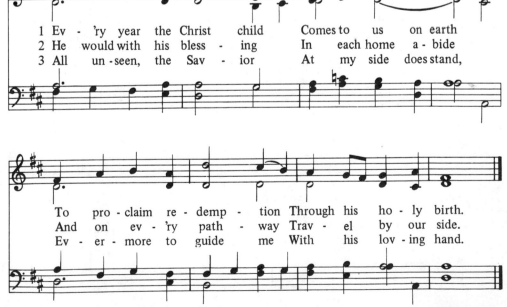

1 Ev - 'ry year the Christ child Comes to us on earth
2 He would with his bless - ing In each home a - bide
3 All un - seen, the Sav - ior At my side does stand,

To pro - claim re - demp - tion Through his ho - ly birth.
And on ev - 'ry path - way Trav - el by our side.
Ev - er - more to guide me With his lov - ing hand.

© *Text: Johann Wilhelm Hey, 1789–1854; tr. Erich B. Allwardt, b. 1905, st. 1; W. Gustave Polack, 1890–1950, sts. 2-3*
Tune: Friedrich Silcher, 1789–1860

ALLE JAHRE WIEDER
6 5 6 5

67 Lo, How a Rose Is Growing

1 Lo, how a rose is grow - ing, A bloom of fin - est grace; The proph - ets had fore - told it: A branch of Jes - se's race Would bear one per - fect flow'r Here in the cold of win - ter And dark - est mid - night hour.

2 The rose of which I'm sing - ing, I - sa - iah had fore - told. He came to us through Mar - y, Who shel - tered him from cold. Through God's e - ter - nal will This child to us was giv - en At mid - night calm and still.

3 The shep - herds heard the sto - ry The an - gels sang that night: How Christ was born of Mar - y; He was the Son of light. To Beth - le - hem they ran To find him in the man - ger As an - gel her - alds sang.

4 This flow'r, so small and ten - der, With fra - grance fills the air; His bright - ness ends the dark - ness That kept the earth in fear. True God and yet true man, He came to save his peo - ple From earth's dark night of sin.

5 O Savior, child of Mary,
   Who felt all human woe;
  O Savior, king of glory,
   Who triumphed o'er our foe:

Bring us at length, we pray,
  To the bright courts of heaven
And into endless day.

© *Text: German, 15th cent.; tr. Gracia Grindal, b. 1943*
  Tune: Alte Catholische Geistliche Kirchengesäng, Köln, 1599

ES IST EIN ROS
76 76 676

Silent Night, Holy Night

68

1 Si - lent night, ho - ly night! All is calm, all is bright Round yon
2 Si - lent night, ho - ly night! Shep-herds quake at the sight; Glo - ries
3 Si - lent night, ho - ly night! Son of God, love's pure light Ra - diant

vir - gin moth - er and child. Ho - ly In - fant, so ten - der and mild,
stream from heav - en a - far, Heav'n - ly hosts . . sing, Al - le - lu - ia!
beams from your ho - ly face With the dawn of re - deem - ing grace,

Sleep in heav - en - ly peace, Sleep in heav - en - ly peace.
Christ, the Sav - ior, is born! Christ, the Sav - ior, is born!
Je - sus, Lord, at your birth, Je - sus, Lord, at your birth.

Text: Joseph Mohr, 1792–1848; tr. John F. Young, 1820–85
Tune: Franz Gruber, 1787–1863

STILLE NACHT
irregular

69 Let Our Gladness Have No End

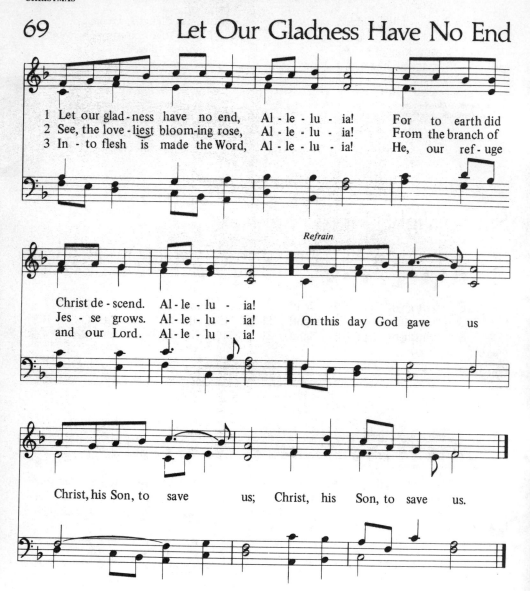

1 Let our glad-ness have no end, Al - le - lu - ia! For to earth did
2 See, the love - liest bloom-ing rose, Al - le - lu - ia! From the branch of
3 In - to flesh is made the Word, Al - le - lu - ia! He, our ref - uge

Christ de - scend. Al - le - lu - ia!
Jes - se grows. Al - le - lu - ia! On this day God gave us
and our Lord. Al - le - lu - ia!

Refrain

Christ, his Son, to save us; Christ, his Son, to save us.

Text: Bohemian carol, 15th cent.; tr. unknown
Tune: Bohemian carol, 15th cent.

NARODIL SE KRISTUS PÁN
7 4 7 4 and refrain

While Shepherds Watched

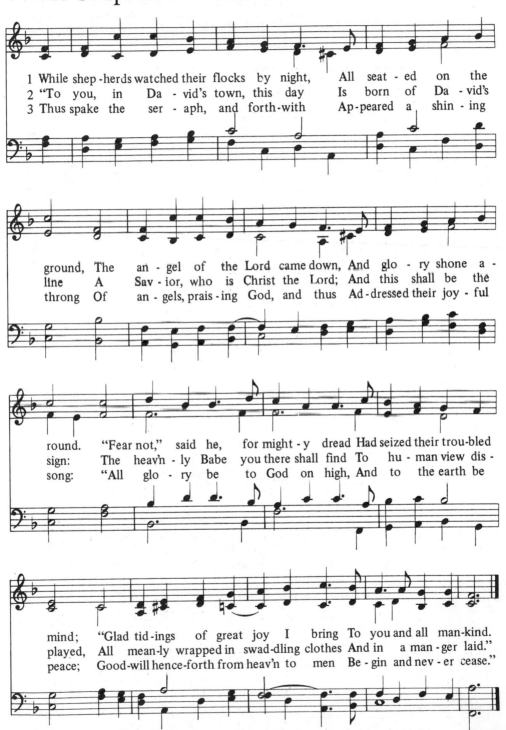

1 While shep-herds watched their flocks by night, All seat-ed on the ground, The an-gel of the Lord came down, And glo-ry shone a-round. "Fear not," said he, for might-y dread Had seized their trou-bled mind; "Glad tid-ings of great joy I bring To you and all man-kind.

2 "To you, in Da-vid's town, this day Is born of Da-vid's line A Sav-ior, who is Christ the Lord; And this shall be the sign: The heav'n-ly Babe you there shall find To hu-man view dis-played, All mean-ly wrapped in swad-dling clothes And in a man-ger laid."

3 Thus spake the ser-aph, and forth-with Ap-peared a shin-ing throng Of an-gels, prais-ing God, and thus Ad-dressed their joy-ful song: "All glo-ry be to God on high, And to the earth be peace; Good-will hence-forth from heav'n to men Be-gin and nev-er cease."

Text: Nahum Tate, 1652–1715
Tune: English carol

WHILE SHEPHERDS WATCHED
C M D

71 From Shepherding of Stars

1 From shep - herd - ing of stars that gaze Toward
2 Your shep - herd King from star - lit hall Bends
3 This night your King brings from a - far The
4 He shep - herds from the this - tled place The

heav'n-ly fields of light, I come with tid - ings to a - maze You
down to wea - ry lands, Lies man-gered low in cat - tle stall. Go
vir - gin's lul - la - by, The Wise Men's faith, a guid - ing star, And
flocks by thick-ets torn; His pierc - ed hands heal all your race Sore

watch-ers in the night, You watch - ers in the night.
touch his in - fant hands, Go touch his in - fant hands.
love from God Most High, And love from God Most High.
wound-ed by the thorn, Sore wound - ed by the thorn.

5 Embrace the Christ child, and with songs
   Bind up the hearts of men.
To shepherd-healer-king let throngs
   Sing glorias again.

© Text: F. Samuel Janzow, b. 1913
© Tune: Richard W. Hillert, b. 1923

SHEPHERDING
86 866

The Only Son from Heaven

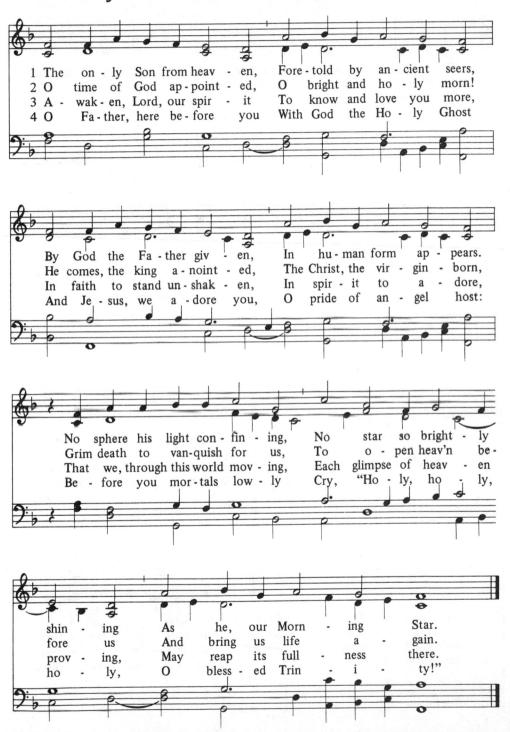

1 The on - ly Son from heav - en, Fore - told by an - cient seers,
2 O time of God ap - point - ed, O bright and ho - ly morn!
3 A - wak - en, Lord, our spir - it To know and love you more,
4 O Fa - ther, here be - fore you With God the Ho - ly Ghost

By God the Fa - ther giv - en, In hu - man form ap - pears.
He comes, the king a - noint - ed, The Christ, the vir - gin - born,
In faith to stand un - shak - en, In spir - it to a - dore,
And Je - sus, we a - dore you, O pride of an - gel host:

No sphere his light con - fin - ing, No star so bright - ly
Grim death to van - quish for us, To o - pen heav'n be -
That we, through this world mov - ing, Each glimpse of heav - en
Be - fore you mor - tals low - ly Cry, "Ho - ly, ho - ly,

shin - ing As he, our Morn - ing Star.
fore us And bring us life a - gain.
prov - ing, May reap its full - ness there.
ho - ly, O bless - ed Trin - i - ty!"

Text: Elizabeth Cruciger, c. 1500–35; tr. Arthur T. Russell, 1806–74, alt.
Tune: Enchiridion, Erfurt, 1524

HERR CHRIST, DER EINIG GOTTS SOHN
76 76 77

73 O Morning Star, How Fair and Bright

1 O Morn - ing Star, how fair and bright! You shine with God's
2 Come, heav'n - ly bride - groom, light di - vine, And deep with - in
3 Lord, when you look on us in love, At once there falls
4 Al - might - y Fa - ther, in your Son You loved us when

own truth and light, A - glow with grace and mer - cy!
our hearts now shine; There light a flame un - dy - ing!
from God a - bove A ray of pur - est plea - sure.
not yet be - gun Was this old earth's foun - da - tion!

Of Ja - cob's race, King Da - vid's son, Our Lord and mas -
In your one bod - y let us be As liv - ing branch -
Your Word and Spir - it, flesh and blood Re - fresh our souls
Your Son has ran - somed us in love To live in him

ter, you have won Our hearts to serve you on - ly!
es of a tree, Your life our lives sup - ply - ing.
with heav'n - ly food. You are our dear - est trea - sure!
here and a - bove: This is your great sal - va - tion.

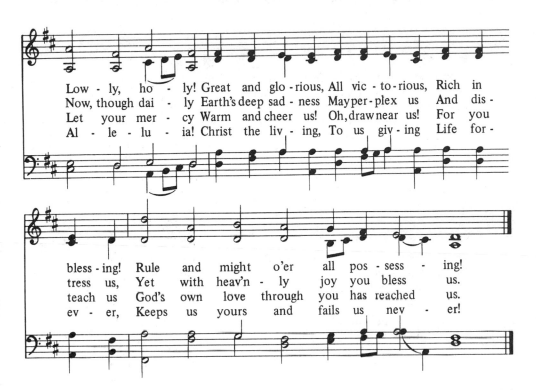

Low - ly, ho - ly! Great and glo - rious, All vic - to - rious, Rich in
Now, though dai - ly Earth's deep sad - ness May per - plex us And dis -
Let your mer - cy Warm and cheer us! Oh, draw near us! For you
Al - le - lu - ia! Christ the liv - ing, To us giv - ing Life for -

bless - ing! Rule and might o'er all pos - sess - ing!
tress us, Yet with heav'n - ly joy you bless us.
teach us God's own love through you has reached us.
ev - er, Keeps us yours and fails us nev - er!

5 What joy to know, when life is past,
  The Lord we love is first and last,
    The end and the beginning!
  He will one day, oh, glorious grace,
  Transport us to that happy place
    Beyond all tears and sinning!
  Amen! Amen!
  Come, Lord Jesus!
  Crown of gladness!
  We are yearning
  For the day of your returning.

6 Oh, let the harps break forth in sound!
  Our joy be all with music crowned,
    Our voices gaily blending!
  For Christ goes with us all the way—
  Today, tomorrow, ev'ry day!
    His love is never ending!
  Sing out! Ring Out!
  Jubilation!
  Exultation!
  Tell the story!
  Great is he, the King of glory!

© Text: Philipp Nicolai, 1556–1608; tr. Lutheran Book of Worship, 1978
Tune: Philipp Nicolai, 1556–1608

WIE SCHÖN LEUCHTET
P M

74 From God the Father, Virgin-Born

1 From God the Fa - ther, vir - gin - born To us the
2 Be - gin - ning from his home on high, In hu - man
3 Glide on, O glo - rious Sun, and bring The gift of
4 A - bide with us, O Lord, we pray; The gloom of

on - ly Son came down; By death the font to con - se -
flesh he came to die; Cre - a - tion by his death re -
heal - ing on your wing; To ev - 'ry dull and cloud - ed
dark - ness chase a - way; Your work of heal - ing, Lord, be -

crate, The faith - ful to re - gen - er - ate.
stored, And shed new joys of life a - broad.
sense The clear - ness of your light dis - pense.
gin, And take a - way the stain of sin.

5 Lord, once you came to earth's domain
   And, we believe, shall come again;
   Be with us on the battlefield,
   From ev'ry harm your people shield.

6 To you, O Lord, all glory be
   For this your blest epiphany;
   To God, whom all his hosts adore,
   And Holy Spirit evermore.

Text: Latin office hymn, c. 11th cent.; tr. John M. Neale, 1818-66, alt.
Tune: Antiphoner, Grenoble, 1753

DEUS TUORUM MILITUM
L M

As with Gladness Men of Old

1 As with glad-ness men of old Did the guid-ing star be-hold;
2 As with joy-ful steps they sped, Sav-ior, to thy low-ly bed,
3 As they of-fered gifts most rare At thy cra-dle, rude and bare,
4 Ho-ly Je-sus, ev-'ry day Keep us in the nar-row way;

As with joy they hailed its light, Lead-ing on-ward, beam-ing bright;
There to bend the knee be-fore Thee, whom heav'n and earth a-dore;
So may we with ho-ly joy, Pure and free from sin's al-loy,
And when earth-ly things are past, Bring our ran-somed souls at last

So, most gra-cious Lord, may we Ev-er-more be led by thee.
So may we with will-ing feet Ev-er seek thy mer-cy seat.
All our cost-liest trea-sures bring, Christ, to thee, our heav'n-ly king.
Where they need no star to guide, Where no clouds thy glo-ry hide.

5 In the heav'nly country bright
Need they no created light;
Thou its light, its joy, its crown,
Thou its sun which goes not down;
There forever may we sing
Alleluias to our King.

Text: William C. Dix, 1837–98, alt.
Tune: Conrad Kocher, 1786–1872

DIX
77 77 77

76 O Chief of Cities, Bethlehem

1 O chief of cit - ies, Beth - le - hem, Of Da - vid's
2 Be - yond the sun in splen - dor bright, A - bove you
3 The Wise Men, see - ing him so fair, Bow low be -
4 The gold - en trib - ute owns him king, But frank - in -

crown the fair - est gem, But more to us than
stands a won - drous light Pro - claim - ing from the
fore him and with prayer Their trea - sured east - ern
cense to God they bring, And last, pro - phet - ic

Da - vid's name, In you, as man, the Sav - ior came.
con - scious skies That here in flesh the God-head lies.
gifts un - fold Of in - cense, myrrh, and roy - al gold.
sign, with myrrh They shad - ow forth his sep - ul - cher.

5 O Jesus, whom the Gentiles see,
With Father, Spirit, One in Three:
To you, O God, be glory giv'n
By saints on earth and saints in heav'n.

Text: Aurelius Prudentius Clemens, 348–c.413; tr. composite
© *Tune: English folk tune*

TRUTH FROM ABOVE
L M

The People That in Darkness Sat

1 The peo - ple that in dark - ness sat A glo - rious light have
2 To hail you, Sun of Righ - teous - ness, The gath - 'ring na - tions
3 To us the Child of hope is born, To us the Son is
4 His name shall be the Prince of Peace, The Ev - er - last - ing

seen; The light has shined on them who long In
come; They joy as when the reap - ers bear Their
giv'n, And on his shoul - der ev - er rests All
Lord, The Won - der - ful, the Coun - sel - or, The

shades of death have been, In shades of death have been.
har - vest trea - sures home, Their har - vest trea - sures home.
pow'r in earth and heav'n, All pow'r in earth and heav'n.
God by all a - dored, The God by all a - dored.

5 His righteous government and pow'r
  Shall over all extend;
On judgment and on justice based,
  His reign shall have no end.

6 Lord Jesus, reign in us, we pray,
  And make us yours alone,
Who with the Father ever are
  And Holy Spirit, one.

Text: John Morison, 1749–98, alt.
Tune: Nikolaus Herman, c. 1480–1561

LOBT GOTT, IHR CHRISTEN
86 866

78 Jesus Has Come and Brings Pleasure

1 Je - sus has come and brings plea - sure e - ter - nal,
2 Je - sus has come! Now see bonds rent a - sun - der!
3 Je - sus has come as the might - y Re - deem - er.
4 Je - sus has come as the King of all glo - ry!

Al - pha, O - me - ga, Be - gin - ning and End;
Fet - ters of death now dis - solve, dis - ap - pear.
See now the threat - en - ing strong one dis - armed!
Heav - en and earth, oh, de - clare his great pow'r,

God - head, hu - man - i - ty, un - ion su - per - nal,
See him burst through with a voice as of thun - der!
Je - sus breaks down all the walls of death's for - tress,
Cap - tur - ing hearts with the heav - en - ly sto - ry.

O great Re - deem - er, you come as our friend!
He sets us free from our guilt and our fear,
Brings forth the pris - 'ners tri - um - phant, un - harmed.
Wel - come him now in this fast - fleet - ing hour!

Heav - en and earth, now pro - claim this great won - der:
Lifts us from shame to the place of his ho - nor.
Sa - tan, you wick - ed one, own now your mas - ter!
Pon - der his love! Take the crown he has for you!

Je - sus has come and brings plea - sure e - ter - nal!
Je - sus has come! Hear the roll of God's thun - der!
Je - sus has come! He, the might - y Re - deem - er!
Je - sus has come! He, the King of all glo - ry!

© Text: Johann L. K. Allendorf, 1693–1773; tr. Oliver C. Rupprecht, b. 1903
Tune: Cöthen, c. 1733

JESUS IST KOMMEN, GRUND EWIGER FREUDE
11 10 11 10 11 11

79

O Jesus, King of Glory

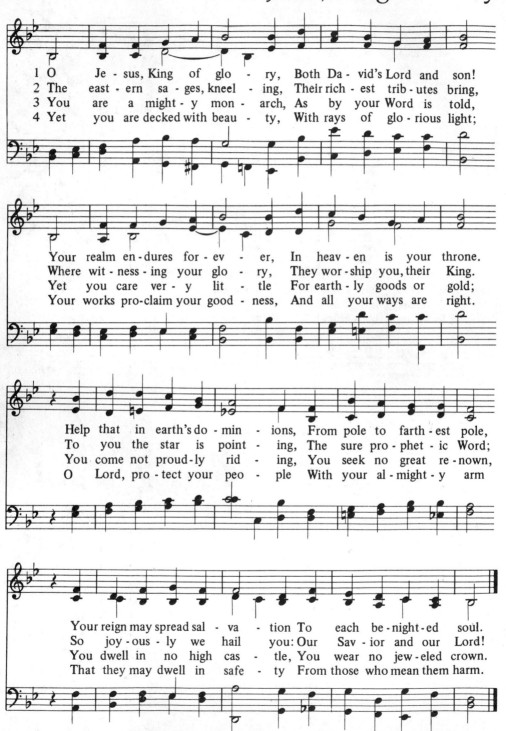

1 O Jesus, King of glory, Both David's Lord and son!
2 The eastern sages, kneeling, Their richest tributes bring,
3 You are a mighty monarch, As by your Word is told,
4 Yet you are decked with beauty, With rays of glorious light;

Your realm endures forever, In heaven is your throne.
Where witnessing your glory, They worship you, their King.
Yet you care very little For earthly goods or gold;
Your works proclaim your goodness, And all your ways are right.

Help that in earth's dominions, From pole to farthest pole,
To you the star is pointing, The sure prophetic Word;
You come not proudly riding, You seek no great renown,
O Lord, protect your people With your almighty arm

Your reign may spread salvation To each benighted soul.
So joyously we hail you: Our Savior and our Lord!
You dwell in no high castle, You wear no jeweled crown.
That they may dwell in safety From those who mean them harm.

5 Oh, look on me with pity
   Though I am weak and poor;
Admit me to your kingdom
   To dwell there, blest and sure.
I pray, Lord, guide and keep me
   Safe from my bitter foes,
From sin and death and Satan;
   Free me from all my woes.

6 Then let your Word within me
   Shine as the fairest star,
Your reign of love revealing
   How wonderful you are.
Help me confess you truly
   And with your Christendom
Here own you King and Savior
   With all the world to come.

Text: Martin Behm, 1557–1622; tr. Catherine Winkworth, 1829–78, alt.
Tune: Melchior Teschner, 1584–1635

VALET WILL ICH DIR GEBEN
76 76 D

Within the Father's House   80

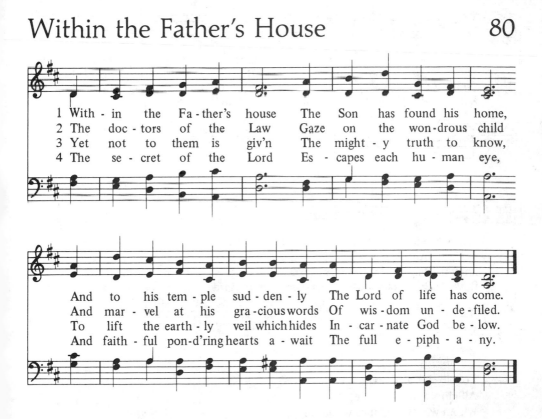

1 With - in the Fa - ther's house The Son has found his home,
2 The doc - tors of the Law Gaze on the won - drous child
3 Yet not to them is giv'n The might - y truth to know,
4 The se - cret of the Lord Es - capes each hu - man eye,

And to his tem - ple sud - den - ly The Lord of life has come.
And mar - vel at his gra - cious words Of wis - dom un - de - filed.
To lift the earth - ly veil which hides In - car - nate God be - low.
And faith - ful pon - d'ring hearts a - wait The full e - piph - a - ny.

5 Lord, enter now our souls
   And teach us by your grace
Each dim revealing of yourself
   With loving awe to trace

6 Till we behold your face
   And know as we are known
You, Father, Son, and Holy Ghost,
   Coequal Three in One.

Text: James R. Woodford, 1820–85, alt.
Tune: Johann B. König, 1691–1758, adapt.

FRANCONIA
S M

When Christ's Appearing Was Made Known

1 When Christ's ap-pear-ing was made known, King Her-od trem-bled for his throne; But he who of-fers heav'n-ly birth Seeks not the king-doms of this earth.

2 The east-ern sa-ges saw from far And fol-lowed on his guid-ing star; By light their way to light they trod, And by their gifts con-fessed their God.

3 With-in the Jor-dan's sa-cred flood The heav'n-ly Lamb in meek-ness stood That he, of whom no sin was known, Might cleanse his peo-ple from their own.

4 And oh, what mir-a-cle di-vine, When wa-ter red-dened in-to wine! He spoke the word, and forth it flowed In streams that na-ture ne'er be-stowed.

5 For this his glad epiphany
All glory unto Jesus be,
Whom with the Father we adore,
And Holy Ghost forevermore.

Text: Coelius Sedulius, 5th cent.; tr. composite
Tune: adapt. Michael Praetorius, 1571-1621

PUER NOBIS
L M

Hail to the Lord's Anointed

1 Hail to the Lord's a - noint - ed, Great Da -vid's great - er son!
2 He comes with res - cue speed - y To those who suf - fer wrong,
3 He shall come down like show - ers Up - on the fruit -ful earth;
4 Kings shall fall down be - fore him And gold and in -cense bring;

Hail, in the time ap - point - ed, His reign on earth be - gun!
To help the poor and need - y And bid the weak be strong;
And love, joy,hope, like flow - ers, Spring in his path to birth.
All na - tions shall a - dore him, His praise all peo - ple sing.

He comes to break op - pres - sion, To set the cap -tive free,
To give them songs for sigh - ing, Their dark -ness turn to light,
Be - fore him on the moun - tains Shall peace, the her -ald, go;
To him shall prayer un - ceas - ing And dai - ly vows as - cend;

To take a - way trans-gres - sion And rule in eq - ui - ty.
Whose souls, con-demned and dy - ing, Were pre-cious in his sight.
And righ-teous-ness in foun - tains From hill to val - ley flow.
His king-dom still in-creas - ing, A king-dom with - out end.

Text: James Montgomery, 1771–1854
Tune: Leonhart Schröter, 1532–1601

FREUT EUCH, IHR LIEBEN
76 76 D

83   O God of God, O Light of Light

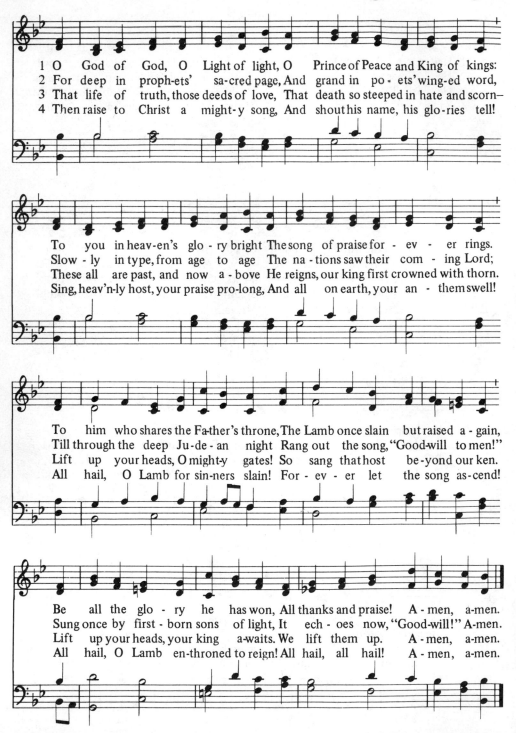

1 O God of God, O Light of light, O Prince of Peace and King of kings:
2 For deep in proph-ets' sa-cred page, And grand in po-ets' wing-ed word,
3 That life of truth, those deeds of love, That death so steeped in hate and scorn—
4 Then raise to Christ a might-y song, And shout his name, his glo-ries tell!

To you in heav-en's glo-ry bright The song of praise for - ev - er rings.
Slow - ly in type, from age to age The na - tions saw their com - ing Lord;
These all are past, and now a - bove He reigns, our king first crowned with thorn.
Sing, heav'n-ly host, your praise pro-long, And all on earth, your an - them swell!

To him who shares the Fa-ther's throne, The Lamb once slain but raised a - gain,
Till through the deep Ju - de - an night Rang out the song, "Good-will to men!"
Lift up your heads, O might-y gates! So sang that host be - yond our ken.
All hail, O Lamb for sin-ners slain! For - ev - er let the song as-cend!

Be all the glo - ry he has won, All thanks and praise! A - men, a-men.
Sung once by first - born sons of light, It ech - oes now, "Good-will!" A-men.
Lift up your heads, your king a-waits. We lift them up. A - men, a-men.
All hail, O Lamb en-throned to reign! All hail, all hail! A - men, a-men.

Text: John Julian, 1839–1913, adapt.
Tune: Schlag-Gesang- und Notenbuch, Stuttgart, 1744

O GROSSER GOTT
LM D

Hail, O Source of Every Blessing 84

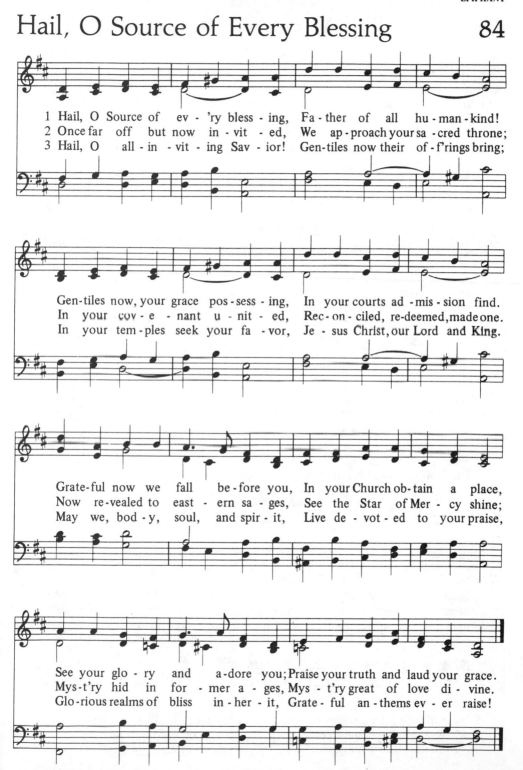

Text: Basil Woodd, 1760–1831, alt.
Tune: Neues geistreiches Gesangbuch, Halle, 1704

O DURCHBRECHER
87 87 D

85 Arise and Shine in Splendor

1 A - rise and shine in splen - dor, Let night to
2 See earth in dark - ness ly - ing, The hea - then
3 The world's re - mot - est rac - es, Up - on whose
4 Lift up your eyes in won - der; See, na - tions

day sur - rend - er; Your light is draw - ing near.
na - tions dy - ing In hope - less gloom and night.
wea - ry fac - es The sun looks from the sky,
gath - er yon - der, They all come to be free.

A - bove, the day is beam - ing, In match - less
To you the Lord of heav - en, Your light, your
Shall run with zeal un - tir - ing, With joy your
The world has heard your sto - ry, Your sons come

beau - ty gleam - ing; The glo - ry of the Lord is here.
hope, has giv - en Great glo - ry, hon - or, and de - light.
light de - sir - ing That breaks up - on them from on high.
to your glo - ry, And daugh - ters haste your light to see.

5 Your heart will leap rejoicing   Your eyes will fill with wonder
When multitudes come voicing   When people without number
Desire to share your peace.   Come thronging to you for God's grace.

Text: Martin Opitz, 1597–1639; tr. Gerhard Gieschen, b. 1899, alt.
Tune: Heinrich Isaac, c. 1450–1517

O WELT, ICH MUSS DICH LASSEN
776 778

Brightest and Best
of the Stars of the Morning

1 Bright-est and best of the stars of the morn-ing,
Dawn on our dark-ness and lend us your aid.
Star of the east, the ho-ri-zon a-dorn-ing,
Guide where our in-fant Re-deem-er is laid.

2 Cold on his cra-dle the dew-drops are shin-ing;
Low lies his head with the beasts of the stall;
An-gels a-dore him in slum-ber re-clin-ing,
Mak-er and Mon-arch and Sav-ior of all.

3 Shall we not yield him, in cost-ly de-vo-tion,
Fra-grance of E-dom and of f'rings di-vine,
Gems of the moun-tain and pearls of the o-cean,
Myrrh from the for-est or gold from the mine?

4 Vain-ly we of-fer each am-ple ob-la-tion,
Vain-ly with gifts would his fa-vor se-cure;
Rich-er by far is the heart's ad-o-ra-tion,
Dear-er to God are the prayers of the poor.

5 Brightest and best of the stars of the morning,
   Dawn on our darkness and lend us your aid.
   Star of the east, the horizon adorning,
   Guide where our infant Redeemer is laid.

Text: Reginald Heber, 1783–1826, alt.
Tune: James P. Harding, 1850–1911, adapt.

MORNING STAR
11 10 11 10

87 Oh, Wondrous Type! Oh, Vision Fair

1 Oh, won - drous type! Oh, vi - sion fair Of
2 With Mo - ses and E - li - jah nigh The in -
3 With shin - ing face and bright ar - ray Christ
4 And faith - ful hearts are raised on high By

glo - ry that the Church may share, Which
car - nate Lord holds con - verse high; And
deigns to man - i - fest to - day What
this great vi - sion's mys - ter - y, For

Christ up - on the moun - tain shows, Where
from the cloud the Ho - ly One Bears
glo - ry shall be theirs a - bove Who
which in joy - ful strains we raise The

bright - er than the sun he glows!
rec - ord to the on - ly Son.
joy in God with per - fect love.
voice of prayer, the hymn of praise.

5 O Father, with th'eternal Son   We pray you, bring us by your grace
  And Holy Spirit ever one,   To see your glory face to face.

Text: Sarum, 15th cent.; tr. John M. Neale, 1818–66, alt.
Tune: English, 15th cent.

DEO GRACIAS
L M

Songs of Thankfulness and Praise 88

1 Songs of thank-ful-ness and praise, Je-sus, Lord, to thee we raise;
2 Man-i-fest at Jor-dan's stream, Proph-et, Priest, and King su-preme;
3 Man-i-fest in mak-ing whole Pal-sied limbs and faint-ing soul;
4 Grant us grace to see thee, Lord, Pres-ent in thy ho-ly Word;

Man-i-fest-ed by the star To the sa-ges from a-far,
And at Ca-na wed-ding guest In thy God-head man-i-fest;
Man-i-fest in val-iant fight, Quell-ing all the dev-il's might;
Grace to im-i-tate thee now And be pure, as pure art thou;

Branch of roy-al Da-vid's stem In thy birth at Beth-le-hem:
Man-i-fest in pow'r di-vine, Chang-ing wa-ter in-to wine;
Man-i-fest in gra-cious will, Ev-er bring-ing good from ill;
That we might be-come like thee At thy great e-piph-a-ny

An-thems be to thee ad-dressed,
An-thems be to thee ad-dressed,
An-thems be to thee ad-dressed, God in flesh made man-i-fest.
And may praise thee, ev-er blest,

Text: Christopher Wordsworth, 1807–85
Tune: George J. Elvey, 1816–93

ST. GEORGE'S, WINDSOR
77 77 D

89 How Good, Lord, to Be Here

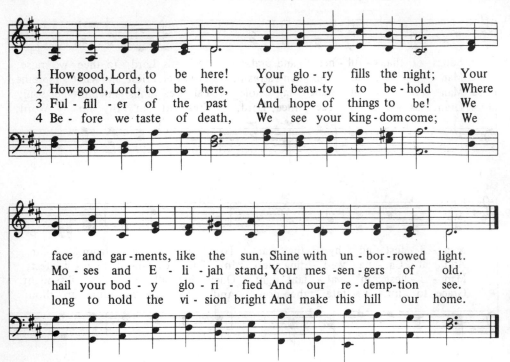

1 How good, Lord, to be here! Your glo-ry fills the night; Your
2 How good, Lord, to be here, Your beau-ty to be-hold Where
3 Ful-fill-er of the past And hope of things to be! We
4 Be-fore we taste of death, We see your king-dom come; We

face and gar-ments, like the sun, Shine with un-bor-rowed light.
Mo-ses and E-li-jah stand, Your mes-sen-gers of old.
hail your bod-y glo-ri-fied And our re-demp-tion see.
long to hold the vi-sion bright And make this hill our home.

5 How good, Lord, to be here!
  Yet we may not remain;
But since you bid us leave the mount,
  Come with us to the plain.

Text: Joseph A. Robinson, 1858-1933, alt.
Tune: J. S. Bach, 1685-1750, adapt.

POTSDAM
S M

Jesus, Refuge of the Weary

1 Je - sus, ref - uge of the wea - ry, Blest re - deem - er, whom we love,
2 Do we pass that cross un - heed - ing, Breath - ing no re - pen - tant vow,
3 Je - sus, may our hearts be burn - ing With more fer - vent love for you;

Foun - tain in life's des - ert drea - ry, Sav - ior from the world a - bove:
Though we see you wound - ed, bleed - ing, See your thorn - en - cir - cled brow?
May our eyes be ev - er turn - ing To be - hold your cross a - new

Of - ten have your eyes, of - fend - ed, Gazed up - on the sin - ner's fall;
Yet your sin - less death has brought us Life e - ter - nal, peace, and rest;
Till in glo - ry, part - ed nev - er From the bless - ed Sav - ior's side,

Yet up - on the cross ex - tend - ed, You have borne the pain of all.
On - ly what your grace has taught us Calms the sin - ner's deep dis - tress.
Grav - en in our hearts for - ev - er, Dwell the cross, the Cru - ci - fied.

Text: Girolamo Savonarola, 1452–98; tr. Jane F. Wilde, 1826–96, alt.
Tune: Herrnhut, c. 1735

O DU LIEBE MEINER LIEBE
87 87 D

91 My Song Is Love Unknown

1 My song is love un-known, My Sav-ior's love to
2 He came from his blest throne Sal-va-tion to be-
3 Some-times they strew his way And his sweet prais-es
4 Why, what hath my Lord done? What makes this rage and

me, Love to the love-less shown That they might love - ly
stow; But men made strange, and none The longed-for Christ would
sing; Re-sound-ing all the day Ho-san-nas to their
spite? He made the lame to run, He gave the blind their

be. Oh, who am I That for my sake
know. But, oh, my friend, My friend in-deed,
King. Then "Cru-ci-fy!" Is all their breath,
sight. Sweet in-ju-ries! Yet they at these

My Lord should take Frail flesh and die?
Who at my need His life did spend!
And for his death They thirst and cry.
Them-selves dis-please And 'gainst him rise.

5 They rise and needs will have
    My dear Lord made away;
A murderer they save,
    The prince of life they slay.
Yet cheerful he
    To suff'ring goes
That he his foes
    From thence might free.

6 In life no house, no home
    My Lord on earth might have;
In death no friendly tomb
    But what a stranger gave.
What may I say?
    Heav'n was his home
But mine the tomb
    Wherein he lay.

7 Here might I stay and sing,
    No story so divine!
Never was love, dear King,
    Never was grief like thine.
This is my friend,
    In whose sweet praise
I all my days
    Could gladly spend!

Text: Samuel Crossman, c. 1624–83
© *Tune: John Ireland, 1879–1962*

LOVE UNKNOWN
66 66 4444

O Lord, Throughout These Forty Days   92

1 O Lord, through-out these for-ty days You prayed and kept the fast;
2 You strove with Sa-tan, and you won; Your faith-ful-ness en-dured;
3 Though parched and hun-gry, yet you prayed And fixed your mind a-bove;
4 Be with us through this sea-son, Lord, And all our earth-ly days,

In-spire re-pen-tance for our sin, And free us from our past.
Lend us your nerve, your skill and trust In God's e-ter-nal Word.
So teach us to de-ny our-selves Since we have known God's love.
That when the fi-nal Eas-ter dawns, We join in heav-en's praise.

© *Text: based on Claudia F. Hernaman, 1838–98; para. Gilbert E. Doan, b. 1930*
Tune: The CL Psalmes of David, Edinburgh, 1635

CAITHNESS
C M

93 Savior, when in Dust to You

1 Sav - ior, when in dust to you Low we bow in hom-age due;
2 By your help-less in - fant years, By your life of want and tears,
3 By your hour of dire de -spair, By your ag - o - ny of prayer,
4 By your deep ex - pir - ing groan, By the sad se - pul - chral stone,

When, re - pen-tant, to the skies Scarce we lift our weep - ing eyes;
By your days of deep dis -tress In the sav - age wil - der - ness,
By the cross, the nail, the thorn, Pierc - ing spear, and tor - turing scorn,
By the vault whose dark a - bode Held in vain the ris - ing God,

Oh, by all your pains and woe Suf - fered once for us be - low,
By the dread, mys - te - rious hour Of the in-sult - ing tempt - er's pow'r,
By the gloom that veiled the skies O'er the dread-ful sac - ri - fice,
Oh, from earth to heav'n re - stored, Might - y, re - as - cend - ed Lord,

Bend-ing from your throne on high, Hear our pen - i - ten - tial cry!
Turn, oh, turn a fa - v'ring eye; Hear our pen - i - ten - tial cry!
Lis - ten to our hum - ble sigh; Hear our pen - i - ten - tial cry!
Bend-ing from your throne on high, Hear our pen - i - ten - tial cry!

Text: Robert Grant, 1779–1838, alt.
Tune: Joseph Parry, 1841–1903

ABERYSTWYTH
77 77 D

Christ, the Life of All the Living

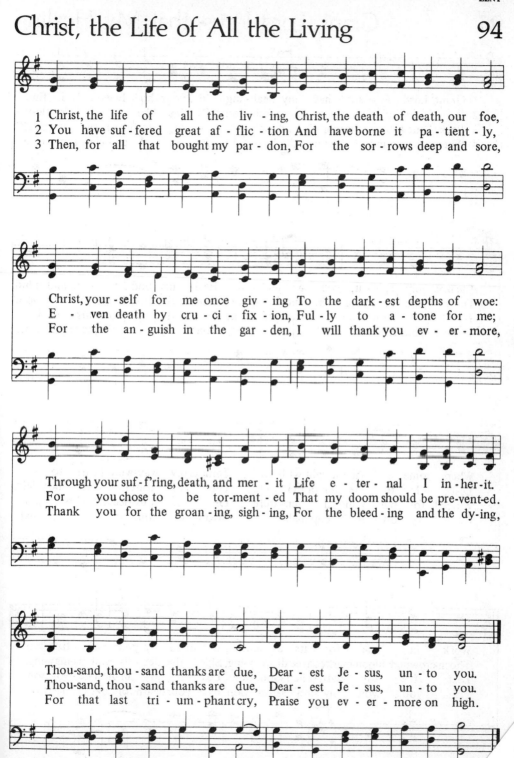

1 Christ, the life of all the liv - ing, Christ, the death of death, our foe,
2 You have suf - fered great af - flic - tion And have borne it pa - tient - ly,
3 Then, for all that bought my par - don, For the sor - rows deep and sore,

Christ, your - self for me once giv - ing To the dark - est depths of woe:
E - ven death by cru - ci - fix - ion, Ful - ly to a - tone for me;
For the an - guish in the gar - den, I will thank you ev - er - more,

Through your suf - f'ring, death, and mer - it Life e - ter - nal I in - her - it.
For you chose to be tor - ment - ed That my doom should be pre - vent - ed.
Thank you for the groan - ing, sigh - ing, For the bleed - ing and the dy - ing,

Thou - sand, thou - sand thanks are due, Dear - est Je - sus, un - to you.
Thou - sand, thou - sand thanks are due, Dear - est Je - sus, un - to you.
For that last tri - um - phant cry, Praise you ev - er - more on high.

Text: Ernst C. Homburg, 1605–81; tr. Catherine Winkworth, 1829–78, alt.
Tune: Kirchengesangbuch, Darmstadt, 1687

JESU, MEINES LEBENS
87 8

95 Grant, Lord Jesus, that My Healing

1 Grant, Lord Je - sus, that my heal - ing In your ho - ly wounds I find.
2 If some lust in cur - rent fash - ion Ris - es like a fi - 'ry flood,
3 Beck - oned by the world's old ques - tion, "Go-ing my broad, eas - y road?"
4 Where the wound is and the hurt - ing, Pour in oil and cleans-ing wine.

Cleanse my spir - it, will, and feel - ing; Heal my bod - y, soul, and mind.
Draw me to your cross and Pas - sion, Quench the fire, Lord, by your blood.
Let me turn from its sug - ges - tion To the ag - o - niz - ing load
Let your cross, its pow'r as - sert - ing, Touch my life with grace di - vine.

When some e - vil thought with - in Tempts my way-ward heart to sin,
Lest I to the tempt - er yield, Let me front him with the shield,
Which for me you did en - dure. Let me thus flee thoughts im-pure
Ev - 'ry bit - ter cup make sweet, Bread of com-fort let me eat.

Work in me for its e - vic-tion, Weight-ed by your cru-ci - fix - ion.
Thorn-crowned, blood-marked tree dis-play-ing, Sign the dev - ils find dis-may-ing.
Lest I toy with soiled e-mo-tions, Los - ing joy in blest de - vo - tions.
For you won my soul's sal-va - tion By your death for ev-'ry na - tion.

5 Jesus, rock of strength, my tower,
  In your death I put my trust.
When you died, death lost its power,
  When you rose, it turned to dust.

Let your bitter agony,
Suffered for us, comfort me.
Dying, Lord, in its protection,
I have life and resurrection.

© *Text: Johann Heermann, 1585-1647; tr. F. Samuel Janzow, b. 1913*
Tune: Johann B. König, Harmonischer Liederschatz, 1738

DER AM KREUZ
87 87 77 88

Come to Calvary's Holy Mountain   96

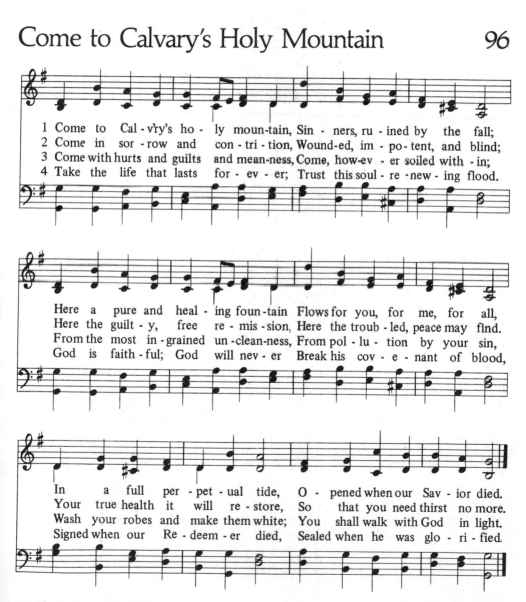

1 Come to Cal-v'ry's ho-ly moun-tain, Sin-ners, ru-ined by the fall;
2 Come in sor-row and con-tri-tion, Wound-ed, im-po-tent, and blind;
3 Come with hurts and guilts and mean-ness, Come, how-ev-er soiled with-in;
4 Take the life that lasts for-ev-er; Trust this soul-re-new-ing flood.

Here a pure and heal-ing foun-tain Flows for you, for me, for all,
Here the guilt-y, free re-mis-sion, Here the troub-led, peace may find.
From the most in-grained un-clean-ness, From pol-lu-tion by your sin,
God is faith-ful; God will nev-er Break his cov-e-nant of blood,

In a full per-pet-ual tide, O-pened when our Sav-ior died.
Your true health it will re-store, So that you need thirst no more.
Wash your robes and make them white; You shall walk with God in light.
Signed when our Re-deem-er died, Sealed when he was glo-ri-fied.

Text: James Montgomery, 1771–1854, alt.
Tune: Ludvig M. Lindeman, 1812–87

NAAR MIT ÖIE
87 87 77

97 Alas! and Did My Savior Bleed

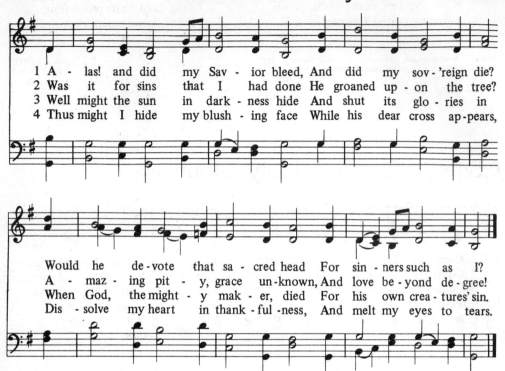

1 A - las! and did my Sav - ior bleed, And did my sov - 'reign die?
2 Was it for sins that I had done He groaned up - on the tree?
3 Well might the sun in dark - ness hide And shut its glo - ries in
4 Thus might I hide my blush - ing face While his dear cross ap - pears,

Would he de - vote that sa - cred head For sin - ners such as I?
A - maz - ing pit - y, grace un - known, And love be - yond de - gree!
When God, the might - y mak - er, died For his own crea - tures' sin.
Dis - solve my heart in thank - ful - ness, And melt my eyes to tears.

5 But tears of grief cannot repay
   The debt of love I owe;
Here, Lord, I give myself away:
   It's all that I can do.

Text: Isaac Watts, 1674–1748, alt.
Tune: Hugh Wilson, 1764–1824

MARTYRDOM
C M

98 Glory Be to Jesus

1 Glo - ry be to Je - sus, Who in bit - ter pains
2 Grace and life e - ter - nal In that blood I find;
3 Blest through end - less a - ges Be the pre - cious stream
4 A - bel's blood for ven - geance Plead - ed to the skies;

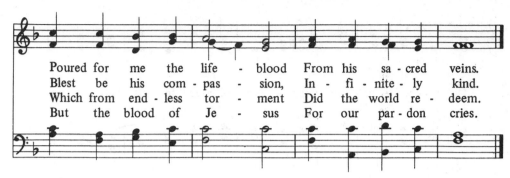

Poured for me the life - blood From his sa - cred veins.
Blest be his com - pas - sion, In - fi - nite - ly kind.
Which from end - less tor - ment Did the world re - deem.
But the blood of Je - sus For our par - don cries.

5 Oft as earth exulting
    Wafts its praise on high,
  Angel hosts rejoicing
    Make their glad reply.

6 Lift we then our voices,
    Swell the mighty flood;
  Louder still and louder
    Praise the precious blood.

Text: Italian, 18th cent.; tr. Edward Caswall, 1814–78
Tune: Friedrich Filitz, 1804–76

WEM IN LEIDENSTAGEN
65 65

Not All the Blood of Beasts 99

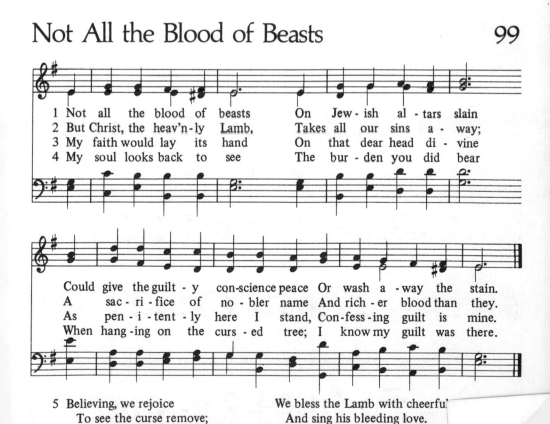

1 Not all the blood of beasts On Jew - ish al - tars slain
2 But Christ, the heav'n - ly Lamb, Takes all our sins a - way;
3 My faith would lay its hand On that dear head di - vine
4 My soul looks back to see The bur - den you did bear

Could give the guilt - y con-science peace Or wash a - way the stain.
A sac - ri - fice of no - bler name And rich - er blood than they.
As pen - i - tent - ly here I stand, Con-fess - ing guilt is mine.
When hang - ing on the curs - ed tree; I know my guilt was there.

5 Believing, we rejoice   We bless the Lamb with cheerful
    To see the curse remove;   And sing his bleeding love.

Text: Isaac Watts, 1674–1748, alt.
Tune: William Daman, The Psalmes of David, 1579

Text: I
Tune: Jon

100 On My Heart Imprint Your Image

On my heart im - print your im - age, Bless-ed Je - sus, king of grace,

That life's rich - es, cares, and plea - sures Nev - er may your work e - rase;

Let the clear in - scrip - tion be: Je - sus, cru - ci - fied for me,

Is my life, my hope's foun-da - tion, And my glo - ry and sal - va - tion!

Thomas H. Kingo, 1634-1703; tr. Peer O. Strömme, 1856-1921, alt.
Johann B. König, Harmonischer Liederschatz, 1738

DER AM KREUZ
87 87 77 88

In the Cross of Christ I Glory

1 In the cross of Christ I glory, Tow'r-ing
2 When the woes of life o'er-take me, Hopes de-
3 When the sun of bliss is beam-ing Light and
4 Bane and bless-ing, pain and plea-sure By the

o'er the wrecks of time. All the light of
ceive, and fears an-noy, Nev-er shall the
love up-on my way, From the cross the
cross are sanc-ti-fied; Peace is there that

sa-cred sto-ry Gath-ers round its head sub-lime.
cross for-sake me; Lo, it glows with peace and joy.
ra-diance stream-ing Adds more lus-ter to the day.
knows no mea-sure, Joys that through all time a-bide.

Text: John Bowring, 1792–1872
Tune: Ithamar Conkey, 1815–67

RATHBUN
87 87

102 All Glory, Laud, and Honor

Refrain

All glo - ry, laud, and hon - or To you, Re - deem - er, King,

To whom the lips of chil - dren Made sweet ho - san - nas ring.

Verse

1 You are the king of Is - rael And Da - vid's roy - al Son,
2 The com - pa - ny of an - gels Are prais - ing you on high;
3 The mul - ti - tude of pil - grims With palms be - fore you went,
4 To you, be - fore your Pas - sion, They sang their hymns of praise.

Refrain

Now in the Lord's name com - ing, Our King and Bless - ed One.
Cre - a - tion and all mor - tals In cho - rus make re - ply.
Our praise and prayer and an - thems Be - fore you we pre - sent.
To you, now high ex - alt - ed, Our mel - o - dy we raise.

5 Their praises you accepted;   Great author of all goodness,
  Accept the prayers we bring,   O good and gracious King. *Refrain*

Text: Theodulf of Orléans, 750/760–821; tr. John M. Neale, 1818–66, alt.
Tune: Melchior Teschner, 1584–1635

VALET WILL ICH DIR GEBEN
76 76 D

The Royal Banners Forward Go

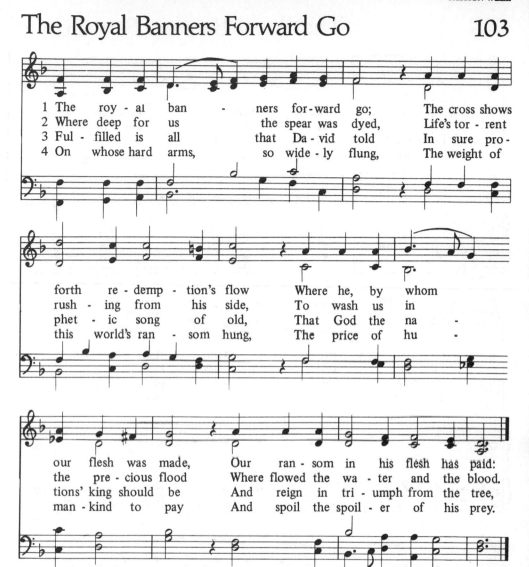

1 The roy - al ban - ners for - ward go; The cross shows
2 Where deep for us the spear was dyed, Life's tor - rent
3 Ful - filled is all that Da - vid told In sure pro -
4 On whose hard arms, so wide - ly flung, The weight of

forth re - demp - tion's flow Where he, by whom
rush - ing from his side, To wash us in
phet - ic song of old, That God the na -
this world's ran - som hung, The price of hu -

our flesh was made, Our ran - som in his flesh has paid:
the pre - cious flood Where flowed the wa - ter and the blood.
tions' king should be And reign in tri - umph from the tree,
man - kind to pay And spoil the spoil - er of his prey.

5 To you, eternal Three in One,
Let homage meet by all be done,
By all you ransomed and restore;
Oh, guide and gladden evermore.

Text: Venantius Honorius Fortunatus, 530–609, sts. 1–4; source unknown, st. 5;   HERR JESU CHRIST, WAHR MENSCH UND GOTT
    tr. composite   LM
Tune: attr. Johann Eccard, 1553–1611

104 The Royal Banners Forward Go

1 The roy - al ban - ners for - ward go;
2 Where deep for us the spear was dyed,
3 Ful - filled is all that Da - vid told
4 On whose hard arms, so wide - ly flung,

The cross shows forth re - demp - tion's flow
Life's tor - rent rush - ing from his side,
In sure pro - phet - ic song of old,
The weight of this world's ran - som hung,

Where he, by whom our flesh was made,
To wash us in the pre - cious flood
That God the na - tions' king should be
The price of hu - man - kind to pay

Our   ran   -   som   in   his   flesh
Where   flowed   the   wa -   ter   and
And   reign   in   tri -   umph from
And   spoil   the   spoil- er   of

has   paid:
the   blood.
the   tree,
his   prey.   A - men

5 To you, eternal Three in One,
  Let homage meet by all be done,
  By all you ransomed and restore;
  Oh, guide and gladden evermore.

For the **Vexilla Celebration** the congregation sings stanzas 1, 3, and 5 to the chorale melody, and the choir sings stanzas 2 and 4 to the plainsong melody.

Text: Venantius Honorius Fortunatus, 530–609, sts. 1-4; source unknown, st. 5; tr. composite
Tune: Sarum plainsong, mode I

VEXILLA REGIS
LM

105 Ride On, Ride On in Majesty

1 Ride on, ride on in maj - es - ty! Hear all the
2 Ride on, ride on in maj - es - ty! In low - ly
3 Ride on, ride on in maj - es - ty! The wing - ed
4 Ride on, ride on in maj - es - ty! Your last and

tribes ho - san - na cry; O Sav - ior meek, pur - sue your
pomp ride on to die. O Christ, your tri - umphs now be -
squad - rons of the sky Look down with sad and won - d'ring
fierc - est strife is nigh. The Fa - ther on his sap - phire

road With palms and scat - tered gar - ments strowed.
gin O'er cap - tive death and con - quered sin.
eyes To see the ap - proach - ing sac - ri - fice.
throne A - waits his own a - noint - ed Son.

5 Ride on, ride on in majesty!
  In lowly pomp ride on to die.

Bow your meek head to mortal pain,
Then take, O Christ, your pow'r and reign!

Text: Henry H. Milman, 1791–1868, alt.
© Tune: Graham George, b. 1912

THE KING'S MAJESTY
L M

Hosanna, Loud Hosanna

1 Ho-san-na, loud ho-san-na, The lit-tle chil-dren sang;
2 From Ol-i-vet they fol-lowed Mid an ex-ul-tant crowd,
3 "Ho-san-na in the high-est!" That an-cient song we sing,

Through pil-lared court and tem-ple The love-ly an-them rang.
The vic-tor palm branch wav-ing And chant-ing clear and loud.
For Christ is our Re-deem-er, The Lord of heav'n our King.

To Je-sus, who had blessed them, Close fold-ed to his breast,
The Lord of men and an-gels Rode on in low-ly state
Oh, may we ev-er praise him With heart and life and voice

The chil-dren sang their prais-es, The sim-plest and the best.
Nor scorned that lit-tle chil-dren Should on his bid-ding wait.
And in his bliss-ful pres-ence E-ter-nal-ly re-joice!

Text: Jeanette Threlfall, 1821–80, alt.
Tune: Gesangbuch der Herzogl. Hofkapelle, *Württemberg*, 1784

ELLACOMBE
76 76 D

107 The Death of Jesus Christ, Our Lord

1 The death of Je - sus Christ, our Lord, We cel - e -
brate with one ac - cord; It is our com - fort in dis -
tress, Our heart's sweet joy and hap - pi - ness.

2 He blot - ted out with his own blood The judg - ment
that a - gainst us stood; He full a - tone - ment for us
made, And all our debt he ful - ly paid.

3 That this is now and ev - er true He gives an
ear - nest ev - er new: In this his ho - ly Sup - per
here We taste his love so sweet, so near.

4 His Word pro - claims and we be - lieve That in this
Sup - per we re - ceive His ver - y bod - y, as he
said, His ver - y blood for sin - ners shed.

5 A precious food is this indeed—
It never fails us in our need—
A heav'nly manna for our soul
Until we safely reach our goal.

6 Oh, blest is each believing guest
Who in this promise finds his rest;
For Jesus will in love abide
With those who do in him confide.

7 The guest that comes with true intent
To turn to God and to repent,
To live for Christ, to die to sin,
Will thus a holy life begin.

8 They who his Word do not believe
This food unworthily receive,
Salvation here will never find—
May we this warning keep in mind!

9 Help us sincerely to believe
That we may worthily receive
Your Supper and in you find rest.
Amen, he who believes is blest.

Text: Haquin Spegel, 1645-1714; tr. Olof Olsson, 1841-1900, alt.
Tune: German, 18th cent.

GOTTLOB, ES GEHT NUNMEHR ZU ENDE
L M

From Calvary's Cross I Heard Christ Say 108

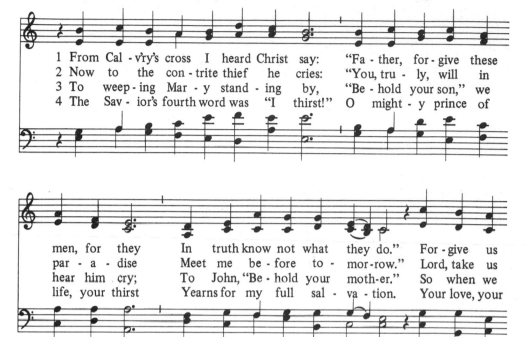

1 From Cal-v'ry's cross I heard Christ say: "Fa-ther, for-give these
2 Now to the con-trite thief he cries: "You, tru-ly, will in
3 To weep-ing Mar-y stand-ing by, "Be-hold your son," we
4 The Sav-ior's fourth word was "I thirst!" O might-y prince of

men, for they In truth know not what they do." For-give us
par-a-dise Meet me be-fore to-mor-row." Lord, take us
hear him cry; To John, "Be-hold your moth-er." So when we
life, your thirst Yearns for my full sal-va-tion. Your love, your

too, for of-ten we In ig-no-rance of-fend you.
soon to heav'n with you, Who lin-ger here in sor-row.
die, let those we leave In love be-friend each oth-er.
mer-cy's sac-ri-fice Com-pel my ad-o-ra-tion.

5 The fifth, "My God, my God, oh, why
  Do you not hear my earnest cry?"
     Lord, you were here forsaken
  That we may never be so lost;
     Let lively faith awaken.

6 With "It is finished!" you have done,
  The course your Father set is run,
     The victory achieving.
  So let us do your work on earth,
     Your promises believing.

7 And last, as life and suff'rings end:
  "O God my Father, I commend
     Into your hands my spirit."
  Be this, dear Lord, my dying prayer;
     O gracious Father, hear it.

8 Our Lord thus spoke these seven times
  When on his cross, for all our crimes,
     He died that we not perish.
  Let us his last and dying words
     In our remembrance cherish.

© Text: Johann Böschenstain, 1472–1539; tr. Henry L. Lettermann, b. 1932
Tune: Adam Reusner, 1496–c. 1575, Babst Gesangbuch, 1545

DA JESUS AN DES KREUZES
887 87

109 Jesus, I Will Ponder Now

1 Je - sus, I will pon - der now On your ho - ly Pas - sion;
2 Make me see your great dis - tress, An - guish, and af - flic - tion,
3 Yet, O Lord, not thus a - lone Make me see your Pas - sion;
4 Grant that I your Pas - sion view With re - pen - tant griev - ing,

With your Spir - it me en - dow For such med - i - ta - tion.
Bonds and stripes and wretch-ed - ness And your cru - ci - fix - ion;
But its cause to me make known And its ter - mi - na - tion.
Let me not bring shame to you By un - ho - ly liv - ing.

Grant that I in love and faith May the im - age cher - ish
Make me see how scourge and rod, Spear and nails did wound you,
For I al - so and my sin Brought your deep af - flic - tion;
How could I re - fuse to shun Ev - 'ry sin - ful plea - sure

Of your suf - f'ring, pain, and death That I may not per - ish.
How you died for those, O God, Who with thorns had crowned you.
This the shame - ful cause has been Of your cru - ci - fix - ion.
Since for me God's on - ly Son Suf - fered with - out mea - sure?

5 If my sins give me alarm
   And my conscience grieve me,
Let your cross my fear disarm,
   Peace and pardon give me.
Grant that I may trust in you
   And your holy Passion;
If his Son forgives anew,
   God must have compassion.

6 Jesus, Lord, my heart renew,
   Let me bear my crosses,
Learning humbleness from you,
   Peace despite my losses.
May I give you love for love!
   Hear me, O my Savior,
That I may in heav'n above
   Sing your praise forever.

Text: Sigismund von Birken, 1626–81; tr. August Crull, 1846–1923, alt.
Tune: Melchior Vulpius, c. 1560–1615

JESU KREUZ, LEIDEN UND PEIN
76 76 D

Go to Dark Gethsemane 110

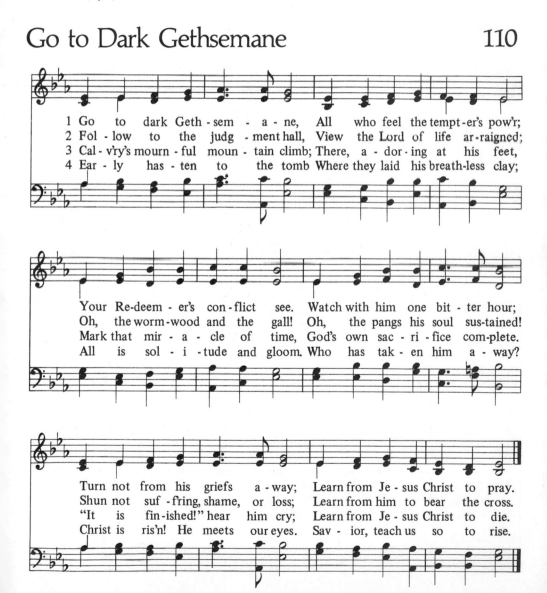

1 Go to dark Geth-sem-a-ne, All who feel the tempt-er's pow'r;
2 Fol-low to the judg-ment hall, View the Lord of life ar-raigned;
3 Cal-v'ry's mourn-ful moun-tain climb; There, a-dor-ing at his feet,
4 Ear-ly has-ten to the tomb Where they laid his breath-less clay;

Your Re-deem-er's con-flict see. Watch with him one bit-ter hour;
Oh, the worm-wood and the gall! Oh, the pangs his soul sus-tained!
Mark that mir-a-cle of time, God's own sac-ri-fice com-plete.
All is sol-i-tude and gloom. Who has tak-en him a-way?

Turn not from his griefs a-way; Learn from Je-sus Christ to pray.
Shun not suf-fring, shame, or loss; Learn from him to bear the cross.
"It is fin-ished!" hear him cry; Learn from Je-sus Christ to die.
Christ is ris'n! He meets our eyes. Sav-ior, teach us so to rise.

Text: James Montgomery, 1771–1854
Tune: Richard Redhead, 1820–1901

GETHSEMANE
77 77 77

111 A Lamb Alone Bears Willingly

1 A lamb a-lone bears will-ing-ly Sin's
2 This lamb is Christ, our soul's great friend, The
3 "Yes, Fa-ther, yes, most will-ing-ly I
4 Then, when we come be-fore God's throne, This

crush-ing weight for sin-ners; He car-ries guilt's
Lamb of God, our Sav-ior, Whom God the Fa-
bear what you com-mand me; My will con-forms
lit-tle lamb shall lead us; His righ-teous-ness

e-nor-mi-ty, Dies shorn of all his
ther chose to send Our reb-el guilt to
to your de-cree, I risk what you have
shall be our crown, His in-no-cence pre-

hon-ors. He goes to slaugh-ter, weak and faint, Is
cov-er. "Go down, my Son," the Fa-ther said, "To
asked me." O won-drous love, what have you done? The
cede us. His grace our dress of roy-al-ty; His

led a - way with no com - plaint His spot - less life to
free my chil - dren from their dread Of death and con - dem-
Fa - ther of - fers up his Son, The Son, con - tent, a -
all - for - giv - ing loy - al - ty U - nites us with our

of - fer. He bears the stripes, the wrath,
na - tion. The wrath and stripes are hard
gree - ing! O Love, how strong you are
Fa - ther, Where we shall stand at Je -

the lies, The mock - er - y, and yet re -
to bear, But in your death they all can
to save, To put God's Son in - to his
sus' side, His Church, re - deemed and glo - ri -

plies, "Will - ing all this I suf - fer."
share The joy of your sal - va - tion!"
grave, All peo - ple there - by free - ing!
fied, Where all his faith - ful gath - er!

© Text: Paul Gerhardt, 1607-76; tr. Henry L. Lettermann, b. 1932
Tune: Wolfgang Dachstein, c. 1487-1553

AN WASSERFLÜSSEN BABYLON
P M

112

Jesus, in Your Dying Woes

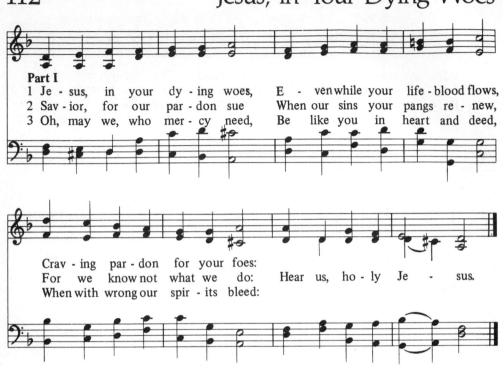

Part I

1 Je - sus, in your dy - ing woes, E - ven while your life - blood flows,
2 Sav - ior, for our par - don sue When our sins your pangs re - new,
3 Oh, may we, who mer - cy need, Be like you in heart and deed,

Crav - ing par - don for your foes:
For we know not what we do: Hear us, ho - ly Je - sus.
When with wrong our spir - its bleed:

Part II

4 Jesus, pitying the sighs
Of the thief, who near you dies,
Promising him paradise:
   Hear us, holy Jesus.

5 May we in our guilt and shame
Still your love and mercy claim,
Calling humbly on your name:
   Hear us, holy Jesus.

6 May our hearts to you incline
And their thoughts your cross entwine.
Cheer our souls with hope divine:
   Hear us, holy Jesus.

Part III

7 Jesus, loving to the end
Her whose heart your sorrows rend,
And your dearest human friend:
   Hear us, holy Jesus.

8 May we in your sorrows share,
For your sake all peril dare,
And enjoy your tender care:
   Hear us, holy Jesus.

9 May we all your loved ones be,
All one holy family,
Loving, since your love we see:
   Hear us, holy Jesus.

Part IV

10 Jesus, whelmed in fears unknown,
   With our evil left alone,
   While no light from heav'n is shown:
      Hear us, holy Jesus.

11 When we seem in vain to pray
   And our hope seems far away,
   In the darkness be our stay:
      Hear us, holy Jesus.

12 Though no Father seem to hear,
   Though no light our spirits cheer,
   May we know that God is near:
      Hear us, holy Jesus.

Part V

13 Jesus, in your thirst and pain,
   While your wounds your lifeblood drain,
   Thirsting more our love to gain:
      Hear us, holy Jesus.

14 Thirst for us in mercy still;
   All your holy work fulfill;
   Satisfy your loving will:
      Hear us, holy Jesus.

15 May we thirst your love to know;
   Lead us in our sin and woe
   Where the healing waters flow:
      Hear us, holy Jesus.

Part VI

16 Jesus, all our ransom paid,
   All your Father's will obeyed;
   By your suff'rings perfect made:
      Hear us, holy Jesus.

17 Save us in our soul's distress;
   Be our help to cheer and bless
   While we grow in holiness:
      Hear us, holy Jesus.

18 Brighten all our heav'nward way
   With an ever holier ray
   Till we pass to perfect day:
      Hear us, holy Jesus.

Part VII

19 Jesus, all your labor vast,
   All your woe and conflict past,
   Yielding up your soul at last:
      Hear us, holy Jesus.

20 When the death shades round us low'r,
   Guard us from the tempter's pow'r,
   Keep us in that trial hour:
      Hear us, holy Jesus.

21 May your life and death supply
   Grace to live and grace to die,
   Grace to reach the home on high:
      Hear us, holy Jesus.

Text: Thomas B. Pollock, 1836–96, alt.
Tune: Bernhard Schumacher, 1886–1978

SEPTEM VERBA
777 6

113   O Sacred Head, Now Wounded

1 O sa - cred head, now wound - ed, With grief and shame weighed down,
2 How pale you are with an - guish, With sore a - buse and scorn!
3 All this for my trans - gres - sion, My way - ward soul to win;
4 Here will I stand be - side you, Your death for me my plea;

Now scorn - ful - ly sur - round - ed With thorns, your on - ly crown.
Your face, your eyes now lan - guish, Which once were bright as morn.
This tor - ment of your Pas - sion, To set me free from sin.
Let all the world de - ride you, I clasp you close to me.

O sa - cred head, what glo - ry And bliss did once com - bine;
Now from your cheeks has van - ished Their col - or once so fair;
I cast my - self be - fore you, Your wrath my right - ful lot;
My awe can - not be spo - ken, To see you cru - ci - fied;

Though now de - spised and gor - y, I joy to call you mine!
From lov - ing lips is ban - ished The splen - dor that was there.
Have mer - cy, I im - plore you, O Lord, con - demn me not!
But in your bod - y bro - ken, Re - deemed, I safe - ly hide!

5 What language can I borrow
    To thank you, dearest friend,
For this your dying sorrow,
    Your mercy without end?
Bind me to you forever,
    Give courage from above;
Let not my weakness sever
    Your bond of lasting love.

6 Lord, be my consolation,
    My constant source of cheer;
Remind me of your Passion,
    My shield when death is near.
I look in faith, believing
    That you have died for me;
Your cross and crown receiving,
    I live eternally.

© *Text: attr. Bernard of Clairvaux, 1091–1153; Paul Gerhardt, 1607–76;*
    tr. Lutheran Worship, 1982
Tune: Hans L. Hassler, 1564–1612

HERZLICH TUT MICH VERLANGEN
76 76 D

When I Survey the Wondrous Cross   114

1 When I sur-vey the won-drous cross On which the prince of glo-ry died, My rich-est gain I count but loss And pour con-tempt on all my pride.

2 For-bid it, Lord, that I should boast Save in the death of Christ, my God; All the vain things that charm me most, I sac-ri-fice them to his blood.

3 See, from his head, his hands, his feet Sor-row and love flow min-gled down. Did e'er such love and sor-row meet Or thorns com-pose so rich a crown?

4 Were the whole realm of na-ture mine, That were a trib-ute far too small; Love so a-maz-ing, so di-vine, De-mands my soul, my life, my all!

Text: Isaac Watts, 1674–1748
Tune: adapt. Edward Miller, 1731–1807

ROCKINGHAM OLD
L M

115 When I Survey the Wondrous Cross

1 When I sur - vey the won - drous
2 For - bid it, Lord, that I should
3 See, from his head, his hands, his
4 Were the whole realm of na - ture

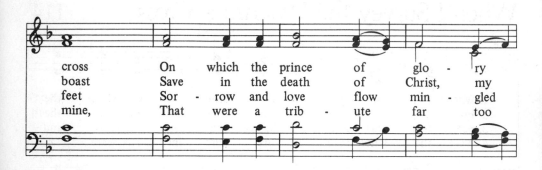

cross On which the prince of glo - ry
boast Save in the death of Christ, my
feet Sor - row and love flow min - gled
mine, That were a trib - ute far too

died, My rich - est gain I count but
God; All the vain things that charm me
down. Did e'er such love and sor - row
small; Love so a - maz - ing, so di -

loss And pour con - tempt on all my pride.
most, I sac - ri - fice them to his blood.
meet Or thorns com - pose so rich a crown?
vine, De - mands my soul, my life, my all!

Text: Isaac Watts, 1674–1748
Tune: Lowell Mason, 1792–1872

HAMBURG
L M

Stricken, Smitten, and Afflicted 116

1 Strick-en, smit-ten, and af-flict-ed, See him dy-ing on the tree!
2 Tell me, all who hear him groan-ing, Was there ev-er grief like this?
3 You who think of sin but light-ly Nor sup-pose the e-vil great
4 Here we have a firm foun-da-tion; Here the ref-uge of the lost;

This is Christ, by man re-ject-ed; Here, my soul, your Sav-ior see.
Friends through fear his cause dis-own-ing, Foes in-sult-ing his dis-tress;
Here may view its na-ture right-ly, Here its guilt may es-ti-mate.
Christ, the rock of our sal-va-tion, His the name of which we boast.

He's the long-ex-pect-ed proph-et, Da-vid's son, yet Da-vid's Lord.
Man-y hands were raised to wound him, None would in-ter-vene to save;
Mark the sac-ri-fice ap-point-ed; See who bears the aw-ful load;
Lamb of God, for sin-ners wound-ed, Sac-ri-fice to can-cel guilt!

Proofs I see suf-fi-cient of it: He's the true and faith-ful Word.
But the deep-est stroke that pierced him Was the stroke that jus-tice gave.
It's the Word, the Lord's A-noint-ed, Son of Man and Son of God.
None shall ev-er be con-found-ed Who on him their hope have built.

Text: Thomas Kelly, 1769–1854, alt.
Tune: Geistliche Volkslieder, Paderborn, 1850

O MEIN JESU, ICH MUSS STERBEN
87 87 D

117 Sing, My Tongue

1 Sing, my tongue, the glo - rious bat - tle; Sing the end - ing
2 Tell how, when at length the full - ness Of the ap-point - ed
3 Thus, with thir - ty years ac - com-plished, He went forth from
4 Faith - ful cross, true sign of tri - umph, Be for all the

of the fray. Now a - bove the cross, the tro - phy,
time was come, He, the Word, was born of wom - an,
Naz - a - reth, Des - tined, ded - i - cat - ed, will - ing,
no - blest tree; None in fo - liage, none in blos - som,

Sound the loud tri - um - phant lay; Tell how Christ, the
Left for us his Fa - ther's home, Blazed the path of
Did his work, and met his death; Like a lamb he
None in fruit your e - qual be; Sym - bol of the

world's re - deem - er, As a vic - tim won the day.
true o - be - dience, Shone as light a - midst the gloom.
hum - bly yield - ed On the cross his dy - ing breath.
world's re - demp - tion, For your bur - den makes us free.

5 Unto God be praise and glory;
　To the Father and the Son,
　To the eternal Spirit honor

Now and evermore be done;
Praise and glory in the highest
While the timeless ages run.

Text: Venantius Honorius Fortunatus, 530–609; tr. John M. Neale, 1818–66, alt.
© *Tune: Carl F. Schalk, b. 1929*

FORTUNATUS NEW
87 87 87

We Sing the Praise of Him Who Died　118

1 We　sing　the　praise　of　him who　died,　Of　him who
2 In - scribed up - on　the　cross we　see　In　shin - ing
3 The　cross! It takes　our　guilt a - way;　It　holds　the
4 It　makes the cow - ard　spir - it brave　And　nerves　the

died　up - on　the cross.　The　sin - ner's hope　let　all　de -
let - ters, "God　is　love."　He　bears our sins　up - on　the
faint - ing　spir - it　up;　It　cheers with hope　the　gloom - y
fee - ble　arm for fight;　It　takes the ter - ror　from the

ride;　For　this　we　count　the　world　but　loss.
tree;　He　brings　us　mer - cy　from　a - bove.
day　And　sweet - ens　ev - 'ry　bit - ter　cup.
grave　And　gilds　the　bed　of　death　with　light;

5 The balm of life, the cure of woe,
　The measure and the pledge of love,

The sinner's refuge here below,
The angels' theme in heav'n above.

Text: Thomas Kelly, 1769–1854
Tune: attr. Daniel Read, 1757–1836

WINDHAM
L M

O Dearest Jesus,
What Law Have You Broken

1 O dear - est Je - sus, what law have you bro - ken
2 They crown your head with thorns, they smite, they scourge you;
3 What is the source of all your mor - tal an - guish?
4 How strange is this great par - a - dox to pon - der:

That such sharp sen - tence should on you be spo - ken?
With cru - el mock - ings to the cross they urge you;
It is my sins for which you, Lord, must lan - guish;
The shep - herd dies for sheep who love to wan - der;

Of what great crime have you to make con -
They give you gall to drink, they still de -
Yes, all the wrath, the woe that you in -
The mas - ter pays the debt his ser - vants

fes - sion, What dark trans - gres - sion?
cry you; They cru - ci - fy you.
her - it, This I do mer - it.
owe him, Who would not know him.

5 The sinless Son of God must die in sadness;
  The sinful child of man may live in gladness;
  We forfeited our lives yet are acquitted;
  God is committed!

6 O wond'rous love, whose depth no heart has sounded,
  That brought you here, by foes and thieves surrounded,
  Conquer my heart, make love its sole endeavor
  Henceforth forever!

7 When, dearest Jesus, at your throne in heaven
  To me the crown of joy at last is given,
  Where sweetest hymns your saints forever raise you,
  I too shall praise you!

Text: Johann Heermann, 1585–1647; tr. Catherine Winkworth, 1829–78, alt.
Tune: Johann Crüger, 1598–1662

HERZLIEBSTER JESU
11 11 11 5

120

Upon the Cross Extended

1 Up - on the cross ex - tend - ed See, world, your Lord sus -
3 Who is it, Lord, that bruised you? Who has so sore a -
5 Your soul in griefs un - bound - ed, Your head with thorns sur -
7 Your cross I place be - fore me; Its sav - ing pow'r re -

pend - ed. Your Sav - ior yields his breath.
bused you And caused you all your woe?
round - ed, You died to ran - som me.
store me, Sus - tain me in the test.

The Prince of Life from heav - en Him - self has free - ly
We all must make con - fes - sion Of sin and dire trans -
The cross for me en - dur - ing, The crown for me se -
It will, when life is end - ing, Be guid - ing and at -

giv - en To shame and blows and bit - ter death.
gres - sion While you no ways of e - vil know.
cur - ing, You healed my wounds and set me free.
tend - ing My way to your e - ter - nal rest.

This hymn is designed to be sung in alternation, stanza by stanza, with choir singing No. 120 and congregation singing No. 121. It may also be sung to No. 121 by singing stanzas 1, 2, 3, etc., in their normal order.

Text: Paul Gerhardt, 1607-76; tr. John Kelly, 1833-90, alt.
Tune: Heinrich Friese, 18th cent.

O WELT, SIEH HIER
776 778

Upon the Cross Extended

121

1 Up - on the cross ex - tend - ed See, world, your Lord sus-
2 Come, see these things and pon - der, Your soul will fill with
4 I caused your grief and sigh - ing By e - vils mul - ti -
6 Your cords of love, my Sav - ior, Bind me to you for -

pend - ed. Your Sav - ior yields his breath. The Prince of
won - der As blood streams from each pore. Through grief be -
ply - ing As count - less as the sands. I caused the
ev - er, I am no long - er mine. To you I

Life from heav - en Him - self has free - ly
yond all know - ing From his great heart came
woes un - num - bered With which your soul is
glad - ly ten - der All that my life can

giv - en To shame and blows and bit - ter death.
flow - ing Sighs well - ing from its deep - est core.
cum - bered, Your sor - rows raised by wick - ed hands.
ren - der And all I have to you re - sign.

This hymn is designed to be sung in alternation, stanza by stanza, with choir singing No. 120 and congregation singing No. 121. It may also be sung to No. 120 by singing stanzas 1, 2, 3, etc., in their normal order.

Text: Paul Gerhardt, 1607–76; tr. John Kelly, 1833–90, alt.
Tune: Heinrich Isaac, c. 1450–1517

O WELT, ICH MUSS DICH LASSEN
7 7 6 7 7 8

122 O Darkest Woe

1 O dark-est woe! Tears, o-ver-flow! What
2 Deep, deep the pain! God's Son is slain, The
3 Our load of sin, Our guilt with-in Brought
4 The Bride-groom dead! The Lamb stained red, His

heav-y grief we car-ry! God the Fa-ther's
Lord, who came from heav-en, Who for us up-
low him who is ly-ing In a stone-cold
life-blood free-ly flow-ing, Wine poured out to

on-ly Son In a grave lies bur-ied.
on the cross His dear life has giv-en.
gar-den tomb, Si-lent mid our sigh-ing.
cleanse our wound, Health on us be-stow-ing.

5 O Ground of faith,
   Brought low in death!
      Fair lips, your silence keeping.
   Must not all throughout the world
      Join in bitter weeping?

6 But how blest he
   Eternally
      Who here will rightly ponder
   Why the Prince of Life has died,
      Why God made this wonder!

7 O Jesus blest,
   My help and rest,
      My tears flow to entreat you:
   Make me love you to the last
      Till in heav'n I greet you.

©Text: Friedrich von Spee, 1591-1635, st. 1; Johann Rist, 1607-67, st. 2-7; tr. F. Samuel Janzow, b. 1913, sts. 1-6;
Catherine Winkworth, 1829-78, st. 7, alt.
Tune: Mainz, 1628

O TRAURIGKEIT
44 776

Christ Jesus Lay in Death's Strong Bands 123

1 Christ Jesus lay in death's strong bands For our offenses given; But now at God's right hand he stands And brings us life from heaven. Therefore let us joyful be And sing to God right thankfully Loud songs of alleluia! Alleluia!

2 It was a strange and dreadful strife When life and death contended; The victory remained with life, The reign of death was ended. Holy Scripture plainly says That death is swallowed up by death, Its sting is lost forever. Alleluia!

3 Here the true Paschal Lamb we see, Whom God so freely gave us; He died on the accursed tree— So strong his love—to save us. See, his blood now marks our door; Faith points to it; death passes o'er, And Satan cannot harm us. Alleluia!

4 So let us keep the festival To which the Lord invites us; Christ is himself the joy of all, The sun that warms and lights us. Now his grace to us imparts Eternal sunshine to our hearts; The night of sin is ended. Alleluia!

5 Then let us feast this Easter Day
 On Christ, the bread of heaven;
 The Word of grace has purged away
 The old and evil leaven.

Christ alone our souls will feed;
He is our meat and drink indeed;
Faith lives upon no other!
Alleluia!

Text: Martin Luther, 1483–1546; tr. Richard Massie, 1800–87, alt.
Tune: Johann Walter, Geystliche gesangk Buchleyn, 1524

CHRIST LAG IN TODESBANDEN
87 87 78 74

124

Christ Is Arisen

Christ is a - ris - en From the grave's dark

pris - on. So let our song ex - ult - ing rise:

Christ with com - fort lights our eyes. Al - le - lu - ia!

All our hopes were end - ed Had Je - sus not as - cend - ed

From the grave tri-um-phant-ly Our nev-er-end-ing life to be.

Al-le-lu-ia! Al-le-lu-ia, al-le-lu-ia,

al-le-lu-ia! So let our song ex-ult-ing rise:

Christ, our com-fort, fills the skies. Al-le-lu-ia!

© Text: German hymn, c. 1100; tr. F. Samuel Janzow, b. 1913
Tune: J. Klug, Geistliche Lieder, 1533

CHRIST IST ERSTANDEN
P M

125
Hail Thee, Festival Day

Refrain

Hail thee, fes - ti - val day! Blest day to be hal-lowed for - ev - er;

1st time | *2nd time*

Day when our Lord was raised, break-ing the king-dom of death. death.

1 All the fair beau - ty of earth from the death of the
3 God the Al-might - y, the Lord, the rul - er of
5 Spir - it of life and of pow'r, now flow in us,

win - ter a - ris - ing! Ev - 'ry good gift of the
earth and the heav - ens, Guard us from harm with -
fount of our be - ing, Light that en - light - ens us

Repeat refrain once after each stanza

year now with its mas - ter re - turns:
out; cleanse us from e - vil with - in:
all, life that in all may a - bide:

2 Rise from the grave now, O Lord, the au - thor of
4 Je - sus, the health of the world, en - light - en our
6 Praise to the giv - er of good! O Lov - er and

life and cre - a - tion. Tread-ing the path-way of
minds, great re - deem - er, Son of the Fa - ther su -
Au - thor of con - cord, Pour out your balm on our

Repeat refrain once after each stanza

death, new life you give to us all:
preme, on - ly - be - got - ten of God:
days; or - der our ways in your peace:

© *Text: Venantius Honorius Fortunatus, 530–609; tr.* Lutheran Book of Worship, *1978*
© *Tune: Ralph Vaughan Williams, 1872–1958*

SALVE FESTA DIES
irregular

126 At the Lamb's High Feast We Sing

1 At the Lamb's high feast we sing
Praise to our victorious king,
Who has washed us in the tide
Flowing from his pierced side. Alleluia!

2 Praise we him, whose love divine
Gives his sacred blood for wine,
Gives his body for the feast—
Christ the victim, Christ the priest. Alleluia!

3 Where the paschal blood is poured,
Death's dread angel sheathes the sword;
Israel's hosts triumphant go
Through the wave that drowns the foe. Alleluia!

4 Praise we Christ, whose blood was shed,
Paschal victim, paschal bread;
With sincerity and love
Eat we manna from above. Alleluia!

5 Mighty Victim from the sky,
Hell's fierce pow'rs beneath you lie;
You have conquered in the fight,
You have brought us life and light.
    Alleluia!

6 Now no more can death appall,
Now no more the grave enthrall;
You have opened paradise,
And your saints in you shall rise.
    Alleluia!

7 Easter triumph, Easter joy!
This alone can sin destroy;
From sin's pow'r, Lord, set us free,
Newborn souls in you to be.
    Alleluia!

8 Father, who the crown shall give,
Savior, by whose death we live,
Spirit, guide through all our days:
Three in One, your name we praise.
    Alleluia!

Text: office hymn, 17th cent.; tr. Robert Campbell, 1814–68, alt.
Tune: Bohemian Brethren, Kirchengeseng, 1566

SONNE DER GERECHTIGKEIT
77 77 4

Jesus Christ Is Risen Today 127

1 Je - sus Christ is ris'n to - day,
2 Hymns of praise then let us sing,
3 But the pains which he en - dured,
4 Sing we to our God a - bove,

Al - le - lu - ia!

Our tri - um - phant ho - ly day,
Un - to Christ, our heav'n - ly king,
Our sal - va - tion have pro - cured;
Praise e - ter - nal as his love;

Al - le - lu - ia!

Who did once up - on the cross,
Who en - dured the cross and grave,
Now a - bove the sky he's king,
Praise him, all you heav'n - ly host,

Al - le - lu - ia!

Suf - fer to re - deem our loss.
Sin - ners to re - deem and save.
Where the an - gels ev - er sing.
Fa - ther, Son, and Ho - ly Ghost.

Al - le - lu - ia!

Text: Latin carol, 14th cent., sts. 1–3; Charles Wesley, 1707–88, st. 4; tr. Lyra Davidica, London, 1708, sts. 1–3
Tune: Lyra Davidica, London, 1708

EASTER HYMN
7 7 7 7 and alleluias

128 Awake, My Heart, with Gladness

1 A - wake, my heart, with glad - ness, See what to - day is done;
2 The foe in tri - umph shout - ed When Christ lay in the tomb;
3 This is a sight that glad - dens— What peace it does im - part!
4 Now hell, its prince, the dev - il, Of all their pow'r are shorn;

Now, af - ter gloom and sad - ness, Comes forth the glo - rious sun.
But lo, he now is rout - ed, His boast is turned to gloom.
Now noth-ing ev - er sad - dens The joy with-in my heart.
Now I am safe from e - vil, And sin I laugh to scorn.

My Sav - ior there was laid Where our bed must be made
For Christ a - gain is free; In glo - rious vic - to - ry
No gloom shall ev - er shake, No foe shall ev - er take
Grim death with all its might Can - not my soul af - fright;

When to the realms of light Our spir - it wings its flight.
He who is strong to save Has tri - umphed o'er the grave.
The hope which God's own Son In love for me has won.
It is a pow'r - less form, How - e'er it rave and storm.

5 Now I will cling forever
  To Christ, my Savior true;
My Lord will leave me never,
  Whate'er he passes through.
He rends death's iron chain;
He breaks through sin and pain;
He shatters hell's grim thrall;
I follow him through all.

6 He brings me to the portal
  That leads to bliss untold,
Whereon this rhyme immortal
  Is found in script of gold:
"Who there my cross has shared
Finds here a crown prepared;
Who there with me has died
Shall here be glorified."

Text: Paul Gerhardt, 1606–76; tr. John Kelly, 1833–90, alt.
Tune: Johann Crüger, 1598–1662

AUF, AUF, MEIN HERZ
76 76 66 66

Good Christian Friends, Rejoice and Sing   129

1 Good Chris - tian friends, re - joice and sing! Now is the
2 The Lord of life is ris'n this day; Bring flow'rs of
3 Praise we in songs of vic - to - ry That love, that
4 Your name we bless, O ris - en Lord, And sing to -

tri - umph of our King! To all the world glad news we bring:
song to strew his way; Let all the world re - joice and say:
life which can - not die, And sing with hearts up - lift - ed high:
day with one ac - cord The life laid down, the life re - stored:

Al - le - lu - ia, al - le - lu - ia, al - le - lu - ia!

© *Text: Cyril A. Alington, 1872–1955, alt.*
Tune: Melchior Vulpius, c. 1570–1615

GELOBT SEI GOTT
8 8 8 and alleluias

130 O Sons and Daughters of the King

Al - le - lu - ia, al - le - lu - ia, al - le - lu - ia!

1 O sons and daugh - ters of the King,
2 That Eas - ter morn, at break of day,
3 An an - gel clad in white they see,
4 That night the a - pos - tles met in fear;

Whom heav'n - ly hosts in glo - ry sing, To - day the
The faith - ful wom - en went their way To seek the
Who sits and speaks un - to the three, "Your Lord will
A - mong them came their mas - ter dear And said, "My

grave has lost its sting! Al - le - lu - ia!
tomb where Je - sus lay. Al - le - lu - ia!
go to Gal - i - lee." Al - le - lu - ia!
peace be with you here." Al - le - lu - ia!

Al - le - lu - ia, al - le - lu - ia, al - le - lu - ia!

5 When Thomas first the tidings heard
   That they had seen the risen Lord,
   He doubted the disciples' word.
      Alleluia!

6 "My pierced side, O Thomas, see,
   And look upon my hands, my feet;
   Not faithless but believing be."
      Alleluia!

7 No longer Thomas then denied;
   He saw the feet, the hands, the side;
   "You are my Lord and God!" he cried.
      Alleluia!

8 How blest are they who have not seen
   And yet whose faith has constant been,
   For they eternal life shall win.
      Alleluia!

9 On this most holy day of days
   Be laud and jubilee and praise:
   To God your hearts and voices raise.
      Alleluia!

Suggested method of singing: All sing st. 1-3 and 8-9; women and children sing st. 4 and 6; men sing st. 5 and 7; all sing alleluias.

Text: attr. Jean Tisserand, d. 1494; tr. John M. Neale, 1818–66, alt.
Tune: French, 15th cent.

O FILII ET FILIAE
8 8 8 and alleluias

131 Now All the Vault of Heaven Resounds

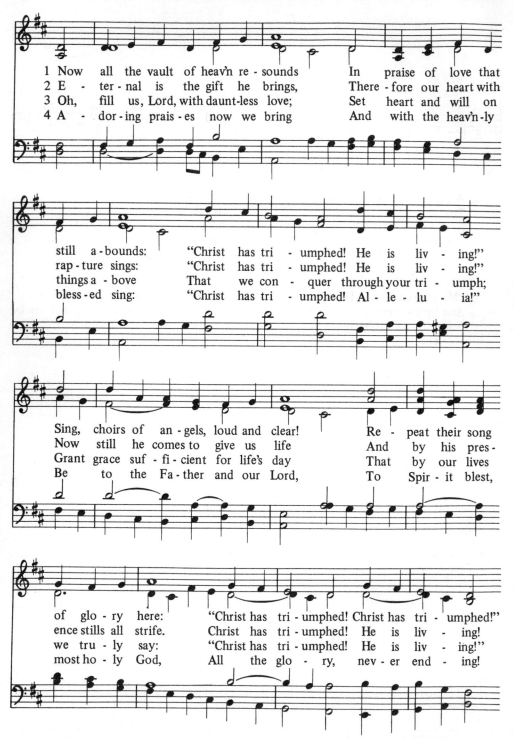

1 Now all the vault of heav'n re-sounds In praise of love that
2 E-ter-nal is the gift he brings, There-fore our heart with
3 Oh, fill us, Lord, with daunt-less love; Set heart and will on
4 A-dor-ing prais-es now we bring And with the heav'n-ly

still a-bounds: "Christ has tri-umphed! He is liv-ing!"
rap-ture sings: "Christ has tri-umphed! He is liv-ing!"
things a-bove That we con-quer through your tri-umph;
bless-ed sing: "Christ has tri-umphed! Al-le-lu-ia!"

Sing, choirs of an-gels, loud and clear! Re-peat their song
Now still he comes to give us life And by his pres-
Grant grace suf-fi-cient for life's day That by our lives
Be to the Fa-ther and our Lord, To Spir-it blest,

of glo-ry here: "Christ has tri-umphed! Christ has tri-umphed!"
ence stills all strife. Christ has tri-umphed! He is liv-ing!
we tru-ly say: "Christ has tri-umphed! He is liv-ing!"
most ho-ly God, All the glo-ry, nev-er end-ing!

Al - le - lu - ia, al - le - lu - ia, al - le - lu - ia!

© *Text:* Paul Z. Strodach, 1876–1947, alt.
  Tune: Geistliche Kirchengesäng, *Köln, 1623*

LASST UNS ERFREUEN
8 8 8 8 8 8 and alleluias

Make Songs of Joy

132

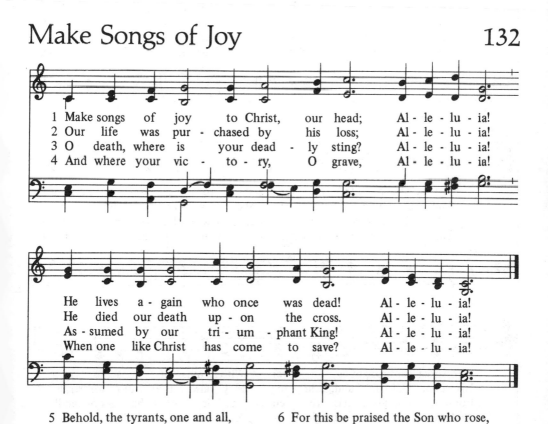

1 Make songs of joy to Christ, our head; Al - le - lu - ia!
2 Our life was pur - chased by his loss; Al - le - lu - ia!
3 O death, where is your dead - ly sting? Al - le - lu - ia!
4 And where your vic - to - ry, O grave, Al - le - lu - ia!

He lives a - gain who once was dead! Al - le - lu - ia!
He died our death up - on the cross. Al - le - lu - ia!
As - sumed by our tri - um - phant King! Al - le - lu - ia!
When one like Christ has come to save? Al - le - lu - ia!

5 Behold, the tyrants, one and all,
  Alleluia!
Before our mighty Savior fall!
  Alleluia!

6 For this be praised the Son who rose,
  Alleluia!
The Father, and the Holy Ghost!
  Alleluia!

© *Text:* Jiři Tranovský, 1591–1637; tr. Jaroslav J. Vajda, b. 1919
  Tune: Chorvát, Velka Partitura, 1936

ZPIVEJMEŽ VŠICKNI VESELE
84 84

133 The Day of Resurrection

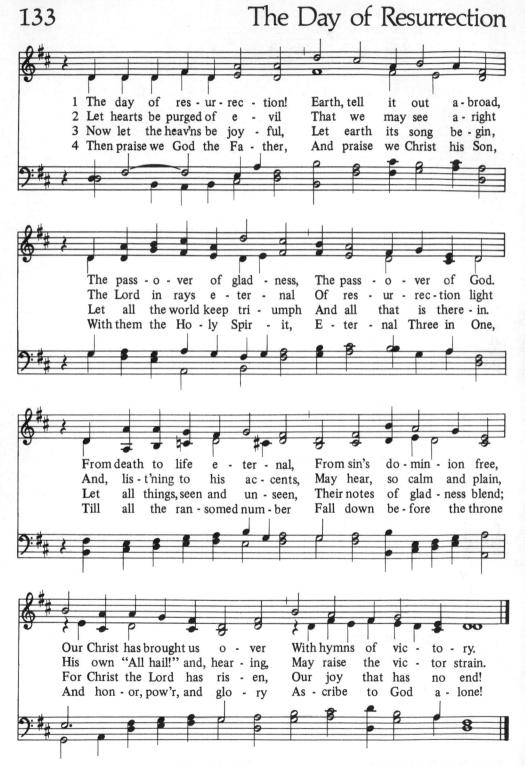

1 The day of res-ur-rec-tion! Earth, tell it out a-broad,
2 Let hearts be purged of e-vil That we may see a-right
3 Now let the heav'ns be joy-ful, Let earth its song be-gin,
4 Then praise we God the Fa-ther, And praise we Christ his Son,

The pass-o-ver of glad-ness, The pass-o-ver of God.
The Lord in rays e-ter-nal Of res-ur-rec-tion light
Let all the world keep tri-umph And all that is there-in.
With them the Ho-ly Spir-it, E-ter-nal Three in One,

From death to life e-ter-nal, From sin's do-min-ion free,
And, lis-t'ning to his ac-cents, May hear, so calm and plain,
Let all things, seen and un-seen, Their notes of glad-ness blend;
Till all the ran-somed num-ber Fall down be-fore the throne

Our Christ has brought us o-ver With hymns of vic-to-ry.
His own "All hail!" and, hear-ing, May raise the vic-tor strain.
For Christ the Lord has ris-en, Our joy that has no end!
And hon-or, pow'r, and glo-ry As-cribe to God a-lone!

Text: John of Damascus, c. 696–c. 754; tr. John M. Neale, 1818–66, alt.
Tune: Johann Walter, Ein schöner Geistlicher Berckreyen, 1552

HERZLICH TUT MICH ERFREUEN
76 76 D

With High Delight Let Us Unite

134

1 With high de-light Let us u-nite In songs of sweet ju-bi-
2 True God, he first From death has burst Forth in-to life, all sub-
3 Let prais-es ring; Give thanks, and bring To Christ our Lord ad-o-

la-tion. You pure in heart, Each take your part, Sing Je-sus Christ,
du-ing. His en-e-my Shall van-quished lie; His death has been
ra-tion. His hon-or speed By word and deed To ev-'ry land,

our sal-va-tion. To set us free For-ev-er, he Is ris'n and
death's un-do-ing. "And yours shall be Like vic-to-ry O'er death and
ev-'ry na-tion. So shall his love Give us a-bove, From mis-er-

sends To all earth's ends Good news to save ev-'ry na-tion.
grave," Said he, who gave His life for us, life re-new-ing.
y And death set free, All joy and full con-so-la-tion.

© Text: Georg Vetter, 1536–99; tr. Martin H. Franzmann, 1907–76
Tune: Trente quatre pseaumes de David, Geneva, 1551

MIT FREUDEN ZART
448 448 44 448 8

135 Welcome, Happy Morning

1 "Wel-come, hap-py morn-ing!" Age to age shall say;
2 Ma - ker and re - deem - er, Life and health of all,
3 Source of all things liv - ing, You came down to die,
4 Free the souls long pris - oned, Bound with Sa - tan's chain;

"Hell to - day is van - quished, Heav'n is won to - day!"
God from heav'n be - hold - ing Hu - man na - ture's fall,
Plumbed the depths of hell to Raise us up on high.
All that once had fall - en Raise to life a - gain;

Christ, once dead, is liv - ing, God for - ev - er - more!
You, the true and on - ly Son of God a - bove,
Come then, true and faith - ful; Come, ful - fill your word;
Show your face in bright - ness, Shine in ev - 'ry land

Him, their true cre - a - tor, All his works a - dore.
Died as mor - tal man to Save us by your love.
This is your third morn - ing: Rise, O bur - ied Lord!
As in E - den's gar - den When the world be - gan.

Refrain

"Wel-come, hap-py morn - ing!" Age to age shall say,

"Hell to - day is van - quished, Heav'n is won to - day!"

Text: Venantius Honorius Fortunatus, 530-609; tr. John Ellerton, 1826-93, adapt.
© *Tune: Old English march, adapt. and arr. Gustav Holst, 1874-1934*

PRINCE RUPERT
65 65 D and refrain

136 Today in Triumph Christ Arose

1 To - day in tri - umph Christ a - rose And con - quered
2 Now hell has lost its pow'r and might; Our Lord puts
3 Though Sa - tan rage, his pow'r is gone; His thun - d'ring
4 O Christ, our Sav - ior, Help - er, Friend, Be with us

all his hell - ish foes.
all its hosts to flight. Al - le - lu - ia, al - le - lu - ia!
roar can harm us none.
till our jour - ney's end.

Great splen - dor marks his vic - to - ry. Sing praise to
He brings the end of all our woe; He routs our
Our strong De - fend - er hurls him down But wins for
In mer - cy guide us by your grace Till we be -

God e - ter - nal - ly!
foes and lays them low. Al - le - lu - ia, al - le - lu - ia!
us a heav'n - ly crown.
hold your glo - rious face.

5 To God the Lord, on highest throne,   To God the Holy Spirit be
To Christ, the Father's own dear Son,   All praise and thanks eternally.
Alleluia, alleluia!   Alleluia, alleluia!

© Text: Kaspar Stolshagen, 1550–94; tr. Oliver C. Rupprecht, b. 1903
Tune: Deutsche geistliche Lieder, Frankfurt a. O., 1601

HEUT TRIUMPHIERET GOTTES SOHN
8 8 8 8 8 8

Christ the Lord Is Risen Today; Alleluia   137

1 Christ the Lord is ris'n to-day;
2 For the sheep the Lamb has bled,
3 Hail, the vic-tim un-de-filed,
4 Chris-tians, on this ho-ly day,

Al - le - lu - ia!

Chris-tians, has-ten on your way;
Sin - less in the sin - ner's stead.
God and sin-ners rec - on - ciled,
All your grate - ful hom - age pay;

Al - le - lu - ia!

Of - fer praise with love re - plete,
Christ the Lord is ris'n on high;
When con-tend - ing death and life,
Christ the Lord is ris'n on high;

Al - le - lu - ia!

At the pas - chal vic - tim's feet.
Now he lives, no more to die.
Met in strange and awe - some strife.
Now he lives, no more to die.

Al - le - lu - ia!

Text: Latin sequence, c. 1100; tr. Jane E. Leeson, 1809–81, alt.
Tune: Robert Williams, c. 1781-1821

LLANFAIR
77 77 and alleluias

138

He's Risen, He's Risen

1 He's ris - en, he's ris - en, Christ Je - sus, the Lord;
2 The foe was tri - um - phant when on Cal - va - ry
3 But short was their tri - umph, the Sav - ior a - rose,
4 Oh, where is your sting, death? We fear you no more;

Death's pris - on he o - pened, in - car - nate, true Word.
The Lord of cre - a - tion was nailed to the tree.
And death, hell, and Sa - tan he van - quished, his foes;
Christ rose, and now o - pen is fair E - den's door.

Break forth, hosts of heav - en, in ju - bi - lant song
In Sa - tan's do - main his hosts shout - ed and jeered,
The con - quer - ing Lord lifts his ban - ner on high.
For all our trans - gres - sions his blood does a - tone;

While earth, sea, and moun - tain the prais - es pro - long.
For Je - sus was slain, whom the e - vil ones feared.
He lives, yes, he lives, and will nev - er - more die.
Re - deemed and for - giv - en, we now are his own.

5 Then sing your hosannas and raise your glad voice;
  Proclaim the blest tidings that all may rejoice.
  Laud, honor, and praise to the Lamb that was slain;
  In glory he reigns, yes, and ever shall reign.

Text: C. Ferdinand Walther, 1811–87; tr. Anna M. Meyer, 1867–1941, alt.
Tune: C. Ferdinand Walther, 1811–87

WALTHER
11 11 11 11

Jesus Lives! The Victory's Won — 139

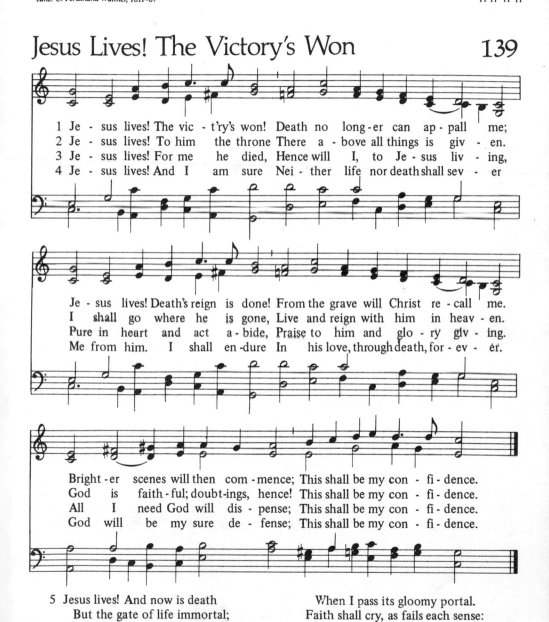

1 Je - sus lives! The vic - t'ry's won! Death no long - er can ap - pall me;
2 Je - sus lives! To him the throne There a - bove all things is giv - en.
3 Je - sus lives! For me he died, Hence will I, to Je - sus liv - ing,
4 Je - sus lives! And I am sure Nei - ther life nor death shall sev - er

Je - sus lives! Death's reign is done! From the grave will Christ re - call me.
I shall go where he is gone, Live and reign with him in heav - en.
Pure in heart and act a - bide, Praise to him and glo - ry giv - ing.
Me from him. I shall en - dure In his love, through death, for - ev - er.

Bright - er scenes will then com - mence; This shall be my con - fi - dence.
God is faith - ful; doubt - ings, hence! This shall be my con - fi - dence.
All I need God will dis - pense; This shall be my con - fi - dence.
God will be my sure de - fense; This shall be my con - fi - dence.

5 Jesus lives! And now is death   When I pass its gloomy portal.
  But the gate of life immortal;   Faith shall cry, as fails each sense:
  This shall calm my trembling breath Jesus is my confidence!

Text: Christian F. Gellert, 1715-69; tr. Frances E. Cox, 1812-97, alt.
Tune: Johann Crüger, 1598-1662

JESUS, MEINE ZUVERSICHT
78 78 77

140

This Joyful Eastertide

1 This joy - ful Eas - ter - tide   A - way   with sin and
2 Death's flood has lost its chill   Since Je - sus crossed the
3 My flesh in hope shall rest   And for a sea - son

sor - row! My love, the Cru - ci - fied,
riv - er; Lov - er of souls, from ill
slum - ber Till trump from east to west

Has sprung to life this mor - row:
My pass - ing soul de - liv - er:
Shall wake the dead in num - ber:

Refrain

Had Christ, who once was slain, Not burst his three - day pris - on,

Our faith had been in vain: But now has Christ a - ris - en, a -

ris - en, a - ris - en; But now has Christ a - ris - en!

© Text: George R. Woodward, 1848–1934
Tune: Dutch, 17th cent.

VRUECHTEN
67 67 and refrain

141 Come, You Faithful, Raise the Strain

1 Come, you faith-ful, raise the strain   Of tri - um-phant glad - ness!
2 This   the spring of souls to - day: Christ has   burst his pris - on
3 Now   the queen of   sea - sons, bright   With the   day of splen - dor,
4 For   to - day a - mong his own   Christ ap - peared, be - stow - ing

God   has brought his   Is - ra - el   In - to   joy from sad - ness,
And   from three days' sleep in death   As   a   sun has ris - en;
With   the   roy - al   feast of feasts   Comes its   joy to ren - der;
His   deep peace, which ev - er - more   Pass - es   hu - man know - ing.

Loosed from Phar - aoh's bit - ter yoke   Ja - cob's sons   and daugh - ters,
All   the   win - ter   of our sins,   Long   and dark,   is fly - ing
Comes to   glad - den faith - ful hearts   Which with true   af - fec - tion
Nei - ther could the gates of death   Nor   the tomb's dark por - tal

Led   them with   un - moist - ened foot   Through the   Red Sea wa - ters.
From   his light, to whom is giv'n   Laud   and   praise un - dy - ing.
Wel - come in   un - wea - ried strain   Je - sus'   res - ur - rec - tion!
Nor   the watch - ers nor   the seal   Hold   him   as   a mor - tal.

5 Alleluia! Now we cry
    To our King immortal,
    Who, triumphant, burst the bars
    Of the tomb's dark portal.

Come, you faithful, raise the strain
    Of triumphant gladness!
    God has brought his Israel
    Into joy from sadness!

Text: John of Damascus, c. 696–c. 754; tr. John M. Neale, 1818–66, alt.
Tune: Johann Horn, c. 1490–1547

GAUDEAMUS PARITER
76·76 D

Christ the Lord Is Risen Today 142

1 "Christ the Lord is ris'n to-day!" All on earth with an-gels say;
2 Love's re-deem-ing work is done, Fought the fight, the bat-tle won;
3 Vain the stone, the watch, the seal; Christ has burst the gates of hell.
4 Lives a-gain our glo-rious king! Where, O death, is now thy sting?

Raise your joys and tri-umphs high; Sing, ye heav'ns;and earth, re-ply.
Lo! Our sun's e-clipse is o'er. Lo! He sets in blood no more.
Death in vain for-bids his rise; Christ has o-pened par-a-dise.
Once he died our souls to save; Where thy vic-to-ry, O grave?

5 Hail the Lord of earth and heav'n!
    Praise to thee by both be giv'n.
    Thee we greet triumphant now;
    Hail, the resurrection, thou!

6 King of glory, soul of bliss,
    Everlasting life is this:
    Thee to know, thy pow'r to prove,
    Thus to sing, and thus to love!

Text: Charles Wesley, 1707–88, alt.
Tune: French, 13th cent.

ORIENTIS PARTIBUS
77 77

143   The Strife Is O'er, the Battle Done

Alleluia, alleluia, alleluia!

1 The strife is o'er, the battle done; Now is the victor's
2 The pow'rs of death have done their worst, But Christ their legions
3 The three sad days have quickly sped, He rises glorious
4 He broke the age-bound chains of hell; The bars from heav'n's high

triumph won; Now be the song of praise begun. Alleluia!
has dispersed. Let shouts of holy joy outburst. Alleluia!
from the dead. All glory to our risen head! Alleluia!
portals fell. Let hymns of praise his triumph tell. Alleluia!

Alleluia, alleluia, alleluia!

5 Lord, by the stripes which wounded you
From death's sting free your servants too
That we may live and sing to you.
Alleluia!

Text: Symphonia Sirenum, *Köln, 1695; tr. Francis Pott, 1832–1909, alt.*
Tune: Giovanni P. da Palestrina, 1525–94, adapt.

VICTORY
8 8 8 and alleluias

Triumphant from the Grave

1 Tri - um-phant from the grave   Rose   Je - sus strong to   save.
2 Bur - ied like sin - ful man   Who ends his mor - tal span,
3 Fierce though God's wrath had been, Af - flict - ing him for men,
4 Nailed fast   to yon - der tree   See   your in - iq - ui - ty!

He crushed—O Chris-tian, mark it well!— Sin, Sa - tan, death,   and hell.
Our Lord could not for long lie there, De - cay of men   to share.
The   fi - 'ry judg-ment burned no more; Its fu - ry had   passed o'er.
His   cross has ban-ished all your sin,   Your par-don has   brought in.

Refrain

Now sing your glad song And   joy - ous praise   to him pro-long!

5 Sure bond and guarantee
   God gave to you and me:
   The Father has raised up his Son
   To seal redemption won. *Refrain*

6 Now Satan is undone!
   Now death's dread pow'r is gone!
   From fear of hell you are set free
   Through Jesus' victory! *Refrain*

© *Text: Werner H. Franzmann, b. 1905*
© *Tune: Bruce Backer, b. 1929*

TRIUMPH
S M and refrain

145 I Am Content! My Jesus Ever Lives

1 I am con-tent! My Je-sus ev-er lives, In
2 I am con-tent! My Je-sus is my head; His
3 I am con-tent! My Je-sus is my light, My
4 I am con-tent! At length I shall be free, A-

whom my heart is pleased. He has ful-filled the
mem-ber I shall be. He bowed his head when
ra-diant sun of grace. His cheer-ing rays beam
wak-ened from the dead, A-ris-ing glo-rious

law of God for me, God's wrath he has ap-
on the cross he died With cries of ag-o-
bless-ings forth for all, Sweet com-fort, hope, and
ev-er-more to be With you, my liv-ing

peased. Since he in death could per-ish
ny. Now death is brought in-to sub-
peace. This Eas-ter sun has brought sal-
head. My Lord, earth's bind-ing fet-ters

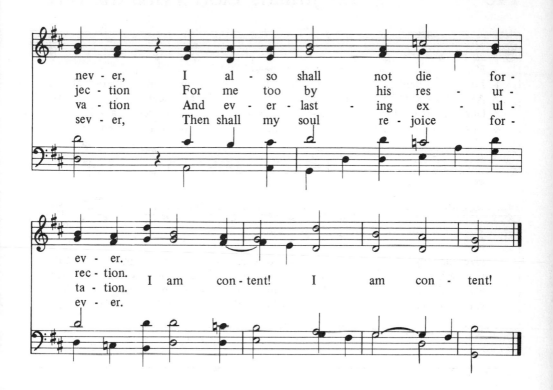

never, I also shall not die for-
jection For me too by his res - ur-
vation And ever-last - ing ex - ul-
sever, Then shall my soul re-joice for-

ever.
rec - tion.
ta - tion. I am con-tent! I am con-tent!
ever.

Text: attr. Johann J. Möller, 1660–1733; tr. August Crull, 1845–1923, alt.
Tune: Drittes Zehn neuer geistlicher Arien, Mühlhausen, 1672

ES IST GENUG
10 6 10 6 99 44

146 Lo, Judah's Lion Wins the Strife

1 Lo, Judah's Li - on wins the strife And con - quers death to
2 As Da - vid, so our Da - vid too The jeer - ing huge Go -
3 Our strong-est, fierc - est foe he foils And waves a - loft the
4 Our Sam - son storms death's cit - a - del And car - ries off the

give us life. Al - le - lu - ia! Come, join in joy - ful
li - ath slew. Al - le - lu - ia! Oh, sing with fes - tive
vic - tor's spoils. Al - le - lu - ia! Now let us sing his
gates of hell. Al - le - lu - ia! Oh, praise him for his

Stanzas 1-7

prais - es!
voic - es!
prais - es!
con - quest!

Stanza 8

A - men.

5 The pow'r of death he broke in two
   When he arose to life anew.
      Alleluia!
   To him all praise be given!

6 He frees the prisoned and oppressed
   And pardons all whom sin possessed.
      Alleluia!
   Oh, praise him for his mercy!

7 In festal spirit, song, and word,
   To Jesus, our victorious Lord,
      Alleluia!
   All praise and thanks be rendered.

8 Praise God, all-holy and triune,
   For this all-gracious, glorious boon;
      Alleluia!
   Now gladly sing we Amen.

© Text: Bohemian, c. 1650; tr. John Bajus, 1901–71, alt.
© Tune: Ralph Schultz, b. 1932

BRONXVILLE
88 47

That Easter Day with Joy Was Bright 147

1 That Eas-ter day with joy was bright; The sun shone
2 O Je-sus, king of gen-tle-ness, With con-stant
3 O Christ, you are the Lord of all In this our
4 All praise, O ris-en Lord, we give To you, once

out with fair-er light, When, to their long-ing eyes re-
love our hearts pos-sess; To you our lips will ev-er
Eas-ter fes-ti-val, For you will be our strength and
dead but now a-live! To God the Fa-ther e-qual

stored, The a-pos-tles saw their ris-en Lord!
raise The trib-ute of our grate-ful praise.
shield From ev-'ry weap-on death can wield. Al-le-lu-ia!
praise, And God the Ho-ly Ghost, we raise!

Text: Latin hymn, 4th or 5th cent.; tr. John M. Neale, 1818–66, alt.
Tune: Nikolaus Herman, c. 1480–1561

ERSCHIENEN IST DER HERRLICH TAG
L M and allelulia

148   Hail Thee, Festival Day

Refrain

Hail thee, fes - ti - val day!   Blest day to be hal-lowed for - ev - er;

Day when our ris - en Lord   rose in the heav - ens   to reign.   reign.

1st time   *2nd time*

1 He   who was nailed   to   the cross   is   rul - er and
3 God   the Al - might - y,   the Lord,   the   rul - er of
5 Spir - it   of   life   and   of pow'r,   now   flow   in   us,

Lord   of   all   peo - ple.   All   things   cre - at - ed on
earth   and the heav - ens,   Guard   us   from harm   with -
fount   of   our   be - ing,   Light   that   en - light - ens us

Repeat refrain once after each stanza

earth   sing   to the glo - ry   of   God:
out;   cleanse us from e - vil   with - in:
all,   life   that in all may   a - bide:

2 Dai - ly   the love - li - ness grows, a - dorned with the
4 Je - sus,   the health of   the world, en - light - en our
6 Praise to   the giv - er of good! O Lov - er and

glo - ry of blos - som; Heav - en her gates un - bars,
minds,   great re - deem - er,   Son of the Fa - ther su -
Au - thor of con - cord, Pour out your balm on our

Repeat refrain once after each stanza

fling - ing her . . in - crease of light:
preme, on - ly - be - got - ten of God:
days;   or - der our ways in your peace:

© Text: Venantius Honorius Fortunatus, 530–609; tr. Lutheran Book of Worship, 1978
© Tune: Ralph Vaughan Williams, 1872–1958

SALVE FESTA DIES
irregular

149 A Hymn of Glory Let Us Sing

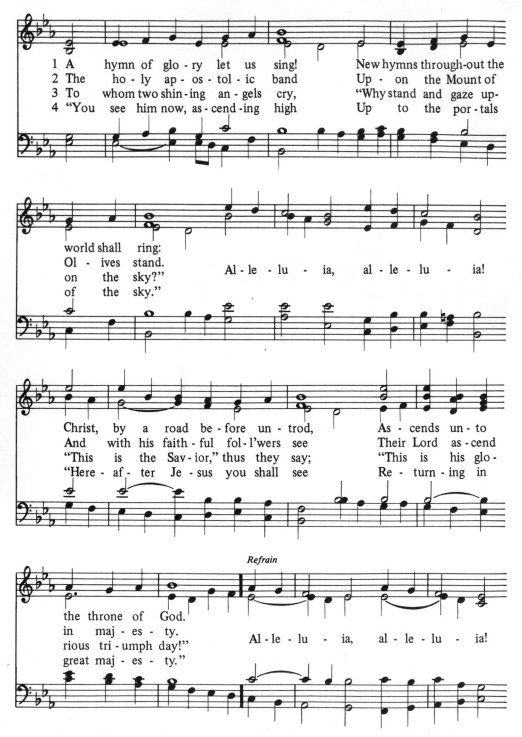

1 A hymn of glo-ry let us sing! New hymns through-out the
2 The ho-ly ap-os-tol-ic band Up-on the Mount of
3 To whom two shin-ing an-gels cry, "Why stand and gaze up-
4 "You see him now, as-cend-ing high Up to the por-tals

world shall ring:
Ol-ives stand.
on the sky?"   Al-le-lu-ia, al-le-lu-ia!
of the sky."

Christ, by a road be-fore un-trod, As-cends un-to
And with his faith-ful fol-l'wers see Their Lord as-cend
"This is the Sav-ior," thus they say; "This is his glo-
"Here-af-ter Je-sus you shall see Re-turn-ing in

Refrain

the throne of God.
in maj-es-ty.
rious tri-umph day!"   Al-le-lu-ia, al-le-lu-ia!
great maj-es-ty."

Al-le - lu - ia,   al - le - lu - ia,   al - le - lu - ia!

5 O Lord, our homeward pathway bend
That our unwearied hearts ascend,
Alleluia, alleluia!
Where, seated on your Father's throne,
You reign as King of kings alone.
Alleluia, alleluia!
Alleluia, alleluia, alleluia!

6 Give us your joy on earth, O Lord,
In heav'n to be our great reward,
Alleluia, alleluia!
Where, throned with you forever, we
Shall praise your name eternally.
Alleluia, alleluia!
Alleluia, alleluia, alleluia!

7 O risen Christ, ascended Lord,
All praise to you let earth accord:
Alleluia, alleluia!
You are, while endless ages run,
With Father and with Spirit one.
Alleluia, alleluia!
Alleluia, alleluia, alleluia!

© Text: The Venerable Bede, 673-735; tr. Lutheran Book of Worship, 1978
Tune: Geistliche Kirchengesäng, Köln, 1623

LASST UNS ERFREUEN
888 888 and alleluias

150 On Christ's Ascension I Now Build

1 On Christ's as - cen - sion I now build The hope of
2 Since Christ re - turned to claim his throne, Great gifts for
3 Oh, grant, dear Lord, this grace to me, Re - call - ing

my as - cen - sion; This hope a - lone has
me ob - tain - ing, My heart will rest in
your as - cen - sion, That I may serve you

al - ways stilled All doubt and ap - pre - hen - sion;
him a - lone, No oth - er rest re - main - ing;
faith - ful - ly, A - dorn - ing your re - demp - tion;

For where the head is, there as well I know his
For where my trea - sure went be - fore, There all my
And then, when all my days will cease, Let me de -

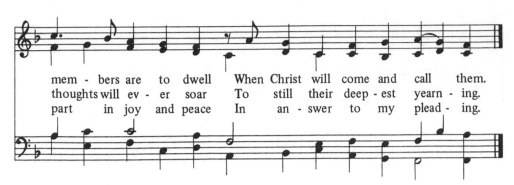

mem - bers are to dwell When Christ will come and call them.
thoughts will ev - er soar To still their deep - est yearn - ing.
part in joy and peace In an - swer to my plead - ing.

Text: Josua Wegelin, 1604–40; tr. William M. Czamanske, 1873–1964, alt.
Tune: Etlich Christlich lider, Wittenberg, 1524

NUN FREUT EUCH
87 87 887

O Christ, Our Hope 151

1 O Christ, our hope, our hearts' de - sire, Cre - a - tion's might-y Lord,
2 How vast your mer - cy to ac - cept The bur - den of our sin
3 But now the bonds of death are burst, The ran - som has been paid;
4 Oh, let your might-y love pre - vail To purge us of our pride

Re - deem - er of the fall - en world, By ho - ly love out - poured:
And bow your head in cru - el death To make us clean with - in.
You now as - cend the Fa - ther's throne In robes of light ar - rayed.
That we may stand be - fore your throne By mer - cy pu - ri - fied.

5 Christ Jesus, be our present joy,
   Our future great reward;
   Our only glory, may it be
   To glory in the Lord!

6 All praise to you, ascended Lord;
   All glory ever be
   To Father, Son, and Holy Ghost
   Through all eternity!

Text: Latin hymn, c. 8th cent.; tr. John Chandler, 1806-76, adapt.
Tune: Johann B. König, Harmonischer Lieder-Schatz, 1738

ICH SINGE DIR
CM

152 Up Through Endless Ranks of Angels

1 Up through end - less ranks of an - gels, Cries of tri - umph
2 Death-de - stroy - ing, life re - stor - ing, Prov - en e - qual
3 To our lives of wan - ton wan - d'ring Send your prom - ised
4 Al - le - lu - ia, al - le - lu - ia! Oh, to breathe the

in his ears, To his heav'n - ly throne as - cend - ing,
to our need, Now for us be - fore the Fa - ther
Spir - it guide; Through our lives of fear and fail - ure
Spir - it's grace! Al - le - lu - ia, al - le - lu - ia!

Hav - ing van - quished all their fears, Christ looks down up -
As our broth - er in - ter - cede; Flesh that for our
With your pow'r and love a - bide; Wel - come us, as
Oh, to see the Fa - ther's face! Al - le - lu - ia,

on his faith - ful, Leav - ing them in hap - py tears.
world was wound - ed, Liv - ing, for the wound - ed plead!
you were wel - comed, To an end - less Eas - ter - tide.
al - le - lu - ia! Oh, to feel the Son's em - brace!

© Text: Jaroslav J. Vajda, b. 1919
© Tune: Henry V. Gerike, b. 1948

ASCENDED TRIUMPH
87 87 87

Draw Us to You

1 Draw us to you, And we will do What you have taught for - ev - er And hast - en on Where you have gone To be with you, dear Sav - ior.

2 Draw us to you Each day a - new. Let us de - part with glad - ness That we may be For - ev - er free From sor - row, grief, and sad - ness.

3 Draw us to you That we stay true And walk the road to heav - en. Di - rect our way Lest we should stray And from your paths be driv - en.

4 Draw us to you; Our hope re - new; In - to your king - dom take us. Let us all there Your glo - ry share; Your saints and joint heirs make us.

Text: Friedrich Funcke, 1642–99; tr. August Crull, 1845–1923, alt.
Tune: Christoph Peter, Andachts-Zymbeln, Freyberg, 1655

ACH GOTT UND HERR
447 447

154 Come, Holy Ghost, God and Lord

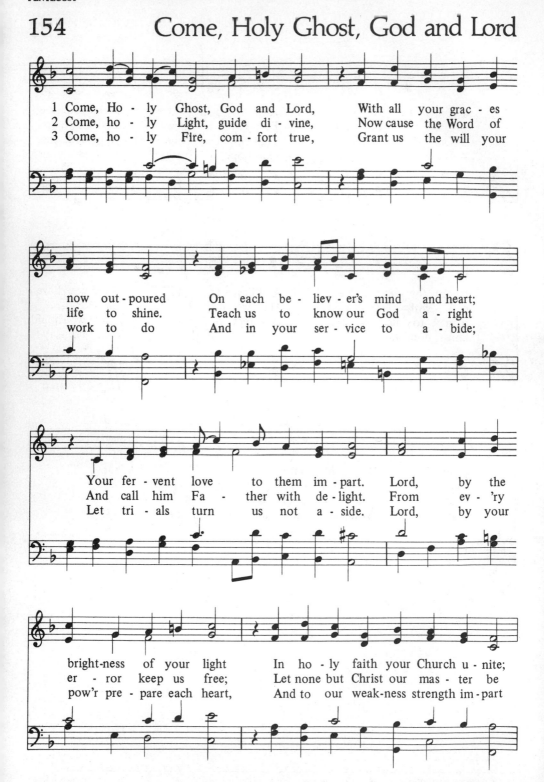

1 Come, Ho - ly Ghost, God and Lord, With all your grac - es
2 Come, ho - ly Light, guide di - vine, Now cause the Word of
3 Come, ho - ly Fire, com - fort true, Grant us the will your

now out - poured On each be - liev - er's mind and heart;
life to shine. Teach us to know our God a - right
work to do And in your ser - vice to a - bide;

Your fer - vent love to them im - part. Lord, by the
And call him Fa - ther with de - light. From ev - 'ry
Let tri - als turn us not a - side. Lord, by your

bright-ness of your light In ho - ly faith your Church u - nite;
er - ror keep us free; Let none but Christ our mas - ter be
pow'r pre - pare each heart, And to our weak-ness strength im - part

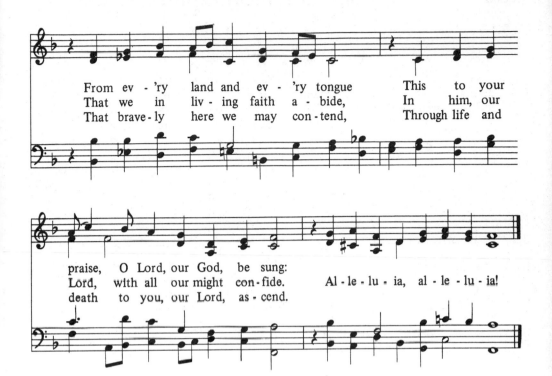

From ev - 'ry land and ev - 'ry tongue
That we in liv - ing faith a - bide,
That brave - ly here we may con - tend,

This to your
In him, our
Through life and

praise, O Lord, our God, be sung:
Lord, with all our might con - fide.
death to you, our Lord, as - cend.

Al - le - lu - ia, al - le - lu - ia!

Text: German hymn, 15th cent., st. 1; Martin Luther, 1483–1546, sts. 2, 3;
 tr. The Lutheran Hymnal, 1941, alt.
Tune: Enchiridion, Erfurt, 1524

KOMM, HEILIGER GEIST, HERRE GOTT
78 88 88 8 10 8

155 To God the Holy Spirit Let Us Pray

1 To God the Holy Spirit let us pray
2 O sweetest Love, your grace on us bestow;
3 Transcendent Comfort in our every need,
4 Shine in our hearts, O Spirit, precious light;

Most of all for faith upon our way
Set our hearts with sacred fire aglow
Help us neither scorn nor death to heed
Teach us Jesus Christ to know aright

That he may defend us when life is ending
That with hearts united we love each other,
That we may not falter nor courage fail us
That we may abide in the Lord who bought us,

And from exile home we are wending.
Ev'ry stranger, sister, and brother.
When the foe shall taunt and assail us.
Till to our true home he has brought us.

Lord, have mercy!

© Text: German folk hymn, st. 1; Martin Luther, 1483–1546, sts. 2–4; tr. Worship Supplement, 1969, adapt.
Tune: Johann Walter, Geystliche gesangk Buchleyn, 1524

NUN BITTEN WIR
109 119 4

Creator Spirit, Heavenly Dove

1 Cre - a - tor Spir - it, heav'n - ly dove, De - scend
2 To you, the Com - fort - er, we cry, To you,
3 In you, with grac - es sev - en - fold, We God's
4 Your light to ev - 'ry sense im - part, And shed

up - on us from a - bove; With grac - es man - i -
the gift of God most high, True fount of life, the
al - might - y hand be - hold While you with tongues of
your love in ev - 'ry heart; Your own un - fail - ing

fold re - store Your crea - tures as they were be - fore.
fire of love, The soul's a - noint - ing from a - bove.
fire pro - claim To all the world his ho - ly name.
might sup - ply To strength - en our in - fir - mi - ty.

5 Keep far from us our cruel foe,
And peace from your own hand bestow;
If you be our protecting guide,
No evil can our steps betide.

6 Oh, make to us the Father known;
Teach us the eternal Son to own;
And you, whose name we ever bless,
Of both the Spirit, to confess.

7 Praise we the Father and the Son
And Holy Spirit, with them one;
And may the Son on us bestow
The gifts that from the Spirit flow.

Text: attr. Rhabanus Maurus, 776–856; tr. composite, alt.
Tune: J. Klug, Geistliche Lieder, 1533

KOMM, GOTT SCHÖPFER
L M

157 Come, Holy Ghost, Our Souls Inspire

1 Come, Holy Ghost, our souls inspire, Ignite them with celestial fire; Spirit of God, you have the art Your gifts, the sev'nfold, to impart.

2 Your blest outpouring from above Is comfort, life, and fire of love. Illumine with perpetual light The dullness of our blinded sight.

3 Anoint and cheer our much-soiled face With the abundance of your grace. Keep far our foes; give peace at home; Where you guide us, no ill can come.

4 Teach us to know the Father, Son, And you, of both, to be but one That, as the ceaseless ages throng, Your praise may be our endless song!

Text: attr. Rhabanus Maurus, 776–856; tr. John Cosin, 1594–1672, alt.
Tune: Joseph Klug, Geistliche Lieder, 1533

KOMM, GOTT SCHÖPFER
L M

Come, Holy Ghost, Our Souls Inspire 158

1 Come, Ho - ly Ghost, our souls in - spire, Ig - nite them with ce -
2 Your blest out - pour - ing from a - bove Is com - fort, life, and
3 A - noint and cheer our much-soiled face With the a - bun - dance
4 Teach us to know the Fa - ther, Son, And you, of both, to

les - tial fire; Spir - it of God, you have the art
fire of love. Il - lu - mine with per - pet - ual light
of your grace. Keep far our foes; give peace at home;
be but one That, as the cease - less a - ges throng,

Your gifts, the sev'n - fold, to im - part.
The dull - ness of our blind - ed sight.
Where you guide us, no ill can come.
Your praise may be our end - less song! A - men

Text: attr. Rhabanus Maurus, 776–856; tr. John Cosin, 1594–1672, alt.
Tune: Sarum plainsong, mode VIII

VENI CREATOR SPIRITUS
L M

159

Hail Thee, Festival Day

Refrain

Hail thee, fes - ti - val day!   Blest day to be hal-lowed for-ev - er;

Day when the Ho - ly Ghost   shone in the world with his grace.   grace.

1st time   *2nd time*

1 Bright and in like - ness of fire,   on   those   who a -
3 God the Al -might - y, the Lord,   the   rul - er of
5 Spir - it of life and of pow'r,   now   flow   in us,

wait his ap-pear   -   ing,   He   whom   the   Lord had fore-
earth and the heav   -   ens,   Guard   us   from   harm with -
fount of our be   -   ing,   Light   that   en - light - ens us

Repeat refrain once after each stanza

told sud - den -ly, swift -ly de - scends:
out; cleanse us from e - vil with - in:
all, life that in all may a - bide:

2 Dai - ly the love - li - ness grows, a - dorned with the
4 Je - sus, the health of the world, en - light - en our
6 Praise to the giv - er of good! O Lov - er and

glo - ry of blos - som; Heav - en her gates un - bars,
minds, great re - deem - er, Son of the Fa - ther su -
Au - thor of con - cord, Pour out your balm on our

Repeat refrain once after each stanza

fling - ing her . . in - crease of light:
preme, on - ly - be - got - ten of God:
days; or - der our ways in your peace:

© *Text: Venantius Honorius Fortunatus, 530–609; tr. Lutheran Book of Worship, 1978*
© *Tune: Ralph Vaughan Williams, 1872–1958*

SALVE FESTA DIES
irregular

160 O Holy Spirit, Enter In

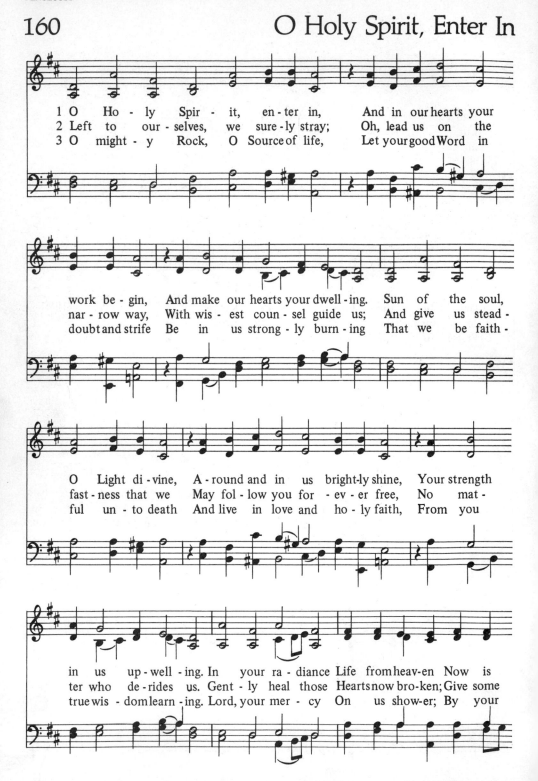

1 O Ho - ly Spir - it, en - ter in, And in our hearts your
2 Left to our - selves, we sure - ly stray; Oh, lead us on the
3 O might - y Rock, O Source of life, Let your good Word in

work be - gin, And make our hearts your dwell - ing. Sun of the soul,
nar - row way, With wis - est coun - sel guide us; And give us stead -
doubt and strife Be in us strong - ly burn - ing That we be faith -

O Light di - vine, A - round and in us bright-ly shine, Your strength
fast - ness that we May fol - low you for - ev - er free, No mat -
ful un - to death And live in love and ho - ly faith, From you

in us up - well - ing. In your ra - diance Life from heav-en Now is
ter who de - rides us. Gent - ly heal those Hearts now bro-ken; Give some
true wis - dom learn - ing. Lord, your mer - cy On us show-er; By your

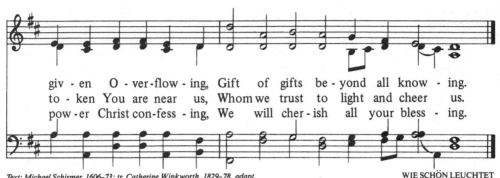

giv - en O - ver-flow - ing, Gift of gifts be - yond all know - ing.
to - ken You are near us, Whom we trust to light and cheer us.
pow - er Christ con-fess - ing, We will cher - ish all your bless - ing.

Text: Michael Schirmer, 1606–73; tr. Catherine Winkworth, 1829–78, adapt.
Tune: Philipp Nicolai, 1556–1608

WIE SCHÖN LEUCHTET
P M

Come, Gracious Spirit, Heavenly Dove 161

1 Come, gra - cious Spir - it, heav'n - ly dove, With light and
2 The light of truth to us dis - play, And make us
3 Lead us to Christ, the liv - ing way, Nor let us
4 Lead us to heav'n that we may share The full - est

com - fort from a - bove. Come, be our guard - ian
know and choose your way; Plant ho - ly fear in
from his pas - tures stray; Lead us to ho - li -
joy for - ev - er there; Lead us to our e -

and our guide; At ev - 'ry thought and step pre - side.
ev - 'ry heart That we from God may not de - part.
ness, the road That we must take to dwell with God.
ter - nal rest, To be with God for - ev - er blest.

Text: Simon Browne, 1680–1732, alt.
Tune: William Knapp, 1698–1768

WAREHAM
L M

162   Come Down, O Love Divine

1 Come down, O Love di - vine; Seek out this soul of mine.
2 Oh, let it free - ly burn Till world - ly pas - sions turn
3 Let ho - ly char - i - ty My out - ward ves - ture be
4 And so the yearn - ing strong, With which the soul will long,

And vis - it it with your own ar - dor glow - ing;
To dust and ash - es in its heat con - sum - ing;
And low - li - ness be - come my in - ner cloth - ing—
Shall far out - pass the pow'r of hu - man tell - ing;

O Com - fort - er, draw near; With - in my heart ap - pear,
And let your glo - rious light Shine ev - er on my sight
True low - li - ness of heart, Which takes the hum - bler part
No soul can guess his grace Till it be - come the place

And kin - dle it, your ho - ly flame be - stow - ing.
And clothe me round, the while my path il - lum - ing.
And ov - er its short - com-ings weeps with loath - ing.
Where - in the Ho - ly Spir - it makes his dwell - ing.

Text: Bianco da Siena, d. 1434; tr. Richard F. Littledale, 1833–90, alt.
© *Tune: Ralph Vaughan Williams, 1872–1958*

DOWN AMPNEY
66 11 66 11

O Day Full of Grace

1 O day full of grace that now we see Appearing on earth's horizon, Bring light from our God that we may be Replete in his joy this season. God, shine for us now in this dark place; Your name on our hearts emblazon.

2 O day full of grace, O blessed time, Our Lord on the earth arriving; Then came to the world that light sublime, Great joy for us all retrieving; For Jesus all mortals did embrace, All darkness and shame removing.

3 For Christ bore our sins, and not his own, When he on the cross was hanging; And then he arose and moved the stone That we might no more from him be lost, All we, unto him belonging, Might join with angelic hosts to raise Our voices in endless singing.

4 God came to us then at Pentecost, His Spirit new life revealing, That we might no more from him be lost, All darkness for us dispelling. His flame will the mark of sin efface And bring to us all his healing.

5 When we on that final journey go
   That Christ is for us preparing,
   We'll gather in song, our hearts aglow,
   All joy of the heavens sharing,
   And walk in the light of God's own place,
   With angels his name adoring.

© Text: Danish folk hymn, c. 1450; tr. Gerald Thorson, b. 1921
Tune: Christoph E. F. Weyse, 1774–1842

DEN SIGNEDE DAG
98 98 98

164

Holy Spirit, Ever Dwelling

1 Ho - ly Spir - it, ev - er dwell - ing In the ho - liest
2 Ho - ly Spir - it, ev - er liv - ing As the Church's
3 Ho - ly Spir - it, ev - er work - ing Through the Church's

realms of light; Ho - ly Spir - it, ev - er brood - ing
ver - y life; Ho - ly Spir - it, ev - er striv - ing
min - is - try; Quick - 'ning, strength-'ning, and ab - solv - ing,

O'er a world of gloom and night; Ho - ly Spir - it, ev - er
Through us in a cease - less strife; Ho - ly Spir - it, ev - er
Set - ting cap - tive sin - ners free; Ho - ly Spir - it, ev - er

rais - ing Those of earth to thrones on high; Liv - ing, life - im -
form - ing In the Church the mind of Christ: You we praise with
bind - ing Age to age and soul to soul In com - mu - nion

part - ing Spir - it, You we praise and mag - ni - fy.
end - less wor - ship For your gifts and fruits un - priced.
nev - er end - ing, You we wor - ship and ex - tol.

© Text: Timothy Rees, 1874–1939, alt.
Tune: Dutch folk tune, 18th cent.

IN BABILONE
87 87 D

Come, Oh, Come, O Quickening Spirit 165

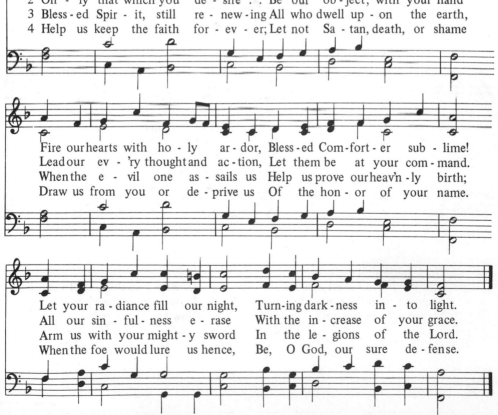

1 Come, oh come, O quick - 'ning Spir - it, God be - fore the dawn of time!
2 On - ly that which you de - sire .. Be our ob - ject; with your hand
3 Bless - ed Spir - it, still re - new-ing All who dwell up - on the earth,
4 Help us keep the faith for - ev - er; Let not Sa - tan, death, or shame

Fire our hearts with ho - ly ar - dor, Bless - ed Com-fort - er sub - lime!
Lead our ev - 'ry thought and ac - tion, Let them be at your com - mand.
When the e - vil one as - sails us Help us prove our heav'n - ly birth;
Draw us from you or de - prive us Of the hon - or of your name.

Let your ra - diance fill our night, Turn-ing dark - ness in - to light.
All our sin - ful - ness e - rase With the in - crease of your grace.
Arm us with your might - y sword In the le - gions of the Lord.
When the foe would lure us hence, Be, O God, our sure de - fense.

© Text: Heinrich Held, 1620-59; tr. Edward T. Horn III, b. 1909, alt.
Tune: Neu-vermehrtes Gesangbuch, Meiningen, 1693

KOMM, O KOMM, DU GEIST DES LEBENS
87 87 77

166

Holy Spirit, Light Divine

1 Ho - ly Spir - it, light di - vine, Dawn up - on this
2 Ho - ly Spir - it, grace di - vine, Cleanse this sin - ful
3 Ho - ly Spir - it, truth di - vine, Shine up - on these
4 Ho - ly Spir - it, pow'r di - vine, For - ti - fy this

soul of mine; Let your word dis - pel the night,
heart of mine; In your mer - cy look on me,
eyes of mine; Send your ra - diance from a - bove,
will of mine; Bend it to your own pure will,

Wake my spir - it, clear my sight.
From sin's bond - age set me free.
Let me know my Sav - ior's love.
All my life with grac - es fill.

5 Holy Spirit, peace divine,
Still this restless heart of mine;
Speak to calm the tossing sea,
Stayed in your tranquility.

6 Holy Spirit, all divine,
Dwell within this self of mine;
I your temple pure would be
Now and for eternity.

Text: Andrew Reed, 1788–1862, and Samuel Longfellow, 1819–92, alt.
Tune: Orlando Gibbons, 1583–1625

SONG 13
77 77

Creator Spirit, by Whose Aid

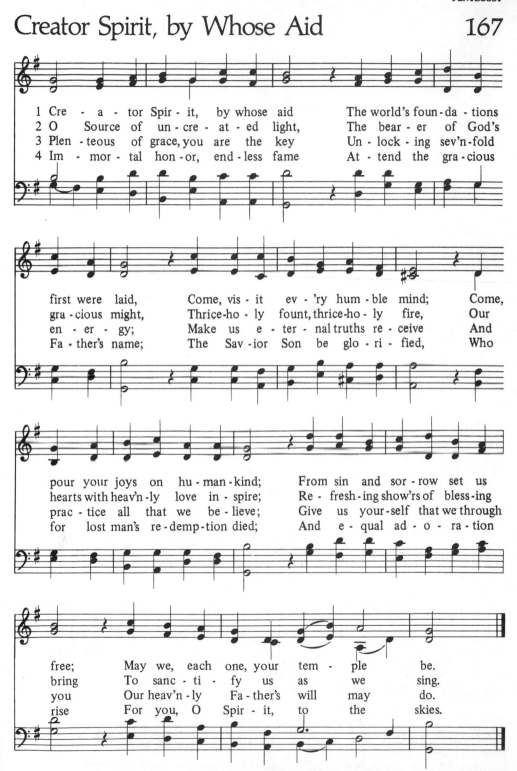

1 Cre - a - tor Spir - it, by whose aid The world's foun - da - tions first were laid, Come, vis - it ev - 'ry hum - ble mind; Come, pour your joys on hu - man - kind; From sin and sor - row set us free; May we, each one, your tem - ple be.

2 O Source of un - cre - at - ed light, The bear - er of God's gra - cious might, Thrice-ho - ly fount, thrice-ho - ly fire, Our hearts with heav'n -ly love in - spire; Re - fresh-ing show'rs of bless-ing bring To sanc - ti - fy us as we sing.

3 Plen - teous of grace, you are the key Un - lock - ing sev'n-fold en - er - gy; Make us e - ter - nal truths re - ceive And prac - tice all that we be - lieve; Give us your-self that we through you Our heav'n - ly Fa - ther's will may do.

4 Im - mor - tal hon - or, end - less fame At - tend the gra - cious Fa - ther's name; The Sav - ior Son be glo - ri - fied, Who for lost man's re - demp -tion died; And e - qual ad - o - ra - tion rise For you, O Spir - it, to the skies.

Text: attr. Rhabanus Maurus, 776–856; tr. John Dryden, 1631–1700, alt.
Tune: Kirchengesangbuch, Strassburg, 1541

ALL EHR UND LOB
88 88 88

Holy, Holy, Holy

1 Ho - ly, ho - ly, ho - ly, Lord God Al - might - y!
2 Ho - ly, ho - ly, ho - ly! All the saints a - dore thee,
3 Ho - ly, ho - ly, ho - ly! Though the dark - ness hide thee,
4 Ho - ly, ho - ly, ho - ly! Lord God Al - might - y!

Ear - ly in the morn - ing our song shall rise to thee.
Cast - ing down their gold - en crowns a - round the glass - y sea;
Though the eye made blind by sin thy glo - ry may not see,
All thy works shall praise thy name in earth and sky and sea.

Ho - ly, ho - ly, ho - ly, mer - ci - ful and might - y!
Cher - u - bim and ser - a - phim fall - ing down be - fore thee,
On - ly thou art ho - ly; there is none be - side thee,
Ho - ly, ho - ly, ho - ly, mer - ci - ful and might - y!

God in three Per - sons, bless - ed Trin - i - ty!
Which wert and art and ev - er - more shalt be.
Per - fect in pow'r, in love and pu - ri - ty.
God in three Per - sons, bless - ed Trin - i - ty!

Text: Reginald Heber, 1783–1826, alt.
Tune: John B. Dykes, 1823–76

NICAEA
11 12 12 10

Come, O Almighty King

1 Come, O al - might-y King,   Help us your   name   to   sing;
2 Come, O in - car - nate Word,   Gird on your   might - y   sword;
3 Come, ho - ly   Com - fort - er,   Your sa - cred   wit - ness   bear
4 To   the great   One   in Three   E - ter - nal   prais - es   be

Help   us   to praise;   Fa - ther all - glo - ri - ous,   In   all   vic -
Our prayer at - tend.   Come and your peo - ple bless,   And give your
In   this glad hour!   Your sev'n - fold gifts   im - part;   Rule now in
Hence ev - er - more!   Your sov - 'reign maj - es - ty   May we in

to - ri - ous,   Come and reign   o - ver us,   An - cient of   Days.
Word suc - cess,   And let   your righ - teous - ness   On   us   de - scend.
ev - 'ry heart;   Nev - er   from us   de - part,   Spir - it   of   pow'r.
glo - ry   see   And to   e - ter - ni - ty   Love and   a - dore.

Text: source unknown, c. 1757, alt.
Tune: Felice de Giardini, 1716–96

ITALIAN HYMN
664 6664

170 Triune God, Oh, Be Our Stay

Tri - une God, oh, be our stay; Oh, let us per - ish nev - er!

Cleanse us from our sins, we pray, And grant us life for - ev - er.

Keep us from the e - vil one; Up-hold our faith most ho - ly,

And let us trust you sole - ly With hum - ble hearts and low - ly.

Let us put God's ar-mor on, With all true Chris-tians run - ning

Our heav'n-ly race and shun - ning The de-vil's wiles and cun - ning.

A - men, a - men! This be done; So sing we, "Al - le - lu - ia!"
(Lent) So sing we all, "Ho - san - na!"

This hymn may be sung in three stanzas in the following form:
1 God the Father, be our stay. . .
2 Jesus Christ, oh, be our stay. . .
3 Holy Spirit, be our stay. . .

Text: adapt. Martin Luther, 1483–1546; tr. Richard Massie, 1800–87, alt.
Tune: Johann Walter, Geystliche gesangk Buchleyn, 1524

GOTT DER VATER WOHN UNS BEI
77 77 77 7 D

171 Holy God, We Praise Your Name

1 Holy God, we praise your name; Lord of all, we bow be-fore you. All on earth your scep-ter claim, All in heav'n a-bove a-dore you. In-fi-nite your vast do-main, Ev-er-last-ing is your reign.

2 Hark! The glad ce-les-tial hymn An-gel choirs a-bove are rais-ing; Cher-u-bim and ser-a-phim, In un-ceas-ing cho-rus prais-ing, Fill the heav'ns with sweet ac-cord: "Ho-ly, ho-ly, ho-ly Lord!"

3 Lo, the ap-os-tol-ic train Join your sa-cred name to hal-low; Proph-ets swell the glad re-frain, And the white-robed mar-tyrs fol-low; And from morn to set of sun Through the Church the song goes on.

4 You are King of Glo-ry, Christ; Son of God, yet born of Ma-ry. For us sin-ners sac-ri-ficed, As to death a Trib-u-tar-y, First to break the bars of death, You have o-pened heav'n to faith.

5 Holy Father, holy Son,
   Holy Spirit, three we name you,
Though in essence only one;
   Undivided God we claim you
And, adoring, bend the knee
While we own the mystery.

Text: source unknown; tr. Clarence A. Walworth, 1820–1900, alt.
Tune: Maria Theresa, Katholisches Gesangbuch, 1774

GROSSER GOTT
78 78 77

I Bind unto Myself Today   172

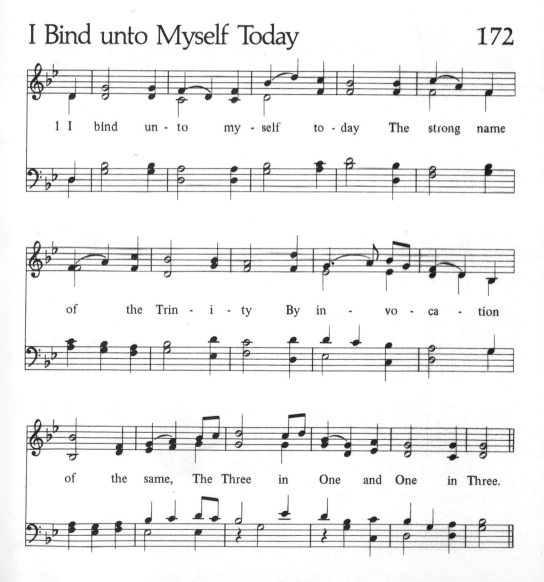

1 I bind un - to my - self to - day The strong name

of the Trin - i - ty By in - vo - ca - tion

of the same, The Three in One and One in Three.

Hymn continues on next page

2 I bind this day to me forever, By
3 I bind un-to my-self to-day The
4 I bind un-to my-self to-day The
5 I bind un-to my-self the name, The

pow'r of faith, Christ's in - car - na - tion, His
vir - tues of the star - lit heav - en, The
pow'r of God to hold and lead, His
strong name of the Trin - i - ty By

bap - tism in the Jor - dan Riv - er, His
glo - rious sun's life - giv - ing ray, · · The
eye to watch, his might to stay, · · His
in - vo - ca - tion of the same, · · The

cross of death for my sal - va - tion, His
white - ness of the moon at e - ven, The
ear to hear - ken to my need, The
Three in One and One in Three, Of

burst - ing from the spic - ed tomb, His
flash - ing of the light - ning free, The
wis - dom of my God to teach, His
whom all na - ture has cre - a - tion, E -

rid - ing up the heav'n - ly way, His
whirl - ing wind's tem - pes - tuous shocks, The
hand to guide, his shield to ward, The
ter - nal Fa - ther, Spir - it, Word. Praise

com - ing at the day of doom, .
sta - ble earth, the deep salt sea, . .
Word of God to give me speech, .
to the Lord of my sal - va - tion;

I bind un - to my - self to - day.
A - round the old e - ter - nal rocks.
His heav'n - ly host to be my guard.
Sal - va - tion is of Christ the Lord!

Text: attr. St. Patrick, c 372–466; para. Cecil F. Alexander, 1823–95
Tune: Irish

ST. PATRICK'S BREASTPLATE
irregular

173 Glory Be to God the Father

1 Glo - ry be to God the Fa - ther, Glo - ry be to
2 Glo - ry be to him who loved us, Washed us from each
3 Glo - ry to the King of an - gels, Glo - ry to the
4 Glo - ry, bless - ing, praise e - ter - nal! Thus the choir of

God the Son, Glo - ry be to God the Spir - it:
spot and stain; Glo - ry be to him who bought us,
Church's King, Glo - ry to the King of na - tions;
an - gels sings; Hon - or, rich - es, pow'r, do - min - ion!

Great Je - ho - vah, Three in One! Glo - ry, glo - ry
Made us kings with him to reign! Glo - ry, glo - ry
Heav'n and earth, your prais - es bring! Glo - ry, glo - ry
Thus its praise cre - a - tion brings. Glo - ry, glo - ry,

While e - ter - nal a - ges run!
To the Lamb that once was slain!
To the King of glo - ry sing!
Glo - ry to the King of kings!

Text: Horatius Bonar, 1808–99
Tune: Walter G. Whinfield, 1865–1919

WORCESTER
87 87 47

The Lord, My God, Be Praised

1 The Lord, my God, be praised, My light, my life from heav - en;
2 The Lord, my God, be praised, My trust, my life from heav - en,
3 The Lord, my God, be praised, My hope, my light from heav - en,
4 The Lord, my God, be praised, My God, the ev - er - liv - ing,

My mak - er, who to me Has soul and bod - y giv - en;
The Fa - ther's own dear Son, Whose life for me was giv - en,
The Spir - it, whom the Son In love to me has giv - en.
To whom the heav - 'nly host Their laud and praise are giv - ing.

My Fa - ther, who will shield And keep me day by day
Who for my sin a - toned With his most pre - cious blood
His grace re - vives my heart And gives my spir - it pow'r,
The Lord, my God, be praised, In whose great name I boast,

And make each mo - ment yield New bless - ings on my way.
And gives to me by faith The high - est heav'n - ly good.
Help, com - fort, and sup - port In sor - row's gloom - y hour.
God Fa - ther, God the Son, And God the Ho - ly Ghost.

Text: Johann Olearius, 1611–84; tr. August Crull, 1845–1923, alt.
Tune: Johann Crüger, 1598–1662

NUN DANKET ALLE GOTT
67 67 66 66

175

Father Most Holy

1 Fa - ther most ho - ly, mer - ci - ful, and ten - der; Je - sus, our
2 Trin - i - ty bless - ed, u - ni - ty un - shak - en; Good - ness un -
3 Mak - er of all things, all thy crea - tures praise thee; All for thy
4 Lord God Al - might - y, un - to thee be glo - ry, One in three

Sav - ior, with the Fa - ther reign - ing; Spir - it of com - fort,
bound - ed, ver - y God of heav - en, Light of the an - gels,
wor - ship were and are cre - at - ed; Now, as we al - so
per - sons, o - ver all ex - alt - ed! Glo - ry we of - fer,

ad - vo - cate, de - fend - er, Light nev - er wan - ing.
joy of those for - sak - en, Hope of all liv - ing.
wor - ship thee de - vout - ly, Hear thou our voic - es.
praise thee and a - dore thee, Now and for - ev - er.

© Text: Latin hymn, 10th cent.; based on tr. by Percy Dearmer, 1867–1936
Tune: Antiphoner, Paris, 1681

CHRISTE SANCTORUM
11 11 11 5

The Bridegroom Soon Will Call Us 176

1 The Bride-groom soon will call us, "Come to the wed - ding
2 Then, oh, what jub - i - la - tion To see our Sav - ior's
3 Then Christ, his glo - ry shar - ing, Will give us crowns of
4 Like skies in joy - ous mo - tion Or mu - sic af - ter

feast." May slum - ber not be - fall us Nor watch-ful-ness de -
face, His glo - rious ex - al - ta - tion Since win-ning us God's
gold He won for us by wear - ing Thorned ag - o - nies un -
tears, New song will fill the o - cean Of heav-en's age - less

crease. But may our lamps be burn - ing With oil e - nough and
grace. Then kings will come to meet us And psalm - ists rich in
told. The Fa - ther with em - brac - es Will wel - come us, each
years While an - gel hosts are rais - ing With saints from great to

more That, with our Lord re - turn - ing, We find an o - pen door.
song, A - pos - tles, proph-ets greet us, A great and splen-did throng.
one, Robed in the Spir - it's grac - es As prince - ly as God's Son.
least The an - them tides for prais - ing The Giv - er of this feast.

Text: Johann Walter, 1496–1570; tr. F. Samuel Janzow, b. 1913
Tune: Michael Praetorius' Musae Sionae, VII, 1609

ACH GOTT VOM HIMMELREICHE
76 76 D

177 Wake, Awake, for Night Is Flying

1 "Wake, a - wake, for night is fly - ing," The watch-men
2 Zi - on hears the watch-men sing - ing, And in her
3 Now let all the heav'ns a - dore you, Let saints and

on the heights are cry - ing; "A - wake, Je - ru - sa - lem, a - rise!"
heart new joy is spring-ing. She wakes, she ris - es from her gloom.
an - gels sing be - fore you With harp and cym-bals' clear - est tone.

Mid - night hears the wel - come voic - es And at the
For her Lord comes down all glo - rious, The strong in
Of one pearl each shin - ing por - tal, Where, join - ing

thrill - ing cry re - joic - es: "Where are the vir - gins, pure and wise?
grace, in truth vic - to - rious. Her star's a - ris - ing light has come!
with the choir im - mor - tal, We gath - er round your ra - diant throne.

The bride - groom comes, a - wake! Your lamps with glad - ness take!
"Now come, O bless - ed one, Lord Je - sus, God's own Son.
No eye has seen that light, No ear the ech - oed might

Al - le - lu - ia! With bri - dal care And faith's bold
Hail! Ho - san - na! We an - swer all In joy your
Of your glo - ry; Yet there shall we In your vic -

prayer, To meet the bride - groom, come, pre - pare!"
call, We fol - low to the wed - ding hall."
t'ry Sing shouts of praise e - ter - nal - ly!

Text: Philipp Nicolai, 1556–1608; tr. Catherine Winkworth, 1829–78, alt.
Tune: Philipp Nicolai, 1556–1608

WACHET AUF
P M

178 At the Name of Jesus

1 At the name of Je - sus Ev - 'ry knee shall bow,
2 At his voice cre - a - tion Sprang at once to sight,
3 Hum - bled for a sea - son, To re - ceive a name
4 Bore it up tri - um - phant With its hu - man light,

Ev - 'ry tongue con - fess him King of glo - ry now.
All the an - gel fac - es, All the hosts of light,
From the lips of sin - ners Un - to whom he came,
Through all ranks of crea - tures To the cen - tral height,

'Tis the Fa - ther's plea - sure We should call him Lord,
Thrones and dom - i - na - tions, Stars up - on their way,
Faith - ful - ly he bore it Spot-less to the last,
To the throne of God - head, To the Fa - ther's breast,

Who from the be - gin - ning Was the might - y Word.
All the heav'n - ly or - ders In their great ar - ray.
Brought it back vic - to - rious When from death he passed;
Filled it with the glo - ry Of that per - fect rest.

5 In your hearts enthrone him;
    There let him subdue
All that is not holy,
    All that is not true:
Crown him as your captain
    In temptation's hour;
Let his will enfold you
    In its light and pow'r.

6 Christians, this Lord Jesus
    Shall return again
In his Father's glory,
    With his angel train;
For all wreaths of empire
    Meet upon his brow,
And our hearts confess him
    King of glory now.

7 Glory then to Jesus,
    Who, the Prince of light,
To a world in darkness
    Brought the gift of sight;
Praise to God the Father;
    In the Spirit's love
Praise we all together
    Him who reigns above.

Text: Caroline M. Noel, 1817–77
© Tune: Ralph Vaughan Williams, 1872–1958

KING'S WESTON
65 65 D

179 Rejoice, the Lord Is King

1 Re-joice, the Lord is King! Your Lord and King a-dore;
2 Our Sav-ior Je-sus reigns, The God of truth and love;
3 His king-dom can-not fail; He rules o'er earth and heav'n;
4 He sits at God's right hand Till all his foes sub-mit

Re-joice, give thanks, and sing, And tri-umph ev - er -more:
When he had purged our stains, He took his seat a - bove:
The keys of death and hell Are to our Je - sus giv'n:
And bow to his com- mand And fall be - neath his feet:

Refrain

Lift up your heart, lift up your voice; Re - joice; a - gain I say, Re - joice!

Text: Charles Wesley, 1707–88, alt.
Tune: John Darwall, 1731–89

DARWALL'S 148TH
66 66 88

Our God, Our Help in Ages Past

180

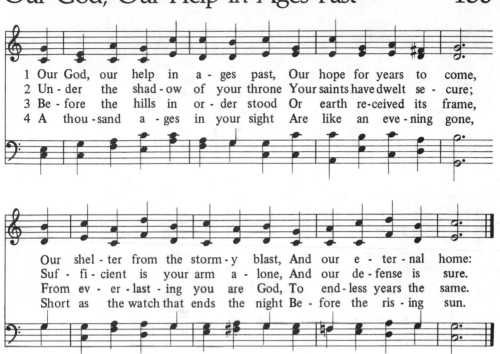

1 Our God, our help in a - ges past, Our hope for years to come,
2 Un - der the shad - ow of your throne Your saints have dwelt se - cure;
3 Be - fore the hills in or - der stood Or earth re-ceived its frame,
4 A thou - sand a - ges in your sight Are like an eve - ning gone,

Our shel - ter from the storm - y blast, And our e - ter - nal home:
Suf - fi - cient is your arm a - lone, And our de - fense is sure.
From ev - er - last - ing you are God, To end - less years the same.
Short as the watch that ends the night Be - fore the ris - ing sun.

5 Time, like an ever-rolling stream,
   Soon bears us all away;
  We fly forgotten, as a dream
    Dies at the op'ning day.

6 Our God, our help in ages past,
   Our hope for years to come,
  Still be our guard while troubles last
    And our eternal home!

Text: Isaac Watts, 1674–1748, alt.
Tune: William Croft, 1678–1727

ST. ANNE
CM

181 Across the Sky the Shades of Night

1 A - cross the sky the shades of night This New Year's
2 Be - fore the cross sub - dued we bow, To you our
3 We gath - er up in this brief hour The mem - 'ry
4 Then, gra - cious God, in years to come, We pray your

Eve are fleet - ing. We deck your al - tar, Lord, with
prayer ad - dress - ing, Re - count - ing all your mer - cies
of your mer - cies: Your won - drous good - ness, love, and
hand may guide us, And, on - ward through our jour - ney

light, In sol - emn wor - ship meet - ing; And as the
now, And all our sins con - fess - ing, Be - seech - ing
pow'r Our grate - ful song re - hears - es; For you have
home, Your mer - cy walk be - side us Un - til at

year's last hours go by, We raise to you our ear - nest
you this com - ing year To keep us in your faith and
been our strength and stay In man - y a dark and drear - y
last our ran - somed life Is safe from per - il, toil, and

cry, Once more your love en - treat - ing.
fear, To crown us with your bless - ing.
day Of sor - row and re - vers - es.
strife When heav'n it - self shall hide us.

Text: James Hamilton, 1819–96, alt.
Tune: attr. Nikolaus Decius, c. 1485–aft. 1546

ALLEIN GOTT IN DER HÖH
87 87 887

Jesus! Name of Wondrous Love   182

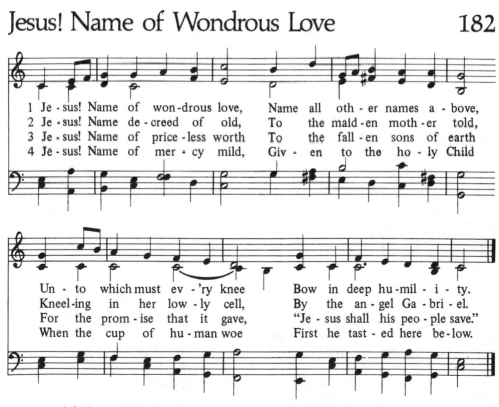

1 Je - sus! Name of won-drous love, Name all oth - er names a - bove,
2 Je - sus! Name de - creed of old, To the maid-en moth-er told,
3 Je - sus! Name of price - less worth To the fall - en sons of earth
4 Je - sus! Name of mer - cy mild, Giv - en to the ho - ly Child

Un - to which must ev - 'ry knee Bow in deep hu - mil - i - ty.
Kneel-ing in her low - ly cell, By the an - gel Ga - bri - el.
For the prom - ise that it gave, "Je - sus shall his peo - ple save."
When the cup of hu - man woe First he tast - ed here be - low.

5 Jesus! Only name that's given
Under all the mighty heaven
Whereby man, to sin enslaved,
Bursts his fetters and is saved.

6 Jesus! Name of wondrous love,
Human name of God above;
Pleading your redemption true,
We flee, helpless, Lord, to you.

Text: William W. How, 1823–97, alt.
Tune: J. A. Freylinghausen, Geistreiches Gesang-Buch, 1704

GOTT SEI DANK
77 77

183 Greet Now the Swiftly Changing Year

1 Greet now the swift-ly chang - ing year With
2 Re - mem - ber now the Son of God And
3 This Je - sus came to end sin's war; This
4 His love a - bun - dant far ex - ceeds The

joy and pen - i - tence sin - cere. Re - joice! Re-joice! With
how he shed his in - fant blood. Re - joice! Re-joice! With
name of names for us he bore. Re - joice! Re-joice! With
vol - ume of a whole year's needs. Re - joice! Re-joice! With

thanks em - brace An - oth - er year of grace.
thanks em - brace An - oth - er year of grace.
thanks em - brace An - oth - er year of grace.
thanks em - brace An - oth - er year of grace.

5 With him as Lord to lead our way
In want and in prosperity,
What need we fear in earth or space
In this new year of grace!

6 "All glory be to God on high,
And peace on earth!" the angels cry.
Rejoice! Rejoice! With thanks embrace
Another year of grace.

7 God, Father, Son, and Spirit, hear!
To all our pleas incline your ear;
Upon our lives rich blessing trace
In this new year of grace.

© Text: *Tranoscius; tr. Jaroslav J. Vajda, b. 1919, alt.*
Tune: *T. Závorka, Kancional, 1602*

ROK NOVÝ
88 86

Now Let Us Come Before Him

184

1 Now let us come before him, With
2 The storms in bat - tle clash - ing, The
3 So when e - vents are fright - 'ning And
4 God helps all those for - sak - en When

song and prayer a - dore him Who for our life has
hooves of thun - der crash - ing, True moth - ers guard the
slash like lu - rid light - ning, God hides us in em -
to their plight they wak - en, Our coun - sel - or, our

giv - en The strength we need from heav - en.
slum - ber Of chil - dren with - out num - ber.
brac - es To shield his chil - dren's fac - es.
trea - sure, Our friend in pain or plea - sure.

5 Lord, show your tender feeling;
For sickness give your healing;
To minds, when dark thoughts frighten,
Come with your joy, bring light in.

6 Above all else, Lord, send us
Your Spirit to attend us,
His peace in us abiding,
Our footsteps heav'nward guiding.

© *Text: Paul Gerhardt, 1607–76; tr. F. Samuel Janzow, b. 1913*
Tune: Johann Crüger, 1598–1662

NUN LASST UNS GOTT DEM HERREN
77 77 Iambic

185   In Peace and Joy I Now Depart

1 In peace and joy I now de-part Since God so
2 This is what you have done for me, My faith-ful
3 It was God's love that sent you forth As man's sal-
4 You are the health and sav-ing light Of lands in

wills it. Se-rene and con-fi-dent my heart;
Sav-ior. In you, Lord, I was made to see
va-tion, In-vit-ing to your-self the earth,
dark-ness; You feed and light-en those in night

Still-ness fills it. For God prom-ised
All God's fa-vor. I now know you
Ev-'ry na-tion, By your whole-some
With your kind-ness. All God's peo-ple

death would be No more than qui-et slum-ber.
as my life, My help when I am dy-ing.
heal-ing Word Re-sound-ing round our plan-et.
find in you Their trea-sure, joy and glo-ry.

© Text: Martin Luther, 1483–1546; tr. F. Samuel Janzow, b. 1913
   Tune: Martin Luther, 1483–1546

MIT FRIED UND FREUD
85 84 77

In His Temple Now Behold Him

186

1 In his tem - ple now be-hold him, See the long - ex-
2 In the arms of her who bore him, Vir - gin pure, be-
3 Je - sus, by your pre - sen - ta - tion, When they blessed you,

pect - ed Lord; An - cient proph - ets had fore-told him,
hold him lie While his a - ged saints a - dore him
weak and poor, Make us see your great sal - va - tion,

God has now ful - filled his word. Now to praise him,
Ere in per - fect faith they die. Al - le - lu - ia,
Seal us with your prom - ise sure; And pre - sent us

his re - deem - ed Shall break forth with one ac - cord.
al - le - lu - ia! Lo, th'in - car - nate God Most High!
in your glo - ry To your Fa - ther, cleansed and pure.

Text: Henry J. Pye, 1825–1903, alt.
Tune: adapt. from an anthem of Henry Purcell, 1658–95

WESTMINSTER ABBEY
87 87 87

187 When All the World Was Cursed

1 When all the world was cursed By Mo-ses' con-dem-na-tion,
2 Be-fore he yet was born, He leaped in joy-ful meet-ing,
3 Be-hold the Lamb of God That bears the world's trans-gres-sion,
4 Thrice blest is ev-'ry-one Who heeds the proc-la-ma-tion

Saint John the Bap-tist came With words of con-so-la-tion.
Con-fess-ing him as Lord Whose moth-er he was greet-ing.
Whose sac-ri-fice re-moves The en-e-my's op-pres-sion.
Which John the Bap-tist brought, Ac-cept-ing Christ's sal-va-tion.

With true fore-run-ner's zeal The great-er one he named,
By Jor-dan's roll-ing stream, A new E-li-jah bold,
Be-hold the Lamb of God, The bear-er of our sin,
He who be-lieves this truth And comes with love un-feigned

And him, as yet un-known, As Sav-ior he pro-claimed.
He tes-ti-fied of him Of whom the proph-ets told:
Who for our peace and joy Will full a-tone-ment win.
Has righ-teous-ness and peace In full-est mea-sure gained.

5 Our Lord of love, oh, grant
   That we receive, rejoicing,
   The word proclaimed by John,
   Our true repentance voicing,

That gladly we may walk
   Upon our Savior's way
Until we live with him
   In his eternal day.

Text: Johann G. Olearius, 1635–1711; tr. Paul E. Kretzmann, 1883–1965, alt.
Tune: Ahasverus Fritsch, 1629–1701

WAS FRAG ICH NACH DER WELT
67 67 66 66

Sweet Flowerets of the Martyr Band   188

1 Sweet flow - 'rets of the mar - tyr band, Plucked by the ty - rant's ruth - less hand Up - on the thresh - old of the morn, Like rose - buds by a temp - est torn;

2 First vic - tims for th'in - car - nate Lord, A ten - der flock to feel the sword; Be - side the al - tar's rud - dy ray, With palm and crown, you seemed to play.

3 Ah, what a - vailed King Her - od's wrath? He could not stop the Sav - ior's path. A - lone, while oth - ers mur - dered lay, In safe - ty Christ is borne a - way.

4 O Lord, the vir - gin - born, we sing E - ter - nal praise to you, our King, Whom with the Fa - ther we a - dore And Ho - ly Spir - it ev - er - more.

Text: Aurelius Prudentius Clemens, 348–c. 413, cento; tr. Henry W. Baker, 1821–77, alt.
Tune: Daniel Vetter, d. 1721

DAS WALT GOTT VATER
LM

189 Lord God, to You We All Give Praise

1 Lord God, to you we all give praise,
To you with joy our thanks we raise
For an - gel mul - ti - tudes that shine
In your great throne room crys - tal - line.

2 From them flow light and heav'n - ly grace
Re - flect - ing splen - dors of your face.
They heed your voice, they know it well,
In god - ly wis - dom they ex - cel.

3 They nev - er rest nor sleep as we;
Their whole de - light is but to be
With you, Lord Je - sus, and to keep
Your lit - tle flock, your lambs and sheep.

4 In - crease, we plead, our song of praise
For an - gel hosts that guard our days;
Teach us to cease - less - ly a - dore,
To serve as they do ev - er - more.

Text: Philipp Melanchthon, 1497–1560; German tr. Paul Eber, 1511–69; English tr.
    Emanuel Cronenwett, 1841–1931, alt.
Tune: J. Klug, Geistliche Lieder, 1533

KOMM, GOTT SCHÖPFER
L M

Stars of the Morning, So Gloriously Bright

1 Stars of the morn - ing, so glo - rious - ly bright,
2 These are your min - is - ters, these are your own,
3 Then, when the earth was first poised in mid space,
4 Still let them be with us, still let them fight,

Filled with ce - les - tial re - splen - dence and light,
Lord God of Sab - a - oth, near - est your throne;
Then, when the plan - ets first sped on their race,
Lord of an - gel - ic hosts, bat - tling for right,

These, where no dark - ness the glo - ry can dim,
These are your mes - sen - gers, these whom you send,
Then, when were end - ed the six days' em - ploy,
Till, where their an - thems they cease - less - ly pour,

Praise the Thrice Ho - ly One, serv - ing but him.
Help - ing your help - less ones, Help - er and Friend.
Then all the sons of God shout - ed for joy.
We with the an - gels may bow and a - dore.

Text: St. Joseph the Hymnographer, c. 800–83; tr. John M. Neale, 1818–66, alt.
Tune: Antiphoner, Paris, 1681

O QUANTA QUALIA
10 10 10 10

191

For All the Saints

1 For all the saints who from their la - bors rest,
2 You were their rock, their for - tress, and their might;
3 Oh, may your sol - diers, faith - ful, true, and bold,
7 But then there breaks a yet more glo - rious day: The
8 From earth's wide bounds, from o - cean's far - thest coast, Through

All who by faith be - fore the world con - fessed,
You, Lord, their cap - tain in the well - fought fight;
Fight as the saints who no - bly fought of old
saints tri - um - phant rise in bright ar - ray;
gates of pearl streams in the count - less host,

Your name, O Je - sus, be for - ev - er blest.
You, in the dark - ness drear, their one true light.
And win with them the vic - tor's crown of gold.
The King of glo - ry pass - es on his way.
Sing - ing to Fa - ther, Son, and Ho - ly Ghost:

Al - le - lu - ia! Al - le - lu - ia!

4 Oh, blest com - mu - nion, fel - low-ship di - vine, We fee - bly strug-gle,
5 And when the strife is fierce, the war - fare long, Steals on the ear the
6 The gold - en eve - ning bright - ens in the west; Soon, soon to faith - ful

they in glo - ry shine; Yet all are one with - in your great de -
dis - tant tri - umph song, And hearts are brave a - gain and arms are
war - riors comes their rest; Sweet is the calm of par - a - dise the

sign.
strong. Al - le - lu - ia! Al - le - lu - ia!
blest.

Text: William W. How, 1923-97, alt.
© Tune: Ralph Vaughan Williams, 1872-1958

SINE NOMINE
10 10 10 and alleluias

192 Behold a Host Arrayed in White

1 Be - hold a host ar - rayed in white Like thou - sand
2 On earth their work was not thought wise, But see them
3 O bless - ed saints, now take your rest; A thou - sand

snow - clad moun - tains bright. They stand with palms And
now in heav - en's eyes; Be - fore God's throne Of
times shall you be blest For keep - ing faith Firm

sing their psalms Be - fore the throne of light. These are the
pre - cious stone They shout their vic - t'ry cries. On earth they
un - to death And scorn - ing world - ly trust. For now you

saints who kept God's Word; They are the hon - ored
wept through bit - ter years; Now God has wiped a -
live at home with God; You har - vest seeds once

of the Lord. He is their prince Who drowned their sins,
way their tears, Trans-formed their strife To heav'n-ly life,
cast a-broad In tears and sighs. See with new eyes

So they were cleansed, re-stored. They now serve God both
And freed them from their fears. For now they have the
The pat-tern in the seed. The myr-iad an-gels

day and night; They sing their songs in end-less light. Their
best at last; They keep their sweet e-ter-nal feast. At
raise their song. O saints, sing with that hap-py throng; Lift

an-thems ring When they all sing With an-gels shin-ing bright.
God's right hand Our Lord com-mands; He is both host and guest.
up one voice; Let heav'n re-joice In our Re-deem-er's song!

© Text: Hans A. Brorson, 1694–1764; tr. Gracia Grindal, b. 1943, alt.
Tune: Norwegian folk tune, 17th cent.

DEN STORE HVIDE FLOK
P M

193 By All Your Saints in Warfare

1 By all your saints in war - fare, For all your saints at
2 *(Insert the stanza appropriate to the day.)*
3 Then let us praise the Fa - ther And wor - ship God the

rest, Your ho - ly name, O Je - sus, For - ev - er - more be
Son And sing to God the Spir - it, E - ter - nal Three in

blest! For you have won the bat - tle That they might wear the
One, Till all the ran - somed num - ber Fall down be - fore the

crown; And now they shine in glo - ry Re - flect - ed from your throne.
throne, As - crib - ing pow'r and glo - ry And praise to God a - lone.

Saints and martyrs (general)

4 Apostles, prophets, martyrs,
   And all the noble throng
Who wear the spotless raiment
   And raise the ceaseless song—
For these, passed on before us,
   We offer praises due
And, walking in their footsteps,
   Would live our lives for you.

St. Andrew, Apostle

5 All praise, O Lord, for Andrew,
   The first to welcome you,
Whose witness to his brother
   Named you Messiah true.
May we, with hearts kept open
   To you throughout the year,
Confess to friend and neighbor
   Your advent ever near.

St. Thomas, Apostle

6 All praise for your apostle
   Whose short-lived doubtings prove
Your perfect twofold nature
   And all your depth of love.
We who await your coming
   Desire your peace, O Lord;
Grant us true faith to know you,
   Made flesh, yet God and Lord.

St. Stephen, Deacon and Martyr

7 Praise for the first of martyrs
   Who saw you ready stand
To help in time of torment,
   To plead at God's right hand.
They share with him who, steadfast,
   In death their master own,
On earth the faithful witness,
   On high the martyr's crown.

St. John, Apostle and Evangelist

8 For your beloved disciple
   Exiled to Patmos' shore,
And for his faithful record,
   We praise you evermore.
Praise for the mystic vision
   His words to us unfold.
Instill in us his longing
   Your glory to behold.

The Holy Innocents, Martyrs

9 All praise for infant martyrs
   Whom your mysterious love
Called early from their warfare
   To share your home above.
O Rachel, cease your weeping;
   They rest from earthbound cares.
Lord, grant us hearts as guileless
   And crowns as bright as theirs.

The Confession of St. Peter

10 Praise for your great apostle
   So eager and so bold,
Thrice falling, yet repentant,
   Thrice charged to feed your fold.
Lord, make your pastors faithful
   To guard your flock from harm,
And hold them when they waver
   With your almighty arm.

The Conversion of St. Paul

11 All praise for light from heaven
   And for the voice of awe,
All praise for glorious versions
   The persecutor saw.
O Lord, for Paul's conversion
   We bless your name today;
Come, lighten all our darkness,
   And guide us on our way.

St. Matthias, Apostle

12 Lord, your abiding presence
   Mysterious made the choice;
For one in place of Judas
   The faithful now rejoice.
From all such false apostles
   Your holy Church defend,
And by your parting promise
   Be with us to the end.

Text: Horatio Bolton Nelson, 1823-1913, alt.
© Tune: English folk tune; coll., arr., and harm. Ralph Vaughan Williams, 1872-1958

KING'S LYNN
76 76 D

194   By All Your Saints in Warfare

1 By all your saints in war - fare, For all your saints at
2 *(Insert the stanza appropriate to the day.)*
3 Then let us praise the Fa - ther And wor - ship God the

rest, Your ho - ly name, O Je - sus, For - ev - er - more be

Son And sing to God the Spir - it, E - ter - nal Three in

blest! For you have won the bat - tle That they might wear the

One, Till all the ran - somed num - ber Fall down be - fore the

crown; And now they shine in glo - ry Re - flect - ed from your throne.

throne, As - crib - ing pow'r and glo - ry And praise to God a - lone.

St. Mark, Evangelist

13 For him, O Lord, we praise you,
   Whose fainting heart, made strong,
Poured forth his faithful Gospel
   To animate our song.
May we in all our weakness
   Receive your pow'r divine
And all as faithful branches
   Grow strong in you, the vine.

St. Philip and St. James, Apostles

14 We praise your name, for Philip,
   Blest guide to Greek and Jew,
And for young James the faithful,
   Who heard and followed you.
Oh, grant us grace to know you,
   The way, the truth, the life,
And wrestle with temptation
   Till victors in the strife.

The Nativity of St. John the Baptist

15 We praise you for the Baptist,
   Forerunner of the Word,
Our true Elijah, making
   A highway for the Lord.
The last and greatest prophet,
   He saw the dawning ray
Of light that grows in splendor
   Until the perfect day.

St. James the Elder, Apostle

16 For him, O Lord, we praise you,
   Who fell to Herod's sword.
He drank your cup of suff'ring
   And thus fulfilled your word.
Lord, curb our vain impatience
   For glory and for gain,
And nerve us for such suff'rings
   As glorify your name.

St. Bartholomew, Apostle

17 All praise for him whose candor
   Through all his doubt you saw
When Philip at the fig tree
   Disclosed you in the law.
Discern, beneath our surface,
   O Lord, what we can be,
That by your truth made guileless,
   Your glory we may see.

St. Matthew, Apostle and Evangelist

18 Praise, Lord, for him whose Gospel
   Your human life declared,
Who, worldly gain forsaking,
   Your path of suff'ring shared.
From all unrighteous mammon,
   Oh, raise our eyes anew
That we, whate'er our station,
   May rise and follow you.

St. Luke, Evangelist

19 For that beloved physician
   All praise, whose Gospel shows
The healer of the nations,
   The one who shares our woes.
Your wine and oil, O Savior,
   Upon our spirits pour,
And with true balm of Gilead
   Anoint us evermore.

St. Simon and St. Jude, Apostles

20 Praise, Lord, for your apostles
   Who sealed their faith today;
One love, one hope impelled them
   To tread the sacred way.
May we with zeal as earnest
   The faith of Christ maintain
And, foll'wing these our brothers,
   At length your rest attain.

Text: Horatio Bolton Nelson, 1823-1913, alt.
© *Tune: English folk tune; coll. Ralph Vaughan Williams, 1872-1958*

KING'S LYNN
76 76 D

195 For All Your Saints, O Lord

1 For all your saints, O Lord, Who strove in you to live,
2 For all your saints, O Lord, Who strove in you to die,
3 They all in life and death, With you, their Lord, in view,
4 For this your name we bless And hum - bly pray a - new

Who fol - lowed you, o - beyed, a - dored, Our grate-ful hymn re - ceive.
Who count-ed you their great re - ward, Ac - cept our thank - ful cry.
Learned from your Ho - ly Spir - it's breath To suf - fer and to do.
That we like them in ho - li - ness May live and die in you.

5 To God, the Father, Son,
  And Spirit, ever blest,
The One in Three, the Three in One,
  Be endless praise addressed.

Text: Richard Mant, 1776–1848, alt.
Tune: William H. Walter, 1825–93

FESTAL SONG
S M

196 When All Your Mercies, O My God

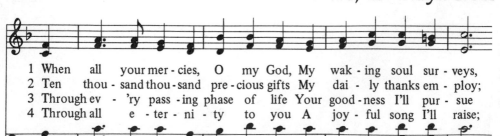

1 When all your mer - cies, O my God, My wak - ing soul sur - veys,
2 Ten thou - sand thou - sand pre - cious gifts My dai - ly thanks em - ploy;
3 Through ev - 'ry pass - ing phase of life Your good - ness I'll pur - sue
4 Through all e - ter - ni - ty to you A joy - ful song I'll raise;

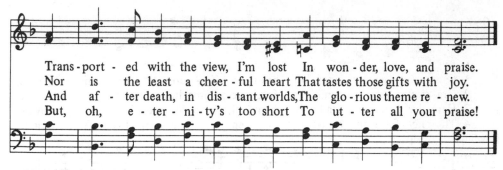

Trans - port - ed with the view, I'm lost In won - der, love, and praise.
Nor is the least a cheer - ful heart That tastes those gifts with joy.
And af - ter death, in dis - tant worlds, The glo - rious theme re - new.
But, oh, e - ter - ni - ty's too short To ut - ter all your praise!

Text: Joseph Addison, 1672–1719, alt.
Tune: attr. George Kirbye, c. 1560–1634

WINCHESTER OLD
C M

Lord, Open Now My Heart to Hear   197

1 Lord, o - pen now my heart to hear, And through your
2 Your Word it is that heals my heart, That makes me
3 To God the Fa - ther, God the Son, To God the

Word to me draw near; Pre - serve that Word in pu - ri -
whole in ev - 'ry part; Your Word of joy with - in me
Spir - it, three in one, Hon - or and praise for - ev - er

ty That I your child and heir may be.
sings, True peace and bless - ed - ness it brings.
be Now and through all e - ter - ni - ty!

© Text: Johannes Olearius, 1611–84; tr. Henry L. Lettermann, b. 1932
Tune: J. Klug, Geistliche Lieder, 1543

ERHALT UNS, HERR
L M

198 Open Now Thy Gates of Beauty

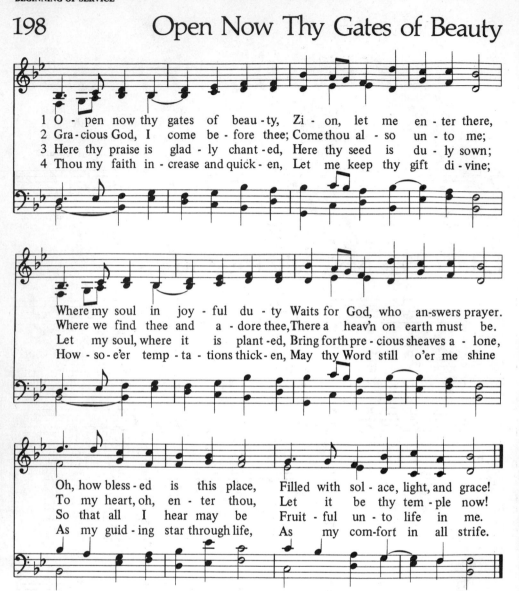

1 O - pen now thy gates of beau - ty, Zi - on, let me en - ter there,
2 Gra - cious God, I come be - fore thee; Come thou al - so un - to me;
3 Here thy praise is glad - ly chant - ed, Here thy seed is du - ly sown;
4 Thou my faith in - crease and quick - en, Let me keep thy gift di - vine;

Where my soul in joy - ful du - ty Waits for God, who an - swers prayer.
Where we find thee and a - dore thee, There a heav'n on earth must be.
Let my soul, where it is plant - ed, Bring forth pre - cious sheaves a - lone,
How - so - e'er temp - ta - tions thick - en, May thy Word still o'er me shine

Oh, how bless - ed is this place, Filled with sol - ace, light, and grace!
To my heart, oh, en - ter thou, Let it be thy tem - ple now!
So that all I hear may be Fruit - ful un - to life in me.
As my guid - ing star through life, As my com - fort in all strife.

5 Speak, O God, and I will hear thee,
    Let thy will be done indeed;
  May I undisturbed draw near thee
    While thou dost thy people feed.
  Here of life the fountain flows;
  Here is balm for all our woes.

Text: Benjamin Schmolck, 1672–1737; tr. Catherine Winkworth, 1829–78, alt.
Tune: Joachim Neander, 1650–80

UNSER HERRSCHER
87 87 77

We Worship You, O God of Might 199

1 We wor - ship you, O God of might,
2 Your faith - ful care your Church pro - tects
3 Your will is that your Church em - brace
4 A - round your throne the count - less throng

Great Lord of all, be - yond our sight!
And shields from harm, from sin's ef - fects
All peo - ple, ev - 'ry land and race,
At last in tri - umph swells the song

You make your Word in heav'n and earth be heard,
Till judg - ment day; your pow'r will be its stay.
That all may bring their praise to Christ and sing,
While cher - u - bim re - ply to ser - a - phim:

Ho - ly, ho - ly, ho - ly is God Most High!

© Text: Johan Olof Wallin, 1779–1836; tr. Joel W. Lundeen, b. 1918, alt.
Tune: Een ny Handbog, Rostock, 1529

VI LOVA DIG, O STORE GUD
8 8 10 10

200 This Is the Day the Lord Has Made

1 This is the day the Lord has made;
He calls the hours his own.
Let heav'n rejoice, let earth be glad,
Let praise surround the throne.

2 Today Christ rose and left the dead,
And Satan's empire fell.
Today the saints his triumphs spread,
They all his wonders tell.

3 Hosanna to the King of kings,
To David's holy son!
He helps us, he descends and brings
Salvation from the throne.

4 Blest be the Lord, who comes to us
With messages of grace;
Who comes in God his Father's name
To save our sinful race.

5 Hosanna in the highest strains
The church on earth can raise.
The highest heavens, where he reigns,
Will give him nobler praise.

Text: Isaac Watts, 1674–1748, alt.
Tune: Johann Crüger, 1598–1662

NUN DANKET ALL
C M

Lord Jesus Christ, Be Present Now 201

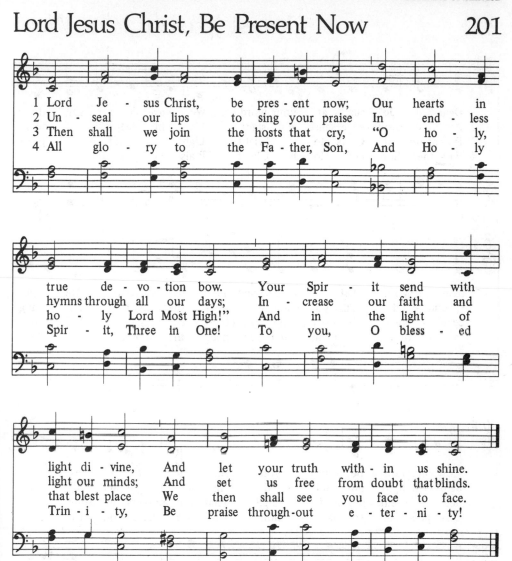

1 Lord Jesus Christ, be pres - ent now; Our hearts in
2 Un - seal our lips to sing your praise In end - less
3 Then shall we join the hosts that cry, "O ho - ly,
4 All glo - ry to the Fa - ther, Son, And Ho - ly

true de - vo - tion bow. Your Spir - it send with
hymns through all our days; In - crease our faith and
ho - ly Lord Most High!" And in the light of
Spir - it, Three in One! To you, O bless - ed

light di - vine, And let your truth with - in us shine.
light our minds; And set us free from doubt that blinds.
that blest place We then shall see you face to face.
Trin - i - ty, Be praise through-out e - ter - ni - ty!

Text: author unknown, 1648/51; tr. Catherine Winkworth, 1829-78, adapt.
Tune: Cantionale Germanicum, *Gochsheim,* 1628

HERR JESU CHRIST, DICH ZU UNS WEND
LM

202   Dearest Jesus, at Your Word

1 Dear-est Je-sus, at your word We have come a-gain to
2 All our knowl-edge, sense, and sight Lie in deep-est dark-ness
3 Ra-diance of God's glo-ry bright, Light of light from God pro-
4 Fa-ther, Son, and Ho-ly Ghost, Praise to you and ad-o-

hear you; Let our thoughts and hearts be stirred And in
shroud-ed Till your Spir-it breaks the night, Fill-ing
ceed-ing, Je-sus, send your bless-ed light; Help our
ra-tion! Grant us what we need the most: Your blest

glow-ing faith be near you As the prom-is-es here
us with light un-cloud-ed. All good thoughts and all good
hear-ing, speak-ing, heed-ing, That our prayers and songs may
Gos-pel's con-so-la-tion While we here on earth a-

giv-en Draw us whol-ly up to heav-en.
liv-ing Come but by your gra-cious giv-ing.
please you As with grate-ful hearts we praise you.
wait you Till in heav'n with praise we greet you.

Text: Tobias Clausnitzer, 1619–84, sts. 1-3; Berliner Gesangbuch, 1707, st. 4;
    tr. Catherine Winkworth, 1829–78, adapt.
Tune: Johann R. Ahle, 1625–73

LIEBSTER JESU, WIR SIND HIER
78 78 88

O Day of Rest and Gladness 203

1 O day of rest and glad - ness, O day of joy and light,
2 On you at earth's cre - a - tion The light first had its birth;
3 To - day on wea - ry na - tions The heav'n-ly man - na falls;
4 New gra - ces ev - er gain - ing From this our day of rest,

O balm for care and sad - ness, Most beau - ti - ful, most bright:
On you for our sal - va - tion Christ rose from depths of earth;
To ho - ly con - vo - ca - tions The sil - ver trum - pet calls,
We reach the rest re - main - ing To spir - its of the blest.

On you the high and low - ly, Through a - ges joined in tune,
On you our Lord vic - to - rious The Spir - it sent from heav'n;
Where Gos-pel light is glow - ing With pure and ra - diant beams
To Ho - ly Ghost be prais - es, To Fa - ther, and to Son;

Sing, "Ho - ly, ho - ly, ho - ly," To the great God tri - une.
And thus on you, most glo - rious, A three - fold light was giv'n.
And liv - ing wa - ter flow - ing With soul - re - fresh - ing streams.
The Church its voice up - rais - es To you, blest Three in One.

Text: Christopher Wordsworth, 1807-85, alt.
Tune: Gesangbuch der Herzogl. Hofkapelle, Württemberg, 1784

ELLACOMBE
76 76 D

204 Come, Let Us Join Our Cheerful Songs

1 Come, let us join our cheer - ful songs With
2 "Wor - thy the Lamb that died," they cry, "To
3 Je - sus is wor - thy to re - ceive Hon -
4 Let all cre - a - tion join in one To

an - gels round the throne; Ten thou-sand thou - sand
be ex - alt - ed thus!" "Wor - thy the Lamb," our
or and pow'r di - vine; And bless - ings more than
bless the sa - cred name Of him who sits up -

are their tongues, But all their joys are one.
lips re - ply, "For he was slain for us!"
we can give Be, Lord, for - ev - er thine.
on the throne And to a - dore the Lamb.

Text: Isaac Watts, 1674-1748
Tune: Johann Crüger, 1598-1662

NUN DANKET ALL
C M

Oh, Sing Jubilee to the Lord

205

1 Oh, sing ju-bi-lee to the Lord, ev - 'ry land:
2 He made us his own and has giv - en us breath;
3 Oh, come to his feast with thanks-giv - ing and praise;
4 His mer - cy is ours; he is Lord o - ver all;

Glo - ry be to God! Oh, serve him with glad - ness as
Glo - ry be to God! The sheep of his pas - ture, we
Glo - ry be to God! Give glo - ry to him, and your
Glo - ry be to God! May all gen - er - a - tions find

in his halls we stand;
need not fear our death;
bright - est ban-ners raise;   Sing prais - es to God out of Zi - on!
pow - er in his call;

© Text: Ulrik V. Koren, 1826–1910; tr. Lutheran Book of Worship, 1978
Tune: Erik C. Hoff, 1832–94

GUDS MENIGHED, SYNG
11 5 12 9

206 God Himself Is Present

1 God him-self is pres-ent; Let us now a-dore him And with awe ap-
2 God him-self is pres-ent; Hear the harps re-sound-ing; See the hosts the
3 Light of light e-ter-nal, All things pen-e-trat-ing, For your rays our
4 Come, ce-les-tial Be-ing, Make our hearts your dwell-ing, Ev-'ry car-nal

pear be-fore him. God is in his tem-ple; All with-in keep si-lence,
throne sur-round-ing! "Ho-ly, ho-ly, ho-ly!" Hear the hymn as-cend-ing,
soul is wait-ing, As the ten-der flow-ers, Will-ing-ly un-fold-ing,
thought dis-pel-ling. By your Ho-ly Spir-it Sanc-ti-fy us tru-ly,

Pros-trate lie with deep-est rev-'rence. Him a-lone God we own,
Songs of saints and an-gels blend-ing. Bow your ear To us here:
To the sun their fac-es hold-ing: E-ven so Would we do,
Teach-ing us to love you on-ly. Where we go Here be-low,

Him, our God and Sav-ior; Praise his name for-ev-er!
Hear, O Christ, the prais-es That your Church now rais-es.
Light from you ob-tain-ing, Strength to serve you gain-ing.
Let us bow be-fore you And in truth a-dore you.

© Text: Gerhard Tersteegen, 1697–1769; tr. composite
Tune: Joachim Neander, 1650–80

WUNDERBARER KÖNIG
668 668 33 66

To Your Temple, Lord, I Come

1 To your tem-ple, Lord, I come, For it is my wor-ship home.
2 I through him am rec-on-ciled, I through him be-come your child.
3 While your glo-rious praise is sung, Touch my lips, un-loose my tongue
4 While the prayers of saints as-cend, God of love, to mine at-tend.

This earth has no bet-ter place, Here I see my Sav-ior's face.
Ab-ba, Fa-ther, give me grace In your courts your love to trace.
That my joy-ful soul may bless Christ the Lord, my Righ-teous-ness.
Hear me, for your Spir-it pleads; Hear, for Je-sus in-ter-cedes.

5 While I listen to your Law,
   Fill my soul with humble awe
   Till your Gospel bring to me
   Life and immortality.

6 While your ministers proclaim
   Peace and pardon in your name,
   Through their voice, by faith, may I
   Hear you speaking from the sky.

7 From your house when I return,
   May my heart within me burn,
   And at evening let me say,
   "I have walked with God today."

Text: James Montgomery, *1771–1854, alt.*
Tune: J. A. Freylinghausen, Geistreiches Gesang-Buch, *1704*

GOTT SEI DANK
77 77

208   Lamb of God, Pure and Sinless

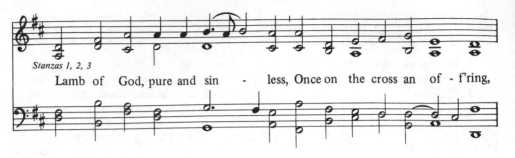

Stanzas 1, 2, 3

Lamb of God, pure and sin - less, Once on the cross an of - f'ring,

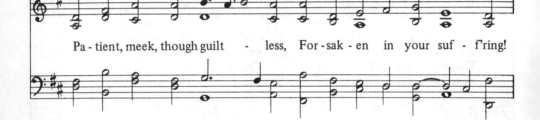

Pa - tient, meek, though guilt - less, For-sak-en in your suf - f'ring!

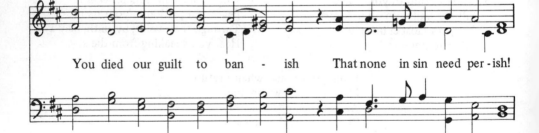

You died our guilt to ban - ish   That none in sin need per - ish!

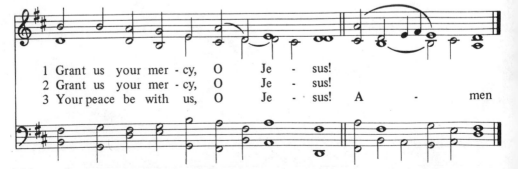

1 Grant us your mer - cy,   O   Je - sus!
2 Grant us your mer - cy,   O   Je - sus!
3 Your peace be with us,   O   Je - sus!   A - men

© Text: Nikolaus Decius, 1485–aft. 1546; tr. Joel W. Lundeen, b. 1918
Tune: Nikolaus Decius, 1485–aft. 1546

O LAMM GOTTES, UNSCHULDIG
77 67 778

Kyrie, God Father

Ky - ri - e, God Fa - ther in heav'n a - bove, You a - bound in gra - cious love,

Of all things the mak - er and pre - serv - er. E - le - i - son, e - le - i - son!

Ky - ri - e, O Christ, our king, Sal - va - tion for all you came to bring.

Hymn continues on next page

O Lord Je - sus, God's own Son, Our me - di - a - tor at the heav'n - ly throne,

Hear our cry and grant our sup - pli - ca - tion. E - le - i - son, e - le - i - son!

Ky - ri - e, O God the Ho - ly Ghost, Guard our faith, the

gift we need the most,   And bless our life's last hour   That we leave this

sin-ful world with glad - ness.   E - le - i - son, e - le - i - son!

Text: Latin, c. 1100; tr. W. Gustave Polack, 1890–1950, alt.
Tune: "Kyrie fons bonitatis," c. 800, adapt.

KYRIE, GOTT VATER
P M

210 All Glory Be to God Alone

1 All glo-ry be to God a-lone, For-ev-er-more the
2 We praise you, God; your name we bless And wor-ship you in
3 Lord God, our King on heav-en's throne, Our Fa-ther, the Al-
4 You take the whole world's sin a-way; Have mer-cy on us,

High-est One. He is our sin-ful ra-ce's friend; His
hum-ble-ness; From day to day we glo-ri-fy Our
might-y One. O Lord, the Sole-be-got-ten One, Lord
Lord, we pray. You take the whole world's sin a-way; Oh,

grace and peace to us ex-tend. May hu-man-kind see his good-
ev-er-last-ing God on high. Your splen-dor's glo-rious light we
Je-sus Christ, the Fa-ther's Son, True God from all e-ter-ni-
lis-ten to the prayer we say. From God's right hand, oh, send to-

will, May hearts with deep thanks-giv-ing fill.
sing, And to your throne our thanks we bring.
ty, O Lamb of God, to you we flee.
day Your mer-cy on us, Lord, we pray.

5 You are the only Holy One,
  The Lord of all things, you alone.
  O Jesus Christ, we glorify
  You and the Spirit, Lord Most High;
  With him you evermore will be
  One in the Father's majesty.

6 This truth divine, this mystery
  The angels sing adoringly.
  By all creation, far and wide,
  You, Lord, are ever glorified;
  For all your people sing your praise
  Now and through everlasting days.

Text: Martin Luther, 1483-1546; tr. W. Gustave Polack, 1890-1950, alt.
Tune: Kirchengesangbuch, Strassburg, 1541

ALL EHR UND LOB
88 88 88

My Soul Now Magnifies the Lord 211

1 My soul now mag - ni - fies the Lord; My spir - it leaps
2 For he a - lone who shows such might Has done a - maz -
3 His arm is strong; his strength is great. He scat - ters those
4 He feeds the hun - gry as his own; The wealth - y leave

for joy in him. He keeps me in his kind re -
ing things to me. His mer - cy flows; his name like
of proud in - tent And casts them down from high es -
with emp - ty hands. He gives his help to Is - ra -

gard, And I am blest for time to come.
light Re - mains in time per - pet - ual - ly.
tate, Then gives the low his nour - ish - ment.
el; His gra - cious prom - ise al - ways stands.

© *Text: Luke 1:46-55; versification, Stephanie K. Frey, b. 1952*
  Tune and bass line: Orlando Gibbons, 1583-1625

SONG 34
LM

We All Believe
in One True God, Father

212

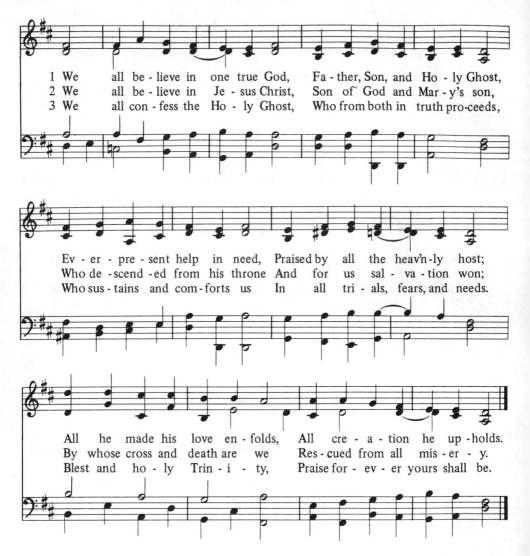

1 We   all be - lieve in   one true God,   Fa - ther, Son, and Ho - ly Ghost,
2 We   all be - lieve in   Je - sus Christ,   Son of God and Mar - y's son,
3 We   all con - fess the Ho - ly Ghost,   Who from both in truth pro - ceeds,

Ev - er - pre - sent help in need, Praised by all the heav'n - ly host;
Who de - scend - ed from his throne And for us sal - va - tion won;
Who sus - tains and com - forts us   In   all tri - als, fears, and needs.

All he made his love en - folds, All cre - a - tion he up - holds.
By whose cross and death are we   Res - cued from all mis - er - y.
Blest and ho - ly Trin - i - ty,   Praise for - ev - er yours shall be.

Text: Tobias Clausnitzer, 1619–84; tr. Catherine Winkworth, 1829–78, alt.
Tune: Kirchengesangbuch, Darmstadt, 1699

WIR GLAUBEN ALL AN EINEN GOTT
87 77 77

We All Believe in One True God, Maker

1 We all be - lieve in one true God,
2 We all be - lieve in Christ, his Son,
3 We all con - fess the Ho - ly Ghost,

Mak - er of the earth and heav - en. "Our Fa-ther," he would
Whom as Lord we are ad - dress - ing, Of e - qual God-head,
Who grants com - fort, grace, and pow - er. He, with the Fa - ther

have us say; Chil - dren's place to us has giv - en.
throne, and might, Source of ev - 'ry grace and bless - ing.
and the Son, Robes us for the tri - umph hour, . . .

Hymn continues on next page

He has pledged al - ways to feed us, Bod - y, soul, to
Born of Ma - ry, vir - gin moth - er, By the pow - er
Keeps the Church, his own cre - a - tion, In true u - ni -

keep, to nour - ish. Through all e - vil he will lead us,
of the Spir - it, Made true man, our hu - man broth - er
ty of spir - it; Here for - give - ness and sal - va - tion

Guards us well that we may flour - ish. He cares
Through whom son - ship we in - her - it; He, cru -
Come to us through Je - sus' mer - it. The bod -

for us   by   day and night   And
ci - fied for   sin - ful men,   Through
y ris'n, we   then shall be   In

gov - erns all things by his might.
God's pow'r rose to   life a - gain.
life with God e - ter - nal - ly.   A -   men,

OR

a -   men   A -   men

OR

© Text: Martin Luther, 1483–1546; tr. F. Samuel Janzow, b. 1913
Tune: Latin credo, c. 1300

WIR GLAUBEN ALL
8 8 8 8 8 8 8 8 88

214 Isaiah, Mighty Seer, in Spirit Soared

I - sa-iah, might-y seer, in spir-it soared And saw en-throned in

maj-es-ty the Lord, A - round whose throne shone glo-ry from his face,

Whose robe of light filled all the ho-ly place. Be - side the throne two

six - winged ser - a - phim, Who with their wings showed rev-er -ence to him.

With two each hid his face in ho- ly awe, With two his feet, these

an - gels with - out flaw, And with the third wing pair as - cend - ed high

Hymn continues on next page

To span the heav-ens with this might-y cry: "Ho - ly is God, the

Lord of Sab - a - oth! Ho - ly is God, the Lord of Sab - a - oth!

Ho - ly is God, the Lord of Sab - a - oth! His grace and might and

glo - ry fill the earth!" Then shook the roof beam and the lin - tel

stone, And smoke of in - cense swirled a - round the throne.

© Text: Martin Luther, 1483–1546; tr. F. Samuel Janzow, b. 1913, alt.
Tune: Martin Luther, 1483–1546

JESAIA, DEM PROPHETEN
P M

215 All Glory Be to God on High

1 All glo - ry be to God on high And thanks to
2 O Fa - ther, for your lord - ship true We give you
3 Lord Je - sus Christ, the on - ly Son Of God, cre -
4 O Ho - ly Spir - it, per - fect gift, Who brings us

him for - ev - er! What-ev - er Sa - tan's host may try,
praise and hon - or; We wor - ship you, we trust in you,
a - tion's au - thor, Re - deem - er of your wan - d'ring ones,
con - so - la - tion: To men and wom - en saved by Christ

God foils their dark en - deav - or. He bends his ear
We give you thanks for - ev - er. Your will is per -
And source of all true plea - sure: O Lamb of God,
As - sure your in - spi - ra - tion. Through sick - ness, need,

to ev - 'ry call And of - fers peace, good -
fect, and your might Re - lent - less - ly con -
O Lord di - vine, Con - form our lives to
and bit - ter death, Grant us your warm, life -

will   to   all,   And calms   the   trou - bled spir   -   it.
firms   the right;   Your lord - ship is   our bless   -   ing.
your   de - sign,   And   on   us   all   have mer   -   cy.
giv - ing breath;   Our lives   are   in   your keep   -   ing.

© *Text: Nikolaus Decius, c. 1485–aft. 1546; tr. Gilbert E. Doan, b. 1930*
Tune: attr. Nikolaus Decius, c. 1485–aft. 1546.

ALLEIN GOTT IN DER HÖH
87 87 887

Almighty Father, Bless the Word   216

1 Al - might - y Fa - ther, bless the   Word   Which through your
2 We praise you for the means of   grace As   home - ward

grace we   now   have heard.   Oh,   may the pre - cious seed   take
now our   steps we   trace.   Grant, Lord, that we   who wor - shiped

root, Spring up,   and   bear a - bun - dant fruit!
here May   all   at   last in   heav'n ap - pear.

Text: author unknown, Scandinavian; tr. The Lutheran Hymnary, 1913
Tune: Louis Bourgeois, c. 1510–c. 1561

OLD HUNDREDTH
L M

217 On What Has Now Been Sown

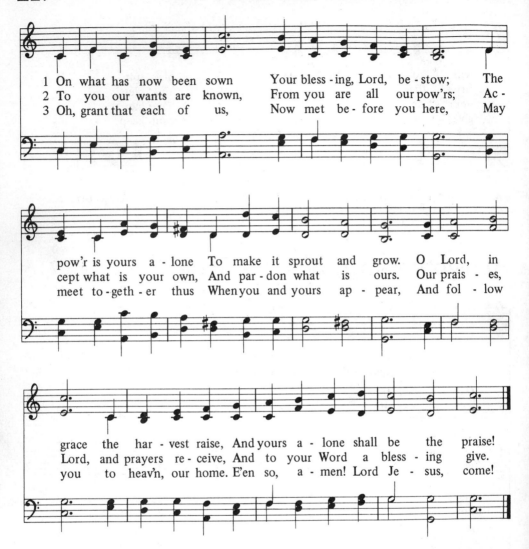

1 On what has now been sown Your bless-ing, Lord, be-stow; The
2 To you our wants are known, From you are all our pow'rs; Ac-
3 Oh, grant that each of us, Now met be-fore you here, May

pow'r is yours a-lone To make it sprout and grow. O Lord, in
cept what is your own, And par-don what is ours. Our prais-es,
meet to-geth-er thus When you and yours ap-pear, And fol-low

grace the har-vest raise, And yours a-lone shall be the praise!
Lord, and prayers re-ceive, And to your Word a bless-ing give.
you to heav'n, our home. E'en so, a-men! Lord Je-sus, come!

Text: John Newton, 1725–1807, alt.
Tune: John Darwall, 1731–89

DARWALL'S 148TH
66 66 88

Lord, Dismiss Us with Your Blessing 218

1 Lord, dis - miss us with your bless - ing, Fill our hearts with
2 Thanks we give and a - dor - a - tion For your Gos - pel's
3 Sav - ior, when your love shall call us From our strug - gling

joy and peace; Let us each, your love pos - sess - ing,
joy - ful sound. May the fruits of your sal - va - tion
pil - grim way, Let not fear of death ap - pall us,

Tri - umph in re - deem - ing grace. Oh, re - fresh us;
In our hearts and lives a - bound. Ev - er faith - ful,
Glad your sum - mons to o - bey. May we ev - er,

oh, re - fresh us, Trav - 'ling through this wil - der - ness.
ev - er faith - ful To your truth may we be found.
may we ev - er Reign with you in end - less day.

Text: attr. John Fawcett, 1740–1817, sts. 1–2; Godfrey Thring, 1823–1903, st. 3, alt.
Tune: Henry T. Smart, 1813–79

REGENT SQUARE
87 87 87

219 Grant Peace, We Pray, in Mercy, Lord

Grant peace, we pray, in mer-cy, Lord; Peace in our time, oh, send us!

For there is none on earth but you, None oth-er to de-fend us.

You on-ly, Lord, can fight for us. A - men

© Text: medieval antiphon, adapt. Martin Luther, 1483–1546; tr. Laudamus, 1952
Tune: mode I; Jobst Gutknecht, Kirchen gesenge, Nürnberg, 1531

VERLEIH UNS FRIEDEN
87 87 8

Guide Me Ever, Great Redeemer

1 Guide me ev - er, great Re - deem - er, Pil - grim through this
2 O - pen now the crys - tal foun - tain Where the heal - ing
3 When I tread the verge of Jor - dan, Bid my anx - ious

bar - ren land. I am weak, but you are might - y; Hold me
wa - ters flow; Let the fire and cloud - y pil - lar Lead me
fears sub - side; Death of death and hell's de - struc - tion, Land me

with your pow'r - ful hand. Bread of heav - en, bread of heav - en,
all my jour - ney through. Strong de - liv - 'rer, strong de - liv - 'rer,
safe on Ca - naan's side. Songs and prais - es, songs and prais - es

Feed me now and ev - er - more; Feed me now and ev - er - more.
Shield me with your might - y arm; Shield me with your might - y arm.
I will raise for - ev - er - more; I will raise for - ev - er - more.

Text: William Williams, 1717–91; tr. composite, alt.
© Tune: John Hughes, 1873–1932

CWM RHONDDA
87 87 877

221 Savior, Again to Your Dear Name

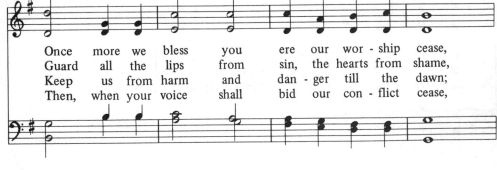

1 Sav - ior, a - gain to your dear name we raise
2 Grant us your peace up - on our home - ward way;
3 Grant us your peace, Lord, through the com - ing night;
4 Grant us your peace through - out our earth - ly life,

With one ac - cord our part - ing hymn of praise;
With you be - gan, with you shall end the day;
For us trans - form its dark - ness in - to light.
Our balm in sor - row and our stay in strife;

Once more we bless you ere our wor - ship cease,
Guard all the lips from sin, the hearts from shame,
Keep us from harm and dan - ger till the dawn;
Then, when your voice shall bid our con - flict cease,

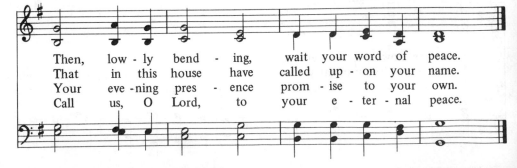

Then, low - ly bend - ing, wait your word of peace.
That in this house have called up - on your name.
Your eve - ning pres - ence prom - ise to your own.
Call us, O Lord, to your e - ter - nal peace.

Text: John Ellerton, 1826–93, alt.
Tune: Edward J. Hopkins, 1818–1901

ELLERS
10 10 10 10

How Blest Are They
Who Hear God's Word

1 How blest are they who hear God's Word, Who keep in faith what
2 Through sor-row's night my sun shall be God's Word, a trea-sure
3 To-day his voice with joy I heard And fed up-on his

they have heard, Who dai-ly grow in wis-dom. From light to
dear to me, My shield and buck-ler ev - er. My ti-tle
ho-ly Word, That bread so free-ly giv - en. May grace a

light they shall in-crease And jour-ney on life's way in peace;
as his child and heir The Fa-ther's hand has writ-ten there,
strong-er faith main-tain So that its fruit shall all re-main

They have the oil of glad-ness To soothe their pain and sad-ness.
His prom-ise fail-ing nev-er: "You will be mine for-ev-er."
When my ac-count is giv - en Be-fore God's throne in heav-en.

© Text: Johan Nordahl Brun, 1745–1816; tr. Service Book and Hymnal, 1958, alt.
Tune: H. Thomissön, Den danske Psalmebog, 1569

OM HIMMERIGES RIGE
8 8 7 88 77

223 To Jordan Came the Christ, Our Lord

1 To Jordan came the Christ, our Lord, To do his Father's
2 Oh, hear and mark the message well, For God himself has
3 These truths on Jordan's banks were shown By mighty word and
4 There stood the Son of God in love, His grace to us ex-

pleasure; Baptized by John, the Father's Word Was
spoken. Let faith, not doubt, among us dwell And
wonder. The Father's voice from heav'n came down, Which
tending; The Holy Spirit like a dove Up-

giv-en us to treasure. This heav'nly washing now shall be
so re-ceive this token. Our Lord here with his Word endows
we do well to ponder: "This man is my belov-ed Son,
on the scene descending; The tri-une God assuring us,

A cleansing from transgression And by his blood and agony
Pure water, freely flowing. God's Holy Spirit here avows
In whom my heart has pleasure. Him you must hear, and him alone,
With promises compelling, That in our baptism he will thus

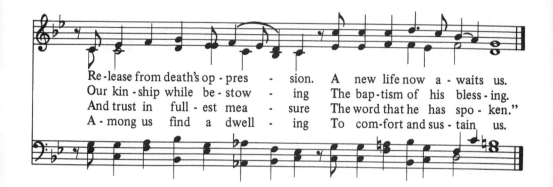

Re-lease from death's op - pres - sion. A new life now a - waits us.
Our kin - ship while be - stow - ing The bap-tism of his bless - ing.
And trust in full - est mea - sure The word that he has spo - ken."
A - mong us find a dwell - ing To com-fort and sus - tain us.

5 To his disciples spoke the Lord,
   "Go out to ev'ry nation,
And bring to them the living Word
   And this my invitation:
Let ev'ryone abandon sin
   And come in true contrition
To be baptized and thereby win
   Full pardon and remission
   And heav'nly bliss inherit."

6 But woe to those who cast aside
   This grace so freely given;
They shall in sin and shame abide
   And to despair be driven.
For born in sin, their works must fail,
   Their striving saves them never;
Their pious acts do not avail,
   And they are lost forever,
   Eternal death their portion.

7 All that the mortal eye beholds
   Is water as we pour it.
Before the eye of faith unfolds
   The pow'r of Jesus' merit,
For here it sees the crimson flood
   To all our ills bring healing;
The wonders of his precious blood
   The love of God revealing,
   Assuring his own pardon.

© Text: Martin Luther, 1483–1546; tr. Elizabeth Quitmeyer, b. 1911, alt.
Tune: Johann Walter, Geystliche gesangk Buchleyn, 1524

CHRIST, UNSER HERR
87 87 87 877

224 Baptized into Your Name Most Holy

1 Bap-tized in - to your name most ho - ly, O Fa - ther, Son, and
2 My lov - ing Fa - ther, here you take me Hence-forth to be your
3 O faith - ful God, you nev - er fail me; Your cov-'nant sure - ly
4 All that I am and love most dear - ly, Re - ceive it all, O

Ho - ly Ghost, I claim a place, though weak and low - ly,
child and heir; My faith - ful Sav - ior, here you make me
will a - bide. Let not e - ter - nal death as - sail me
Lord, from me. Oh, let me make my vows sin - cere - ly,

A - mong your seed, your cho - sen host. Bur - ied with Christ and
The fruit of all your sor - rows share; O Ho - ly Ghost, you
Should I trans-gress it on my side! Have mer - cy when I
And help me your own child to be! Let noth - ing that I

dead to sin, I have your Spir - it now with - in.
com - fort me Though threat-'ning clouds a - round I see.
come de - filed; For - give, lift up, re - store your child.
am or own Serve an - y will but yours a - lone.

Text: Johann J. Rambach, 1693-1735; tr. Catherine Winkworth, 1829-78, alt.
Tune: Kornelius Heinrich Dretzel, 1697-1775

O DASS ICH TAUSEND ZUNGEN HÄTTE
98 98 88

All Who Believe and Are Baptized

1 All who be - lieve and are bap - tized Shall see the Lord's sal - va - tion;
2 With one ac - cord, O God, we pray, Grant us your Ho - ly Spir - it;

Bap - tized in - to the death of Christ, They are a new
Help us in our in - fir - mi - ty Through Je - sus' blood

cre - a - tion; Through Christ's re - demp - tion they will stand A -
and mer - it; Grant us to grow in grace each day By

mong the glo - rious heav'n - ly band Of ev - 'ry tribe and na - tion.
ho - ly Bap - tism that we may E - ter - nal life in - her - it.

Text: Thomas H. Kingo, 1634–1703; tr. George A. T. Rygh, 1860–1943, alt.
Tune: Etlich Christlich lider, Wittenberg, 1524

ES IST DAS HEIL
87 87 887

226

Dearest Jesus, We Are Here

1 Dear-est Je - sus, we are here, Glad - ly your com-mand o-
2 Your com-mand is clear and plain, And we would o - bey it
3 This is why we come to you, In our arms this in - fant
4 Gra - cious head, your mem-ber own; Shep -herd, take your lamb and

bey - ing. With this child we now draw near In re-
du - ly: "You must all be born a - gain, Heart and
bear - ing; Lord, to us your glo - ry show; Let this
feed it; Prince of Peace, make here your throne; Way of

sponse to your own say - ing That to you it shall be
life re - new - ing tru - ly, Born of wa - ter and the
child, your mer - cy shar - ing, In your arms be shield - ed
life, to heav - en lead it; Pre - cious vine, let noth - ing

giv - en As a child and heir of heav - en.
Spir - it, And my king - dom thus in - her - it."
ev - er, Yours on earth and yours for - ev - er.
sev - er From your side this branch for - ev - er.

5 Now into your heart we pour
   Prayers that from our hearts proceeded.
  Our petitions heav'nward soar;

May our fond desires be heeded!
Write the name we now have given;
Write it in the book of heaven!

Text: Benjamin Schmolck, 1672–1737; tr. Catherine Winkworth, 1829–78, alt.
Tune: Johann R. Ahle, 1625–73

LIEBSTER JESU, WIR SIND HIER
78 78 88

This Child We Now Present to You   227

1 This child we now pre-sent to you, O gra-cious God; its
2 Oh, may your Spir-it gent-ly draw Its will-ing soul to
3 We too be-fore your gra-cious sight Once shared the blest bap-
4 Grant that with true and faith-ful heart We still may act the

heart make new; Shield it from sin and threat-'ning
keep your Law! May vir-tue, pi-e-ty, and
tis-mal rite; Its cov-e-nant we here re-
Chris-tian's part, Cheered by each prom-ise you have

wrong, And let your love its life pro-long.
truth Dawn e-ven with its dawn-ing youth!
new With love and thanks and praise to you.
giv'n And la-b'ring for the prize in heav'n.

Text: author unknown, German, 18th cent.; tr. Samuel Gilman, 1791–1858, alt.
Tune: Lowell Mason, 1792–1872

UXBRIDGE
L M

228 Our Children Jesus Calls

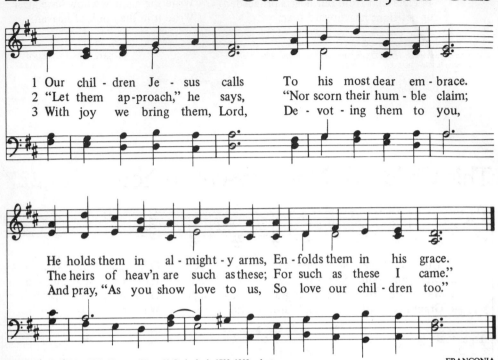

1 Our chil - dren Je - sus calls To his most dear em - brace.
2 "Let them ap-proach," he says, "Nor scorn their hum - ble claim;
3 With joy we bring them, Lord, De - vot - ing them to you,

He holds them in al - might - y arms, En - folds them in his grace.
The heirs of heav'n are such as these; For such as these I came."
And pray, "As you show love to us, So love our chil - dren too."

Text: Philip Doddridge, 1702–51, cento; Henry U. Onderdonk, 1789–1858, adapt.
Tune: Johann B. König, 1691–1758, adapt.

FRANCONIA
S M

229 Jesus Sinners Will Receive

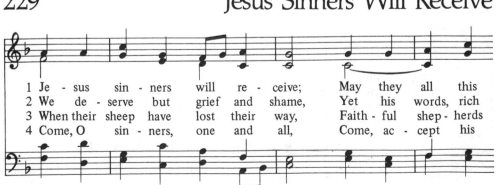

1 Je - sus sin - ners will re - ceive; May they all this
2 We de - serve but grief and shame, Yet his words, rich
3 When their sheep have lost their way, Faith - ful shep - herds
4 Come, O sin - ners, one and all, Come, ac - cept his

say - ing pon - der Who in sin's de - lu - sions
grace re - veal - ing, Par - don, peace, and life pro-
go to seek them; Je - sus watch - es all who
in - vi - ta - tion; Come, o - bey his gra - cious

live And from God and heav - en wan - der! Here is
claim. Here our ills have per - fect heal - ing; We with
stray, Faith-ful - ly to find and take them In his
call, Come and take his free sal - va - tion! Firm - ly

hope for all who grieve:
hum - ble hearts be - lieve
arms that they may live—   Je - sus sin - ners will re - ceive.
in these words be - lieve:

5 Jesus sinners will receive.
   Even me he has forgiven;
And when I this earth must leave,
   I shall find an open heaven.
Dying, still to him I cleave—
Jesus sinners will receive.

Text: Erdmann Neumeister, *1671–1756; tr.* The Lutheran Hymnal, *1941, alt.*
Tune: Johann Ulich, *1634–1712*

MEINEN JESUM LASS ICH NICHT
78 78 77

230 From Depths of Woe I Cry to You

1 From depths of woe I cry to you. O Lord, my
2 Your grace and love a - lone a - vail To blot out
3 In God I an - chor all my trust, Dis - card - ing
4 Though help de - lays un - til the night Or waits till

voice is try - ing To reach your heart and, Lord, break
sin with par - don. In your gaze our best ef - forts
my own mer - it. His love holds firm; I there - fore
morn - ing wak - en, My heart shall nev - er doubt his

through With these my cries and sigh - ing. If you
pale, De - vel - op pride, and hard - en. Be - fore
must His full - est grace in - her - it. He tells
might Nor think it - self for - sak - en. All you

keep re - cord of our sin And hold a - gainst us
your throne no one can boast That he es - caped sin's
me, and my heart has heard, The stead - fast prom - ise
who are God's own in - deed, Born of the Spir - it's

what we've been, Who then can stand be - fore you?
dead - ly coast. Our ha - ven is your mer - cy.
of his Word, That he's my help and ha - ven.
Gos - pel seed, A - wait his prom - ised res - cue.

5 Though sins arise like dunes of sand,
   God's mercy-tides submerge them.
   Like oceans pouring from his hand,
   Strong flows the grace to purge them.

Our shepherd will his Israel lead
To uplands out of every need
And ransom us from sinning.

© Text: Martin Luther, 1483–1546; tr. F. Samuel Janzow, b. 1913, alt.
Tune: Martin Luther, 1483–1546

AUS TIEFER NOT I
87 87 887

Lord Jesus, Think on Me   231

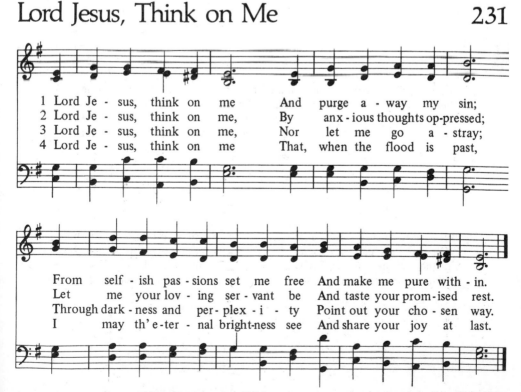

1 Lord Je - sus, think on me And purge a - way my sin;
2 Lord Je - sus, think on me, By anx - ious thoughts op-pressed;
3 Lord Je - sus, think on me, Nor let me go a - stray;
4 Lord Je - sus, think on me That, when the flood is past,

From self - ish pas - sions set me free And make me pure with - in.
Let me your lov - ing ser - vant be And taste your prom - ised rest.
Through dark - ness and per - plex - i - ty Point out your cho - sen way.
I may th' e - ter - nal bright-ness see And share your joy at last.

Text: Synesius of Cyrene, c. 370/375–c. 414; tr. Allen W. Chatfield, 1808–96, alt.
Tune: William Daman, The Psalmes of David, 1579

SOUTHWELL
S M

232 Alas, My God, My Sins Are Great

1 A-las, my God, my sins are great, My con-science
2 Were I to flee in my de-spair In some lone
3 I must, O Lord, by you be sought; Oh, pit-y
4 If pain and woe must fol-low sin, Then be my

must up-braid me; And now I find that in my
spot to hide me, My grief would still be with me
and re-store me. Just God, make not your wrath my
path still rough-er. Here spare me not; if heav'n I

strait No hu-man pow'r can aid me.
there And peace still be de-nied me.
lot; Your Son has suf-fered for me.
win, On earth I glad-ly suf-fer.

5 But curb my heart, forgive me still,
   Oh, make my patience firmer;
For they ignore your kindly will
   Who at your chast'nings murmur.

6 All that you do is for my best;
   Your grace will help me bear it
If but at last I see your rest
   And with my Savior share it.

Text: Johann Major, 1564-1654; tr. Catherine Winkworth, 1829-78, alt.
Tune: Christoph Peter, Andachts-Zymbeln, Freyberg, 1655

ACH GOTT UND HERR
447 447

Lord, to You I Make Confession

1 Lord, to you I make con-fes - sion: I have sinned and
2 Though my con - science' voice ap - pall me, Fa - ther, I will
3 Your Son came to suf - fer for me, Gave him - self to
4 Lord, on you I cast my bur - den. Sink it to the

gone a - stray, I have mul - ti - plied trans - gres - sion,
seek your face; Though your child I dare not call me,
res - cue me, Died to heal me and re - store me,
depths be - low. Let me know your gra - cious par - don,

Cho - sen for my - self my way. Led by you to see my
Yet re - ceive me in your grace. Do not for my sins for -
Rec - on - ciled and set me free. Je - sus' cross a - lone can
Wash me, make me white as snow. Let your Spir - it leave me

er - rors, Lord, I trem - ble at your ter - rors.
sake me; Let your wrath not o - ver - take me.
van - quish These dark fears and soothe this an - guish.
nev - er; Make me on - ly yours for - ev - er.

Text: Johann Franck, 1618–77; tr. Catherine Winkworth, 1829–78, alt.
Tune: Johann Crüger, 1598–1662

HERR, ICH HABE MISSGEHANDELT
87 87 88

234 To You, Omniscient Lord of All

1 To you, om-ni-scient Lord of all, With grief and shame I
2 My Lord and God, to you I pray, Oh, cast me not in
3 O Je-sus, let your pre-cious blood Be to my soul a

hum-bly call; I see my sins a-gainst you, Lord,
wrath a-way; Let your good Spir-it ne'er de-part,
cleans-ing flood. Turn not, O Lord, your guest a-way,

The sins of thought, of deed and word. They press me sore; to
But let him draw to you my heart That tru-ly pen-i-
But grant that jus-ti-fied I may Go to my house, at

you I flee:
tent I be: O God, be mer-ci-ful to me!
peace to be:

Text: Magnus B. Landstad, 1802–80; tr. Carl Doving, 1867–1937, alt.
Tune: Martin Luther, 1483–1546

VATER UNSER
88 88 88

As Surely as I Live, God Said

1 As sure-ly as I live, God said, I would not see the
2 To us there-fore Christ gave com-mand: "Go forth and preach in
3 "All those whose sins you thus re-mit I tru-ly par-don
4 "What you will bind, that bound shall be; What you will loose, that

sin - ner dead. I want him turned from er - ror's ways,
ev - 'ry land; Be - stow on all my par - d'ning grace
and ac - quit, And those whose sins you will re - tain
shall be free; To my dear Church the keys are giv'n

Re - pent - ant, liv - ing end - less days.
Who will re - pent and mend their ways.
Con - demned and guilt - y shall re - main.
To o - pen, close the gates of heav'n."

5 The words which absolution give
Are his who died that we might live;
The minister whom Christ has sent
Is but his humble instrument.

6 When ministers lay on their hands,
Absolved by Christ the sinner stands;
He who by grace the Word believes
The purchase of his blood receives.

7 All praise to you, O Christ, shall be
For absolution full and free,
In which you show your richest grace;
From false indulgence guard our race.

8 Praise God the Father and the Son
And Holy Spirit, Three in One,
As was, is now, and so shall be
World without end, eternally!

Text: Nikolaus Herman, c. 1480–1561; tr. Matthias Loy, 1828–1915, alt.
Tune: Jeremiah Clarke, 1669–1707

ST. LUKE
L M

236 Jesus Christ, Our Blessed Savior

1 Je - sus Christ, our bless - ed Sav - ior, Turned a - way
3 Ban - quet gifts God here is shar - ing; Take them— af -
5 Firm - ly hold with faith un - shak - en That this food
7 Christ says: "Come, all you that la - bor, And re - ceive

God's wrath for - ev - er; By his bit - ter grief
ter well pre - par - ing; For if one does not
is to be tak - en By the sick who are
my grace and fa - vor: They that feel no want

and woe He saved us from the e - vil foe.
be - lieve, Then death for life he shall re - ceive.
dis - tressed, By hearts that long for peace and rest.
nor ill Need no phy - si - cian's help nor skill."

9 Let this food your faith so nourish
That by love its fruit may flourish
And your neighbor learn from you
How much God's wondrous love can do.

The nine stanzas of these two hymns may be sung in numerical order to either tune, or they may be sung in alternation as the stanza numbers indicate.

© Text: John Hus, c. 1369-1415; tr. F. Samuel Janzow, b. 1913
Tune: J. Klug, Geistliche Lieder, 1533

JESUS CHRISTUS, UNSER HEILAND
88 78

Jesus Christ, Our Blessed Savior

237

2 He,   to   pledge   his love   un - dy - ing,
4 Praise the   Fa - ther, who   from   heav - en
6 Ag - on - y   and   bit - ter   la - bor
8 If   your   heart   this truth   pro - fes - ses

Spreads this ta - ble, grace   sup - ply - ing,
To   his own   this food   has   giv - en,
Were   the cost   of God's   high   fa - vor;
And   your mouth your sin   con - fes - ses,

Gives his bod - y   with   the   bread,   And   with the
Who,   to mend what we   have   done,   Gave   in - to
Do   not come if   you   sup - pose   You   need not
You will   be your Sav - ior's   guest,   Be   at his

stanzas 1-8   *stanza 9*

wine   the   blood   he   shed.
death   his   on - ly   Son.
him   who   died   and   rose.
ban - quet   tru - ly   blest.   do.

The nine stanzas of these two hymns may be sung in numerical order to either tune, or they may be sung in alternation as the stanza numbers indicate.

© *Text: John Hus, c. 1369–1415; tr. F. Samuel Janzow, b. 1913*
Tune: 15th cent., Erfurt, 1524

JESUS CHRISTUS, UNSER HEILAND
88 78

238 O Lord, We Praise You

1 O Lord, we praise you, bless you, and a-dore you, In thanks-giv - ing bow be - fore you. Here with your bod - y and your blood you nour - ish Our weak souls that they may flour - ish.

2 Your ho - ly bod - y in - to death was giv - en, Life to win for us in heav - en. No great - er love than this to you could bind us; May this feast of that re - mind us! O Lord, have mer - cy!

3 May God be - stow on us his grace and fa - vor To please him with our be - hav - ior And live to - geth - er here in love and u - nion Nor re - pent this blest com - mu - nion.

May your bod - y, Lord, born of Mar - y, That our
Lord, your kind - ness so much did move you That your
Let not your good Spir - it for - sake us, But that

sins and sor - rows did car - ry, And your blood for us plead
blood now moves us to love you. All our debt you have paid;
heav'n-ly - mind - ed he make us; Give your Church, Lord, to see

In all tri - al, fear, and need:
Peace with God once more is made. O Lord, have mer - cy!
Days of peace and u - ni - ty.

Text: *German folk hymn, 15th cent., st. 1; Martin Luther, 1483–1546, sts. 2-3;*
  tr. The Lutheran Hymnal, *1941, alt.*
Tune: Johann Walter, Geystliche gesangk Buchleyn, *1524*

GOTT SEI GELOBET UND GEBENEDEIET
P M

239 Soul, Adorn Yourself with Gladness

1 Soul, a - dorn your - self with glad - ness, Leave the
2 Has - ten as a bride to meet him, Ea - ger -
3 Now in faith I hum - bly pon - der O - ver
4 Je - sus, source of last - ing plea - sure, Tru - est

gloom - y haunts of sad - ness, Come in - to the day-light's
ly and glad - ly greet him. There he stands al - read - y
this sur - pass - ing won - der That the bread of life is
friend, and dear - est trea - sure, Peace be - yond all un - der-

splen - dor, There with joy your prais - es ren - der.
knock - ing; Quick - ly, now, your gate un - lock - ing,
bound - less Though the souls it feeds are count - less:
stand - ing, Joy in - to all life ex - pand - ing:

Bless the one whose grace un - bound - ed This a - maz -
O - pen wide the fast - closed por - tal, Say - ing to
With the choic - est wine of heav - en Christ's own blood
Hum - bly now, I bow be - fore you; Love in - car -

ing   ban-quet found - ed;   He,   though heav'n - ly, high, and
the   Lord im - mor - tal: "Come, and   leave your loved one
to   us   is giv - en.   Oh,   most   glo - rious con - so -
nate, I   a - dore you;   Wor - thi - ly   let   me   re -

ho - ly,   Deigns to   dwell with you most low - ly.
nev - er;   Dwell   with - in   my   heart for - ev - er."
la - tion, Pledge and   seal of   my sal - va - tion.
ceive you   And,   so   fa - vored, nev - er leave you.

5 Jesus, sun of life, my splendor,
  Jesus, friend of friends, most tender,
  Jesus, joy of my desiring,
  Fount of life, my soul inspiring:
  At your feet I cry, my maker,
  Let me be a fit partaker
  Of this blessed food from heaven,
  For our good, your glory, given.

6 Jesus, Bread of Life, I pray you,
  Let me gladly here obey you.
  By your love I am invited,
  By your love with love requited;
  By this Supper let me measure,
  Lord, how vast and deep love's treasure.
  Through the gift of grace you give me
  As your guest in heaven receive me.

© *Text: Johann Franck, 1618-77; tr. Lutheran Book of Worship, 1978, sts. 1-4;*
The Lutheran Hymnal, 1941, sts. 5-6
Tune: Johann Crüger, 1598-1662

SCHMÜCKE DICH
L M D

Draw Near and Take the Body of the Lord

1 Draw near and take the bod-y of the Lord,
2 He who his saints in this world rules and shields,
3 Come for-ward then with faith-ful hearts sin - cere,

And drink the ho - ly blood for you out-poured;
To all be - liev - ers life e - ter - nal yields;
And take the pledg - es of sal - va - tion here.

Of - fered was he for great - est and for least,
With heav'n - ly bread he makes the hun - gry whole,
O Lord, our hearts with grate - ful thanks en - dow

Him - self the vic - tim and him - self the priest.
Gives liv - ing wa - ters to the thirst - ing soul.
As in this feast of love you bless us now.

Text: Latin hymn, 7th cent.; tr. John M. Neale, 1818–66, alt.
Tune: Trente quatre pseaumes de David, Geneva, 1551

OLD 124TH abbr.
10 10 10 10

Let All Mortal Flesh Keep Silence

241

1 Let all mor-tal flesh keep si-lence And with fear and
2 King of kings yet born of Mar - y, As of old on
3 Rank on rank the host of heav - en Spreads its van-guard
4 At his feet the six - winged ser - aph, Cher-u-bim with

trem-bling stand; Pon-der noth-ing earth-ly - mind-ed,
earth he stood, Lord of lords in hu - man ves-ture,
on the way As the Light of Light, de - scend-ing
sleep-less eye, Veil their fac-es to the pres-ence

For with bless-ing in his hand Christ our God to earth de-
In the bod-y and the blood, He will give to all the
From the realms of end-less day, Comes the pow'rs of hell to
As with cease-less voice they cry: "Al - le-lu-ia, al - le-

scend - ing Comes our hom-age to de - mand.
faith - ful His own self for heav'n-ly food.
van - quish As the dark-ness clears a - way.
lu - ia! Al - le-lu-ia, Lord Most High!"

Text: Liturgy of St. James; tr. Gerard Moultrie, 1829–85, alt.
Tune: French folk tune, 17th cent.

PICARDY
87 87 87

242 I Come, O Savior, to Your Table

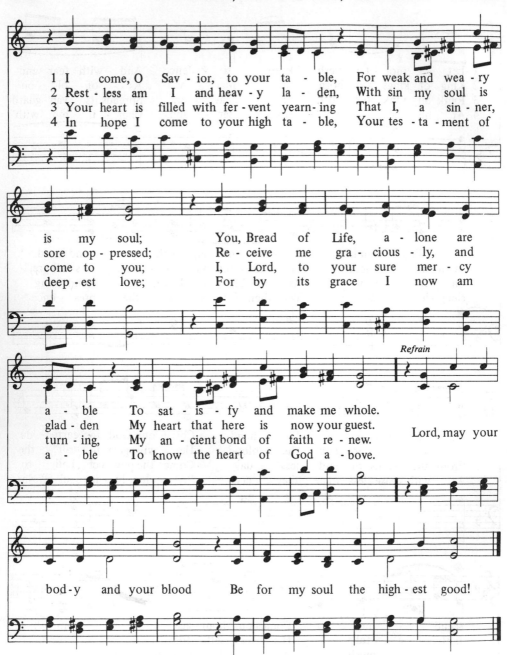

1 I come, O Savior, to your table, For weak and weary is my soul;
You, Bread of Life, alone are able To satisfy and make me whole.

2 Restless am I and heavy laden, With sin my soul is sore oppressed;
Receive me graciously, and gladden My heart that here is now your guest.

3 Your heart is filled with fervent yearning That I, a sinner, come to you;
I, Lord, to your sure mercy turning, My ancient bond of faith renew.

4 In hope I come to your high table, Your testament of deepest love;
For by its grace I now am able To know the heart of God above.

Refrain

Lord, may your body and your blood Be for my soul the highest good!

5 What greater gift can I inherit?
 It is faith's bonded solid base;
 It is the strength of heart and spirit,
 The covenant of hope and grace. *Refrain*

6 Your body crucified, O Savior,
 Your blood which once for me was shed,
 These are my life and strength forever,
 By them my hungry soul is fed. *Refrain*

Text: Friedrich C. Heyder, 1677–1754; tr. The Lutheran Hymnal, 1941, alt.
Tune: Ms., Municipal Library, Leipzig, 1756

ICH STERBE TÄGLICH
9 8 9 8 and refrain

Here, O My Lord, I See You Face to Face

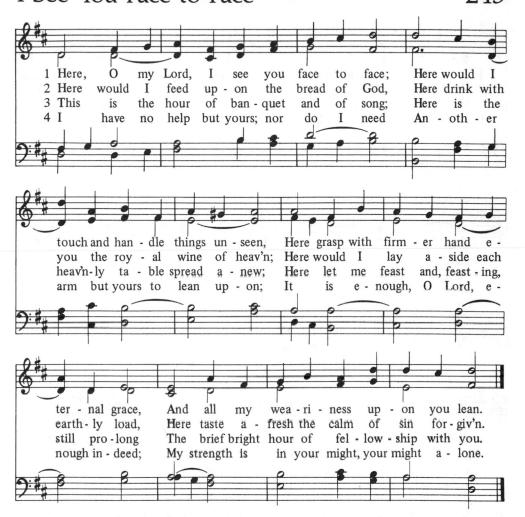

1 Here, O my Lord, I see you face to face;
 Here would I touch and han - dle things un - seen,
 Here grasp with firm - er hand e - ter - nal grace,
 And all my wea - ri - ness up - on you lean.

2 Here would I feed up - on the bread of God,
 Here drink with you the roy - al wine of heav'n;
 Here would I lay a - side each earth - ly load,
 Here taste a - fresh the calm of sin for - giv'n.

3 This is the hour of ban - quet and of song;
 Here is the heav'n - ly ta - ble spread a - new;
 Here let me feast and, feast - ing, still pro - long
 The brief bright hour of fel - low - ship with you.

4 I have no help but yours; nor do I need
 An - oth - er arm but yours to lean up - on;
 It is e - nough, O Lord, e - nough in - deed;
 My strength is in your might, your might a - lone.

5 Mine is the sin but yours the righteousness;
   Mine is the guilt but yours the cleansing blood;
 Here is my robe, my refuge, and my peace:
   Your blood, your righteousness, O Lord, my God.

6 Too soon we rise; the vessels disappear;
   The feast, though not the love, is past and gone.
 The bread and wine remove, but you are here,
   Nearer than ever, still my shield and sun.

7 Feast after feast thus comes and passes by,
   Yet, passing, points to that glad feast above,
 Giving sweet foretaste of the festal joy,
   The Lamb's great marriage feast of bliss and love.

Text: Horatius Bonar, 1808–89, alt.
Tune: attr. Henry Lawes, 1595–1662

FARLEY CASTLE
10 10 10 10

244   O Living Bread from Heaven

1 O liv - ing Bread from heav - en, How well you feed your
2 My Lord, you here have led me With - in your ho - liest
3 You gave me all I want - ed; This food can death de -
4 Lord, grant me then, thus strength - ened With heav'n - ly food, while

guest! The gifts that you have giv - en Have
place And here your - self have fed me With
stroy. And you have free - ly grant - ed The
here My course on earth is length - ened, To

filled my heart with rest. Oh, won - drous food of
trea - sures of your grace; For you have free - ly
cup of end - less joy. My Lord, I do not
serve with ho - ly fear. And when you call my

bless - ing, Oh, cup that heals our woes! My
giv - en What earth could nev - er buy, The
mer - it The fa - vor you have shown, And
spir - it To leave this world be - low, I

heart, this gift pos - sess - ing, With prais - es o - ver - flows.
bread of life from heav - en, That now I shall not die.
all my soul and spir - it Bow down be - fore your throne.
en - ter, through your mer - it, Where joys un - min - gled flow.

Text: Johann Rist, 1606–67; tr. Catherine Winkworth, 1829–78, alt.
Tune: Michael Praetorius, Musae Sionae, VII, 1609

ACH GOTT VOM HIMMELREICHE
76 76 D

O Jesus, Blessed Lord, My Praise 245

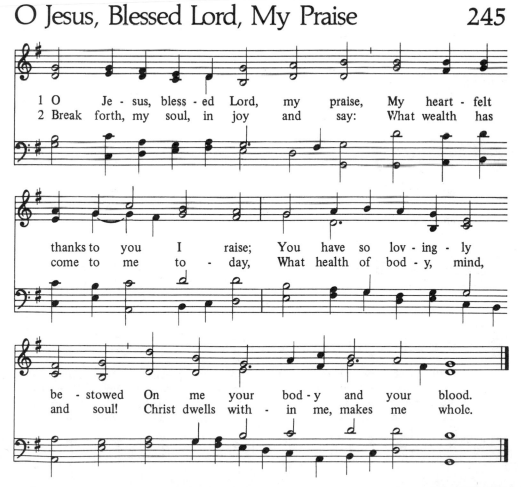

1 O Je - sus, bless - ed Lord, my praise, My heart - felt
2 Break forth, my soul, in joy and say: What wealth has

thanks to you I raise; You have so lov - ing - ly
come to me to - day, What health of bod - y, mind,

be - stowed On me your bod - y and your blood.
and soul! Christ dwells with - in me, makes me whole.

Text: Thomas H. Kingo, 1634–1703; tr. Arthur J. Mason, 1851–1928, alt.
Tune: Louis Bourgeois, c. 1510–c. 1561

OLD HUNDREDTH
L M

246 Lord Jesus Christ, You Have Prepared

1 Lord Jesus Christ, you have pre-pared This feast for
2 Though in-to heav-en you have gone, As-cend-ing
3 I eat this bread, I drink this cup, Your prom-ise
4 Un-aid-ed rea-son can-not see What ea-ger

my sal-va-tion, Your ve-ry bod-y
far a-bove me, Yet here in earth-ly
firm be-liev-ing; In truth your bod-y
faith em-brac-es, But this con-sol-ing

and your blood; Thus, at your in-vi-ta-tion,
food I see How much in-deed you love me.
and your blood My lips are here re-ceiv-ing.
sup-per, Lord, Each rest-less doubt dis-plac-es.

With wea-ry heart, by sin op-pressed, I come to
You are not bound to an-y place; No con-trite
Your word re-mains for-ev-er true; All things are
Your won-drous ways are not con-fined With-in the

you for need-ed rest;   I need your peace, your par - don.
heart es - capes your grace;   Your love un - sought sur - rounds me.
pos - si - ble for you;   Your search-ing love has found me.
lim - its of my mind;   Your prom - ise whol - ly tri - umphs.

5 I should have died eternally,
    But here, repentant kneeling,
Newborn I rise to live the love
    Found in your strength, your healing.
Lord, in this sacrament impart
Your joy and courage to my heart;
    Dead yet alive I praise you!

© Text: Samuel Kinner, 1603–68; tr. Henry L. Lettermann, b. 1932
Tune: Peter Sohren, c. 1630–c. 1692

DU LEBENSBROT, HERR JESU CHRIST
87 87 887

247

Sent Forth by God's Blessing

1 Sent forth by God's bless - ing, Our true faith con - fess - ing, The
2 With praise and thanks - giv - ing To God ev - er - liv - ing, The

peo - ple of God from his dwell - ing take leave.
tasks of our ev - 'ry - day life we will face.

The sup - per is end - ed. Oh, now be ex - tend - ed The
Our faith ev - er shar - ing, In love ev - er car - ing, Em -

fruits of this ser - vice in all who be - lieve. The
brac - ing his chil - dren of each tribe and race. With

seed of his teach-ing, Re-cep-tive souls reach-ing, Shall
your feast you feed us, With your light now lead us; U-

blos-som in ac-tion for God and for all. His
nite us as one in this life that we share. Then

grace did in-vite us, His love shall u-nite us To
may all the liv-ing With praise and thanks-giv-ing Give

work for God's king-dom and an-swer his call.
hon-or to Christ and his name that we bear.

© Text: Omer Westendorf, b. 1916, alt.
Tune: Welsh folk tune

THE ASH GROVE
66 11 66 11 D

248 Lord Jesus Christ, Life-Giving Bread

1 Lord Jesus Christ, life-giving bread, May I in grace
2 To pastures green, Lord, safely guide, To restful wa-
3 O bread of heav'n, my soul's delight, For full and free
4 I do not merit favor, Lord, My weight of sin

possess you. Let me with holy food be fed,
ters lead me; Your table well for me provide,
remission I come with prayer before your sight
would break me; In all my guilty heart's discord,

In hunger I address you. Prepare me well
Your wounded hand now feed me. Though weary, sin-
In sorrow and contrition. Your righteousness,
O Lord, do not forsake me. In my distress

for you, O Lord, And, humbly by my prayer implored,
ful, sick, and weak, Refuge in you alone I seek,
Lord, cover me That I receive you worthily,
this comforts me That you receive me graciously,

Give me your grace and mer - cy.
To share your cup of heal - ing.
As - sured of your full par - don.
O Christ, my Lord of mer - cy!

Text: Johann Rist, 1607–67; tr. Arthur T. Russell, 1806–74, alt.
Tune: Strassburg, 1525

AUS TIEFER NOT II
87 87 887

Your Table I Approach 249

1 Your ta - ble I ap - proach; Dear Sav - ior, hear my prayer. Oh,
2 Lord, I con - fess my sins And mourn their wretch - ed bands; A
3 Your bod - y and your blood, Once slain and shed for me, Are
4 Search not how this takes place, This won - drous mys - ter - y; God

let no un - re - pent - ed sin Prove hurt - ful to me there.
con - trite heart is sure to find For - give - ness at your hands.
tak - en at your ta - ble, Lord, In blest re - al - i - ty.
can ac - com - plish vast - ly more Than what we think could be.

5 Oh, grant, most blessed Lord,
   That earth and hell combined
May not about this sacrament
   Raise doubt within my mind.

6 Oh, may I never fail
   To thank you day and night
For your true body and true blood,
   O God, my peace and light.

Text: Gerhard W. Molanus, 1633–1722; tr. Matthias Loy, 1828–1915, alt.
Tune: Trente quatre pseaumes de David, Geneva, 1551

ST. MICHAEL
SM

250 Lord Jesus Christ, We Humbly Pray

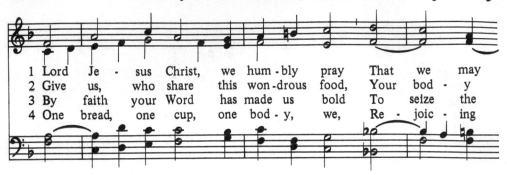

1 Lord Je - sus Christ, we hum - bly pray That we may
2 Give us, who share this won - drous food, Your bod - y
3 By faith your Word has made us bold To seize the
4 One bread, one cup, one bod - y, we, Re - joic - ing

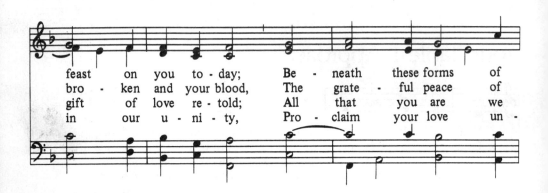

feast on you to - day; Be - neath these forms of
bro - ken and your blood, The grate - ful peace of
gift of love re - told; All that you are we
in our u - ni - ty, Pro - claim your love un -

bread and wine En - rich us with your grace di - vine.
sins for - giv'n, The cer - tain joys of heirs of heav'n.
here re - ceive, And all we are to you we give.
til you come To bring your scat - tered loved ones home.

5 Lord Jesus Christ, we humbly pray:
Oh, keep us steadfast till that day
When each will be your welcomed guest
In heaven's high and holy feast.

Text: Henry E. Jacobs, 1844-1932, alt.
Tune: Cantionale Germanicum, Gochsheim, 1628

HERR JESU CHRIST, DICH ZU UNS WEND
I.M

O Father, All Creating

1 O Father, all creating, Whose wisdom, love, and pow'r
2 With good wine, Lord, at Cana The wedding feast you blessed.
3 O Spirit of the Father, Breathe on them from above,
4 Unless you build it, Father, The house is built in vain;

First bound two lives together In Eden's primal hour,
Grant also these your presence, And be their dearest guest.
So mighty in your pureness, So tender in your love
Unless you, Savior, bless it, The joy will turn to pain.

Today to these your children Your earliest gifts renew:
Their store of earthly gladness Transform to heav'nly wine,
That, guarded by your presence And kept from strife and sin,
But nothing breaks a marriage Of hearts in you made one;

A home by you made happy, A love by you kept true.
And teach them, in the testing, To know the gift divine.
Their hearts may sense your guidance And know you dwell within.
The love your Spirit hallows Is endless love begun.

Text: John Ellerton, 1826–93, alt.
Tune: Samuel S. Wesley, 1810–76

AURELIA
76 76 D

Lord, when You Came
as Welcome Guest

252

1 Lord, when you came as wel - come guest To
2 Pre - serve the vow these two shall make, This
3 On all who thus be - fore you kneel Your

Ca - na's wed - ding feast, The
cir - cle round their life, This
joy - ous Spir - it pour That

brid - al pair, di - vine - ly blest, Found
gold - en ring that none may break Which
each may wake the oth - er's zeal To

all their joy in - creased. Now
makes them man and wife. Your
love you more and more. Oh,

© Text: F. Samuel Janzow, b. 1913
Tune: W. Walker, Southern Harmony, 1835

RESIGNATION
C M D

253 O Perfect Love

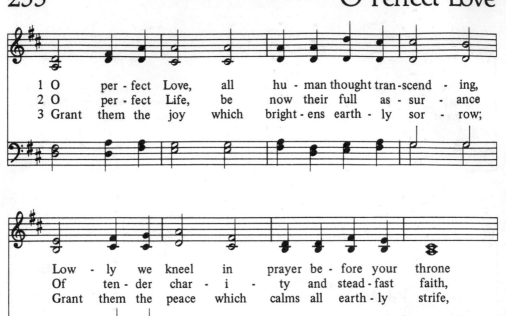

1 O per - fect Love, all hu - man thought tran - scend - ing,
2 O per - fect Life, be now their full as - sur - ance
3 Grant them the joy which bright - ens earth - ly sor - row;

Low - ly we kneel in prayer be - fore your throne
Of ten - der char - i - ty and stead - fast faith,
Grant them the peace which calms all earth - ly strife,

That theirs may be the love which knows no end - ing,
Of pa - tient hope and qui - et, brave en - dur - ance,
And to life's day the glo - rious un - known mor - row

Whom you for - ev - er - more u - nite in one.
With child - like trust that fears no pain or death.
That dawns up - on e - ter - nal love and life.

© Text: Dorothy F. Gurney, 1858–1932
Tune: Joseph Barnby, 1838–96, adapt.

O PERFECT LOVE
11 10 11 10

May God the Father of Our Lord

1 May God the Fa-ther of our Lord, Who called you by his
[2] may you be blest And brought to his e-
[3] it give you pow'r, The strength of prayer in
[4] ther, God the Son, And God the Spir-it,

ho-ly Word, Per-fect, es-tab-lish, set-tle you, Keep you through
ter-nal rest. The work he has in you be-gun He will per-
ev-'ry hour, The wis-dom, knowl-edge, fear of God That lifts a-
Three in One, Pre-serve you blame-less till in grace You stand be-

Stanzas 1-3   *Stanza 4*

faith for-ev-er true. 2 In Je-sus Christ
form till all is done. 3 The Ho-ly Spir-
bove his chas-t'ning rod. 4 May God the Fa-
fore his ho-ly face.

This setting is organized as a canon between congregation and organ. The text may also be sung to the straight TALLIS' CANON setting (Hymn 484).

© Text: Dorothy Hoyer Scharlemann, b. 1912
Tune: Thomas Tallis, c. 1505-85

TALLIS' CANON
L M

255

My Maker, Now Be Nigh

1 My Mak - er, now be nigh The light of life to give,
2 My Sav - ior, wash me clean With your most pre - cious blood,
3 My Com-fort - er, give pow'r That I may stand se - cure
4 O Ho - ly Trin - i - ty, To whom I all things owe,

And guide me with your eye While here on earth I live.
That takes a - way all sin And seals my peace with God.
When in temp - ta-tion's hour The world and sin al - lure.
Your im - age gra-cious - ly With - in my heart be - stow.

To you my heart I ten - der And all my pow'rs sur - ren - der;
My soul in peace a - bid-ing, With - in your deep wounds hid - ing,
The Son to me re - veal-ing, In - spire my thought and feel-ing,
Choose me, though weak and low - ly, To be your tem - ple ho - ly

Make it my one en - deav - or To love and serve you ev - er.
I there find full sal - va - tion And free-dom from dam - na - tion.
His Word of grace to pon - der, Nor let me from Him wan - der.
Where praise shall rise un - end - ing For grace so con - de - scend - ing.

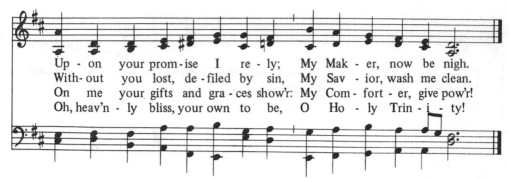

Up - on your prom - ise I re - ly; My Mak - er, now be nigh.
With- out you lost, de - filed by sin, My Sav - ior, wash me clean.
On me your gifts and gra - ces show'r: My Com - fort - er, give pow'r!
Oh, heav'n - ly bliss, your own to be, O Ho - ly Trin - i - ty!

Text: Johann J. Rambach, 1693–1735; tr. R. E. Taylor, d. 1938, alt.
Tune: Franz H. Meyer, 1705–67

MEIN SCHÖPFER, STEH MIR BEI
66 66 77 77 86

Yours Forever, God of Love 256

1 Yours for - ev - er, God of love! Hear us from your throne a - bove.
2 Yours for - ev - er! Oh, how blest They who find in you their rest!
3 Yours for - ev - er! Lord of life, Shield us through our earth - ly strife.
4 Yours for - ev - er! Shep - herd, save This your flock that you for - gave.

Yours for - ev - er may we be Here and in e - ter - ni - ty.
Sav - ior, Guard - ian, heav'n - ly friend, Oh, de - fend us to the end.
You, the life, the truth, the way, Guide us to the realms of day.
Keep us safe with - in your care, Let us all your good - ness share.

5 Yours forever! You our guide,
All our wants by you supplied,
All our sins by you forgiven,
Lead us, Lord, from earth to heaven.

Text: Mary F. Maude, 1819–1913, alt.
Tune and bass line: Orlando Gibbons, 1583–1625

SONG 13
77 77

257

Let Me Be Yours Forever

1 Let me be yours for-ev-er, My gra-cious God and Lord;
2 Lord Je-sus, boun-teous giv-er Of light and life di-vine,
3 O Ho-ly Spir-it, pour-ing Sweet peace in-to my heart

May I for-sake you nev-er Nor wan-der from your Word.
You did my soul de-liv-er; To you I all re-sign.
And all my soul re-stor-ing, Let me in grace de-part.

Pre-serve me from the maz-es Of er-ror and dis-trust,
You have in mer-cy bought me With blood and bit-ter pain;
And while his name con-fess-ing Whom I by faith have known,

And I shall sing your prais-es For-ev-er with the just.
Let me, since you have sought me, E-ter-nal life ob-tain.
Grant me your con-stant bless-ing And take me as your own.

Text: Nikolaus Selnecker, 1532-92, st. 1; Rudolstädter Gesangbuch, 1688, sts. 2-3;
    tr. Matthias Loy, 1828-1915, alt.
Tune: Ein Gesangbuch der Brüder, Nürnberg, 1544

LOB GOTT GETROST MIT SINGEN
76 76 D

God of the Prophets,
Bless the Prophets' Sons

1 God of the proph - ets, bless the proph-ets' sons;
2 A - noint them proph - ets, men who are in - tent
3 A - noint them priests; strong in - ter - ces - sors, they,
4 Make them a - pos - tles, her - alds of your cross;

E - li - jah's man - tle on E - li - sha cast.
To hear and share your Word; their hearts a - wake
For par - don and for love and hope and peace.
Forth let them go to tell all lands your grace.

Each age its sol - emn task may claim but once;
To hu - man need; their lips make el - o - quent
Oh, if with them the world might, now a - stray,
By you in - spired, they count all else but loss

Make each one no - bler, strong - er than the last.
To gird the right and ev - 'ry e - vil break.
Find, Lord, in you from all their woes re - lease.
And stand at last with joy be - fore your face.

Text: Denis Wortman, 1835-1922, alt.
Tune: Trente quatre pseaumes de David, Geneva, 1551

OLD 124TH, abbr.
10 10 10 10

Preach You the Word

1 Preach you the Word and plant it home To men who
2 We know how hard, O Lord, the task Your ser-vant
3 The sow-er sows; his reck-less love Scat-ters a-
4 Though some be snatched and some be scorched And some be

like or like it not, The Word that shall en-dure and
bade us un-der-take: To preach your Word and nev-er
broad the good-ly seed, In-tent a-lone that men may
choked and mat-ted flat, The sow-er sows; his heart cries

stand When flow'rs and men shall be for-got.
ask What pride-ful prof-it it may make.
have The whole-some loaves that all men need.
out, "Oh, what of that, and what of that?"

5 Preach you the Word and plant it home
   And never faint; the Harvest Lord
Who gave the sower seed to sow
   Will watch and tend his planted Word.

© Text: Martin H. Franzmann, 1907–76
Tune: Rheinfelsisches Gesangbuch, Augsburg, 1666

O HEILAND, REISS DIE HIMMEL AUF
L M

Lord of the Living Harvest

1 Lord of the liv-ing har - vest That whit-ens on the plain,
2 As la-b'rers in your vine - yard, Help them be ev - er true,
3 Be with them, God the Fa - ther, Be with them, God the Son

Where an-gels soon shall gath - er Their sheaves of gold-en grain,
Con - tent to bear the bur - den Of wea - ry days for you,
And God the Ho-ly Spir - it, Most bless - ed Three in One.

Ac - cept these hands to la - bor, These hearts to trust and love,
To ask no oth - er wa - ges When you will call them home
Teach them, as faith-ful ser - vants You right - ly to a - dore,

And with them ev - er has - ten Your king-dom from a - bove.
Than to have shared the la - bor That makes your king-dom come.
And fill them with your full - ness Both now and ev - er - more.

Text: John S. B. Monsell, 1811–75, alt.
Tune: Samuel S. Wesley, 1810–76

AURELIA
76 76 D

261 Lord of the Church, We Humbly Pray

1 Lord of the Church, we hum-bly pray For those who
2 Help them to preach your truth, O God, Re - demp -tion
3 So may they live to you a - lone, Then hear the

guide us in your way And speak your ho - ly Word.
through the Sav - ior's blood, Nor let the Spir - it cease
wel - come word "Well done," And take their crown a - bove,

With love di - vine their hearts in - spire, And touch their
On all the Church his gifts to show'r: To them a
En - ter in - to their Mas - ter's joy And all e -

lips with hal - lowed fire, And need - ful strength af - ford.
mes - sen - ger of pow'r; To us, of life and peace.
ter - ni - ty em - ploy In praise and bliss and love.

Text: Edward Osler, 1798–1863
Tune: Nürnberg, 1534

KOMMT HER ZU MIR
886 886

We Bid You Welcome in the Name

262

1 We bid you wel - come in the name
2 Come as a shep - herd, guard and keep
3 Come as a teach - er sent from God,
4 Come as a mes - sen - ger of peace,

Of Je - sus, our ex - alt - ed head.
This fold from hell and world and sin;
Charged his whole coun - sel to de - clare.
Filled with the Spir - it, fired with love.

Come as a ser - vant— so he came—
Nour - ish the lambs and feed the sheep;
Our ranks en - cour - age, lag - gards prod
Live to en - joy our large in - crease,

And we re - ceive you in his stead.
The wound - ed heal, the lost bring in.
While we up - hold your hands with prayer.
And die to meet us all a - bove.

Text: James Montgomery, 1771–1854, alt.
Tune: As hymnodus sacer, Leipzig, 1625

HERR JESU CHRIST, MEINS
L M

263 Send, O Lord, Your Holy Spirit

1 Send, O Lord, your Ho-ly Spir-it On your ser-vant now, we pray;
2 You, O Lord, your-self have called him For your pre-cious lambs to care;
3 Help, Lord Je-sus, help him nour-ish All our chil-dren with your Word

Let him prove a faith-ful shep-herd That no lamb is led a-stray.
But to pros-per in his call-ing, He the Spir-it's gifts must share.
That in fer-vent love they serve you Till in heav'n their song is heard.

Your pure teach-ing to pro-claim, To ex-tol your ho-ly name,
Give him wis-dom from a-bove, Fill his heart with ho-ly love;
Bound-less bless-ings, Lord, be-stow On his faith-ful toil be-low

And to feed your lambs, dear Sav-ior, Make his aim and sole en-deav-or.
In his weak-ness, Lord, be near him, In his prayers, Good Shep-herd, hear him.
Till by grace to him be giv-en His re-ward, the crown of heav-en.

Text: author unknown, 19th cent.; tr. Frederick W. Herzberger, 1859–1930, alt.
Tune: Johann Schop, c. 1595–1667

WERDE MUNTER
87 87 77 88

I Know that My Redeemer Lives

264

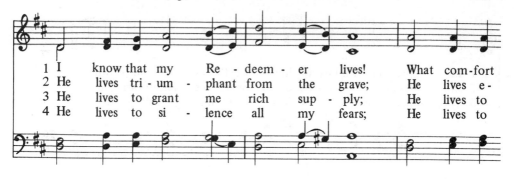

1 I know that my Re - deem - er lives! What com-fort
2 He lives tri - um - phant from the grave; He lives e -
3 He lives to grant me rich sup - ply; He lives to
4 He lives to si - lence all my fears; He lives to

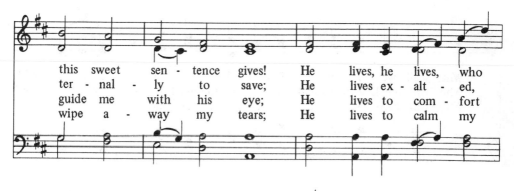

this sweet sen - tence gives! He lives, he lives, who
ter - nal - ly to save; He lives ex - alt - ed,
guide me with his eye; He lives to com - fort
wipe a - way my tears; He lives to calm my

once was dead; He lives, my ev - er - liv - ing head!
throned a - bove; He lives to rule his Church in love.
me when faint; He lives to hear my soul's com - plaint.
trou - bled heart; He lives all bless - ings to im - part.

5 He lives to bless me with his love;
He lives to plead for me above;
He lives my hungry soul to feed;
He lives to help in time of need.

6 He lives, my kind, wise, heav'nly friend;
He lives and loves me to the end;
He lives, and while he lives, I'll sing;
He lives, my Prophet, Priest, and King!

7 He lives and grants me daily breath;
He lives, and I shall conquer death;
He lives my mansion to prepare;
He lives to bring me safely there.

8 He lives, all glory to his name!
He lives, my Savior, still the same;
What joy this blest assurance gives:
I know that my Redeemer lives!

Text: Samuel Medley, 1738–99, alt.
Tune: attr. John Hatton, d. 1793

DUKE STREET
L M

265 In the Very Midst of Life

1 In the ver - y midst of life Death has us sur - round - ed.
2 In the midst of bit - ter death, Sharp the hell-drawn har - row.
3 Through the midst of hells of fear Our trans - gres - sions drive us.

When shall we a help - er find, Hear his com - ing sound - ed?
Who will break its teeth and save Faith's most in - ner mar - row?
Who will help us to es - cape, Shield us, and re - vive us?

For you, our Lord, we're wait - ing. We sor - row that we left your
Lord, you a - lone, our Sav - ior. Though you were grieved by our mis -
Lord, you a - lone, our Sav - ior. Your shed blood our sal - va - tion

path, Do - ing what de - serves your wrath.
deed, Pit - y drew you to our need. Ho - ly, most righ - teous God!
won; Sin, death, hell are now un - done.

Ho - ly, most might - y God! Ho - ly and most mer - ci - ful

Sav - ior! For - ev - er our Lord!

Keep us from de - spair - ing
Let de-spair not bind us
Give us grace a - bound - ing;

In the bit - ter pain of death.
With its threats of deep - est hell.
Keep us, keep us in the faith.

Have mer - cy, O Lord!

© Text: Martin Luther, 1483–1546; tr. F. Samuel Janzow, b. 1913
Tune: Johann Walter, Geystliche gesangk Buchleyn, 1524

MITTEN WIR IM LEBEN SIND
P M

266 Jesus Christ, My Sure Defense

1 Je - sus Christ, my sure de - fense And my Sav - ior,
2 Je - sus, my re - deem - er, lives; Like - wise I to
3 No, I am too close - ly bound By my hope to
4 I am flesh and must re - turn To the dust, whence

now is liv - ing! Know - ing this, my con - fi - dence
life shall wak - en. He will bring me where he is;
Christ for - ev - er; Faith's strong hand the rock has found,
I am tak - en; But by faith I now dis - cern

Rests up - on the hope here giv - en Though the
Shall my cour - age then be shak - en? Shall I
Grasped it, and will leave it nev - er; E - ven
That from death I will a - wak - en With my

night of death be caught Still in man - y an anx - ious thought.
fear, or could the head Rise and leave his mem - bers dead?
death now can - not part From its Lord the trust - ing heart.
Sav - ior to a - bide In his glo - ry, at his side.

5 Then these eyes my Lord will know,
 My redeemer and my brother;
In his love my soul will glow—
 I myself and not another!
Then the weakness I feel here
Will forever disappear.

6 Then take comfort and rejoice,
 For his members Christ will cherish.
Fear not, they will hear his voice;
 Dying, they will never perish;
For the very grave is stirred
When the trumpet's blast is heard.

7 Oh, then, draw away your hearts
 From all pleasures base and hollow.
Strive to share what he imparts
 While you here his footsteps follow.
As you now still wait to rise,
Fix your hearts beyond the skies.

Text: Berlin, 1653; tr. Catherine Winkworth, 1829–78, alt.
Tune: Johann Crüger, 1598–1662

JESUS, MEINE ZUVERSICHT
78 78 77

For Me to Live Is Jesus 267

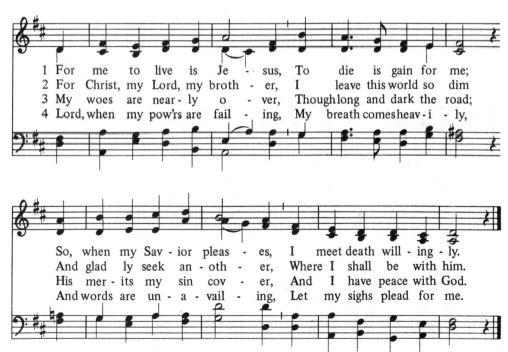

1 For me to live is Je - sus, To die is gain for me;
2 For Christ, my Lord, my broth - er, I leave this world so dim
3 My woes are near - ly o - ver, Though long and dark the road;
4 Lord, when my pow'rs are fail - ing, My breath comes heav - i - ly,

So, when my Sav - ior pleas - es, I meet death will - ing - ly.
And glad - ly seek an - oth - er, Where I shall be with him.
His mer - its my sin cov - er, And I have peace with God.
And words are un - a - vail - ing, Let my sighs plead for me.

5 In my last hour, oh, grant me
 A slumber soft and still,
No doubts to vex or haunt me,
 Safe anchored in your will;

6 This anchor of your making
 Forever holding me,
I will, in heav'n awaking,
 Sing heaven's melody.

Text: author unknown; tr. The Lutheran Hymnal, 1941, alt.
Tune: Melchior Vulpius, c. 1560–1615

CHRISTUS, DER IST MEIN LEBEN
76 76

268   Oh, How Blest Are You

1 Oh, how blest are you whose toils are end - ed, Who
2 We are still as in a dun-geon liv - ing, Still
3 You mean-while are in your cham-bers sleep - ing, Qui -
4 Christ has wiped a - way your tears for - ev - er; You

through death have to our God as - cend - ed! You have a -
op - pressed with sor - row and mis - giv - ing; Our un - der -
et and set free from all our weep - ing; No cross or
have that for which we still en - deav - or; To you are

ris - en From the cares which keep us still in pris - on.
tak - ings Are but toils and trou-bles and heart - break - ings.
sad - ness There can hin - der your un - trou - bled glad - ness.
chant - ed Songs that to no mor - tal ear are grant - ed.

5 Ah, who would, then, not depart with gladness
   To inherit heav'n for earthly sadness?
   Who here would languish
   Longer in bewailing and in anguish?

6 Come, O Christ, and loose the chains that bind us;
   Lead us forth and cast this world behind us.
   With you, th' Anointed,
   Finds the soul its joy and rest appointed.

Text: Simon Dach, 1605–59; tr. Henry W. Longfellow, 1807–92, alt.
Tune: J. Georg Stoezel's Choralbuch, Stuttgart, 1744

O WIE SELIG
10 10 5 10

Jesus, Shepherd, in Your Arms

1 Je - sus, Shep-herd, in your arms / You have held this child once weep - ing, / Willed it should be free from harm / And the moan-ing end in sleep - ing, / Car - ried it then through the door / To where cry - ing is no more.

2 There your peace ends ev - 'ry care; / No more wail of wind through stub - ble. / There bloom on - ly mead - ows fair, / Nev - er chilled by an - y trou - ble. / Your lamb, robed in ra - diant white, / Lives there, Lord, now crowned with light.

3 Shep - herd us to that bright place, / In - to fields where joy is ring - ing, / Where this lamb, in your em - brace, / Has its sighs all turned to sing - ing. / Bring us, like this child we love, / To that life in heav'n a - bove.

© Text: Johann W. Meinhold, 1797–1851; tr. F. Samuel Janzow, b. 1913
Tune: Neuverfertigtes Gesangbuch, Darmstadt, 1699

MEINEN JESUM LASS ICH NICHT
78 78 77

270   Jesus, Priceless Treasure

1 Jesus, priceless treasure, Source of purest pleasure, Truest friend to me, Long my heart was burning, And my soul was yearning, Lord, with you to be!

2 In your arms I rest me; Foes who would molest me Cannot reach me here. Though the earth be shaking, Ev'ry heart be quaking, Jesus calms my fear.

3 Satan, I defy you; Death, I now defy you; Fear, I bid you cease. World, you cannot harm me Nor your threats alarm me While I sing of peace.

4 Hence, all earthly treasure! Jesus is my pleasure, Jesus is my choice. Hence, all empty glory! What to me your story Told with tempting voice?

Yours I am, O spot - less Lamb; Noth - ing I'll al -
Sin and hell in con - flict fell With their bit - ter
God's great pow'r guards ev - 'ry hour; Earth and all its
Pain or loss or shame or cross Shall not from my

low to hide you, Noth - ing ask be - side you.
storms as - sail me; Je - sus will not fail me.
depths a - dore him, Si - lent bow be - fore him.
Sav - ior move me Since he chose to love me.

5 Hence, all fears and sadness,
For the Lord of gladness,
   Jesus, enters in.
Those who love the Father,
Though the storms may gather,
   Still have peace within.
For, whatever I must bear,
   Still in you lies purest pleasure,
   Jesus, priceless treasure!

Text: Johann Franck, 1618–77; tr. Catherine Winkworth, 1829–78, alt.
Tune: Johann Crüger, 1598–1662

JESU, MEINE FREUDE
665 665 786

271   Christ Is the World's Redeemer

1 Christ is the world's Redeemer, The lov-er of the pure,
2 Christ has our host sur-round-ed With clouds of mar-tyrs bright,
3 Down in the realm of dark-ness He lay, a cap-tive bound,
4 Glo-ry to God the Fa-ther, The un-be-got-ten One,

The font of heav'n-ly wis-dom, Our trust and hope se-cure,
Who wave their palms in tri-umph And fire us for the fight.
But at the hour ap-point-ed He rose, a vic-tor crowned.
All hon-or be to Je-sus, His sole-be-got-ten Son;

The ar-mor of his sol-diers The Lord of earth and sky,
Then Christ the cross as-cend-ed To save a world un-done
And now, to heav'n as-cend-ed, He sits up-on the throne
And to the Ho-ly Spir-it, The per-fect Trin-i-ty,

Our health while we are liv-ing, Our life when we shall die.
And, suf-f'ring for the sin-ful, Our full re-demp-tion won.
Whence he had ne'er de-part-ed, His Fa-ther's and his own.
Let all the worlds give an-swer, A-men— so let it be.

Text: attr. St. Columba, 521–597; tr. Duncan MacGregor, 1854–1923
Tune: Irish traditional melody

MOVILLE
76 76 D

All Hail the Power of Jesus' Name

1 All hail the pow'r of Jesus' name! Let angels prostrate fall;
2 Crown him, you martyrs of our God, Who from his altar call;
3 O seed of Israel's chosen race, Now ransomed from the fall,
4 Hail him, you heirs of David's line, Whom David Lord did call,

Bring forth the royal diadem And crown him Lord of all.
Extol the stem of Jesse's rod And crown him Lord of all.
Hail him who saves you by his grace And crown him Lord of all.
The God Incarnate, man divine, And crown him Lord of all.

Bring forth the royal diadem And crown him Lord of all.
Extol the stem of Jesse's rod And crown him Lord of all.
Hail him who saves you by his grace And crown him Lord of all.
The God Incarnate, man divine, And crown him Lord of all.

5 Sinners, whose love can ne'er forget
   The wormwood and the gall,
Go, spread your trophies at his feet
   And crown him Lord of all.

6 Let ev'ry kindred, ev'ry tribe
   On this terrestrial ball
To him all majesty ascribe
   And crown him Lord of all.

7 Oh, that with yonder sacred throng
   We at his feet may fall!
We'll join the everlasting song
   And crown him Lord of all.

Text: Edward Perronet, 1726-92, sts. 1-5, alt.; John Rippon, A Selection of Hymns, 1787, sts. 6, 7, alt.
Tune: Oliver Holden, 1765-1844

CORONATION
86 86 86

273 Amid the World's Bleak Wilderness

1 A - mid the world's bleak wil - der - ness A vine - yard grows with
2 His love se - lect - ed this ter - rain; His vine with love he
3 We are his branch - es, cho - sen, dear, And though we feel the
4 From him we draw the juice of life, For him sup - ply his

prom - ise green, The plant - ing of the Lord him - self.
plant - ed here To bear the choic - est fruit for him.
dress - er's knife, We are the ob - jects of his care.
win - er - y With fruit from which true joys de - rive.

5 Vine, keep what I was meant to be:

Your branch, with your rich life in me.

© Text: Jaroslav J. Vajda, b. 1919
© Tune: Richard W. Hillert, b. 1923

GRANTON
irregular

O Jesus, King Most Wonderful 274

1 O Je - sus, King most won - der - ful! O Con-quer-or re-nowned!
2 When once you vis - it dark - ened hearts,Then truth be-gins to shine,
3 O Je - sus, light of all be - low, The fount of life and fire,
4 May ev - 'ry heart con - fess your name, For-ev-er you a-dore,

O Source of peace in - ef - fa - ble, In whom all joys are found:
Then earth - ly van - i - ty de-parts, Then kin-dles love di - vine.
Sur - pass - ing all the joys we know, All that we can de-sire:
And, seek - ing you, it - self in-flame To seek you more and more!

5 Oh, may our tongues forever bless,
May we love you alone
And ever in our lives express
The image of your own!

Text: attr. Bernard of Clairvaux, 1091–1153; tr. Edward Caswall, 1814–78, alt.
Tune: J. Leavitt, Christian Lyre, 1831

HIDING PLACE
C M

275 Oh, Love, How Deep

1 Oh, love, how deep, how broad, how high,
Beyond all thought and fantasy,
That God, the Son of God, should take
Our mortal form for mortal's sake!

2 He sent no angel to our race,
Of higher or of lower place,
But wore the robe of human frame,
And to this world himself he came.

3 For us baptized, for us he bore
His holy fast and hungered sore;
For us temptation sharp he knew;
For us the tempter overthrew.

4 For us he prayed; for us he taught;
For us his daily works he wrought,
By words and signs and actions thus
Still seeking not himself but us.

5 For us by wickedness betrayed,
    For us, in crown of thorns arrayed,
    He bore the shameful cross and death;
    For us he gave his dying breath.

6 For us he rose from death again;
    For us he went on high to reign;
    For us he sent his Spirit here
    To guide, to strengthen, and to cheer.

7 All glory to our Lord and God
    For love so deep, so high, so broad;
    The Trinity whom we adore
    Forever and forevermore.

Text: attr. Thomas à Kempis, 1380-1471; tr. Benjamin Webb, 1819-85, alt.
Tune: English, 15th cent.

DEO GRACIAS
L M

Oh, for a Thousand Tongues to Sing   276

1 Oh, for a thou-sand tongues to sing My great Re-deem-er's praise,
2 My gra-cious Mas-ter and my God, As-sist me to pro-claim,
3 The name of Je-sus charms our fears And bids our sor-rows cease,
4 He breaks the pow'r of can-celed sin; He sets the pris-'ner free.

The glo-ries of my God and King, The tri-umphs of his grace!
To spread through all the earth a-broad The hon-ors of your name.
Sings mu-sic in the sin-ner's ears, Brings life and health and peace.
His blood can make the foul-est clean; His blood a-vails for me.

5 Look to the Lord, who did atone
    For sin, O fallen race.
    Look and be saved through faith alone,
    Be justified by grace.

6 See all our sins on Jesus laid;
    The Lamb has made us whole.
    His soul was once an off'ring made
    For ev'ry human soul.

7 To God all glory, praise, and love
    Be now and ever giv'n
    By saints below and saints above,
    The Church in earth and heav'n.

Text: Charles Wesley, 1707–88, alt.
Tune: John B. Dykes, 1823–76

BEATITUDO
C M

277 One Thing's Needful

1 One thing's need-ful; Lord, this trea-sure Teach me high-ly to re-
2 If you seek this one thing need-ful, Turn from all cre-at-ed
3 How were Mar-y's thoughts de-vot-ed Her e-ter-nal joy to
4 So my long-ings, up-ward tend-ing, Je-sus, rest a-lone on

gard; All else, though it first give plea-sure, Is a yoke
things; Turn to Je-sus and be heed-ful Of the peace
find As in-tent each word she not-ed At her Sav-
you. All my life on you de-pend-ing, Teach me what

that press-es hard. Be-neath it the heart is still fret-ting
and joy he brings. For where God and man both in one are
ior's feet re-clined! How kin-dled her heart, how de-vout was
to will and do. Al-though all the world should for-sake and

and striv-ing, No true, last-ing hap-pi-ness ev-er
u-nit-ed, With love and for-give-ness the heart is
its feel-ing While hear-ing the wis-dom that Christ was
for-get you, In love I would fol-low, I'll nev-er

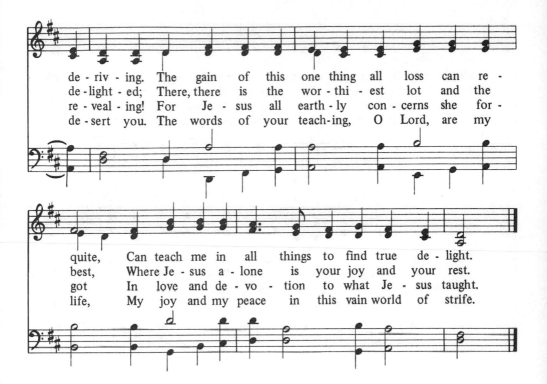

de - riv - ing. The gain of this one thing all loss can re -
de - light - ed; There, there is the wor - thi - est lot and the
re - veal - ing! For Je - sus all earth - ly con - cerns she for -
de - sert you. The words of your teach - ing, O Lord, are my

quite, Can teach me in all things to find true de - light.
best, Where Je - sus a - lone is your joy and your rest.
got In love and de - vo - tion to what Je - sus taught.
life, My joy and my peace in this vain world of strife.

5 Wisdom's highest, noblest treasure,
    Jesus, is revealed in you.
Let me find in you my pleasure,
    Make my will and actions true,
Humility there and simplicity reigning,
In paths of true wisdom my steps ever training.
If I learn from Jesus this knowledge divine,
The blessing of heavenly wisdom is mine.

6 Therefore you alone, my Savior,
    Shall be all in all to me;
Search my heart and my behavior,
    Root out all hypocrisy.
Through all my life's pilgrimage, guard and uphold me,
In loving forgiveness, O Jesus, enfold me.
This one thing is needful, all others are vain;
I count all but loss that I Christ may obtain!

Text: Johann H. Schröder, 1667–99; tr. Frances E. Cox, 1812–97, alt.
Tune: Adam Krieger, 1657; Halle, 1704

EINS IST NOT
87 87 12 12 11 11

278

Crown Him with Many Crowns

1 Crown him with man - y crowns, The Lamb up - on his throne; Hark
2 Crown him the vir - gin's Son, The God in - car - nate born, Whose
3 Crown him the Lord of love. Be - hold his hands and side, Rich
4 Crown him the Lord of life, Who tri-umphed o'er the grave And

how the heav'n - ly an - them drowns All mu - sic but its own. A -
arm those crim - son tro - phies won Which now his brow a - dorn; Fruit
wounds, yet vis - i - ble a - bove, In beau - ty glo - ri - fied. No
rose vic - to - rious in the strife For those he came to save. His

wake, my soul, and sing Of him who died for thee, And
of the mys - tic rose, Yet of that rose the stem, The
an - gels in the sky Can ful - ly bear that sight, But
glo - ries now we sing, Who died and rose on high, Who

hail him as thy match-less king Through all e - ter - ni - ty.
root whence mer - cy ev - er flows, The babe of Beth - le - hem.
down - ward bend their burn - ing eyes At mys - ter - ies so bright.
died e - ter - nal life to bring And lives that death may die.

5 Crown him the Lord of years,
  The potentate of time,
Creator of the rolling spheres,
  Ineffably sublime.
All hail, Redeemer, hail!
  For thou hast died for me;
Thy praise and glory shall not fail
  Throughout eternity.

6 Crown him the Lord of heav'n,
  Enthroned in worlds above,
Crown him the king to whom is giv'n
  The wondrous name of Love.
Crown him with many crowns
  As thrones before him fall;
Crown him, ye kings, with many crowns,
  For he is king of all.

Text: Matthew Bridges, 1800–94; Godfrey Thring, 1823–1903, alt.
Tune: George J. Elvey, 1816–93

DIADEMATA
S M D

How Sweet the Name of Jesus Sounds 279

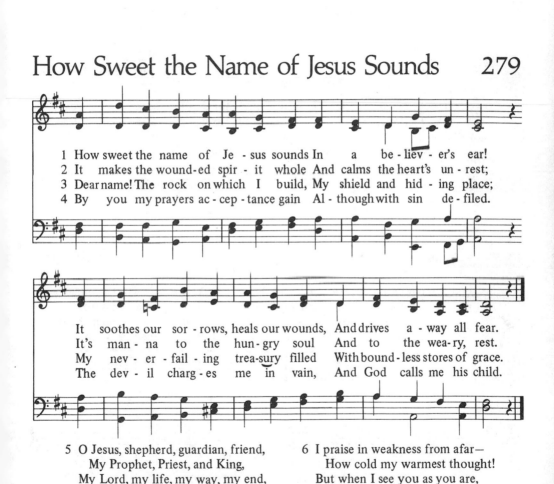

1 How sweet the name of Je - sus sounds In a be - liev - er's ear!
2 It makes the wound-ed spir - it whole And calms the heart's un - rest;
3 Dear name! The rock on which I build, My shield and hid - ing place;
4 By you my prayers ac - cep -tance gain Al - though with sin de - filed.

It soothes our sor - rows, heals our wounds, And drives a - way all fear.
It's man - na to the hun - gry soul And to the wea - ry, rest.
My nev - er - fail - ing trea-sury filled With bound - less stores of grace.
The dev - il charg - es me in vain, And God calls me his child.

5 O Jesus, shepherd, guardian, friend,
  My Prophet, Priest, and King,
My Lord, my life, my way, my end,
  Accept the praise I bring.

6 I praise in weakness from afar—
  How cold my warmest thought!
But when I see you as you are,
  I'll praise you as I ought.

7 Till then I would your love proclaim
  With ev'ry fleeting breath;
And may the music of your name
  Refresh my soul in death!

Text: John Newton, 1725–1807, alt.
Tune: Alexander R. Reinagle, 1799–1877

ST. PETER
C M

280 Jesus, Your Boundless Love So True

1 Jesus, your boundless love so true No thought can reach, no tongue declare; Unite my thankful heart to you, And reign without a rival there. Yours wholly, yours alone I am; Be you alone my sacred flame.

2 Oh, grant that nothing in my soul May dwell but your pure love alone; Oh, may your love possess me whole, My joy, my treasure, and my crown! All coldness from my heart remove; My ev'ry act, word, thought be love.

3 This love unwearied I pursue And dauntlessly to you aspire. Oh, may your love my hope renew, Glow in my soul like heav'nly fire! And day and night be all my care To guard this sacred treasure there.

4 In suff'ring be your love my peace, In weakness be your love my pow'r; And when the storms of life shall cease, O Jesus, in that final hour Be then my rod and staff and guide And draw me safely to your side.

Text: Paul Gerhardt, 1607–76; tr. John Wesley, 1703–91, alt.
Tune: Martin Luther, 1483–1546

VATER UNSER
88 88 88

Lord, Enthroned in Heavenly Splendor 281

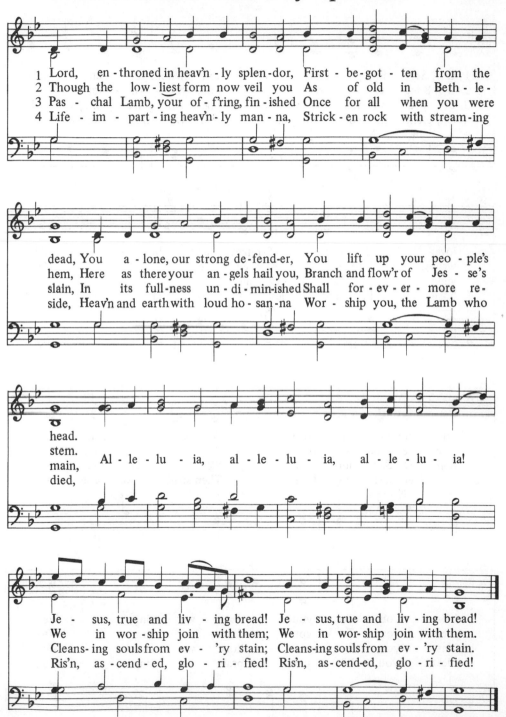

1 Lord, en-throned in heav'n-ly splen-dor, First-be-got-ten from the
2 Though the low-liest form now veil you As of old in Beth-le-
3 Pas-chal Lamb, your of-f'ring, fin-ished Once for all when you were
4 Life-im-part-ing heav'n-ly man-na, Strick-en rock with stream-ing

dead, You a-lone, our strong de-fend-er, You lift up your peo-ple's
hem, Here as there your an-gels hail you, Branch and flow'r of Jes-se's
slain, In its full-ness un-di-min-ished Shall for-ev-er-more re-
side, Heav'n and earth with loud ho-san-na Wor-ship you, the Lamb who

head.
stem.
main, Al-le-lu-ia, al-le-lu-ia, al-le-lu-ia!
died,

Je-sus, true and liv-ing bread! Je-sus, true and liv-ing bread!
We in wor-ship join with them; We in wor-ship join with them.
Cleans-ing souls from ev-'ry stain; Cleans-ing souls from ev-'ry stain.
Ris'n, as-cend-ed, glo-ri-fied! Ris'n, as-cend-ed, glo-ri-fied!

Text: George H. Bourne, 1840–1925, alt.
Tune: William Owen, 1814–93

BRYN CALFARIA
87 87 444 77

282   O Savior, Precious Savior

1 O Sav - ior, pre - cious Sav - ior, Whom yet un - seen we
2 O Bring - er of sal - va - tion, So mar - vel - ous - ly
3 In you all full - ness dwell - ing, All grace and pow'r di -
4 Oh, grant the con - sum - ma - tion Of this our song a -

love; O name of might and fa - vor, All
wrought, Your - self the rev - e - la - tion Of
vine; Your glo - ry all ex - cel - ling, God's
bove In end - less ad - o - ra - tion And

oth - er names a - bove: We wor - ship you; we
love be - yond our thought: We wor - ship you; we
Son, O Sav - ior mine. We wor - ship you; we
ev - er - last - ing love; Then shall we praise and

bless you; To you a - lone we sing; We
bless you; To you a - lone we sing; We
bless you; To you a - lone we sing; We
bless you Where per - fect prais - es ring And

praise you and con‑fess you, Our ho‑ly Lord and King.
praise you and con‑fess you, Our ho‑ly Lord and King.
praise you and con‑fess you, Our ho‑ly Lord and King.
ev‑er‑more con‑fess you, Our Sav‑ior and our King!

Text: Frances R. Havergal, 1836–79, alt.
Tune: Arthur H. Mann, 1850–1929

ANGEL'S STORY
76 76 D

You Are the Way; to You Alone   283

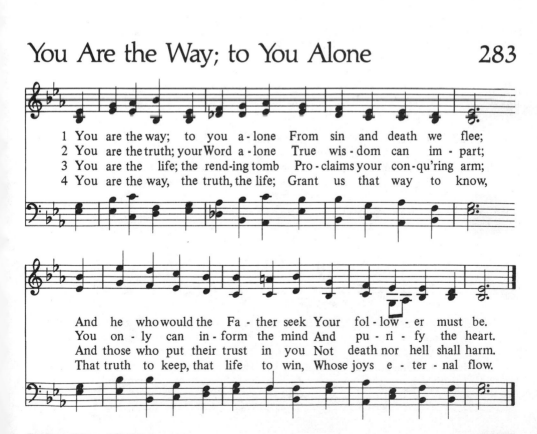

1 You are the way; to you a‑lone From sin and death we flee;
2 You are the truth; your Word a‑lone True wis‑dom can im‑part;
3 You are the life; the rend‑ing tomb Pro‑claims your con‑qu'ring arm;
4 You are the way, the truth, the life; Grant us that way to know,

And he who would the Fa‑ther seek Your fol‑low‑er must be.
You on‑ly can in‑form the mind And pu‑ri‑fy the heart.
And those who put their trust in you Not death nor hell shall harm.
That truth to keep, that life to win, Whose joys e‑ter‑nal flow.

Text: George W. Doane, 1799–1859, alt.
Tune: The CL Psalmes of David, Edinburgh, 1615

DUNDEE
CM

284 Hail, O Once Rejected Jesus

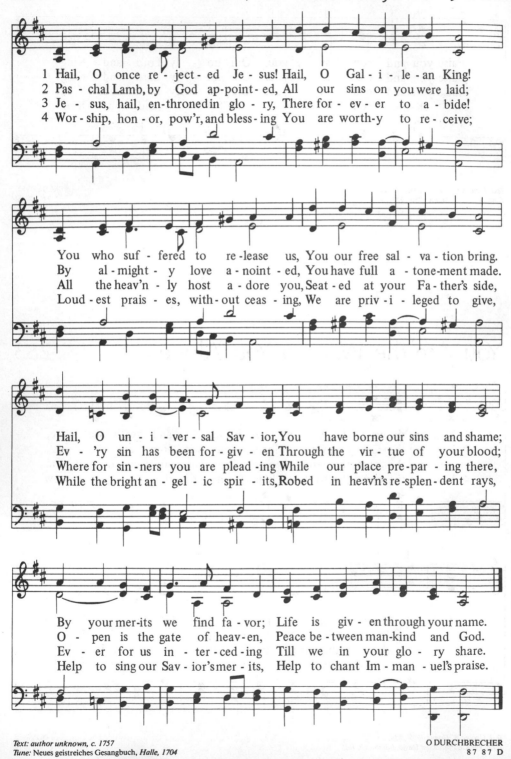

1 Hail, O once re - ject - ed Je - sus! Hail, O Gal - i - le - an King!
2 Pas - chal Lamb, by God ap-point - ed, All our sins on you were laid;
3 Je - sus, hail, en-throned in glo - ry, There for - ev - er to a - bide!
4 Wor - ship, hon - or, pow'r, and bless - ing You are worth-y to re - ceive;

You who suf - fered to re - lease us, You our free sal - va - tion bring.
By al - might - y love a - noint - ed, You have full a - tone-ment made.
All the heav'n - ly host a - dore you, Seat - ed at your Fa - ther's side,
Loud - est prais - es, with - out ceas - ing, We are priv - i - leged to give,

Hail, O un - i - ver - sal Sav - ior, You have borne our sins and shame;
Ev - 'ry sin has been for - giv - en Through the vir - tue of your blood;
Where for sin - ners you are plead - ing While our place pre-par - ing there,
While the bright an - gel - ic spir - its, Robed in heav'n's re-splen - dent rays,

By your mer-its we find fa - vor; Life is giv - en through your name.
O - pen is the gate of heav-en, Peace be - tween man-kind and God.
Ev - er for us in - ter - ced - ing Till we in your glo - ry share.
Help to sing our Sav - ior's mer - its, Help to chant Im - man - uel's praise.

Text: author unknown, c. 1757
Tune: Neues geistreiches Gesangbuch, Halle, 1704

O DURCHBRECHER
87 87 D

Chief of Sinners Though I Be

1 Chief of sin-ners though I be, Je - sus shed his blood for me,
2 Oh, the height of Je - sus' love, High-er than the heav'ns a - bove,
3 On - ly Je - sus can im-part Balm to heal the wound-ed heart,
4 Chief of sin-ners though I be, Christ is all in all to me;

Died that I might live on high, Lives that I might nev - er die.
Deep - er than the depths of sea, Last-ing as e - ter - ni - ty!
Peace that flows from sin for-giv'n, Joy that lifts the soul to heav'n,
All my wants to him are known, All my sor-rows are his own.

As the branch is to the vine, I am his, and he is mine.
Love that found me—won-drous thought—Found me when I sought him not.
Faith and hope to walk with God In the way that E - noch trod.
He sus-tains the hid - den life Safe with him from earth - ly strife.

5 O my Savior, help afford
By your Spirit and your Word!
When my wayward heart would stray,
Keep me in the narrow way;
Grace in time of need supply
While I live and when I die.

Text: William McComb, 1793–1873
Tune: Richard Redhead, 1820–1901

GETHSEMANE
77 77 77

286 Love Divine, All Love Excelling

1 Love di-vine, all love ex-cel-ling, Joy of heav'n, to earth come
2 Breathe, oh, breathe thy lov-ing Spir-it In-to ev-'ry trou-bled
3 Come, Al-might-y, to de-liv-er; Let us all thy life re-
4 Fin-ish then thy new cre-a-tion, Pure and spot-less let us

down! Fix in us thy hum-ble dwell-ing, All thy faith-ful
breast; Let us all in thee in-her-it; Let us find thy
ceive; Sud-den-ly re-turn, and nev-er, Nev-er-more thy
be; Let us see thy great sal-va-tion Per-fect-ly re-

mer-cies crown. Je-sus, thou art all com-pas-sion,
prom-ised rest. Take a-way the love of sin-ning;
tem-ples leave. Thee we would be al-ways bless-ing,
stored in thee, Changed from glo-ry in-to glo-ry,

Pure, un-bound-ed love thou art; Vis-it us with
Al-pha and O-me-ga be; End of faith, as
Serve thee as thy hosts a-bove, Pray and praise thee
Till in heav'n we take our place, Till we cast our

thy sal - va - tion, En - ter ev - 'ry trem - bling heart.
its be - gin - ning, Set our hearts at lib - er - ty.
with - out ceas - ing, Glo - ry in thy per - fect love.
crowns be - fore thee, Lost in won - der, love, and praise.

Text: Charles Wesley, 1707–88
Tune: Rowland H. Prichard, 1811–87

HYFRYDOL
87 87 D

Abide with Us, Our Savior

287

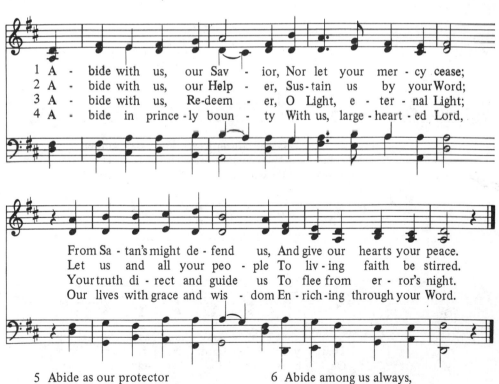

1 A - bide with us, our Sav - ior, Nor let your mer - cy cease;
2 A - bide with us, our Help - er, Sus - tain us by your Word;
3 A - bide with us, Re-deem - er, O Light, e - ter - nal Light;
4 A - bide in prince - ly boun - ty With us, large - heart - ed Lord,

From Sa - tan's might de - fend us, And give our hearts your peace.
Let us and all your peo - ple To liv - ing faith be stirred.
Your truth di - rect and guide us To flee from er - ror's night.
Our lives with grace and wis - dom En - rich - ing through your Word.

5 Abide as our protector
   Among us, Lord, our strength;
  Let world and wily Satan
   Be overcome at length.

6 Abide among us always,
   O Lord, our faithful friend,
  And take us to your mansions
   When time and world shall end.

Text: Josua Stegmann, 1588–1632; tr. composite, alt.
Tune: Melchior Vulpius, c. 1560–1615

CHRISTUS, DER IST MEIN LEBEN
76 76

288 May God Embrace Us with His Grace

1 May God em - brace us with his grace, Pour bless - ings
2 All peo - ple liv - ing on his globe, Praise God with
3 Our prais - es grow from liv - ing roots When we thank

from his foun - tains, And by the bright - ness
ex - ul - ta - tion! The world puts on a
God by ac - tion, Im - prove the field, grow

of his face Guide toward ce - les - tial moun -
fes - tive robe And sings its ju - bi - la -
righ - teous fruits Drawn by the Word's at - trac -

tains, So that his sav - ing acts we see
tion That your rule, Lord, is strong and true
tion. Oh, bless us, Fa - ther and the Son

Where - in his love takes plea - sure. Let Je - sus'
And curbs sin's e - vil hour. . . . . Your Word stands
And Spir - it, ev - er ho - ly. May peo - ple

heal - ing pow - er be Re - vealed in rich - est
guard and will re - new Your peo - ple's health and
ev - 'ry - where be won To love and praise you

mea - sure, Con - vert - ing ev - 'ry na - tion.
pow - er To live, Lord, in your pres - ence.
tru - ly. To this our heart - felt a - men.

© Text: Martin Luther, 1483–1546; tr. F. Samuel Janzow, b. 1913, alt.
Tune: 15th cent.; Magdeburg, 1524

ES WOLLE GOTT UNS GNÄDIG SEIN
87 87 87 87 7

289 The Church's One Foundation

1 The Church's one foun - da - tion Is Je - sus Christ, her Lord;
2 E - lect from ev - 'ry na - tion, Yet one o'er all the earth;
3 Through toil and trib - u - la - tion And tu - mult of her war
4 Yet she on earth has un - ion With God, the Three in One,

She is his new cre - a - tion By wa - ter and the Word.
Her char - ter of sal - va - tion: One Lord, one faith, one birth.
She waits the con - sum - ma - tion Of peace for - ev - er - more
And mys - tic sweet com - mun - ion With those whose rest is won.

From heav'n he came and sought her To be his ho - ly bride;
One ho - ly name she bless - es, Par - takes one ho - ly food,
Till with the vi - sion glo - rious Her long - ing eyes are blest,
O bless - ed heav'n - ly cho - rus! Lord, save us by your grace

With his own blood he bought her, And for her life he died.
And to one hope she press - es With ev - 'ry grace en - dued.
And the great Church vic - to - rious Shall be the Church at rest.
That we, like saints be - fore us, May see you face to face.

Text: Samuel J. Stone, 1839–1900
Tune: Samuel S. Wesley, 1810–76

AURELIA
76 76 D

Christ Is Our Cornerstone

1 Christ is our cor - ner - stone, On him a - lone we build;
2 Oh, then, with hymns of praise These hal - lowed courts shall ring;
3 Here, gra - cious God, do now And ev - er - more draw near;
4 Here may we gain from heav'n The grace which we im - plore,

With his true saints a - lone The courts of heav'n are filled. On his
Our voic - es we will raise The Three in One to sing And thus
Ac - cept each faith - ful vow, And ev - 'ry sup - pliant hear. In co -
And may that grace, once giv'n, Be with us ev - er - more Un - til

great love Our hopes we place Of pres - ent grace And joys a - bove.
pro - claim In joy - ful song, Both loud and long, That glo - rious name.
pious show'r On all who pray Each ho - ly day Your bless - ing pour.
that day When all the blest To end - less rest Are called a - way.

Text: author unknown, Latin, c. 700; tr. John Chandler, 1806–76, alt.
Tune: John Darwall, 1731–89

DARWALL'S 148TH
66 66 4444

291

Built on the Rock

1 Built on the Rock the Church shall stand, E - ven when stee - ples are fall -
2 Not in our tem - ples made with hands God, the Al - might - y, is dwell -
3 We are God's house of liv - ing stones, Built for his own hab - i - ta -
4 Yet in this house, an earth - ly frame, Je - sus the chil - dren is bless -

ing; Crum - bled have spires in ev - 'ry land, Bells still are chim - ing and
ing; High in the heav'ns his tem - ple stands, All earth - ly tem - ples ex -
tion; He fills our hearts, his hum - ble thrones, Grant - ing us life and sal -
ing; Hith - er we come to praise his name, Faith in our Sav - ior con -

call - ing, Call - ing the young and old to rest, Call - ing the
cel - ling. Yet he who dwells in heav'n a - bove Deigns to a -
va - tion. Were two or three to seek his face, He in their
fess - ing. Je - sus to us his Spir - it sent, Mak - ing with

souls of those dis - tressed, Long - ing for life ev - er - last - ing.
bide with us in love, Mak - ing our bod - ies his tem - ple.
midst would show his grace, Bless - ings up - on them be - stow - ing.
us his cov - e - nant, Grant - ing his chil - dren the King - dom.

5 Through all the passing years, O Lord,
    Grant that, when church bells are ringing,
Many may come to hear God's Word
    Where he this promise is bringing:
I know my own, my own know me;
You, not the world, my face shall see;
    My peace I leave with you. Amen.

© Text: Nikolai F. S. Grundtvig, 1783–1872; tr. Carl Doving, 1867–1937, adapt.
Tune: Ludvig M. Lindeman, 1812–87

KIRKEN DEN ER ET GAMMELT HUS
88 88 88 8

In Adam We Have All Been One 292

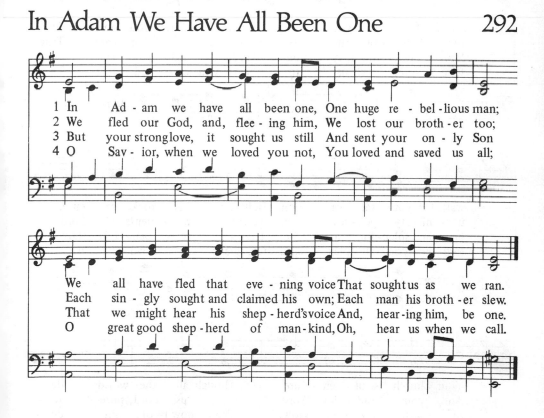

1 In Adam we have all been one, One huge rebellious man;
We all have fled that evening voice That sought us as we ran.

2 We fled our God, and, fleeing him, We lost our brother too;
Each singly sought and claimed his own; Each man his brother slew.

3 But your strong love, it sought us still And sent your only Son
That we might hear his shepherd's voice And, hearing him, be one.

4 O Savior, when we loved you not, You loved and saved us all;
O great good shepherd of mankind, Oh, hear us when we call.

5 Send us your Spirit, teach us truth
    To purge our vanity;
From fancied wisdom, self-sought ways,
    O Savior, set us free.

6 Then shall our song united rise
    To your eternal throne,
Where with the Father evermore
    And Spirit you are one.

© Text: Martin H. Franzmann, 1907–76, alt.
Tune: W. Walker, Southern Harmony, 1835

THE SAINTS' DELIGHT
C M

293 Lord Jesus Christ, the Church's Head

1 Lord Je - sus Christ, the Church's head, You are her one foun -
2 O Lord, let this your lit - tle flock, Your name a - lone con -
3 Help us to serve you ev - er-more With hearts both pure and
4 And for your Gos - pel let us dare To sac - ri - fice all

da - tion; In you she trusts, be - fore you bows, And
fess - ing, Con - tin - ue in your lov - ing care, True
low - ly; And may your Word, that light di - vine, Shine
trea - sure; Teach us to bear your bless - ed cross, To

waits for your sal - va - tion. Built on this rock se - cure,
u - ni - ty pos - sess - ing. Your sac - ra - ments, O Lord,
on in splen-dor ho - ly That we re - pen-tance show,
find in you all plea - sure. Oh, grant us stead - fast - ness

Your Church shall en - dure Though all the world de -
And your sav - ing Word To us, Lord, pure re -
In faith ev - er grow; The pow'r of sin de -
In joy and dis - tress, Lest we, Lord, you for -

cay   And   all   things   pass   a - way.
tain.   Grant   that   they   may   re - main
stroy   And   e - vils   that   an - noy.
sake.   Let   us   by   grace   par - take

Oh,   hear,   oh,   hear   us,   Je - sus!
Our   on - ly   strength   and   com - fort.
Oh,   make   us   faith - ful   Chris - tians.
Of   end - less   joy   and   glad - ness.

Text: Johann Mentzer, 1658–1734; tr. William J. Schaefer, 1891–1976
Tune: Friedrich O. Reuter, 1863–1924

REUTER
87 87 65 66 7

294 Glorious Things of You Are Spoken

1 Glo - rious things of you are spo - ken, Zi - on, cit - y
2 See, the streams of liv - ing wa - ters, Spring-ing from e -
3 Round each hab - i - ta - tion hov - 'ring, See the cloud and
4 Sav - ior, since of Zi - on's cit - y I through grace a

of our God; He whose word can - not be bro - ken
ter - nal love, Well sup - ply your sons and daugh - ters
fire ap - pear For a glo - ry and a cov - 'ring,
mem - ber am, Let the world de - ride or pit - y,

Formed you for his own a - bode. On the Rock of
And all fear of want re - move. Who can faint while
Show - ing that the Lord is near. Thus de - riv - ing
I will glo - ry in your name. Fad - ing are the

A - ges found - ed, What can shake your sure re - pose? With sal -
such a riv - er Ev - er will their thirst as - suage— Grace which,
from their ban - ner Light by night and shade by day, Safe they
world - lings' plea - sures, All their boast - ed pomp and show; Sol - id

va - tion's walls sur - round-ed, You may smile at all your foes.
like the Lord, the giv - er, Nev - er fails from age to age?
feed up - on the man - na Which God gives them on their way.
joys and last - ing trea - sures None but Zi - on's chil - dren know.

Text: John Newton, 1725–1807, alt.
Tune: Franz Joseph Haydn, 1732–1809

AUSTRIA
87 87 D

Blest Be the Tie That Binds 295

1 Blest be the tie that binds Our hearts in Chris - tian love;
2 Be - fore our Fa - ther's throne We pour our ar - dent prayers;
3 We share our mu - tual woes, Our mu - tual bur - dens bear,
4 From sor - row, toil, and pain And sin we shall be free,

The u - ni - ty of heart and mind Is like to that a - bove.
Our fears, our hopes, our aims are one, Our com-forts and our cares.
And of - ten for each oth - er flows The sym - pa - thiz - ing tear.
And per - fect love and friend - ship reign Through all e - ter - ni - ty.

Text: John Fawcett, 1740–1817, alt.
Tune: Lowell Mason, 1792–1872

BOYLSTON
S M

296   I Love Your Kingdom, Lord

1 I love your king-dom, Lord, The place of your a - bode;
2 I love your Church, O God! Its walls be-fore you stand,
3 Be-yond my high-est joy I prize its heav'n-ly ways,
4 Sure as your truth shall last, To Zi-on shall be giv'n

The Church our blest Re-deem-er saved With his own pre-cious blood.
Dear as the ap-ple of your eye And grav-en on your hand.
Its sweet com-mu-nion, sol-emn vows, Its hymns of love and praise.
The bright-est glo-ries earth can yield And bright-er bliss of heav'n.

Text: Timothy Dwight, 1752–1817, alt.
Tune: Aaron Williams, 1731–76

ST. THOMAS
S M

297   A Mighty Fortress Is Our God

1 A might-y for-tress is our God, A sword and shield vic-
2 No strength of ours can match his might. We would be lost, re-
3 Though hordes of dev-ils fill the land All threat-'ning to de-
4 God's Word for-ev-er shall a-bide, No thanks to foes, who

© Text: Martin Luther, 1483–1546; tr. Lutheran Book of Worship, 1978
Tune: Martin Luther, 1483–1546

EIN FESTE BURG
87 87 66 667

298 A Mighty Fortress Is Our God

1 A might - y for - tress is our God,
2 With might of ours can naught be done,
3 Though dev - ils all the world should fill,
4 The Word they still shall let re - main

A trust - y shield and weap - on;
Soon were our loss ef - fect - ed;
All ea - ger to de - vour us,
Nor an - y thanks have for it;

He helps us free from ev - 'ry need
But for us fights the val - iant One,
We trem - ble not, we fear no ill,
He's by our side up - on the plain

That hath us now o'er - tak - en.
Whom God him - self e - lect - ed.
They shall not o - ver - pow'r us.
With his good gifts and Spir - it.

The old   e -   vil foe   Now means
Ask ye,   Who   is this?   Je - sus
This world's   prince   may still Scowl fierce
And take   they   our life, Goods, fame,

dead - ly   woe;   Deep guile   and   great   might
Christ it   is,   Of sab - a - oth   Lord,
as   he   will,   He can harm us   none,
child, and   wife,   Though these all   be   gone,

Are his   dread arms   in   fight;   On   earth
And there's none oth - er   God;   He   holds
He's judged; the deed   is   done;   One lit -
Our vic - t'ry has   been won;   The King -

is   not   his   e   -   qual.
the   field   for - ev   -   er.
tle   word   can   fell   him.
dom   ours   re - main   -   eth.

Text: Martin Luther, 1483–1546; tr. composite
Tune: Martin Luther, 1483–1546

EIN FESTE BURG
87 87 55 56 7

299

Fight the Good Fight

1 Fight the good fight with all your might; Christ is your
2 Run the straight race through God's good grace; Lift up your
3 Cast care a - side, lean on your guide; His bound - less
4 Faint not nor fear, his arms are near; He chang - es

strength, and Christ your right. Lay hold on life, and
eyes, and seek his face. Life with its way be -
mer - cy will pro - vide. Trust, and en - dur - ing
not who holds you dear; On - ly be - lieve, and

it shall be Your joy and crown e - ter - nal - ly.
fore us lies; Christ is the path, and Christ the prize.
faith shall prove Christ is your life and Christ your love.
you will see That Christ is all e - ter - nal - ly.

Text: John S. B. Monsell, 1811–75, alt.
© *Tune: Graham George, b. 1912*

GRACE CHURCH, GANANOQUE
L M

Do Not Despair, O Little Flock

300

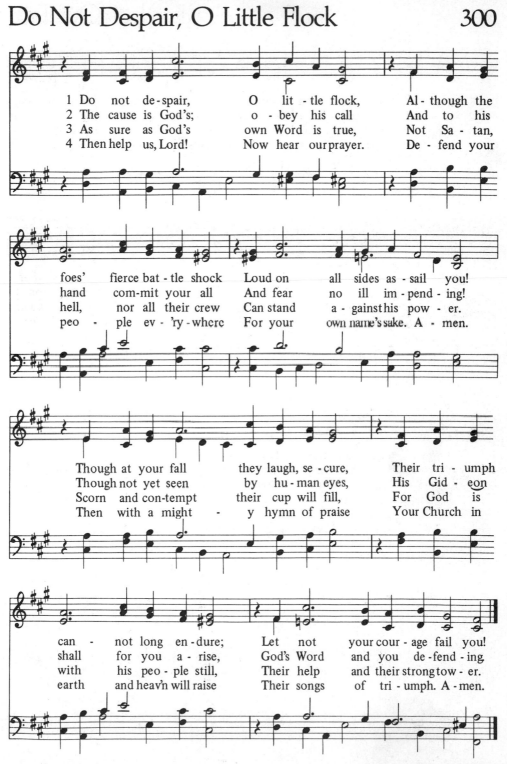

1 Do not de-spair, O lit-tle flock, Al-though the
2 The cause is God's; o-bey his call And to his
3 As sure as God's own Word is true, Not Sa-tan,
4 Then help us, Lord! Now hear our prayer. De-fend your

foes' fierce bat-tle shock Loud on all sides as-sail you!
hand com-mit your all And fear no ill im-pend-ing!
hell, nor all their crew Can stand a-gainst his pow-er.
peo-ple ev-'ry-where For your own name's sake. A-men.

Though at your fall they laugh, se-cure, Their tri-umph
Though not yet seen by hu-man eyes, His Gid-eon
Scorn and con-tempt their cup will fill, For God is
Then with a might-y hymn of praise Your Church in

can-not long en-dure; Let not your cour-age fail you!
shall for you a-rise, God's Word and you de-fend-ing,
with his peo-ple still, Their help and their strong tow-er.
earth and heav'n will raise Their songs of tri-umph. A-men.

© Text: Jacob Fabricius, 1593–1654; tr. Lutheran Book of Worship, 1978
Tune: Nürnberg, 1534

KOMMT HER ZU MIR
887 887

301

Lord of Our Life

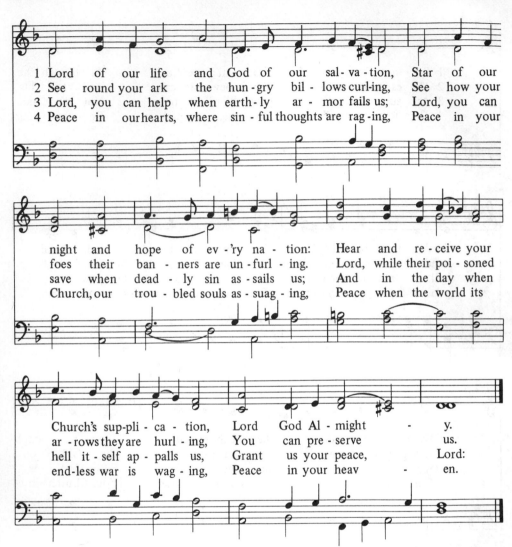

1 Lord of our life and God of our sal-va-tion, Star of our night and hope of ev-'ry na-tion: Hear and re-ceive your Church's sup-pli-ca-tion, Lord God Al-might-y.

2 See round your ark the hun-gry bil-lows curl-ing, See how your foes their ban-ners are un-furl-ing. Lord, while their poi-soned ar-rows they are hurl-ing, You can pre-serve us.

3 Lord, you can help when earth-ly ar-mor fails us; Lord, you can save when dead-ly sin as-sails us; And in the day when hell it-self ap-palls us, Grant us your peace,

4 Peace in our hearts, where sin-ful thoughts are rag-ing, Peace in your Church, our trou-bled souls as-suag-ing, Peace when the world its end-less war is wag-ing, Peace in your heav-en.

Text: Matthäus A. von Löwenstern, 1594–1648; tr. Philip Pusey, 1799–1855, alt.
Tune: Antiphoner, Poitiers, 1746

ISTE CONFESSOR
11 11 11 5

Rise, My Soul, to Watch and Pray

302

1 Rise, my soul, to watch and pray; From your sleep a-
2 Watch a - gainst the world that frowns Dark - ly to dis-
3 Watch a - gainst your - self, my soul, Lest with grace you
4 But while watch - ing, al - so pray To the Lord un-

wak - en; Be not by the e - vil day Un - a-
may you; Watch when it your wish - es crowns, Smil - ing
tri - fle; Let not self your thoughts con - trol Nor God's
ceas - ing. God a - lone can make you free, Strength and

wares o'er - tak - en. Sa - tan's prey Oft are they Who se-
to be - tray you. Watch and see, You are free From false
mer - cy sti - fle. Pride and sin Lurk with - in, All your
faith in - creas - ing, So that still Mind and will Heart - felt

cure are sleep - ing And no watch are keep - ing.
friends who charm you While they seek to harm you.
hopes to shat - ter; Heed not when they flat - ter.
prais - es ten - der And true ser - vice ren - der.

Text: Johann B. Freystein, 1671–1718; tr. Catherine Winkworth, 1829–78, adapt.
Tune: Hundert geistliche Arien, Dresden, 1694

STRAF MICH NICHT
76 76 33 66

303 Rise! To Arms! With Prayer Employ You

1 Rise! To arms! With prayer em-ploy you, O Chris - tians,
2 Cast a - far this world's vain plea - sure And bold - ly
3 Wise - ly fight, for time is fleet - ing; The hours of

lest the foe de-stroy you; For Sa - tan has de-signed your fall.
strive for heav'n -ly trea -sure. Be stead -fast in the Sav - ior's might.
grace are fast re -treat -ing; Short, short is this our earth - ly way.

Wield God's Word, the weap -on glo - rious; A - gainst all
Trust the Lord, who stands be - side you, For Je - sus
When the Lord the dead will wak - en And sin - ners

foes be thus vic - to - rious. God will set you a - bove them all.
from all harm will hide you. By faith you con - quer in the fight.
all by fear are shak - en, The saints with joy will greet that day.

Fear not the hordes of hell, Here is Em-man-u-el.
Take cour - age, wea - ry soul! Look for - ward to the goal!
Praise God, our tri - umph's sure. We need not long en-dure

Hail the Sav - ior! The strong foes yield To Christ, our shield,
Joy a - waits you. The race well run, Your long war won,
Scorn and tri - al. Our Sav - ior King His own will bring

And we, the vic - tors, hold the field.
Your crown shines splen - did as the sun.
To that great glo - ry which we sing.

Text: Wilhelm E. Arends, 1677–1721; tr. John M. Sloan, b. 1835, alt.
Tune: Philipp Nicolai, 1556–1608

WACHET AUF
P M

304 The Son of God Goes Forth to War

1 The Son of God goes forth to war A king-ly crown to gain.
2 The mar-tyr first, whose ea-gle eye Could pierce be-yond the grave,
3 A glo-rious band, the cho-sen few, On whom the Spir-it came,
4 A no-ble ar-my, men and boys, The ma-tron and the maid,

His blood-red ban-ner streams a-far; Who fol-lows in his train?
Who saw his mas-ter in the sky And called on him to save.
Twelve val-iant saints; their hope they knew And mocked the cross and flame.
A-round the Sav-ior's throne re-joice, In robes of light ar-rayed.

Who best can drink his cup of woe, Tri-um-phant o-ver pain,
Like him, with par-don on his tongue In midst of mor-tal pain,
They met the ty-rant's bran-dished steel, The li-on's gor-y mane;
They climbed the steep as-cent of heav'n Through per-il, toil, and pain.

Who pa-tient bears his cross be-low— He fol-lows in his train.
He prayed for those who did the wrong—Who fol-lows in his train?
They bowed their necks the death to feel — Who fol-lows in their train?
O God, to us may grace be giv'n To fol-low in their train!

Text: Reginald Heber, 1783–1826, alt.
Tune: Henry S. Cutler, 1824–1902

ALL SAINTS NEW
C M D

Stand Up, Stand Up for Jesus

305

1 Stand up, stand up for Je - sus As sol - diers of the cross.
2 Stand up, stand up for Je - sus; The trum-pet call o - bey;
3 Stand up, stand up for Je - sus; Stand in his strength a - lone;
4 Stand up, stand up for Je - sus; The strife will not be long;

Lift high his roy - al ban - ner; It must not suf - fer loss.
Stand forth in might - y con - flict In this his glo-rious day.
The arm of flesh will fail you, You dare not trust your own.
This day the din of bat - tle, The next the vic -tor's song.

From vic - t'ry un - to vic - t'ry His ar - my he shall lead
Let all his faith - ful serve him A - gainst un-num-bered foes;
Put on the Gos - pel ar - mor; Each piece put on with prayer.
The sol - diers, o - ver-com - ing, Their crown of life shall see

Till ev - 'ry foe is van -quished And Christ is Lord in - deed.
Let cour - age rise with dan - ger And strength to strength op - pose.
Where du - ty calls or dan - ger, Be nev - er want - ing there.
And with the King of glo - ry Shall reign e - ter - nal - ly.

Text: George Duffield, 1818–88, alt.
Tune: George J. Webb, 1803–87

WEBB
76 76 D

306 Jerusalem, O City Fair and High

1 Je - ru - sa - lem, O cit - y fair and high, Your tow'rs I
2 O hap - py day, O yet far hap-pier hour, When will you
3 The pa - tri - archs' and proph-ets' no - ble train, With all Christ's
4 Un - num - bered choirs be - fore the shin-ing throne Their joy - ful

yearn to see; My long - ing heart to you would glad - ly
come at last, When by my gra - cious Fa - ther's love and
fol - l'wers true, Who washed their robes and cleansed sin's guilt - y
an - thems raise Till heav - en's arch - es ech - o with the

fly, It will not stay with me. E - li - jah's char - iot
pow'r I see that por - tal vast? From heav - en's shin - ing
stain, Sing prais - es ev - er new! I see them shine for -
tone Of that great hymn of praise. And all its host re -

take me A - bove the low - er skies, To
re - gions To greet me glad - ly come Your
ev - er, Re - splen - dent as the sun, In
joic - es, And all its bless - ed throng U -

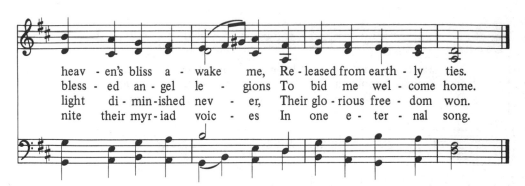

heav - en's bliss a - wake   me,   Re - leased from earth - ly   ties.
bless - ed an - gel   le - gions   To   bid   me   wel - come   home.
light   di - min -ished   nev - er,   Their glo - rious free - dom   won.
nite   their myr - iad   voic - es   In   one   e - ter - nal   song.

Text: Johann M. Meyfart, 1590–1642; tr. Catherine Winkworth, 1829–78, alt.
Tune: Melchior Franck, c. 1573–1639

JERUSALEM, DU HOCHGEBAUTE STADT
106 106 76 76

Jerusalem, My Happy Home   307

1 Je - ru - sa - lem, my hap - py home, When shall I come to thee?
2 O   hap - py har - bor of   the saints, O   sweet and pleas - ant soil!
3 Thy gar - dens and thy gal - lant walks Con - tin - ual - ly   are green;
4 There trees for-ev - er - more bear fruit And ev - er - more do spring;

When shall   my sor - rows have   an end? Thy joys when shall I see?
In   thee   no sor - row   may   be found, No grief,   no care, no toil.
There grow   such sweet and   pleas - ant flow'rs As no - where else are seen.
There ev - er - more   the   an - gels sit   And ev - er - more do sing.

5 Jerusalem, my happy home,   Would God my woes were at an end,
   Would God I were in thee!   Thy joys that I might see!

Text: F.B.P., 16th cent.
Tune: American folk hymn

LAND OF REST
C M

308 Ye Watchers and Ye Holy Ones

1 Ye watch-ers and ye ho-ly ones, Bright ser-aphs, cher-u-bim, and
2 Re-spond, O souls in end-less rest, Ye pa-tri-archs and proph-ets
3 O friends, in glad-ness let us sing, E-ter-nal an-thems ech-o-

thrones, Raise the glad strain: "Al-le-lu-ia!" Cry
blest: "Al-le-lu-ia, al-le-lu-ia!" Ye
ing: "Al-le-lu-ia, al-le-lu-ia!" To

out, do-min-ions, prince-doms, pow'rs, Arch-an-gels, vir-tues, an-gel
ho-ly twelve, ye mar-tyrs strong, All saints tri-um-phant, raise the
God the Fa-ther, God the Son, And God the Spir-it, Three in

choirs:
song: "Al - le - lu – ia, al - le - lu – ia!" Al - le -
One:

lu – ia, al - le - lu – ia, al - le - lu – ia!

© *Text:* J. Athelstan Riley, 1858–1945
Tune: Geistliche Kirchengesäng, *Köln, 1623*

LASST UNS ERFREUEN
8 8 8 8 8 8 and alleluias

309   Jerusalem the Golden

1 Je - ru - sa - lem the gold - en, With milk and hon - ey blest,
2 They stand, those halls of Zi - on, Con - ju - bi - lant with song
3 There is the throne of Da - vid, And there, from care re - leased,
4 Oh, sweet and bless - ed coun - try, The home of God's e - lect!

Be - neath your con - tem - pla - tion Sink heart and voice op - pressed.
And bright with man - y an an - gel And all the mar - tyr throng.
The shout of those who tri - umph, The song of those who feast.
Oh, sweet and bless - ed coun - try That ea - ger hearts ex - pect!

I know not, oh, I know not What joys a - wait us there,
The prince is ev - er in them; The day - light is se - rene;
And they, who with their lead - er Have con - quered in the fight,
In mer - cy, Je - sus, bring us To that dear land of rest!

What ra - dian - cy of glo - ry, What bliss be - yond com - pare.
The pas - tures of the bless - ed Are decked in glo - rious sheen.
For - ev - er and for - ev - er Are clad in robes of white.
You are, with God the Fa - ther And Spir - it, ev - er blest.

Text: Bernard of Cluny, 12th cent.; tr. John M. Neale, 1818-66, alt.   EWING
Tune: Alexander C. Ewing, 1830-95   76 76 D

Look Toward the Mountains

310

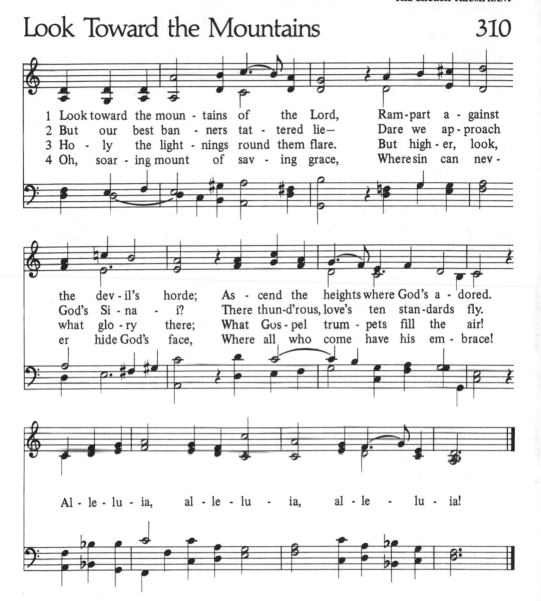

1 Look toward the mountains of the Lord, Rampart against
2 But our best banners tattered lie— Dare we approach
3 Holy the lightnings round them flare. But higher, look,
4 Oh, soaring mount of saving grace, Where sin can nev-

the devil's horde; Ascend the heights where God's adored.
God's Sinai? There thund'rous, love's ten standards fly.
what glory there; What Gospel trumpets fill the air!
er hide God's face, Where all who come have his embrace!

Alleluia, alleluia, alleluia!

5 Christ is the way to that blest height!
Our wayward steps he sets aright,
He takes us up into the light.
Alleluia, alleluia, alleluia!

6 Follow the cross where God the Lord,
His Son, who life and joy restored,
And their blest Spirit are adored.
Alleluia, alleluia, alleluia!

© Text: F. Samuel Janzow, b. 1913
Tune: Nikolaus Herman, c. 1480-1561

ERSCHIENEN IST DER HERRLICH TAG
L M and alleluia

311 Lift High the Cross

Refrain

Lift high the cross, the love of Christ pro - claim Till
all the world a - dore his sa - cred name.

1 Come, Chris - tians, fol - low where our cap - tain trod,
2 Led on their way by this tri - um - phant sign,
3 All new - born sol - diers of the cru - ci - fied
4 O Lord, once lift - ed on the glo - rious tree,

Refrain

Our king vic - to - rious, Christ, the Son of God.
The hosts of God in con - qu'ring ranks com - bine.
Bear on their brows the seal of him who died.
Raise us, and let your cross the mag - net be.

5 So shall our song of triumph ever be:
Praise to the Crucified for victory! *Refrain*

© Text: George W. Kitchin, 1827–1912; Michael R. Newbolt, 1874–1956, alt.
© Tune: Sydney H. Nicholson, 1875–1947

CRUCIFER
10 10 10 10

Jesus Shall Reign

1 Je - sus shall reign wher - e'er the sun Does its suc-
2 To him shall end - less prayer be made, And prais - es
3 Peo - ple and realms of ev - 'ry tongue Dwell on his
4 Bless - ings a - bound wher - e'er he reigns: The pris-'ners

ces - sive jour - neys run; His king - dom stretch from
throng to crown his head; His name like sweet per -
love with sweet - est song; And in - fant voic - es
leap to lose their chains, The wea - ry find e -

shore to shore Till moons shall wax and wane no more.
fume shall rise With ev - 'ry morn - ing sac - ri - fice.
shall pro - claim Their ear - ly bless - ings on his name.
ter - nal rest, And all who suf - fer want are blest.

5 Let ev'ry creature rise and bring
Honors peculiar to our King;
Angels descend with songs again,
And earth repeat the loud amen.

Text: Isaac Watts, 1674–1748, alt.
Tune: attr. John Hatton, d. 1793

DUKE STREET
L M

313

Rise, Crowned with Light

1 Rise, crowned with light, im - pe - rial Sa - lem, rise!
2 See a long race thy tem - ple courts a - dorn;
3 See bar - b'rous na - tions at thy gates at - tend,
4 The seas shall waste, the skies in smoke de - cay,

Ex - alt thy tow - 'ring head and lift thine eyes;
See fu - ture sons and daugh - ters, yet un - born,
Walk in the light, and in thy tem - ple bend;
Rocks fall to dust, and moun - tains melt a - way;

See heav'n its spar - kling por - tals wide dis - play
In crowd - ing ranks on ev - 'ry side a - rise,
See thy bright al - tars thronged with pros - trate kings
But fixed this Word, this sav - ing pow'r, re - mains;

And break up - on thee in a flood of day.
De - mand - ing life, im - pa - tient for the skies.
While ev - 'ry land its joy - ful trib - ute brings.
Thy realms shall last, thine own Mes - si - ah reigns.

Text: Alexander Pope, 1688-1744, alt.
Tune: Trente quatre pseaumes de David, Geneva, 1551

OLD 124TH, abbr.
10 10 10 10

O Christ, Our Light, O Radiance True   314

1 O   Christ, our light,   O   Ra - diance true,   Shine forth   on
2 Fill   with   the   ra - diance of   your grace   The   wan - d'rers
3 Lord,   o - pen all   re - luc - tant ears,   And   take   a-
4 Lord,   let   your mer - cy's gen - tle   ray   Shine down   on

those   es - tranged   from   you,   And   bring them   to   your
lost   in   er - ror's   maze.   En - light - en   those   whose
way   the   child - ish   fears   Of   those who   trem - ble
oth - ers   strayed   a - **way.**   To   those in   con - science

home   a - gain,   Where their de - light   shall nev - er   end.
se - cret minds   Some deep de - lu - sion haunts   and   blinds.
to   ex - press   The   faith their se - cret hearts   con - fess.
wound - ed   sore   Show heav-en's wait - ing,   o - pen   door.

5 Make theirs with ours a single voice
Uplifted, ever to rejoice
With wond'ring gratitude and praise
To you, O Lord, for boundless grace.

Text: Johann Heermann, 1585–1647; tr. composite
Tune: Gesang-Buch, Nürnberg, 1676

O JESU CHRISTE, WAHRES LICHT
L M

315 Awake, Thou Spirit of the Watchmen

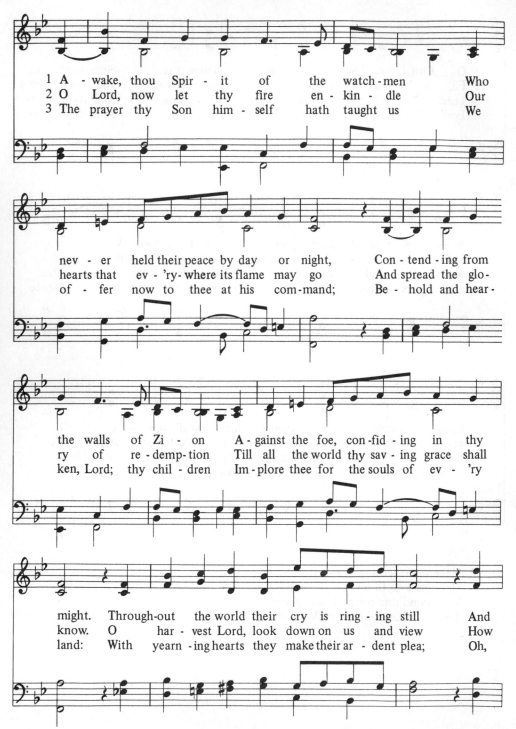

1 A - wake, thou Spir - it of the watch-men Who
2 O Lord, now let thy fire en - kin - dle Our
3 The prayer thy Son him - self hath taught us We

nev - er held their peace by day or night, Con - tend - ing from
hearts that ev - 'ry-where its flame may go And spread the glo -
of - fer now to thee at his com-mand; Be - hold and hear-

the walls of Zi - on A - gainst the foe, con-fid - ing in thy
ry of re - demp-tion Till all the world thy sav - ing grace shall
ken, Lord; thy chil - dren Im - plore thee for the souls of ev - 'ry

might. Through-out the world their cry is ring - ing still And
know. O har - vest Lord, look down on us and view How
land: With yearn - ing hearts they make their ar - dent plea; Oh,

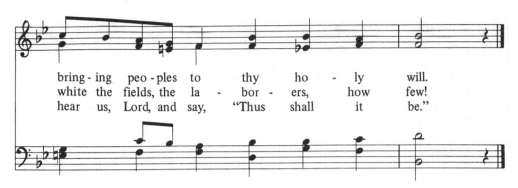

bring-ing peo-ples to thy ho - ly will.
white the fields, the la - bor - ers, how few!
hear us, Lord, and say, "Thus shall it be."

© Text: Karl H. von Bogatzky, 1690–1774; tr. C. Winfred Douglas, 1867–1944, and Arthur W. Farlander, 1898–1952
Tune: J. A. Freylinghausen, Geistreiches Gesang-Buch, 1704

DIR, DIR, JEHOVA
9 10 9 10 10 10

Send Now, O Lord, to Every Place 316

1 Send now, O Lord, to ev - 'ry place Swift mes - sen - gers be - fore your face,
2 Send men whose eyes have seen the King, Men in whose ears his sweet words ring;
3 To bring good news to souls in sin, The bruised and bro - ken hearts to win;
4 Lord, since you died, your vic - t'ry claim; As - sert, O Christ, your glo - ry's name

The her - alds of your won - drous grace, Where you your - self will come.
Send such your lost ones home to bring; Send them where you will come—
In ev - 'ry place to bring them in Where you your - self will come.
And far to lands of pa - gan shame Send men where you will come.

5 Gird each one with the Spirit's sword,
The sword of your own deathless Word,
And make them conqu'rors, conqu'ring Lord,
Where you yourself will come.

6 Raise up, O Lord the Holy Ghost,
From this broad land a mighty host;
Their war cry, "We will seek the lost
Where you, O Christ, will come."

Text: Mary C. Gates, 1842–1905, alt.
Tune: Samuel Howard, 1710–82

ISLEWORTH
888 6

317 God, Whose Almighty Word

1 God, whose al - might - y word
2 Lord, who once came to bring,
3 Spir - it of truth and love,
4 Ho - ly and bless - ed Three,

Cha - os and
On your re -
Life - giv - ing,
Glo - ri - ous

dark - ness heard And took their flight:
deem - ing wing, Heal - ing and sight,
ho - ly dove, Speed forth your flight;
Trin - i - ty, Wis - dom, love, might!

Hear us, we hum - bly pray, And where the Gos - pel day
Health to the sick in mind, Sight to the in - ly blind:
Move on the wa - ter's face, Bear - ing the lamp of grace,
Bound - less as o - cean's tide, Roll - ing in full - est pride,

Sheds not its glo - rious ray,
Oh, now to hu - man - kind
And in earth's dark - est place Let there be light!
Through the earth, far and wide,

Text: John Marriott, 1780–1825, alt.
Tune: Felice de Giardini, 1716–96

ITALIAN HYMN
664 6664

Hark, the Voice of Jesus Calling

1 Hark, the voice of Je-sus call-ing, "Who will go and work to-day?
2 If you can-not speak like an-gels, If you can-not preach like Paul,
3 If you can-not be a watch-man, Stand-ing high on Zi-on's wall,
4 Let none hear you i-dly say-ing, "There is noth-ing I can do,"

Fields are white and har-vests wait-ing, Who will bear the sheaves a-way?"
You can tell the love of Je-sus; You can say he died for all.
Point-ing out the path to heav-en, Of-f'ring life and peace to all,
While the mul-ti-tudes are dy-ing And the mas-ter calls for you.

Loud and long the mas-ter calls you; Rich re-ward he of-fers free.
If you can-not rouse the wick-ed With the judg-ment's dread a-larms,
With your prayers and with your boun-ties You can do what God de-mands;
Take the task he gives you glad-ly; Let his work your plea-sure be.

Who will an-swer, glad-ly say-ing, "Here am I. Send me, send me"?
You can lead the lit-tle chil-dren To the Sav-ior's wait-ing arms.
You can be like faith-ful Aar-on, Hold-ing up the proph-et's hands.
An-swer quick-ly when he calls you, "Here am I. Send me, send me!"

Text: Daniel March, 1816–1909, alt.
Tune: Joseph Barnby, 1838–96

GALILEAN
87 87 D

319 O God, O Lord of Heaven and Earth

1 O God, O Lord of heav'n and earth, Your living fin - ger nev - er wrote That life should be an aim - less mote, A death - ward drift from fu - tile birth. Your Word meant life tri - um - phant hurled

2 In blind re - volt we would not see That reb - el wills wrought death and night. We seized and used in fear and spite Your won - drous gift of lib - er - ty. We walled us in this house of doom,

3 You came in - to our hall of death, O Christ, to breathe our poi - soned air, To drink for us the deep de - spair That stran - gled our re - luc - tant breath. How beau - ti - ful the feet that trod

4 O Spir - it, who did once re - store The Church that it might yet re - call The bring - er of good news to all: Breathe on your clo - ven Church once more That in these gray and lat - ter days

In splen-dor through your bro-ken world; Since light a-
Where death had roy - al scope and room, Un - til your
The road to bring good news from God! How beau - ti-
There may be those whose life is praise, Each life a

woke and life be - gan, You made for us
ser - vant, Prince of Peace, Broke down its walls
ful the feet that bring Good tid - ings of
high dox - ol - o - gy Un - to the ho -

a ho - ly plan.
for our re - lease.
our sav - ing king!
ly Trin - i - ty.

© Text: Martin H. Franzmann, 1907–76, alt.
© Tune: Jan O. Bender, b. 1909

WITTENBERG NEW
L M D

320 On Galilee's High Mountain

1 On Gal - i - lee's high moun - tain Christ gave the great com - mand
2 The Lord who, born of Mar - y, Came down as man and died,
3 His strength with - in my weak - ness Will make me bold to say
4 And not a - lone to na - tions In far - a - way re - treats,

In words of strength and prom - ise Which all can un - der - stand:
Who preached to all who lis - tened, For us was cru - ci - fied—
How his re - deem - ing pow - er Trans - forms my stub - born clay;
But ev - 'ry-where I broad-cast His love through crowd - ed streets:

"All pow'r to me is giv - en To do what I shall choose;
This Lord, our liv - ing broth - er, In pow'r at God's right hand,
His touch of fire ig - nites me, With cour - age I am sent,
The lives that my life touch - es, How - ev - er great or small—

There - fore I send my chil - dren, Their wit - ness I will use."
Has cho - sen us to car - ry His truth to ev - 'ry land.
My tongue - tied si - lence bro - ken, With grace made el - o - quent.
Let them through me see Je - sus, Who served and saved us all.

5 That ev'ryone he chooses,
    For reasons of his own,
Will find in Christ his calling
    To live his love alone.
His presence always leads us
    Till time no more shall be;
Christ's strength, his love, his comfort
    Gives us his victory.

6 Lord, gather all your children,
    Wherever they may be,
And lead them on to heaven
    To live eternally
With you, our loving Father,
    And Christ, our brother dear,
Whose Spirit guards and gives us
    The joy to persevere.

© *Text: Henry L. Lettermann, b. 1932*
Tune: Lowell Mason, 1792–1872

MISSIONARY HYMN
76 76 D

Spread the Reign of God the Lord   321

1 Spread the reign of God the Lord,
  Spo - ken, writ - ten, might - y Word;
2 Tell how God the Fa - ther's will
  Made the world, up - holds it still,
3 Tell of our Re - deem - er's grace,
  Who, to save our hu - man race
4 Tell of God the Spir - it giv'n
  Now to guide us on to heav'n,

Ev - 'ry - where his crea - tures call
  To his heav'n - ly ban - quet hall.
How his own dear Son he gave
  Us from sin and death to save.
And to pay re - bel - lion's price,
  Gave him - self as sac - ri - fice.
Strong and ho - ly, just and true,
  Work - ing both to will and do.

5 Enter, mighty Word, the field;
  Ripe the promise of its yield.
But the reapers, oh, how few
  For the work there is to do!

6 Lord of harvest, great and kind,
  Rouse to action heart and mind;
Let the gath'ring nations all
  See your light and heed your call.

© *Text: Jonathan F. Bahnmaier, 1774–1841, alt.; tr.* composite
Tune: J. A. Freylinghausen, Geistreiches Gesang-Buch, 1704

GOTT SEI DANK
77 77

322 From Greenland's Icy Mountains

1 From Green - land's i - cy moun - tains To In - dia's cor - al strand,
2 Our own land's fair - est breez - es Bear sounds of stee - ple bells,
3 Can we whose souls are light - ed With wis - dom from on high,

From Af - ri - ca's bright foun - tains To A - sia's gold - en sand,
All na - ture's beau - ty pleas - es, Yet man builds count - less hells.
Can we to those be - night - ed The lamp of life de - ny?

From man - y an up - land riv - er To man - y a coast - al plain,
In vain with lav - ish kind - ness The gifts of God are strown;
Sal - va - tion! Oh, sal - va - tion! The joy - ful sound pro - claim

God would the lost de - liv - er From er - ror's e - vil chain.
Throngs turn from him in blind - ness To false gods of their own.
Till those of ev - 'ry na - tion Have learned Mes - si - ah's name.

Text: Reginald Heber, 1783–1826, alt.
Tune: Lowell Mason, 1792–1872

MISSIONARY HYMN
76 76 D

Only-Begotten, Word of God Eternal 323

1 On - ly - be - got - ten, Word of God e - ter - nal, Lord of cre -
2 Ho - ly this tem - ple where our Lord is dwell-ing; This is none
3 Hear us, O Fa - ther, as we throng your tem - ple. By your past
4 God in three Per - sons, Fa - ther ev - er - last - ing, Son co - e -

a - tion, mer - ci - ful and might - y: Hear us, your ser - vants,
oth - er than the gate of heav - en. Ev - er your chil - dren,
bless - ings, by your pre - sent boun - ty, Smile on your chil - dren,
ter - nal, ev - er bless - ed Spir - it: To you be prais - es,

as our tune - ful voic - es Rise in your pres - ence.
year by year re - joic - ing, Chant in your tem - ple.
and in grace and mer - cy Hear our pe - ti - tion.
thanks, and ad - o - ra - tion, Glo - ry for - ev - er.

Text: Bern, 9th cent.; tr. Maxwell J. Blacker, 1822–88, alt.
Tune: Antiphoner, Poitiers, 1746

ISTE CONFESSOR
11 11 11 5

324 As Moses, Lost in Sinai's Wilderness

1 As Moses, lost in Sinai's wilderness, Was
2 As priests a - cross the surging Jor - dan bore With
3 As Sol - o - mon with gold and ce - dar wood Was
4 As in the vi - sion of the mir - a - cle Our

led in awe be - fore the burn - ing bush, So
trem - bling hands the Ark of Cov - e - nant, So
bold to make your house with hu - man hands, So
fa - thers ven - tured far in Je - sus' name, So

have our fa - thers walked the ho - ly ground, And
have our fa - thers walked, by you com - pelled, The
have our fa - thers built these walls in faith, Your
touch the hearts that rise to you in praise, And

stam - mered out God's thoughts and seen his will:
way of sor - rows to the sa - cred hill:
name up - on each lin - tel, sash, and sill:
let the song of faith your tem - ple fill:

Refrain

God of our fa - thers, God of

love, Re - mem - ber us still!

© Text: Henry Lettermann, b. 1932
© Tune: Richard Hillert, b. 1923

RIVER FOREST
10 10 10 10 and refrain

325   For Many Years, O God of Grace

1 For man - y years, O God of grace, This church has
2 Here chil - dren have been born a - new As man - i-
3 Here when the mar - riage vows were made, Both bride and

been your dwell - ing place And we your con - gre - ga-
fold as morn - ing dew, Their vows to you con - fess-
groom be - sought your aid, Your love their own tran - scend-

tion. On Christ, our pre - cious cor - ner - stone,
ing. Here man - y found a ta - ble spread,
ing. Here mourn - ers, with their trou - bled hearts,

Our faith is built, and Christ a - lone Is still
They ate Christ's bod - y with the bread And drank
Have found the peace your Word im - parts, The joy

our one foun - da - tion. This day We pray:
the cup of bless - ing. This day We pray:
that has no end - ing. This day We pray:

"Let us greet you, Lord, and meet you Here with sing - ing,
"Let none fal - ter At your al - tar. We a - dore you,
"May the sto - ry Of your glo - ry Here re - sound - ing

All our prais - es to you bring - ing."
Glad - ly wor - ship here be - fore you."
Be a song of grace a - bound - ing!"

Text: William M. Czamanske, 1873–1964, alt.
Tune: Philipp Nicolai, 1556–1608

WIE SCHÖN LEUCHTET
P M

326 Our Fathers' God in Years Long Gone

1 Our fa-thers' God in years long gone, Our God for all the years to be,
2 You led our fa-thers to this land, A land of beau-ty, boun-ty, pow'r;
3 Make us the chan-nels of your love, Your end-less mer-cy, pow'r, and peace.
4 Grant us your mer-cy to the end, With all your Spir-it's pow'r and grace,

Ac-cept the sac-ri-fice of praise We bring to you on bend-ed knee.
You blessed the la-bors of their hands, Up-held them in each tri-al hour.
So build your Church in ev-'ry place, And day by day her strength in-crease.
Till with the ran-somed, white-robed throng We stand at last be-fore your face,

For mer-cies to our fa-thers shown, For all your grace, so rich and free,
You kept them faith-ful to your Word, Were not a-shamed their God to be.
May we hold high the cross of Christ, Who rose and lives e-ter-nal-ly,
Where we with bright an-gel-ic choirs And all who served you faith-ful-ly

To you, great God, the One in Three, We sing the hymn of ju-bi-lee.
To you their sons sing grate-ful-ly The joy-ful hymn of ju-bi-lee.
That all in him their Sav-ior see And sing the hymn of ju-bi-lee.
Will blend our voic-es end-less-ly In one un-end-ing ju-bi-lee.

© Text: W. Harry Krieger, 1914–74
Tune: Schlag-Gesang- und Notenbuch, Stuttgart, 1744

O GROSSER GOTT
LM D

How Blessed Is This Place, O Lord   327

1 How bless-ed is this place, O Lord, Where you are wor-shiped and a-dored!
2 Here let your sa-cred fire of old De-scend to kin-dle spir-its cold;
3 Here let the wea-ry one find rest, The trou-bled heart, your com-fort blest,
4 Here your an-gel-ic spir-its send Their sol-emn praise with ours to blend,

In faith we here an al-tar raise To your great glo-ry, God of praise.
And may our prayers, when here we bend, Like in-cense sweet to you as-cend.
The guilt-y one, a sure re-treat, The sin-ner, par-don at your feet.
And grant the vi-sion in-ly giv'n Of this your house, the gate of heav'n.

© Text: Ernest E. Ryden, b. 1886, alt.
Tune: Nikolaus Herman, c. 1480–1561

STEHT AUF, IHR LIEBEN KINDERLEIN
L M

328

Thy Strong Word

1 Thy strong word did cleave the dark-ness; At thy
2 Lo, on those who dwelt in dark-ness, Dark as
3 Thy strong Word be-speaks us righ-teous; Bright with
4 From the cross thy wis-dom shin-ing Break-eth

speak-ing it was done. For cre - at - ed
night and deep as death, Broke the light of
thine own ho - li - ness, Glo - rious now, we
forth in con - qu'ring might; From the cross for-

light we thank thee, While thine or-dered sea-sons run.
thy sal - va - tion, Breathed thine own life - giv - ing breath.
press toward glo - ry, And our lives our hopes con - fess.
ev - er beam-eth All thy bright re - deem-ing light.

Al - le - lu - ia, al - le - lu - ia! Praise to

thee who light dost send! Al - le - lu - ia,

al - le - lu - ia! Al - le - lu - ia with - out end!

5 Give us lips to sing thy glory,
    Tongues thy mercy to proclaim,
  Throats that shout the hope that fills us,
    Mouths to speak thy holy name.
  Alleluia, alleluia!
    May the light which thou dost send
  Fill our songs with alleluias,
    Alleluias without end!

6 God the Father, light-creator,
    To thee laud and honor be.
  To thee, Light of Light begotten,
    Praise be sung eternally.
  Holy Spirit, light-revealer,
    Glory, glory be to thee.
  Mortals, angels, now and ever
    Praise the holy Trinity!

© Text: Martin H. Franzmann, 1907–76
© Tune: Thomas J. Williams, 1869–1944

EBENEZER
87 87 D

329   The Law of God Is Good and Wise

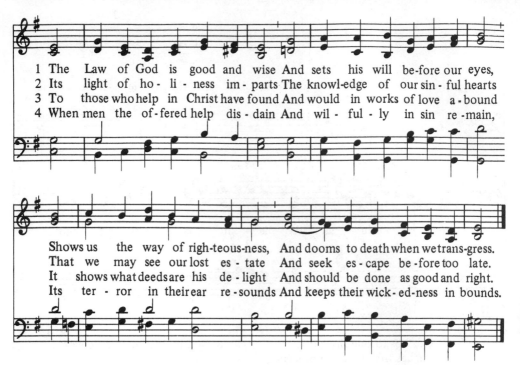

1 The Law of God is good and wise And sets his will be-fore our eyes,
2 Its light of ho - li - ness im - parts The knowl-edge of our sin - ful hearts
3 To those who help in Christ have found And would in works of love a - bound
4 When men the of - fered help dis - dain And wil - ful - ly in sin re - main,

Shows us the way of righ-teous-ness, And dooms to death when we trans-gress.
That we may see our lost es - tate And seek es - cape be - fore too late.
It shows what deeds are his de - light And should be done as good and right.
Its ter - ror in their ear re - sounds And keeps their wick - ed-ness in bounds.

5 The Law is good; but since the fall
  Its holiness condemns us all;
  It dooms us for our sin to die
  And has no pow'r to justify.

6 To Jesus we for refuge flee,
  Who from the curse has set us free,
  And humbly worship at his throne,
  Saved by his grace through faith alone.

The stanzas of this and the following hymn may be sung in alternation.

Text: Matthias Loy, 1828–1915
Tune: J. Klug, Geistliche Lieder, 1543

ERHALT UNS, HERR
L M

The Gospel Shows the Father's Grace 330

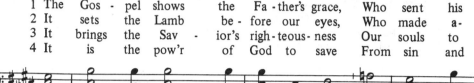

1 The Gos - pel shows the Fa -ther's grace, Who sent his
2 It sets the Lamb be - fore our eyes, Who made a -
3 It brings the Sav - ior's righ-teous- ness Our souls to
4 It is the pow'r of God to save From sin and

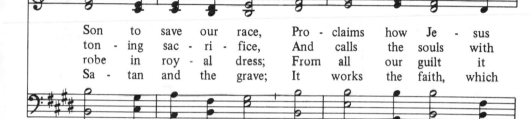

Son to save our race, Pro - claims how Je - sus
ton - ing sac - ri - fice, And calls the souls with
robe in roy - al dress; From all our guilt it
Sa - tan and the grave; It works the faith, which

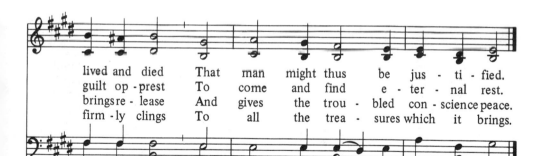

lived and died That man might thus be jus - ti - fied.
guilt op - prest To come and find e - ter - nal rest.
brings re - lease And gives the trou - bled con - science peace.
firm -ly clings To all the trea - sures which it brings.

5 It bears to all the tidings glad
And bids their hearts no more be sad;
The heavy-laden souls it cheers
And banishes their guilty fears.

6 May we in faith its tidings learn
Nor thanklessly its blessings spurn;
May we in faith its truth confess
And praise the Lord our Righteousness.

The stanzas of this and the previous hymn may be sung in alternation.

Text: Matthias Loy, 1828-1915
Tune: Cantionale Germanicum, *Gochsheim, 1628*

HERR JESU CHRIST, DICH ZU UNS WEND
LM

331 Here Is the Tenfold Sure Command

1 Here is the ten-fold sure com-mand God gave to
2 I, I a - lone, am God, your Lord; All i - dols
3 Do not my ho - ly name dis - grace, Do not my
4 And cel - e - brate the wor - ship day That peace may

men of ev - 'ry land Through faith-ful Mo - ses stand-ing high
are to be ab-horred. Trust me, step bold - ly to my throne,
Word of truth de - base. Praise on - ly that as good and true
fill your home, and pray, And put a - side the work you do,

On ho - ly Mount Si - na - i. Have mer - cy, Lord!
Sin - cere - ly love me a - lone. Have mer - cy, Lord!
Which I my - self say and do. Have mer - cy, Lord!
So that God may work in you. Have mer - cy, Lord!

5 You are to honor and obey
   Your parents, masters, ev'ry day,
   Serve them each way that comes to hand;
   You'll then live long in the land.
      Have mercy, Lord!

6 Curb anger, do not harm or kill,
   Hate not, repay not ill with ill.
   Be patient and of gentle mind,
   Convince your foe you are kind.
      Have mercy, Lord!

7 Be faithful, keep the marriage vow;
   The straying thought do not allow.
   Keep all your conduct free from sin
   By self-controlled discipline.
      Have mercy, Lord!

8 You shall not steal or cheat away
   What others worked for night and day,
   But open up a gen'rous hand
   To feed the poor in the land.
      Have mercy, Lord!

9 A lying witness never be,
 Nor foul your tongue with calumny.
 The cause of innocence embrace,
 The fallen shield from disgrace.
  Have mercy, Lord!

10 The portion in your neighbor's lot,
 His goods, home, wife, desire not.
 Pray God he would your neighbor bless
 As you yourself wish success.
  Have mercy, Lord!

11 You have this law to see therein
 That you have not been free from sin
 But also that you clearly see
 How pure toward God life should be.
  Have mercy, Lord!

12 Lord Jesus, help us in our need;
 Christ, you our go-between indeed.
 Our works, how sinful, marred, unjust!
 Christ, you our one hope and trust.
  Have mercy, Lord!

© Text: Martin Luther, 1483–1546; tr. F. Samuel Janzow, b. 1913
Tune: German, 13th cent.; Wittenberg, 1524

IN GOTTES NAMEN FAHREN WIR
88 87 4

How Precious Is the Book Divine   332

1 How pre-cious is the book di-vine, By in-spi-ra-tion giv'n!
2 Its light, de-scend-ing from a-bove, Our gloom-y world to cheer,
3 It shows to us our wan-d'ring ways And where our feet have trod
4 On all the straight and nar-row way Its ra-diant beams are cast,

Bright as a lamp its teach-ings shine To guide our souls to heav'n.
Dis-plays our Sav-ior's bound-less love And brings his glo-ries near.
And brings to view the match-less grace Of our for-giv-ing God.
A light whose nev-er wea-ry ray Grows bright-est at the last.

5 It gladly cheers our drooping hearts
 In this dark vale of tears.
 Life, peace, and joy its light imparts
 And quells our rising fears.

6 This lamp through all the tedious night
 Of life shall guide our way
 Till we behold the clearer light
 Of an eternal day.

Text: John Fawcett, 1740–1817, alt.
Tune: Johann J. Walder, 1750–1817

WALDER
CM

333 God's Word Is Our Great Heritage

God's Word is our great her - i - tage And shall be ours for-

ev - er; To spread its light from age to age Shall

be our chief en - deav - or. Through life it guides our way,

In death it is our stay. Lord, grant, while worlds en-

dure, We keep its teach - ings pure Through-

out all gen - er - a - tions.

Text: Nikolai F. S. Grundtvig, 1783–1872; tr. Ole G. Belsheim, 1861–1925, alt.
Tune: Friedrich O. Reuter, 1863–1924

REUTER
87 87 66 66 7

Lord, Keep Us Steadfast in Your Word   334

1 Lord, keep us stead - fast in your Word; Curb those who
2 Lord Je - sus Christ, your pow'r make known, For you are
3 O Com - fort - er of price - less worth, Send peace and

by de - ceit or sword Would wrest the king - dom from your
Lord of lords a - lone; De - fend your ho - ly Church that
u - ni - ty on earth; Sup - port us in our fi - nal

Son And bring to nought all he has done.
we May sing your praise tri - um - phant - ly.
strife And lead us out of death to life.

Text: Martin Luther, 1483–1546; tr. Catherine Winkworth, 1829–78, alt.
Tune: J. Klug, Geistliche Lieder, 1543

ERHALT UNS, HERR
L M

335

O Word of God Incarnate

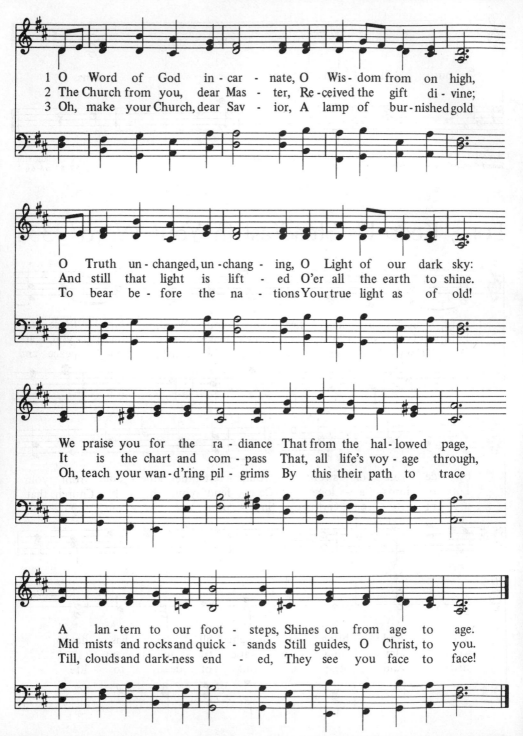

1 O Word of God in-car-nate, O Wis-dom from on high,
2 The Church from you, dear Mas-ter, Re-ceived the gift di-vine;
3 Oh, make your Church, dear Sav-ior, A lamp of bur-nished gold

O Truth un-changed, un-chang-ing, O Light of our dark sky:
And still that light is lift-ed O'er all the earth to shine.
To bear be-fore the na-tions Your true light as of old!

We praise you for the ra-diance That from the hal-lowed page,
It is the chart and com-pass That, all life's voy-age through,
Oh, teach your wan-d'ring pil-grims By this their path to trace

A lan-tern to our foot-steps, Shines on from age to age.
Mid mists and rocks and quick-sands Still guides, O Christ, to you.
Till, clouds and dark-ness end-ed, They see you face to face!

Text: William W. How, 1823–97, alt.
Tune: Neu-vermehrtes Gesangbuch, Meiningen, 1693

MUNICH
76 76 D

Grant, Holy Ghost, that We Behold

336

1 Grant, Ho - ly Ghost, that we be - hold   The   grace   of Christ our
2 Your liv - ing Word shine   in   our heart   And   to   a   new life
3 Then when our earth - ly course is run,   Death's bit - ter hour im -

Sav - ior,   Whose wounds and ag - o - ny un-told   Made   good for
win   us.   With   seed   of light im - plant the start   Of   Christ - like
pend - ing,   May   your good work in   us   be-gun   Bring peace to

our   be - hav - ior.   The last hour can - not bring us   loss   When
deeds with - in   us.   Help us up - root what   is   im - pure,   And
our   life's   end - ing,   The joy of sure - ly   be - ing brought,   By

we   are   shel - tered by the cross   That can - celed our trans - gres - sions.
while faith's fruits in   us ma - ture,   Pre - pare us for your har - vest.
Christ, who   our   sal - va - tion bought,   In - to   our Fa - ther's man - sion.

© Text: Bartholomäus Ringwaldt, 1530–99; tr. F. Samuel Janzow, b. 1913
Tune: J. Klug, Geistliche Lieder, 1529

ES IST GEWISSLICH
87 87 887

337 Preserve Your Word, O Savior

1 Pre-serve your Word, O Sav - ior, To us this lat - ter day,
2 Pre-serve, O Lord, your hon - or, The bold blas-phem - er smite;
3 Pre-serve, O Lord, your Zi - on, Bought dear-ly with your blood;
4 Pre-serve your Word and preach - ing, The truth that makes us whole,

And let your king-dom flour - ish; En - large your Church, we pray.
Con - vince, con - vert, en -light - en The souls in er - ror's night.
Pro - tect what you have cho - sen A -gainst the hell - ish flood.
The mir - ror of your glo - ry, The pow'r that saves the soul.

Oh, keep our faith from fail - ing; Keep hope's bright star a - glow.
Re - veal your will, dear Sav - ior, To all who dwell be - low,
Be al - ways our de -fend - er When dan - gers gath - er round;
Oh, may this liv - ing wa - ter, This dew of heav'n- ly grace,

Let noth - ing from truth turn us While liv - ing here be - low.
Great light of all the liv - ing, That all your name may know.
When all the earth is crum - bling, Safe may your Church be found.
Sus - tain us while here liv - ing Un - til we see your face.

5 Preserve in wave and tempest
   Your storm-tossed little flock;
  Assailed by wind and weather,
   May it endure each shock.

Stand at the helm, our pilot,
   And set the course aright;
  Then we will reach the harbor
   In your eternal light.

Text: Andreas Gryphius, 1616-64; tr. William J. Schaefer, 1891-1976, alt.
Tune: David Spaiser, Vier und zwantzig Geystliche Lieder, Augsburg, 1609

IST GOTT FÜR MICH
76 76 D

When Seed Falls on Good Soil

338

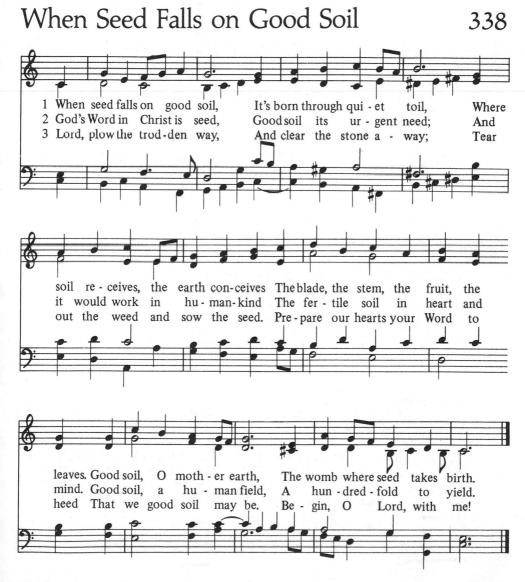

1 When seed falls on good soil, It's born through qui-et toil, Where
2 God's Word in Christ is seed, Good soil its ur-gent need; And
3 Lord, plow the trod-den way, And clear the stone a-way; Tear

soil re-ceives, the earth con-ceives The blade, the stem, the fruit, the
it would work in hu-man-kind The fer-tile soil in heart and
out the weed and sow the seed. Pre-pare our hearts your Word to

leaves. Good soil, O moth-er earth, The womb where seed takes birth.
mind. Good soil, a hu-man field, A hun-dred-fold to yield.
heed That we good soil may be. Be-gin, O Lord, with me!

© *Text: Norman P. Olsen, b. 1932*
© *Tune: Frederick F. Jackisch, b. 1922*

WALHOF
66 88 66

339 Speak, O Lord, Your Servant Listens

1 Speak, O Lord, your ser - vant lis - tens, Let your Word to
2 Oh, what bless - ing to be near you And to lis - ten
3 Lord, your words are wa - ters liv - ing, When my thirst - ing
4 Pre - cious Je - sus, I en - treat you, Let your words in

me come near; New - born life and spir - it give me, Let each
to your voice; Let me ev - er love and hear you, Let your
spir - it pleads; Lord, your words are bread life - giv - ing, On your
me take root; Let this gift of heav'n en - rich me So that

prom - ise still my fear. Death's dread pow'r, its in - ward strife,
Word be now my choice! Man - y hard - ened sin - ners, Lord,
words my spir - it feeds. Lord, your words will be my light
I bring gen - 'rous fruit: Nev - er take them from my heart

Wars a - gainst your Word of life; Fill me, Lord, with love's strong
Flee in ter - ror at your Word, But to me, who know my
Through death's vale, its drear - y night; Yes, they are my sword pre -
Till I see you as you are, When in heav'n - ly bliss and

fer - vor   That I cling   to   you for - ev - er!
bur - den,   Show me now   your Word of par - don!
vail - ing,   And my cup   of   joy un - fail - ing!
glo - ry   I will meet you   and a - dore you!

Text: Anna Sophia of Hesse-Darmstadt, 1638–83; tr. George T. Rygh, 1860–1942, alt.
Tune: Johann Schop, c. 1595–1667

WERDE MUNTER
87 87 77 88

We Have a Sure Prophetic Word   340

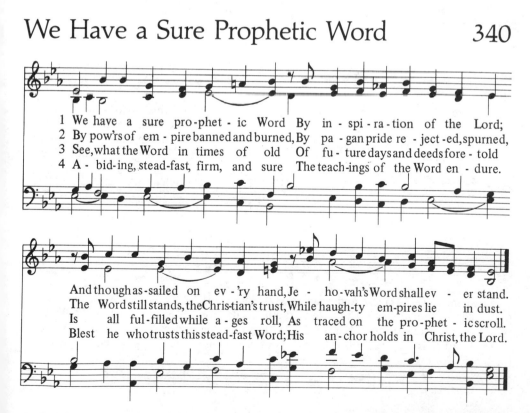

1 We have a sure pro-phet-ic Word By in - spi - ra - tion of the Lord;
2 By pow'rs of em - pire banned and burned, By pa - gan pride re - ject -ed, spurned,
3 See, what the Word in times of old Of fu - ture days and deeds fore - told
4 A - bid-ing, stead-fast, firm, and sure The teach-ings of the Word en - dure.

And though as - sailed on ev - 'ry hand, Je - ho-vah's Word shall ev - er stand.
The Word still stands, the Chris-tian's trust, While haugh-ty em-pires lie in dust.
Is   all ful-filled while a - ges roll, As traced on the pro-phet - ic scroll.
Blest he who trusts this stead-fast Word; His an - chor holds in Christ, the Lord.

Text: Emanuel Cronenwett, 1841–1931
Tune: J. Klug, Geistliche Lieder, 1533

WO GOTT ZUM HAUS
L M

341 O God, Our Lord, Your Holy Word

1 O God, our Lord, Your ho-ly Word Was long a hid-den
2 Sal - va-tion true By faith in you, That is your Gos-pel's
3 Lord, you a-lone This work have done By your free grace and
4 You are my Lord, And by your Word Death holds no dread-ful

trea - sure Till to its place It was by grace Re-
preach - ing, The heart and core Of Bi-ble lore In
fa - vor. All who be-lieve Will grace re-ceive Through
ter - rors; Your pre-cious blood, My high-est good, Has

stored in full - est mea - sure. For this to-day Our
all its sa - cred teach - ing. In Christ we must Put
Je - sus Christ, our Sav - ior. And though the foe Would
blot - ted out my er - rors. My thanks to you! Your

thanks we say And glad - ly glo - ri - fy you. Your
all our trust, Not in our deeds or la - bor; With
o - ver - throw Your Word with grim en - deav - or, What
Word is true, You keep your prom - ise ev - er. While

mer - cy show And grace be - stow On all who still de - ny you.
con - science pure And heart se - cure Love you, Lord, and our neigh - bor.
plan he tries, It al - ways dies; Your Word will stand for - ev - er.
here I live, Your grace you give And heav-en's bliss for - ev - er.

Text: author unknown, 1527, cento; tr. W. Gustave Polack, 1890–1950, alt.
Tune: Enchiridion, Erfurt, 1527

O HERRE GOTT
447 447 D

Almighty God, Your Word Is Cast 342

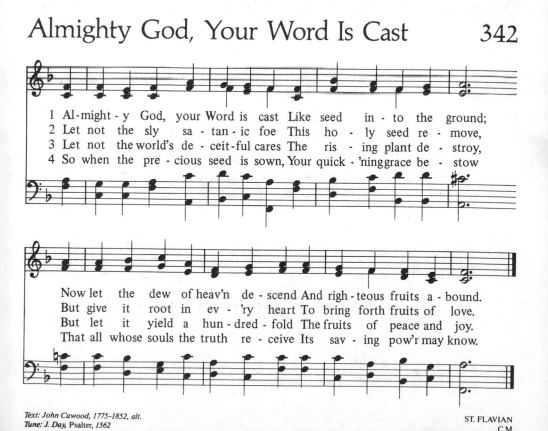

1 Al - might - y God, your Word is cast Like seed in - to the ground;
2 Let not the sly sa - tan - ic foe This ho - ly seed re - move,
3 Let not the world's de - ceit-ful cares The ris - ing plant de - stroy,
4 So when the pre - cious seed is sown, Your quick - 'ning grace be - stow

Now let the dew of heav'n de - scend And righ - teous fruits a - bound.
But give it root in ev - 'ry heart To bring forth fruits of love.
But let it yield a hun - dred - fold The fruits of peace and joy.
That all whose souls the truth re - ceive Its sav - ing pow'r may know.

Text: John Cawood, 1775–1852, alt.
Tune: J. Day, Psalter, 1562

ST. FLAVIAN
CM

343 God Has Spoken by His Prophets

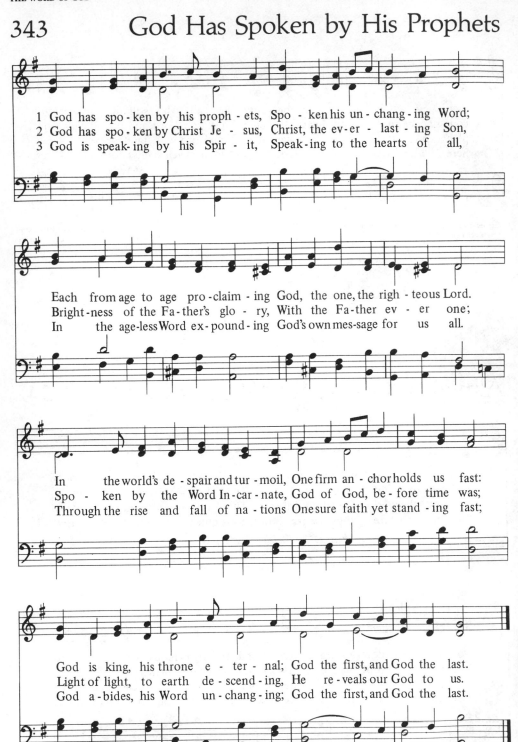

1 God has spo-ken by his proph-ets, Spo-ken his un-chang-ing Word;
2 God has spo-ken by Christ Je - sus, Christ, the ev-er - last-ing Son,
3 God is speak-ing by his Spir - it, Speak-ing to the hearts of all,

Each from age to age pro-claim-ing God, the one, the righ-teous Lord.
Bright-ness of the Fa-ther's glo - ry, With the Fa-ther ev - er one;
In the age-less Word ex-pound-ing God's own mes-sage for us all.

In the world's de-spair and tur-moil, One firm an-chor holds us fast:
Spo - ken by the Word In-car-nate, God of God, be-fore time was;
Through the rise and fall of na-tions One sure faith yet stand-ing fast;

God is king, his throne e - ter - nal; God the first, and God the last.
Light of light, to earth de-scend-ing, He re-veals our God to us.
God a-bides, his Word un-chang-ing; God the first, and God the last.

© Text: George W. Briggs, 1875-1959, alt.
Tune: Henry Smart, 1813-79

REX GLORIAE
87 87 D

Lord Jesus Christ, Will You Not Stay   344

1 Lord Je - sus Christ, will you not stay? It is now
2 Re - kin - dle for this end - time stress Faith's an - cient
3 To hope grown dim, To hearts turned cold Speak tongues of
4 May glo - rious truths that we have heard, The bright lance

toward the end of day. Oh, let your Word,
strength and stead - fast - ness That we keep pure
fire and make us bold To shine your Word
of your might - y Word, Spurn Sa - tan that

that sav - ing light, Shine forth un-dimmed in - to the night.
till life is spent Your ho - ly Word and Sac - ra - ment.
of sav - ing grace In - to each dark and love - less place.
your Church be strong, Bold, u - ni - fied in act and song.

5 Restrain, O Lord, the human pride
That seeks to thrust your truth aside
Or with some man-made thoughts or things
Would dim the words your Spirit sings.

6 The cause is yours, the glory too.
Then hear us, Lord, and keep us true,
Your Word alone our heart's defense,
The Church's glorious confidence.

© Text: Nikolaus Selnecker, 1532-92, et al.; tr. F. Samuel Janzow, b. 1913
Tune: Geistliche Lieder, Leipzig, 1589

ACH BLEIB BEI UNS
L M

345 # Come unto Me, Ye Weary

1 "Come un-to me, ye wea - ry, And I will give you rest."
2 "Come un-to me, ye wan - d'rers, And I will give you light."
3 "Come un-to me, ye faint - ing, And I will give you life."
4 "And who-so-ev-er com - eth, I will not cast him out."

O bless-ed voice of Je - sus, Which comes to hearts op -prest!
O lov-ing voice of Je - sus, Which comes to cheer the night!
O cheer-ing voice of Je - sus, Which comes to aid our strife!
O pa-tient love of Je - sus, Which drives a - way our doubt,

It tells of ben-e-dic-tion, Of par - don, grace, and peace,
Our hearts were filled with sad - ness, And we had lost our way;
The foe is stern and ea - ger, The fight is fierce and long;
Which, though we be un-wor - thy Of love so great and free,

Of joy that has no end - ing, Of love that can-not cease.
But thou hast brought us glad - ness And songs at break of day.
But thou hast made us might - y And strong-er than the strong.
In - vites us ver-y sin - ners To come, dear Lord, to thee!

Text: William C. Dix, 1837–98
Tune: J. A. Anthes, 1789–1842

ANTHES
76 76 D

O Kingly Love, That Faithfully

1 O king-ly Love, that faith-ful-ly Didst keep thine an-cient prom-is-es,
2 O lav-ish Love, that didst pre-pare A ta-ble boun-teous as thy heart,
3 O seek-ing Love, thy hur-rying feet Go search-ing still to urge and call
4 O ho-ly Love, thou canst not brook Man's cool and care-less en-mi-ty;

Didst bid the bid-den come to thee, The peo-ple thou didst choose to
That men might leave their pu-ny care And taste and see how good thou
The bad and good on ev-'ry street To fill thy bound-less ban-quet
O ruth-less Love, thou wilt not look On man robed in con-tempt of

bless, This day we raise Our song of praise, A-dor-ing thee,
art, This day we raise Our song of praise, A-dor-ing thee,
hall. This day we raise Our song of praise, A-dor-ing thee,
thee. Thine ech-oes die; Our deeds de-ny Thy sum-mon-ing:

Hymn continues on next page

Thy liv - ing breath did blow for all the world to hear,
Thy liv - ing breath did blow for all the world to hear,
Thy liv - ing breath did blow for all the world to hear,
And blow once more for us and all the world to hear,

Liv - ing and clear:
Liv - ing and clear:
Liv - ing and clear:
Liv - ing and clear: The feast is read - y. Come to the feast, The good

and the bad. Come and be glad! Great - est and least, Come to the feast!

© Text: Martin H. Franzmann, 1907–76
© Tune: Richard W. Hillert, b. 1923

KINGLY LOVE
P M

347 Today Your Mercy Calls Us

1 To-day your mer-cy calls us To wash a-way our
2 To-day your gate is o-pen, And all who en-ter
3 To-day our Fa-ther calls us; His Ho-ly Spir-it
4 O all-em-brac-ing Mer-cy, O ev-er-o-pen

sin. How-ev-er great our tres-pass, What-ev-er we have
in Shall find a Fa-ther's wel-come And par-don for their
waits; His bless-ed an-gels gath-er A-round the heav'n-ly
Door, What should we do with-out you When heart and eye run

been, How-ev-er long from mer-cy Our hearts have turned a-
sin. The past shall be for-got-ten, A pres-ent joy be
gates. No ques-tion will be asked us, How of-ten we have
o'er? When all things seem a-gainst us, To drive us to de-

way, Your pre-cious blood can wash us And make us clean to-day.
giv'n, A fu-ture grace be prom-ised, A glo-rious crown in heav'n.
come; Al-though we oft have wan-dered, It is our Fa-ther's home.
spair, We know one gate is o-pen, One ear will hear our prayer.

Text: Oswald Allen, 1816–78, alt.
Tune: J. A. Anthes, 1789–1842

ANTHES
76 76 D

I Heard the Voice of Jesus Say

1 I heard the voice of Je-sus say, "Come un - to me and rest;
2 I heard the voice of Je-sus say, "Be - hold, I free - ly give
3 I heard the voice of Je-sus say, "I am this dark world's light;

Lay down, O wea - ry one, lay down Your head up - on my breast."
The liv - ing wa - ter, thirst - y one; Stoop down and drink and live."
Look un - to me, your morn shall rise, And all your day be bright."

I came to Je - sus as I was, So wea - ry, worn, and sad;
I came to Je - sus, and I drank Of that life - giv - ing stream;
I looked to Je - sus, and I found In him my star, my sun;

I found in him a rest - ing-place, And he has made me glad.
My thirst was quenched, my soul re-vived, And now I live in him.
And in that light of life I'll walk Till trav-'ling days are done.

Text: Horatius Bonar, 1808–89
Text: Thomas Tallis, c. 1505–85

THIRD MODE MELODY
CM D

Delay Not, Delay Not, O Sinner, Draw Near

349

1 De - lay not, de - lay not, O sin - ner, draw near;
2 De - lay not, de - lay not, O sin - ner, to come;
3 De - lay not, de - lay not! The Spir - it of grace,
4 De - lay not, de - lay not! The hour is at hand;

The wa - ters of life are now flow - ing for you.
For mer - cy still lin - gers and calls you to - day.
Long grieved and re - sist - ed, may take his sad flight
The earth will dis - solve, and the heav - ens will fade.

No price is de - mand - ed, the Sav - ior is here,
Its voice is not heard in the vale of the tomb;
And leave you in dark - ness to fin - ish your race,
The dead, small and great, in the judg - ment must stand.

Re - demp - tion is pur - chased, God's prom - ise is true.
Its mes - sage, un - heed - ed, will soon pass a - way.
To sink in the gloom of e - ter - ni - ty's night.
What pow'r, then, O sin - ner, can lend you its aid?

5 Delay not, delay not! Why longer abuse
   The love and compassion of Jesus, your God?
   A fountain is opened; how can you refuse
   To wash and be cleansed in his pardoning blood?

Text: Thomas Hastings, 1784–1872, alt.
Tune: Welsh, c. 1600

MALDWYN
11 11 11 11

The Savior Calls; Let Every Ear   350

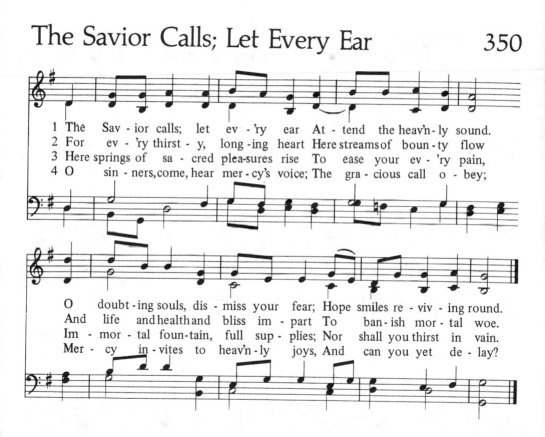

1 The Sav-ior calls; let ev-'ry ear At-tend the heav'n-ly sound.
2 For ev-'ry thirst-y, long-ing heart Here streams of boun-ty flow
3 Here springs of sa-cred plea-sures rise To ease your ev-'ry pain,
4 O sin-ners, come, hear mer-cy's voice; The gra-cious call o-bey;

O doubt-ing souls, dis-miss your fear; Hope smiles re-viv-ing round.
And life and health and bliss im-part To ban-ish mor-tal woe.
Im-mor-tal foun-tain, full sup-plies; Nor shall you thirst in vain.
Mer-cy in-vites to heav'n-ly joys, And can you yet de-lay?

5 Dear Savior, draw reluctant hearts;
   To you let sinners fly
And take the bliss your love imparts,
   Revive, and never die.

Text: Anne Steele, 1716–78, alt.
Tune: Carl G. Gläser, 1784–1829

AZMON
C M

351

By Grace I'm Saved

1 By grace I'm saved, grace free and bound-less; My soul, be-lieve and
2 By grace God's Son, our on-ly Sav-ior, Came down to earth to
3 By grace! This ground of faith is cer-tain; As long as God is
4 By grace to tim-id hearts that trem-ble, In trib-u-la-tion's

doubt it not. Why stag-ger at this word of prom-ise?
bear our sin. Was it be-cause of your own mer-it
true, it stands. What saints have penned by in-spi-ra-tion,
fur-nace tried, By grace, in spite of fear and trou-ble,

Has Scrip-ture ev-er false-hood taught? No; then this word must
That Je-sus died your soul to win? No, it was grace, and
What in his Word our God com-mands, Our faith in what our
The Fa-ther's heart is o-pen wide. Where could I help and

true re-main: By grace you too will life ob-tain.
grace a-lone, That brought him from his heav'n-ly throne.
God has done De-pends on grace— grace through his Son.
strength se-cure If grace were not my an-chor sure?

5 By grace! On this I'll rest when dying;
   In Jesus' promise I rejoice;
   For though I know my heart's condition,

I also know my Savior's voice.
My heart is glad, all grief has flown
Since I am saved by grace alone.

Text: Christian L. Scheidt, 1709–61; tr. The Lutheran Hymnal, 1941, alt.
Tune: Kornelius Heinrich Dretzel, 1705–73

O DASS ICH TAUSEND ZUNGEN HÄTTE
98 98 88

God Loved the World So that He Gave   352

1 God loved the world so that he gave His only
Son the lost to save That all who would in him believe
Should everlasting life receive.

2 Christ Jesus is the ground of faith, Who was made
flesh and suffered death; All who confide in Christ
alone Are built on this chief cornerstone.

3 If you are sick, if death is near, This truth your
troubled heart can cheer: Christ Jesus saves your soul
from death; That is the firmest ground of faith.

4 Be of good cheer, for God's own Son Forgives all
sins which you have done; You're justified by Jesus' blood;
Baptized, you have the highest good.

5 Glory to God the Father, Son,
   And Holy Spirit, Three in One!

To you, O blessed Trinity,
Be praise now and eternally!

Text: L. Bollhagen, Heiliges Lippen- und Herzens-Opfer, c. 1778; tr. August Crull, 1845–1923, alt.
Tune: Melchior Vulpius, c. 1560–1615

DIE HELLE SONN LEUCHT
L M

353   Dear Christians, One and All

1 Dear Chris - tians, one and all, re - joice, With ex - ul -
2 Fast bound in Sa - tan's chains I lay, Death brood - ed
3 My own good works all came to naught, No grace or
4 But God had seen my wretch - ed state Be - fore the

ta - tion spring - ing, And with u - nit - ed
dark - ly o'er me, Sin was my tor - ment
mer - it gain - ing; Free will a - gainst God's
world's foun - da - tion, And mind - ful of his

heart and voice And ho - ly rap - ture sing - ing,
night and day; In sin my moth - er bore me.
judg - ment fought, Dead to all good re - main - ing.
mer - cies great, He planned for my sal - va - tion.

Pro - claim the won - ders God has done, How his right
But dai - ly deep - er still I fell; My life be -
My fears in - creased till sheer de - spair Left on - ly
He turned to me a fa - ther's heart; He did not

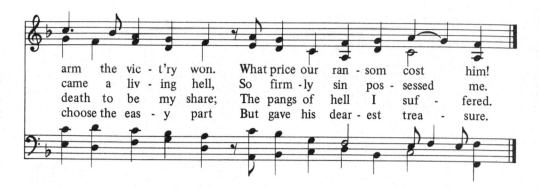

arm the vic - t'ry won. What price our ran - som cost him!
came a liv - ing hell, So firm - ly sin pos - sessed me.
death to be my share; The pangs of hell I suf - fered.
choose the eas - y part But gave his dear - est trea - sure.

5 God said to his beloved Son:
   "It's time to have compassion.
   Then go, bright jewel of my crown,
   And bring to all salvation;
   From sin and sorrow set them free;
   Slay bitter death for them that they
   May live with you forever."

6 The Son obeyed his Father's will,
   Was born of virgin mother;
   And God's good pleasure to fulfill,
   He came to be my brother.
   His royal pow'r disguised he bore,
   A servant's form, like mine, he wore
   To lead the devil captive.

7 To me he said: "Stay close to me,
   I am your rock and castle.
   Your ransom I myself will be;
   For you I strive and wrestle;
   For I am yours, and you are mine,
   And where I am you may remain;
   The foe shall not divide us.

8 "Though he will shed my precious blood,
   Of life me thus bereaving,
   All this I suffer for your good;
   Be steadfast and believing.
   Life will from death the vict'ry win;
   My innocence shall bear your sin;
   And you are blest forever.

9 "Now to my Father I depart,
   From earth to heav'n ascending,
   And, heav'nly wisdom to impart,
   The Holy Spirit sending;
   In trouble he will comfort you
   And teach you always to be true
   And into truth shall guide you.

10 "What I on earth have done and taught
   Guide all your life and teaching;
   So shall the kingdom's work be wrought
   And honored in your preaching.
   But watch lest foes with base alloy
   The heav'nly treasure should destroy;
   This final word I leave you."

Text: Martin Luther, 1483–1546; tr. Richard Massie, 1800–87, alt.
Tune: Etlich Christlich lider, *Wittenberg, 1524*

NUN FREUT EUCH
87 87 887

354 I Know My Faith Is Founded

1 I know my faith is found - ed On Je - sus Christ, my
2 In - crease my faith, dear Sav - ior, For Sa - tan seeks by
3 In faith, Lord, let me serve you; When per - se - cu - tion,

God and Lord; And this my faith con - fess - ing, Un -
night and day To rob me of this trea - sure And
grief, and pain From you, Lord, seek to swerve me, Let

moved I stand on his sure Word. Man's rea - son can - not
take my hope of bliss a - way. But, Lord, with you be -
me a stead - fast trust re - tain; And then at my de -

fath - om The truth of God pro - found;
side me, I shall be un - dis - mayed;
par - ture, Lord, take me home to you

Who trusts its sub-tle wis-dom Re-lies on shift-ing
And led by your good Spir-it, I shall be un-a-
Your rich-es to in-her-it As all you said holds

ground. God's Word is all-suf-fi-cient, It
fraid. A-bide with me, O Sav-ior, A
true. In life and death, Lord, keep me Un-

makes di-vine-ly sure, And trust-ing in its
firm-er faith be-stow; Then I shall bid de-
til your heav'n I gain, Where I by your great

wis-dom, My faith shall rest se-cure.
fi-ance To ev-'ry e-vil foe.
mer-cy The end of faith at-tain.

Text: Erdmann Neumeister, 1671-1756; *tr.* The Lutheran Hymnal, *1941, alt.*
Tune: Hans Kugelmann, Concentus novi, *1540*

NUN LOB, MEIN SEEL
P M

355 Salvation unto Us Has Come

1 Sal - va - tion un - to us has come By God's free grace and
2 What God did in his Law de - mand And none to him could
3 It was a false, mis-lead-ing dream That God his Law had
4 Since Christ has full a -tone-ment made And brought to us sal -

fa - vor; Good works can - not a - vert our doom, They help and
ren - der Caused wrath and woe on ev -'ry hand For man, the
giv - en That sin - ners could them-selves re-deem And by their
va - tion, Each Chris - tian there-fore may be glad And build on

save us nev - er. Faith looks to Je - sus Christ a - lone, Who
vile of - fend - er. Our flesh has not those pure de - sires The
works gain heav - en. The Law is but a mir - ror bright To
this foun - da - tion. Your grace a - lone, dear Lord, I plead, Your

did for all the world a - tone; He is our one re - deem-er.
spir - it of the Law re-quires, And lost is our con - di - tion.
bring the in - bred sin to light That lurks with - in our na - ture.
death is now my life in - deed, For you have paid my ran - som.

5 Faith clings to Jesus' cross alone
   And rests in him unceasing;
   And by its fruits true faith is known,
     With love and hope increasing.
   For faith alone can justify;
   Works serve our neighbor and supply
     The proof that faith is living.

6 All blessing, honor, thanks, and praise
   To Father, Son, and Spirit,
   The God who saved us by his grace;
     All glory to his merit.
   O triune God in heav'n above,
   You have revealed your saving love;
     Your blessed name we hallow.

Text: Paul Speratus, 1484–1531; tr. The Lutheran Hymnal, *1941, alt.*
Tune: Etlich Christlich lider, *Wittenberg, 1524*

ES IST DAS HEIL
87 87 887

Drawn to the Cross, Which You Have Blessed

356

1 Drawn to the cross, which you have blessed With heal-ing
2 How well you know my griefs and fears, Your grace a-
3 Wash me and take a-way each stain; Let noth-ing
4 Then all that you would have me do Shall such glad

gifts for souls dis-tressed, To find in you my
bused, my mis-spent years! Yet now to you with
of my sin re-main. For cleans-ing, though it
ser-vice be for you That an-gels wish to

life, my rest,
con-trite tears,
be through pain,
do it too.

Christ Cru-ci-fied, I come.

Text: Genevieve Irons, b. 1855, alt.
Tune: Joseph Barnby, 1838–96

DUNSTAN
888 6

357 I Trust, O Christ, in You Alone

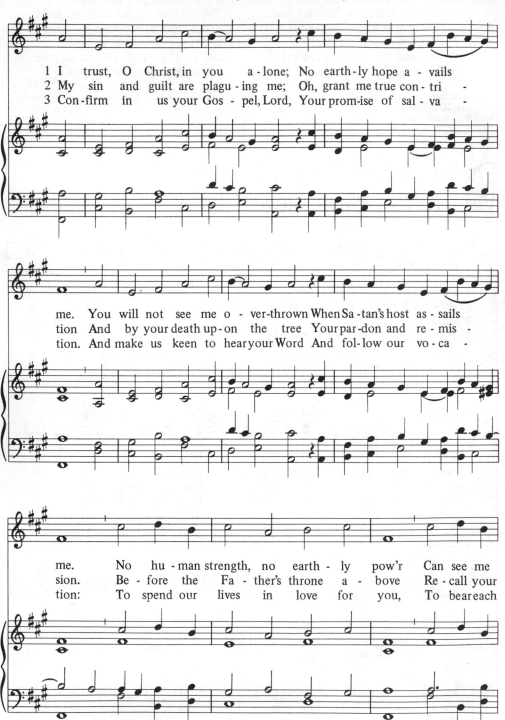

1 I trust, O Christ, in you a - lone; No earth-ly hope a - vails
2 My sin and guilt are plagu-ing me; Oh, grant me true con - tri -
3 Con-firm in us your Gos - pel, Lord, Your prom-ise of sal - va -

me. You will not see me o - ver-thrown When Sa-tan's host as-sails
tion And by your death up-on the tree Your par-don and re - mis -
tion. And make us keen to hear your Word And fol-low our vo - ca -

me. No hu - man strength, no earth - ly pow'r Can see me
sion. Be - fore the Fa - ther's throne a - bove Re - call your
tion: To spend our lives in love for you, To bear each

through the e - vil hour, For you a - lone my strength re - new.
match - less deed of love That he may lift my dread - ful load,
oth - er's bur - dens too. And then, at last, when death shall loom,

I cry to you! I trust, O Lord, your prom - ise true.
O Son of God! I plead the grace your death be - stowed.
O Sav - ior, come And bear your loved ones safe - ly home.

© Text: Konrad Hubert, 1507–77; tr. Gilbert E. Doan, b. 1930
Tune: Eyn schönn Lied, Wittenberg, 1541

ALLEIN ZU DIR
87 87 888 48

358 Seek Where You May to Find a Way

1 Seek where you may To find a way, Rest-less, toward your sal-
2 Seek whom you may To be your stay, None can re-deem his
3 Seek him a-lone, Do not post-pone; Let him your soul de-
4 My heart's de-light, My crown most bright, O Christ, my joy for-

va - tion. My heart is stilled, On Christ I build, He
broth - er. All help-ers failed; This man pre-vailed, The
liv - er. All you who thirst, Go to him first, Whose
ev - er. Not wealth nor pride Nor for-tune's tide Our

is the one foun-da - tion. His Word is sure, His
God - man and none oth - er, Our Ser-vant-King Of
grace flows like a riv - er. Seek him in-deed In
bonds of love shall sev - er. You are my Lord; Your

works en - dure; He o-ver-throws All e-vil foes;
whom we sing. We're jus-ti-fied Be-cause he died,
ev - 'ry need; He will im-part To ev-'ry heart
pre - cious Word Shall guide my way And help me stay

Through him   I   more   than   con   -   quer.
The   guilt - y   be - ing   guilt   -   less.
The   full - ness   of   his   trea   -   sure.
For - ev - er   in   your   pres   -   ence.

Text: Georg Weissel, 1590–1635; tr. Arthur Voss, 1899–1955, alt.
Tune: Johann Stobäus, 1580–1646

SUCH, WER DA WILL
447 447 44447

Just as I Am, Without One Plea   359

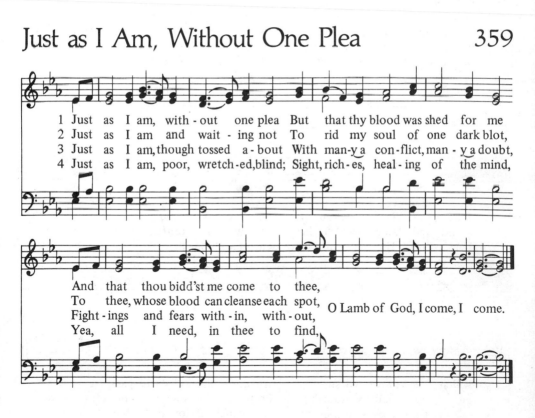

1 Just   as   I   am, with - out   one plea   But   that thy blood was shed   for   me
2 Just   as   I   am   and   wait - ing not   To   rid my soul of one   dark blot,
3 Just   as   I   am, though tossed a - bout   With man-y a con - flict, man - y a doubt,
4 Just   as   I   am, poor, wretch - ed, blind; Sight, rich - es, heal - ing of   the mind,

And   that   thou bidd'st me come   to   thee,
To   thee, whose blood can cleanse each spot,   O Lamb of God, I come, I   come.
Fight - ings   and fears with - in,   with - out,
Yea,   all   I   need,   in   thee   to   find,

5 Just as I am, thou wilt receive,
Wilt welcome, pardon, cleanse, relieve;
Because thy promise I believe,
O Lamb of God, I come, I come.

6 Just as I am; thy love unknown
Has broken ev'ry barrier down;
Now to be thine, yea, thine alone,
O Lamb of God, I come, I come.

Text: Charlotte Elliott, 1789–1871
Tune: William B. Bradbury, 1816–68

WOODWORTH
L M

Now I Have Found the Firm Foundation

1 Now I have found the firm foun - da - tion Which holds my
2 It is that mer - cy nev - er end - ing Which far our
3 Our ru - in God has not in - tend - ed; For our sal -
4 O depth of love, to me re - veal - ing The sea where

an - chor ev - er sure, Laid long be - fore the world's cre -
hu - man thought tran - scends Of him who, lov - ing arms ex -
va - tion he has yearned; For this his Son to earth de -
my sins dis - ap - pear! In Christ my wounds find per - fect

a - tion In Christ my Sav - ior's wounds se - cure, Foun - da - tion
tend - ing, To wretch - ed sin - ners con - de - scends; His heart with
scend - ed And now to heav - en has re - turned. Thus he is
heal - ing, There is no con - dem - na - tion here; For Je - sus'

which un - moved will stay When all this world will pass a - way.
pit - y still will break Both if we seek him or for - sake.
pa - tient ev - er - more And knocks at our heart's bolt - ed door.
blood through earth and skies For - ev - er "Mer - cy! Mer - cy!" cries.

5 I never will forget this crying;
 In faith I trust it all my days,
And when because of sins I'm sighing,
 Into my Father's heart I gaze,
For in his heart is surely found
Free mercy without end and bound.

6 Lord, I will stand on this foundation
 As long as I on earth remain;
This will engage my meditation
 While I the breath of life retain.
And then, when face to face with you,
I'll sing your mercy great and true.

Text: Johann A. Rothe, 1688–1758; tr. The Lutheran Hymnal, *1941, alt.*
Tune: Johann B. König, Harmonischer Lieder-Schatz, *1738*

O DASS ICH TAUSEND ZUNGEN HÄTTE
98 98 88

Rock of Ages, Cleft for Me 361

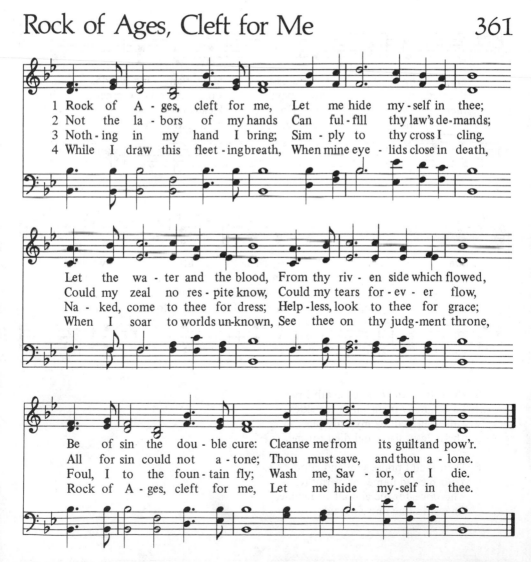

1 Rock of Ages, cleft for me, Let me hide myself in thee;
2 Not the labors of my hands Can fulfill thy law's demands;
3 Nothing in my hand I bring; Simply to thy cross I cling.
4 While I draw this fleeting breath, When mine eyelids close in death,

Let the water and the blood, From thy riven side which flowed,
Could my zeal no respite know, Could my tears forever flow,
Naked, come to thee for dress; Helpless, look to thee for grace;
When I soar to worlds unknown, See thee on thy judgment throne,

Be of sin the double cure: Cleanse me from its guilt and pow'r.
All for sin could not atone; Thou must save, and thou alone.
Foul, I to the fountain fly; Wash me, Savior, or I die.
Rock of Ages, cleft for me, Let me hide myself in thee.

Text: Augustus M. Toplady, 1740–78
Tune: Thomas Hastings, 1784–1872

TOPLADY
77 77 77

362 Jesus, Your Blood and Righteousness

1 Je - sus, your blood and righ - teous-ness My beau - ty are, my glo - rious dress; Mid flam - ing worlds, in these ar - rayed, With joy shall I lift up my head.

2 Bold shall I stand in that great day, Cleansed and re - deemed, no debt to pay; For by your cross ab - solved I am From sin and guilt, from fear and shame.

3 Lord, I be - lieve your pre - cious blood, Which at the mer - cy - seat of God Pleads for the cap - tives' lib - er - ty, Was al - so shed in love for me.

4 Lord, I be - lieve, were sin - ners more Than sands up - on the o - cean shore, You have for all a ran - som paid, For all a full a - tone - ment made.

5 When from the dust of death I rise
To claim my mansion in the skies,
This then shall be my only plea:
Christ Jesus lived and died for me.

6 Then shall I praise you and adore
Your blessed name forevermore,
Who once, for me and all you made,
An everlasting ransom paid.

Text: Nicolaus L. von Zinzendorf, 1700–60; tr. John Wesley, 1703–91, alt.
Tune: George J. Elvey, 1816–93

ST. CRISPIN
L M

All Mankind Fell in Adam's Fall

1 All mankind fell in Adam's fall,
One common sin infects us all;
From sire to son the bane descends,
And over all the curse impends.

2 Through humankind corruption creeps
And them in dreadful bondage keeps;
In guilt they draw the infant breath
And reap its fruits of woe and death.

3 From hearts depraved, to evil prone,
Flow thoughts and deeds of sin alone;
God's image lost, the darkened soul
Seeks not nor finds its heav'nly goal.

4 But Christ, the second Adam, came
To bear our sin and woe and shame,
To be our life, our light, our way,
Our only hope, our only stay.

5 As by one man all mankind fell
And, born in sin, was doomed to hell,
So by one Man, who took our place,
We all received the gift of grace.

6 We thank you, Christ; new life is ours,
New light, new hope, new strength, new pow'rs:
This grace our ev'ry way attend
Until we reach our journey's end.

Text: Lazarus Spengler, 1479–1534; tr. Matthias Loy, 1828–1915, alt.
Tune: Louis Bourgeois, c. 1510 –c. 1561

WENN WIR IN HÖCHSTEN NÖTEN SEIN
L M

364 Oh, How Great Is Your Compassion

1 Oh, how great is your com - pas - sion, Faith - ful Fa - ther,
2 Your great love for this has striv - en That we may, from
3 Firm - ly to our soul's sal - va - tion Wit - ness - es your
4 Lord, your mer - cy will not leave me; Ev - er will your

God of grace, That with all our fall - en race
sin made free, Live with you e - ter - nal - ly.
Spir - it, Lord, In your sac - ra - ments and Word.
truth a - bide. Then in you I will con - fide.

In our depth of deg - ra - da - tion You had mer - cy
Your dear Son him - self has giv - en And ex - tends his
There he sends true con - so - la - tion, Giv - ing us the
Since your Word can - not de - ceive me, My sal - va - tion

so that we Might be saved e - ter - nal - ly!
gra - cious call, To his sup - per calls us all.
gift of faith That we fear not hell nor death.
is to me Safe and sure e - ter - nal - ly.

5 I will praise your great compassion,
  Faithful Father, God of grace,
  That with all our fallen race
In our depth of degradation
  You had mercy so that we
  Might be saved eternally.

Text: Johannes Olearius, 1611–84; tr. August Crull, 1845–1923, alt.
Tune: Hirthenlieder, Altdorf, 1653

ACH, WAS SOLL ICH SÜNDER MACHEN
877 877

Christ Be My Leader

365

1 Christ be my lead-er by night as by day; Safe through the
2 Christ be my teach-er in age as in youth, Drift-ing or
3 Christ be my sav-ior in calm as in strife; Death can-not

dark-ness, for he is the way. Glad-ly I fol-low, my
doubt-ing, for he is the truth. Grant me to trust him; though
hold me, for he is the life. Nor dark-ness nor doubt-ing nor

fu-ture his care; ... Dark-ness is day-light when Je-sus is there.
shift-ing as sand, ... Doubt can-not daunt me; in Je-sus I stand.
sin and its stain Can touch my sal-va-tion: with Je-sus I reign.

© Text: Timothy Dudley-Smith, b. 1926
Tune: Irish folk tune

SLANE
irregular

366　　　　　　　　　　　　　I Lay My Sins on Jesus

1 I lay my sins on Jesus, The spot-less Lamb of God;
2 I lay my wants on Jesus; All full-ness dwells in him;
3 I rest my soul on Jesus, This wea-ry soul of mine;

He bears them all and frees us From the ac-curs-ed load.
He heals all my dis-eas-es; My soul he does re-deem.
His right hand me em-brac-es; I on his breast re-cline.

I bring my guilt to Jesus To wash my crim-son stains
I lay my griefs on Jesus, My bur-dens and my cares;
I love the name of Jesus, Im-man-uel, Christ, the Lord;

Clean in his blood most pre-cious Till not a spot re-mains.
He from them all re-leas-es; He all my sor-rows shares.
Like fra-grance on the breez-es His name a-broad is poured.

Text: Horatius Bonar, 1808–89
Tune: Neu-vermehrtes Gesangbuch, *Meiningen, 1693*

MUNICH
76 76 D

When over Sin I Sorrow

367

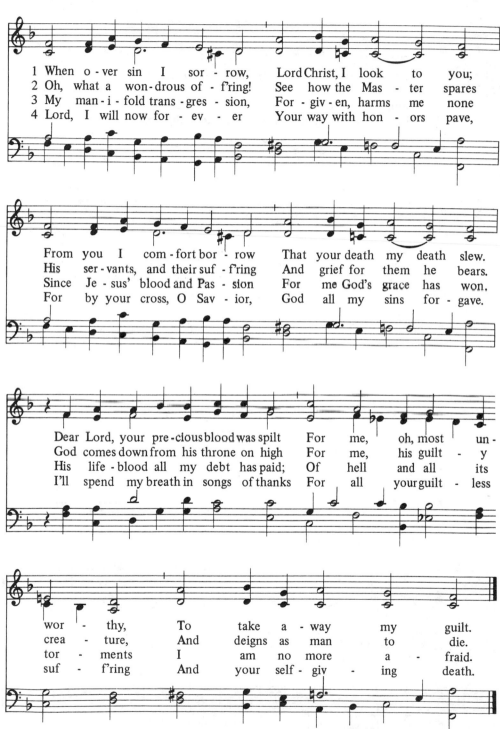

1 When o-ver sin I sor-row, Lord Christ, I look to you;
2 Oh, what a won-drous of-f'ring! See how the Mas-ter spares
3 My man-i-fold trans-gres-sion, For-giv-en, harms me none
4 Lord, I will now for-ev-er Your way with hon-ors pave,

From you I com-fort bor-row That your death my death slew.
His ser-vants, and their suf-f'ring And grief for them he bears.
Since Je-sus' blood and Pas-sion For me God's grace has won.
For by your cross, O Sav-ior, God all my sins for-gave.

Dear Lord, your pre-cious blood was spilt For me, oh, most un-
God comes down from his throne on high For me, his guilt-y
His life-blood all my debt has paid; Of hell and all its
I'll spend my breath in songs of thanks For all your guilt-less

wor-thy, To take a-way my guilt.
crea-ture, And deigns as man to die.
tor-ments I am no more a-fraid.
suf-f'ring And your self-giv-ing death.

Text: Justus Gesenius, 1601–73; tr. Catherine Winkworth, 1829–78, st. 1;
   The Lutheran Hymnal, *1941, sts. 2–4, alt.*
Tune: Enchiridion, Erfurt, 1524

HERR CHRIST, DER EINIG GOTTS SOHN
76 76 876

368 My Hope Is Built on Nothing Less

1 My hope is built on noth-ing less Than Je - sus' blood and righ-teous-ness; No mer - it of my own I claim But whol - ly lean on Je - sus' name.

2 When dark - ness veils his love - ly face, I rest on his un - chang - ing grace; In ev - 'ry high and storm - y gale My an - chor holds with - in the veil.

3 His oath, his cov - e - nant, his blood Sus - tain me in the rag - ing flood; When all sup - ports are washed a - way, He then is all my hope and stay.

4 When he shall come with trum - pet sound, Oh, may I then in him be found, Clothed in his righ - teous - ness a - lone, Re - deemed to stand be - fore the throne!

Refrain

On Christ, the sol - id rock, I stand; All oth - er ground is sink - ing sand.

Text: Edward Mote, 1797–1874, alt.
Tune: John Stainer, 1840–1901

MAGDALEN
L M and refrain

Through Jesus' Blood and Merit

1 Through Jesus' blood and merit | I am at peace with God;
2 There's nothing that can sever | From this great love of God;
3 Oh, neither life's temptation | Nor death's so trying hour
4 Nor any creature ever | Shall from the love of God

What, then, can daunt my spirit, | However dark my road?
No want, no pain whatever, | No famine, peril, flood.
Nor angels of high station | Nor any other pow'r
This wretched sinner sever; | For in my Savior's blood

My courage shall not fail me, | For God is on my side;
Though thousand foes surround me, | For slaughter mark his sheep,
Nor things that now are present | Nor things that are to come
This love has its foundation; | God hears my faithful prayer

Though hell itself assail me, | Its rage I may deride.
They never shall confound me, | The vic-t'ry I shall reap.
Nor height, however pleasant, | Nor depth of deepest gloom
And long before creation | Owns me his child and heir.

Text: Simon Dach, 1605–59; tr. The Lutheran Hymnal, 1941, alt.
Tune: Bohemian Brethren, Ein Gesangbuch der Brüder, 1544

LOB GOTT GETROST MIT SINGEN
76 76 D

370 Blest the Children of Our God

1 Blest the chil - dren of our God, They are bought with
2 They are jus - ti - fied by grace, They en - joy the
3 They are lights up - on the earth, Chil - dren of a

Christ's own blood; They are ran - somed from the grave,
Sav - ior's peace; All their sins are washed a - way,
heav'n - ly birth; One with God, with Je - sus one;

Life e - ter - nal they will have:
They will stand in God's great day: With them num - bered
Glo - ry is in them be - gun:

may we be Here and in e - ter - ni - ty!

Text: Joseph Humphreys, b. 1720, alt.
Tune: Johann G. Ebeling, 1637–76

VOLLER WUNDER
77 77 77

O God, My Faithful God

1 O God, my faithful God, True foun-tain ev-er flow-ing,
2 Give me the strength to do With read-y heart and will-ing
3 Keep me from say-ing words That lat-er need re-call-ing;
4 When dan-gers gath-er round, Oh, keep me calm and fear-less;

With-out whom noth-ing is, All per-fect gifts be-stow-ing:
What-ev-er you com-mand, My call-ing here ful-fill-ing.
Guard me lest i-dle speech May from my lips be fall-ing;
Help me to bear the cross When life seems dark and cheer-less;

Give me a health-y frame, And may I have with-in
Help me do what I should With all my might, and bless
But when with-in my place I must and ought to speak,
Help me, as you have taught, To love both great and small

A con-science free from blame, A soul un-stained by sin.
The out-come for my good, For you must give suc-cess.
Then to my words give grace Lest I of-fend the weak.
And by your Spir-it's might To live at peace with all.

Text: Johann Heermann, 1585–1647; tr. Catherine Winkworth, 1829–78, alt.
Tune: Ahasverus Fritsch, 1629–1701

WAS FRAG ICH NACH DER WELT
67 67 66 66

372 O God, Forsake Me Not

1 O God, for - sake me not! Your gra - cious pres - ence
2 O God, for - sake me not! Take not your Spir - it
3 O God, for - sake me not! Lord, hear my sup - pli -
4 O God, for - sake me not! My heart your grace ad -

lend me; Oh, lead your help - less child; Your
from me; Do not al - low the night Of
ca - tion! In ev - 'ry e - vil hour Help
dress - ing, O Fa - ther, God of love, Grant

Ho - ly Spir - it send me That I my course may
sin to o - ver - come me. In - crease my fee - ble
me re - sist temp - ta - tion; And when the prince of
me your heav'n - ly bless - ing To do when du - ty

run. Be you my light, my lot, My
faith, Which you your - self have wrought. Be
hell My con - science seeks to blot, Be
calls What - ev - er you al - lot, To

staff, my rock, my shield. O God, for - sake me not!
you my strength and pow'r. O God, for - sake me not!
then not far from me. O God, for - sake me not!
do what pleas - es you. O God, for - sake me not!

5 O God, forsake me not!
   Lord, I am yours forever.
The true faith grant to me;
   Grant that I leave you never.
Grant me a blessed end
   When my good fight is fought;
Help me in life and death.
   O God, forsake me not!

Text: Salomo Franck, 1659–1725; tr. August Crull, 1845–1923, alt.
Tune: Ahasverus Fritsch, 1629–1701

WAS FRAG ICH NACH DER WELT
67 67 66 66

373 Renew Me, O Eternal Light

1 Re - new me, O e - ter - nal Light,
2 Re - move the pow'r of sin from me
3 Cre - ate in me a new heart, Lord,
4 Grant that I on - ly you may love

And let my heart and soul be bright,
And cleanse all my im - pu - ri - ty
That glad - ly I o - bey your Word.
And seek those things which are a - bove

Il - lu - mined with the light of grace
That I may have the strength and will
Let what you will be my de - sire,
Till I be - hold you face to face,

That is - sues from your ho - ly face.
Temp - ta - tions of the flesh to still.
And with new life my soul in - spire.
O Light e - ter - nal, through your grace.

Text: Johann F. Ruopp, 1672–1708; tr. August Crull, 1845–1923, alt.
Tune: As hymnodus sacer, Leipzig, 1625

HERR JESU CHRIST, MEINS
L M

Savior, Thy Dying Love

374

1 Sav - ior, thy dy - ing love Thou gav - est me;
2 O'er the blest mer - cy seat, Plead - ing for me,
3 Give me a faith - ful heart, Like - ness to thee,
4 All that I am and have, Thy gifts so free,

Nor should I aught with - hold, Dear Lord, from thee.
My fee - ble faith looks up, Je - sus, to thee.
That each de - part - ing day Hence-forth may see
In joy, in grief, through life, Dear Lord, for thee!

In love my soul would bow, My heart ful - fill its vow,
Help me the cross to bear, Thy won - drous love de - clare,
Some work of love be - gun, Some deed of kind - ness done,
And when thy face I see, My ran - somed soul shall be

Some of - f'ring bring thee now, Some - thing for thee.
Some song to raise or prayer, Some - thing for thee.
Some wan - d'rer sought and won, Some - thing for thee.
Through all e - ter - ni - ty Some - thing for thee.

Text: Sylvanus D. Phelps, 1816–95
Tune: Joseph Barnby, 1838–96

WINTERTON
64 64 6664

375 You Will I Love, My Strength

1 You will I love, my strength, my tow - er; You will I love, my
2 You will I love, my life, my Sav - ior, You are my best, my
3 I thank you, Je - sus, sun from heav - en, Whose ra - diance has brought
4 Oh, keep me watch - ful, then, and hum - ble, And nev - er suf - fer

hope, my joy; You will I love with all my pow - er,
tru - est friend; You will I love and praise for - ev - er,
light to me; I thank you, who has rich - ly giv - en
me to stray; Up - hold me when my feet would stum - ble,

With fer - vor time can - not de - stroy. You will I
For nev - er shall your kind - ness end. Your love for
All that could make me glad and free. I thank you
And keep me faith - ful to your way. Fill all my

love, O Light di - vine, So long as life is mine.
me casts out my fear, You are my Sav - ior dear.
that my soul is healed With love that you re - vealed.
na - ture with your light, O Ra - diance strong and bright!

5 You will I love, my crown of gladness;
   You will I love, my God and Lord,
Within the darkest depths of sadness,
   And not for hope of high reward—
For your own sake, O Light divine,
   So long as life is mine!

Text: Johann Scheffler, 1624–77; tr. Catherine Winkworth, 1829–78, alt.
Tune: Johann B. König, Harmonischer Lieder-Schatz, 1738

ICH WILL DICH LIEBEN
88 88 88

Love in Christ Is Strong and Living 376

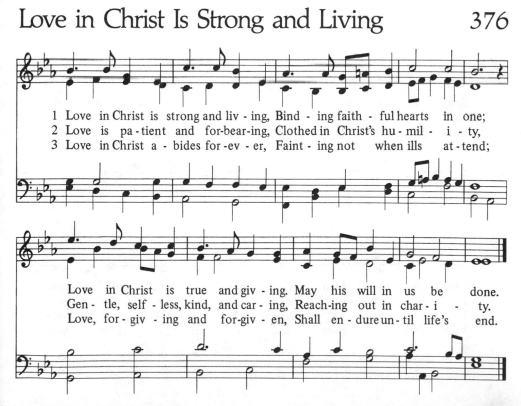

1 Love in Christ is strong and liv - ing, Bind - ing faith - ful hearts in one;
2 Love is pa - tient and for-bear-ing, Clothed in Christ's hu - mil - i - ty,
3 Love in Christ a - bides for -ev - er, Faint - ing not when ills at -tend;

Love in Christ is true and giv - ing. May his will in us be done.
Gen - tle, self - less, kind, and car - ing, Reach-ing out in char - i - ty.
Love, for - giv - ing and for-giv - en, Shall en - dure un - til life's end.

© Text: Dorothy R. Schultz, b. 1934
© Tune: Ralph C. Schultz, b. 1932

DOROTHY
87 87

377 Hope of the World

1 Hope of the world, thou Christ of great com-pas - sion;
2 Hope of the world, God's gift from high - est heav - en,
3 Hope of the world, a - foot on dust - y high - ways,
4 Hope of the world, who by thy cross didst save us

Speak to our fear - ful hearts by con - flict rent.
Bring - ing to hun - gry souls the bread of life,
Show - ing to wan - d'ring souls the path of light,
From death and dark de - spair, from sin and guilt,

Save us, thy peo - ple, from con - sum - ing pas - sion,
Still let thy Spir - it un - to us be giv - en
Walk thou be - side us lest the tempt - ing by - ways
We ren - der back the love thy mer - cy gave us;

Who by our own false hopes and aims are spent.
To heal earth's wounds and end our bit - ter strife.
Lure us a - way from thee to end - less night.
Take thou our lives and use them as thou wilt.

5 Hope of the world, O Christ, o'er death victorious,
    Who by this sign didst conquer grief and pain,
  We would be faithful to thy Gospel glorious;
    Thou art our Lord! Thou dost forever reign!

© *Text: Georgia Harkness, 1891–1974*
Tune: Trente quatre pseaumes de David, Geneva, 1551

DONNE SECOURS
11 10 11 10

My Faith Looks Trustingly

378

1 My faith looks trust-ing-ly To Christ of Cal-va-ry,
2 May your rich grace im-part Strength to my faint-ing heart,
3 While life's dark maze I tread And griefs a-round me spread,
4 When ends life's tran-sient dream, When death's cold, sul-len stream

My Sav-ior true! Lord, hear me while I pray, Take all my
My zeal in-spire; As you have died for me, My love, a-
Oh, be my guide; Make dark-ness turn to day, Wipe sor-row's
Rolls o-ver me, Blest Sav-ior, then in love Fear and dis-

guilt a-way, Strength-en in ev-'ry way My love for you!
dor-ing-ly, Pure, warm, and change-less be, A liv-ing fire!
tears a-way, Nor let me ev-er stray From you a-side.
trust re-move; Oh, bear me safe a-bove, Re-deemed and free!

Text: Ray Palmer, 1808–87, alt.
Tune: Lowell Mason, 1792–1872

OLIVET
664 6664

"Come, Follow Me"
Said Christ, the Lord

379

1 "Come, fol - low me," said Christ, the Lord, "All in my way a-
2 "I am the light; I light the way, A god - ly life dis-
3 "My heart is rich in low - li - ness; My soul with love is
4 "I teach you how to shun and flee What harms your soul's sal-

bid - ing; Your self - ish - ness throw o - ver - board, O-
play - ing; I help you walk as in the day; I
glow - ing; My lips the words of grace ex - press, Their
va - tion; Your heart from ev - 'ry guile to free, From

bey my call and guid - ing. Oh, bear your cross - es,
keep your feet from stray - ing. I am the way, and
tones all gen - tly flow - ing. My heart, my mind, my
sin and its temp - ta - tion. I am the ref - uge

and con - fide In my ex - am - ple as your guide.
well I show How you should jour - ney here be - low.
strength, my all To God I yield; on him I call.
of the soul And lead you to your heav'n - ly goal."

5 Then let us follow Christ, our Lord,
   And take the cross appointed
And, firmly clinging to his word,
   In suff'ring be undaunted.
For those who bear the battle's strain
The crown of heav'nly life obtain.

Text: Johann Scheffler, 1624–77; tr. Charles W. Schaeffer, 1813–96, alt.
Tune: Bartholomäus Gesius, c. 1555–1613, adapt.

MACHS MIT MIR, GOTT
87 87 88

Forth in Your Name, O Lord, I Go   380

1 Forth in your name, O Lord, I go,   My dai-ly
2 The task your wis-dom has as-signed,   Oh, let me
3 You may I find at my right hand,   Whose eyes see
4 Give me to bear your eas-y yoke   And ev-'ry

la-bor to pur-sue,   You, on-ly you,   re-
cheer-ful-ly ful-fill; In all my works   your
tru-ly what I do,   And la-bor on   at
mo-ment watch and pray And still to things   e-

solved to know   In all I think or speak or do.
pres-ence find   And prove your good and per-fect will.
your com-mand   And of-fer all my works to you.
ter-nal look   And has-ten to your glo-rious day.

5 For you I joyously employ   I run my course with even joy,
   Whatever you in grace have giv'n;   I closely walk with you to heav'n.

Text: Charles Wesley, 1707–88, alt.
© *Tune: Barry L. Bobb, b. 1951*

LAKEWOOD
L M

381

Let Us Ever Walk with Jesus

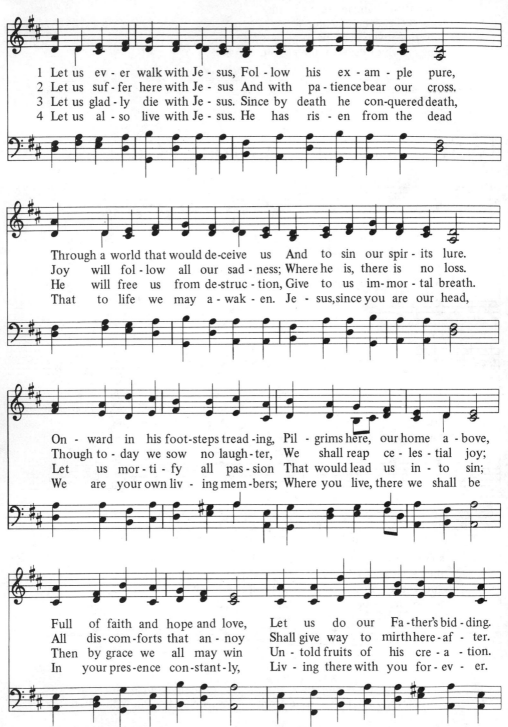

1 Let us ev-er walk with Je-sus, Fol-low his ex-am-ple pure,
2 Let us suf-fer here with Je-sus And with pa-tience bear our cross.
3 Let us glad-ly die with Je-sus. Since by death he con-quered death,
4 Let us al-so live with Je-sus. He has ris-en from the dead

Through a world that would de-ceive us And to sin our spir-its lure.
Joy will fol-low all our sad-ness; Where he is, there is no loss.
He will free us from de-struc-tion, Give to us im-mor-tal breath.
That to life we may a-wak-en. Je-sus, since you are our head,

On-ward in his foot-steps tread-ing, Pil-grims here, our home a-bove,
Though to-day we sow no laugh-ter, We shall reap ce-les-tial joy;
Let us mor-ti-fy all pas-sion That would lead us in-to sin;
We are your own liv-ing mem-bers; Where you live, there we shall be

Full of faith and hope and love, Let us do our Fa-ther's bid-ding.
All dis-com-forts that an-noy Shall give way to mirth here-af-ter.
Then by grace we all may win Un-told fruits of his cre-a-tion.
In your pres-ence con-stant-ly, Liv-ing there with you for-ev-er.

Faith - ful Lord, with me a - bide; I shall fol - low where you guide.
Je - sus, here I share your woe; Help me there your joy to know.
Je - sus, un - to you I die, There to live with you on high.
Je - sus, let me faith - ful be, Life e - ter - nal grant to me.

© *Text: Sigismund von Birken, 1626–81; tr. Lutheran Book of Worship, 1978, alt.*
Tune: Georg G. Boltze, 1788

LASSET UNS MIT JESU ZIEHEN
P M

"Take Up Your Cross," the Savior Said   382

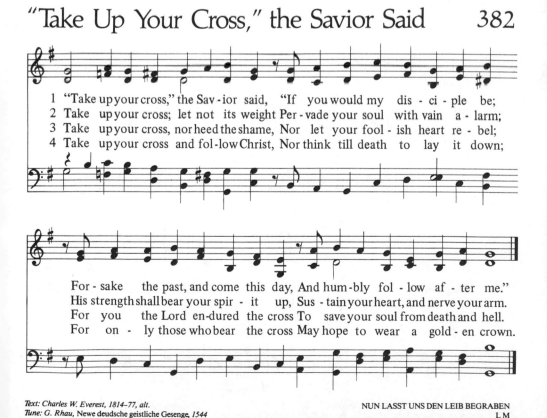

1 "Take up your cross," the Sav - ior said, "If you would my dis - ci - ple be;
2 Take up your cross; let not its weight Per - vade your soul with vain a - larm;
3 Take up your cross, nor heed the shame, Nor let your fool - ish heart re - bel;
4 Take up your cross and fol - low Christ, Nor think till death to lay it down;

For - sake the past, and come this day, And hum - bly fol - low af - ter me."
His strength shall bear your spir - it up, Sus - tain your heart, and nerve your arm.
For you the Lord en - dured the cross To save your soul from death and hell.
For on - ly those who bear the cross May hope to wear a gold - en crown.

Text: Charles W. Everest, 1814–77, alt.
Tune: G. Rhau, Newe deudsche geistliche Gesenge, 1544

NUN LASST UNS DEN LEIB BEGRABEN
L M

383 All Who Would Valiant Be

1 All who would val - iant be 'Gainst all di - sas - ter,
2 Who - so be - set them round With dis - mal sto - ries
3 Since, Lord, you will de - fend Us with your Spir - it,

Let them in con - stan - cy Fol - low the mas - ter.
Do but them - selves con - found; Their strength the more is.
We know we at the end Shall life in - her - it.

There's no dis - cour - age - ment Shall make them once re - lent
No foes shall stay their might; Though they with gi - ants fight,
Then fan - cies flee a - way! We'll fear not what they say,

Their first a - vowed in - tent To be true pil - grims.
They will make good their right To be true pil - grims.
We'll la - bor night and day To be true pil - grims.

© Text: Percy Dearmer, 1867-1936; after John Bunyan
© Tune: English traditional melody; coll., adapt., and arr. Ralph Vaughan Williams, 1872-1958

MONKS GATE
65 65 6665

All Who Would Valiant Be

384

1 All who would valiant be 'Gainst all di - sas - ter,
2 Who - so be - set them round With dis - mal sto - ries
3 Since, Lord, you will de - fend Us with your Spir - it,

Let them in con - stan - cy Fol - low the mas - ter.
Do but them - selves con - found; Their strength the more is.
We know we at the end Shall life in - her - it.

There's no dis - cour - age - ment Shall make them once re - lent
No foes shall stay their might; Though they with gi - ants fight,
Then fan - cies flee a - way! We'll fear not what they say,

Their first a - vowed in - tent To be true pil - grims.
They will make good their right To be true pil - grims.
We'll la - bor night and day To be true pil - grims.

© Text: Percy Dearmer, 1867-1936; after John Bunyan
Tune: C. Winfred Douglas, 1867-1944

ST. DUNSTAN'S
65 65 6665

385　　　　　　　　　　　How Can I Thank You, Lord

1 How can I thank you, Lord, For all your lov-ing-kind-ness,
2 It is your work a - lone That I am now con - vert - ed;
3 Lord, you have raised me up To joy and ex - ul - ta - tion
4 Grant that your Spir - it's help To me be al - ways giv - en

That you have pa - tient - ly En - dured my sin - ful blind - ness!
A - gainst the sin in me You have the pow'r as - sert - ed.
And clear - ly shown the way That leads me to sal - va - tion.
Lest I should fall a - gain And lose the way to heav - en.

When dead in man - y sins And tres - pass - es I lay,
Your mer - cy and your grace, Which rise a - fresh each morn,
My sins are washed a - way; For this I thank you, Lord,
Grant that he give me strength A - gainst in - fir - mi - ty;

I kin - dled, ho - ly God, Your an - ger ev - 'ry day.
Have turned my ston - y heart In - to a heart new - born.
That in my heart and soul I have all sin ab - horred.
May he re - new my heart To serve you will - ing - ly.

5 O Father, God of love,
   Accept my supplication;
O Savior, Son of God,
   Grant me your full salvation;

O Holy Spirit, be
   My ever faithful guide
That I may serve you here
   And there with you abide.

Text: David Denicke, 1603–80; tr. August Crull, 1845–1923, alt.
Tune: Neu-vermehrtes Gesangbuch, Meiningen, 1693

O GOTT, DU FROMMER GOTT
67 67 66 66

Jesus, Still Lead On 386

1 Je - sus, still lead on / Till our rest be won; / And al - though the way be cheer - less, / We will fol - low calm and fear - less; / Guide us by your hand / To our fa - ther - land.

2 If the way be drear, / If the foe be near, / Let no faith - less fears o'er-take us, / Let not faith and hope for-sake us; / Safe - ly past the foe / To our home we go.

3 When we seek re - lief / From a long - felt grief, / When temp-ta - tions come al - lur - ing, / Make us pa - tient and en-dur - ing; / Show us that bright shore / Where we weep no more.

4 Je - sus, still lead on / Till our rest be won; / Heav'n - ly lead - er, still di - rect us, / Still sup - port, con - sole, pro-tect us, / Till we safe - ly stand / In our fa - ther - land.

Text: Nicolaus L. von Zinzendorf, 1700–60; tr. Jane L. Borthwick, 1813–97, alt.
Tune: Adam Drese, 1620–1701

SEELENBRÄUTIGAM
55 88 55

387 Praise and Thanks and Adoration

1 Praise and thanks and ad - o - ra - tion, Son of God, to
2 Hold me ev - er in your keep - ing, Com - fort me in

you we give, For you chose to serve cre - a - tion,
pain and strife; Through my laugh - ter and my weep - ing

Died that Ad - am's heirs might live. Dear Lord Je - sus,
Lift me to a no - bler life. Draw my fer - vent

guide my way; Faith - ful let me day by day Fol - low where
love to you; Con - stant faith and hope re - new In your birth,

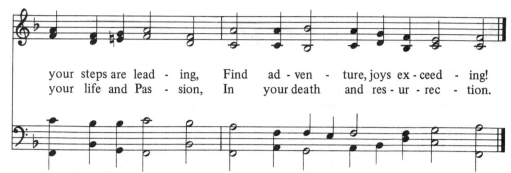

your steps are lead - ing, Find ad - ven - ture, joys ex - ceed - ing!
your life and Pas - sion, In your death and res - ur - rec - tion.

© *Text:* Thomas H. Kingo, 1634–1703; *tr.* Lutheran Book of Worship, 1978
Tune: Trente quatre pseaumes de David, *Geneva, 1551*

FREU DICH SEHR
87 87 77 88

The Man Is Ever Blessed 388

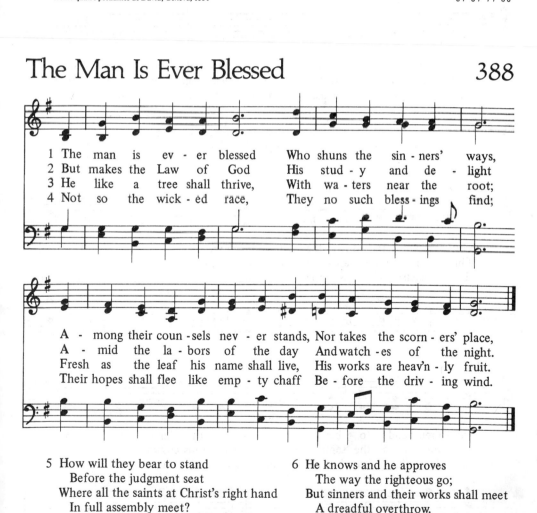

1 The man is ev - er blessed Who shuns the sin - ners' ways,
2 But makes the Law of God His stud - y and de - light
3 He like a tree shall thrive, With wa - ters near the root;
4 Not so the wick - ed race, They no such bless - ings find;

A - mong their coun - sels nev - er stands, Nor takes the scorn - ers' place,
A - mid the la - bors of the day And watch - es of the night.
Fresh as the leaf his name shall live, His works are heav'n - ly fruit.
Their hopes shall flee like emp - ty chaff Be - fore the driv - ing wind.

5 How will they bear to stand
  Before the judgment seat
Where all the saints at Christ's right hand
  In full assembly meet?

6 He knows and he approves
  The way the righteous go;
But sinners and their works shall meet
  A dreadful overthrow.

Text: Isaac Watts, 1674–1748
Tune: Trente quatre pseaumes de David, *Geneva, 1551*

ST. MICHAEL
S M

389   May We Your Precepts, Lord, Fulfill

1 May we your pre - cepts, Lord, ful - fill And do on
2 So may we join your name to bless, Your grace a -
3 Spir - it of life, of love and peace, Our hearts u -

earth our Fa - ther's will As an - gels do a - bove;
dore, your pow'r con - fess, To flee from sin and strife.
nite, our joy in - crease, Your gra - cious help sup - ply.

Still walk in Christ, the liv - ing way, With all your
One is our call - ing, one our name, The end of
To each of us the bless - ing give In Chris - tian

chil - dren and o - bey The law of Chris - tian love.
all our hopes the same, A glo - rious crown of life.
fel - low - ship to live, In joy - ful hope to die.

Text: Edward Osler, 1798–1863, alt.
Tune: Lowell Mason, 1792–1872

MERIBAH
886 886

For Jerusalem You're Weeping

390

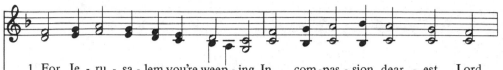

1 For Je - ru - sa - lem you're weep - ing In com - pas - sion, dear - est Lord.
2 By the love your tears are tell - ing, Lamb of God for sin - ners slain,
3 O dear Lord of my sal - va - tion, Grant my soul your blood-bought peace,

Love di - vine—your prom - ise keep - ing—O - ver err - ing Is - rael poured,
Make my heart your tem - ple dwell - ing, Purged from ev - 'ry guilt - y stain.
By your tears of lam - en - ta - tion Bid my faith and love in - crease.

Cries a - loud its bit - ter moan: "O loved cit - y, had you known
Oh, for - give, for-give my sin! Cleanse me, cleanse me, Lord, with - in!
Grant me grace to love your Word, Grace to keep the mes - sage heard,

This your day of vis - i - ta - tion, You would not re - ject sal - va - tion."
I am yours since you have sought me, Since your pre - cious blood has bought me,
Grace to hold you as my trea - sure, Grace to love you with - out mea - sure.

Text: Anna B. D. Hoppe, 1889–1941, alt.
Tune: Trente quatre pseaumes de David, *Geneva, 1551*

FREU DICH SEHR
87 87 77 88

391 I Walk in Danger All the Way

1 I walk in dan-ger all the way. The thought shall nev-er leave me
2 I pass through tri-als all the way, With sin and ills con-tend - ing;
3 And death pur-sues me all the way, No-where I rest se-cure - ly;
4 I walk with an-gels all the way, They shield me and be-friend me;

That Sa-tan, who has marked his prey, Is plot-ting to de-ceive me.
In pa-tience I must bear each day The cross of God's own send - ing.
He comes by night, he comes by day, He takes his prey most sure - ly.
All Sa-tan's pow'r is held at bay When heav'n-ly hosts at-tend me;

This foe with hid - den snares May seize me un - a - wares If
When in ad - ver - si - ty I know not where to flee, When
A fail - ing breath, and I In death's strong grasp may lie To
They are my sure de - fense, All fear and sor - row, hence! Un -

I should fail to watch and pray. I walk in dan - ger all the way.
storms of woe my soul dis - may, I pass through tri - als all the way.
face e - ter - ni - ty to - day As death pur - sues me all the way.
harmed by foes, do what they may, I walk with an - gels all the way.

5 I walk with Jesus all the way,
  His guidance never fails me;
Within his wounds I find a stay
  When Satan's pow'r assails me;
And by his footsteps led,
My path I safely tread.
No evil leads my soul astray;
I walk with Jesus all the way.

6 My walk is heav'nward all the way;
  Await, my soul, the morrow,
When God's good healing shall allay
  All suff'ring, sin, and sorrow.
Then, worldly pomp, begone!
To heav'n I now press on.
For all the world I would not stay;
My walk is heav'nward all the way.

Text: Hans A. Brorson, 1694–1764; tr. Ditlef G. Ristad, 1863–1938, alt.
Tune: Geistreiches Gesangbuch, *Halle, 1704*

DER LIEBEN SONNE LICHT UND PRACHT
87 87 66 88

Oh, that the Lord Would Guide My Ways

392

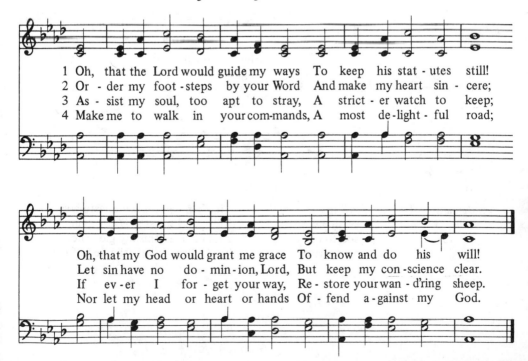

1 Oh, that the Lord would guide my ways To keep his stat-utes still!
2 Or-der my foot-steps by your Word And make my heart sin-cere;
3 As-sist my soul, too apt to stray, A strict-er watch to keep;
4 Make me to walk in your com-mands, A most de-light-ful road;

Oh, that my God would grant me grace To know and do his will!
Let sin have no do-min-ion, Lord, But keep my con-science clear.
If ev-er I for-get your way, Re-store your wan-d'ring sheep.
Nor let my head or heart or hands Of-fend a-gainst my God.

Text: Isaac Watts, 1674–1748, alt.
Tune: William H. Havergal, 1793–1870

EVAN
CM

393 Jesus! Oh, How Could It Be True

1 Je - sus! Oh, how could it be true, A mor-tal
2 A - shamed of Je - sus? Soon - er far Let eve-ning
3 A - shamed of Je - sus? Just as soon Let mid-night
4 A - shamed of Je - sus, that dear friend On whom my

man a - shamed of you? A - shamed of you, whom an -
blush to own a star. He sheds the beams of light
be a - shamed of noon. There's mid-night in my soul
hopes of heav'n de - pend? No; when I blush, be this

gels praise, Whose glo - ries shine through end - less days?
di - vine, On this be - night - ed soul of mine.
till he, Bright Morn - ing Star, bids dark - ness flee.
my shame, That I no more re - vere his name.

5 Ashamed of Jesus? Yes, I may
When I've no guilt to wash away,
No tear to wipe, no good to crave,
No fear to quell, no soul to save.

6 Till then— nor is my boasting vain—
Till then I boast a Savior slain;
And oh, may this my glory be,
That Christ is not ashamed of me!

Text: Joseph Grigg, c. 1722-68; Benjamin Francis, 1734-99, alt.
Tune: Henry K. Oliver, 1800-85

FEDERAL STREET
L M

Son of God, Eternal Savior

394

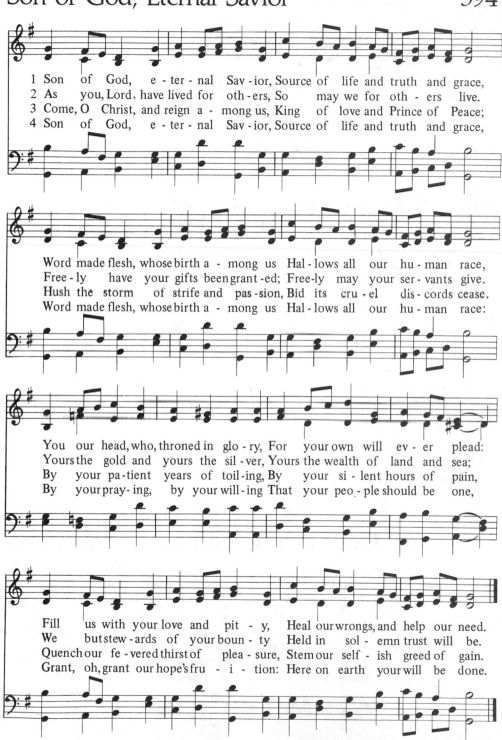

1 Son of God, e-ter-nal Sav-ior, Source of life and truth and grace,
2 As you, Lord, have lived for oth-ers, So may we for oth-ers live.
3 Come, O Christ, and reign a-mong us, King of love and Prince of Peace;
4 Son of God, e-ter-nal Sav-ior, Source of life and truth and grace,

Word made flesh, whose birth a-mong us Hal-lows all our hu-man race,
Free-ly have your gifts been grant-ed; Free-ly may your ser-vants give.
Hush the storm of strife and pas-sion, Bid its cru-el dis-cords cease.
Word made flesh, whose birth a-mong us Hal-lows all our hu-man race:

You our head, who, throned in glo-ry, For your own will ev-er plead:
Yours the gold and yours the sil-ver, Yours the wealth of land and sea;
By your pa-tient years of toil-ing, By your si-lent hours of pain,
By your pray-ing, by your will-ing That your peo-ple should be one,

Fill us with your love and pit-y, Heal our wrongs, and help our need.
We but stew-ards of your boun-ty Held in sol-emn trust will be.
Quench our fe-vered thirst of plea-sure, Stem our self-ish greed of gain.
Grant, oh, grant our hope's fru-i-tion: Here on earth your will be done.

© Text: Somerset T. C. Lowry, 1855-1932
Tune: Dutch folk tune, 18th cent.

IN BABILONE
87 87 D

395   O Fount of Good, for All Your Love

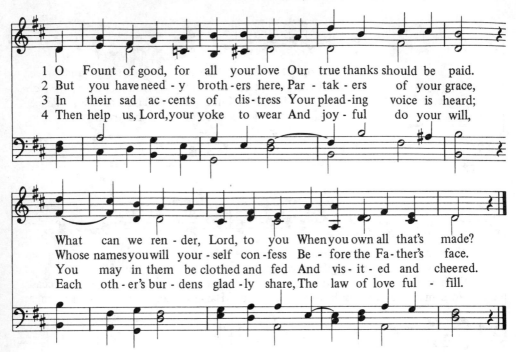

1 O Fount of good, for all your love Our true thanks should be paid.
2 But you have need-y broth-ers here, Par-tak-ers of your grace,
3 In their sad ac-cents of dis-tress Your plead-ing voice is heard;
4 Then help us, Lord, your yoke to wear And joy-ful do your will,

What can we ren-der, Lord, to you When you own all that's made?
Whose names you will your-self con-fess Be-fore the Fa-ther's face.
You may in them be clothed and fed And vis-it-ed and cheered.
Each oth-er's bur-dens glad-ly share, The law of love ful-fill.

5 Your face with rev'rence and with love
   We in your poor would view,
And while we minister to them
   Would do it as to you.

Text: Philip Doddridge, 1702–51, and Edmund Osler, 1798–1863, alt.
Tune and bass line: Orlando Gibbons, 1583–1625

SONG 67
C M

396   O God, Whose Will Is Life and Good

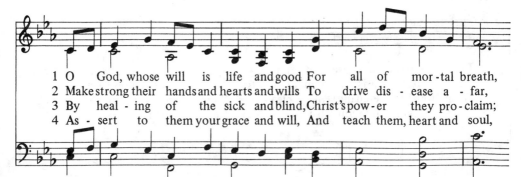

1 O God, whose will is life and good For all of mor-tal breath,
2 Make strong their hands and hearts and wills To drive dis-ease a-far,
3 By heal-ing of the sick and blind, Christ's pow-er they pro-claim;
4 As-sert to them your grace and will, And teach them, heart and soul,

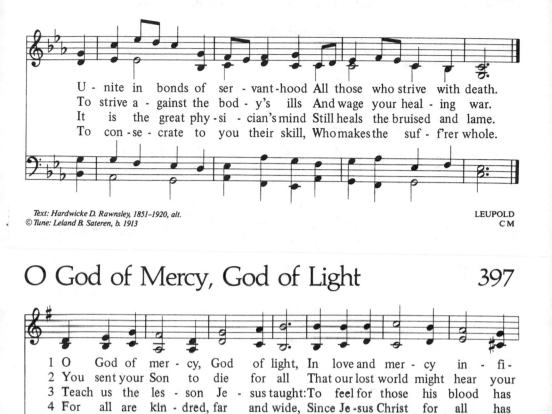

U - nite in bonds of ser - vant-hood All those who strive with death.
To strive a - gainst the bod - y's ills And wage your heal - ing war.
It is the great phy -si - cian's mind Still heals the bruised and lame.
To con -se - crate to you their skill, Who makes the suf - f'rer whole.

Text: Hardwicke D. Rawnsley, 1851–1920, alt.
© Tune: Leland B. Sateren, b. 1913

LEUPOLD
C M

O God of Mercy, God of Light 397

1 O God of mer - cy, God of light, In love and mer - cy in - fi -
2 You sent your Son to die for all That our lost world might hear your
3 Teach us the les - son Je - sus taught: To feel for those his blood has
4 For all are kin - dred, far and wide, Since Je -sus Christ for all has

nite, Teach us, as ev - er in your sight, To live our lives in you.
call; Oh, hear us lest we stray and fall! We rest our hope in you.
bought, That ev - 'ry deed and word and thought May work a work for you.
died; Grant us the will and grace pro - vide To love them all in you.

5 In sickness, sorrow, want, or care,
Each other's burdens help us share;
May we, where help is needed, there
Give help as though to you.

6 And may your Holy Spirit move
All those who live to live in love
Till you receive in heav'n above
Those who have lived to you.

Text: Godfrey Thring, 1823–1903, alt.
Tune: Joseph Barnby, 1838–96, adapt.

JUST AS I AM
888 6

398 God of Grace and God of Glory

1 God of grace and God of glory, On your people pour your pow'r; Crown your ancient church's story; Bring its bud to glorious flow'r. Grant us wisdom, grant us courage For the facing of this hour, For the facing of this hour.

2 Lo, the hosts of evil round us Scorn the Christ, assail his ways! From the fears that long have bound us Free our hearts to faith and praise. Grant us wisdom, grant us courage For the living of these days, For the living of these days.

3 Cure your children's warring madness; Bend our pride to your control; Shame our wanton, selfish gladness, Rich in things and poor in soul. Grant us wisdom, grant us courage Lest we miss your kingdom's goal, Lest we miss your kingdom's goal.

4 Save us from weak resignation To the evils we deplore; Let the gift of your salvation Be our glory evermore. Grant us wisdom, grant us courage, Serving you whom we adore, Serving you whom we adore.

Text: Harry E. Fosdick, 1878–1969
© Tune: John Hughes, 1873–1932

CWM RHONDDA
87 87 877

Your Hand, O Lord, in Days of Old

399

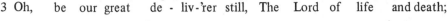

1 Your hand, O Lord, in days of old Was strong to heal and save;
2 Your touch then, Lord, brought life and health, Gave speech and strength and sight;
3 Oh, be our great de-liv-'rer still, The Lord of life and death;

It tri-umphed o-ver ills and death, All dark-ness and the grave.
And youth re-newed and fren-zy calmed Re-vealed you, Lord of light.
Re-store and quick-en, soothe and bless, With your life-giv-ing breath.

To you they came, the blind, the dumb, The pal-sied and the lame,
And now, O Lord, be near to bless, Al-might-y as be-fore,
To hands that work and eyes that see Give wis-dom's heal-ing pow'r

The lep-ers in their mis-er-y, The sick with fe-vered frame.
In crowd-ed street, by beds of pain, As by Gen-nes-'ret's shore.
That whole and sick and weak and strong May praise you ev-er-more.

Text: Edward H. Plumptre, 1821–91, alt.
Tune: Marot, Trente Pseaulmes de David, 1542

OLD 107TH
CM D

400

O Son of God, in Galilee

1 O Son of God, in Gal - i - lee You made the deaf to hear,
2 Oh, lis - ten to the si - lent prayer Of your af - flict - ed ones.
3 The speech - less tongue, the life - less ear You can re - store, O Lord;
4 Mean - while to them the lis - t'ning ear Of stead - fast faith im - part,

The mute to speak, the blind to see; O bless - ed Lord, be near.
Oh, bid them cast on you their care; Your grace to them make known.
Your "Eph - pha - tha," O Sav - ior dear, Can in - stant help af - ford.
And let your Word bring light and cheer To ev - 'ry trou - bled heart.

5 Then in your promised happy land
Each loss will prove a gain;

All myst'ries we shall understand,
For you will make them plain.

© Text: Anna B. D. Hoppe, 1889–1941, alt.
Tune: attr. Lucius Chapin, 1760–1842

TWENTY-FOURTH
C M

401

Forgive Us, Lord, for Shallow Thankfulness

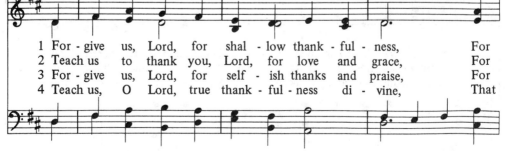

1 For - give us, Lord, for shal - low thank - ful - ness, For
2 Teach us to thank you, Lord, for love and grace, For
3 For - give us, Lord, for self - ish thanks and praise, For
4 Teach us, O Lord, true thank - ful - ness di - vine, That

dull con-tent with warmth and shel-tered care, For
life and vi-sion, for a pur-pose clear, For
words that speak at var-i-ance with deeds; Forgives as Christ gave, nev-er count-ing cost, That

songs of praise for world-ly wealth-i-ness, While
Christ your Son, and for each hu-man face That
give our thanks for walk-ing pleas-ant ways Un-
knows no bar-ri-er of "yours" and "mine," As-

of your rich-er gifts we're un-a-ware:
shows your mes-sage ev-er new and near.
mind-ful of a bro-ken broth-er's needs:
sured that on-ly what's with-held is lost.

5 Forgive us, Lord, for feast that knows not fast,
    For joy in things that meanwhile starve the soul,
For walls and wars that hide your mercies vast
    And blur our vision of the Kingdom goal:

6 Open our eyes to see your love's intent,
    To know with minds and hearts its depth and height;
Let thankful days in loving labor spent
    Reflect the truly Christ-like life and light.

© Text: William W. Reid Sr., b. 1890, alt.
© Tune: Alfred M. Smith, 1879–1971

SURSUM CORDA
10 10 10 10

402 Lord of Glory, You Have Bought Us

1 Lord of glo - ry, you have bought us With your
2 Grant us hearts, dear Lord, to give you Glad - ly,
3 Won - drous hon - or you have giv - en To our
4 Yes, the sor - row and the suf - f'rings Which on

life - blood as the price, Nev - er grudg - ing
free - ly of your own. With the sun - shine
hum - blest char - i - ty In your own mys -
ev - 'ry hand we view Chan - nels are for

for the lost ones That tre - men - dous sac - ri - fice;
of your good - ness Melt our thank - less hearts of stone
te - rious sen - tence, "You have done it all to me."
gifts and of - f'rings Due by sol - emn right to you;

And with that have free - ly giv - en Bless - ings
Till our cold and self - ish na - tures, Warmed by
Can it be, O gra - cious Mas - ter, That you
Right of which we may not rob you, Debt we

count - less as the sand To th'un - thank - ful
you, at length be - lieve That more hap - py
deign for alms to sue, Say - ing by your
may not choose but pay Lest that face of

and the e - vil With your own un - spar - ing hand.
and more bless - ed 'Tis to give than to re - ceive.
poor and need - y, "Give as I have giv'n to you"?
love and pit - y Turn from us an - oth - er day.

5 Lord of glory, you have bought us
With your lifeblood as the price,
Never grudging for the lost ones
That tremendous sacrifice.
Give us faith to trust you boldly,
Hope, to stay our souls on you;
But, oh, best of all your graces,
With your love our love renew.

Text: Eliza S. Alderson, 1818–89, alt.
Tune: Rowland H. Prichard, 1811–87

HYFRYDOL
87 87 D

403 Praise and Thanksgiving

1 Praise and thanks-giv - ing, Fa - ther, we of - fer For all things
2 Bless, Lord, the la - bor We bring to serve you That with our
3 Fa - ther, pro - vid - ing Food for your chil - dren, By your wise

liv - ing, Cre - at - ed good: Har - vest of sown fields, Fruits of the
neigh - bor We may be fed. Sow - ing or till - ing, We would work
guid - ing Teach us to share One with an - oth - er, So that, re -

or - chard, Hay from the mown fields, Blos - som and wood.
with you, Har - vest - ing, mill - ing For dai - ly bread.
joic - ing With us, all oth - ers May know your care.

© *Text: Albert F. Bayly, b. 1901, alt.*
Tune: Gaelic

BUNESSAN
55 54 D

Take My Life, O Lord, Renew

404

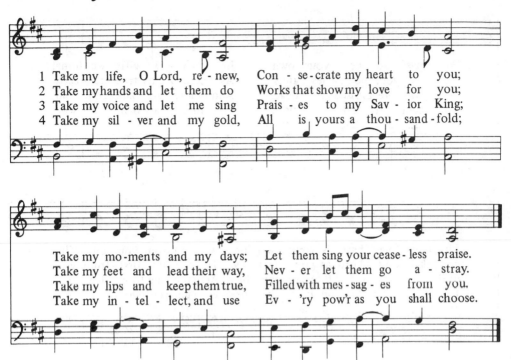

1 Take my life, O Lord, re-new, Con-se-crate my heart to you;
2 Take my hands and let them do Works that show my love for you;
3 Take my voice and let me sing Prais-es to my Sav-ior King;
4 Take my sil-ver and my gold, All is yours a thou-sand-fold;

Take my mo-ments and my days; Let them sing your cease-less praise.
Take my feet and lead their way, Nev-er let them go a-stray.
Take my lips and keep them true, Filled with mes-sag-es from you,
Take my in-tel-lect, and use Ev-'ry pow'r as you shall choose.

5 Make my will your holy shrine,
It shall be no longer mine.
Take my heart, it is your own;
It shall be your royal throne.

6 Take my love; my Lord, I pour
At your feet its treasure store;
Take my self, Lord, let me be
Yours alone eternally.

Text: Frances R. Havergal, 1836–79, alt.
Tune: William H. Havergal, 1793–1870

PATMOS
77 77

405 We Give You But Your Own

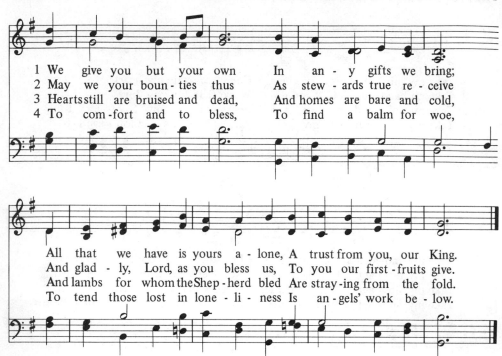

1 We give you but your own In an - y gifts we bring;
2 May we your boun - ties thus As stew - ards true re - ceive
3 Hearts still are bruised and dead, And homes are bare and cold,
4 To com - fort and to bless, To find a balm for woe,

All that we have is yours a - lone, A trust from you, our King.
And glad - ly, Lord, as you bless us, To you our first - fruits give.
And lambs for whom the Shep - herd bled Are stray - ing from the fold.
To tend those lost in lone - li - ness Is an - gels' work be - low.

5 The captive to release,
   The lost to God to bring,
To teach the way of life and peace,
   It is a Christlike thing.

6 And we believe your word,
   Though dim our faith, it's true:
What we do for your people, Lord,
   We do it all for you.

Text: William W. How, 1823–97, alt.
Tune: William H. Monk, 1823–89

ENERGY
S M

406 In You, Lord, I Have Put My Trust

1 In you, Lord, I have put my trust; Leave
2 Oh, lis - ten, Lord, most gra - cious - ly And
3 You are my strength, my shield, my rock, My
4 With you, Lord, I have cast my lot; O

me not help-less in the dust, Let me not
hear my cry, my prayer, my plea, Make haste for
for-tress that with-stands each shock, My help, my
faith-ful God, for-sake me not, To you my

be con-found-ed. Let in your Word My faith, O
my pro-tect-tion; For woes and fear Sur-round me
life, my tow-er, My bat-tle sword, Al-might-y
soul com-mend-ing. Lord, be my stay And lead the

Lord, Be al-ways firm-ly ground - ed.
here. Help me in my af-flic - tion.
Lord, What can re-sist your pow - er?
way Now and when life is end - ing.

5 All honor, praise, and majesty
 To Father, Son, and Spirit be,
  Our God forever glorious,
 In whose rich grace
 We run our race
  Till we depart victorious.

Text: Adam Reusner, 1496–1575; tr. Catherine Winkworth, 1829–78, alt.
Tune: Leipzig, 1573; Nürnberg, 1581

IN DICH HAB ICH GEHOFFET
887 447

407   If God Himself Be for Me

1 If God him-self be for me, I may a host de-fy;
2 I build on this foun-da - tion, That Je - sus and his blood
3 Christ Je - sus is my splen - dor, My sun, my light, a - lone;
4 Though earth, Lord, break a - sun - der, You are my Sav-ior true;

For when I pray, be - fore me My foes, con - found-ed, fly.
A - lone are my sal - va - tion, The true, e - ter - nal good.
Were he not my de - fend - er Be - fore God's awe-some throne,
No fire or sword or thun - der Shall sev - er me from you;

If Christ, my head and mas - ter, Be - friend me from a - bove,
With - out him all that pleas - es Will vain and emp - ty prove.
I nev - er should find fa - vor And mer - cy in his sight
No dan - ger, thirst, or hun - ger, No pain or pov - er - ty,

What foe or what di - sas - ter Can drive me from his love?
The gifts I have from Je - sus A - lone are worth my love.
But be de-stroyed for - ev - er As dark - ness by the light.
No might - y princ - es' an - ger Shall ev - er van - quish me.

5 No angel and no gladness,
　　No high place, pomp, or show,
　No love, no hate, no badness,
　　No sadness, pain, or woe,
　No scheming, no contrivance,
　　No subtle thing or great
　Shall draw me from your guidance
　　Nor from you separate.

6 For joy my heart is ringing;
　　All sorrow disappears;
　And full of mirth and singing,
　　It wipes away all tears.
　The sun that cheers my spirit
　　Is Jesus Christ, my king;
　The heav'n I shall inherit
　　Makes me rejoice and sing.

Text: Paul Gerhardt, 1607–76; tr. Richard Massie, 1800–87, adapt., alt.
Tune: David Spaiser, Vier und zwantzig Geystliche Lieder, Augsburg, 1609

IST GOTT FÜR MICH
76 76 D

I Am Trusting You, Lord Jesus   408

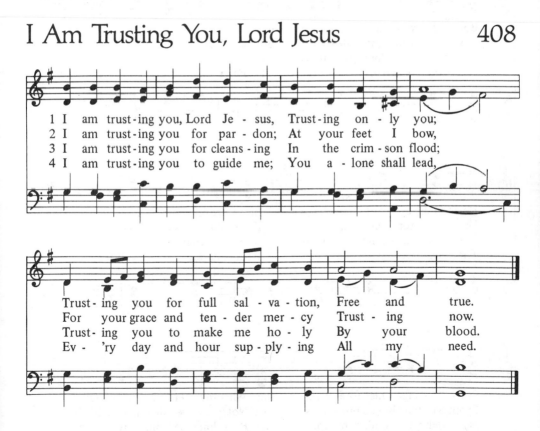

1 I am trust-ing you, Lord Je - sus, Trust-ing on - ly you;
2 I am trust-ing you for par - don; At your feet I bow,
3 I am trust-ing you for cleans - ing In the crim - son flood;
4 I am trust-ing you to guide me; You a - lone shall lead,

Trust-ing you for full sal - va - tion, Free and true.
For your grace and ten - der mer - cy Trust - ing now.
Trust-ing you to make me ho - ly By your blood.
Ev - 'ry day and hour sup - ply - ing All my need.

5 I am trusting you for power;
　　You can never fail.
　Words which you yourself shall give me
　　Must prevail.

6 I am trusting you, Lord Jesus;
　　Never let me fall.
　I am trusting you forever
　　And for all.

Text: Frances R. Havergal, 1836–79, alt.
Tune: Henry W. Baker, 1821–77

STEPHANOS
85 83

409 From God Can Nothing Move Me

1 From God can noth-ing move me; He will not step a-side
2 When those whom I re-gard - ed As trust-wor-thy and sure
3 When in my dark-est hour, ... I can on him re - ly;
4 Praise God with hearts and voic - es, For both are gifts from him;

But al - ways will re - prove me And be my con - stant guide.
Have long from me de - part - ed, God's grace shall still en - dure.
I have from him the pow - er All e - vil to de - fy.
A trou - bled world re - joic - es Each time we wor - ship him.

He stretch - es out his hand In eve-ning and in morn - ing,
He cares for all my needs, From sin and shame cor-rects me,
For God a - lone has might, And I shall nev - er fear it;
The days we spend on earth With-out our God are wast - ed,

Pro - vid - ing his fore-warn - ing Wher-ev - er I may stand.
From Sa - tan's bonds pro - tects me; Not e - ven death suc - ceeds.
My bod - y, soul, and spir - it Be - long to him by right.
For we shall not have tast - ed His joy in end - less birth.

5 Yet even though I suffer
  The world's unpleasantness,
  And though the days grow rougher
  And bring me great distress,
  That day of bliss divine,
  Which knows no end or measure,
  And Christ, who is my pleasure,
  Forever shall be mine.

6 We were by God created
  In his own time and place
  And by his Son persuaded
  To follow truth and grace.
  The Spirit guides our ways
  And faithfully will lead us
  That nothing can impede us.
  To God be all our praise!

© *Text: Ludwig Helmbold, 1532–98; tr. Gerald Thorson, b. 1921*
Tune: 16th cent.; sacred use, Erfurt, 1563

VON GOTT WILL ICH NICHT LASSEN
76 76 67 76

Have No Fear, Little Flock 410

1 Have no fear, lit-tle flock; Have no fear, lit-tle
2 Have good cheer, lit-tle flock; Have good cheer, lit-tle
3 Praise the Lord high a - bove; Praise the Lord high a-
4 Thank-ful hearts raise to God; Thank-ful hearts raise to

flock, For the Fa - ther has cho - sen To
flock, For the Fa - ther will keep you In
bove, For he stoops down to heal you, Up -
God, For he stays close be - side you, In

give you the King - dom; Have no fear, lit - tle flock!
his love for - ev - er; Have good cheer, lit - tle flock!
lift and re - store you; Praise the Lord high a - bove!
all things works with you; Thank-ful hearts raise to God!

© *Text: Luke 12:32, st. 1; Marjorie Jillson, b. 1931, sts. 2-4*
© *Tune: Heinz Werner Zimmermann, b. 1930*

LITTLE FLOCK
66 76 6

411 How Firm a Foundation

1 How firm a foun-da-tion, O saints of the Lord,
2 Fear not, I am with you, oh, be not dis-mayed,
3 When through fi-ery tri-als your path-way will lie,
4 Through-out all their life-time my peo-ple will prove

Is laid for your faith in his ex-cel-lent Word!
For I am your God and will still give you aid;
My grace, all-suf-fi-cient, will be your sup-ply.
My sov-'reign, e-ter-nal, un-change-a-ble love;

What more can he say than to you he has said
I'll strength-en you, help you, and cause you to stand,
The flames will not hurt you; I on-ly de-sign
And then, when gray hairs will their tem-ples a-dorn,

Who un-to the Sav-ior for ref-uge have fled?
Up-held by my righ-teous, om-nip-o-tent hand.
Your dross to con-sume and your gold to re-fine.
Like lambs they will still in my bo-som be borne.

Text: John Rippon, A Selection of Hymns, 1787, alt.
Tune: J. Funk, Genuine Church Music, 1832

FOUNDATION
11 11 11 11

The King of Love My Shepherd Is

1 The King of love my shep-herd is, Whose good-ness
2 Where streams of liv-ing wa-ter flow, My ran-somed
3 Per-verse and fool-ish oft I strayed, But yet in
4 In death's dark vale I fear no ill With thee, dear

fail-eth nev-er; I noth-ing lack if
soul he lead-eth And, where the ver-dant
love he sought me And on his shoul-der
Lord, be-side me, Thy rod and staff my

I am his And he is mine for-ev-er.
pas-tures grow, With food ce-les-tial feed-eth.
gent-ly laid And home re-joic-ing brought me.
com-fort still, Thy cross be-fore to guide me.

5 Thou spreadst a table in my sight;
   Thine unction grace bestoweth;
And, oh, what transport of delight
   From thy pure chalice floweth!

6 And so through all the length of days
   Thy goodness faileth never.
Good Shepherd, may I sing thy praise
   Within thy house forever.

Text: Henry W. Baker, 1821–77
Tune: Irish

ST. COLUMBA
87 87

413 Lord, You I Love with All My Heart

1 Lord, you I love with all my heart;
Oh, let me not from
you de - part, With ten - der mer - cy cheer me. Earth
has no joy for which I care, Heav - en it - self were
void and bare If I can't have you near me. And should my

2 Lord, all I am or have, you gave;
From stub - born e - go,
Lord, you save, My self - ish ways re - ject - ing. So
let me give my - self to you, To all my fel - low
crea - tures too, Your grace, your love re - flect - ing. Let no false

3 Then let at last your an - gels come,
To A - bram's bo - som
bear me home That I may die un - fear - ing. With -
in my earth - en cham - ber keep My bod - y safe in
peace - ful sleep Un - til your re - ap - pear - ing. And then from

guilt my heart sub-due, Let noth-ing shake my trust in you.
teach-ing me be-guile Nor Sa-tan's lies my soul de-file;
death a-wak-en me That my own eyes with joy may see,

You are the por-tion I de-sire; Your sac-ri-
In all my cross-es com-fort me That I may
O Son of God, your glo-rious face, My Sav-ior

fice my soul in-spire. Lord Je-sus Christ, My God and
bear them pa-tient-ly. Lord Je-sus Christ, My God and
and my ground of grace! Lord Je-sus Christ, Oh, hear my

Lord, my God and Lord, For-sake me not! I trust your Word.
Lord, my God and Lord, Let me be yours, my soul re-stored!
prayer; oh, hear my prayer, Your love sur-round me ev-'ry-where!

© *Text: Martin Schalling, 1532–1608; tr. Henry L. Lettermann, b. 1932*
Tune: Bernhard Schmid, Orgeltabulatur-Buch, 1577

HERZLICH LIEB
P M

414 Who Trusts in God a Strong Abode

1 Who trusts in God a strong a - bode In heav'n and
2 Though Sa - tan's wrath be - set our path And world - ly
3 In all the strife of mor - tal life Our feet will

earth pos - sess - es; Who looks in love to
scorn as - sail us, While you are near, we
stand se - cure - ly; Temp - ta - tion's hour will

Christ a - bove, No fear that heart op - press - es.
shall not fear; Your strength will nev - er fail us.
lose its pow'r, For you will guard us sure - ly.

In you a - lone, dear Lord, we own Sweet hope and con - so -
Your rod and staff will keep us safe And guide our steps for -
Our God, re - new with heav'n - ly dew Our bod - y, soul, and

la - tion,   Our shield from foes, our balm for woes,
ev - er;   Nor shades of   death nor hell be - neath,
spir - it   Un - til we stand at your right hand

Our great and sure sal - va - tion.
Our lives from you will sev - er.
Through Je - sus' sav - ing mer - it.

Text: Joachim Magdeburg, c. 1525–c. 1583, st. 1; Harmonia Cantionum, Leipzig, 1597, sts. 2–3;
tr. Benjamin H. Kennedy, 1804–99, alt.
Tune: Claudin de Sermisy, c. 1490–1562

WAS MEIN GOTT WILL
87 87 D

415 All Depends on Our Possessing

1 All de-pends on our pos-sess-ing God's free grace and
2 He who to this day has fed me And to man-y
3 Man-y spend their lives in fret-ting O-ver tri-fles
4 When with sor-row I am strick-en, Hope a-new my

con-stant bless-ing, Though all earth-ly wealth de-part.
joys has led me Is and ev-er shall be mine.
and in get-ting Things that lack all sol-id ground.
heart will quick-en, All my long-ing shall be stilled.

They who trust with faith un-shak-en By their God are
He who did so gent-ly school me, He who dai-ly
I shall strive to win a trea-sure That will bring me
To his lov-ing-kind-ness ten-der Soul and bod-y

not for-sak-en And will keep a daunt-less heart.
guides and rules me Will re-main my help di-vine.
last-ing plea-sure And that now is sel-dom found.
I sur-ren-der, For on God a-lone I build.

5 Well he knows what best to grant me;
   All the longing hopes that haunt me,
      Joy and sorrow, have their day.
   I shall doubt his wisdom never;
   As God wills, so be it ever;
      I commit to him my way.

6 If my days on earth he lengthen,
   God my weary soul will strengthen;
      All my trust in him I place.
   Earthly wealth is not abiding,
   Like a stream away is gliding;
      Safe I anchor in his grace.

Text: Gesang-Buch, *Nürnberg, 1676; tr. Catherine Winkworth, 1829–78, alt.*
Tune: Johann Löhner, 1645–1705; adapt. Johann B. König, 1691–1758.

ALLES IST AN GOTTES SEGEN
887 887

The Lord's My Shepherd, I'll Not Want

416

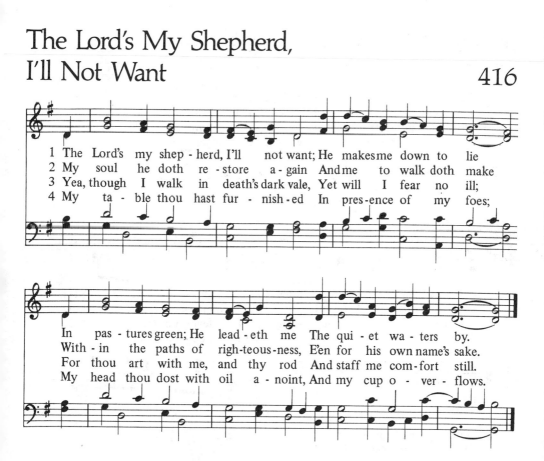

1 The Lord's my shep-herd, I'll not want; He makes me down to lie
2 My soul he doth re-store a-gain And me to walk doth make
3 Yea, though I walk in death's dark vale, Yet will I fear no ill;
4 My ta-ble thou hast fur-nish-ed In pres-ence of my foes;

In pas-tures green; He lead-eth me The qui-et wa-ters by.
With-in the paths of right-teous-ness, E'en for his own name's sake.
For thou art with me, and thy rod And staff me com-fort still.
My head thou dost with oil a-noint, And my cup o-ver-flows.

5 Goodness and mercy all my life
      Shall surely follow me;
   And in God's house forevermore
      My dwelling place shall be.

Text: The Psalms of David in Meeter, *Edinburgh, 1650*
Tune: William Gardiner, 1770–1853

BELMONT
CM

417 The Lord's My Shepherd, Leading Me

1 The Lord's my shep-herd, lead-ing me To pas-tures new-ly green;
2 My hun-gry soul he fills a-gain With man-na from a-bove;
3 E-ven with-in the vale of death I feel no threat-'ning chill,
4 How he con-founds my en-e-mies By rich-ly bless-ing me;

Deep flow the wa-ters of his care, His mer-cies un-fore-seen.
He sets my foot-steps right a-gain In path-ways of his love.
His rod and staff pro-tect-ing me, His love be-side me still.
His cup of prom-ise o-ver-flows With gen-er-os-i-ty.

He loves me so, he leads me to His pas-tures gent-ly green.
For his name's sake he nur-tures me With man-na from a-bove.
His guard-ian love pro-tect-ing me, I fear no threat of ill.
A-noint-ing me his cho-sen one, He rich-ly bless-es me.

5 I take my stand forevermore
   Within my shepherd's fold,
Secure in his forgiving love.
   How gently strong his hold!
He loves me so, he leads me to
   His blessings rich and bold.

© Text: Henry L. Lettermann, b. 1932
Tune: J. L. Macbeth Bain, c. 1840–1925, adapt.

BROTHER JAMES' AIR
86 86 86

What Is the World to Me

1 What is the world to me With all its vaunt-ed plea-sure
2 The world seeks to be praised And hon-ored by the might-y
3 The world seeks af-ter wealth And all that mam-mon of-fers
4 What is the world to me! My Je-sus is my trea-sure,

When you, and you a-lone, Lord Je-sus, are my trea-sure!
Yet nev-er once re-flects That they are frail and flight-y.
Yet nev-er is con-tent Though gold should fill its cof-fers.
My life, my health, my wealth, My friend, my love, my plea-sure,

You on-ly, dear-est Lord, My soul's de-light shall be;
But what I tru-ly prize A-bove all things is he,
I have a high-er good, Con-tent with it I'll be:
My joy, my crown, my all, My bliss e-ter-nal-ly.

You are my peace, my rest. What is the world to me!
My Je-sus, he a-lone. What is the world to me!
My Je-sus is my wealth. What is the world to me!
Once more, then, I de-clare: What is the world to me!

Text: Georg M. Pfefferkorn, 1645–1732; tr. August Crull, 1845–1923, alt.
Tune: Ahasverus Fritsch, 1629–1701

WAS FRAG ICH NACH DER WELT
67 67 66 66

419

Evening and Morning

1 Eve - ning and morn - ing, Sun - set and dawn - ing,
2 Fa - ther, oh, hear me, Par - don and spare me;
3 Ills that still grieve me Soon are to leave me;
4 To God in heav - en All praise be giv - en!

Wealth, peace, and glad - ness, Com - fort in sad - ness:
Calm all my ter - rors, Blot out my er - rors,
Though bil - lows tow - er And winds gain pow - er,
Come, let us of - fer And glad - ly prof - fer

These are your works and bring glo - ry to you.
That by your eyes they may no more be scanned.
Af - ter the storm the fair sun shows its face.
To the Cre - a - tor the gifts he will prize,

Times with - out num - ber, We wake or we slum - ber,
Or - der my go - ings, Di - rect all my do - ings;
My joys in - creas - ing, My peace nev - er ceas - ing,
Glad - ly re - ceiv - ing Our fruits of be - liev - ing.

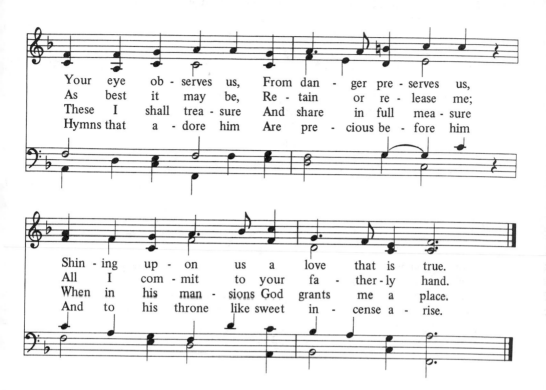

Your eye ob - serves us, From dan - ger pre - serves us,
As best it may be, Re - tain or re - lease me;
These I shall trea - sure And share in full mea - sure
Hymns that a - dore him Are pre - cious be - fore him

Shin - ing up - on us a love that is true.
All I com - mit to your fa - ther - ly hand.
When in his man - sions God grants me a place.
And to his throne like sweet in - cense a - rise.

© Text: Paul Gerhardt, 1607–76; tr. Richard Massie, 1800–87, sts. 1–2; Herman Brueckner, 1866–1942, sts. 3–4, alt.
Tune: Johann G. Ebeling, 1637–76

DIE GÜLDNE SONNE
P M

420 If You But Trust in God to Guide You

1 If you but trust in God to guide you, And place your
2 What gain is there in fu - tile weep - ing, In help - less
3 In pa - tient trust a - wait his lei - sure In cheer - ful
4 Sing, pray, and keep his ways un - swerv - ing, Of - fer your

con - fi - dence in him, You'll find him al - ways there be -
an - ger and dis - tress? If you are in his care and
hope, with heart con - tent To take what - e'er your Fa - ther's
ser - vice faith - ful - ly, And trust his word; though un - de -

side you To give you hope and strength with - in. For those who
keep - ing, In sor - row will he love you less? For he who
plea - sure And all - dis - cern - ing love have sent; Doubt not your
serv - ing, You'll find his prom - ise true to be. God nev - er

trust God's change - less love Build on the rock that will not move.
took for you a cross Will bring you safe through ev - 'ry loss.
in - most wants are known To him who chose you for his own.
will for - sake in need The soul that trusts in him in - deed.

© Text: Georg Neumark, 1621–81; tr. composite, alt.
Tune: Georg Neumark, 1621–81

WER NUR DEN LIEBEN GOTT
98 98 88

In God, My Faithful God

1 In God, my faith-ful God, I trust when dark my
2 My sins fill me with care, Yet I will not de -
3 If death my por - tion be, It brings great gain to
4 "So be it," then, I say With all my heart each

road; Great woes may o - ver - take me, Yet
spair. I build on Christ, who loves me; From
me; It speeds my life's en - deav - or To
day. Dear Lord, we all a - dore you, We

he will not for - sake me. It is his love that
this rock noth - ing moves me. To him I will sur -
live with Christ for - ev - er. He gives me joy in
sing for joy be - fore you. Guide us while here we

sends them; At his best time he ends them.
ren - der, To him, my soul's de - fend - er.
sor - row, Come death now or to - mor - row.
wan - der Un - til we praise you yon - der.

Text: Leipzig, before 1603; Wittenberg and Nürnberg, 1607; tr. Catherine Winkworth, 1829-78, alt.
Tune: Jacob Regnart, c. 1540-99; Bartholomäus Gesius, c. 1560-1613; Johann Schein, 1586-1630

AUF MEINEN LIEBEN GOTT
66 77 77

422 What God Ordains Is Always Good

1 What God or-dains is al - ways good: His will is
2 What God or-dains is al - ways good: He nev - er
3 What God or-dains is al - ways good: His lov - ing
4 What God or-dains is al - ways good: He is my

just and ho - ly. As he di - rects my life for me,
will de - ceive me; He leads me in his own right way,
thought at - tends me; No poi - son can be in the cup
friend and fa - ther; He suf - fers naught to do me harm

I fol - low meek and low - ly. My God in - deed
And nev - er will he leave me. I take con - tent
That my phy - si - cian sends me. My God is true;
Though man - y storms may gath - er. Now I may know

In ev - 'ry need Knows well how he will shield me;
What he has sent; His hand that sends me sad - ness
Each morn - ing new I trust his grace un - end - ing,
Both joy and woe; Some - day I shall see clear - ly

To him, then, I will yield me.
Will turn my tears to glad - ness.
My life to him com - mend - ing.
That he has loved me dear - ly.

5 What God ordains is always good:
    Though I the cup am drinking
Which savors now of bitterness,
    I take it without shrinking.
For after grief
God gives relief,
My heart with comfort filling
And all my sorrow stilling.

6 What God ordains is always good:
    This truth remains unshaken.
Though sorrow, need, or death be mine,
    I shall not be forsaken.
I fear no harm,
For with his arm
He shall embrace and shield me;
So to my God I yield me.

Text: Samuel Rodigast, 1649–1708; tr. The Lutheran Hymnal, 1941, alt.
Tune: Severus Gastorius, c. 1650–c. 1693

WAS GOTT TUT
87 87 888

423 When I Suffer Pains and Losses

1 When I suf - fer pains and loss - es,
2 Un - der bur - dens of cross-bear - ing,
3 Chris - tians, let us be un - daunt - ed.
4 What at last does this world leave us

Lord, be near, Let me hear Com-fort un - der cross - es.
Though the weight May be great, Yet I'm not de - spair - ing.
Ev - 'ry day Hurl a - way That which us once haunt - ed.
But a hand Full of sand Or some loss to grieve us?

Point me, Fa - ther, to the heav - en
You de - signed the cross you gave me;
Is it true that death de - feats us?
See what rich and no - ble gra - ces

Which your Son For me won When his life was giv - en.
Thus you know All my woe And how best to save me.
No! Re - joice, For Christ's voice Then in peace will greet us.
Our Lord shares With his heirs In the heav'n-ly pla - ces.

5 Savior, Shepherd, my Defender,
   I belong To the throng
Blood-bought for that splendor.
   Having you, I want no other
Light of heav'n To be giv'n,
   My dear God and Brother.

© Text: Paul Gerhardt, 1607–76; tr. F. Samuel Janzow, b. 1913
Tune: Johann G. Ebeling, 1620–76

WARUM SOLLT ICH MICH DENN GRÄMEN
8 3 3 6 D

Rejoice, My Heart, Be Glad 424

1 Re - joice, my heart, be glad and sing, A cheer-ful trust main - tain;
2 He is your trea-sure, he your joy, Your life and light and Lord,
3 Why spend the day in blank de-spair, In rest - less thought the night?
4 Did not his love and truth and pow'r Guard ev - 'ry child - hood day?

For God, the source of ev - 'ry-thing, Your por - tion shall re - main.
Your coun-sel - or when doubts an - noy, Your shield and great re - ward.
On your cre - a - tor cast your care; He makes your bur-dens light.
And did he not in threat-'ning hour Turn dread - ed ills a - way?

5 He only will with patience chide,
   His rod falls gently down,
And all your sins he casts aside;
   In ocean depth they drown.

6 His wisdom never plans in vain
   Nor falters nor mistakes.
All that his counsels may ordain
   A happy ending makes.

7 Upon your lips, then, lay your hand,
   And trust his guiding love;
Then like a rock your peace shall stand
   Here and in heav'n above.

Text: Paul Gerhardt, 1607–76; tr. John Kelly, 1833–90, alt.
Tune: Johann B. König, Harmonischer Liederschatz, 1738

ICH SINGE DIR
C M

425 The Will of God Is Always Best

1 The will of God is al-ways best And shall be done for-
2 God is my com-fort and my trust, My hope and life a-
3 Lord, this I ask, oh, hear my plea, De-ny me not this
4 When life's brief course on earth is run And I this world am

ev - er; And they who trust in him are blest, He
bid - ing; And to his coun - sel, wise and just, I
fa - vor: When Sa - tan sore - ly trou - bles me, Then
leav - ing, Grant me to say, "Your will be done," Your

will for-sake them nev - er. He helps in-deed In time of need,
yield, in him con-fid - ing. The ver - y hairs, His Word de-clares,
do not let me wav - er. Oh, guard me well, My fear dis-pel,
faith-ful Word be-liev - ing. My dear-est friend, I now com-mend

He chas-tens with for-bear - ing; They who de-pend
Up - on my head he num - bers. By night and day
Ful - fill your faith-ful say - ing: He who be-lieves
My soul in - to your keep - ing, From sin and hell,

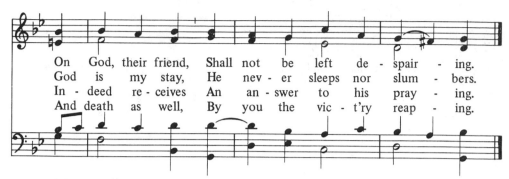

On God, their friend, Shall not be left de - spair - ing.
God is my stay, He nev - er sleeps nor slum - bers.
In - deed re - ceives An an - swer to his pray - ing.
And death as well, By you the vic - t'ry reap - ing.

Text: Albrecht von Brandenburg, 1522–57; tr. The Lutheran Hymnal, 1941, alt.
Tune: Claudin de Sermisy, c. 1490–1562

WAS MEIN GOTT WILL
87 87 D

God Moves in a Mysterious Way   426

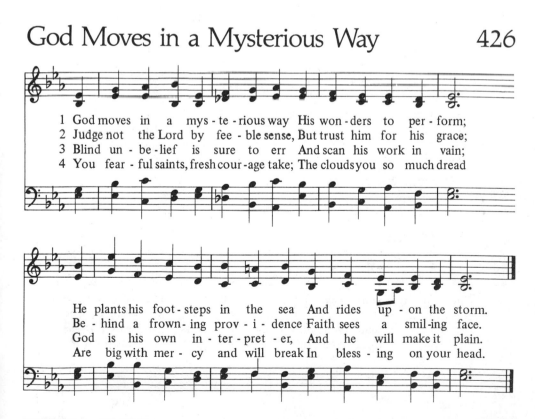

1 God moves in a mys - te - rious way His won - ders to per - form;
2 Judge not the Lord by fee - ble sense, But trust him for his grace;
3 Blind un - be - lief is sure to err And scan his work in vain;
4 You fear - ful saints, fresh cour - age take; The clouds you so much dread

He plants his foot - steps in the sea And rides up - on the storm.
Be - hind a frown - ing prov - i - dence Faith sees a smil - ing face.
God is his own in - ter - pret - er, And he will make it plain.
Are big with mer - cy and will break In bless - ing on your head.

Text: William Cowper, 1731–1800, alt.
Tune: The CL Psalmes of David, Edinburgh, 1615

DUNDEE
C M

427 Entrust Your Days and Burdens

1 En - trust your days and bur - dens To God's most lov - ing hand;
2 Re - ly on God your Sav - ior And find your life se - cure.
3 Take heart, have hope, my spir - it, And do not be a - fraid.
4 Leave all to God's di - rec - tion; His wis - dom rules for you

He cares for you while rul - ing The sky, the sea, the land.
Make his work your foun - da - tion That your work may en - dure.
From an - y low de - pres - sion, Where ag - o - nies are made,
In ways to rouse your won - der At all his love can do.

He that in clouds and tem - pest Finds break-through for the sun
No anx - ious thought, no wor - ry, No self - tor - ment - ing care
God's grace will lift you up - ward On arms of sav - ing might
When his plans are ma - tur - ing, Then won - der - work - ing pow'rs

Will find right path - ways for you Till trav - 'ling days are done.
Can win your Fa - ther's fa - vor; His heart is moved by prayer.
Un - til the sun you hoped for De - lights your ea - ger sight.
Will ban - ish from your spir - it What gave you trou - bled hours.

5 How blest you heir of heaven
   To hear the song resound
Of thanks and jubilation
   When you with life are crowned.
In your right hand your maker
   Will place the victor's palm,
And for God's great deliv'rance
   You'll sing the vict'ry psalm.

6 Lord, till we see the ending
   Of all this life's distress,
Faith's hand, love's sinews strengthen,
   With joy our spirits bless.
As yours, we have committed
   Ourselves into your care
On ways made sure to bring us
   To heav'n to praise you there.

© *Text: Paul Gerhardt, 1607–76; tr. F. Samuel Janzow, b. 1913*
Tune: Hans L. Hassler, 1564–1612

HERZLICH TUT MICH VERLANGEN
76 76 D

When in the Hour of Deepest Need   428

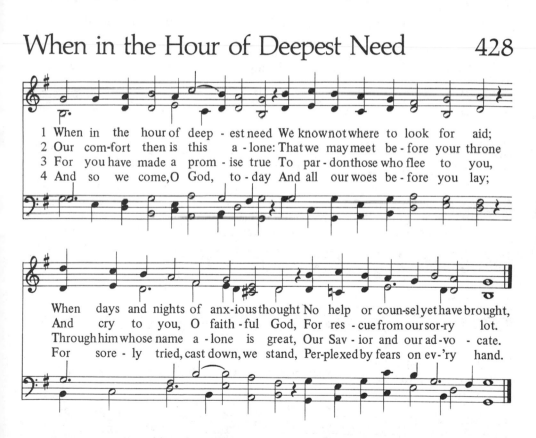

1 When in the hour of deep-est need We know not where to look for aid;
2 Our com-fort then is this a-lone: That we may meet be-fore your throne
3 For you have made a prom-ise true To par-don those who flee to you,
4 And so we come, O God, to-day And all our woes be-fore you lay;

When days and nights of anx-ious thought No help or coun-sel yet have brought,
And cry to you, O faith-ful God, For res-cue from our sor-ry lot.
Through him whose name a-lone is great, Our Sav-ior and our ad-vo-cate.
For sore-ly tried, cast down, we stand, Per-plexed by fears on ev-'ry hand.

5 Oh, from our sins hide not your face;
   Absolve us through your boundless grace!
   Be with us in our anguish still!
   Free us at last from ev'ry ill!

6 So we with all our hearts each day
   To you our glad thanksgiving pay,
   Then walk obedient to your Word,
   And now and ever praise you, Lord.

Text: Paul Eber, 1511–69; tr. Catherine Winkworth, 1829–78, alt.
Tune: Louis Bourgeois, c. 1510–c. 1561

WENN WIR IN HÖCHSTEN NÖTEN SEIN
LM

429   I Leave All Things to God's Direction

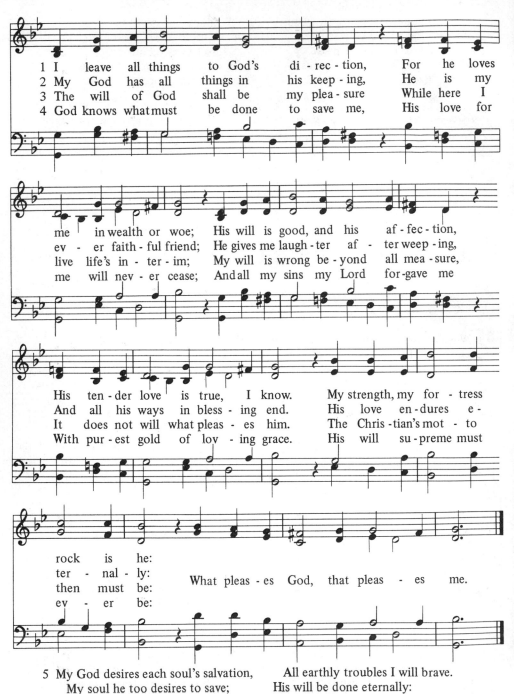

1 I leave all things to God's di-rec-tion, For he loves me in wealth or woe; His will is good, and his af-fec-tion, His ten-der love is true, I know. My strength, my for-tress rock is he: What pleas-es God, that pleas-es me.

2 My God has all things in his keep-ing, He is my ev-er faith-ful friend; He gives me laugh-ter af-ter weep-ing, And all his ways in bless-ing end. His love en-dures e-ter-nal-ly: What pleas-es God, that pleas-es me.

3 The will of God shall be my plea-sure While here I live life's in-ter-im; My will is wrong be-yond all mea-sure, It does not will what pleas-es him. The Chris-tian's mot-to then must be: What pleas-es God, that pleas-es me.

4 God knows what must be done to save me, His love for me will nev-er cease; And all my sins my Lord for-gave me With pur-est gold of lov-ing grace. His will su-preme must ev-er be: What pleas-es God, that pleas-es me.

5 My God desires each soul's salvation,   All earthly troubles I will brave.
My soul he too desires to save;   His will be done eternally:
Therefore with Christian resignation   What pleases God, that pleases me.

Text: Salomo Franck, 1659–1725; tr. August Crull, 1845–1923, alt.
Tune: Georg Neumark, 1621–81

WER NUR DEN LIEBEN GOTT
98 98 88

Our Father, Who from Heaven Above

430

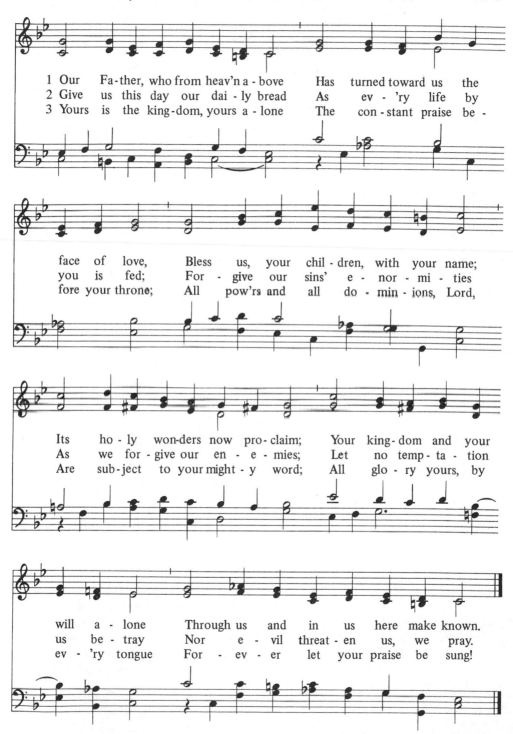

1 Our Fa-ther, who from heav'n a-bove Has turned toward us the face of love, Bless us, your chil-dren, with your name; Its ho-ly won-ders now pro-claim; Your king-dom and your will a-lone Through us and in us here make known.

2 Give us this day our dai-ly bread As ev-'ry life by you is fed; For-give our sins' e-nor-mi-ties As we for-give our en-e-mies; Let no temp-ta-tion us be-tray Nor e-vil threat-en us, we pray.

3 Yours is the king-dom, yours a-lone The con-stant praise be-fore your throne; All pow'rs and all do-min-ions, Lord, Are sub-ject to your might-y word; All glo-ry yours, by ev-'ry tongue For-ev-er let your praise be sung!

© Text: Henry L. Lettermann, b. 1932
Tune: Martin Luther, 1483–1546

VATER UNSER
88 88 88

431 Our Father, Who from Heaven Above

1 Our Fa - ther, who from heav'n a - bove Has told us here to live in love And with our fel - low Chris - tians share Our mu - tual bur - dens and our prayer, Teach us no thought - less word to say But from our in - most heart to pray.

2 Your name be hal - lowed. Help us, Lord, In pu - ri - ty to keep your Word That to the glo - ry of your name We walk be - fore you free from blame. Let no false teach - ing us per - vert; All poor de - lud - ed souls con - vert.

3 Your king - dom come. Guard your do - main And your e - ter - nal righ - teous reign. The Ho - ly Ghost en - rich our day With gifts at - ten - dant on our way. Break Sa - tan's pow'r, de - feat his rage; Pre - serve your Church from age to age.

4 Your gra - cious will on earth be done As it is done be - fore your throne, That pa - tient - ly we may o - bey In good or bad times all you say. Curb flesh and blood and ev - 'ry ill That sets it - self a - gainst your will.

5 Give us this day our daily bread
   And let us all be clothed and fed.
   From warfare, rioting, and strife,
   Disease, and famine save our life
   That we in honest peace may live,
   To care and greed no entrance give.

6 Forgive our sins, let grace outpour
   That they may trouble us no more;
   We too will gladly those forgive
   Who harm us by the way they live.
   Help us in each community
   To serve with love and unity.

7 Lead not into temptation, Lord,
   Where our grim foe and all his horde
   Would vex our souls on ev'ry hand.
   Help us resist, help us to stand
   Firm in the faith, armed with your might;
   Your Spirit gives your children light.

8 Deliver us from evil days,
   From every dark and trying maze;
   Redeem us from eternal death,
   Console us when we yield our breath.
   Give us at last a blessed end;
   Receive our souls, O faithful friend.

9 Amen, that is, it shall be so.
   Make our faith strong that we may know
   We need not doubt but shall receive
   All that we ask, as we believe.
   On your great promise we lay claim.
   Our faith says amen in your name.

© Text: Martin Luther, 1483–1546; tr. F. Samuel Janzow, b. 1913, alt.
Tune: Martin Luther, 1483–1546

VATER UNSER
88 88 88

432 Eternal Spirit of the Living Christ

1 E - ter - nal Spir - it of the liv - ing Christ,
2 Come, pray in me the prayer I need this day;
3 Come with the strength I lack, bring vi - sion clear

I know not how to ask or what to say;
Help me to see your pur - pose and your will
Of hu - man need; oh, give me eyes to see

I on - ly know my need, as deep as life,
Where I have failed, what I have done a - miss;
Ful - fill - ment of my life in love out - poured;

And on-ly you can teach me how to pray.
Held in for-giv - ing love, let me be still.
My life in you, O Christ; your love in me. A - men

© Text: Frank von Christierson, b. 1900
Tune: mode V; Processionale, Paris, 1697

ADORO TE DEVOTE
10 10 10 10

Come, My Soul, with Every Care 433

1 Come, my soul, with ev - 'ry care,   Je - sus loves to an - swer prayer;
2 You are com-ing to your King,   Large pe - ti - tions with you bring;
3 With my bur - den I be - gin: Lord, re - move this load of sin;
4 Lord, your rest to me im - part,   Take pos - ses - sion of my heart;

He him - self bids you to pray,   There - fore will not turn a - way.
For his grace and pow'r are such   None can ev - er ask too much.
Let your blood, for sin - ners spilt,   Set my con-science free from guilt.
There your blood-bought right main - tain   And with-out a ri - val reign.

5 While I am a pilgrim here,
   Let your love my spirit cheer;
   As my guide, my guard, my friend,
   Lead me to my journey's end.

6 Show me what I am to do;
   Ev'ry hour my strength renew.
   Let me live a life of faith;
   Let me die your people's death.

Text: John Newton, 1725–1807, alt.
Tune: Justin Heinrich Knecht, 1752–1817

VIENNA
77 77

434 Christians, While on Earth Abiding

1 Chris-tians, while on earth a - bid - ing, Let us nev - er cease to pray,
2 Bless us, Fa - ther, and pro - tect us From all harm in all our ways;

Firm-ly in the Lord con - fid - ing As our par - ents in their day.
Pa - tient - ly, O Lord, di - rect us Safe - ly through these fleet-ing days.

Be the chil - dren's voic - es raised To the God their par - ents praised.
Let your face up - on us shine, Fill us with your peace di - vine.

May his bless-ing, fail - ing nev - er, Rest up - on his peo - ple ev - er.
Praise the Fa-ther, Son, and Spir - it! Praise him, all who life in - her - it!

Text: Johan Olof Wallin, 1779–1839, st. 1; Jesper Svedberg, 1653–1735, st. 2; tr. unknown, adapt.
Tune: Johann Schop, 1595–1667

WERDE MUNTER
87 87 77 88

All People That on Earth Do Dwell 435

1 All peo-ple that on earth do dwell, Sing to the
2 Know that the Lord is God in-deed; With-out our
3 Oh, en-ter then his gates with praise; Ap-proach with
4 For why? The Lord our God is good: His mer-cy

Lord with cheer-ful voice; Him serve with mirth, his praise
aid he did us make. We are his folk, he doth
joy his courts un-to; Praise, laud, and bless his name
is for-ev-er sure; His truth at all times firm-

forth-tell; Come ye be-fore him and re-joice.
us feed, And for his sheep he doth us take.
al-ways, For it is seem-ly so to do.
ly stood And shall from age to age en-dure.

5 To Father, Son, and Holy Ghost,
    The God whom heav'n and earth adore,
From us and from the angel host
    Be praise and glory evermore.

Text: William Kethe, d. c. 1593
Tune: Louis Bourgeois, c. 1510–c. 1561

OLD HUNDREDTH
L M

436 All Creatures of Our God and King

1 All crea-tures of our God and King, Lift up your voice with
2 O rush-ing wind and breez-es soft, O clouds that ride the
3 O flow-ing wa-ters, pure and clear, Make mu-sic for your
4 Dear moth-er earth, who day by day Un-folds rich bless-ings

us and sing: Al - le - lu - ia, al - le - lu - ia!
winds a - loft: Oh, . . praise him! Al - le - lu - ia!
Lord to hear. Oh, . . praise him! Al - le - lu - ia!
on our way, Oh, . . praise him! Al - le - lu - ia!

O burn-ing sun with gold-en beam And sil - ver moon
O ris-ing morn, in praise re-joice, O lights of eve -
O fire so mas-ter-ful and bright, Pro - vid-ing us
The fruits and flow'rs that ver-dant grow, Let them his praise

Refrain

with soft-er gleam:
ning, find a voice. Oh, praise him! Oh, praise him!
with warmth and light,
a - bun - dant show.

Al - le - lu - ia, al - le - lu - ia, al - le - lu - ia!

5 O ev'ryone of tender heart,
Forgiving others, take your part,
Oh, praise him! Alleluia!
All you who pain and sorrow bear,
Praise God and lay on him your care. *Refrain*

6 And you, most kind and gentle death,
Waiting to hush our final breath,
Oh, praise him! Alleluia!
You lead to heav'n the child of God,
Where Christ our Lord the way has trod. *Refrain*

7 Let all things their Creator bless
And worship God in humbleness.
Oh, praise him! Alleluia!
Oh, praise the Father, praise the Son,
And praise the Spirit, Three in One, *Refrain*

© *Text:* Francis of Assisi, 1182–1226; tr. William H. Draper, 1855–1933, alt.
Tune: Geistliche Kirchengesäng, *Köln, 1623*

LASST UNS ERFREUEN
8 8 8 8 8 8 and alleluias

437 Alleluia! Let Praises Ring

1 Alleluia! Let praises ring! To God the Father let us bring Our songs of adoration. To him through ever-lasting days Be worship, honor, pow'r, and praise,

2 Alleluia! Let praises ring! Unto the Lamb of God we sing, In whom we are elected. He bought his Church with his own blood, He cleansed her in that blessed flood,

3 Alleluia! Let praises ring! Unto the Holy Ghost we sing For our regeneration. The saving faith in us he wrought, And us unto the Bridegroom brought,

4 Alleluia! Let praises ring! Unto our triune God we sing; Blest be his name forever! With angel hosts let us adore And sing his praises more and more

Whose hand sus-tains cre - a - tion. Sing - ing, Ring - ing:
And as his bride se - lect - ed. Ho - ly, Ho - ly
Made us his cho - sen na - tion. Glo - ry! Glo - ry!
For all his grace and fa - vor! Sing - ing, Ring - ing:

Ho - ly, ho - ly, God is ho - ly; Spread the sto - ry
Is our un - ion And com - mu - nion. His be - friend - ing
Joy e - ter - nal, Bliss su - per - nal; There is man - na
Ho - ly, ho - ly, God is ho - ly; Spread the sto - ry

Of our God, the Lord of glo - ry.
Gives us joy and peace un - end - ing.
And an end - less, glad ho - san - na.
Of our God, the Lord of glo - ry!

Text: author unknown, 1698; tr. The Lutheran Hymnal, 1941
Tune: Philipp Nicolai, 1556–1608

WIE SCHÖN LEUCHTET
P M

438

Earth and All Stars

1 Earth and all stars! Loud rush-ing plan-ets! Sing to the
2 Hail, wind, and rain! Loud blow-ing snow-storm! Sing to the
3 Trum-pet and pipes! Loud clash-ing cym-bals! Sing to the
4 En-gines and steel! Loud pound-ing ham-mers! Sing to the

Lord a new song! Oh, vic-to-ry! Loud shout-ing
Lord a new song! Flow-ers and trees! Loud rus-tling
Lord a new song! Harp, lute, and lyre! Loud hum-ming
Lord a new song! Lime-stone and beams! Loud build-ing

ar-my! Sing to the Lord a new song!
dry leaves! Sing to the Lord a new song!
cel-los! Sing to the Lord a new song!
work-ers! Sing to the Lord a new song!

Refrain

He has done mar - vel-ous things.

I too will praise him with a new song!

5 Classrooms and labs!
   Loud boiling test tubes!
   Sing to the Lord a new song!
   Athlete and band!
   Loud cheering people!
   Sing to the Lord a new song! *Refrain*

6 Knowledge and truth!
   Loud sounding wisdom!
   Sing to the Lord a new song!
   Daughter and son!
   Loud praying members!
   Sing to the Lord a new song! *Refrain*

7 Children of God,
   Dying and rising,
   Sing to the Lord a new song!
   Heaven and earth,
   Hosts everlasting,
   Sing to the Lord a new song! *Refrain*

© *Text: Herbert F. Brokering, b. 1926*
© *Tune: David N. Johnson, b. 1922*

EARTH AND ALL STARS
457 457 and refrain

439 I Will Sing My Maker's Praises

1 I will sing my Mak - er's prais - es And in him most joy - ful be, For in all things I see tra - ces Of his ten - der love to me. Noth - ing else than love could move him

2 He so cared for and es - teemed me That the Son he loved so well He gave for me to re - deem me From the quench - less flames of hell. O Lord, spring of bound - less bless - ing,

3 All that for my soul is need - ful He with lov - ing care pro - vides, Nor is he of that un - heed - ful Which my bod - y needs be - sides. When my strength can - not a - vail me,

4 Since there's nei - ther change nor cold - ness In God's love that on me smiled, I now lift my hands in bold - ness, Com - ing to you as your child. Grant me grace, O God, I pray you,

With such deep and ten - der care Ev - er -
How then could my fi - nite mind Of your
When my pow'rs can do no more, Then will
That I may with all my might, All my

more to raise and bear All who try to
love the lim - it find Though my ef - forts
God his strength out - pour; In my need he
life - time, day and night, Love and trust you

serve and love him. All things else have but their
were un - ceas - ing? All things else have but their
will not fail me. All things else have but their
and o - bey you And then, af - ter this life's

hour, God's great love re - tains its pow'r.
hour, God's great love re - tains its pow'r.
hour, God's great love re - tains its pow'r.
end, Ev - er praise you, God, my friend.

Text: Paul Gerhardt, 1607–76; tr. The Lutheran Hymnal, 1941, alt.
Tune: Johann Schop, c.1600–65

SOLLT ICH MEINEM GOTT
87 87 87 78 77

440 From All That Dwell Below the Skies

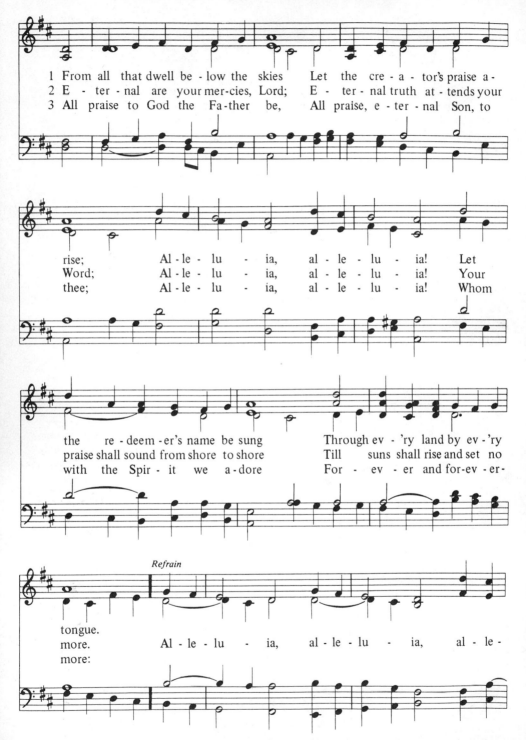

1 From all that dwell be - low the skies Let the cre - a - tor's praise a -
2 E - ter - nal are your mer-cies, Lord; E - ter - nal truth at - tends your
3 All praise to God the Fa-ther be, All praise, e - ter - nal Son, to

rise; Al - le - lu - ia, al - le - lu - ia! Let
Word; Al - le - lu - ia, al - le - lu - ia! Your
thee; Al - le - lu - ia, al - le - lu - ia! Whom

the re - deem - er's name be sung Through ev - 'ry land by ev - 'ry
praise shall sound from shore to shore Till suns shall rise and set no
with the Spir - it we a - dore For - ev - er and for - ev - er -

Refrain

tongue.
more. Al - le - lu - ia, al - le - lu - ia, al - le -
more:

lu - ia, al - le - lu - ia, al - le - lu - ia!

Text: Isaac Watts, 1674–1748; doxology by William W. How, 1823–97, added
Tune: Geistliche Kirchengesäng, Köln, 1623

LASST UNS ERFREUEN
8 8 8 8 8 8 and alleluias

We Sing the Almighty Power of God 441

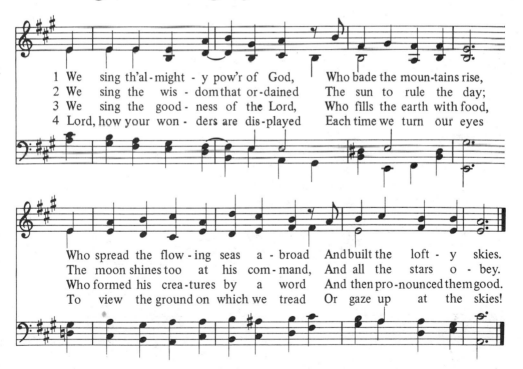

1 We   sing th'al - might - y pow'r of God,   Who bade the moun-tains rise,
2 We   sing the   wis - dom that or - dained   The sun to rule the day;
3 We   sing the   good - ness of the Lord,   Who fills the earth with food,
4 Lord, how your won - ders are dis - played   Each time we turn our eyes

Who spread the flow - ing seas   a - broad   And built the   loft - y   skies.
The moon shines too   at   his com - mand,   And all the   stars   o - bey.
Who formed his crea - tures by   a   word   And then pro - nounced them good.
To   view the ground on which we   tread   Or gaze up   at   the skies!

5 There's not a plant or flow'r below
   But makes your glories known;
   And clouds arise and tempests blow
   By order from your throne.

6 On you each moment we depend;
   If you withdraw, we die.
   Oh, may we never God offend,
   Our God, forever nigh!

Text: Isaac Watts, 1674–1748, alt.
Tune: Johann B. König, Harmonischer Liederschatz, 1738

ICH SINGE DIR
C M

442

In You Is Gladness

1 In you is glad - ness A - mid all sad - ness, Je - sus,
2 If he is ours, ... We fear no pow - ers, Not of

sun - shine of my heart. By you are giv - en The gifts of
earth or sin or death. He sees and bless - es In worst dis -

heav - en, You the true Re - deem - er are. Our souls are
tress - es; He can change them with a breath. Where - fore the

wak - ing; Our bonds are break - ing. Who trusts you sure - ly Has built se -
sto - ry Tell of his glo - ry With hearts and voic - es; All heav'n re -

cure - ly And stands for - ev - er. Al - le - lu - ia! Our hearts are
joic - es In him for - ev - er. Al - le - lu - ia! We shout for

pin - ing To see your shin - ing, Dy - ing or liv - ing To you are
glad - ness, Win o - ver sad - ness, Love him and praise him And still shall

cleav - ing Now and for - ev - er. Al - le - lu - ia!
raise him Glad hymns for - ev - er. Al - le - lu - ia!

Text: Johann Lindemann, 1549–1631; tr. Catherine Winkworth, 1829–78, alt.
Tune: Giovanni Giacomo Gastoldi, c. 1556–1622

IN DIR IST FREUDE
P M

443 Now Thank We All Our God

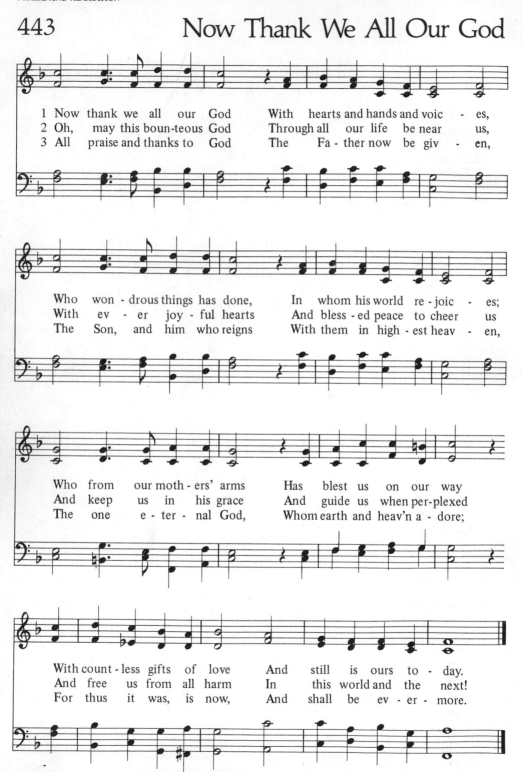

1 Now thank we all our God With hearts and hands and voic - es,
2 Oh, may this boun-teous God Through all our life be near us,
3 All praise and thanks to God The Fa - ther now be giv - en,

Who won - drous things has done, In whom his world re - joic - es;
With ev - er joy - ful hearts And bless - ed peace to cheer us
The Son, and him who reigns With them in high - est heav - en,

Who from our moth - ers' arms Has blest us on our way
And keep us in his grace And guide us when per-plexed
The one e - ter - nal God, Whom earth and heav'n a - dore;

With count - less gifts of love And still is ours to - day.
And free us from all harm In this world and the next!
For thus it was, is now, And shall be ev - er - more.

Text: Martin Rinckart, 1586-1649; tr. Catherine Winkworth, 1829-78
Tune: Johann Crüger, 1598-1662

NUN DANKET ALLE GOTT
67 67 66 66

Praise to the Lord, the Almighty 444

1 Praise to the Lord, the Al-might-y, the King of cre-a - tion! O my soul, praise him, for he is your health and sal-va - tion! Let all who hear Now to his tem - ple draw near, Join-ing in glad ad-o-ra - tion!

2 Praise to the Lord, who o'er all things is won-drous-ly reign - ing And, as on wings of an ea-gle, up-lift-ing, sus-tain - ing. Have you not seen All that is need-ful has been Sent by his gra-cious or-dain - ing?

3 Praise to the Lord, who will pros-per your work and de-fend you; Sure-ly his good-ness and mer-cy shall dai-ly at-tend you. Pon-der a-new What the Al-might-y can do As with his love he be-friends you.

4 Praise to the Lord! Oh, let all that is in me a - dore him! All that has life and breath, come now with prais-es be-fore him! Let the a-men Sound from his peo-ple a - gain. Glad-ly for-ev-er a-dore him!

Text: Joachim Neander, 1650–80; tr. Catherine Winkworth, 1829–78, alt.
Tune: Ernewertes Gesangbuch, Stralsund, 1665

LOBE DEN HERREN
14 14 478

445   Praise the Almighty

1 Praise the Al - might - y, my soul, a - dore him! Yes, I will laud him un - til death; With songs and an - thems I come be - fore him As long as he al - lows me

2 Trust not in rul - ers; they are but mor - tal; Earth-born they are and soon de - cay. Vain are their coun - sels at life's last por - tal, When the dark grave en - gulfs its

3 Bless - ed, oh, bless - ed are they for - ev - er Whose help is from the Lord most high, Whom from sal - va - tion noth - ing can sev - er, And who in hope to Christ draw

4 Pen - i - tent sin - ners, for mer - cy cry - ing, Par - don and peace from him ob - tain; Ev - er the wants of the poor sup - ply - ing, Their faith - ful God he will re -

breath. From him my life and all things
prey. Since mor - tals can no help af -
nigh. To all who trust in him, our
main. He helps his chil - dren in dis -

came; Bless, O my soul, his ho - ly name.
ford, Place all your trust in Christ, our Lord.
Lord Will aid and coun - sel now af - ford.
tress, The wid - ows and the fa - ther - less.

Al - le - lu - ia, al - le - lu - ia!

5 Praise, all you people, the name so holy
  Of him who does such wondrous things!
All that has being, to praise him solely,
  With happy heart its amen sings.
Children of God, with angel host
Praise Father, Son, and Holy Ghost!
  Alleluia, alleluia!

Text: Johann D. Herrnschmidt, 1675–1723; tr. Alfred E. R. Brauer, 1866–1949, alt.
Tune: Seelenharpf, *Ansbach, 1664*

LOBE DEN HERREN, O MEINE SEELE
108 108 88 8

446 Jehovah, Let Me Now Adore You

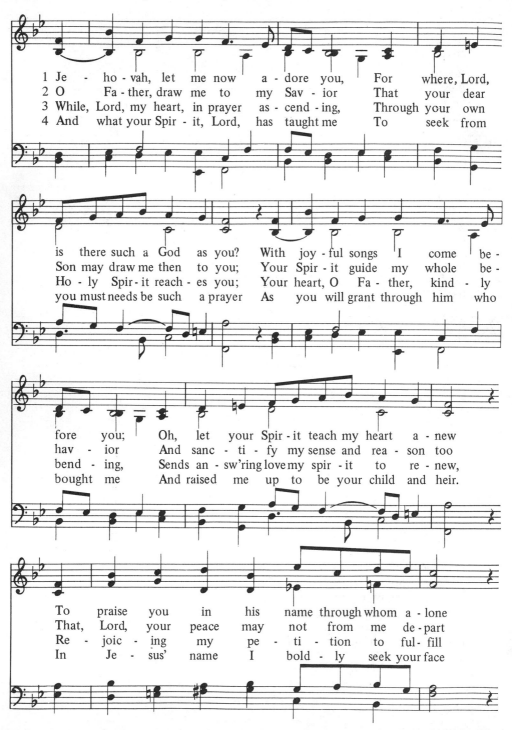

1 Je - ho - vah, let me now a - dore you, For where, Lord,
2 O Fa - ther, draw me to my Sav - ior That your dear
3 While, Lord, my heart, in prayer as - cend - ing, Through your own
4 And what your Spir - it, Lord, has taught me To seek from

is there such a God as you? With joy - ful songs I come be -
Son may draw me then to you; Your Spir - it guide my whole be -
Ho - ly Spir - it reach - es you; Your heart, O Fa - ther, kind - ly
you must needs be such a prayer As you will grant through him who

fore you; Oh, let your Spir - it teach my heart a - new
hav - ior And sanc - ti - fy my sense and rea - son too
bend - ing, Sends an - sw'ring love my spir - it to re - new,
bought me And raised me up to be your child and heir.

To praise you in his name through whom a - lone
That, Lord, your peace may not from me de - part
Re - joic - ing my pe - ti - tion to ful - fill
In Je - sus' name I bold - ly seek your face

Our   songs can please you through your   bless - ed   Son!
But   wake sweet mel - o - dies   with - in   my   heart.
Which   I   have made ac - cord - ing   to   your   will.
And   take from you, my   Fa - ther,   grace   for   grace.

Text: Bartholomäus Crasselius, 1667–1724; tr. Catherine Winkworth, 1829–78, alt.
Tune: J.A. Freylinghausen, Geistreiches Gesang-Buch, 1704

DIR, DIR, JEHOVAH
9 10 9 10 10 10

Songs of Praise the Angels Sang 447

1 Songs   of praise the an - gels   sang,   Heav'n   with   al - le - lu - ias rang
2 Songs   of praise a - woke the morn   When   the   Prince of   Peace was born;
3 Heav'n and earth must pass   a - way;   Songs   of   praise shall crown that day.
4 And   shall man a - lone   be   still   Till   he   stand   on   heav - en's hill?

When cre - a - tion was   be - gun,   When God spoke and   it   was done.
Songs of   praise a - rose when he   Cap - tive   led   cap - tiv - i - ty.
God   will make new heav'ns and earth;   Songs   of   praise shall hail   their birth.
No;   the Church de - lights to raise   Psalms and hymns and songs   of   praise.

5 Saints below, with heart and voice,
   Still in songs of praise rejoice,
   Learning here, by faith and love,
   Songs of praise to sing above.

6 Carried by their final breath,
   Songs of praise shall conquer death;
   Then, amid eternal joy,
   Songs of praise their powers employ.

Text: James Montgomery, 1771–1854, alt.
Tune: French melody, 13th cent.

INNOCENTS
7 7 7 7

448 Oh, that I Had a Thousand Voices

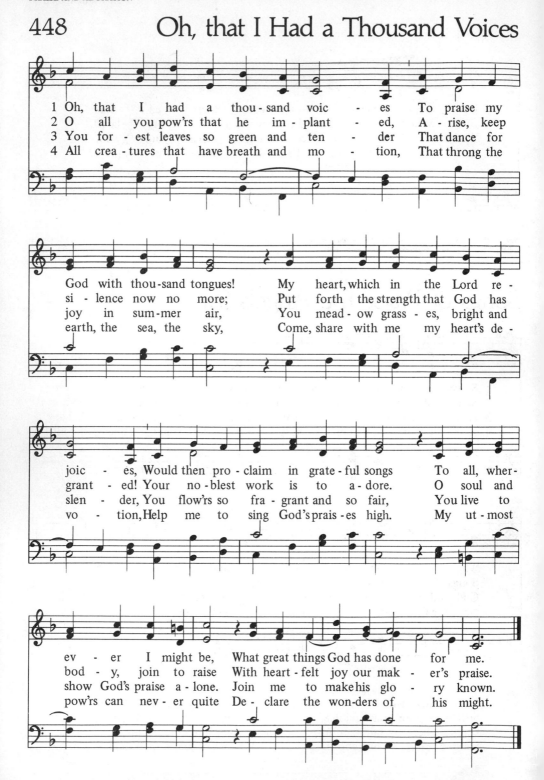

1 Oh, that I had a thou-sand voic - es To praise my
2 O all you pow'rs that he im - plant - ed, A - rise, keep
3 You for - est leaves so green and ten - der That dance for
4 All crea - tures that have breath and mo - tion, That throng the

God with thou-sand tongues! My heart, which in the Lord re -
si - lence now no more; Put forth the strength that God has
joy in sum-mer air, You mead - ow grass - es, bright and
earth, the sea, the sky, Come, share with me my heart's de -

joic - es, Would then pro - claim in grate - ful songs To all, wher -
grant - ed! Your no - blest work is to a - dore. O soul and
slen - der, You flow'rs so fra - grant and so fair, You live to
vo - tion, Help me to sing God's prais - es high. My ut - most

ev - er I might be, What great things God has done for me.
bod - y, join to raise With heart - felt joy our mak - er's praise.
show God's praise a - lone. Join me to make his glo - ry known.
pow'rs can nev - er quite De - clare the won-ders of his might.

5 Creator, humbly I implore you
   To listen to my earthly song
   Until that day when I adore you,

When I have joined the angel throng
And learned with choirs of heav'n to sing
Eternal anthems to my king.

Text: Johann Mentzer, 1658–1734; *tr.* The Lutheran Hymnal, *1941, alt.*
Tune: Johann B. König, Harmonischer Lieder-Schatz, *1738*

O DASS ICH TAUSEND ZUNGEN HÄTTE
98 98 88

When in Our Music God Is Glorified 449

1 When in our mu-sic God is glo-ri-fied And ad-o-ra-tion
2 How oft, in mak-ing mu-sic, we have found A new di-men-sion
3 So has the Church, in lit-ur-gy and song, In faith and love, through
4 And did not Je-sus sing a psalm that night When ut-most e-vil

leaves no room for pride, It is as though the whole cre-a-tion cried:
in the world of sound As wor-ship moved us to a more pro-found
cen-tu-ries of wrong, Borne wit-ness to the truth in ev-'ry tongue:
strove a-gainst the light? Then let us sing, for whom he won the fight:

Al-le-lu-ia, al-le-lu-ia, al-le-lu-ia!

5 Let ev'ry instrument be tuned for praise;
   Let all rejoice who have a voice to raise;

And may God give us faith to sing always:
Alleluia, alleluia, alleluia!

© *Text:* F. Pratt Green, b. 1903
© *Tune:* Charles R. Anders, b. 1929

FREDERICKTOWN
10 10 10 and alleluias

450 The God of Abraham Praise

1 The God of A - br'am praise, Who reigns en - throned a - bove;
2 The God of A - br'am praise, At whose su - preme com - mand
3 The God of A - br'am praise, Whose all - suf - fi - cient grace
4 He by him - self has sworn; I on his oath de - pend.

An - cient of ev - er - last - ing days And God of love.
From earth I rise and seek the joys At his right hand.
Shall guide me all my pil - grim days In all my ways.
I shall, on ea - gle wings up - borne, To heav'n as - cend.

Je - ho - vah, great I Am! By earth and heav'n con - fessed;
I all on earth for - sake, Its wis - dom, fame, and pow'r,
He deigns to call me friend; He calls him - self my God.
I shall be - hold his face; I shall his pow'r a - dore

I bow and bless the sa - cred name For - ev - er blest.
And him my on - ly por - tion make, My shield and tow'r.
And he shall save me to the end Through Je - sus' blood.
And sing the won - ders of his grace For - ev - er - more.

5 Though nature's strength decay,
   And earth and hell withstand,
To Canaan's bounds I urge my way
   At his command.
The wat'ry deep I pass,
   With Jesus in my view,
And through the howling wilderness
   My way pursue.

6 The goodly land I see,
   With peace and plenty blest;
A land of sacred liberty
   And endless rest.
There milk and honey flow,
   And oil and wine abound,
And trees of life forever grow
   With mercy crowned.

7 There dwells the Lord our king,
   The Lord our righteousness,
Triumphant o'er the world and sin,
   The Prince of Peace.
On Zion's sacred height
   His kingdom he maintains
And glorious with his saints in light
   Forever reigns.

8 The God who reigns on high
   The great archangels sing,
And "Holy, holy, holy!" cry,
   "Almighty King!
Who was and is the same
   And evermore shall be:
Jehovah, Father, great I Am!
   We worship thee!"

9 The whole triumphant host
   Give thanks to God on high.
"Hail, Father, Son, and Holy Ghost!"
   They ever cry.
Hail, Abr'am's God and mine!
   I join the heav'nly lays:
All might and majesty are thine
   And endless praise!

Text: Thomas Olivers, 1725-99, alt.
Tune: Hebrew, arr. Meyer Lyon, c. 1751-97

YIGDAL
6684 D

451 Immortal, Invisible, God Only Wise

1 Im - mor - tal, in - vis - i - ble, God on - ly wise,
2 Un - rest - ing, un - hast - ing, and si - lent as light,
3 All life you en - gen - der in great and in small;
4 Great Fa - ther of glo - ry, pure Fa - ther of light,

In
Not
To
Your

light in - ac - ces - si - ble hid from our eyes,
want - ing nor wast - ing, you rule in your might;
all life be - friend - er, the true life of all.
an - gels a - dore you, en - veil - ing their sight.

Most
Your
We
All

bless - ed, most glo - rious, O An - cient of Days,
jus - tice like moun - tains high soar - ing a - bove,
blos - som and flour - ish in rich - ness and range,
laud we would ren - der; oh, lead us to see

Al -
Your
We
The

might - y, vic - to - rious, your great name we praise!
clouds which are foun - tains of good - ness and love.
with - er and per - ish, but you nev - er change.
light of your splen - dor, your love's maj - es - ty!

Text: W. Chalmers Smith, 1824-1908, alt.
Tune: Welsh folk tune

ST. DENIO
11 11 11 11

Sing Praise to God, the Highest Good 452

1 Sing praise to God, the high - est good, The au - thor of cre -
2 What God's al - might - y pow'r has made, In mer - cy he is
3 We sought the Lord in our dis - tress; O God, in mer - cy
4 All who con - fess Christ's ho - ly name, Give God the praise and

a - tion, The God of love who un - der - stood Our need for
keep - ing; By morn - ing glow or eve - ning shade His eye is
hear us. Our Sav - ior saw our help - less - ness And came with
glo - ry. Let all who know his pow'r pro - claim A - loud the

his sal - va - tion. With heal - ing balm our souls he fills
nev - er sleep - ing; With - in the king - dom of his might
peace to cheer us. For this we thank and praise the Lord,
won - drous sto - ry. Cast ev - 'ry i - dol from its throne,

And ev - 'ry faith - less mur - mur stills:
All things are just and good and right:
Who is by one and all a - dored: To God all praise and glo - ry!
For God is God, and he a - lone:

Text: Johann J. Schütz, 1640–90; tr. Frances E. Cox, 1812–97, adapt.
Tune: Melchior Vulpius, c. 1560–1615

LOBT GOTT DEN HERREN, IHR
87 87 887

453 My Soul, Now Praise Your Maker

1 My soul, now praise your Mak - er! Let all with - in me
2 He of - fers all his trea - sure Of jus - tice, truth, and
3 For as a lov - ing moth - er Has pit - y on her
4 His grace re - mains for - ev - er, And chil - dren's chil - dren

bless his name Who makes you full par - tak - er Of
righ - teous - ness, His love be - yond our mea - sure, His
chil - dren here, God in his arms will gath - er All
yet shall prove That God for - sakes them nev - er Who

mer - cies more than you dare claim. For - get him not whose
yearn - ing pit - y o'er dis - tress; Nor treats us as we
those who him like chil - dren fear. He knows how frail our
in true fear shall seek his love. In heav'n is fixed his

meek - ness Still bears with all your sin, Who
mer - it But sets his an - ger by. The
pow - ers, Who but from dust are made. We
dwell - ing, His rule is o - ver all; You

heals your ev - 'ry weak - ness, Re - news your life with -
poor and con - trite spir - it Finds his com - pas - sion
flour - ish as the flow - ers, And e - ven so we
hosts with might ex - cel - ling, With praise be - fore him

in; Whose grace and care are end - less And
nigh; And high as heav'n a - bove us, As
fade; The wind but o'er them pass - es, And
fall. Praise him for - ev - er reign - ing, All

saved you through the past; Who leaves no suf - f'rer
break from close of day, So far, since he has
all their bloom is o'er. We with - er like the
here who hear his Word— Our life and all sus -

friend - less But rights the wronged at last.
loved us, He puts our sins a - way.
grass - es; Our place knows us no more.
tain - ing. My soul, oh, praise the Lord!

Text: Johann Gramann, 1487–1541; tr. Catherine Winkworth, 1829–78, alt.
Tune: Hans Kugelmann, Concentus novi, 1540

NUN LOB, MEIN SEEL
PM

454 Before Jehovah's Awesome Throne

1 Be - fore Je - ho - vah's awe - some throne, O na - tions,
2 His sov - 'reign pow'r with -out our aid Made us of
3 We are his peo - ple, we his care, Our souls and
4 We'll crowd your gates with thank - ful songs, High as the

bow with sa - cred joy; Know that the Lord is God
clay and formed us men; And when like wan - d'ring sheep
all our mor - tal frame. What last - ing hon - ors shall
heav'ns our voic - es raise; And earth with all its thou-

a - lone, He can cre - ate, and he de - stroy.
we strayed, He brought us to his fold a - gain.
we rear, Al - might - y Mak - er, to your name?
sand tongues Shall fill your courts with sound - ing praise.

5 Wide as the world is your command,
   Vast as eternity your love;
Firm as a rock your truth shall stand
   When rolling years shall cease to move.

Text: Isaac Watts, 1674–1748, adapt.
Tune: Louis Bourgeois, c. 1510–c. 1561

OLD HUNDREDTH
L M

Rejoice, O Pilgrim Throng

455

1 Re - joice, O pil - grim throng! Re - joice, give thanks, and sing;
2 With voice as full and strong As o - cean's surg - ing praise,
3 With all the an - gel choirs, With all the saints on earth
4 Yet on and on - ward still, With hymn and chant and song,

Your fes - tal ban - ner wave on high, The cross of Christ your king.
Send forth the stur - dy hymns of old, The psalms of an - cient days.
Pour out the strains of joy and bliss, True rap - ture, no - blest mirth.
Through gate and porch and col - umned aisle The hal-lowed path-ways throng.

Refrain

Re - joice! Re - joice! Re - joice, give thanks, and sing!

5 Still lift your standard high,
　　Still march in firm array,
　As pilgrims through the darkness wend
　　Till dawns the golden day. *Refrain*

6 At last the march shall end;
　　The wearied ones shall rest;
　The pilgrims find their home at last,
　　Jerusalem the blest. *Refrain*

7　　Praise him who reigns on high,
　　　The Lord whom we adore:
　　The Father, Son, and Holy Ghost,
　　　One God forevermore. *Refrain*

Text: Edward H. Plumptre, 1821–91, alt.
Tune: Arthur H. Messiter, 1834–1916

MARION
S M and refrain

God Brought Me
to This Time and Place

1 God brought me to this time and place Sur-round-ed
2 All hon-or, thanks, and praise to you, O Fa-ther,
3 Oh, help me ev-er, God of grace, Through ev-'ry

by his fa-vor. He guard-ed all my nights and
God of heav-en, For mer-cies ev-'ry morn-ing
time and sea-son, At ev-'ry turn, in ev-'ry

days, His kind-ness did not wa-ver. His peace as
new, Which you have free-ly giv-en. In-scribe this
place—Re-demp-tive love the rea-son. Through joy and

sen-ti-nel he gave My spir-it's health and joy to
on my mem-o-ry: My Lord has done great things for
pain and fi-nal breath By Je-sus' life and sav-ing

save. | To this | day | he | has | blessed | me.
me; | To this | day | he | has | helped | me.
death | Help me | as | you | have | helped | me.

© Text: Emilie Juliane, 1637–1706; tr. F. Samuel Janzow, b. 1913
Tune: attr. Nikolaus Decius, c. 1485–aft. 1546

ALLEIN GOTT IN DER HÖH
87 87 887

Oh, Bless the Lord, My Soul   457

1 Oh, bless the Lord, my soul! Let all in me com-bine To
2 Oh, bless the Lord, my soul, Nor let his mer-cies lie For-
3 The Lord for-gives my sins, And he re-lieves my pain; The
4 He crowns my life with love, He ran-soms from the grave; He

aid my tongue to bless his name Whose fa-vor is di-vine.
got-ten in un-thank-ful-ness And with-out prais-es die.
Lord has healed my sick-ness-es And made me whole a-gain.
that re-deemed my soul from hell Has sov-'reign pow'r to save.

5 He fills the poor with good;
   He gives the suff'rers rest;
   The Lord has judgments for the proud,
   Relief for those oppressed.

6 His works and laws and ways
   He made by Moses known
   But showed the world his loving heart
   In Christ, his only Son.

Text: Isaac Watts, 1674–1748, alt.
Tune: Aaron Williams, 1731–76

ST. THOMAS
SM

458   Oh, Worship the King

1 Oh, worship the King, all-glorious above.
2 Oh, tell of his might; oh, sing of his grace,
3 The earth with its store of wonders untold,
4 Your bountiful care what tongue can recite?

Oh, gratefully sing his pow'r and his love;
Whose robe is the light, whose canopy space;
Almighty, your pow'r has founded of old,
It breathes in the air, it shines in the light,

Our shield and defender, the Ancient of Days,
His chariots of wrath the deep thunderclouds form,
Established it fast by a changeless decree,
It streams from the hills, it descends to the plain

Pavilioned in splendor and girded with praise.
And dark is his path on the wings of the storm.
And round it has cast, like a mantle, the sea.
And sweetly distills in the dew and the rain.

5 Frail children of dust, and feeble as frail,
In you do we trust, nor find you to fail;
Your mercies, how tender, how firm to the end,
Our maker, defender, redeemer, and friend!

6 O measureless Might, ineffable Love,
  While angels delight to hymn you above,
  The humbler creation, though feeble their lays,
  With true adoration shall sing to your praise.

Text: Robert Grant, 1779–1838, alt.
Tune: William Croft, 1678–1727

HANOVER
10 10 11 11

Forth in the Peace of Christ 459

1 Forth in the peace of Christ we go; Christ to the
2 King of our hearts, Christ makes us kings; King - ship with
3 Priests of the world, Christ sends us forth This world of
4 Christ's are our lips, his Word we speak, Proph - ets are

world with joy we bring; Christ in our minds, Christ
him his ser - vants gain; With Christ the Ser - vant -
time to con - se - crate, This world of sin by
we whose deeds pro - claim Christ's truth in love that

on our lips, Christ in our hearts, the world's true king.
Lord of all, Christ's world we serve to share Christ's reign.
grace to heal, Christ's world in Christ to re - cre - ate.
we may be Christ in the world, to spread Christ's name.

5 We are the Church; Christ bids us show
  That in his Church all nations find
  Their hearth and home where Christ restores
  True peace, true love to all mankind.

© Text: James Quinn, b. 1919
Tune: traditional Welsh hymn melody

LLEDROD
LM

460 When Morning Gilds the Skies

1 When morn-ing gilds the skies, My heart a-wak-ing cries:
2 When mirth for mu-sic longs, This is my song of songs:
3 To him, my highest and best, I sing when love-pos-sessed:
4 No love-lier an-ti-phon In all high heav'n is known

May Je-sus Christ be praised! When eve-ning shad-ows fall,
May Je-sus Christ be praised! God's ho-ly house of prayer
May Je-sus Christ be praised! What-e'er my hands be-gin,
Than "Je-sus Christ be praised!" There to th'e-ter-nal Word

This rings my cur-few call: May Je-sus Christ be praised!
Has none that can com-pare With "Je-sus Christ be praised!"
This bless-ing shall break in: May Je-sus Christ be praised!
Th'e-ter-nal psalm is heard: Oh, Je-sus Christ be praised!

5 Let all of humankind
In this their concord find:
    May Jesus Christ be praised!
Let all the earth around
Ring joyous with the sound:
    May Jesus Christ be praised!

6 Sing, sun and stars of space,
Sing, all who see his face,
    Sing, "Jesus Christ be praised!"
God's whole creation o'er,
Today and evermore
    Shall Jesus Christ be praised!

Text: German hymn, 19th cent.; tr. Robert Bridges, 1844–1930, alt.
Tune: Joseph Barnby, 1838–96

LAUDES DOMINI
666 666

Praise God, from Whom All Blessings Flow

461

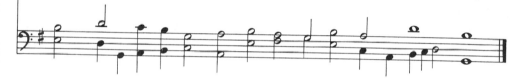

Praise God, from whom all bless - ings flow; Praise him, all crea - tures here be - low;

Praise him a - bove, O heav'n - ly host; Praise Fa - ther, Son, and Ho - ly Ghost.

Text: Thomas Ken, 1637–1711
Tune: Louis Bourgeois, c. 1510– c. 1561

OLD HUNDREDTH
L M

The Day Is Surely Drawing Near

462

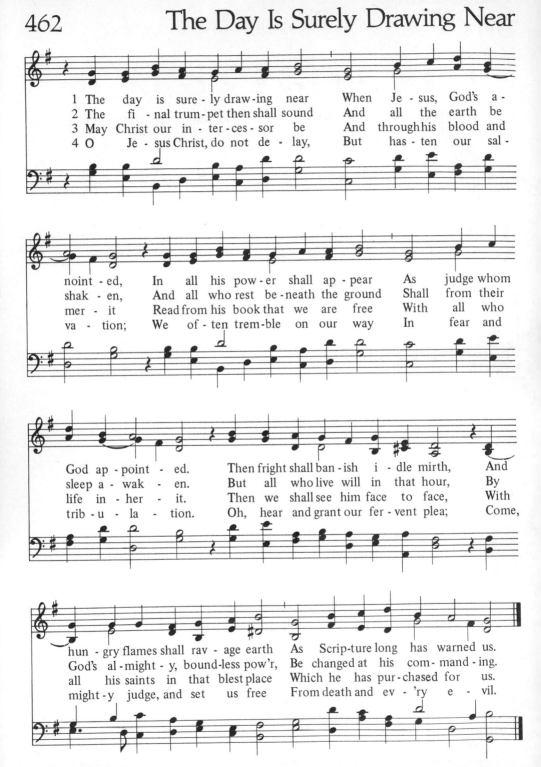

1 The day is sure-ly draw-ing near When Je-sus, God's a-
2 The fi-nal trum-pet then shall sound And all the earth be
3 May Christ our in-ter-ces-sor be And through his blood and
4 O Je-sus Christ, do not de-lay, But has-ten our sal-

noint-ed, In all his pow-er shall ap-pear As judge whom
shak-en, And all who rest be-neath the ground Shall from their
mer-it Read from his book that we are free With all who
va-tion; We of-ten trem-ble on our way In fear and

God ap-point-ed. Then fright shall ban-ish i-dle mirth, And
sleep a-wak-en. But all who live will in that hour, By
life in-her-it. Then we shall see him face to face, With
trib-u-la-tion. Oh, hear and grant our fer-vent plea; Come,

hun-gry flames shall rav-age earth As Scrip-ture long has warned us.
God's al-might-y, bound-less pow'r, Be changed at his com-mand-ing.
all his saints in that blest place Which he has pur-chased for us.
might-y judge, and set us free From death and ev-'ry e-vil.

Text: Bartholomäus Ringwaldt, 1532-c. 1600; tr. Philip A. Peter, 1832-1919, adapt.
Tune: Joseph Klug, Geistliche Lieder, 1529

ES IST GEWISSLICH
87 87 887

The Clouds of Judgment Gather

463

1 The clouds of judg - ment gath - er, The time is grow - ing late;
2 A - rise, O true dis - ci - ples; Let wrong give way to right,
3 The home of fade - less splen - dor, Of blooms that bear no thorn,
4 Oh, hap - py, ho - ly por - tion, Re - lief for all dis - tressed,

Be so - ber and be watch - ful, Our judge is at the gate:
And pen - i - ten - tial shad - ow To Je - sus' bless - ed light:
Where they shall dwell as chil - dren Who here as ex - iles mourn;
True vi - sion of true beau - ty, Re - fresh - ment for the blest!

The judge who comes in mer - cy, The judge who comes in might
The light that has no eve - ning, That knows no moon or sun,
The peace of all the faith - ful, The calm of all the blest,
Strive now to win that glo - ry, Toil now to gain that light;

To put an end to e - vil And di - a - dem the right.
The light so new and gold - en, The light that is but one.
In - vi - o - late, un - fad - ing, Di - vin - est, sweet - est, best.
Send hope a - head to grasp it Till hope be lost in sight.

© Text: Bernard of Cluny, 12th cent.; tr. Lutheran Book of Worship, 1978
Tune: Irish

DURROW
76 76 D

464

A Multitude Comes

1 A mul-ti-tude comes from the east and the west To
2 O God, let us hear when our shep-herd shall call In
3 All tri-als shall be like a dream that is past; For-
4 The heav-ens shall ring with an an-them more grand Than

sit at the feast of sal-va-tion With A-bra-ham,
ac-cents per-sua-sive and ten-der, That while there is
got-ten all trou-ble and mourn-ing. All ques-tions and
ev-er on earth was re-cord-ed; The blest of the

I-saac, and Ja-cob, the blest, O-bey-ing the Lord's in-vi-
time we make haste, one and all, And find him, our might-y de-
doubts have been an-swered at last, When ris-es the light of that
Lord shall re-ceive at his hand The crown to the vic-tors a-

ta-tion.
fend-er.
morn-ing.   Have mer-cy up-on us, O Je-sus!
ward-ed.

Text: Magnus B. Landstad, 1802–80; tr. Peer O. Strömme, 1856–1921, adapt.
Tune: Swedish, 1694

DER MANGE SKAL KOMME
11 9 11 9 9

Our Father, by Whose Name

465

1 Our Fa-ther, by whose name   All fa-ther-hood is known,
2 O Christ, thy-self   a child   With-in an earth-ly home,
3 O Spir-it, who dost bind Our hearts in u - ni - ty,

Who dost in love pro-claim   Each fam - i - ly thine own,
With heart still un-de-filed,   Thou didst to man-hood come;
Who teach-est us to find   The love from self set free,

Bless thou all par-ents, guard - ing   well,   With con-stant love as
Our chil-dren bless in ev - 'ry   place   That they may all be-
In all our hearts such love   in - crease   That ev - 'ry home by

sen - ti - nel, The homes in which thy peo - ple   dwell.
hold thy face, And know-ing thee may grow   in   grace.
this re - lease May be the dwell-ing place   of   peace.

© Text: F. Bland Tucker, b. 1895
Tune: John Edwards, 1806–85

RHOSYMEDRE
66 66 888

Oh, Blessed Home
Where Man and Wife

1 Oh, bless - ed home where man and wife To - geth - er
2 If they have giv - en him their heart, The place of
3 And if their home be dark and drear, The cruse be
4 O Lord, we come be - fore your face; In ev - 'ry

lead a god - ly life, By deeds their faith con - fess - ing!
hon - or set a - part For him each night and mor - row,
emp - ty, hun - ger near, All hope with - in them dy - ing,
home be - stow your grace On chil - dren, fa - ther, moth - er.

There man - y hap - py days are spent, There Je - sus
Then he the storms of life will calm, Will bring for
Let them de - spair not in dis - tress; See, Christ is
Re - lieve their wants, their bur - dens ease, Let them to -

glad - ly will con - sent To tar - ry with his bless - ing.
ev - 'ry wound a balm, And change to joy their sor - row.
there the bread to bless, The frag - ments mul - ti - ply - ing.
geth - er dwell in peace And love to one an - oth - er.

Text: Magnus B. Landstad, 1802–80; tr. Ole T. Arneson, 1853–1917, alt.
Tune: Nürnberg, 1534

KOMMT HER ZU MIR
887 887

Oh, Blest the House

467

1 Oh, blest the house, what-e'er be-fall, Where Je-sus Christ is all in all! For if he were not dwell-ing there, How dark and poor and void it were!

2 Oh, blest that house where faith is found And all in char-i-ty a-bound To trust their God and serve him still And do in all his ho-ly will!

3 Oh, blest that house; it pros-pers well! In peace and joy the par-ents dwell, And in their chil-dren's lives is shown How rich-ly God can bless his own.

4 Then here will I and mine to-day A sol-emn cov-'nant make and say: Though all the world for-sake his Word, My house and I will serve the Lord.

Text: Christoph C. L. von Pfeil, 1712–84; tr. Catherine Winkworth, 1829–78, alt.
Tune: Joseph Klug, Geistliche Lieder, 1533

WO GOTT ZUM HAUS
LM

468 Feed Your Children, God Most Holy

Feed your chil - dren, God most ho - ly, Com-fort sin - ners poor and low - ly;

You our Bread of Life from heav - en, Bless the food you here have giv - en!

As these gifts the bod-y nour - ish, May our souls in gra - ces flour - ish

Till with saints in heav'n-ly splen-dor At your feast our thanks we ren - der.

Text: Johann Heermann, 1585–1647; tr. The Lutheran Hymnal, *1941, alt.*
Tune: Johann Crüger, 1598–1662

SCHMÜCKE DICH
LM D

Holy Father, in Your Mercy

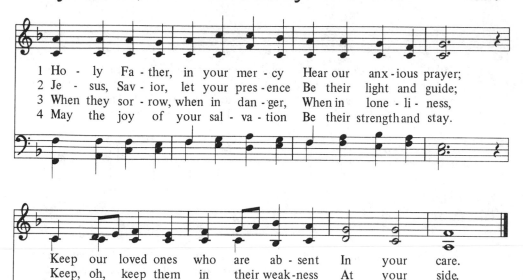

1 Ho - ly Fa - ther, in your mer - cy Hear our anx - ious prayer;
2 Je - sus, Sav - ior, let your pres - ence Be their light and guide;
3 When they sor - row, when in dan - ger, When in lone - li - ness,
4 May the joy of your sal - va - tion Be their strength and stay.

Keep our loved ones who are ab - sent In your care.
Keep, oh, keep them in their weak - ness At your side.
In your love look down and com - fort Their dis - tress.
May they love you, may they praise you Day by day.

5 Holy Spirit, let your teaching
   Sanctify their life;
Send your grace that they may conquer
   In the strife.

6 Father, Son, and Holy Spirit,
   You are God alone;
Bless them, guide them, save them, keep them,
   All you own.

Text: Isabella S. Stevenson, 1843–90, alt.
Tune: Henry W. Baker, 1821–77

STEPHANOS
8 5 8 3

470 Lord Jesus Christ, the Children's Friend

1 Lord Jesus Christ, the children's friend, To each of
2 In Christian homes, Lord, let them be Your blessing
3 That caring parents, gracious Lord, And faithful
4 For by your Word we clearly see That we have

them your presence send; Call them by name and keep them
to their family; Let Christian schools your work ex-
teachers find reward In leading these, to whom you
sinned continually; But show us too, for giving

true In loving faith, dear Lord, to you.
tend In living truth as you intend.
call, To find in Christ their all in all.
Lord, Your saving Gospel's great reward.

5 That all of us, your children dear,
By Christ redeemed, may Christ revere;
Lead us in joy that all we do
Will witness to our love for you.

6 Then guard and keep us to the end,
Secure in you, our gracious friend,
That in your heav'nly family
We sing your praise eternally.

© Text: Henry L. Lettermann, b. 1932
Tune: Thomas Tallis, c. 1505-85

TALLIS' CANON
LM

Shepherd of Tender Youth

471

1 Shep-herd of tend - er youth, Guid-ing in love and truth
2 You are our ho - ly Lord, O all-sub - du - ing Word,
3 You are the great high priest; You have pre - pared the feast
4 Oh, ev - er be our guide, Our shep-herd, and our pride,

Through de - vious ways; Christ, our tri - um - phant king, We come your
Heal - er of strife. Your-self you did a - base That from sin's
Of ho - ly love; And in our mor - tal pain None calls on
Our staff and song. Je - sus, O Christ of God, By your en-

name to sing And here our chil - dren bring To join your praise.
deep dis-grace You so might save our race And give us life.
you in vain; Our plea do not dis - dain; Help from a - bove.
dur - ing Word Lead us where you have trod; Make our faith strong.

5 So now, and till we die,
  Sound we your praises high
    And joyful sing:
  Infants and the glad throng
  Who to the Church belong
  Unite to swell the song
    To Christ, our king.

Text: attr. Clement of Alexandria, c 170–c 220; tr. Henry M. Dexter, 1821–90, alt.
Tune: Felice de Giardini, 1716–96

ITALIAN HYMN
664 6664

472   Let Children Hear the Mighty Deeds

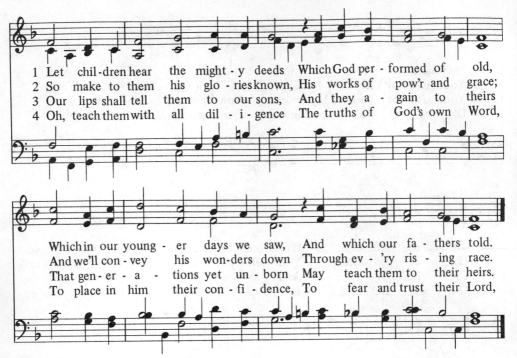

1 Let chil-dren hear the might-y deeds Which God per-formed of old,
2 So make to them his glo-ries known, His works of pow'r and grace;
3 Our lips shall tell them to our sons, And they a-gain to theirs
4 Oh, teach them with all dil-i-gence The truths of God's own Word,

Which in our young-er days we saw, And which our fa-thers told.
And we'll con-vey his won-ders down Through ev-'ry ris-ing race.
That gen-er-a-tions yet un-born May teach them to their heirs.
To place in him their con-fi-dence, To fear and trust their Lord,

5 To learn that in our God alone
    Their hope securely stands,
That they may never doubt his love
    But walk in his commands.

Text: Isaac Watts, 1674–1748, sts. 1, 2, 3, 5, alt.; Bernhard Schumacher, 1886–1978, st. 4
Tune: Johann Crüger, 1598–1662

NUN DANKET ALL
CM

473   You Parents, Hear What Jesus Taught

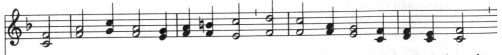
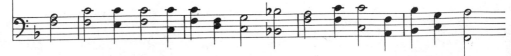

1 You par-ents, hear what Je-sus taught When lit-tle ones to him were brought:
2 O-bey your Lord and let his truth Be taught your chil-dren in their youth
3 For if you love them as you ought, To Christ your chil-dren will be brought.

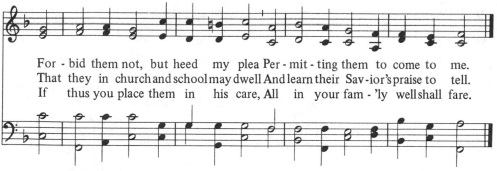

For - bid them not, but heed my plea Per - mit - ting them to come to me.
That they in church and school may dwell And learn their Sav - ior's praise to tell.
If thus you place them in his care, All in your fam - 'ly well shall fare.

Text: Ludwig Helmbold, 1532-98; tr. William M. Czamanske, 1873-1964, alt.
Tune: Cantionale Germanicum, Gochsheim, 1628

HERR JESU CHRIST, DICH ZU UNS WEND
LM

How Shall the Young Secure Their Hearts

474

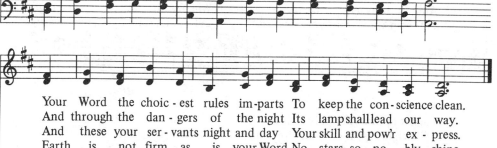

1 How shall the young se - cure their hearts And guard their lives from sin?
2 It's like the sun, a heav'n - ly light That guides us all the day,
3 The star - ry heav'ns your rule o - bey, The earth main - tains its place;
4 But still your Law and Gos - pel, Lord, Have les - sons more di - vine;

Your Word the choic - est rules im-parts To keep the con - science clean.
And through the dan - gers of the night Its lamp shall lead our way.
And these your ser - vants night and day Your skill and pow'r ex - press.
Earth is not firm as is your Word, No stars so no - bly shine.

5 Your Word is everlasting truth.
How pure its every page!

That holy book shall guide our youth
And well support our age.

Text: Isaac Watts, 1674–1748, alt.
Tune: Alexander R. Reinagle, 1799–1877

ST. PETER
CM

475 Gracious Savior, Gentle Shepherd

1 Gra - cious Sav - ior, gen - tle Shep - herd, Chil-dren all are dear to you;
2 Ten - der Shep-herd, nev - er leave them, Nev - er let them go a - stray;
3 Cleanse their hearts from sin - ful fol - ly In the stream your love sup-plied,
4 By your ho - ly Word in-struct them; Fill their minds with heav'n-ly light;

May your lov - ing arms en - fold them In your care their whole life through;
By your warn - ing love di - rect - ed, May they walk the nar - row way!
Min - gled stream of blood and wa - ter Flow-ing from your wound-ed side;
By your pow'r - ful grace con-strain them Al - ways to ap - prove what's right;

Fond-ly tend and safe - ly keep them In your mer - cy strong and true.
Thus di - rect them, thus de - fend them Lest they fall an eas - y prey.
And to heav'n-ly pas-tures lead them, Where your own still wa - ters glide.
Let them know your yoke is eas - y, Let them prove your bur - den light.

5 Taught to lisp your holy praises,
  Which on earth your children sing,
With their lips and hearts, sincerely,
  Glad thank off'rings may they bring,
Then with all the saints in glory
  Join to praise their Lord and King.

Text: Jane E. Leeson, 1807–82; Jonathan Whittemore, 1802–60, cento, alt.
Tune: Geistreiches Gesangbuch, Darmstadt, 1698

SIEH, HIER BIN ICH
87 87 87

I Pray You, Dear Lord Jesus 476

I pray you, dear Lord Jesus, My heart to keep and train

That I your holy temple From youth to age remain.

Oh, turn my thoughts forever From worldly wisdom's lore;

If I but learn to know you, I shall not want for more.

Text: Thomas H. Kingo, 1634–1703; tr. Norman A. Madson, 1886–1962
Tune: Hartnack Zinck's Koralbog, 1801

JEG VIL MIG HERREN LOVE
76 76 D

477

Lord, Help Us Ever to Retain

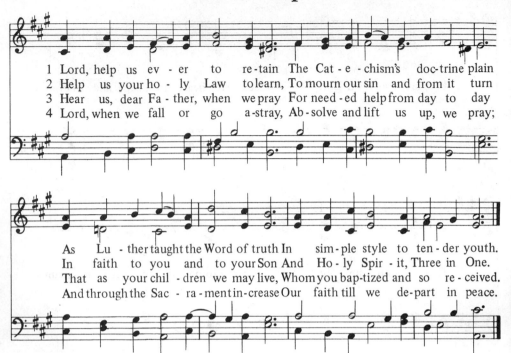

1 Lord, help us ev - er to re - tain The Cat - e - chism's doc - trine plain
2 Help us your ho - ly Law to learn, To mourn our sin and from it turn
3 Hear us, dear Fa - ther, when we pray For need - ed help from day to day
4 Lord, when we fall or go a - stray, Ab - solve and lift us up, we pray;

As Lu - ther taught the Word of truth In sim - ple style to ten - der youth.
In faith to you and to your Son And Ho - ly Spir - it, Three in One.
That as your chil - dren we may live, Whom you bap - tized and so re - ceived.
And through the Sac - ra - ment in - crease Our faith till we de - part in peace.

Text: Ludwig Helmbold, 1532-98; tr. Matthias Loy, 1828-1915, alt.
Tune: As hymnodus sacer, Leipzig, 1625

HERR JESU CHRIST, MEINS
L M

478

Awake, My Soul, and with the Sun

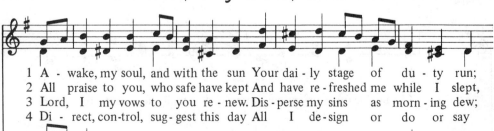

1 A - wake, my soul, and with the sun Your dai - ly stage of du - ty run;
2 All praise to you, who safe have kept And have re - freshed me while I slept.
3 Lord, I my vows to you re - new. Dis - perse my sins as morn - ing dew;
4 Di - rect, con - trol, sug - gest this day All I de - sign or do or say

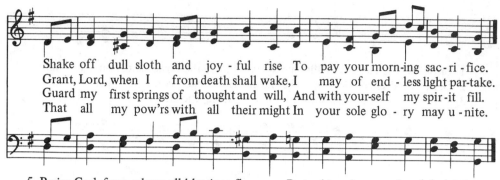

Shake off dull sloth and joy-ful rise To pay your morn-ing sac-ri-fice.
Grant, Lord, when I from death shall wake, I may of end-less light par-take.
Guard my first springs of thought and will, And with your-self my spir-it fill.
That all my pow'rs with all their might In your sole glo-ry may u-nite.

5 Praise God, from whom all blessings flow;   Praise him above, ye heav'nly host;
Praise him, all creatures here below;   Praise Father, Son, and Holy Ghost.

Text: Thomas Ken, 1637–1711
Tune: François H. Barthélémon, 1741–1808

MORNING HYMN
L M

O Holy, Blessed Trinity 479

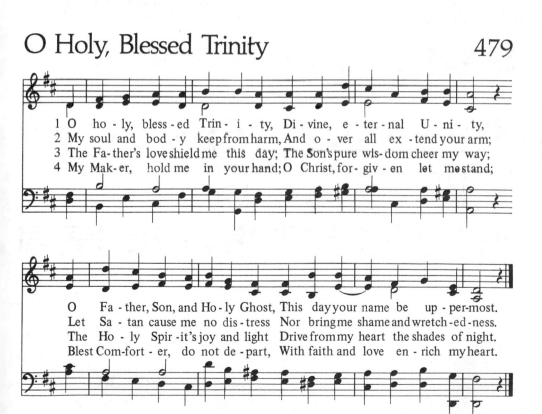

1 O ho-ly, bless-ed Trin-i-ty, Di-vine, e-ter-nal U-ni-ty,
2 My soul and bod-y keep from harm, And o-ver all ex-tend your arm;
3 The Fa-ther's love shield me this day; The Son's pure wis-dom cheer my way;
4 My Mak-er, hold me in your hand; O Christ, for-giv-en let me stand;

O Fa-ther, Son, and Ho-ly Ghost, This day your name be up-per-most.
Let Sa-tan cause me no dis-tress Nor bring me shame and wretch-ed-ness.
The Ho-ly Spir-it's joy and light Drive from my heart the shades of night.
Blest Com-fort-er, do not de-part, With faith and love en-rich my heart.

5 Lord, bless and keep me as your own;   Lord, shine unfailing peace on me
Lord, look in kindness from your throne;   By grace surrounded; set me free.

Text: Martin Behm, 1557–1622; tr. Conrad H. L. Schuette, 1843–1926, alt.
Tune: Nikolaus Herman, c. 1480–1561

STEHT AUF, IHR LIEBEN KINDERLEIN
L M

480 Christ, Whose Glory Fills the Skies

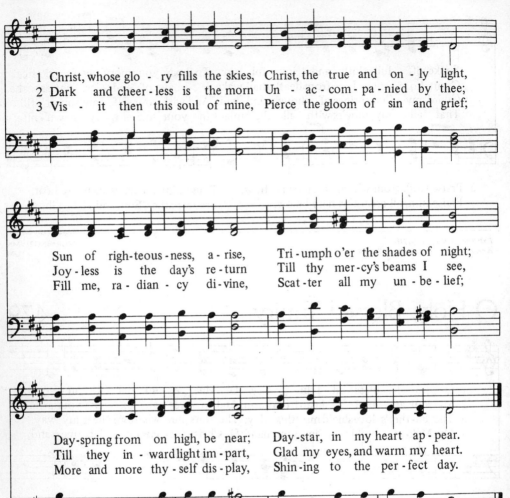

1 Christ, whose glo - ry fills the skies, Christ, the true and on - ly light,
2 Dark and cheer - less is the morn Un - ac - com - pa - nied by thee;
3 Vis - it then this soul of mine, Pierce the gloom of sin and grief;

Sun of righ - teous - ness, a - rise, Tri - umph o'er the shades of night;
Joy - less is the day's re - turn Till thy mer - cy's beams I see,
Fill me, ra - dian - cy di - vine, Scat - ter all my un - be - lief;

Day-spring from on high, be near; Day-star, in my heart ap - pear.
Till they in - ward light im - part, Glad my eyes, and warm my heart.
More and more thy - self dis - play, Shin - ing to the per - fect day.

Text: Charles Wesley, 1707–88
Tune: J. G. Werner, Choral-Buch, 1815

RATISBON
77 77 77

O Splendor of the Father's Light

1 O Splen-dor of the Fa-ther's light That makes our day-light lu-cid,
2 O Fa-ther, fash-ion love in us; Drive en-vy from the en-vi-
3 True Sun, break out on earth and shine In ra-diance with your light di-
4 The Fa-ther sends his Son, our Lord, To be his bright and shin-ing

bright; O Light of light and sun of day, Now
ous; And may you pros-per all our days With
vine; By daz-zling of your Spir-it's might, Oh,
Word; Come, Lord, ride out your gleam-ing course And

shine on us your bright-est ray.
strength to live in your pure grace.
give our jad-ed sens-es light.
be our dawn, our light's true source. A - men

© Text: St. Ambrose, 340–397; tr. Gracia Grindal, b. 1943
Tune: mode I; Antiphoner, Sarum

SPLENDOR PATERNAE
L M

482

Father, We Praise You

1 Fa - ther, we praise you, now the night is o - ver, Ac - tive and
2 Mon - arch of all things, fit us for your man - sions; Ban - ish our
3 All - ho - ly Fa - ther, Son, and e - qual Spir - it, Trin - i - ty

watch-ful, stand - ing now be - fore you; Sing - ing, we of - fer
weak-ness, health and whole-ness send - ing; Bring us to heav - en,
bless - ed, send us your sal - va - tion; Yours is the glo - ry,

prayer and med - i - ta - tion; Thus we a - dore you.
where your saints u - nit - ed Joy with - out end - ing.
gleam - ing and re - sound-ing Through all cre - a - tion.

© *Text: attr. Gregory I, 540–604; tr. Percy Dearmer, 1867–1936, alt.*
Tune: Antiphoner, Paris, 1681

CHRISTE SANCTORUM
11 11 11 5

With the Lord Begin Your Task

1 With the Lord be-gin your task; Je - sus will di - rect it.
2 Let each day be - gin with prayer, Praise, and ad - o - ra - tion.
3 With your Sav-ior at your side, Foes need not a - larm you;
4 If your task be thus be - gun With the Sav-ior's bless - ing,

For his aid and coun - sel ask; Je - sus will per - fect it.
On the Lord cast ev - 'ry care; He is your sal - va - tion.
In his prom - is - es con - fide, And no ill can harm you.
Safe - ly then your course will run, Toward the prom - ise press - ing.

Ev - 'ry morn with Je - sus rise, And when day is end - ed,
Morn-ing, eve - ning, and at night Je - sus will be near you,
All your trust and hope re - pose In the might - y mas - ter,
Good will fol - low ev - 'ry - where While you here must wan - der;

In his name then close your eyes; Be to him com - mend - ed.
Save you from the tempt - er's might, With his pres - ence cheer you.
Who in wis - dom tru - ly knows How to stem di - sas - ter.
You at last the joy will share In the man - sions yon - der.

Text: Morgen- und Abend-segen, *Waldenburg, 1734; tr. W. Gustave Polack, 1890–1950*
Tune: Peter Frank, 1616–75

FANG DEIN WERK
76 76 D

484 All Praise to Thee, My God, This Night

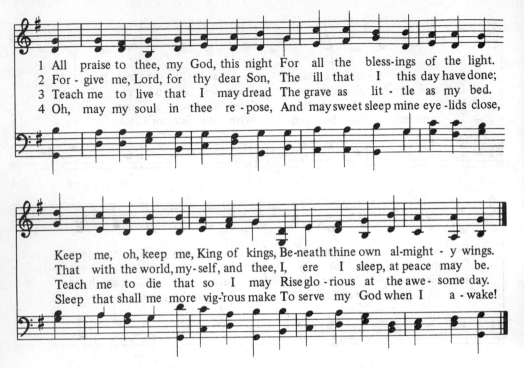

1 All praise to thee, my God, this night For all the bless-ings of the light.
2 For - give me, Lord, for thy dear Son, The ill that I this day have done;
3 Teach me to live that I may dread The grave as lit - tle as my bed.
4 Oh, may my soul in thee re - pose, And may sweet sleep mine eye-lids close,

Keep me, oh, keep me, King of kings, Be-neath thine own al-might - y wings.
That with the world, my-self, and thee, I, ere I sleep, at peace may be.
Teach me to die that so I may Rise glo - rious at the awe-some day.
Sleep that shall me more vig-'rous make To serve my God when I a - wake!

5 When in the night I sleepless lie,
My soul with heav'nly thoughts supply;
Let no ill dreams disturb my rest,
No pow'rs of darkness me molest.

6 Praise God, from whom all blessings flow;
Praise him, all creatures here below;
Praise him above, ye heav'nly host;
Praise Father, Son, and Holy Ghost.

Text: Thomas Ken, 1637–1711
Tune: Thomas Tallis, c. 1505–85

TALLIS' CANON
L M

485 Now Rest Beneath Night's Shadow

1 Now rest be - neath night's shad - ow The wood-land, field,
2 The ra - diant sun has van - ished, Its gold - en rays
3 Now all the heav'n - ly splen - dor Breaks forth in star -
4 Lord Je - sus, since you love me, Now spread your wings

and mead - ow; The world in slum - ber lies. But you,
are ban - ished From dark - 'ning skies of night; But Christ,
light ten - der From myr - iad worlds un - known; And we,
a - bove me And shield me from a - larm. Though Sa -

my heart, a - wak - ing And prayer and mus - ic mak -
the sun of glad - ness, Dis - pel - ling all our sad -
this mar - vel see - ing, For - get our self - ish be -
tan would de - vour me, Let an - gel guards sing o'er

ing, Let praise to your cre - a - tor rise.
ness, Shines down on us in warm - est light.
ing For joy of beau - ty not our own.
me: This child of God shall meet no harm.

5 My loved ones, rest securely,
   For God this night will surely
   From peril guard your heads.
   Sweet slumbers may he send you
   And bid his hosts attend you
   And through the night watch o'er your beds.

Text: Paul Gerhardt, 1607–76; tr. The Lutheran Hymnal, 1941, alt.
Tune: Heinrich Isaac, c. 1450–1517

O WELT, ICH MUSS DICH LASSEN
776 778

486   # O Gladsome Light, O Grace

1 O glad-some Light, O Grace Of God the Fa-ther's face, E-
2 Day has not fad-ed quite; We see the sun-set light, Our
3 Glo-ry to you be-longs And praise of ho-ly songs, O

ter-nal splen-dor wear - ing: Ce - les-tial, ho-ly, blest, Our
eve-ning hymn out-pour - ing, Fa - ther, in-car-nate Son, Who
Three in One, Life-giv - er; There-fore, our God most high, We

Sav-ior and our guest, Joy - ful in your ap-pear - ing.
our re - demp-tion won, Spir - it of both a - dor - ing.
wor-ship, glo - ri - fy, And praise your name for-ev - er.

Text: Greek hymn, 3rd cent.; tr. Robert Bridges, 1844–1930, alt.
Tune: Louis Bourgeois, c. 1510–c. 1561, adapt.

NUNC DIMITTIS
667 667

O Trinity, O Blessed Light

487

1 O Trin - i - ty, O bless - ed Light, O U - ni - ty of prince-ly might:
2 To you our morn-ing song of praise, To you our eve-ning prayer we raise;
3 All glo - ry be to God a - bove And to the Son, the prince of love,

The fi - 'ry sun is go-ing down; Shed light up - on us through your Son.
We praise your light in ev-'ry age, The glo - ry of our pil - grim-age.
And to the Spir -it, One in Three! We praise you, bless - ed Trin - i - ty

© Text: attr. St. Ambrose, 340–397; tr. Gracia Grindal, b. 1943
Tune: Nikolaus Herman, c. 1480–1561

STEHT AUF, IHR LIEBEN KINDERLEIN
L M

488

Sun of My Soul, O Savior Dear

1 Sun of my soul, O Savior dear, It is not
   night if you are near. Oh, may no earth-born cloud a-
   rise To hide you from your servant's eyes.

2 When the soft dews of kindly sleep My wearied
   eyelids gently steep, Be my last thought how, safe from
   harm, I rest within my Savior's arm.

3 Abide with me from morn till eve, For without
   you I cannot live; Abide with me when night is
   nigh, For without you I dare not die.

4 If some poor wand'ring child of God Has spurned to-
   day your shepherd's rod, Now, Lord, the gracious work be-
   gin; Let him no more lie down in sin.

5 Watch by the sick; enrich the poor
   With blessings from your boundless store;
   Be ev'ry mourner's sleep tonight,
   Like infant's slumbers, pure and light.

6 Come near and bless us when we wake,
   As through the world our way we take,
   Till in the ocean of your love
   We lose ourselves in heav'n above.

Text: John Keble, 1792–1866, alt.
Tune: Katholisches Gesangbuch, Vienna, c. 1774—80, adapt.

HURSLEY
L M

Before the Ending of the Day

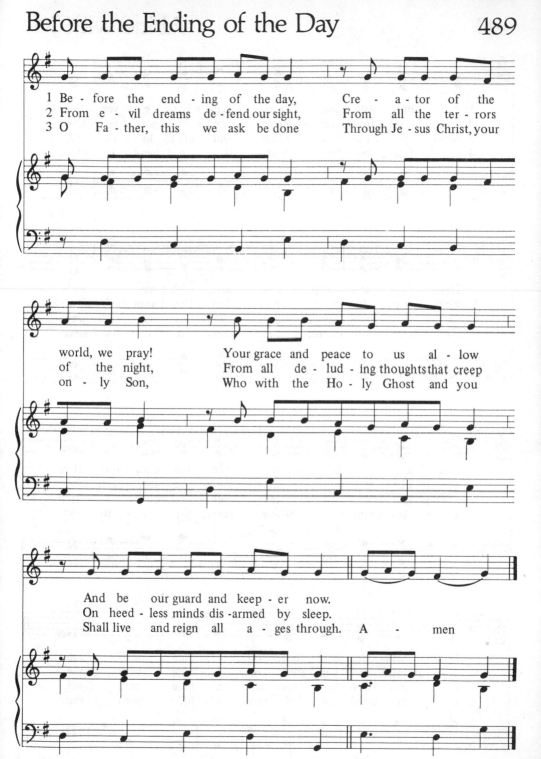

489

1 Be - fore the end - ing of the day, Cre - a - tor of the
2 From e - vil dreams de - fend our sight, From all the ter - rors
3 O Fa - ther, this we ask be done Through Je - sus Christ, your

world, we pray! Your grace and peace to us al - low
of the night, From all de - lud - ing thoughts that creep
on - ly Son, Who with the Ho - ly Ghost and you

And be our guard and keep - er now.
On heed - less minds dis - armed by sleep.
Shall live and reign all a - ges through. A - men

Text: compline office hymn, c. 8th cent.; tr. John M. Neale, 1818-66, adapt.
Tune: Benedictine plainsong, mode VI

JAM LUCIS
L M

490

Abide with Me

1 A - bide with me, fast falls the e - ven - tide.
2 I need thy pres - ence ev - 'ry pass - ing hour;
3 Swift to its close ebbs out life's lit - tle day;
4 I fear no foe with thee at hand to bless;

The dark - ness deep - ens; Lord, with me a - bide.
What but thy grace can foil the tempt - er's pow'r?
Earth's joys grow dim, its glo - ries pass a - way;
Ills have no weight, and tears no bit - ter - ness.

When oth - er help - ers fail and com - forts flee,
Who like thy - self my guide and stay can be?
Change and de - cay in all a - round I see;
Where is death's sting? Where, grave, thy vic - to - ry?

Help of the help - less, oh, a - bide with me.
Through cloud and sun - shine, oh, a - bide with me.
O thou who chang - est not, a - bide with me.
I tri - umph still if thou a - bide with me!

5 Hold thou thy cross before my closing eyes,
  Shine through the gloom, and point me to the skies;
  Heav'n's morning breaks, and earth's vain shadows flee;
  In life, in death, O Lord, abide with me.

Text: Henry F. Lyte, 1793–1847
Tune: William H. Monk, 1823–89

EVENTIDE
10 10 10 10

Now the Day Is Over 491

1 Now the day is o - ver; Night is draw - ing nigh;
2 Je - sus, give the wea - ry Calm and sweet re - pose;
3 Com - fort ev - 'ry suf - f'rer Watch-ing late in pain;
4 Through the long night - watch - es May your an - gels spread

Shad - ows of the eve - ning Steal a - cross the sky.
With your ten -d'rest bless - ing May our eye - lids close.
Those who plan some e - vil, From their sin re - strain.
Their bright wings a - bove me, Watch - ing round my bed.

Shad - ows of the eve -ning Steal a - cross the sky.

5 When the morning wakens,
  Then may I arise
  Pure and fresh and sinless
  In your holy eyes.

6 Glory to the Father,
  Glory to the Son,
  And to you, blest Spirit,
  While the ages run.

Text: Sabine Baring-Gould, 1834–1924, alt.
Tune: Joseph Barnby, 1838–96

MERRIAL
65 65

492 God, Who Made the Earth and Heaven

1 God, who made the earth and heav-en, Dark-ness and light:
2 And when morn a-gain shall call us To run life's way,
3 Guard us wak-ing, guard us sleep-ing, And when we die,
4 Ho-ly Fa-ther, throned in heav-en, All-ho-ly Son,

You the day for work have giv-en, For rest the night.
May we still, what-e'er be-fall us, Your will o-bey.
May we in your might-y keep-ing All peace-ful lie.
Ho-ly Spir-it, free-ly giv-en, Blest Three in One:

May your an-gel guards de-fend us, Slum-ber sweet your mer-cy send us,
From the pow'r of e-vil hide us, In the nar-row path-way guide us,
When the last dread call shall wake us, Then, O Lord, do not for-sake us,
Grant us grace, we now im-plore you, Till we lay our crowns be-fore you

Ho-ly dreams and hopes at-tend us All through the night.
Nev-er be your smile de-nied us All through the day.
But to reign in glo-ry take us With you on high.
And in wor-thier strains a-dore you While a-ges run.

Text: Reginald Heber, 1783–1826, st. 1; William Mercer, 1811–73, sts. 2, 4; Richard Whately, 1787–1863, st. 3; alt.
Tune: Welsh

AR HYD Y NOS
84 84 88 84

Sing to the Lord of Harvest

493

1 Sing to the Lord of har-vest, Sing songs of love and praise;
2 God makes the clouds rain good-ness, The des-erts bloom and spring,
3 Bring to this sa-cred al-tar The gifts his good-ness gave,

With joy-ful hearts and voic-es Your al-le-lu-ias raise.
The hills leap up in glad-ness, The val-leys laugh and sing.
The gold-en sheaves of har-vest, The souls Christ died to save.

By him the roll-ing sea-sons In fruit-ful or-der move;
God fills them with his full-ness, All things with large in-crease;
Your hearts lay down be-fore him When at his feet you fall,

Sing to the Lord of har-vest A joy-ous song of love.
He crowns the year with bless-ing, With plen-ty and with peace.
And with your lives a-dore him Who gave his life for all.

Text: John S. B. Monsell, 1811–75, alt.
Tune: Johann Steurlein, 1546–1613

WIE LIEBLICH IST DER MAIEN
76 76 D

494

We Praise You, O God

1 We praise you, O God, our re-deem - er, cre - a - tor;
2 We wor - ship you, God of our fa - thers, we bless you;
3 With voic - es u - nit - ed our prais - es we of - fer

In grate - ful de - vo - tion our trib - ute we bring.
Through tri - al and tem - pest our guide you have been.
And glad - ly our songs of thanks - giv - ing we raise.

We lay it be - fore you, we kneel and a - dore you;
When per - ils o'er - take us, you will not for - sake us,
With you, Lord, be - side us, your strong arm will guide us.

We bless your ho - ly name, glad prais - es we sing.
And with your help, O Lord, our strug - gles we win.
To you, our great re - deem - er, for - ev - er be praise!

Text: Julia C. Cory, 1882–1963, alt.
Tune: A. Valerius, Nederlandtsch Gedenckclanck, 1626

KREMSER
12 11 12 11

Come, You Thankful People, Come

495

1 Come, you thank-ful peo-ple, come; Raise the song of har-vest home.
2 All the world is God's own field, Fruit un-to his praise to yield.
3 For the Lord our God shall come And shall take his har-vest home,
4 E-ven so, Lord, quick-ly come To your fi-nal har-vest home.

All is safe-ly gath-ered in Ere the win-ter storms be-gin.
Wheat and tares to-geth-er sown, Un-to joy or sor-row grown.
From his field shall in that day All of-fens-es purge a-way,
Gath-er all your peo-ple in, Free from sor-row, free from sin,

God, our mak-er, does pro-vide For our wants to be sup-plied.
First the blade and then the ear, Then the full corn shall ap-pear.
Give his an-gels charge at last In the fire the tares to cast
There, for-ev-er pu-ri-fied, In your gar-ner to a-bide.

Come to God's own tem-ple, come, Raise the song of har-vest home.
Lord of har-vest, grant that we Whole-some grain and pure may be.
But the fruit-ful ears to store In his gar-ner ev-er-more.
Come, with all your an-gels, come, Raise the glo-rious har-vest home.

Text: Henry Alford, 1810–71, alt.
Tune: George J. Elvey, 1816–93

ST. GEORGE'S, WINDSOR
77 77 D

496   Lord, to You Immortal Praise

1 Lord, to you im - mor - tal praise For the love that crowns our days;
2 All the plen - ty sum - mer pours; Au - tumn's rich, a - bun - dant stores,
3 Peace, pros-per - i - ty, and health, Pri - vate bliss and pub - lic wealth,
4 As your pros-p'ring hand has blest, May we give you of the best

Boun - teous Source of ev - 'ry joy, Let your praise our tongues em - ploy.
Flocks that whit - en all the plain, Yel - low sheaves of rip - ened grain:
Knowl-edge with its glad-d'ning streams, True re - li - gion's ho - lier beams:
And by deeds of kind - ly love For your mer - cies grate - ful prove,

All to you, our God, we owe, Source whence all our bless-ings flow.
Lord, for these our souls shall raise Grate - ful vows and sol - emn praise.
Lord, for these our souls shall raise Grate - ful vows and sol - emn praise.
Sing - ing thus through all our days: "Lord, to you im - mor - tal praise."

xt: Anna L. Barbauld, 1743–1825, alt.
ne: Conrad Kocher, 1786–1872

DIX
77 77 77

God Bless Our Native Land

497

1 God bless our na - tive land; Firm may it ev - er stand
2 So shall our prayers a - rise To God a - bove the skies,

Through storm and night. When the wild tem - pests rave, Rul - er of
On whom we wait. Thou who art ev - er nigh, Guard - ing with

wind and wave, Do thou our coun - try save By thy great might.
watch - ful eye, To thee a - loud we cry: God save the state!

Text: Charles T. Brooks, 1812–83, st. 1; John S. Dwight, 1813–93, st. 2; alt.
Tune: Thesaurus Musicus, *London, 1744*

NATIONAL ANTHEM
664 6664

498   # O God of Love, O King of Peace

1 O God of love, O King of peace, Make wars through-
2 Re - mem - ber, Lord, your works of old, The won - ders
3 Whom shall we trust but you, O Lord? Where rest but
4 Where saints and an - gels dwell a - bove, All hearts are

out the world to cease; Our greed and sin - ful
that our el - ders told; Re - mem - ber not our
on your faith - ful Word? None ev - er called on
knit in ho - ly love; Oh, bind us in that

wrath re - strain.
sins' dark stain.   Give peace, O God, give peace a - gain.
you in vain.
heav'n - ly chain.

Text: Henry W. Baker, 1821–77
Tune: Swenska Psalm Boken, Stockholm, 1697

ACK, BLIV HOS OSS
L M

Christ, by Heavenly Hosts Adored

1 Christ, by heav'n-ly hosts a-dored, Gra-cious, might-y, sov-'reign Lord,
2 On our fields of grass and grain Send, O Lord, the kind-ly rain,
3 Give us rul-ers faith-ful, true, Such as love and hon-or you;

God of na-tions, King of kings, Head of all cre-a-ted things,
And through-out this spa-cious land Crown the la-bors of each hand.
Let the pow-ers you or-dained Be in right-teous-ness main-tained.

By the Church with joy con-fessed, God the Son for-ev-er blessed,
Let your kind pro-tec-tion be O-ver com-merce on the sea.
In the peo-ple's hearts in-crease Love of pi-e-ty and peace.

Plead-ing at your throne we stand, Save your peo-ple, bless our land.
O-pen, Lord, your boun-teous hand; Bless your peo-ple, bless our land.
Thus u-nit-ed, we shall stand One wide, free, and hap-py land.

Text: Henry Harbaugh, 1817–67, alt.
Tune: George J. Elvey, 1816–93

ST. GEORGE'S, WINDSOR
77 77 D

500

Before You, Lord, We Bow

1 Be - fore you, Lord, we bow, Our God who reigns a - bove And
2 The na - tion you have blest May well your love de - clare, From
3 May ev - 'ry moun-tain height, Each vale and for - est green, Shine
4 Earth, hear your Mak - er's voice; Your great Re - deem - er own; Be -

rules the world be - low, Bound-less in pow'r and love. Our thanks we
foes and fears at rest, Pro - tect - ed by your care. For this bright
in your Word's pure light, And its rich fruits be seen! May ev - 'ry
lieve, o - bey, re - joice, And wor-ship him a - lone. Cast down your

bring In joy and praise, Our hearts we raise To you, our king!
day, For this fair land— Gifts of your hand— Our thanks we pay.
tongue Be tuned to praise And join to raise A grate - ful song.
pride, Your sin de - plore, And bow be - fore The Cru - ci - fied.

5 And when in pow'r he comes,
   Oh, may our native land
From all its rending tombs
   Send forth a glorious band,
A countless throng,
   With joy to sing
   To heav'n's high king
Salvation's song!

Text: Francis S. Key, 1779–1843, alt.
Tune: John Darwall, 1731–89

DARWALL'S 148TH
66 66 4444

God of Our Fathers

1 God of our fa - thers, whose al - might - y hand
2 Your love di - vine has led us in the past;
3 From war's a - larms, from dead - ly pes - ti - lence
4 Re - fresh your peo - ple on their toil - some way;

Leads forth in beau - ty all the star - ry band
In this free land by you our lot is cast;
Make your strong arm our ev - er sure de - fense.
Lead us from night to nev - er - end - ing day;

Of shin - ing worlds in splen - dor through the skies:
Oh, be our rul - er, guard - ian, guide, and stay;
Your true re - li - gion in our hearts in - crease;
Fill all our lives with heav'n - born love and grace

Our grate - ful songs be - fore your throne a - rise.
Your Word our law, your paths our cho - sen way.
Your boun - teous good - ness nour - ish us in peace.
Un - til at last we meet be - fore your face.

Text: Daniel C. Roberts, 1841–1907, alt.
Tune: George W. Warren, 1828–1902

NATIONAL HYMN
10 10 10 10

502   Lord, While for Humankind We Pray

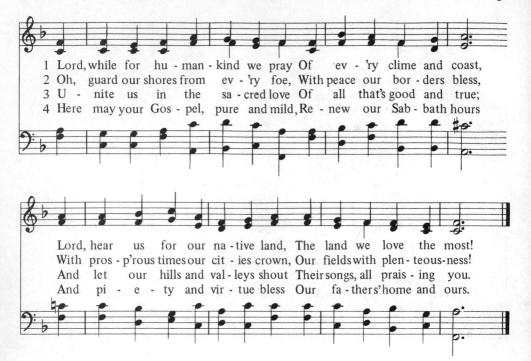

1 Lord, while for hu-man-kind we pray Of ev-'ry clime and coast,
2 Oh, guard our shores from ev-'ry foe, With peace our bor-ders bless,
3 U-nite us in the sa-cred love Of all that's good and true;
4 Here may your Gos-pel, pure and mild, Re-new our Sab-bath hours

Lord, hear us for our na-tive land, The land we love the most!
With pros-p'rous times our cit-ies crown, Our fields with plen-teous-ness!
And let our hills and val-leys shout Their songs, all prais-ing you.
And pi-e-ty and vir-tue bless Our fa-thers' home and ours.

5 Lord of the nations, thus to you
   Our country we commend.
Oh, be her refuge and her trust,
   Her everlasting friend.

Text: John R. Wreford, 1800–81, alt.
Tune: J. Day, Psalter, 1562

ST. FLAVIAN
CM

SPIRITUAL SONGS

Now the Light Has Gone Away   503

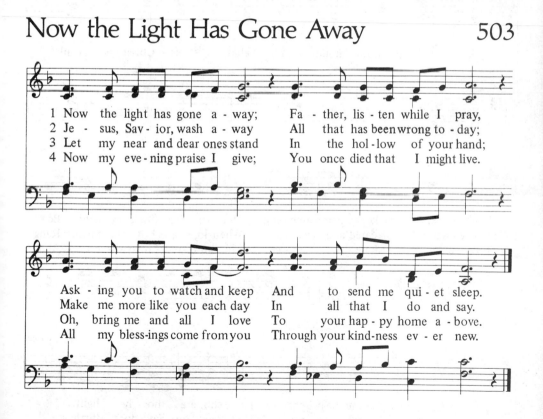

1 Now the light has gone a-way; Fa-ther, lis-ten while I pray,
2 Je - sus, Sav-ior, wash a-way All that has been wrong to-day;
3 Let my near and dear ones stand In the hol-low of your hand;
4 Now my eve-ning praise I give; You once died that I might live.

Ask - ing you to watch and keep And to send me qui-et sleep.
Make me more like you each day In all that I do and say.
Oh, bring me and all I love To your hap-py home a-bove.
All my bless-ings come from you Through your kind-ness ev-er new.

5 O my blest and dearest Friend,
You will love me to the end.
Let me love you more and more,
Always better than before.

Text: Frances R. Havergal, 1836–79, alt.
Tune: Liederbuch für Kleinkinder-Schulen, *Kaiserswerth, 1842*

MÜDE BIN ICH
7 7 7 7

504 Go Tell It on the Mountain

Refrain

Go tell it on the moun - tain, O - ver the hills and ev - 'ry - where;

Go tell it on the moun - tain That Je - sus Christ is born!

1 While shep - herds kept their watch - ing O'er si - lent flocks by night, Be -
2 The shep - herds feared and trem - bled When lo, a - bove the earth Rang
3 Down in a lone - ly man - ger The hum - ble Christ was born; And

Refrain

hold, through - out the heav - ens There shone a ho - ly light.
out the an - gel cho - rus That hailed our Sav - ior's birth.
God sent us sal - va - tion That bless - ed Christ - mas morn.

© Text: Negro spiritual, refrain; John W. Work II, 1871–1925, stanzas, alt.
Tune: Negro spiritual

GO TELL IT
78 76 76 76

Were You There

505

1 Were you there when they cru - ci - fied my Lord? Were you
2 Were you there when they nailed him to the tree? Were you
3 Were you there when they laid him in the tomb? Were you
4 Were you there when God raised him from the tomb? Were you

there when they cru - ci - fied my Lord? Oh,
there when they nailed him to the tree? Oh,
there when they laid him in the tomb? Oh,
there when God raised him from the tomb? Oh,

some - times it caus - es me to trem - ble, trem - ble, trem - ble.
some - times it caus - es me to trem - ble, trem - ble, trem - ble.
some - times it caus - es me to trem - ble, trem - ble, trem - ble.
some - times it caus - es me to trem - ble, trem - ble, trem - ble.

Were you there when they cru - ci - fied my Lord?
Were you there when they nailed him to the tree?
Were you there when they laid him in the tomb?
Were you there when God raised him from the tomb?

Text: Negro spiritual, alt.
Tune: Negro spiritual

WERE YOU THERE
10 10 14 10

506 There Stands a Fountain Where for Sin

1 There stands a foun - tain where for sin Im - man - u - el was slain, And sin - ners who are washed there -in Are cleansed from ev - 'ry stain, Are cleansed from ev - 'ry stain.

2 The dy - ing thief re - joiced to see That foun - tain in his day; And there have I, as vile as he, Washed all my sins a - way, Washed all my sins a - way.

3 Dear dy - ing Lamb, thy pre - cious blood Shall nev - er lose its pow'r Till all the ran - somed Church of God Be saved to sin no more, Be saved to sin no more.

4 E'er since by faith I saw the stream Thy flow - ing wounds sup - ply, Re - deem - ing love has been my theme And shall be till I die, And shall be till I die.

5 When this poor lisping, stamm'ring tongue
   Lies silent in the grave,
Then in a nobler, sweeter song
   I'll sing thy pow'r to save.

Text: William Cowper, 1731–1800, alt.
Tune: Lowell Mason, 1792–1872

COWPER
C M

Beautiful Savior

1 Beau - ti - ful Sav - ior, King of cre - a - tion, Son of
2 Fair are the mead - ows, Fair are the wood - lands, Robed in
3 Fair is the sun - shine, Fair is the moon - light, Bright the
4 Beau - ti - ful Sav - ior, Lord of the na - tions, Son of

God and Son of Man! Tru - ly I'd love thee, Tru - ly I'd
flow'rs of bloom - ing spring; Je - sus is fair - er, Je - sus is
spar - kling stars on high; Je - sus shines bright - er, Je - sus shines
God and Son of Man! Glo - ry and hon - or, Praise, ad - o -

serve thee, Light of my soul, my joy, my crown.
pur - er, He makes our sor - r'wing spir - it sing.
pur - er Than all the an - gels in the sky.
ra - tion Now and for - ev - er - more be thine!

Text: Gesangbuch, Münster, 1677; tr. Joseph A. Seiss, 1823–1904
Tune: Silesian folk tune, 1842

SCHÖNSTER HERR JESU
557 558

508   Jesus, Lover of My Soul

1 Jesus, lover of my soul,   Let me to thy mercy fly
2 Other refuge have I none;   Hangs my helpless soul on thee.
3 Wilt thou not regard my call,   Wilt thou not accept my prayer?
4 Thou, O Christ, art all I want;   More than all in thee I find.

While the nearer waters roll,   While the tempest still is high.
Leave, ah, leave me not alone,   Still support and comfort me!
Lo, I sink, I faint, I fall;   Lo, on thee I cast my care;
Raise the fallen, cheer the faint,   Heal the sick, and lead the blind.

Hide me, O my Savior, hide   Till the storm of life is past;
All my trust on thee is stayed,   All my help from thee I bring;
Reach me out thy gracious hand!   While I of thy strength receive,
Just and holy is thy name;   I am all unrighteousness,

Safe into the haven guide.   Oh, receive my soul at last!
Cover my defenseless head   With the shadow of thy wing.
Hoping against hope I stand,   Dying, and behold, I live!
False and full of sin I am;   Thou art full of truth and grace.

5 Plenteous grace with thee is found,
    Grace to cover all my sin.
  Let the healing streams abound;
    Make and keep me pure within.

Thou of life the fountain art,
  Freely let me take of thee;
Spring thou up within my heart,
  Rise to all eternity.

Text: Charles Wesley, 1707–88, alt.
Tune: Joseph Parry, 1841–1903

ABERYSTWYTH
77 77 D

Amazing Grace, How Sweet the Sound   509

1 A - maz - ing grace! How sweet the sound That
2 The Lord has prom - ised good to me, His
3 Through man - y dan - gers, toils, and snares I
4 Yes, when this flesh and heart shall fail And

saved a wretch like me! I once was lost but
word my hope se - cures; He will my shield and
have al - read - y come; His grace has brought me
mor - tal life shall cease, A - maz - ing grace shall

now am found, Was blind but now I see!
por - tion be As long as life en - dures.
safe so far, His grace will see me home.
then pre - vail In heav - en's joy and peace.

Text: John Newton, 1725–1807, alt.
Tune: J. Carrell and D. Clayton, Virginia Harmony, 1831

NEW BRITAIN
C M

510

Be Still, My Soul

1 Be still, my soul; the Lord is on your side; Bear pa-tient-ly the
2 Be still, my soul; your God will un-der-take To guide the fu-ture
3 Be still, my soul; though dear-est friends de-part And all is dark-ened
4 Be still, my soul; the hour is has-t'ning on When we shall be for-

cross of grief or pain; Leave to your God to or-der and pro-vide;
as he has the past. Your hope, your con-fi-dence let noth-ing shake;
in the vail of tears; Then you will bet-ter know his love, his heart,
ev-er with the Lord, When dis-ap-point-ment, grief, and fear are gone,

In ev-'ry change he faith-ful will re-main. Be still, my soul; your
All now mys-te-rious shall be bright at last. Be still, my soul; the
Who comes to soothe your sor-rows and your fears. Be still, my soul; your
Sor-row for-got, love's pur-est joys re-stored. Be still, my soul; when

best, your heav'n-ly Friend Through thorn-y ways leads to a joy-ful end.
waves and winds still know His voice who ruled them while he dwelt be-low.
Je-sus can re-pay From his own full-ness all he takes a-way.
change and tears are past, All safe and bless-ed we shall meet at last.

Text: Catharina von Schlegel, b. 1697; tr. Jane Borthwick, 1813–97, alt.
Tune: Jean Sibelius, 1865–1957, arr. from Finlandia

FINLANDIA
10 10 10 10 10 10

In the Hour of Trial

1 In the hour of tri - al, Je - sus, plead for me
2 With for - bid - den plea - sures Should this vain world charm
3 Should thy mer - cy send me Sor - row, toil, and woe,
4 When my last hour com - eth, Fraught with strife and pain,

Lest by base de - ni - al I de - part from thee.
Or its tempt - ing trea - sures Spread to work me harm,
Or should pain at - tend me On my path be - low,
When my dust re - turn - eth To the dust a - gain,

When thou see'st me wa - ver, With a look re - call
Bring to my re - mem - brance Sad Geth - sem - a - ne
Grant that I may nev - er Fail thy hand to see;
On thy truth re - ly - ing, Through that mor - tal strife,

Nor for fear or fa - vor Suf - fer me to fall.
Or, in dark - er sem - blance, Cross - crowned Cal - va - ry.
Grant that I may ev - er Cast my care on thee.
Je - sus, take me, dy - ing, To e - ter - nal life.

Text: James Montgomery, 1771–1854, alt.
Tune: John B. Dykes, 1823–76, alt.

ST. MARY MAGDALENE
65 65 D

512   Lord, Take My Hand and Lead Me

1 Lord, take my hand and lead me Up-on life's way;
2 Lord, when the tem-pest ra-ges, I need not fear;
3 Lord, when the shad-ows length-en And night has come,

Di-rect, pro-tect, and feed me From day to day.
For you, the Rock of A-ges, Are al-ways near.
I know that you will strength-en My steps toward home,

With-out your grace and fa-vor I go a-stray;
Close by your side a-bid-ing, I fear no foe,
And noth-ing can im-pede me, O bless-ed Friend!

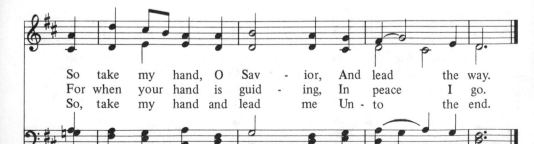

So take my hand, O Sav-ior, And lead the way.
For when your hand is guid-ing, In peace I go.
So, take my hand and lead me Un-to the end.

© Text: Julie von Hausmann, 1825–1901; tr. Lutheran Book of Worship, 1978   SO NIMM DENN MEINE HÄNDE
Tune: Friedrich Silcher, 1789–1860   74 74 D

Jesus, Savior, Pilot Me

513

1 Je - sus, Sav - ior, pi - lot me   O - ver life's tem - pes - tuous
2 As   a moth - er stills her child,   Thou canst hush the o - cean
3 When at last I near the shore   And the fear - ful break - ers

sea;   Un - known waves   be - fore me roll,   Hid - ing
wild;   Bois-t'rous waves   o - bey thy will   When thou
roar   'Twixt me and   the peace - ful rest,   Then, while

rock   and treach-'rous shoal.   Chart and com - pass come from
say'st   to them, "Be still!"   Won-drous Sov - 'reign of the
lean - ing on thy breast,   May I hear   thee say to

thee.   Je - sus, Sav - ior, pi - lot me.
sea,   Je - sus, Sav - ior, pi - lot me.
me,   "Fear not, I   will pi - lot thee."

Text: Edward Hopper, 1818–88
Tune: John E. Gould, 1822–75

PILOT
77 77 77

514 Nearer, My God, to Thee

1 Near - er, my God, to thee, Near - er to thee!
2 Near - er, my Lord, to thee, Near - er to thee,
3 Near - er, O Com - fort - er, Near - er to thee,
4 But to be near - er still, Bring me, O God,

E'en though it be a cross That rais - eth me;
Who to thy cross didst come, Dy - ing for me!
Who with my lov - ing Lord Dwell - est with me!
Not by the vi - sioned steeps An - gels have trod.

Still all my song shall be: Near - er, my God, to thee,
Strength-en my will - ing feet, Hold me in ser - vice sweet
Grant me thy fel - low - ship! Help me each day to keep
Here where thy cross I see, Je - sus, I wait for thee,

Near - er, my God, to thee, Near - er to thee!
Near - er, O Christ, to thee, Near - er to thee!
Near - er, my Guide, to thee, Near - er to thee!
Then ev - er - more to be Near - er to thee!

Text: Sarah F. Adams, 1805–48, st. 1; Hervey D. Ganse, 1822-91, sts. 2-4
Tune: Lowell Mason, 1792–1872

BETHANY
64 64 6664

516 What a Friend We Have in Jesus

1 What a friend we have in Je - sus, All our sins and griefs to bear!
2 Have we tri - als and temp - ta - tions? Is there trou - ble an - y - where?
3 Are we weak and heav - y - lad - en, Cum - bered with a load of care?

What a priv - i - lege to car - ry Ev - 'ry-thing to God in prayer!
We should nev - er be dis - cour - aged— Take it to the Lord in prayer.
Pre - cious Sav - ior, still our ref - uge— Take it to the Lord in prayer.

Oh, what peace we of - ten for - feit; Oh, what need-less pain we bear—
Can we find a friend so faith - ful Who will all our sor - rows share?
Do your friends de - spise, for - sake you? Take it to the Lord in prayer.

All be - cause we do not car - ry Ev - 'ry-thing to God in prayer!
Je - sus knows our ev - 'ry weak - ness— Take it to the Lord in prayer.
In his arms he'll take and shield you; You will find a sol - ace there.

Text: Joseph Scriven, 1820–86
Tune: Charles C. Converse, 1832–1918

CONVERSE
87 87 D

I'm But a Stranger Here

1 I'm but a stran-ger here, Heav'n is my home;
2 What though the tem-pest rage, Heav'n is my home;
3 There-fore I mur-mur not, Heav'n is my home;

Earth is a des-ert drear, Heav'n is my home.
Short is my pil-grim-age, Heav'n is my home;
What-e'er my earth-ly lot, Heav'n is my home;

Dan-ger and sor-row stand Round me on ev-'ry hand;
And time's wild win-try blast Soon shall be o-ver-past;
And I shall sure-ly stand There at my Lord's right hand.

Heav'n is my fa-ther-land, Heav'n is my home.
I shall reach home at last, Heav'n is my home.
Heav'n is my fa-ther-land, Heav'n is my home.

Text: Thomas R. Taylor, 1807–1835
Tune: Arthur S. Sullivan, 1842–1900

HEAVEN IS MY HOME
64 64 6664

I Am Jesus' Little Lamb

1 I am Je - sus' lit - tle lamb, Ev - er glad at heart I am; For my Shep - herd gent - ly guides me, Knows my need and well pro - vides me, Loves me ev - 'ry day the same, E - ven calls me by my name.

2 Day by day, at home, a - way, Je - sus is my staff and stay. When I hun - ger, Je - sus feeds me, In - to pleas - ant pas - tures leads me; When I thirst, he bids me go Where the qui - et wa - ters flow.

3 Who so hap - py as I am, E - ven now the Shep - herd's lamb? And when my short life is end - ed, By his an - gel host at - tend - ed, He shall fold me to his breast, There with - in his arms to rest.

Text: Henrietta L. von Hayn, 1724–82; tr. composite
Tune: Brüder Choral-Buch, 1784

WEIL ICH JESU SCHÄFLEIN BIN
778 877

518 Onward, Christian Soldiers

1 On - ward, Chris - tian sol - diers, March-ing as to war,
2 Like a might - y ar - my Moves the Church of God;
3 Crowns and thrones may per - ish, King-doms rise and wane,
4 On - ward, then, ye faith - ful, Join our hap - py throng,

With the cross of Je - sus Go - ing on be - fore.
Broth-ers, we are tread - ing Where the saints have trod.
But the Church of Je - sus Con-stant will re - main.
Blend with ours your voic - es In the tri - umph song:

Christ, the roy - al mas - ter, Leads a - gainst the foe;
We are not di - vid - ed, All one bod - y we,
Gates of hell can nev - er 'Gainst that Church pre - vail;
Glo - ry, laud, and hon - or Un - to Christ, the king;

For - ward in - to bat - tle See his ban - ners go!
One in hope and doc - trine, One in char - i - ty.
We have Christ's own prom - ise, And that can - not fail.
This through count - less a - ges Men and an - gels sing.

On-ward, Chris-tian sol - diers, March-ing as to war,

With the cross of Je - sus Go - ing on be - fore.

Text: Sabine Baring-Gould, 1834–1924
Tune: Arthur S. Sullivan, 1842–1900

ST. GERTRUDE
65 65 65 D

519

How Great Thou Art

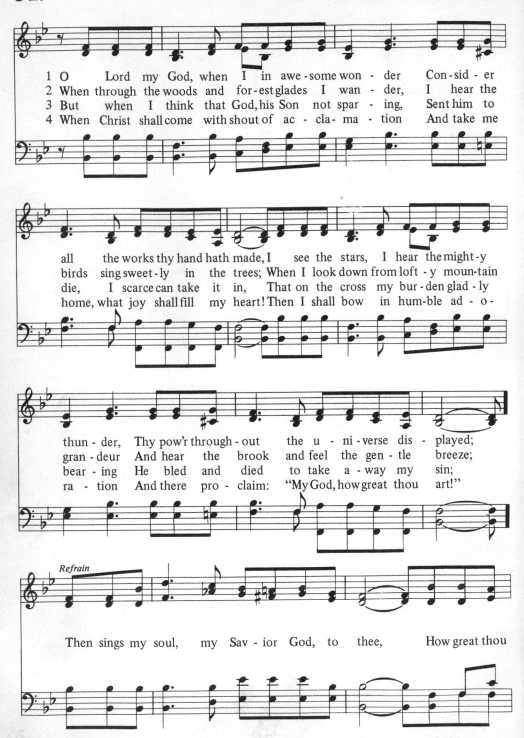

1 O Lord my God, when I in awe-some won - der Con-sid - er
2 When through the woods and for-est glades I wan - der, I hear the
3 But when I think that God, his Son not spar - ing, Sent him to
4 When Christ shall come with shout of ac - cla - ma - tion And take me

all the works thy hand hath made, I see the stars, I hear the might-y
birds sing sweet-ly in the trees; When I look down from loft - y moun-tain
die, I scarce can take it in, That on the cross my bur-den glad-ly
home, what joy shall fill my heart! Then I shall bow in hum-ble ad - o-

thun - der, Thy pow'r through - out the u - ni-verse dis - played;
gran - deur And hear the brook and feel the gen - tle breeze;
bear - ing He bled and died to take a - way my sin;
ra - tion And there pro - claim: "My God, how great thou art!"

Refrain

Then sings my soul, my Sav - ior God, to thee, How great thou

art! How great thou art! Then sings my soul, my Sav - ior God, to

thee, How great thou art! How great thou art!

© Text: Carl Boberg, 1859–1940 (Swedish); Stuart K. Hine, b. 1899 (English)
© Tune: Swedish folk tune; arr. Stuart K. Hine, b. 1899

© Copyright 1953 by Stuart K. Hine, assigned to Manna Music, Inc.
© Copyright 1955 by Manna Music, Inc.

O STORE GUD
11 10 11 10 and refrain

Rejoice, Rejoice This Happy Morn
He Is Arisen! Glorious Word!

520

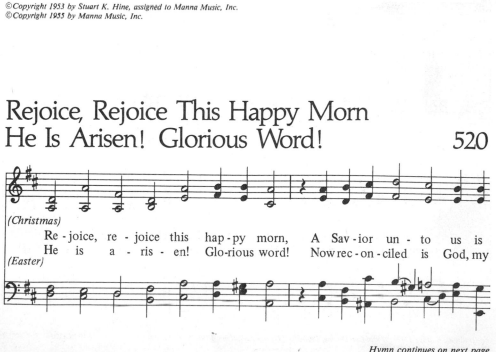

(Christmas)
Re - joice, re - joice this hap-py morn, A Sav - ior un - to us is
He is a - ris - en! Glo-rious word! Now rec - on - ciled is God, my
(Easter)

Hymn continues on next page

born, The Christ, the Lord of glo - ry! His low - ly birth at
Lord; The gates of heav'n are o - pen. My Je - sus did tri -

Beth-le - hem The an-gels from on high pro-claim And sing re -
um-phant die, And Sa-tan's ar - rows bro-ken lie, De -stroyed hell's

demp - tion's sto - ry! My soul, Ex - tol God's great fa - vor; Bless him
fierc - est weap - on. Oh, hear What cheer! Christ vic - to - rious, Ris - ing

ev - er For sal - va - tion; Give him praise and ad - o - ra - tion!
glo - rious, Life is giv - ing. He was dead but now is liv - ing!

Texts: *Birgitte K. Boye, 1742–1824; tr. Carl Doving, 1867–1937; George A. T. Rygh, 1860–1942, alt.*
Tune: *Philipp Nicolai, 1556–1608*

WIE SCHÖN LEUCHTET
P M

INDEXES

ACKNOWLEDGMENTS

The liturgical material on pages 8-384 is covered by the copyright of this book.

Material from the following sources is acknowledged:

International Consultation on English Texts: the preface dialog; the canticle texts "Glory to God in the highest," "Holy, holy, holy Lord," "Lamb of God," "Lord, now you let your servant go in peace," "You are God; we praise you," and "My soul proclaims the greatness of the Lord."

Book of Common Prayer The Episcopal Church 1979. Reprinted by permission: the canticle text "Let my prayer rise before you as incense."

Holy Bible: *New International Version*, copyright © 1978 by the New York International Bible Society. Used by permission of Zondervan Bible Publishers: The Psalmody.

Lutheran Book of Worship, copyright © 1978 by Lutheran Church in America, The American Lutheran Church, The Evangelical Lutheran Church of Canada, The Lutheran Church—Missouri Synod. From *The Holy Communion:* music, Setting One and Setting Two; liturgical texts: "Alleluia, Lord, to whom shall we go," "Return to the Lord your God," "What shall I render to the Lord," "Thank the Lord and sing his praise." Liturgical texts and music: Morning Prayer, Evening Prayer and Prayer at the Close of the Day; the canticle text "All you works of the Lord, bless the Lord"; and the Lectionaries.

Composers / arrangers of liturgical music are acknowledged: Paul G. Bunjes, b. 1914— Divine Service I, Matins, Vespers, The Litany; harmonizations for Evening Prayer (Litany, responses), Prayer at the Close of the Day. Gerhard M. Cartford, b. 1923— Litany (Evening Prayer). Richard W. Hillert, b. 1923— Divine Service II, First Setting, alt.; "Create in me a clean heart, O God," "Oh, come, let us sing to the Lord," alt., and "You are God; we praise you" (Morning Prayer). Carlos R. Messerli, b. 1927— Prayer at the Close of the Day, alt. Ronald A. Nelson, b. 1927— Divine Service II, Second Setting, alt. Roger T. Petrich, b. 1938— "Joyous light of glory" (Evening Prayer). David Schack, b. 1947— "Let my prayer rise before you as incense" (Evening Prayer). Dale Wood,

b. 1934— "Blessed be the Lord, the God of Israel," alt. (Morning Prayer); "My soul proclaims the greatness of the Lord," alt. (Evening Prayer).

Authors / translators of liturgical texts are acknowledged: John W. Arthur, 1922-80— "Worthy Is Christ" and "Let the vineyards be fruitful." Roger T. Petrich, b. 1938— "Joyous light of glory."

The preparation of the collects is acknowledged: Charles J. Evanson, b. 1936.

The preparation of the Daily Lectionary is acknowledged: Robert C. Sauer, b. 1921.

The composer / arranger of the psalm tones and the settings of canticles 1-11 is acknowledged: Paul G. Bunjes, b. 1914.

The Commission on Worship of The Lutheran Church—Missouri Synod: Paul G. Bunjes*, Alfred Fremder*, F. Samuel Janzow*, Edward Klammer*, Robert D. Koeppen, Henry L. Lettermann*, Norman E. Nagel*, Roger D. Pittelko, Ralph C. Schultz*, Norman Troyke, Willis Wright. **Additional members of standing committees:** M. Alfred Bichsel, Charles J. Evanson, Hugo J. Gehrke, Jaroslav J. Vajda. **Church staff:** Fred L. Precht, executive secretary, Commission on Worship; Ruth Eckert, office secretary. **Synodical president's representative:** Robert C. Sauer, first vice-president.

Music composition and typesetting: Capital Music Service, Inc., Washington, D.C.

Composers of hymn tune settings are acknowledged: Charles R. Anders, b. 1929; Edward Shippen Barnes, 1887-1958; Theodore A. Beck, b. 1929; Jan O. Bender, b. 1909; Barry L. Bobb, b. 1951; Paul B. Bouman, b. 1918; Annabel Morris Buchanan, b. 1888; Paul G. Bunjes, b. 1914; Donald A. Busarow, b. 1934; Robert Carwithen, b. 1933; William H. Cummings, 1831-1915; C. Winfred Douglas, 1867-1944; John B. Dykes, 1823-76; James Engel, b. 1925; William E. France, b. 1912; Alfred Fremder, b. 1920;

Indicates service on one of the standing committees

969

Johann A. Freylinghausen, 1670-1739; Graham George, b. 1912; Henry V. Gerike, b. 1948; Orlando Gibbons, 1583-1625; Thomas Gieschen, b. 1931; Richard W. Gieseke, b. 1952; Herbert Gotsch, b. 1926; Claude Goudimel, 1505-72; Walter Gresens, b. 1937; Edvard Grieg, 1843-1907; Andreas Hammerschmidt, c. 1611-75; Basil Harwood, 1859-1949; Charles H. Heaton, b. 1928; Richard W. Hillert, b. 1923; Gustav Holst, 1874-1934; John Ireland, 1879-1962; Frederick F. Jackisch, b. 1922; Charles Herbert Kitson, 1874-1944; George Leonard, b. 1914; Paul O. Manz, b. 1919; Lowell Mason, 1792-1872; Felix Mendelssohn, 1809-47; Sydney Hugo Nicholson, 1875-1947; Giovanni P. da Palestrina, 1524-94; Hugh Porter, 1897-1960; Michael Praetorius, c. 1571-1621; Fred L. Precht, b. 1916; Wilhelm Quampen, b. 1914; William J. Reynolds, b. 1920; John Roberts, 1822-77; Julius Röntgen, 1855-1932; Melvin Rotermund, b. 1927; Leland B. Sateren, b. 1913; Carl F. Schalk, b. 1929; Ralph Schultz, b. 1932; Ralph Vaughan Williams, 1872-1958; Samuel S. Wesley, 1810-76; George R. Woodward, 1848-1939.

The following canticle and hymn copyrights are acknowledged:

1-11 **Settings:** Copyright © 1982 Concordia Publishing House.

13 **Text:** Copyright 1978 Concordia Publishing House. **Setting:** Copyright 1982 Concordia Publishing House.

14 **Setting:** From the *Cowley Carol Book* by permission of A. R. Mowbray & Co. Ltd., Oxford, England.

15 **Setting:** Copyright 1982 Concordia Publishing House.

16 **Setting:** Copyright 1982 Concordia Publishing House.

17 **Text:** © Copyright 1961-62 World Library Publications. Reprinted with permission. **Setting:** Copyright 1978 *Lutheran Book of Worship*.[1]

18 **Setting:** Copyright 1969 Concordia Publishing House.

19 **Setting:** Copyright 1982 Concordia Publishing House.

20 **Setting:** Copyright 1982 Concordia Publishing House.

21 **Text and setting:** Copyright 1982 Concordia Publishing House. **Tune:** From *Evangelisches Kirchengesangbuch*, Bärenreiter-Verlag, Kassel and Basel. Used by permission.

22 **Setting:** Copyright 1978 *Lutheran Book of Worship*.[1]

23 **Text:** Copyright 1982 Concordia Publishing House.

24 **Text:** Copyright 1982 Concordia Publishing House.

25 **Text and setting:** Copyright 1982 Concordia Publishing House.

26 **Setting:** Copyright 1969 Concordia Publishing House.

27 **Text:** Copyright 1978 *Lutheran Book of Worship*.[1] **Setting:** Copyright 1981 Richard W. Gieseke. Used by permission.

28 **Setting:** Copyright 1981 Richard W. Gieseke. Used by permission.

30 **Setting:** Copyright 1982 Concordia Publishing House.

31 **Setting:** Copyright 1982 Concordia Publishing House.

32 **Text and setting:** Copyright 1969 Concordia Publishing House.

33 **Setting:** Copyright 1982 Concordia Publishing House.

35 **Text:** Copyright 1978 Concordia Publishing House. **Setting:** Copyright 1982 Concordia Publishing House.

36 **Setting:** Copyright 1982 Concordia Publishing House.

37 **Text:** Copyright 1978 *Lutheran Book of Worship*.[1]

Setting: Copyright 1982 Concordia Publishing House.

38 **Text:** Copyright 1978 *Lutheran Book of Worship*.[1] **Setting:** Copyright 1982 Concordia Publishing House.

39 **Setting:** Copyright 1982 Concordia Publishing House.

40 **Setting:** Copyright 1982 Concordia Publishing House.

43 **Setting:** Copyright 1969 Concordia Publishing House.

44 **Text:** Copyright 1969 Concordia Publishing House. **Setting:** Copyright 1953 *Württembergisches Choralbuch*.[2]

45 **Text:** Copyright 1978 *Lutheran Book of Worship*.[1] **Setting:** Copyright 1982 Concordia Publishing House.

46 **Setting:** Copyright 1982 Concordia Publishing House.

47 **Text:** Copyright 1982 Concordia Publishing House. **Setting:** Copyright 1969 Concordia Publishing House.

48 **Setting:** Copyright 1982 Concordia Publishing House.

50 **Setting:** Copyright 1982 Concordia Publishing House.

52 **Text:** Copyright 1978 Concordia Publishing House. **Setting:** Copyright 1982 Concordia Publishing House.

54 **Text, tune, and setting:** Copyright 1969 Concordia Publishing House.

56 **Text:** Copyright © 1982 Concordia Publishing House.

57 **Text:** Copyright © 1956, 1958 Gordon V. Thompson, Limited, Toronto, Canada. International Copyright Secured. Used by permission of Carl Fischer, Inc., New York, Agents on behalf of Alta Lind Cook and Gordon V. Thompson, Limited. **Setting:** Copyright 1969 Concordia Publishing House.

58 **Setting:** Copyright 1982 Concordia Publishing House.

59 **Tune and setting:** From the *English Hymnal* by permission of Oxford University Press.

63 **Text and setting:** Copyright 1969 Concordia Publishing House.

64 **Setting:** Harmonized by Ralph Vaughan Williams. From *Enlarged Songs of Praise* by permission of Oxford University Press.

65 **Text, tune, and setting:** Copyright Stainer & Bell Ltd. All rights reserved. Used by permission.

66 **Text and setting:** Copyright 1982 Concordia Publishing House.

67 **Text:** Copyright 1978 *Lutheran Book of Worship*.[1]

69 **Setting:** Copyright 1978 *Lutheran Book of Worship*.[1]

70 **Setting:** Copyright 1982 Concordia Publishing House.

71 **Text, tune, and setting:** Copyright 1969 Concordia Publishing House.

72 **Setting:** Copyright 1978 *Lutheran Book of Worship*.[1]

73 **Text:** Copyright 1978 *Lutheran Book of Worship*.[1] **Setting:** Copyright 1955 *Choralbuch*.[4]

74 **Setting:** Printed by permission of Dr. Basil Harwood's Executors. Copyright The Public Trustee. Used by permission.

76 **Tune and setting:** Copyright Stainer and Bell Ltd. All rights reserved. Used by permission of Galaxy Music Corp., NY, sole U.S. agent.

77 **Setting:** Copyright 1982 Concordia Publishing House.

78 **Text and setting:** Copyright 1982 Concordia Publishing House.

79 **Setting:** Copyright 1982 Concordia Publishing House.

81 **Setting:** From the *Cowley Carol Book* by permission of A. R. Mowbray & Co. Ltd., Oxford, England.

82 **Setting:** Copyright 1982 Concordia Publishing House.

83 **Setting:** Copyright 1978 *Lutheran Book of Worship*.[1]

84 **Setting:** Copyright 1982 Concordia Publishing House.

85 **Setting:** Copyright 1982 Concordia Publishing House.

87 **Setting:** Copyright 1982 Concordia Publishing House.

91 **Tune and setting:** By permission of the Successor to Dr. John Ireland.

92 **Text:** Copyright 1978 *Lutheran Book of Worship*.[1]

95 **Text and setting:** Copyright 1982 Concordia Publishing House.

100 **Setting:** Copyright 1982 Concordia Publishing House.

102 **Setting:** Copyright 1976 Concordia Publishing House.

103 **Setting:** Copyright 1969 Concordia Publishing House.

104 **Setting:** Copyright 1982 Concordia Publishing House.

105 **Tune and setting:** Copyright © 1941 H. W. Gray Co., Inc. Copyright renewed. Used with permission. All rights reserved.

106 **Setting:** Copyright 1982 Concordia Publishing House.

107 **Setting:** Copyright 1982 Concordia Publishing House.

108 **Text and setting:** Copyright 1982 Concordia Publishing House.

111 **Text and setting:** Copyright 1982 Concordia Publishing House.

113 **Text and setting:** Copyright 1982 Concordia Publishing House.

116 **Setting:** Copyright 1982 Concordia Publishing House.

117 **Tune and setting:** Copyright 1967 Concordia Publishing House.

119 **Setting:** Copyright 1982 Concordia Publishing House.

120 **Setting:** Copyright 1981 Richard W. Gieseke. Used by permission.

121 **Setting:** Copyright 1981 Richard W. Gieseke. Used by permission.

122 **Text:** Copyright 1982 Concordia Publishing House, sts. 1-6. **Setting:** Copyright 1982 Concordia Publishing House.

123 **Setting:** Copyright 1981 Richard W. Gieseke. Used by permission.

124 **Text and setting:** Copyright 1982 Concordia Publishing House.

125 **Text:** Copyright 1978 *Lutheran Book of Worship*.[1] **Tune and setting:** From the *English Hymnal* by permission of Oxford University Press.

126 **Setting:** Copyright 1969 Concordia Publishing House.

129 **Text:** Copyright 1952. By permission of Hymns Ancient and Modern, Ltd. From *Hymns Ancient and Modern Revised*. **Setting:** Copyright 1969 Concordia Publishing House.

130 **Setting:** Copyright 1969 Concordia Publishing House.

131 **Text:** Copyright 1958 *Service Book and Hymnal*.[3] **Setting:** Arr. and harm. by Ralph Vaughan Williams. From the *English Hymnal* by permission of Oxford University Press.

132 **Text:** Copyright 1978 *Lutheran Book of Worship*.[1]

133 **Setting:** Copyright 1969 Concordia Publishing House.

134 **Text and setting:** Copyright 1969 Concordia Publishing House.

135 **Tune and setting:** From *Songs of Praise* by permission of Oxford University Press.

136 **Text and setting:** Copyright 1982 Concordia Publishing House.

139 **Setting:** Copyright 1953 *Württembergisches Choralbuch*.[2]

140 **Text:** From the *Cowley Carol Book* by permission of A. R. Mowbray & Co. Ltd., Oxford, England. **Setting:** Copyright 1969 Concordia Publishing House.

141 **Setting:** Copyright 1969 Concordia Publishing House.

142 **Setting:** Copyright 1978 *Lutheran Book of Worship*.[1]

144 **Text, tune, and setting:** Copyright 1982 Concordia Publishing House.

145 **Setting:** Copyright 1982 Concordia Publishing House.

146 **Tune and setting:** Copyright 1982 Concordia Publishing House.

147 **Setting:** Copyright 1982 Concordia Publishing House.

148 **Text:** Copyright 1978 *Lutheran Book of Worship*.[1] **Tune and setting:** From the *English Hymnal* by permission of Oxford University Press.

149 **Text:** Copyright 1978 *Lutheran Book of Worship*.[1] **Setting:** Arr. and harm. by Ralph Vaughan Williams. From the *English Hymnal* by permission of Oxford University Press.

150 **Setting:** Copyright 1982 Concordia Publishing House.

151 **Setting:** Copyright 1981 Richard W. Gieseke. Used by permission.

152 **Text:** Copyright 1974 Augsburg Publishing House. Used by permission. **Tune and setting:** Copyright Henry V. Gerike. Used by permission.

153 **Setting:** Copyright 1982 Concordia Publishing House.

154 **Setting:** Copyright 1982 Concordia Publishing House.

155 **Text:** Copyright 1969 Concordia Publishing House. **Setting:** Copyright 1953 *Württembergisches Choralbuch*.[2]

157 **Setting:** Copyright 1982 Concordia Publishing House.

158 **Setting:** Copyright 1982 Concordia Publishing House.

159 **Text:** Copyright 1978 *Lutheran Book of Worship*.[1] **Tune and setting:** From the *English Hymnal* by permission of Oxford University Press.

160 **Setting:** Copyright 1955 *Choralbuch*.[4]

162 **Tune and setting:** From the *English Hymnal* by permission of Oxford University Press.

163 **Text:** Copyright 1978 *Lutheran Book of Worship*.[1] **Setting:** Copyright 1982 Concordia Publishing House.

164 **Text:** The text by Timothy Rees is reprinted by permission of A. R. Mowbray & Co. Ltd., Oxford, England. **Setting:** Copyright 1969 Concordia Publishing House.

165 **Text:** Copyright 1958 *Service Book and Hymnal*.[3] **Setting:** Copyright 1982 Concordia Publishing House.

166 **Setting:** Copyright 1981 Richard W. Gieseke. Used by permission.

169 **Setting:** Music copyright 1972 The Westminster Press; from *The Worshipbook—Services and Hymns*. Used by permission.

170 **Setting:** Copyright 1982 Concordia Publishing House.

172 **Setting:** Copyright 1969 Concordia Publishing House.

173 **Setting:** Copyright 1982 Concordia Publishing House.
174 **Setting:** Copyright 1981 Richard W. Gieseke. Used by permission.
175 **Text:** From the *English Hymnal* by permission of Oxford University Press. **Setting:** Copyright 1969 Concordia Publishing House.
176 **Text and setting:** Copyright 1982 Concordia Publishing House.
177 **Setting:** Copyright 1982 Concordia Publishing House.
178 **Tune and setting:** From *Enlarged Songs of Praise* by permission of Oxford University Press.
181 **Setting:** Copyright 1982 Concordia Publishing House.
182 **Setting:** Copyright 1982 Concordia Publishing House.
183 **Text and setting:** Copyright 1969 Concordia Publishing House.
184 **Text and setting:** Copyright 1982 Concordia Publishing House.
185 **Text:** Copyright 1978 Concordia Publishing House. **Setting:** Copyright 1982 Concordia Publishing House.
186 **Setting:** Copyright 1981 Richard W. Gieseke. Used by permission.
187 **Setting:** Copyright 1982 Concordia Publishing House.
189 **Setting:** Copyright 1982 Concordia Publishing House.
191 **Tune and setting:** From the *English Hymnal* by permission of Oxford University Press.
192 **Text:** Copyright 1978 *Lutheran Book of Worship.*[1]
193 **Tune and setting:** From the *English Hymnal* by permission of Oxford University Press.
194 **Tune:** From the *English Hymnal* by permission of Oxford University Press. **Setting:** Copyright 1969 Concordia Publishing House. This setting allowed by permission of Oxford University Press.
195 **Setting:** Copyright 1978 *Lutheran Book of Worship.*[1]
197 **Text and setting:** Copyright 1982 Concordia Publishing House.
198 **Setting:** Copyright 1976 Concordia Publishing House.
199 **Text:** Copyright 1978 *Lutheran Book of Worship.*[1] **Setting:** Copyright 1969 Concordia Publishing House.
200 **Setting:** Copyright 1982 Concordia Publishing House.
202 **Setting:** Copyright 1982 Concordia Publishing House.
204 **Setting:** Copyright 1955 *Choralbuch.*[4]
205 **Text:** Copyright 1978 *Lutheran Book of Worship.*[1]
206 **Text:** Copyright Augsburg Publishing House, sts. 3-4. Used by permission.
207 **Setting:** Copyright 1982 Concordia Publishing House.
208 **Text:** Copyright 1978 *Lutheran Book of Worship.*[1] **Setting:** Copyright 1953 *Württembergisches Choralbuch.*[2]
209 **Setting:** Copyright 1982 Concordia Publishing House.
211 **Text:** Copyright 1978 *Lutheran Book of Worship.*[1] **Setting:** Copyright 1969 Concordia Publishing House.
212 **Setting:** Copyright 1982 Concordia Publishing House.
213 **Text:** Copyright 1980 Concordia Publishing House. **Setting:** Copyright 1982 Concordia Publishing house.
214 **Text:** Copyright 1978 Concordia Publishing House. **Setting:** Copyright 1982 Concordia Publishing House.

215 **Text and setting:** Copyright 1978 *Lutheran Book of Worship.*[1]
218 **Setting:** Copyright 1982 Concordia Publishing House.
219 **Text:** Copyright Lutheran World Federation. Used by permission. **Setting:** Copyright 1978 *Lutheran Book of Worship.*[1]
220 **Tune:** © Mrs. Dilys Webb c/o Mechanical-Copyright Protection Society Limited and reproduced by permission of the legal representatives of the composer, who reserve all rights therein. **Setting:** Copyright 1982 Concordia Publishing House.
222 **Text:** Copyright 1958 *Service Book and Hymnal.*[3]
223 **Text:** Copyright 1976 Elizabeth Quitmeyer. Used by permission. **Setting:** Copyright 1978 *Lutheran Book of Worship.*[1]
226 **Setting:** Copyright 1982 Concordia Publishing House.
229 **Setting:** Copyright 1953 *Württembergisches Choralbuch.*[2]
230 **Text:** Copyright 1978 Concordia Publishing House. **Setting:** Copyright 1982 Concordia Publishing House.
232 **Setting:** Copyright 1982 Concordia Publishing House.
233 **Setting:** Copyright 1982 Concordia Publishing House.
234 **Setting:** Copyright 1969 Concordia Publishing House.
235 **Setting:** Copyright 1982 Concordia Publishing House.
236 **Text:** Copyright 1980 Concordia Publishing House. **Setting:** Copyright 1976 Concordia Publishing House.
237 **Text:** Copyright 1980 Concordia Publishing House. **Setting:** Copyright 1982 Concordia Publishing House.
238 **Setting:** Copyright 1978 *Lutheran Book of Worship.*[1]
239 **Text:** Copyright 1978 *Lutheran Book of Worship,*[1] sts. 1-4. **Setting:** Copyright 1982 Concordia Publishing House.
241 **Setting:** Copyright 1982 Concordia Publishing House.
242 **Setting:** Copyright 1982 Concordia Publishing House.
243 **Setting:** Copyright 1969 Concordia Publishing House.
244 **Setting:** Copyright 1982 Concordia Publishing House.
245 **Setting:** Copyright 1976 Concordia Publishing House.
246 **Text:** Copyright 1982 Concordia Publishing House. **Setting:** Copyright 1978 *Lutheran Book of Worship.*[1]
247 **Text:** Copyright 1964 World Library Publications, Inc. Reprinted with permisson. **Setting:** Copyright 1972 by the publishers for the Inter-Lutheran Commission on Worship representing the cooperating churches, the copyright holders. Used by permission.
248 **Setting:** Copyright 1982 Concordia Publishing House.
249 **Setting:** Copyright 1982 Concordia Publishing House.
250 **Setting:** Copyright 1982 Concordia Publishing House.
252 **Text and setting:** Copyright 1982 Concordia Publishing House.
253 **Text:** By permission of Oxford University Press.
254 **Text:** Copyright 1978 Dorothy Hoyer Scharlemann. Used by permission.
259 **Text:** Copyright 1971 Mrs. Martin H. Franzmann. Used by permission. **Setting:** Copyright 1982 Concordia Publishing House.

261 **Setting:** Copyright 1982 Concordia Publishing House.
262 **Setting:** Copyright 1982 Concordia Publishing House.
263 **Setting:** Copyright 1981 Richard W. Gieseke. Used by permission.
265 **Text:** Copyright 1978 Concordia Publishing House. **Setting:** Copyright 1953 *Württembergisches Choralbuch.*[2]
266 **Setting:** Copyright 1982 Concordia Publishing House.
267 **Setting:** Copyright 1982 Concordia Publishing House.
269 **Text and setting:** Copyright 1982 Concordia Publishing House.
270 **Setting:** Copyright 1982 Concordia Publishing House.
271 **Tune and setting:** Copyright Association for Promoting Christian Knowledge, Dublin.
273 **Text, tune, and setting:** Copyright 1978 *Lutheran Book of Worship.*[1]
274 **Setting:** Copyright 1982 Concordia Publishing House.
275 **Setting:** Copyright 1969 Concordia Publishing House.
277 **Setting:** Copyright 1982 Concordia Publishing House.
279 **Setting:** Copyright 1982 Concordia Publishing House.
280 **Setting:** Copyright 1953 *Württembergisches Choralbuch.*[2]
281 **Setting:** Copyright 1969 Concordia Publishing House.
282 **Setting:** Copyright 1982 Concordia Publishing House.
284 **Setting:** Copyright 1982 Concordia Publishing House.
288 **Text:** Copyright 1979 Concordia Publishing House. **Setting:** Copyright 1982 Concordia Publishing House.
291 **Text:** Copyright 1958 *Service Book and Hymnal.*[3] **Setting:** Copyright 1982 Concordia Publishing House.
292 **Text:** Copyright 1969 Concordia Publishing House. **Setting:** Copyright 1982 Concordia Publishing House.
297 **Text:** Copyright 1978 *Lutheran Book of Worship.*[1]
298 **Setting:** Copyright 1982 Concordia Publishing House
299 **Tune:** Music copyright © 1964 Abingdon Press. Used by permission.
300 **Text:** Copyright 1978 *Lutheran Book of Worship.*[1] **Setting:** Copyright 1982 Concordia Publishing House.
301 **Setting:** Copyright 1969 Concordia Publishing House.
302 **Setting:** Copyright 1982 Concordia Publishing House.
303 **Setting:** Copyright 1981 Richard W. Gieseke. Used by permission.
306 **Setting:** Copyright 1982 Concordia Publishing House.
307 **Setting:** Copyright 1938 J. Fischer and Bros. Copyright renewed. Used with permission. All rights reserved.
308 **Text:** From the *English Hymnal* by permission of Oxford University Press. St. 2 omitted by permission. **Setting:** Arr. and harm. by Ralph Vaughan Williams. From the *English Hymnal* by permission of Oxford University Press.
309 **Setting:** Copyright 1982 Concordia Publishing House.
310 **Text and setting:** Copyright 1982 Concordia Publishing House.

311 **Text, tune, and setting:** By permission of Hymns Ancient and Modern, Ltd.
314 **Text:** Copyright 1978 *Lutheran Book of Worship,*[1] sts. 1, 3-5. **Setting:** Copyright 1953 *Württembergisches Choralbuch.*[2]
315 **Text:** © The Church Pension Fund. Used by permission. **Setting:** Copyright 1982 Concordia Publishing House.
317 **Setting:** Copyright 1981 Richard W. Gieseke. Used by permission.
319 **Text and tune:** Copyright 1967 Lutheran Council in the U.S.A. Used by permission. **Setting:** Copyright 1969 Concordia Publishing House.
320 **Text:** Copyright 1982 Concordia Publishing House.
321 **Text:** Copyright 1982 Concordia Publishing House, sts. 1, 5; Copyright 1978 *Lutheran Book of Worship,*[1] sts. 3, 4, 6. **Setting:** Copyright 1982 Concordia Publishing House.
323 **Setting:** Copyright 1969 Concordia Publishing House.
324 **Text:** Copyright 1982 Concordia Publishing House. **Tune and setting:** Copyright 1979 Richard W. Hillert. Used by permission.
325 **Setting:** Copyright 1982 Concordia Publishing House.
326 **Text:** Copyright 1972 Concordia Publishing House. **Setting:** Copyright 1981 Richard W. Gieseke. Used by permission.
327 **Text:** Copyright Board of Publication, Lutheran Church in America, sts. 1-3. Used by permission; Copyright 1958 *Service Book and Hymnal,*[3] st. 4. **Setting:** Copyright 1982 Concordia Publishing House.
328 **Text:** Copyright 1969 Concordia Publishing House. **Tune:** Copyright Gwenlyn Evans, Ltd. Used by permission.
329 **Setting:** Copyright 1982 Concordia Publishing House.
331 **Text:** Copyright 1980 Concordia Publishing House. **Setting:** Copyright 1982 Concordia Publishing House.
334 **Setting:** Copyright 1953 *Württembergisches Choralbuch.*[2]
336 **Text and setting:** Copyright 1982 Concordia Publishing House.
337 **Setting:** Copyright 1953 *Württembergisches Choralbuch.*[2]
338 **Text:** Copyright 1976 Norman P. Olsen. Used by permission. **Tune and setting:** Copyright 1978 *Lutheran Book of Worship.*[1]
339 **Setting:** Copyright 1982 Concordia Publishing House.
340 **Setting:** Copyright 1982 Concordia Publishing House.
341 **Setting:** Copyright 1982 Concordia Publishing House.
343 **Text:** Words copyright © 1953 The Hymn Society of America, Wittenberg University, Springfield, OH 45501. Used by permission. **Setting:** Copyright 1981 Richard W. Gieseke. Used by permission.
344 **Text and setting:** Copyright 1982 Concordia Publishing House.
345 **Setting:** Copyright 1982 Concordia Publishing House.
346 **Text, tune, and setting:** Copyright 1969 Concordia Publishing House.
352 **Setting:** Copyright 1982 Concordia Publishing House.
353 **Setting:** Copyright 1978 *Lutheran Book of Worship.*[1]
354 **Setting:** Copyright 1982 Concordia Publishing House.

355 **Setting:** Copyright 1982 Concordia Publishing House.
356 **Setting:** Copyright 1982 Concordia Publishing House.
357 **Text and setting:** Copyright 1978 *Lutheran Book of Worship.*[1]
358 **Setting:** Copyright 1982 Concordia Publishing House.
360 **Setting:** Copyright 1981 Richard W. Gieseke. Used by permission.
363 **Setting:** Copyright 1982 Concordia Publishing House.
364 **Setting:** Copyright 1982 Concordia Publishing House.
365 **Text:** © Timothy Dudley-Smith. Used by permission. **Setting:** Copyright 1982 Concordia Publishing House.
367 **Setting:** Copyright 1982 Concordia Publishing House.
369 **Setting:** Copyright 1982 Concordia Publishing House.
370 **Setting:** Copyright 1982 Concordia Publishing House.
371 **Setting:** Copyright 1981 Richard W. Gieseke. Used by permission.
372 **Setting:** Copyright 1982 Concordia Publishing House.
373 **Setting:** Copyright 1982 Concordia Publishing House.
374 **Setting:** Copyright 1982 Concordia Publishing House.
375 **Setting:** Copyright 1982 Concordia Publishing House.
376 **Text and tune:** Copyright 1980 Concordia Publishing House. **Setting:** Copyright 1982 Concordia Publishing House.
377 **Text:** From *Eleven Ecumenical Hymns.* Copyright 1954 The Hymn Society of America. Used by permission. **Setting:** Copyright 1969 Concordia Publishing House.
379 **Setting:** Copyright 1982 Concordia Publishing House.
380 **Tune:** Copyright 1981 Barry L. Bobb. Used by permission. **Setting:** Copyright 1982 Concordia Publishing House.
381 **Text:** Copyright 1978 *Lutheran Book of Worship.*[1]
382 **Setting:** Copyright 1969 Concordia Publishing House.
383 **Text, tune, and setting:** From the *English Hymnal* by permission of Oxford University Press. Text altered by permission.
384 **Text:** From the *English Hymnal* by permission of Oxford University Press. Text altered by permission.
386 **Setting:** Copyright 1982 Concordia Publishing House.
387 **Text:** Copyright 1978 *Lutheran Book of Worship.*[1] **Setting:** Copyright 1982 Concordia Publishing House.
390 **Text:** Copyright Board of Publication, Lutheran Church in America. Used by permission. **Setting:** Copyright 1982 Concordia Publishing House.
391 **Setting:** Copyright 1982 Concordia Publishing House.
394 **Text:** By permission of Oxford University Press. **Setting:** Copyright 1979 F. E. Röntgen. Used with permission.
395 **Setting:** Copyright 1969 Concordia Publishing House.
396 **Tune:** Copyright 1964 Augsburg Publishing House. Used by permission. **Setting:** Copyright 1978 *Lutheran Book of Worship.*[1]

397 **Setting:** Copyright 1978 *Lutheran Book of Worship.*[1]
398 **Tune:** © by Mrs. Dilys Webb c/o Mechanical-Copyright Protection Society Limited and reproduced by permission of the legal representatives of the composer, who reserve all rights therein. **Setting:** Copyright 1969 Concordia Publishing House.
400 **Text:** Copyright Board of Publication, Lutheran Church in America. Used by permission. **Setting:** Copyright 1978 *Lutheran Book of Worship.*[1]
401 **Text:** Words copyright © 1965 The Hymn Society of America, Wittenberg University, Springfield, OH 45501. Used by permission. **Tune:** Copyright Doris Wright Smith. Used by permission. **Setting:** Copyright 1969 Concordia Publishing House.
402 **Setting:** Copyright 1982 Concordia Publishing House.
403 **Text:** Copyright Albert F. Bayly. Used by permission. **Setting:** Copyright 1982 Concordia Publishing House.
404 **Setting:** Copyright 1982 Concordia Publishing House.
405 **Setting:** Copyright 1982 Concordia Publishing House.
406 **Setting:** Copyright 1982 Concordia Publishing House.
407 **Setting:** Copyright 1953 *Württembergisches Choralbuch.*[2]
408 **Setting:** Copyright 1978 *Lutheran Book of Worship.*[1]
409 **Text:** Copyright 1978 *Lutheran Book of Worship.*[1] **Setting:** Copyright 1953 *Württembergisches Choralbuch.*[2]
410 **Text and tune:** Copyright 1973 Concordia Publishing House.
411 **Setting:** Copyright © 1967 The Bethany Press. Used by permission.
413 **Text and setting:** Copyright 1982 Concordia Publishing House.
414 **Setting:** Copyright 1955 *Choralbuch.*[4]
416 **Setting:** Copyright 1982 Concordia Publishing House.
417 **Text:** Copyright 1981 Henry L. Lettermann. Used by permission. **Setting:** Copyright 1982 Concordia Publishing House.
418 **Setting:** Copyright 1982 Concordia Publishing House.
419 **Text:** Copyright Augsburg Publishing House, sts. 3-4. Used by permission. **Setting:** Copyright 1953 *Württembergisches Choralbuch.*[2]
420 **Text:** Copyright 1978 *Lutheran Book of Worship,*[1] st. 2.
421 **Setting:** Copyright 1982 Concordia Publishing House.
422 **Setting:** Copyright 1982 Concordia Publishing House.
423 **Text and Setting:** Copyright 1982 Concordia Publishing House.
425 **Setting:** Copyright 1982 Concordia Publishing House.
427 **Text and setting:** Copyright 1982 Concordia Publishing House.
428 **Setting:** Copyright 1953 *Württembergisches Choralbuch.*[2]
430 **Text and setting:** Copyright 1982 Concordia Publishing House.
431 **Text:** Copyright 1980 Concordia Publishing House. **Setting:** Copyright 1981 Richard W. Gieseke. Used by permission.
432 **Text:** Words copyright © 1976 The Hymn Society of

America, Wittenberg University, Springfield, OH 45501.
Used by permission. **Setting:** Copyright 1982 Concordia
Publishing House.
434 **Setting:** Copyright 1955 *Choralbuch.*[4]
435 **Setting:** Copyright 1982 Concordia Publishing
House.
436 **Text:** Copyright © 1926 J. Curwen & Sons. Used by
permission. **Setting:** Arr. and harm. by Ralph Vaughan
Williams. From the *English Hymnal* by permission of
Oxford University Press.
437 **Setting:** Copyright 1981 Richard W. Gieseke. Used
by permission.
438 **Text, tune, and setting:** Copyright 1968 Augsburg
Publishing House. Used by permission.
439 **Setting:** Copyright 1981 Richard W. Gieseke. Used
by permission.
440 **Setting:** Arr. and harm. by Ralph Vaughan
Williams. From the *English Hymnal* by permission of
Oxford University Press.
441 **Setting:** Copyright 1982 Concordia Publishing
House.
442 **Setting:** Copyright 1969 Concordia Publishing
House.
443 **Setting:** Copyright 1955 *Choralbuch.*[4]
444 **Setting:** Copyright 1955 *Choralbuch.*[4]
445 **Text:** Copyright Lutheran Publishing House,
Adelaide. Used by permission. **Setting:** Copyright 1978
Lutheran Book of Worship.[1]
446 **Setting:** Copyright 1982 Concordia Publishing
House.
448 **Setting:** Copyright 1953 *Württembergisches
Choralbuch.*[2]
449 **Text:** By permission of Oxford University Press.
Tune and setting: Copyright 1978 *Lutheran Book of
Worship.*[1]
451 **Setting:** Copyright 1969 Concordia Publishing
House.
453 **Setting:** Copyright 1982 Concordia Publishing
House.
454 **Setting:** Copyright 1982 Concordia Publishing
House.
456 **Text and setting:** Copyright 1982 Concordia
Publishing House.
459 **Text:** © 1969 James Quinn, SJ, printed by
permission of Geoffrey Chapman, a division of Cassell
Ltd. **Setting:** Copyright 1982 Concordia Publishing
House.
461 **Setting:** Copyright 1953 *Württembergisches
Choralbuch.*[2]
462 **Setting:** Copyright 1953 *Württembergisches
Choralbuch.*[2]
463 **Text:** Copyright 1978 *Lutheran Book of Worship.*[1]
Setting: Copyright William E. France. Used with
permission.
464 **Setting:** Copyright 1978 *Lutheran Book of
Worship.*[1]
465 **Text:** © The Church Pension Fund. Used by
permission.
466 **Setting:** Copyright 1982 Concordia Publishing
House.
467 **Setting:** Copyright 1982 Concordia Publishing
House.
470 **Text:** Copyright 1982 Concordia Publishing House.
471 **Setting:** Copyright 1982 Concordia Publishing
House.

472 **Setting:** Copyright 1982 Concordia Publishing
House.
475 **Setting:** Copyright 1982 Concordia Publishing
House.
476 **Setting:** Copyright 1982 Concordia Publishing
House.
479 **Setting:** Copyright 1982 Concordia Publishing
House.
481 **Text:** Copyright 1978 *Lutheran Book of Worship.*[1]
482 **Text:** From the *English Hymnal* by permission of
Oxford University Press. **Setting:** Copyright 1969
Concordia Publishing House.
483 **Setting:** Copyright 1978 *Lutheran Book of
Worship.*[1]
485 **Setting:** Copyright 1982 Concordia Publishing
House.
487 **Text:** Copyright 1978 *Lutheran Book of Worship.*[1]
Setting: Copyright 1982 Concordia Publishing House.
488 **Setting:** Copyright 1982 Concordia Publishing
House.
489 **Setting:** Copyright 1969 Concordia Publishing
House.
492 **Setting:** Harmonized by Ralph Vaughan Williams.
From the *English Hymnal* by permission of Oxford
University Press.
493 **Setting:** Copyright 1969 Concordia Publishing
House.
498 **Setting:** Copyright 1969 Concordia Publishing
House.
503 **Setting:** Copyright 1982 Concordia Publishing
House.
504 **Text:** From *American Negro Songs and Spirituals.*
Copyright 1940 Mrs. John W. Work III. Used by
permission.
509 **Setting:** Copyright 1982 Concordia Publishing
House.
510 **Tune:** Copyright Breitkopf & Haertel, Wiesbaden.
Used by permission of Associated Music Publishers, Inc.
Setting: Arrangement copyright 1933 Presbyterian Board
of Christian Education; renewed, 1961. Used by
permission of The Westminster Press.
512 **Text:** Copyright 1978 *Lutheran Book of Worship.*[1]
513 **Setting:** Copyright 1982 Concordia Publishing
House.
517 **Setting:** Copyright 1982 Concordia Publishing
House.
519 **Text, tune, and setting:** © Copyright 1953, 1955
Manna Music, Inc., 2111 Kenmere Ave., Burbank, CA
91504. International copyright secured. All rights
reserved. Used by permission.
520 **Setting:** Copyright 1955 *Choralbuch.*[4]

---

[1] *Copyright administered by Augsburg Publishing House, Board of
Publication of Lutheran Church in America, and Concordia
Publishing House. Used by permission.*

[2] *From* Choralbuch zum Evangelischen Kirchengesangbuch,
Ausgabe für die Evangelische Landeskirche in Württemberg 1953.
*Verlag des Gesangbuchs und Choralbuchs für die Evangelische
Landeskirche in Württemberg, Stuttgart. Used by permission.*

[3] *Copyright administered by Augsburg Publishing House and Board
of Publication, Lutheran Church in America. Used by permission.*

[4] *From* Choralbuch zum Evangelischen Kirchengesangbuch der
Evangelisch-lutherischen Landeskirchen Scheswig-Holstein-
Lauenburg/Hamburg/Lübeck und Eutin 1955. Verlag Merseburger,
Berlin. Used by permission.*

HYMN OF THE DAY

These hymns constitute a selection for the church year based on both the one-year and the three-year lectionaries. In instances where the selected hymn(s) varies for the two lectionaries, the asterisk (*) marks the hymn(s) appropriate to the one-year series. The letters A, B, and C are references to the three-year series.

TOPICAL INDEX OF HYMNS
AND SPIRITUAL SONGS

Bible
See The Word of God, 328-344

Burial
See Death and Burial, 264-269; Easter, 123-147

Celebration

Christ the King

Christmas, 35-71

Church Anniversary

Church Building
See The House of God, 323-327

Church (General), 287-296

Church Militant, 297-305

Church Triumphant, 306-310

Close of Service, 216-222

Comfort and Rest
See Cross and Comfort, 420-429

Commissioning, Lay Ministry

Commitment, 371-378

Communion of Saints

Confession, 229-235

Confirmation, 254-257
See Pentecost, 154-167

982

AUTHORS, TRANSLATORS, AND SOURCES OF HYMNS AND SPIRITUAL SONGS

Italic numbers indicate translations.

987

COMPOSERS AND SOURCES OF HYMNS AND SPIRITUAL SONGS

Italic numbers indicate settings.

TUNES—ALPHABETICAL

*Indented lines indicate names by which some tunes in this book
may also be known.*

TUNES—METRICAL

996

997

FIRST LINES OF HYMNS
AND SPIRITUAL SONGS

* *Indented lines indicate first lines by which some hymns in this
book may also be known.*

1003

CANTICLES AND CHANTS

METRICAL PARAPHRASES OF PSALMS

For hymns which relate to specific psalm verses, see Scriptural References in Hymns, Lutheran Worship, Altar Book.

METRICAL LISTING OF DOXOLOGIES

Meter	Hymn Stanzas	Meter	Hymn Stanzas
S M (Short Meter—66 86)	12, 6	77 77 4	126, 8
	195, 5	78 78 77	171, 5
S M and refrain	455, 7	78 78 88	202, 4
C M (Common Meter—86 86)	292, 6	84 84 88 84	492, 4
	151, 6	86 866	44, 7
L M (Long Meter—88 88)	435, 5		77, 6
	484, 6	87 87	18, 5
	235, 8	87 87 D	328, 6
	478, 5	87 87 and refrain	50, 4
	489, 3	87 87 47	173, 1
	157, 158, 4	87 87 77 88	434, 2
	156, 7	87 87 87	117, 5
	43, 5		152, 4
	74, 6	87 87 877	36, 5
	352, 5	87 87 87 87 7	288, 3
	201, 4	87 87 887	355, 6
	197, 3	88 47	146, 8
	76, 5	887 447	406, 5
	17, 6	888 6	183, 7
	45, 7	88 88 4	310, 6
	487, 3		147, 4
	275, 7	88 88 88	167, 4
	87, 5	888 888	136, 5
	14, 5	888 888 and alleluias	149, 7
	461, 1		436, 7
	103, 104, 5		440, 3
	81, 5		131, 4
L M D (Long Meter Double—88 88 88 88)	319, 4		308, 3
65 65	491, 6	88 88 88	167, 4
65 65 D	178, 7	10 8 10 8 888	445, 5
664 6664	169, 4	10 10 10 and alleluias	191, 8
6684 D	450, 9	11 11 11 5	175, 4
67 67 66 66	443, 3		482, 3
	174, 4		323, 4
76 76 D	193, 194, 3	Irregular	172, 5
	271, 4	P M (Peculiar Meter)	437, 4
	203, 4		
	133, 4		
76 76 776	72, 4		
77 77	13, 8		
77 77 and alleluias	127, 4		